CONTENTS

A Dictionary of

First Names

PATRICK HANKS
and FLAVIA HODGES

Oxford New York
OXFORD UNIVERSITY PRESS

Oxford University Press, Walton Street, Oxford OX2 6DP

Oxford New York
Athens Auckland Bangkok Bogota Bombay
Buenos Aires Calcutta Cape Town Dar es Salaam
Delhi Florence Hong Kong Istanbul Karachi
Kuala Lumpur Madras Madrid Melbourne
Mexico City Nairobi Paris Singapore
Taipei Tokyo Toronto
and associated companies in
Berlin Ibadan

Oxford is a trade mark of Oxford University Press

First published 1990
First issued as an Oxford University Press paperback 1996

British Library Cataloguing in Publication Data
Hanks, Patrick
A dictionary of first names.
1. English forenames—Dictionaries
I. Title II. Hodges, Flavia
929.44
ISBN 0-19-280050-7

Library of Congress Cataloging in Publication Data
Hanks, Patrick.
A dictionary of first names/Patrick Hanks and Flavia Hodges.
p. cm. Includes bibliographical references.
1. Names, Personal—Dictionaries. I. Hodges, Flavia. II. Title.
929.4'4'03—dc20 CS2367.H32 1990 90-7001
ISBN 0-19-280050-7

3 5 7 9 10 8 6 4 2

Printed in Great Britain by
Mackays of Chatham,
Chatham, Kent

INTRODUCTION

SCOPE OF THE WORK

What is a 'first name'? Strictly, it is the first of a sequence of one or more given names borne by an individual. A given name is one that is bestowed on a child by its parents or guardians at birth, as opposed to an inherited surname. More loosely, the term is used with much the same significance as 'given name'. All the names listed in this book can, of course, be used both as first names and as second or subsequent given names. But the range of names used as second, third, or fourth given names is somewhat wider. Typically, for example, a mother's maiden surname, or an unusual personal name with some special family significance, may be found used in this way. In many cases, this has been a first stage in the transfer of a surname to use as a common conventional given name. Those names that have clearly completed the transfer are included in this dictionary. Other, less usual secondary given names are not included here.

A person's given name is a badge of cultural identity. Cultural identity is closely allied to religious identity: religious affiliation and native language are often key factors, overtly or subliminally, in the choice of an appropriate name for a new member of a family. Even agnostics and atheists typically choose names for their children that are common among the sect or religion which they may have rejected but in whose midst they live, rather than totally alien or invented names.

It is difficult to imagine a human culture without personal names. The names that people bear are determined in large part by the culture that they belong to. A woman called *Niamh* can be presumed to be Irish; at the very least, her parents, in choosing this name for her, were announcing some sort of cultural identification with Ireland and Irish culture.

Even the commonest names are to some extent culture-specific in form. *John* is one of the commonest first names in Europe, but it is still a reasonable guess that a man called *John* is English-speaking and Christian. If he is German, we expect him to be called *Johann* or *Hans*: the choice of the form *John* for a German is unusual and suggestive of Anglophilia. At the very least, it would invite comment or explanation. Names such as *Maria*, which are shared in the same form by several languages, are the exception rather than the rule in Europe, despite the shared cultural history and the cross-fertilization that are characteristic of Europe and that have played such an important part in determining choices of names.

For underlying the differences are deeper unities, connecting naming practices across linguistic boundaries. *John*, *Seán*, *Ia(i)n*, *Giovanni*, *Johann*, *Jean*, *Jan*, *Ivan*, and so on are in one sense all variants of the same name, with the same 'meaning'. A description that is relevant to one will be in large part relevant to another.

The purpose of this dictionary is to record and explain these similarities and differences in the names of Europe and the English-speaking world, giving the forms, linguistic origins, cultural peculiarities, and cognate relationships of each. Where a name that is essentially 'the same name' is found in many different forms in the different languages of Europe, the main entry is placed under the usual English spelling. There are cross-references, in small capitals, where differences in spelling mean that two names are more than a few entries apart.

Also included are two supplements on naming traditions that up to now have been largely independent of the European tradition, but that are of increasing interest among English speakers and others. The first of these describes the most frequent given names in the Arab world. These are important not only in their own right, but also because they are the source of the most common Islamic names in every part of the globe where Islam is practised. They provide a striking parallel to the Judaeo-Christian tradition. The other supplement records and explains the most common Indian names. The ancient religions and culture of India have long attracted interest in the West, and the need for summary information on the names from this rich and varied culture is reinforced now by immigration. Each of the supplements is preceded by a short introduction explaining the principal features of naming practices in the two cultures.

THE SET OF CONVENTIONAL GIVEN NAMES

Conventional given names constitute quite a small set of items (compared, say, with surnames or vocabulary words). In each of the main European languages, only a few hundred male names, and even fewer female names, form the inventory from which children's names are ordinarily chosen. This set of common conventional names is supplemented in various ways, for example by the use of surnames and vocabulary words as given names. Some of these new coinages in turn achieve conventional status.

In most European languages, over half of the common conventional names (in some cases, almost all of them) owe their importance to Christian tradition. These common Christian names usually have numerous cognates in the other European languages. In some countries, for example post-revolutionary France and pre-revolutionary Russia, there were official sanctions against straying outside the set of names sanctioned by the Church or the State. Christian names taken from the Old Testament overlap to a large extent with Jewish names of biblical origin, although there are often distinct Jewish forms, either representing the ancient Hebrew more closely or existing in a specific Yiddish, Judezmo, or other form.

This small, central set of Christian and Judaeo-Christian names is usually augmented by a much more language-specific set of survivals of very ancient names from a pre-Christian past. Many of these owe their long-continuing popularity to having been borne by royalty or by members of the aristocracy. In English, for example, such names as *William* and *Richard* are of Germanic origin, while *Malcolm* and *Brian* are from Gaelic. In Scandinavia many ancient Norse names (e.g. *Sigurd*, *Gunnar*, and *Torsten*) can be found in modern use. In Poland the names *Stanisław*, *Kazimierz*, and *Wojciech* represent survivals of a pre-Christian tradition. Polish names of this type very often have Czech cognates, while some Old Slavonic names have survived in Czech but not in Polish. In Russia, on the other hand, the use of such pre-Christian names was forbidden by the Orthodox Church; on the whole, those that are now in use are recent reintroductions from a pre-Christian past, often borrowed under the influence of some other Slavonic language. Conventional Russian names are typically of Byzantine Greek origin, being those bestowed in honour of saints venerated by the Orthodox Church.

The set of conventional Christian, Judaeo-Christian, and pre-Christian names is further augmented in other ways. Typically, vocabulary words, surnames, topographic terms, and placenames may be found pressed into service as given names. Some of these are so rare that they have no place in a dictionary. Others are found over the centuries mainly in just one family, and a few of these (for example *Fulk* and *Kenelm*) are recorded here. Finally, we must mention the class of 'made-up' names, usually blends of parts of other names, such as *Charlene* and *Raelene*. A few of these have become used conventionally and are recorded here.

GIVEN NAMES IN USE OVER THE CENTURIES

In some cultures, the relationship between names and vocabulary words is generally transparent: that is, the names are just special uses of ordinary words. In such cultures, a name can be chosen on account of its meaning, as well as on grounds of its historical or religious associations or euphony. This is not the case with English, nor with most of the languages of Western Europe. English names are mostly opaque: that is, the 'meaning' of almost all of them is to be sought in languages other than modern English, often ancient languages no longer spoken and only studied by specialists.

Because of this, among English speakers (and indeed among speakers of French, German, Spanish, and so on) there can rarely be any question of choosing a name for a child on the basis of its meaning. A name is chosen either on ornamental grounds—'because it sounds nice'—or in honour of some close relative. These are private reasons for choice, which cannot be recorded in a dictionary.

There are, however, other, more public reasons for choosing one name rather than another, and these have clearly affected the continued popularity of certain names over the centuries. There are definite vogues for given names; they come into fashion and go out again for reasons that can sometimes be recorded: for example, a name may experience a sudden increase in use after it has been used for a character in a popular book, film, or television series. More seriously (but less noticeably), a particular set of names may be associated with a religious sect or cult, which will affect the popularity of those names. In other cases, the popularity of certain names seems to ebb and flow with the generations, so that (for example) some of the names that came into vogue in the seventies can be expected to go out again during the nineties. Some have already gone. Leslie Dunkling has carried out a most interesting partial survey of the rise and fall in the popularity of English names.

Not all names undergo significant fluctuations in popularity. Some, such as *John* and *Mary*, are so widespread that any factor that might diminish their popularity for one reason is offset by other factors increasing their popularity. These are the hardy perennials of nomenclature.

BIBLICAL NAMES

The most widespread of all given names are those taken from a biblical original. Names derived from the major characters whose story is told in the Old Testament (and indeed many of the minor ones) are borne by Jews and Christians alike in every country of Europe, in the United States, Canada, Australia, New Zealand, the West Indies, South Africa, and elsewhere. This dictionary records the various forms in which such names appear in different vernacular languages: names such as *Adam* and *Eve; Benjamin, Joseph*, and *Jacob; David; Sarah, Deborah, Rebecca*, and *Ruth*.

Some of these Old Testament names are rare now. Among non-Jews, names such as *Reuben, Seth, Hezekiah* and *Caleb, Bathsheba, Zillah*, and *Beulah* are associated particularly with Nonconformist sects of the 17th century. *Adam* was a popular name among such groups, but *Eve* was shunned, on the grounds that the biblical Eve brought sin into the world.

Many of these Old Testament biblical names were revived among Christian fundamentalists of the 19th century. A few, especially female names such as *Abigail*, have survived or been revived in modern use, but others have once again dropped out of fashion. Some of them, for example *Moses, Solomon*, and *Zipporah*, are now found almost exclusively among Jews.

David is one of the most common names among English speakers of all creeds. It is borne by Christians and Jews alike. As well as being the name of the greatest of all the biblical kings of Israel, it was also borne by the patron saint of Wales and by two kings of Scotland. These are among the reasons why *David* is freely used as a Gentile name in the English-speaking world. In other countries, however, there is no such tradition of Gentile use, and the name is regarded as characteristically Jewish. In general, Old Testament names are found among both Jews and Protestants, but are uncommon among Roman Catholics.

New Testament names are shared by Christians of all sects and persuasions, and their overwhelming frequency in all the countries of Europe, as well as in North and South America, Australasia, and elsewhere, bears witness to the pervasive influence of Christianity over the past millennium. It is only in the Islamic world and the Far East that New Testament names are rare or not used.

The most important names in the New Testament are those of the four evangelists, *Matthew, Mark, Luke*, and *John*, and the apostles, principally *Peter, James, Andrew, Thomas, Philip, Bartholomew, John, Matthew*, and *Simon*. The gospels agree that there were twelve apostles (twelve was a number with symbolic significance in Judaic tradition, as witness the twelve tribes of Israel). However, they do not agree on the precise identity of the twelve names. The picture is further complicated by the fact that in at least one case (*James*) the same name was shared by two different apostles, and by the fact that St Paul is generally regarded as an apostle, and indeed refers to himself in his letters as 'an apostle, not of men, neither by men, but by Jesus Christ, and God the Father, who raised him from the dead' (Galatians 1: 1). There is no evidence that St Paul knew Christ personally before the Crucifixion, so he was not one of the original twelve.

John is trebly important as a Christian name based on the New Testament: it was borne by an apostle (the son of Zebedee), by the author of the fourth gospel, and by the forerunner of Christ, John the Baptist. In France, Italy, and elsewhere, compound names such as *Jean-Baptiste* and *Giambattista* distinguish the Baptist from the apostle and the evangelist. The frequency of forms of *John* among early Christians ensured that it would be borne by some early saints, which further reinforced its conventional status.

With the exception of Mary, the mother of Jesus, very few women play a major role in the gospels. This helps to explain why the set of conventional female Christian names is even smaller than that for males, and why *Mary* has been so enormously popular.

In Roman Catholic countries the Virgin Mary is the subject of a religious cult of great importance and influence. In Spain, in particular, a set of female names has grown up associated with different aspects of this cult: names such as *Dolores*, *Mercedes*, *Concepción*, *Presentación*, and *Candelaria*. In some cases, for example *Pilar* and *Rosario*, these are used as female names even though the vocabulary word from which each is derived is masculine.

The name *Mary* is borne by others in the New Testament—principally Mary Magdalene, a woman who 'had been healed of evil spirits and infirmities' (Luke 8), and who was identified in Christian tradition with the repentant sinner of Luke 7. The French name *Madeleine* was coined with reference to this particular Mary, although in fact *Magdalene* in the New Testament is not a personal name, but refers to a placename. Other important New Testament female names from the gospels are *Martha* and *Elizabeth*. The latter was borne by the mother of John the Baptist (Luke 1: 5), although the name of his father, *Zacharias*, never achieved similar popularity.

Some equally popular Christian names are derived from Christian folk tradition rather than from the Bible itself. For example, *Anne* was, according to an ancient tradition, borne by the mother of the Virgin Mary. There is, however, no support for this story in the New Testament itself.

The stock of Christian names, especially female names, was augmented from the early centuries AD onwards by use of names found in the Acts of the Apostles and St Paul's Epistles. One of the best known is *Timothy*, the name of St Paul's companion, but even the names of characters who are no more than mentioned in passing were picked up eagerly in the Christian naming tradition. Among female names so transmitted are *Berenice, Chloe, Dorcas, Drusilla, Julia, Lois, Lydia, Priscilla,* and *Rhoda*. A few male names also fall into this category, notably *Felix* and *Jason*. However, it will readily be seen that names borne by minor characters in the Acts and the Epistles have achieved only a fraction of the popularity of the names of the apostles and other principal characters of the gospels.

SAINTS' NAMES

A very large number of European names owe their importance to the fact that they were borne by early, famous, or canonized Christians. These include an extraordinarily wide variety of different personalities, ranging from learned Church fathers (*Athanasius, Basil, Ambrose, Jerome, Augustine,* and *Gregory*) through innumerable martyrs (*Agatha, Agnes, Anastasia, Lucilla, Lucia; Lucian, Laurence, Sebastian*), mystics, ascetics, and visionaries (*Anthony, Simeon, Francis, Teresa*), founders of religious orders (*Benedict, Bernard, Dominic*), to the simple 19th-century French peasant girl (*Bernadette*), whose visions of the Virgin Mary led to the foundation of a healing shrine at Lourdes.

What they all have in common is that at some time during the past two millennia a cult grew up around them. In some cases (*Christopher, George, Blaise*) the legends of the cult have obscured any basis of historical fact that may once have existed. In other cases the facts about the lives and doings of the early saints are well known and well documented.

NAMES OF CLASSICAL ANTIQUITY

Christian sainthood is almost the only channel by which old Roman names have been transmitted to present-day use as given names. In spite of the pervasive use of Latin during most of the Christian era, Roman names that were not borne by early saints have almost entirely dropped out of use. This is because, officially at any rate, the early Church made repeated attempts to suppress classical literature and to obliterate all memory of pagan classical history. The role of Latin before the Reformation was as a liturgical language and lingua franca, not as the language of pagan civilization and literature. In the Christian era, therefore, there has been almost no tradition of naming children in honour of the great and admired figures of classical antiquity. Where a

Roman name such as *Antonius*, *Claudius*, *Julius*, or *Marcus* has yielded modern derivatives, we may look with confidence for an early saint or martyr somewhere along the road.

The same is even more true of ancient Greek names, although since modern Greece took up and won the struggle for independence from Turkey, ancient Greek names such as *Sophocles*, *Socrates*, *Aristotle*, and *Thucydides* have become commonplace in Greece itself. They also now occur occasionally, rather surprisingly, in South America, so that combinations such as *Epaminondas López* may be found. However, these are still the exceptions rather than the rule. Insofar as they are not common and conventional at the present time outside Greece, classical Greek names have not been included in this book.

LOCAL CULTS AND PATRON SAINTS

In many places in Europe, the name of a local saint is regularly used within a small community, but has not spread far beyond it. St Leocadia of Toledo, St Godleva of Flanders, St Pons of Cimiez, and St Brizio of Spoleto are examples of saints whose cults are highly localized, and with them their names.

In other cases a local saint's name has become much more widespread. Because of the cultural importance of Paris, the names of its patron saints, *Denis* and *Geneviève*, have become popular far beyond the French capital, and indeed beyond the boundaries of France itself. *Didier* is widespread in France, having been borne by at least four different early saints and bishops, in Langres, Auxerre, Cahors, and Vienne. Similarly, *Gennaro*, the name of the patron saint of Naples, is found mainly in the south of Italy, but has certainly spread beyond Naples itself.

Status as a national patron saint is even more influential, as can be seen in the cases of St George of England, St Andrew of Scotland, St David of Wales, St Patrick of Ireland, and St Birgit of Sweden. This explains why *Beat* is still found in use as a Swiss male given name: St Beatus is venerated as the apostle of Switzerland, although he is a shadowy figure—even his dates are uncertain.

Saints can also function as patrons of particular occupations, and we find cases where this, too, influences the choice of a name. It is not unusual for the daughter of music-loving parents to be named after St Cecilia, the patron saint of music. A more mundane example is the choice of *Baldomero* as a name for the son of a Spanish locksmith, after St Baldomar, the patron of locksmiths in Provence and Iberia.

NAMES ASSOCIATED WITH PARTICULAR RELIGIOUS DENOMINATIONS

A number of given names are associated with particular Christian groups: *Calvin*, *Luther*, and *Wesley* are the main examples borne by Protestants. Among Mormons, *Brigham* is sometimes used in honour of their early leader Brigham Young. By contrast, certain names are found exclusively or almost exclusively among Roman Catholics: examples are *Aloysius*, *Xavier*, and *Ignatius*.

ROYAL AND ARISTOCRATIC NAMES

A name that is borne by a member of a royal family, especially a successful and much-admired monarch, invariably rapidly increases its currency among his or her subjects. Thus, the popularity of the New Testament name *Elizabeth* was enormously enhanced by the fact that it was borne by the enlightened and skilful queen of England who reigned 1558–1603. It has remained popular, partly because of that association, ever since. Its popularity increased again in the 20th century, after it became clear in 1936 that the then Princess Elizabeth would be heir to the throne.

Elizabeth, like *James* and *John*, is a biblical name, firmly rooted in the Christian tradition. However, the majority of English, and indeed European, royal names derive from a pre-Christian, pagan tradition. English speakers are sometimes surprised to discover that ordinary, everyday names such as *William*, *Henry*, *Richard*, and *Robert*, not to mention *Charles*, have their origin in a distant, pre-Christian Germanic past. Moreover, these names have not even been transmitted to us through Old English. With the exception of *Edward*, most names of Old English derivation, even royal names, went out of use some time after the Norman Conquest. *Edward* survived, mainly because King Edward the Confessor was venerated by Normans and Saxons alike. Other names derived from Old English, such as *Alfred* and *Edwin*, *Audrey* and *Elfreda*, were revived in the Victorian period. Many of them now once again seem somewhat old-fashioned.

A few modern English first names reflect Old Norse personal names established in England before the Norman Conquest, such as *Harold*. However, the Normans themselves had abandoned their Norse language and pagan culture when they settled in northern France in the 10th century. Even more surprisingly, they abandoned their traditional Norse names. Within a few decades, they adopted the Christian religion, the French language, and French names. It so happens that although the French language is mainly derived from Latin, many French names are derived from Germanic. These are survivals of the ancient names that were used in the Germanic languages once spoken in France, in particular Frankish, the vernacular of the court of Charlemagne. Thus, *William* is from *wil* meaning 'will' plus *helm* meaning 'helmet'. Its cognates, French *Guillaume* and German *Wilhelm*, are from the same source. Germanic names are normally 'dithematic': that is, they consist of two vocabulary elements. These names are often extremely ancient, the elements reflecting qualities that were prized in prehistoric Germanic society: they have meanings such as 'war', 'strife', 'battle'; 'protection', 'rule', 'counsel'; 'raven', 'wolf', and 'bear'.

Many, but not all, of the most common male names of Germanic origin that are used in Britain today owe their importance to having been royal names: they were borne by one or more kings of England (or, as in the case of *Robert*, Scotland). But some, such as *Gerald*, *Hugh*, and *Roger*, were borne by members of the aristocracy rather than royalty.

Rather fewer Germanic female names, such as *Alice*, *Emma*, and *Matilda*, have survived into modern English. Generally, they are no less warlike in meaning than their male counterparts. The origins of these Germanic names owe nothing to Christianity, although in some cases, for example *Bernard*, their survival does: many such names were borne by people who became Christian saints, after whom children were named in succeeding generations.

Elsewhere in Europe the story is similar. *Louis*, *Charles*, and *Henri* became well established as French given names because from an early period they were borne by kings of France. *Hugues* is an ancient royal and aristocratic name, which was borne by Hugues Capet, founder of the Capetian dynasty.

In the German kingdoms and principalities the most popular names, alongside those of Christian origin, were those borne by royalty and princes: *Otto*, *Ludwig*, *Friedrich*, *Albrecht*, and *Wilhelm*, for example. In the Austro-Hungarian Empire we find extensive use of names favoured by the Habsburgs, such as *Rudolf*, *Franz*, and *Josef*. When a name of Spanish origin, *Ferdinand*, was brought by marriage into the imperial family, it soon came into use among their subjects as well.

Likewise in Eastern Europe, the traditional names once borne by famous kings are firmly established and continue to enjoy great popularity. Examples are *Kazimierz* and *Władysław* in Poland and *László* in Hungary.

THE CELTIC TRADITION

After Christianity and Germanic royalty, the greatest influence on the stock of names in the English-speaking world has been the Celtic tradition. Its influence has sometimes been underestimated. Many names are now used throughout the world by people who may be only vaguely aware, if at all, of their derivation from Irish or Scottish Gaelic or from Welsh. Examples are *Barry, Brian, Bridget, Donald, Duncan, Ian, Kenneth, Kevin, Neil,* and *Sheila* from Irish and Scottish Gaelic, and *Gareth, Gladys, Gwendolen,* and *Trevor* from Welsh. These are all Anglicizations of Celtic names. Other Celtic names exist in an Anglicized form, but are still used mainly by people conscious of their Celtic ancestry. Examples are *Brendan, Connor, Cormac, Declan,* and *Rory* from Gaelic and *Branwen, Dylan, Dilys, Gwyneth, Olwen,* and *Wyn* from Welsh.

In Ireland, Gaelic names such as *Aodh, Conchúr, Meadhbh,* and *Naoise* have survived in Gaelic-speaking areas from generation to generation among a rural community who were normally illiterate in Irish, English being the only language permitted for education. Increasingly now, the same is true of Scottish Gaelic names in the Highlands and Islands of Scotland. It is now fashionable, especially in Ireland, even among city-dwellers to revive such names in their original form, unscrambling the garblings due to Anglicization. It is also fashionable to bestow Gaelic names such as *Fiona* on children, and this has led not only to revivals but also to new coinages based on Gaelic, widely used by the Irish and by Highland Scots, including those who no longer speak the ancient language of their forebears.

The phonology of Gaelic is very different from that of English, and the spelling system of the Gaelic languages has its own logic. The medieval Gaelic spelling system is largely preserved, so that etymological connections can normally be perceived, which would not be apparent if a purely phonetic modern orthography were adopted. Gaelic names can therefore look very different from English names, even when they are quite closely equivalent. For example, the Irish Gaelic form of *George* is *Seoirse.* Irish *Séamas* and Scottish *Seumas* are the Gaelic equivalents of English *James.* The vocative case of the latter, *Sheumais*, has been re-Anglicized as *Hamish.* The Irish name *Siobhán* (Scottish Gaelic *Siubhan*), related to English *Jane*, has in recent years been Anglicized as *Shevaun* and *Chevonne*; its cognate *Síne* is found in the Anglicized form *Sheena.*

Thanks to the generous help of two leading Gaelic scholars, Professor Tomás de Bhaldraithe and Mr Ronald Black, this dictionary has attempted to unravel some of the complexities of Gaelic personal names, showing both the Gaelic versions of common European names and the unique contribution of the Gaelic tradition. We have also recorded new coinages where we have encountered them. In 1981 an excellent small book on *Gaelic Personal Names*, by Donnchadh Ó Corráin and Fidelma Maguire, was published in Dublin; this has a strong orientation towards Irish history. An equivalent work on Scottish Gaelic names is still wanting: until such time as a specialist study can be undertaken, Mr Black's contribution to the present work will, it is hoped, help to go some way towards supplying the deficiency.

A striking feature of the Gaelic naming tradition is the antiquity of its independence and folklore. It seems to predate the royal names of English by a millennium and more. *Meadhbh* (*Maeve*) recalls a 1st-century queen of Connacht, leader of 'the Cattle Raid of Cooley'. The name *Deirdre* recalls the tragic story of a beautiful girl betrothed against her will to Conchobhar (*Connor*) and her elopement with her beloved Naoise, who is eventually caught and killed by Conchobhar. The historical events on which this famous story is based probably took place at around the time of Christ.

Other names recall pre-Christian beliefs that vanished some fourteen hundred years ago. *Aodh* (the Anglicized form of which is *Hugh*) is the name of a Celtic sun god. *Niamh* is the daughter of the sea god, who falls in love with the hero Oisín, son of Finn MacCool, and carries him off to her kingdom beyond the sea. Several Irish and Scottish Gaelic names currently in use are associated with ancient myths such as these.

The influence of Christianity has been as profound on Irish names as on any naming tradition in Europe. The names of St Patrick (*Pádraig*) and St Bridget (*Brighid*) are characteristically Irish names bestowed in honour of the Christian saints who bore them. The Irish saint who brought Christianity to the Gaels and Picts of Scotland in the 6th century is commemorated both in the name *Calum* and in *Malcolm* ('servant of Calum'). The name, which is traditionally given as *Columba* 'dove' in Latin, reminds us of the influence of Latin on early Christian names in Ireland. *Patrick* itself is derived via Irish *Pádraig* from Latin *Patricius* 'nobleman'.

During the Dark Ages, Christianity was as firmly established in Ireland as it was in Rome, and Irishmen were appointed to bishoprics in every part of Europe. Many of them set out as missionaries to pagan areas, and this explains, for example, why the Irish name *Colmán* (*Columbanus*, *Kálmán*) is popular in Hungary, and *Gall* (*Gaweł*) in Poland.

In Scotland, where the Gaels settled from the 5th century onwards, particular names are sometimes associated with particular clans. So, for example, the name *Somerled* (*Somhairle* in Scottish Gaelic, Anglicized as *Sorley*) is traditionally associated with Clan Macdonald, the kindred of the Lords of the Isles. Mention of this name reminds us of the interplay between Gaelic names and Norse names. Gaelic *Amhlaoibh/Amhlaidh, Somhairle, Tormod, Ùisdean, Sgàire*, and even *Raghnall* (*Ronald*) are from Norse, while Norse names such as *Njall* and *Birgit* are from Gaelic.

In the 18th century, the rise of fashionable interest in the Celtic twilight led James Macpherson to compose a series of 'ancient epic poems' (1762–3) purporting to be by Ossian (*Oisín, Oisein*), son of Fingal. These poems were admired by Goethe and Schiller amongst others, and by Napoleon, with a curious sequel for the history of personal names. Some of Napoleon's godchildren were christened with 'Ossianic' names such as *Oscar, Selma, Morna*, and *Malvina*. When Napoleon's marshal Bernadotte accepted the invitation to take the throne of Sweden, the Ossianic name *Oscar* became established as a Scandinavian royal name.

Welsh names are of similar antiquity, though there are fewer traditional names surviving in Welsh than in Gaelic. Many of the old Welsh names that are now in use or being revived are found in the *Mabinogi*, a medieval collection of ancient legends. These names include *Branwen, Lleu, Geraint, Heilyn, Iorwerth, Rhiannon, Urien, Ynyr*, and *Pryderi*. Another group of traditional Welsh names commemorates heroes and princes who led resistance variously to the Romans (*Caradoc*), the Saxons (*Cadwaladr*), and the English (*Llewelyn, Glyndŵr*). Also found are Welsh forms of Norman and English names introduced in the Middle Ages and later (*Siôn, Siân, Siarl*).

By far the most important Welsh source of names, in many different European languages, is the cycle of Arthurian legends. The historical Arthur is a shadowy, legendary figure who led British resistance to the Saxon invasions of Britain in the 5th or 6th century AD. From the Middle Ages onwards a vast body of European literature grew up around the subject of King Arthur and his knights. Names derived from this tradition include *Elaine, Enid, Gavin* (*Gawain*), *Guinevere, Lancelot, Merlin* (*Myrddin*), *Percival*, and *Tristram* (*Tristan*) and *Isolde* (*Yseult*, Welsh *Esyllt*).

The present century is witnessing not only a revival of traditional Welsh names but also an influx of new coinages. These are mainly from vocabulary elements (e.g. *Eirwen* 'snow-pure', *Glenda* 'clean-good'), but also from placenames such as *Arfon, Eifion, Dyfed*, and *Trefor*.

We are grateful to Professor Gwynedd Pierce for his advice on Welsh names.

THE INFLUENCE OF LITERATURE, FILM, AND POPULAR CULTURE

Works of literature can have a profound influence on name choices. The widespread influence of Arthurian legend on European naming has already been mentioned. The names of some of Shakespeare's heroines have been used as given names, for example *Rosalind, Olivia, Portia, Perdita, Imogen, Juliet,* and *Cordelia.* However, on the whole, the names of Shakespeare's characters have been less influential than might have been expected. Many Shakespearean names are those of historical or supposedly historical characters (*Hal, Troilus, Macbeth*); others are Italianate (*Antonio, Claudio, Viola*); others, especially male names (*Florizel, Prospero, Hamlet*), seem to have been simply too outlandish to have achieved popular status.

Other writers have influenced particular names. Thus, *Pamela* and *Clarissa* probably owe much if not all of their popularity to novels by Samuel Richardson; *Amelia* to Henry Fielding; *Nicol* to Sir Walter Scott; *Justine* to Lawrence Durrell; *Leila* to Byron and Lord Lytton; *Christabel* to Samuel Taylor Coleridge; *Maud* and *Vivien* to Alfred, Lord Tennyson; and *Pippa* to Browning. In the 19th century, the given name *Shirley* (which is derived via a surname from a placename) changed sex, becoming a conventional female name after publication of Charlotte Brontë's novel *Shirley* in 1849.

Literary influence is not, of course, confined to the English language. In Italy, for example, the same phenomenon may be observed in the name *Loredana*, which was coined by Luciano Zuccoli for a novel published in 1908, and *Ornella*, in Gabriele d'Annunzio's *Figlia de Ioro* (1904). The phenomenon is long established, as the influence of Dante and Petrarch on the names *Beatrice* and *Laura* bears witness.

The literary quality of a work is a less influential factor than its wide readership and ability to capture the popular imagination. All the writers mentioned above have enjoyed perennial popularity, but in addition some more ephemeral works have played a major part in establishing certain names. Paul Leicester Ford's novel *Janice Meredith*, published in 1899, is little read nowadays, but the name *Janice* owes its popularity to that work.

The most striking example of the influence of a work of literature on the choice of names is Margaret Mitchell's novel *Gone with the*

Wind (1936), which was made into a popular film in 1939. The names of most of the characters were invented by the author, and so their adoption as conventional given names can be pinpointed precisely and attributed to this work. It was largely or wholly responsible for the names *Bonnie*, *Rhett*, *Scarlett*, and *Careen* among others.

In the 20th century, films have had a considerable influence on the choice of names. *Tracy*, for example, underwent a great increase in popularity as a female name from the late 1950s onwards, after release of the 1956 film *High Society*, in which Grace Kelly played the character of Tracy Lord.

Not only fictional characters but also the actors who portray them can have an influence on the popularity of a name. *Greer*, *Cary*, and *Spencer*, for example, have been chosen as names in honour of the film stars Greer Garson, Cary Grant, and Spencer Tracy. *Claudette* increased in popularity in the English-speaking world because of the fame of the film actress Claudette Colbert. Where a film star, or a character in film or popular fiction, bears a name that is already well established the influence is more difficult to trace. However, the influence of glamour is undeniable: it seems very likely that the popular status of *Humphrey* was improved by Bogart, *Clark* by Gable, *Trevor* by Howard, *James* by Cagney and Dean, *Jean* by Harlow, *Jane* by Russell, and *Marilyn* by Monroe.

Another characteristically 20th-century influence is that of rock and pop music: the rise of *Elvis* is clearly traceable, but we can only guess how many present-day Johns and Pauls owe their name to Lennon and McCartney.

Soap operas, too, influence the choice of names, as witness the rise during the late 1980s of *Charlene*, in Britain as well as Australia. This is the name of a character played by Kylie Minogue in the Australian soap opera *Neighbours*. And of course the popularity of *Kylie* itself derives from the same source.

SURNAMES AS GIVEN NAMES

In the English-speaking world a large number of surnames are in use as given names: only those are recorded here that have acquired conventional status.

Surnames had been sporadically used as first names for several centuries, mainly among landed families: for example the Skeffingtons, among whom the surname *Clotworthy* was in regular use as a first name. In the 19th century, however, this phenomenon became more frequent. In most cases it originated because of a close relationship or connection between families—usually by marriage. A bride from a rich and powerful family would christen her first-born with her own maiden surname; the conjunction of the two names would be taken as symbolic of the union between the two families. Gradually, the practice became more and more widespread. Use of the mother's maiden name as a *second* given name has been an especially common practice among English speakers in the 20th century.

Some given names that were derived originally from surnames have become fully established as freely used first names in their own right (e.g. *Clifford*, *Dudley*, *Stanley*). Many more are fairly frequently used as such (e.g. *Kendal*, *Kingsley*, *Marshall*). In Britain such names are almost always borne by males, apart from a few conventionalized exceptions (e.g. *Shirley*, *Beverley*, *Kimberley*).

A number of Scottish surnames have become very common as conventional English given names, including *Keith*, *Douglas*, *Fraser*, *Graham*, and *Leslie*. The latter, in the *-ie* spelling, has become conventionalized as a female name. The spelling *Lesley* is used for both sexes.

Some Old English personal names have become modern first names by an indirect route, i.e. through the transferred use of surnames that were derived from them during the early Middle Ages. Examples are *Goddard*, *Goodwin*, and *Osborn*.

OTHER SOURCES OF GIVEN NAMES

We have now mentioned the main sources of traditional given names, but there are many other sources from which a personal name may be derived. Some of these can be rather ephemeral.

Since the 19th century, several different types of vocabulary word have been used as given names: in particular, words denoting precious stones (*Beryl*, *Ruby*) and flowers (*Daisy*, *Primrose*). Sometimes a vocabulary word denoting a desirable quality for the life ahead is bestowed on a baby, as in the case of the names *Joy*, *Happy; Fortunato*, *Bonifacio*, and *Felix*.

Occasionally, a placename will be found in use as a given name. Several of the Western Isles and other parts of Scotland have been used in this way, notably *Isla(y)* and *Iona*, less commonly *Lewis* and *Uist*, *Lorne* and *Athol*, and the river name *Clyde*. Otherwise, this source of given names is unusual except through the mediation of a surname.

Nicknames rarely become established as personal names, but pet forms such as *Peggy* and *Bill* can take on a life of their own. American examples include *Chuck* and *Bud*. Some short forms or pet forms are more commonly used than the more formal version, as in the case of *Reg/Reginald*. In other cases, a short name such as *Max* or *Kim* may be used in its own right, and strangers may wrongly identify it as a 'short form' of a longer name such as *Maxwell* or *Kimberley*.

The Slavonic languages are particularly rich in pet forms, and use of the official version of a person's name can sound cold and formal. However, there is very rarely any confusion in such languages as to what is an appropriate pet form and what is the full form to which each belongs. In English, by contrast, a name such as *Jack* can be taken variously as a pet form of *John* or *James* or as a name in its own right.

MASCULINE AND FEMININE

Many female names in Christian cultures are derived from male names—names such as *Joan, Jane, Janet,* and *Seònaid* (all members of the 'John' group), or *Petra, Paula, Georgina,* and *Simone*. One reason for this is that for the past two thousand years and more, European societies have been male-dominated and patrilineal. Another factor is that comparatively few women are mentioned by name in the gospels.

In languages such as Italian, where normally the inflection clearly indicates whether a name is male or female, there is no difficulty in creating a feminine equivalent of a male name, such as *Giovanna* from *Giovanni*, and vice versa in rarer cases such as *Carmela/Carmelo*.

In English and some other languages, certain diminutive suffixes have become conventional signs of feminine gender, for example *-et* as well as *-ette*, and *-een/-ene*, the latter being at least in part derived from Irish *-ín*. These endings are now commonly used as elements in the coining of new female names.

NAMING PRACTICES IN DIFFERENT CULTURES

ENGLISH COINAGES SINCE THE 17TH CENTURY

Some Old Testament names were in occasional use throughout the Middle Ages, but they became far more frequent during the 17th century, and more of them were brought into use under the influence of Puritan reformers. A few, such as *Jabez*, *Saul*, and *Solomon*, became for a while part of the common stock of usual first names. They subsequently declined in popularity, were modestly revived during the Victorian period, and are now once again uncommon, except as Jewish names. At the height of the vogue for Old Testament names in the

17th century, some very unlikely sounding names were taken from incidental mentions and genealogical lists, and even biblical place-names were pressed into service, for example *Ebenezer*. Another innovation of the Puritans was the use of vocabulary words and phrases as first names: *Praisegod*, *Livewell*, *Truth*, *Increase*. These were for the most part nonce coinages, and the vogue quickly passed, but a few names denoting virtuous qualities (*Faith*, *Joy*, *Patience*) have survived from that period as standard female names.

During the 18th century, the stock of first names was modestly increased by the adoption in real life of various consciously literary coinages or far-fetched borrowings, fanciful names bestowed on romantic heroines and then used in real life. Examples are *Clarinda*, *Pamela*, and *Vanessa*.

The Victorian era was a period of further expansion in the stock of first names, which occurred in two principal ways. On the one hand both Old English and Old Testament names were revived, while on the other hand new first names were created from surnames and from vocabulary words.

In the 20th century, the number of names used regularly has continued to grow apace. The use of vocabulary words as first names for women has increased, and the two categories mentioned earlier (gemstones and flowers) have been expanded to include other precious and desirable things (*Amber*, *Jade*, *Crystal*), plants (*Bryony*, *Fern*, *Poppy*), and birds (*Kestrel*, *Teale*). Names from other parts of the world have been enthusiastically adopted, beginning in the early years of the century with Russian names introduced via France (*Vera*, *Tanya*, *Natasha*). A couple of decades later, there was a vogue for names of Scandinavian origin (*Ingrid*, *Astrid*). Currently, certain fanciful inventions, combinations, and respellings are gaining ground, a process formerly more associated with America (see below).

MODERN GIVEN NAMES IN AMERICA

The first European names to be established in America were those in use among Puritan settlers. Some of the more unusual Old Testament names (see above) remain in steady use, especially in rural areas: *Jed* (*Jedidiah*), *Zeke* (*Ezekiel*), *Hephzibah*, *Zillah*.

A later American naming practice, less common in Britain, is the adoption of surnames as first names, not because of any family connection, but out of admiration for some famous contemporary or historical figure so called (*Chauncey*, *Wesley*, *Sandford*). A number of American presidents have been so honoured, in particular *Washington* and *Lin-*

coln. From presidential forenames come the names *Franklin*, *Lyndon*, *Grover*, and *Woodrow*. The last two, incidentally, were surnames given as middle names and later preferred as forenames by their bearers. The full names of the presidents in question were *Stephen Grover Cleveland* and *Thomas Woodrow Wilson*.

Many first names derived from surnames are in America borne by women. A few are conventionalized in this use (*Brooke*, *Paige*) but many more are used equally for either sex, so that it is often not possible to determine the gender of a bearer from the name alone. Even conventional male first names, such as *Sean*, are coming increasingly to be bestowed on girls as well.

Another process of name creation long established in America is that of free invention. Formerly regarded as typical of the southern states, this has in the second half of the present century become more widespread. Most of the coined names are borne by women. Strategies include fanciful respelling (*Kathryn* (now the predominant form in America), *Madalynne*, *Ilayne*); minor alterations in currently popular names (*Jenna*, *Deloris*); the combining of syllables from existing names (*Jolene*, *Lolicia*); elaborations with productive feminine suffixes (such as *-elle*, *-ette*, *-ice*, *-inda*, *-ona*, *-yl*); and outright invention (*Luvenia*, *Tawana*).

Another feature more characteristic of America than Britain is the use of pet forms as fully fledged first names in their own right, so that a *Pam* is not necessarily to be addressed more formally as *Pamela*, nor *Bobby* as *Robert*. President Carter insisted that he be officially known as *Jimmy*, although he was in fact christened *James*. In the same way, some informal nicknames have come to be bestowed as official first names (*Bud*, *Ginger*, *Rusty*). Vocabulary words that denote titles such as *Duke*, *Earl*, and *Prince* are also regularly used as first names.

BLACK NAMES

In both America and Britain, the names borne by Blacks differ to an extent from those of the White population. They contain a high proportion of freely invented names of the kind just mentioned. These are commonly borne by males as well as females.

Characteristic Black names also include adopted European forms (*Antonio*, *Antoine*, *Anton*) and some surname forms that are much less common among the population as a whole (*Curtis*, *Leroy*, *Winston*).

It is possible to detect certain fashionable processes at work in the forming of new Black names, for example the prefixing of *De-* to male names (*Dejuan*, *Deshawn*). This probably originated by extraction from

Italian patronymic surnames such as *Deangelo* and *Demarco*. The practice is matched by the prefixing of *La-* and *Sha-* to female names (*Lashauna*, *Shafaye*).

CANADA, AUSTRALIA, AND NEW ZEALAND

First names in Canada do not differ greatly from those of the United States. There are, however, a few names that are characteristically Canadian: for example *Lorne*, the recent feminine creation *Jaime*, and the hybrid respelling *Meaghan*.

Australia and New Zealand also share the same basic stock of English first names, with a rich admixture of names from other parts of Europe brought by a wide diversity of immigrants. Irish influence is strong in Australia, and the use of the surname *Kelly* as a girl's name seems to be of Australian origin. This in turn may have influenced the coinage of *Kylie*, which is usually said to be of Aboriginal origin.

Australia shares with some parts of America a convention of cheerful creativity in given names, especially female names. A characteristically Australian name is *Raelene*. *Charlene*, which is also sometimes regarded as characteristically Australian, is also found in the southern and western United States. It is not clear whether it was coined independently in the two places or whether it was borrowed by one from the other.

In New Zealand two names of Maori origin, *Ngaio* and *Nyree*, have achieved some currency.

FRENCH NAMES

In France the choice of first name is in theory legally restricted by a law of 1803 to names that have been borne by saints or by figures from ancient history. However, names occurring in the Bible (*Abel*, *Adam*) and in classical mythology (*Achille*, *Hercule*) have long been freely allowed. In the present century a much wider variety of names has become officially acceptable. In particular, words denoting flowers (*Garance*, *Guimauve*, *Pervenche*), largely drawn from the Revolutionary calendar, have passed into occasional use as girls' names. As in other Roman Catholic countries, the veneration of local and national patron saints is an important source of given names in France.

In the south of France a number of traditional Provençal names have long been in use. Some of these, such as *Mireille* and *Magali*, have become fashionable throughout France.

Breton first names are, not surprisingly, very much more restricted in geographical distribution. Although certain names such as *Guen(n)olé*, *Guenaèlle*, *Guyomard*, and *Judicael* have become well established in Brittany, there have been court battles over the more exotic names favoured by some Breton nationalists.

ITALIAN NAMES

The common given names of Italy today are all derived from names borne by saints recognized by the Roman Catholic Church. In the Middle Ages there was a comparatively wide repertoire of names in Italian, including an extensive group of Germanic names of Lombard origin (*Galimberto*, *Garibaldo*). Some of these have given rise to surnames, but most of them are no longer in use as given names.

Vocabulary phrases intended to invoke a good omen (*Benvenuto* 'welcome', *Diotiguardi* 'God preserve you') were also formerly used as given names in Italy.

Many different dialects are spoken, and the sense of regional identity is strong. Regional influences, therefore, such as the veneration of local patron saints, are prominent. For example, *Romolo* is a typical name of the Rome area; *Brizio* is more or less limited to parts of Umbria.

NAMES IN THE IBERIAN PENINSULA

In Spain the influence of the Roman Catholic Church is, if anything, more powerful than it is in Italy. Some of the well-established royal names, for example *Alfonso*, *Hernán* (*Fernando*), and *Rodrigo*, and a few other names, including *Elvira* and *Gonzalo*, are of Visigothic origin. Apart from the royal names, those that survived did so by virtue of having been borne by Christian saints. Veneration of the local patron saint is as strong in Spain as it is in Italy. St Ramiro of León, St Elodia of Huesca, and St Sandalio of Cordoba are examples of local patron saints who happened to bear Visigothic names. Of many of the other Germanic names introduced by the Visigoths (*Amalasunta*, *Sisebuto*) there is now little trace.

A striking feature of Spanish names is the large number of female names that refer to epithets or aspects of the cult of the Virgin Mary, mentioned earlier. Often these are affixed to the overwhelmingly common first name *María*, as, for example, *María de las Mercedes*, *María del Amor*. Some of these references (*Angosto*, *Aranzazu*) are to minor local cults, and many such names are confined to a particular region, within which they may be enormously popular.

A further, related group of names refers to festivals and symbolic objects associated with the Church and particularly with the adoration of the Virgin: *Concepción*, *Anunciación*, *Asunción*, *Resurección*, and *Rosario*. These names may in theory be borne by both men and women, but in practice they are nowadays largely confined to women, and are so marked in the dictionary. Similar names are to a lesser extent found in Italy (*Concetta*, *Assunta*) and Ireland (*Concepta*, *Assumpta*).

The Spanish language is also notable for its extensive use of affective forms of first names, readily employing a variety of diminutives (*Juanito*, *Teresita*), pet forms (*Charo*, *Chus*, *Manolo*, *Quique*), and contractions (*Maripi*, *Maica*).

In western Spain, speakers of Galician use forms such as *Xoán* and *Xosé*.

Catalan names are found in the north-east of Spain. Some of them are closely related to the Provençal names of southern France. The most typical of them is *Jordi*, the name of the patron saint of Catalonia.

In the Basque country are found saints' names (*Txomin*, *Gorka*) and vernacular religious names, some of which (*Jasone*, *Sorne*) have common Spanish equivalents. Others (*Arrene*, *Izaga*) are unique to Basque.

Portuguese names are very similar in character and often in form also to those of Spain. A peculiarly Portuguese feature is the adaptation of names from classical antiquity (*Péricles*, *Pompeu*, *Tucídides*, *Lucrécio*). These are, however, comparatively unusual.

GERMAN NAMES

In Germany and Austria some ancient Germanic names are still in use for which cognates are not found in other parts of Europe (e.g. *Helmut*, *Berthold*). Many of these have been in use continuously from the early Middle Ages to the present day, although they have from time to time faced strong competition from biblical names and the Greek and Latin names of early saints. Nowadays many of the less common Germanic names, especially women's names (*Waltraut*, *Gerlinde*), which were revived during the last century under the influence of Romantic enthusiasm for early Germanic mythology, are again out of fashion.

Names borne by members of the royal and imperial families in German-speaking countries were particularly well established, e.g. *Friedrich* and *Wilhelm* in Prussia, *Ernst* and *August* in Saxony, *Ludwig* in Bavaria, and *Franz*, *Josef*, and *Ferdinand* in Austria. However, the regional loyalties of German names were never as strong as those of Italy.

Another characteristic of German nomenclature is the group of pious names formed during the Reformation on the model of traditional dithematic names, but composed of elements of Christian significance, for example *Gottlob* and *Hilfgott*. These survived through the 19th century, but many of them are now felt to be rather old-fashioned.

Certain linguistic features may be regarded as characteristic of different regions of Germany. The Low German dialects in the north have many hypocoristic forms ending in *-ke*, and some names long common there have in the past couple of decades become more popular throughout both the Federal and the Democratic Republic.

In southern Germany and Austria hypocoristic forms typically end in *-l* and *-i* (*Gretel*, *Poldi*). Certain names are characteristically Austrian, for example *Leopold*, the name of the country's patron saint. In Switzerland hypocoristic forms tend to end in *-i* and *-li* (*Mitzi*, *Resli*). Several names of local saints (*Regula*, *Reto*, *Pirmin*) are scarcely used outside Switzerland. The influence of the Roman Catholic Church, too, is strong in south Germany and in Austria, encouraging the use of names such as *Alois* and *Theresia*.

In the eastern regions of Germany, Slavonic influence can be observed on the choice of first names (*Wenzel*, *Stenzel*) and on hypocoristic forms (*Anja*, *Anke*, *Annuschke*).

NAMES IN THE NETHERLANDS AND BELGIUM

Some of the first names of the Netherlands are similar to the Low German names of north Germany. They are distinguished by a large number of pet forms, which are only with difficulty to be related to the base form (*Jaap*, *Joop*, *Mies*). Considering the small size of the country, Dutch has a particularly rich variety of different local forms of personal names.

Some Frisian names preserve what appear to be old Germanic monothematic bynames, often of uncertain derivation (*Boje*, *Ibbe*).

Among the Flemish-speakers of Belgium, substantially the same names are used as in the Netherlands, often with slight differences in spelling, for example *Blaes* instead of the usual Dutch *Blaas*. Certain typically Belgian names of Germanic origin have been adopted by French-speaking Walloons in a French spelling, for example *Baudouin*.

SCANDINAVIAN NAMES

The most striking aspect of names in Scandinavia, outside Finland, is that a large number of Old Norse names have survived to the present day. Names of Christian origin are indeed found in Scandinavia, such as *Anders* (Andrew), *Johan* (John), and *Anna*, but they are rivalled by more ancient Norse names, which it has been fashionable to revive in all parts of Scandinavia since the 19th century. In some cases this revival has led to the coinage of new names not actually attested in Old Norse literature or inscriptions, but made up from combinations of elements found in the ancient names.

Many of these names go back to the characters of Norse legends and sagas (*Sigurd*, *Gunnar*, *Gudrun*). Generally they are dithematic—that is, they are composed of two parts etymologically, using such elements as *arn* eagle, *björn* bear, *úlfr* wolf, *sigr* victory, *gunr* strife, and *rún* secret lore. Names of the old gods are found as elements too: in particular *Þórr*, the god of thunder.

In Scandinavia, as elsewhere, use of a name by a monarch has had a profound influence on its popularity: this is true not only of comparatively recent royal names such as *Gustav* and *Margrethe*, but also of more ancient ones such as *Knut*, *Olav*, and *Håkon*.

Some of the names derived from Old Norse forms are monothematic: these represent in part historic or modern shortenings of the more usual dithematic names (*Stein*, *Tor*), in part ancient or medieval bynames formed from vocabulary words (*Frode*, *Bror*).

Some Celtic influence on Scandinavian names is detectable, too. The patron saint of Sweden, *Birgit*, is one example, being of Irish origin. The influence of Ossianic names has already been mentioned in the section on the Celtic tradition.

There are few differences in most Scandinavian names between Danish, Swedish, and Norwegian forms, and those that exist are often no more than reflections of the different orthographic systems of the languages, e.g. Swedish *Björn* for Norwegian *Bjørn*. By the same token, we find Danish *Torbe(r)n* for Norwegian *Torbjørn*. However, not all Scandinavian names have cognate forms in all three languages. Examples of names that are characteristically Danish include *Abelone* and *Jytte*. Names found normally only in Norway include *Gro* and *Terje*, while typically Swedish names include *Birger* and *Göran*.

The given names of Finland differ greatly from those in use in the rest of Scandinavia, as a result of the distinct character of the Finnish language and culture. Finnish is not an Indo-European language. It is distantly related to Hungarian, and is quite unlike the Germanic and

Slavonic languages that are its neighbours. A few common first names in use in Finland have been borrowed from Swedish (*Pirjo*, *Pirkko*, *Oskari*). Others are derived from the names of saints, often in a heavily altered form (*Pentti*, *Ransu*). Others again are derived from vocabulary words of religious or ornamental significance (*Toivo*, *Usko*).

Our thanks are due to Docent Lena Peterson for her advice on Scandinavian names.

RUSSIAN NAMES

The overwhelming influence on Russian names has been the Orthodox Church. From an early date, the Church forbade the use of native Slavonic names, and insisted on names that had been borne by saints of the Eastern Church. This had the curious effect of ensuring that the Russian naming tradition was derived mainly from Byzantine Greek, whence such names as *Arkadi*, *Gennadi*, and *Prokop*.

Names of the traditional Slavonic dithematic type became more common towards the end of the 19th century, for example *Vsevolod*, *Vyacheslav*, either from a reading of ancient literature or by borrowing from other Slavonic languages. However, they are not widespread. A few modern names (*Ninel*, *Melor*) were created after the Revolution by enthusiasts for the new Socialist order, but these never achieved much currency either, and they are now felt to be rather dated.

A noticeable feature of Russian naming practice is the very large number of pet forms of first names in familiar use, many of them differing greatly from the base form (e.g. *Dunya* from *Avdotya*, *Sasha* from *Aleksandr*). These in turn may have further hypocoristic suffixes added to them (*Dunyasha*, *Sashura*).

Our thanks are due to Mr Paul Falla for his advice on Russian and Eastern European names.

POLISH NAMES

In Poland, by contrast, the majority of the population is staunchly Catholic. The names of the most popular saints are very often those familiar in the West, albeit in an unfamiliar spelling. In addition, a number of traditional dithematic Slavonic names are in common use (e.g. *Bogdan*, *Bronisław*, *Jaromierz*). Typical name-forming elements include *-sław* glory, *-mierz* famous, *rad-* glad, and *jaro-* spring. As in other Slavonic countries, short forms and pet forms (*Basia*, *Jarek*, *Stanek*) are very widely used in Polish. In general, everyday conversation people normally use a pet form, while the full form of a name is usually reserved for formal and official situations.

Polish royal names include *Kazimierz, Mieczysław, Zygmunt* and *Władysław*. All except *Zygmunt* are dithematic Slavonic names. *Stanisław* is famous both as a royal name and as the name of a martyred 11th-century bishop of Cracow.

CZECH NAMES

The historic former kingdom of Bohemia (*Čechy*) forms the western part of modern Czechoslovakia. The eastern part is Slovakia, whose language is closely related to Czech. The majority of common Czech given names are vernacular spellings of the saints' names that are the common heritage of the Western Church (*Ondřej* (Andrew), *Antonín* (Anthony), *Blažej* (Blaise), *Brož* (Ambrose), etc.). As in the case of Polish, there is also a substantial admixture of Slavonic dithematic names (*Bohumíl, Břetislav, Dobroslav*, etc.).

Two names of special importance to Czechs are *Ludmila*, the name of a 10th-century Bohemian saint, and *Václav* (*Wenceslaus*), the name borne by five rulers of Bohemia, including the pious Duke of Bohemia known to English carol singers as 'Good King Wenceslas'.

HUNGARIAN NAMES

Hungarian, like Finnish, to which it is distantly related, is a non-Indo-European language. Its form and structure are quite unlike those of the Indo-European languages by which it is surrounded (German, Czech, Slovak, Russian, Serbo-Croatian, Slovene, and Romanian). However, its position as the language of a major central European power, which for many years was politically united to German-speaking Austria, ensured that its names would be strongly influenced by the traditions of Western Christianity and of German-speakers, as well as by those of the Slavonic communities, many of which were at one time ruled from Budapest.

Even when they are of Latin, German, or Slavonic origin, the given names of Hungary are often far removed from the forms they have in those languages. For example, among the most common male names are *István* (from Latin *Stephanus*), *Imre* (corresponding to German *Heinrich*), *László* (from Slavonic *Vladislav*), and *Kálmán* (from Irish *Colman*, Latin *Columbānus*). Not one of these names is native to Hungary. In addition, a few given names based on Hungarian vocabulary elements have been formed as calques on names of Latin origin (e.g.

Virág on *Flora*, *Vidor* on *Hilarius*). In Hungary, uniquely in Europe, the given name follows the surname.

ROMANIAN NAMES

In spite of its location in eastern Europe, the language of Romania is of Romance origin, and the forms of the given names in use there are often quite similar to those of Italy and Spain (*Anghel*, *Ignatie*, *Rafail*, *Silvestru*). In addition, there are several names drawn from the neighbouring Slavonic areas (*Cislau*, *Ladislau*, *Mirca*).

MODERN JEWISH NAMES

Traditional Jewish names, in every country of Europe where there were Jewish communities, were and are the names of the Bible. In many places these were altered in form to conform to the phonology of the local language, in particular Yiddish in northern and eastern Europe.

Many Jewish names are common to Gentiles and Jews alike (*Joseph*, *Deborah*). Others are traditional Hebrew names (*Asher*, *Baruch*, *Hyam*), Hebrew forms (*Moshe*, *Shelomo*), Yiddish forms (*Issur*, *Motke*), and Anglicized forms (*Morton*, *Milton*). The latter two examples are used for reasons of alliteration in place of *Mordecai* or *Moshe*. There are also modern revivals of biblical Hebrew names (*Ehud*, *Yael*) and modern Hebrew coinages (*Ilan*, *Semadar*).

Our thanks are due to Dr Joseph A. Reif for his contribution to the Jewish names in this dictionary.

P.W.H., F.M.H.
January 1990

ACKNOWLEDGEMENTS

A comparative work of this kind can only hope to succeed by drawing on the expertise of scholars from many different disciplines. Advisers for particular aspects have been mentioned in the course of the introduction; a summary list is given here of those scholars who kindly gave up a great deal of their time to read the first draft of this dictionary, giving detailed comments and suggestions for additions and improvements. We are profoundly grateful to them for their efforts, which have enabled us to improve the accuracy and usefulness of the book greatly. Any errors or shortcomings that remain are of course the responsibility of the authors.

Professor Tomás de Bhaldraithe, Royal Irish Academy
Ronald Black, Lecturer in Celtic, University of Edinburgh
P. S. Falla, Editor, *Oxford English–Russian Dictionary*
Docent Lena Peterson, University of Uppsala
Professor Emeritus Gwynedd Pierce, University of Wales College of Cardiff
Dr Joseph A. Reif, Bar-Ilan University

BIBLIOGRAPHY

Albaigés Olivart, José María: *Diccionario de nombres de personas* (Barcelona, 1984).

Allén, Sture, and Staffan Wåhlin: *Förnamnsboken* (Stockholm, 1979).

Attwater, Donald: *The Penguin Dictionary of Saints* (London, 1965).

Bahlow, Hans: *Deutsches Namenlexikon* (Munich, 1967).

Baker, Glenn: *The Name Game* (London, 1986).

Barbé, Jean-Maurice, and Jean-Pierre Nortel: *Dictionnaire de prénoms* (Paris, 1980).

Benedictine Monks of St Augustine's Abbey, Ramsgate: *The Book of Saints* (London, 1947).

Benson, Morton: *Dictionary of Russian Personal Names* (Philadelphia, 1964).

Bernage, Georges: *Prénoms normands et vikings* (Paris, 1981).

Beuque, Boris, and Michèle Labracherie: *Dictionnaire pour choisir son prénom* (Paris, 1978).

Brandt, Mogens: *Hvad skal barnet hedde?* (Copenhagen, 1972).

Brice, Christopher: *Names for the Cornish* (Truro, 1970).

Brookes, Reuben and Blanche: *A Guide to Jewish Names* (Birmingham, 1967).

Brown, Michèle: *The New Book of First Names* (London, 1985).

Burgio, Alfonso: *Dizionario dei nomi propri di persona* (Rome, 1970).

Burkhart, Walter: *Neues Lexikon der Vornamen* (Köln, 1987).

Coghlan, Ronan: *Irish Christian Names* (London, 1987).

Comrie, B., and G. Stone: *The Russian Language since the Revolution* (Oxford, 1978), 179–84, 187–92.

Dauzat, Albert: *Dictionnaire étymologique des noms de famille et prénoms de France* (Paris, 1951; revised edn 1977).

Davies, Trefor: *A Book of Welsh Names* (London, 1952).

Drosdowski, Günther: *Lexikon der Vornamen* (Mannheim, 1968).

Dunkling, Leslie: *First Names First* (London, 1977).

——: *Scottish Christian Names* (London, 1979).

——, and William Gosling: *Everyman's Dictionary of First Names* (London, 1983).

Eder, Angelika: *Vornamen für Jungen und Mädchen* (Köln, 1987).

Egger, Carl: *Lexicon nominum virorum et mulierum* (Rome, 1963).

Fekete, Antal: *Keresztneveink, Védószentjeink* (Budapest, 1974).

Fergusson, Rosalind: *Choose Your Baby's Name* (London, 1987).

Freeman, William: *Dictionary of Fictional Characters* (London, 1967).

Gauk, Roma: *Ukrainian Christian Names* (Edmonton, 1961).

Gerr, Elke: *Das grosse Vornamenbuch* (Munich, 1985).

Gruffudd, Heini: *Enwau i'r Cymry/Welsh Personal Names* (Talybont, 1980).

Hanks, Patrick, and Flavia Hodges: *A Dictionary of Surnames* (Oxford, 1988).

Heller, M.: *Black Names in America* (Chicago, 1975).

Janowowa, Wanda, *et al.*: *Slownik Imion* (Warsaw, 1975).

Johnson, Charles, and Linwood Sleigh: *The Harrap Book of Boys' and Girls' Names* (London, 1983).

Kaganoff, Benzion C.: *A Dictionary of Jewish Names and their History* (New York, 1977).

Kalman, Béla: *The World of Names: A Study in Hungarian Onomatology* (Budapest, 1978).

Knappová, Miloslava: *Jak se bude jmenovat?* (Prague, 1978).

Kupis, Bogdan, *et al.*: *Księga imion* (Warsaw, 1975).

Lebel, Paul: *Les noms de personnes* (Paris, 1968).

Levchenko, S. P., *et al.*: *Slovnik vlasnikh imen lyudey* (Kiev, 1961).

Merkle, Elli and Ludwig: *Vornamen in Bayern* (Munich, 1981).

Moll, Francesc de B.: *Els llinatges catalans* (Mallorca, 1982).

Nunes, J. J.: 'Os nomes de baptismo', *Revista lusitana*, 32 (1934), 56–160; 33 (1935), 5–72; 34 (1936), 105–64; 35 (1937), 5–37.

Ó Corráin, Donnchadh, and Fidelma Maguire: *Gaelic Personal Names* (Dublin, 1981).

Otterbjörk, Roland: *Svenska förnamn* (Stockholm, 1964; 3rd edn 1979).

Pálsson, Hermann: *Íslenzk Mannanöfn* (Reykjavik, 1960).

Partridge, Eric: *Name This Child* (London, 1951).

Petrovsky, N. A.: *Slovar' russkikh lichnykh imen* (Moscow, 1966).

Raveling, Irma: *Die ostfriesischen Vornamen* (Aurich, 1972).

Satrustegi, J. M.: *Euskal izedengia* (Bilbao, 1983).

Schaar, J. van der: *Woordenboek van Voornamen* (Utrecht/Antwerp, 1981).

Seibicke, Wilfried: *Vornamen* (Wiesbaden, 1977).

Serdoch, Pedro, and Marcelo Igonda: *Diccionario Onomatologico* (Mendoza, Argentina, 1952).

Stemshaug, Ola: *Norsk Personnamnleksikon* (Oslo, 1982).

Stephens, Ruth: *Welsh Names for Children* (Talybont, 1970).

Stewart, George R.: *American Given Names* (New York, 1979).

Tagliavini, Carlo: *Origine e stori dei nomi de persona* (Bologna, 1976 and 1982).

Vasseur, Jacques and Johanna: *Grosses Namenlexicon* (Munich, 1982).

Vilkuna, Kustaa: *Etunimet* (Helsinki, 1977).

——, *et al.*: *Suomalainen nimikirja* (Helsinki, 1984).

Weekly, Ernest: *Jack and Jill* (London, 1939 and 1945).

Weitershaus, Friedrich Wilhelm: *Das neue Vornamenbuch* (Munich, 1988).

Withycombe, E. G.: *The Oxford Dictionary of English Christian Names* (Oxford, 1945; 3rd edn 1977).

Woods, Richard: *Hispanic First Names* (Chicago, 1984).

Woulfe, Patrick: *Irish Names for Children* (Dublin, 1923; revised edn 1974).

A

Aaltje (f.) Low German, Dutch, and Frisian: pet form derived from *Aalt*, a contracted form of ADELHEID.

Aaltruide (f.) Dutch form of ADELTRAUD.

Aaron (m.) Biblical: name of the brother of Moses, who was appointed by God to be Moses' spokesman, and became the first high priest of the Israelites (Exodus 4: 14–16; 7: 1–2). It is of uncertain origin and meaning but most probably, like MOSES, of Egyptian rather than Hebrew origin. The traditional derivation from Hebrew *har-on* 'mountain of strength' is no more than a folk etymology. The name has been used fairly infrequently by Christians, rather more commonly by Jews.

Variants: Jewish: **Aharon** (Hebrew); **Arn** (Yiddish).

Pet form: Yiddish: **Arke**.

Aatami (m.) Finnish form of ADAM.

Abbie (f.) 1. English: pet form of ABIGAIL, now used as an independent given name.

2. Irish: Anglicized form of GOBNAIT.

Variant: **Abbey**.

Abbondio (m.) Italian: from Late Latin *Abundius*, a derivative of *abundans* abundant, copious (genitive *abundantis*). The name was borne by a 5th-century bishop of Como, who is the subject of a local cult. The name is still most common in the Como region.

Abe (m.) 1. Jewish (two syllables): Yiddish name, from Aramaic *abba* father, which was used as a personal name in Talmudic times instead of ABRAHAM.

2. Jewish and English (one syllable): short form of ABRAHAM.

Abel (m.) Biblical: name of the younger son of Adam and Eve, who was murdered out of jealousy by his brother Cain (Genesis 4: 1–8). The Hebrew form is *Hevel*, ostensibly representing the vocabulary word *hevel* breath, vapour, and so taken to imply vanity or worthlessness. Abel is considered by the Christian Church to have been a pre-Christian martyr (cf. Matthew 23: 35), and is invoked as a saint in the litany for the dying. Nevertheless, his name has not been much used either before or after its brief vogue among the Puritans.

Abelone (f.) Danish form of APOLLONIA.

Abigail (f.) Biblical: name (meaning 'father of exaltation' in Hebrew) borne by one of King David's wives, who had earlier been married to Nabal (1 Samuel 25: 3), and by the mother of Absalom's captain Amasa (2 Samuel 1: 25). The name was popular in the 17th century under Puritan influence. It was a common name in literature for a lady's maid, for example in Beaumont and Fletcher's play *The Scornful Lady* (1616), partly no doubt because the biblical Abigail refers to herself as 'thy servant'. In Ireland this name has traditionally been used as an Anglicized form of GOBNAIT, although the reasons for this are not clear.

Pet forms: English, Irish: **Abbie**, **Abbey**.

Abilene (f.) English (U.S.): a comparatively rare name. In the New Testament, Abilene is a region of the Holy Land (Luke 3: 1), whose name is of uncertain origin, but may be derived from a Hebrew element meaning 'grass'. Several places in America have been named from this reference, notably a city in Kansas, which was the boyhood home of President Dwight D. Eisenhower. Its adoption as a female given name was probably encouraged partly by its resemblance to ABBIE and partly by the productive suffix of female names *-lene* (cf. e.g. CHARLENE).

Abishag (f.) Biblical: name (possibly meaning 'wise, educated' in Hebrew) borne by a beautiful Shunammite virgin who was brought to the dying King David in a vain attempt to restore him to health and vigour. She was later used by David's son and successor Solomon as a reason for executing his half-brother and rival Adonijah (1 Kings 1–2): Adonijah had wanted to marry Abishag.

Variant: Jewish: **Avishag**.

Abner (m.) Biblical: name (meaning 'father of light' in Hebrew) of a relative of King Saul, who was in command of Saul's army (1 Samuel 14: 50; 26: 5). It is not common as a given name in England, but has enjoyed a steady, modest popularity in America, where it was brought in at the time of the earliest Puritan settlements.

Variant: Jewish: **Avner**.

Abraham (m.) Biblical: name of the first of the Jewish patriarchs, who entered into a covenant with God that his descendants should possess the land of Canaan. The Hebrew form is *Avraham*, of uncertain derivation. In Genesis 17: 5 it is explained as 'father of a multitude (of nations)' (Hebrew *av hamon* (*goyim*)). It has always been a popular given name among Jews, and was also chosen by Christians, especially among 17th-century Puritans and other fundamentalists. Various early saints of the Eastern Roman Empire also bore this name. Its currency in the United States was greatly enhanced by the fame of President Abraham Lincoln (1809–65).

Variants: Jewish: **Avraham** (Hebrew); **Avrom** (Yiddish).

Short form: English: **Abe**.

Abram (m.) Biblical: variant of ABRAHAM. It was probably originally a distinct name (meaning 'high father' in Hebrew). According to Genesis 17: 5, the patriarch's name was changed by divine command from *Abram* to *Abraham*. From the Middle Ages, however, if not before, it was taken to be a contracted version.

Absalom (m.) Biblical: name (probably meaning 'father of peace' in Hebrew) of the third son of King David, who rebelled against him and was eventually killed when he was caught by the hair in an oak tree as he fled, to the great grief of his father (2 Samuel 15–18). The name has never been particularly common in the English-speaking world, but the Scandinavian form AXEL is familiar in the United States.

Achilles (m.) From Greek mythology. Achilles, son of the sea nymph Thetis and the mortal Peleus, was the leading warrior of the Greek army attacking Troy. In the *Iliad*, Homer relates how he withdrew from the siege as a result of a slight to his honour, until his lover Patroclus was killed wearing his armour, whereupon he rejoined the fray in order to avenge him. The Greek form of his name is *Akhilleus*, and is of unknown, possibly pre-Greek, origin; it may be connected with that of the River *Akheloös*. The name has been used only rarely in the English-speaking world, usually as a result of recent Continental influence. Although there were various minor early saints so named, it has normally been chosen by parents who wished to take advantage of the licence given by the Catholic Church to select names borne by classical heroes as well as those of saints.

Derivatives: French: **Achille**. Italian: **Achilleo**. Spanish: **Aquiles**.

Achim (m.) A German short form of JOACHIM.

Acke (m.) Swedish: pet form of AXEL.

Ada (f.) English: of uncertain origin, apparently not generally bestowed before the late 18th century. In part, this is a pet form of ADELE and ADELAIDE, and so it may go back to a Germanic female personal name, a short form of various compound names with the first element *adal* noble. Ada was the name of a 7th-century abbess of Saint-Julien-des-Prés at Le

Mans. Alternatively, it may represent a variant of ADAH.

Adah (f.) Biblical: Authorized Version spelling of the name (meaning 'adornment' in Hebrew) borne by the wives of Lamech (Genesis 4: 19) and of Esau (Genesis 36: 2). See also ADA.

Adalgisa (f.) Italian: of Germanic origin, composed of the elements *adal* noble + *gisil* pledge or hostage. It died out in the Middle Ages, but has undergone a minor revival since the 19th century as a result of the popularity of Bellini's opera *Norma* (1831), in which it is borne, inappropriately enough, by a Celtic priestess.

Adam (m.) Biblical: name of the first man (Genesis 2–3). It probably derives from Hebrew *adama* earth; it is a common feature of creation legends that the god responsible fashioned the first human beings from earth or clay and breathed life into them. The name was subsequently borne by a 7th-century Irish abbot of Fermo in Italy. It has enjoyed something of a resurgence in the English-speaking world since the 1960s. In Hebrew it is a generic term for 'man' (Genesis 5: 2) and has never been considered a personal name, although *Hava* 'Eve' has enjoyed popularity among Jews.

Derivatives: Irish Gaelic: **Ádhamh**. Scottish Gaelic: **Àdhamh**. Italian: **Adamo**. Spanish: **Adán**. Portuguese: **Adão**. Finnish: **Aatami**.

Pet form: Scottish: ADIE.

Adda (f.) German: pet form of ADELHEID.

Addolorata (f.) Italian equivalent of DOLORES, from Italian *Madonna Addolorata* 'Our Lady of Sorrows'.

Adela (f.) English: Latinate form of ADELE, especially popular in the late 19th century

Adelaide (f.) English (from French **Adélaïde**): of Germanic origin, composed of the elements *adal* noble + *heid* kind, sort. It was borne in the 10th century by the wife of the Holy Roman Emperor Otto the Great. She became regent after his death and was revered as a saint. The given name increased in popularity in England during the 19th century, when it was borne by the wife of King William IV; she was the daughter of the ruler of the German duchy of Saxe-Meiningen. The Australian city of Adelaide was named in her honour.

Pet form: **Addie** (esp. Irish).

Adele (f.) English (from French **Adèle**): of Germanic origin, representing a short form of various compound names with the first element *adal* noble. It was popular among the Normans as a result of the fame of a 7th-century saint, a daughter of the Frankish king Dagobert II. It was also the name of William the Conqueror's youngest daughter (*c.*1062–1137), who became the wife of Stephen of Blois and was likewise revered as a saint. It was revived in England in the late 19th century, being the name of a character in Johann Strauss's opera *Die Fledermaus*. Its popularity was further reinforced in the 1930s as the name of a character in the novels of Dornford Yates.

Adelheid (f.) German, Dutch, and Scandinavian form of ADELAIDE.

Pet forms: German: **Adda**, **Heidi**. Frisian, Dutch: ELKE.

Adeline (f.) French: diminutive of *Adèle* (see ADELE). The Latinate form **Adelina** is also found. Both enjoyed a brief vogue in the 19th century.

Adeltraud (f.) German: cognate of ETHELDREDA and AUDREY. It enjoyed some popularity in the 19th century, but has now fallen back into disuse.

Variants: **Adeltrud**, **Edeltr(a)ud**.

Cognate: Dutch: **Aaltruide**.

Adie (m.) Scottish: pet form of ADAM or, less commonly, of AIDAN. **Adaidh** is a Gaelic spelling of *Adie*, hence the surname *MacAdaidh*, Anglicized as *McCadie*.

Adina (f., m.) Mainly Jewish: in the Bible a male name, derived from Hebrew *adin* slender. It is borne by a soldier in the army of King David, 'Adina the son of Shiza the Reubenite, a captain of the

Reubenites, and thirty with him' (1 Chronicles 11: 42). In modern times it was revived as a male name among Zionists, but is now more commonly a female name, no doubt because of the characteristically feminine *-a* ending.

Adlai (m.) Biblical: name of a very minor character, the father of one of King David's herdsmen (1 Chronicles 27: 29). It represents an Aramaic contracted form of the Hebrew name *Adaliah* 'God is just'. In recent times, it is particularly associated with the American statesman and Democratic presidential candidate Adlai Stevenson (1900–65), in whose family the name was traditional: it was also borne by his grandfather (1835–1914), who was vice-president in 1893–7.

Adolf (m.) German: composed of the Germanic elements *adal* noble + *wolf* wolf. This form of the name was first introduced into Britain by the Normans, displacing the Old English cognate *Æthelwulf*, but it did not become at all common until it was reintroduced by the Hanoverians in the 18th century. The association with Adolf Hitler (1889–1945) has meant that the name has hardly been used since the Second World War.

Adolphus (m.) Latinized form of ADOLF (the *ph* a result of hypercorrection). This has been a recurring name in the Swedish royal family, and this form has also been used occasionally in the English-speaking world.

Adria (f.) English: modern feminine form of ADRIAN.

Adrian (m.) Usual English form of the Latin name *Hadriānus* 'man from Hadria'. Hadria was a town in northern Italy which has given its name to the Adriatic Sea; it is of unknown derivation, and the initial *H-* has always been very volatile. The name was borne by the Roman emperor Publius Aelius Hadrianus, during whose reign (AD 117–38) Hadrian's Wall was built across northern England. The name was later taken by several early popes, including the only English pope, Nicholas Breakspeare (Adrian IV). It has become particularly popular in the English-speaking world during the past thirty years.

Cognates: French: **Adrien**. Italian: **Adriano**. Spanish: **Adrián**. Portuguese: **Adrião**. Hungarian: **Adorjan**.

Adrianne (f.) English: modern feminine form of ADRIAN, less common than ADRIENNE.

Variants: **Adrianna, Adriana**.

Adrienne (f.) French: feminine form of ADRIAN, now also used in the English-speaking world.

Aegidius (m.) Original Latin form of GILES, sometimes used in Germany.

Aegle (f.) From Latin: the name borne in classical mythology by various characters—a daughter of the Sun and sister of Phaeton; one of the Hesperides; and a nymph, daughter of Jupiter and Neaera. It derives from the Greek word *aiglē* brightness, splendour.

Aeneas (m.) British (rare): from the Latin name of the Trojan hero who, according to classical legend, fled after the sack of Troy and sailed eventually to Italy, where he founded the Roman state. This, in essence, is the subject of Virgil's *Aeneid*. The name is of unknown derivation; it appears in Homer as *Aineas*, and was associated by the Romans themselves with Greek *ainein* to praise. As a given name, it used to be quite common in Scotland as an Anglicized form of Gaelic AONGHAS, and in Ireland as an Anglicized form of Gaelic **Éigneachán**, a personal name representing a diminutive of *éigneach* violent fate or death.

Aeron (f.) Welsh: name borne in early Celtic mythology by the goddess of battle and slaughter, *Agrona*. Her name is probably a derivative of the element represented in modern Welsh *aer* battle. In modern use this name may have been selected because of its homonomy with the vocabulary word *aeron* fruit, berries. The extended forms **Aeronwy** (using a name suffix of ancient origin and uncertain derivation) and **Aeronwen** (with Welsh *(g)wen* white, fair, blessed, holy) are also in common use.

Afanasi (m.) Russian form of ATHANASIUS.

Pet form: **Afonya**.

Afonso (m.) Portuguese form of ALFONSO.

Afonya (m.) Russian: pet form of AFANASI.

Africa (f.) English: name adopted in the 20th century among American Blacks, conscious of their ancestral heritage in the continent of Africa. It was also formerly used in Scotland as an Anglicized form of the Gaelic name OIGHRIG, but this use is now completely obsolete.

Agafya (f.) Russian: from Greek *Agapia*, a derivative of *agapē* love. The masculine form *Agapius* was borne by several early saints.

Agatha (f.) English: Latinized version of the Greek name *Agathē*, from the feminine form of the adjective *agathos* good, honourable. This was the name of a Christian saint popular in the Middle Ages; she was a Sicilian martyr of the 3rd century who suffered the fate of having her breasts cut off. According to the traditional iconography, she is depicted holding them on a platter. In some versions they look more like loaves, leading to the custom of blessing bread on her feast day (5 February). The name was revived in the 19th century, but has faded again since.

Cognates: French, German: **Agathe**. Italian, Scandinavian, Polish: **Agata**. Spanish: **Águeda**. Czech: **Agáta**. Hungarian: **Ágota**. Norwegian also: **Ågot**. Swedish also: **Agda**.

Pet form: English: **Aggie**.

Åge (m.) Danish: variant of ÅKE.

Aggie (f.) Scottish and English: pet form of AGNES and AGATHA.

Ägid (m.) German form of the Latin name AEGIDIUS; see GILES.

Aglaia (f.) Russian: from Greek. This was the name in classical mythology of one of the three Graces, but its acceptability for the Orthodox Church was due to the fact that it was also the name of a companion of St Boniface. It is of uncertain derivation, but is probably connected with AEGLE.

Agna (f.) Scandinavian and German: pet form of AGNETHE, also used as an independent given name.

Agnes (f.) English, German, Dutch, and Scandinavian: Latinized version of the Greek name *Hagnē*, from the feminine form of the adjective *hagnos* pure, holy. This was the name of a young Roman virgin martyred in the persecutions instigated by the Roman emperor Diocletian. She became a very popular saint in the Middle Ages. Her name was early associated with Latin *agnus* lamb, leading to the consistent dropping of the initial *H-* and to her representation in art accompanied by a lamb. The name was strongly revived in the 19th century, and has become especially popular in Scotland. In Ireland it has traditionally been used as a 'translation' of ÚNA.

Cognates: Irish Gaelic: **Aignéis**. French: **Agnès**. Italian: **Agnese**. Spanish: **Inés**. Portuguese: **Inês**. Polish: **Agnieszka**. Czech: **Anežka**. Finnish: **Aune**. See also ANNIS.

Pet form: Scottish: **Aggie**.

Agnethe (f.) German and Scandinavian form of AGNES, derived from the Latin genitive case *Agnētis*. It has occasionally been used in the English-speaking world during the 20th century

Variant: Swedish: **Agneta**.

Short form: Swedish: **Neta**.

Pet form: **Agna**.

Agostinho (m.) Portuguese form of AUGUSTINE.

Agostino (m.) Italian form of AUGUSTINE.

Ågot (f.) Norwegian form of AGATHA.

Ágota (f.) Hungarian form of AGATHA.

Agrafena (f.) Russian: vernacular form of *Agrippina*, the name of several prominent women in the Roman imperial family, most notably the mother of Nero, who was murdered by order of her son. As a Russian given name it has been adopted in honour of an early Christian saint of the same name, martyred under the Emperor Valerian. The given name is derived from the old Roman family name *Agrippa*, which is probably of Etruscan origin.

Pet forms: **Grunya, Grusha.**

Águeda (f.) Spanish form of AGATHA.

Agurtzane (f.) Basque equivalent of ROSARIO. The contracted form **Agurne** is also used.

Agustí (m.) Catalan form of AUGUSTINE.

Agustín (m.) Spanish form of AUGUSTINE.

Aharon (m.) Jewish: modern Hebrew form of AARON.

Ahuva (f.) Jewish: modern Hebrew name, coined from the vocabulary word meaning 'beloved'. The Yiddish name LIBE no doubt provided a stimulus for the coining of the Hebrew name.

Aidan (m.) Irish: Anglicized form of the Gaelic name **Aodán**, a diminutive of AODH. This was borne by various early Irish saints, among them the 7th-century apostle of Northumbria. It has been revived in the 20th century, in particular during the past couple of decades, by parents conscious of their Irish ancestry.

Variant: **Edan.**

Cognate: Welsh: **Aeddan.**

Ailbeart (m.) Scottish Gaelic form of ALBERT.

Ailbhe (m., f.) Irish Gaelic: traditional name of uncertain origin, perhaps from an Old Celtic element cognate with Latin *albus* white (cf. ALBINA). It has been Anglicized as **Alby** and, as a male name, ALBERT.

Ailean (m.) Scottish Gaelic form of ALAN.

Aileen (f.) Scottish and English: variant spelling of EILEEN.

Ailie (f.) Scottish: pet form of AILEEN or an Anglicized spelling of EILIDH.

Ailís (f.) Irish Gaelic form of ALICE.

Ailsa (f.) Scottish: modern name derived from that of *Ailsa Craig*, a high rocky islet in the Clyde estuary off the Ayrshire coast, near the traditional estates of the Scottish Kennedys. Its name is derived from Old Norse *Alfsigesey* 'island of *Alfsigr*', a personal name composed of the elements *alf* elf, supernatural being + *sigi* victory. Adoption as a given name probably represents an Anglicized form of EALASAID. Ailsa Craig is known in Gaelic as *Allasa*, or popularly *Creag Ealasaid*.

Aimée (f.) French: originally a vernacular nickname meaning 'beloved', from the past participle of French *aimer* to love (Latin *amāre*; cf. AMY). It has been in use, although never very common, since the Middle Ages. It is now also sometimes used, with or without the accent, as a given name in the English-speaking world.

Aindrea (m.) Scottish Gaelic form of ANDREW; see also ANNDRA.

Aindréas (m.) Irish Gaelic form of ANDREW.

Variants: **Aindrias, Aindriú.**

Áine (f.) Irish Gaelic: traditional name meaning originally 'brightness' or 'radiance'. It is the traditional name of the queen of the fairies, who plays an important and varied role in Celtic mythology. It has also been used as an Irish form of ANNE.

Aingeal (f.) Irish Gaelic form of ANGELA, from the Gaelic vocabulary word *aingeal* angel. The word is masculine in gender but it is used as a female given name.

Aingeru (m.) Basque form of the male name ANGEL; see also GOTZON.

Ainsley (m., occasionally f.) Scottish and English: transferred use of the surname, which is borne by a powerful and ancient family long established in the Scottish borders. It was probably originally a local name, taken north from either *Annesley* in Nottinghamshire or *Ansley* in Warwickshire. The former gets its name from the genitive case of the Old English name *Ān* (a short form of any of various compounds containing as a first element *ān* one, only) + Old English *lēah* wood or clearing. The latter is from Old English *ānsetl* hermitage + *lēah*.

Variant: **Ainslee**.

Aisling (f.) Irish Gaelic: from the vocabulary word meaning 'dream, vision'. This was not in use as a given name during the Middle Ages, but was adopted as part of the Irish revival in the 20th century.

Variants: **Aislinn; Ashling** (Anglicized form).

Aisone (f.) Basque equivalent of ASUNCIÓN.

Aitor (m.) Basque: of unknown origin. It was the name of the legendary founder of the Basque people, and is still bestowed in his honour.

Aizik (m.) Jewish: Yiddish form of *Yitzhak* (see ISAAC).

Åke (m.) Scandinavian: related to the medieval Germanic name *Anicho* (a derivative of the element *ano* ancestor, which is not common as a name element). It has also been associated with the Latin names *Achatius* or *Acacius* (from Greek words meaning 'agate' and 'blameless' respectively).

Variant: Danish: **Åge**.

Akilina (f.) Russian: from the Late Latin woman's personal name *Aquilīna*, a derivative of *Aquila* 'eagle', which had been used as a family name in the classical period. St Aquilina is revered in the Orthodox Church as a young virgin martyr beheaded in Syria at the end of the third century.

Variant: **Akulina** (a vernacular form).

Cognate: Ukrainian: **Kilina**.

Pet forms: Russian: **Akulya; Kilya, Kulya**.

Akim (m.) Scandinavian and Russian form of JOACHIM, traditional in the villages of the Russian countryside, but now rare among city-dwellers. It has become familiar in the English-speaking world through the film actor Akim Tamaroff (1899–1972).

Pet form: **Kima**.

Al (m.) English: short form of any of the English male names beginning with this syllable.

Ala (f.) Polish: pet form of ALICJA.

Variant: **Alinka**.

Alain (m.) French form of ALAN, which originated in Brittany and is now common in all parts of France.

Alan (m.) English and Scottish: of Celtic origin and uncertain derivation (possibly a diminutive of a word meaning 'rock'). It was introduced into England by Breton followers of William the Conqueror, most notably Alan, Earl of Brittany, who was rewarded for his services with vast estates in the newly conquered kingdom.

In Britain the variants **Allan** and **Allen** are considerably less frequent, and generally represent transferred uses of surname forms, whereas in America all three forms of the name are approximately equally common. See also ALUN.

Cognates: Scottish Gaelic: **Ailean**. French: **Alain**.

Alana (f.) English: feminine form of ALAN, a comparatively recent coinage.

Variants: **Alanna**, ALANNAH.

Alanda (f.) English: a recent coinage, a feminine form of ALAN influenced by AMANDA.

Alannah (f.) English (esp. U.S.): respelling of ALANA, possibly influenced by names of Hebrew origin such as HANNAH and *Susannah* (see SUSANNA) and by the Anglo-Irish term of endearment *alannah* (Gaelic *a leanbh* O child).

Alaric (m.) English (rare): from a Germanic personal name composed of the elements *ala* all or *ali* stranger + *rīc* power, ruler, which was introduced to

Britain in this form by the Normans. The first element may also in part derive from a contracted form of the element *adal* noble. The Blessed Alaricus or Adalricus (d. 975) was a Swabian prince who became a monk at the monastery of Einsiedeln in Switzerland.

Alasdair (m.) Scottish Gaelic form of ALEXANDER, often Anglicized as ALISTAIR.

Variants: **Alastair, Alaster.**

Alastar (m.) Irish Gaelic form of ALEXANDER.

Alazne (f.) Basque equivalent of MILAGROS.

Alba (f.) Italian, occasionally used in the English-speaking world. It seems to represent the feminine form of the Latin adjective *alba* white, but may in fact be a derivative of Germanic *alb* elf, supernatural being.

Alban (m.) Mainly English: name of the first British Christian martyr, the Latin form of which is *Albānus*. This may be an ethnic name from one of the numerous places in the Roman Empire called *Alba*. Alternatively, it may represent a Latinized form of a British name derived from the Celtic element *alp* rock, crag. The 3rd- or 4th-century Romano-British saint was executed at the place now known as St Albans, from the Benedictine abbey founded there in his memory by King Offa. The name was in use in the Middle Ages, and was revived in the 19th century. In some people's minds it may have been associated with *Albion*, a poetic name for Britain.

Alberic (m.) English: learned form of AUBREY, derived from the Latin *Albericus* in the 14th century. It enjoyed a slight and brief vogue in the 19th century, but is now once again very rare.

Albert (m.) French and English (Norman): of Germanic origin, composed of the elements *adal* noble + *berht* bright, famous. The Norman form displaced the Old English cognate *Æþelbeorht*. The name is popular in a variety of forms in Western Europe, and has been traditional in a number of European princely families. Its great popularity in England in the 19th century was due largely to Queen Victoria's consort, Prince Albert of Saxe-Coburg-Gotha. In Ireland, it has been used as an Anglicized form of the male name AILBHE.

Cognates: Scottish Gaelic: **Ailbeart.** Italian, Spanish: **Alberto.** German: **Albrecht.**

Short forms: English: **Al, Bert.**

Pet form: English: **Bertie.**

Albina (f.) Latin feminine form of *Albinus*, a derivative of the Roman family name *Albius*, which is from *albus* white. It is the name of a minor saint: St Albina was a young woman martyred at Caesarea in 250. She is particularly venerated in Campania, where her relics are preserved to this day.

Short form: BINA.

Albrecht (m.) German form of ALBERT.

Alby (m., f.) Irish: Anglicized form of AILBHE.

Aldo (m.) Italian: of Germanic origin, possibly from the element *ald* old. More probably it is from a metathesized form of *adal* noble, or rather from any of the two-element names of which this forms the first element (cf. e.g. ALBERT).

Aldous (m.) English: of uncertain origin; probably a short form of any of various Norman names, such as *Aldebrand*, *Aldemund*, and *Alderan*, containing the Germanic element *ald* old. It was relatively common in East Anglia during the Middle Ages, but is now rare, known mainly as the given name of the novelist Aldous Huxley (1894–1963).

Alec (m.) English and Scottish: short form of ALEXANDER, now somewhat less popular in England than ALEX, possibly because of the colloquial pejorative term *smart alec*. See also ALICK.

Aleida (f.) German (esp. N. Germany): form of ADELHEID, influenced by the Low German form ALEIT.

Aleit (f.) Low German: contracted form of ADELHEID.

Aleix (m.) Catalan form of ALEXIUS.

Aleixandre (m.) Catalan form of ALEXANDER.

Aleixo (m.) Portuguese form of ALEXIUS.

Alejandra (f.) Spanish form of ALEXANDRA; feminine of ALEJANDRO.

Alejandro (m.) Spanish form of ALEXANDER.

Alejo (m.) Spanish form of ALEXIUS.

Aleksander (m.) Polish form of ALEXANDER.

Aleksandr (m.) Usual spelling in the Roman alphabet of the Russian form of ALEXANDER.

Feminine form: **Aleksandra**.

Aleksei (m.) Russian form of ALEXIUS.

Pet form: **Alyosha**.

Aleksy (m.) Polish form of ALEXIUS.

Alena (f.) German and Czech: aphetic short form of *Magdalena* (see MAGDALENE).

Aleš (m.) Czech: pet form of ALEXEJ.

Alessandra (f.) Italian form of ALEXANDRA; feminine of ALESSANDRO.

Alessandro (m.) Italian form of ALEXANDER.

Alessia (f.) Italian form of ALEXIA.

Alessio (m.) Italian form of ALEXIUS.

Alethea (f.) English: a learned coinage, not found before the 17th century. It represents the Greek word *alētheia* truth, and seems to have arisen as a result of the Puritan enthusiasm for using terms for abstract virtues as female names. See also ALTHEA.

Alette (f.) French: Gallicized form of the Middle Low German name ALEIT, which is a contracted form of ADELHEID.

Alex (m., f.) English: short form of ALEXANDER, ALEXANDRA, or ALEXIS; also commonly used as a given name in its own right. It is now also sometimes used in France and Germany.

Variant: English: **Alix** (f.).

Short form: English: **Lex**.

Alexa (f.) English: short form of ALEXANDRA or variant of ALEXIS as a female name.

Alexander (m.) English, Dutch, German, and Hebrew: from the Latin form of the Greek name *Alexandros*, which is composed of the elements *alexein* to defend + *anēr* man, warrior (genitive *andros*). The compound was probably coined originally as a title of the goddess Hera, consort of Zeus. It was also borne as a byname by the Trojan prince Paris. The name became extremely popular in the post-classical period, and was borne by several characters in the New Testament and some early Christian saints. Its use as a common given name throughout Europe, however, derives largely from the fame of Alexander the Great, King of Macedon (356–23 BC), around whom a large body of popular legend grew up in late antiquity, much of which came to be embodied in the medieval 'Alexander romances'. It also became a popular Hebrew name under Alexander the Great's benign rule of Palestine.

Cognates: Scottish Gaelic: **Alasdair** (Anglicized as ALISTAIR). Irish Gaelic: **Alastar**. French: **Alexandre**. Italian: **Alessandro**. Spanish: **Alejandro**. Catalan: **Aleixandre**. Portuguese: **Alexandre**. Romanian: **Alexandru**. Russian: **Aleksandr**. Ukrainian: **Oleksander**. Polish: **Aleksander**. Czech: **Alexandr**. Hungarian: **Sándor**. Yiddish: **Sender**.

Short forms: English: **Alex**, **Alec**, **Alick**. Italian: **Sandro**.

Pet forms: English, Scottish: **Sandy** (Gaelic **Sandaidh**). Scottish: **Sawney**. Russian: **Sasha**, **Sanya**, **Shura**. Polish: **Oleś**, **Olech**, **Olek**. Czech: **Olexa**.

Alexandra (f.) Latinate feminine form of ALEXANDER. It was very little used in the English-speaking world before the 20th century, when it was brought in from Scandinavia and Eastern Europe. It owes its sudden rise in popularity in Britain at the end of the 19th century to Queen Alexandra, Danish wife of Edward VII.

Derivatives: Italian: **Alessandra**. Spanish: **Alejandra**. Russian: **Aleksandra**.

Short forms: English: **Alex, Alexa**; SANDRA.

Pet forms: English, Scottish: **Sandy**; **Lexy**. Russian: **Sasha, Sanya, Shura**.

Alexandrina (f.) Latinate derivative of ALEXANDRA. It was most common in the 19th century, and was in fact the first name of Queen Victoria.

Alexej (m.) Czech form of ALEXIUS, or pet form of ALEXANDER.

Pet form: **Aleš**.

Alexia (f.) English and German: variant of ALEXIS as a female name.

Cognate: Italian: **Alessia**.

Alexina (f.) Scottish (Highland): elaborated feminine form of the male name ALEX, used as an unambiguously female name.

Alexis (f., m.) English and German: variant (or female derivative) of ALEXIUS. It was originally a male name, but is now more commonly given to girls.

Alexius (m.) Latin spelling of Greek *Alexios*, derived from a short form of various compound personal names with the first element *alexein* to defend. St Alexius was a 5th-century saint of Edessa, venerated particularly in the Orthodox Church as a 'man of God'. In Eastern European languages here has been some confusion between derivatives of this name and pet forms of ALEXANDER.

Variant: ALEXIS.

Derivatives: Italian: **Alessio**. Spanish: **Alejo**. Catalan: **Aleix**. Portuguese: **Aleixo**. Polish: **Aleksy**. Czech: **Alexej**. Russian: **Aleksei**.

Aleydis (f.) Dutch: from a contracted form of the medieval name *Adalheidis* (see ADELAIDE).

Alf (m.) English: short form of ALFRED.

Pet form: **Alfie**.

Alfa (m., f.) English: variant spelling of ALPHA.

Alfio (m.) Italian: a typically Sicilian name, borne in honour of a saint martyred under the Emperor Decius in 251, together with his brothers Philadelphus and Cyrinus. The name may represent Greek *Alphios*, from *alphos* wheat, or it may be from the Roman family name *Alfius*; this is from an Italic dialectal form, *alfus*, of Latin *albus* white, and is in fact distantly connected with the Greek word.

Alfonso (m.) Spanish: of Germanic (Visigothic) origin, probably composed of the elements *adal* noble + *funs* ready, prompt. Alternatively, the first element may be *ala* all, *hadu* struggle, or *hild* battle; forms are found to support each derivation, so it is possible that several names that were originally distinct in Visigothic have fallen together. St Alphonsus was a 9th-century bishop of Astorga, who spent the last years of his life at the abbey of St Stephen de Ribas de Sil in Galicia. The major influence on the spread and popularity of the name, however, was the fact that it was established as a traditional name in various royal families of the Iberian peninsula from a very early date. Alfonso I (*c.*693–757), King of Asturias, played an important part in establishing Christianity in Spain. By the 14th century, eleven Alfonsos had sat on the throne of Leon and Castile, four on the throne of Aragon, and four *Afonsos* on the throne of Portugal.

Variant: **Alonso**.

Cognates: French: **Alphonse**. Portuguese: **Afonso**. See also ALPHONSUS.

Alfred (m.) English: from Old English, composed of the elements *ælf* elf, supernatural being + *ræd* counsel. It was a relatively common name before the Norman Conquest of Britain, being borne most notably by Alfred the Great (849–99), King of Wessex. After the Conquest it was adopted by the Normans in a variety of more or less radically altered forms, and provides a rare example (see also

Edward) of a distinctively Old English name that has spread widely on the Continent. It was strongly revived in the 19th century, along with other names of pre-Conquest historical figures (such as *Hereward*), but has faded since. See also Avery.

Derivatives: Irish Gaelic: **Ailfrid**. Italian, Spanish: **Alfredo**.

Short forms: English: **Alf, Fred**.

Alger (m.) English: from Old English, composed of the elements *ælf* elf, supernatural being + *gār* spear; it is possible that this form may also have absorbed other names with the first elements *æþel* noble, *ēald* old, and *ēalh* temple. The name was not common either before or after the Norman Conquest, but was revived in the 19th century, along with other Germanic names. It is relatively common in America, where it seems to have been taken up as a more 'manly' short form of Algernon.

Algernon (m.) English: of Norman French origin. In Norman French it was a byname meaning 'moustached' (from *grenon, gernon* moustache, of Germanic origin). The Normans were as a rule clean-shaven, and this formed a suitable distinguishing nickname when it was applied to William de Percy, a companion of William the Conqueror. In the 15th century it was revived, with a sense of family tradition, as a byname or second given name for his descendant Henry Percy (1478–1527), and thereafter regularly used in that family. It was subsequently adopted into other families connected by marriage with the Percys, and eventually became common property.

Pet forms: **Algy, Algie**.

Algot (m.) Scandinavian: from an Old Norse or Old Swedish personal name, *Alfgautr*, composed of the elements *alfr* elf, supernatural being + the tribal name *Gautr* Goth.

Alice (f.) English and French: variant of Adelaide, representing an Old French spelling of a greatly contracted version of Germanic *Adalheidis*. It was regarded as a distinct name when it was revived in the 19th century. It was the name of the child heroine of Lewis Carroll's *Alice's Adventures in Wonderland* (1865) and *Through the Looking Glass* (1872), who was based on his child friend Alice Patience Liddell, daughter of the dean of Christ Church, Oxford.

Variant: **Alys**.

Cognate: Irish Gaelic: **Ailís**.

Alicia (f.) Spanish and English: modern Latinate form of Alice.

Variants: English: **Alissa, Alyssa**.

Alicja (f.) Polish form of Alice.

Pet forms: **Ala, Alinka**.

Alick (m.) Scottish and English: variant of Alec, which has gained some currency as a given name in its own right. In the Highlands the form *Ellic* was also formerly in use; the Gaelic form is **Ailig**.

Feminine form: Scottish (Highland): **Alickina**.

Alida (f.) Hungarian form of Adelaide, now also used in German-speaking countries.

Alina (f.) Used in both English- and German-speaking countries, and of uncertain origin. It is probably a variant of Aline, but could also be of Arabic origin, from a word meaning 'noble' or 'illustrious'. In Scotland it has been used as a feminine form of Alistair.

Alinda (f.) In the English-speaking world this name is of recent origin; apparently it represents an artificial combination of the names Alina and Linda. It is, however, also used in German-speaking countries, where it may be derived from the Germanic personal name *Adelinde*, composed of the elements *adal* noble + *lind* soft, tender, weak.

Aline (f.) English and French: in the Middle Ages this represented a contracted form of Adeline. In modern use it is either a revival of this or a respelling of Aileen. In Scotland and Ireland it has sometimes been chosen as representing an Anglicized spelling of the Gaelic vocabulary word *àlainn* (Scottish), *álainn* (Irish) lovely.

Alinka (f.) Polish: pet form of ALICJA.

Alirio (m.) Spanish: of uncertain origin. It may possibly derive from a popular form of Latin *Hilarius* (see HILARY) or *Hilarion* (see ILLARION). A saint variously known as *Allyre* or *Illidius* was a 4th-century bishop of Clermont: his name may be connected with this one.

Alison (f.) Scottish, English, and French: from a very popular medieval Norman diminutive of ALICE, formed by the addition of the diminutive suffix *-on*. In spite of its medieval popularity, the name virtually died out in England in the 15th century. However, it survived in Scotland, with the result that until its revival in England in the 20th century the name had a strongly Scottish flavour.

Pet forms: English: **Allie, Ally**.

Alissa (f.) English: variant of ALICIA.

Alistair (m.) Scottish: altered spelling of Gaelic **Alasdair**, a form of ALEXANDER. Alexander has long been a popular name in Scotland, having been borne by three early medieval kings of the country.

Variants: **Alisdair, Alastair, Alister, Al(l)aster**.

Pet form: **Aly**.

Alix (f.) English: variant of ALEX, used only as a feminine name. Its formation has probably been influenced by ALICE.

Aliza (f.) Jewish: modern Hebrew name meaning 'gay'. Its popularity has been influenced by the English names GAY and ALICE, and it has also been used as a translation of the Yiddish name FREYDE.

Alke (m.) Low German: popular pet form used as a given name in its own right, derived from a dramatically shortened version of ADELHEID (cf. AALTJE).

Allan (m.) Scottish and English: variant spelling of ALAN.

Allaster (m.) Scottish: variant spelling of ALISTAIR. It is borne, for example, by a minstrel in Sir Walter Scott's *Rob Roy* (1818), which ensured its 19th-century popularity.

Allegra (f.) Italian and English: from the feminine form of the Italian adjective *allegro* gay, jaunty (familiar in English as a musical tempo). It seems to have been an original coinage when it was given to Byron's illegitimate daughter (1817–22), but since then it has been taken up by parents in many English-speaking countries. It is not commonly used as a given name in Italy.

Allen (m.) Scottish and English: variant spelling of ALAN, in Britain generally found only as a surname, but in the United States equally common as a given name.

Allie (f.) English: pet form of ALISON, occasionally used as a given name in its own right.

Variant: **Ally**.

Allina (f.) English and Scottish: variant of ALINA.

Alma (f.) English: a relatively modern creation, of uncertain origin. It had a temporary vogue following the Battle of Alma (1854), which is named from the river in the Crimea by which it took place; similarly *Trafalgar* had occasionally been used as a female name earlier in the century. Nevertheless, the historical event seems only to have increased the popularity of an existing, if rare, name. *Alma* is also the feminine form of the Latin adjective *almus* nourishing, kind (cf. *alma mater* fostering mother, the clichéd phrase for an educational establishment). In Tennessee Williams's play *Summer and Smoke* (1948), a bearer of the name explains that it is 'Spanish for soul' (Latin *anima*), but this seems to be only coincidental.

Alois (m.) German and Czech form of ALOYSIUS.

Aloisia (f.) German and English: Latinate feminine form of ALOYSIUS.

Cognate: Czech: **Aloisie**.

Alojzy (m.) Polish form of ALOYSIUS.

Alonso (m.) Spanish: popular altered form of ALFONSO, with simplification of the consonantal cluster.

Aloysius (m.) English, German, and Dutch: of unknown origin, possibly a Latinized form of a Provençal version of LOUIS. It was relatively common in Italy in the Middle Ages, and has subsequently enjoyed some popularity among Roman Catholics in honour of St Aloysius Gonzaga (1568–91), who was born in Lombardy.

Variant: German: **Alois**.

Cognates: Polish: **Alojzy**. Czech: **Alois**.

Alpha (m., f.) English: name taken from the first letter of the Greek alphabet (ultimately of Semitic origin; cf. Hebrew *āleph* ox). It seems to have been chosen as a given name in the 19th and 20th centuries as a symbol of primacy and excellence, and is used for both boys and girls.

Variant: **Alfa**.

Alphonse (m.) French form of ALFONSO. The *-ph-* spelling is the result of classical influences (or classical pretensions). It has been occasionally used in the English-speaking world, especially among West Indians and American Blacks, but is now out of fashion.

Alphonsine (f.) French: feminine diminutive of ALPHONSE, now also used in the English-speaking world.

Alphonsus (m.) Irish: Latinized form of ALFONSO, used as an equivalent of the Gaelic name **Anluan**. This is of uncertain origin, but could be composed of an intensive prefix + an element meaning 'hound' or 'warrior'.

Pet forms: **Fonsie, Fonso**.

Alpin (m.) Scottish: Anglicized form of Gaelic **Ailpein**, a name widely borne in the Highlands from the time of the earliest historical records. It has no obvious Gaelic etymology, and for that reason, if no other, is often taken to be of Pictish origin.

Variant: **Alpine**.

Alte (f.) Jewish: feminine form of *Alter* (see ALTMAN).

Althea (f.) English: from Greek mythology. Although often considered to be a contracted form of ALETHEA, it is actually a quite distinct name (Greek *Althaia*), of uncertain origin. It was borne in classical legend by the mother of Meleager, who was given a brand plucked from the fire at the instant of her son's birth, with the promise that his life would last as long as the brand did; some twenty years later she destroyed it in a fit of pique. The name was revived by the 17th-century poet Richard Lovelace, as a poetic pseudonym for his beloved.

Althena (f.) English: modern coinage, apparently a blend of ALTHEA and ATHENE.

Altman (m.) Jewish: composed of the Yiddish elements *alt* old + *man* man. Traditionally, it was a name given to children to protect them from the angel of death, who would be confused by the conflict between the name and its infant bearer, or else as an omen name intended to ensure that the bearer would live to a ripe old age. The nominal adjective **Alter** is also used as a given name.

Alton (m.) English: transferred use of the surname, which is of local origin, being derived from any of several places in England so called. These have various origins; the most common is from Old English *ǣwiell* source (of a river) + *tūn* settlement, enclosure. It was borne (but dropped) as a given name by the American bandleader and trombonist Alton Glenn Miller (1904–44).

Alun (m.) Welsh: possibly a cognate of ALAN. It is borne in the *Mabinogi* by Alun of Dyfed, a character mentioned in passing several times. It is also a river name and a regional name in Wales, sometimes spelled *Alyn*. *Alun* was adopted as a bardic name by John Blackwell (1797–1840) and became popular as a result of his fame.

Alva (f.) Irish: Anglicized form of the Gaelic name **Almha**. This is of uncertain origin; it is earlier found in the form *Almu* and was borne, according to legend, by a semi-divine heroine who gave her name to the fortress and hill of Almu in Leinster.

Alvar (m.) English: from a medieval English name, representing an Old English personal name, *Ælfhere*, composed of the elements *ælf* elf, supernatural being + *here* army, warrior. In modern use it is either a revival of this (or a transferred use of the surname derived from it) or an Anglicized form of the Spanish ÁLVARO. A name of the same form is also in occasional use in Scandinavia, in which case it derives from an Old Norse personal name cognate with the Old English form quoted above.

Álvaro (m.) Spanish: of Germanic (Visigothic) origin. It is probably composed of the elements *al* all + *war* guard. The name is now also quite common in Italy, where the accent falls on the second syllable. It seems to have been taken up as a result of the influence of Verdi's opera *The Force of Destiny* (1862), in which a Peruvian character of this name appears.

Alvin (m.) English: from an Old English personal name composed of the elements *ælf* elf, supernatural being + *wine* friend. The medieval name was not especially common in Britain either before or after the Norman Conquest, but the modern form has recently become fairly popular in the United States. The reasons for this are not entirely clear; association with CALVIN may be a factor, but a more plausible (though less elevated) reason may be that it was the name given to the naughty chipmunk in a popular American television cartoon series of the 1960s.

Alwyn (m.) English: variant of ALVIN.
Variant: **Aylwin**.

Alyosha (m.) Russian: pet form of ALEKSEI.

Alys (f.) English: variant spelling of ALICE.

Alyssa (f.) English: variant spelling of ALISSA.

Alžběta (f.) Czech form of ELIZABETH.
Short form: **Běta**.
Pet forms: **Bětka, Betuška**.

Amabel (f.) English: of Old French origin, from Latin *amābilis* lovable. This name is now very rare in the English-speaking world, but lies behind the much commoner ANNABEL and MABEL. It gained some currency from being borne by the character Amabel Rose Adams in Angela Thirkell's *Barsetshire Chronicles* (1933 onwards).

Amadeus (m.) Original Latin form of AMEDEO, famous chiefly as the second name of the composer Wolfgang Amadeus Mozart (1756–91), for whom it was a Latin version of GOTTLIEB. It is still occasionally bestowed by music-loving parents in his honour.

Amado (m.) Spanish form of AMATO.

Amador (m.) Spanish: from the Latin name *Amātor* 'lover' (an agent derivative of *amāre* to love). It was borne by a 9th-century Cordoban priest who was executed by the Moors for his Christian faith.

Amalia (f.) Latinized form of the Germanic name *Amal*, representing the vocabulary element *amal* work. This was a first element in various names—now more or less obsolete—such as *Amalberta*, *Amalfriede*, and *Amalgunde*, for which *Amal* was used as a short form. *Amalia* is chiefly German and Scandinavian, but is also found occasionally in the English-speaking world. Its popularity was enhanced in Germany in the 18th century by the fame of Anna Amalia, Duchess of Saxe-Weimar (1739–1807), a great patron of the arts, whose court attracted Goethe, Schiller, Herder, and many others.
Variant: German: **Amalie**.

Amancio (m.) Spanish: from the Latin name *Amantius* 'loving', a derivative of the present participle of *amāre* to love. This name was borne by some half-dozen minor early saints, but there has been much confusion in the sources with the name *Amandus* 'lovable'.

Cognates: Catalan: **Amans, Mans**.

Amanda (f.) A 17th-century literary coinage from the Latin gerundive (feminine) *amanda* lovable, fit to be loved, from *amāre* to love. This is evidently modelled on MIRANDA. The masculine form *Amandus*, borne by various saints from the 4th to the 7th century, seems not to have been the source of the feminine form, and is itself not now used. The female name has enjoyed considerable popularity in the mid-20th century.

Short form: **Manda**.

Pet form: MANDY.

Amans (m.) Catalan form of AMANCIO.

Variant: **Mans**.

Amaryllis (f.) Name borne in classical pastoral poetry, including Virgil's *Eclogues*, by a typical shepherdess or country girl. The name is of Greek origin and uncertain derivation, possibly from *amaryssein* to sparkle. In modern times the name may sometimes have been given because of association with the flower, named in the 19th century from the Arcadian heroine.

Amato (m.) Italian: from the Latin name *Amātus* 'beloved'. There are two saints of this name who have influenced its popularity: the first abbot of Remiremont (*c.*597–*c.*630) and the tenth bishop of Sion (d. *c.*690).

Cognate: Spanish: **Amado**.

Amber (f.) English: from the vocabulary word for the gemstone *amber*, a word derived via Old French and Latin from Arabic *ambar*. This was first used as a given name at the end of the 19th century, but has become particularly popular in the past couple of decades. In part it owes its popularity to Kathleen Winsor's novel *Forever Amber* (1944).

Ambjörn (m.) Swedish: assimilated form of ARNBJÖRN.

Ambrose (m.) English (and Old French) form of the Late Latin name *Ambrosius*, from post-classical Greek *Ambrosios* 'immortal'. This was borne by various early saints, most notably a 4th-century bishop of Milan. The name has never been common in England, but has enjoyed considerably greater popularity in Roman Catholic Ireland, where the surname *Mac Ambrois* is Anglicized as *McCambridge*.

Cognates: Irish Gaelic: **Ambrós**. Welsh: **Emrys**. French: **Ambroise**. Italian: **Ambrogio**. Spanish, Portuguese: **Ambrosio**. Catalan: **Ambròs**. Polish: **Ambroży**. Czech: **Ambrož**. Hungarian: **Ambróz**.

Short forms: Italian: **Brogio**. Czech: **Brož**. Polish: **Mroż**.

Pet forms: Czech: **Brožek**. Polish: **Mrożek**.

Amedeo (m.) Italian: from the medieval Latin name **Amadeus**, composed of the elements *ama-*, from *amāre* to love, + *Deus* God. It was probably originally a deliberate calque of Greek *Theophilos* (see THEOPHILUS). The name has been traditional in the royal house of Savoy; bearers include the Blessed Amadeus IX, Duke of Savoy (1435–72). It is also quite common as an Italian Jewish name; recent bearers include the painter Amedeo Modigliani (1884–1920).

Cognate: French: **Amedée**.

Amelia (f.) English: probably the result of a cross between the Latin-origin *Emilia* (see EMILY) and the Latinized Germanic AMALIA. Its first use seems to have been in the English-speaking world, by Henry Fielding for the heroine of his novel *Amelia* (1751).

Amélie (f.) French form of AMELIA, now sometimes also used in the English-speaking world, with or without the accent.

Amerigo (m.) Italian: an early byform of *Enrico* (see HENRY). *Amerigo* is found in Italian sources from *c.*1100, evidently already well established by that time. It was probably introduced into Italy by the Ostrogoths some six centuries earlier; they controlled Italy from 493 to 552, and the name does not seem to have been in use among the Lombards who succeeded them. Its most famous bearer was Amerigo Vespucci (1454–1512), the Italian explorer and geographer who gave his name to the continent of America; it is sometimes used among Italian Americans in his honour.

Amhlaoibh (m.) Irish Gaelic form of OLAF. The Old Norse name was introduced to Ireland by Viking settlers.

Anglicized forms: **Auliffe**, HUMPHREY.

Cognates: Scottish: **Amhla(i)dh** (Gaelic), **Aulay** (Anglicized).

Amias (m.) English: rare, and of uncertain origin, possibly from the surname *Amias*, which is a local name for someone from Amiens in France. However, both surname and given name are rare. The ending *-ias* is found in biblical names (e.g. TOBIAS), where it represents a Greek form of Hebrew *-iyah* 'God'; *Amias* may sometimes have been chosen in the belief that it was a biblical name, reinforced by the fact that *am-* is the Latin root meaning 'love'. See also AMIAZ and AMYAS.

Amiaz (m.) Jewish: modern Hebrew given name, meaning 'my people is strong'.

Amice (f.) English: from a medieval given name derived from Latin *ami(ci)tia* friendship; see AMITY.

Amilcare (m.) Italian: from the name of the Carthaginian general Hamilcar Barca (d. *c.*228 BC), father of Hannibal. Hamilcar led the Carthaginian army against the Romans in the First Punic War, and was chiefly responsible for establishing Carthaginian influence in Spain. His name is composed of the Phoenician elements *hi* friend + the divine name *Melkar*.

Amita (f.) English: apparently a modern creation, representing an altered form of AMITY. In form it coincides with Latin *amita* maternal aunt.

Amittai (m.) Jewish: biblical name (meaning 'true' or 'honest' in Hebrew), borne by the father of Jonah (2 Kings 14: 25).

Amity (f.) English: comparatively recent coinage from the learned, Latinate vocabulary word meaning 'friendship'. The medieval doublet AMICE has also been occasionally revived.

Amnon (m.) Mainly Jewish: name (meaning 'faithful' in Hebrew) borne in the Bible by King David's eldest son, who raped and abandoned his half-sister Tamar and was killed by her brother Absalom.

Amos (m.) Biblical: name of a Hebrew prophet of the 8th century BC, whose sayings are collected in the book of the Bible that bears his name. This is of uncertain derivation, but may be connected with the Hebrew verb *amos* to carry. In some traditions it is assigned the meaning 'borne by God'. The name is used among Christians as well as Jews, and was popular among the Puritans. In Britain it survived well into the 19th century, but is little used today.

Amparo (f.) Spanish: from the vocabulary word *amparo* protection (from the verb *amparar* to help or protect, Late Latin *anteparāre* to prepare in advance). The given name was coined with reference to the role of the Virgin Mary in affording protection to Christians.

Amshel (m.) Jewish (Yiddish): variant of ANTSHEL.

Amund (m.) Scandinavian (esp. Norwegian): from an Old Norse personal name composed of the elements *ag* awe, fear or edge, point + *mundr* protector. The usual modern spelling is with a boll: **Åmund**.

Amy (f.) English: Anglicized form of Old French *Amee* 'beloved'. This originated in part as a vernacular nickname, in part as a form of Latin *Amāta*. The latter is ostensibly the feminine form of the past participle of *amāre* to love, but in fact it may have had a different, pre-Roman, origin; it was borne in classical mythology by the wife of King Latinus, whose daughter Lavinia married Aeneas and (according to the story in the *Aeneid*) became the mother of the Roman people.

Amyas (m.) English: of uncertain origin; possibly a variant of AMIAS. It first occurs in Spenser's *Faerie Queene*, in which it is the name of a 'squire of low degree'.

Ana (f.) Spanish form of ANNE.
Pet form: ANITA.

Anacleto (m.) Italian, Spanish, and Portuguese: from the Late Latin personal name *Anaclētus*, Greek *Anaklētos*, originally a divine byname meaning 'called on, invoked'. It also seems to have absorbed the personal name *Anengklētos* meaning 'irreproachable'. This was the name of the third pope.
Short form: **Cleto** (also used as a full baptismal name).

Anaïs (f.) Catalan and Provençal derivative of ANA.

Anastasia (f.) Russian: feminine form of the Greek male name *Anastasios* (a derivative of *anastasis* resurrection). It has always been popular in Eastern Europe as a result of the fame of a 4th-century saint who was martyred at Sirmium in Dalmatia, and in the Middle Ages it was in use in England too. One of the daughters of the last tsar of Russia bore this name. She was probably murdered along with the rest of the family by the Bolsheviks in 1918, but in 1920 a woman claiming to be the Romanov princess Anastasia came to public notice in Germany, and a film was subsequently based on this story (1956).
Cognates: Polish: **Anastazja**. Czech: **Anastázie**.
Short form: Russian: **Nastasia**.
Pet forms: Russian: **Nastya, Asya**. Polish: **Nastka, Nastusia**. Czech: **Nast'a**.

Anatole (m.) French: from the Late Latin personal name *Anatolius*, an adjectival derivative of Greek *anatolē* sunrise, dawn. The name was popular among early Christians because of its optimistic associations. It was borne by an early bishop of Cahors and by a 9th-century Scottish bishop, who settled as a hermit at Salins.

Anatoli (m.) Russian form of ANATOLE. The popularity of this name in Russia and in the Eastern Church is largely due to the influence of St Anatolius, bishop of Constantinople from 449 to 458.

Anděl (m.) Czech form of the male name ANGEL.
Pet form: **Andělik**.

Anděla (f.) Czech form of ANGELA.
Pet form: **Andělka**.

Anders (m.) Scandinavian form of ANDREW.

Andoni (m.) Basque form of ANTHONY.

Andor (m.) Scandinavian: from an Old Norse name composed of the elements *arn* eagle + a derivative of *Þorr* Thor, the god of thunder.

Andra (f., m.) 1. (f.) English: modern feminine form of ANDREW.
2. (m.) Scottish: traditional Lowland Scots form of ANDREW.

Andras (m.) Welsh form of ANDREW.

András (m.) Hungarian form of ANDREW. It has been sometimes bestowed in Hungary in honour of a Benedictine monk of Zobor Abbey, who was killed, along with a companion, St Benedict, by marauders in *c.*1020.

Andre (m.) Portuguese form of ANDREW.

André (m.) French form of ANDREW, which has been borrowed into English recently. It was the twenty-seventh most common male name among American Blacks in 1982.

Andrea (m., f.) 1. (m.) Italian equivalent of ANDREW. [*cont.*]

2. (f.) English: of disputed origin. It has been in use since the 17th century, although never common. It is now generally taken as a feminine equivalent of ANDREAS, and this probably represents its actual origin. However, it was not in use in the Middle Ages, and the suggestion has also been made that it represents an independent coinage in English from the Greek vocabulary word *andreia* manliness, virility.

Andreas (m.) The original New Testament Greek form of ANDREW, also found in Latin, and still used in German, and now occasionally in English.

Andrée (f.) French: feminine form of ANDREW, now also occasionally used in the English-speaking world.

Andrei (m.) Russian form of ANDREW. St Andrew is the patron saint of Russia as well as of Greece and Scotland.

Andrej (m.) Czech: 'learned' form of ANDREW. See also ONDŘEJ.

Pet forms: **Andráš, Androušek**.

Andrés (m.) Spanish form of ANDREW.

Andreu (m.) Catalan form of ANDREW.

Andrew (m.) English form of the Greek name *Andreas*, a short form of any of various compound names with the first element *andr-* man or, in particular, warrior. In the New Testament, this is the name of the first disciple to be called by Jesus. After the Resurrection, St Andrew preached in Asia Minor and Greece, and was probably crucified at Patras in Achaia. He was one of the most popular saints of the Middle Ages and was adopted as the patron of Scotland, Russia, and Greece. The name has long been popular in Scotland (in the Lowlands traditionally in the form **Andra**); its popularity in England has been enhanced by its use as a British royal name for Prince Andrew (b. 1960), the Duke of York.

Cognates: Scottish Gaelic: **Aindrea, Anndra**. Irish Gaelic: **Aindrias, Aindréas; Aindriú**. Welsh: **Andras**. French: **André**. Italian: ANDREA. Spanish: **Andrés**. Catalan: **Andreu**. Portuguese: **Andre**. German: **Andreas**. Low German, Dutch: **Andries**. Scandinavian: **Anders**. Polish: **Andrzej, Jędrzej**. Czech: **Andrej, Ondřej**. Russian: **Andrei**. Ukrainian: **Andrei**. Hungarian: **András, Endre**. Finnish: **Antero**.

Short forms: Scottish: **Drew**. Low German, Dutch: **Dries**.

Andriana (f.) English: modern coinage, apparently a blend of ANDREA and *Adriana* (see ADRIANNE) or possibly *Arianna* (see ARIADNE).

Andries (m.) Low German and Dutch form of ANDREW. St Andries Wouters (d. 1572) was a Catholic hanged by Calvinists at Gorkum.

Short form: **Dries**.

Andrine (f.) English: comparatively rare feminine derivative of ANDREW with the characteristically feminine ending *-ine*.

Andrzej (m.) Polish form of ANDREW. St Andrzej Bobola was a Polish Jesuit murdered by Cossacks at Janów in 1657.

Andula (f.) Czech: pet form of ANNA.

Variant: **Andulka**.

Andy (m.) Scottish and English: pet form of ANDREW.

Aneirin (m.) Welsh: of uncertain derivation. The original form of the name was *Neirin*, with the initial *A-* developing in the 13th century; it may be derived from an element cognate with Irish Gaelic *nár* noble, modest. This name was borne by the first known Welsh poet, who lived *c.*600. The 'Book of Aneirin' is a 13th-century manuscript which purports to preserve his work, including the *Gododdin*, a long work about the defeat of the Welsh by the Saxons.

Variant: **Aneurin** (a modern form).

Pet form: **Nye** (popularized as a result of the fame of the statesman Aneurin Bevan, 1897–1960).

Anežka (f.) Czech form of AGNES.

Pet forms: **Aneša, Neš(k)a**.

Anfisa (f.) Russian: from Greek *Anthousa*, a name of uncertain derivation. It may be a derivative of *anthos* flower. St Anthousa was a 9th-century abbess who lived near Constantinople.

Short form: **Fisa**.

Angel (f., formerly also m.) English: originally a male name, as in the case of Angel Clare, the chief male character in Thomas Hardy's novel *Tess of the D'Urbervilles* (1891), and derived from the Church Latin name *Angelus*, from Greek *angelos*. This meant 'messenger' in classical Greek, but in New Testament Greek it had the specialized meaning 'messenger of God', i.e. an angel. It is now completely out of fashion as a male name in English, but is being increasingly bestowed as a female name, especially among American Blacks. It is no doubt influenced strongly by the use of the English vocabulary word *angel* as an affectionate term of address for a good (or pretty) little girl.

Cognates (all m.): Italian: **Angelo**. Spanish: **Ángel**. Basque: **Aingeru**. Polish: **Anioł**. Czech: **Anděl**. Yiddish: **An(t)shel**.

Angela (f.) English and Italian: from Church Latin, feminine form of the male name *Angelus* (see ANGEL), which is from New Testament Greek *angelos* angel, which meant 'messenger' in classical Greek. It has been in use in Britain and America from the 18th century, since when it has increased steadily in popularity.

Cognates: Spanish: **Ángela**. Polish: **Aniela**. Czech: **Anděla**. Irish Gaelic: **Aingeal**.

Pet forms: English: **Angie**. Spanish: **Angelita**. Czech: **Andělka**.

Ángeles (f.) Spanish: from a title of the Virgin Mary, *Maria de los Ángeles*. Mary is revered in Roman Catholic tradition as the Queen of Heaven and mistress of the ranks of angels who wait on the throne of God.

Cognate: French: **Marie-Ange**.

Angelica (f.) English: from Church Latin, from the feminine form of the Latin adjective *angelicus* angelic, or simply a Latinate elaboration of ANGELA.

Cognates: French: **Angélique**. German: **Angelika, Angelike**.

Angelina (f.) English: Latinate elaboration of ANGELA.

Cognate: French: **Angeline** (now also used in the English-speaking world).

Angélique (f.) French form of ANGELICA.

Angelita (f.) Spanish: diminutive pet form of *Ángela* (see ANGELA).

Angelo (m.) Italian form of the male name ANGEL.

Angharad (f.) Welsh: composed of the Old Celtic intensive prefix *an-* + the root *cār* love + the noun suffix *-ad*. This was the name of the mother of the 12th-century chronicler Giraldus Cambrensis ('Gerald the Welshman'). In the *Mabinogi*, Angharad Golden Hand at first rejects Peredur's suit, but later falls in love with him when he comes back as the unknown Mute Knight. The name has been strongly revived in Wales since the 1940s.

Angie (f., m.) 1. (f.) English (pronounced /'ændʒɪ/): pet form of ANGELA.

2. (m.) Scottish (pronounced /'aŋgɪ/): pet form of ANGUS.

Angosto (f.) Spanish (mainly Galician): from a title of the Virgin Mary, *Nuestra Señora de Angosto* 'Our Lady of Angosto'. Angosto is a place in the province of Álava where the Virgin is supposed to have appeared in a vision. The place derives its name from Late Latin *angustum* narrows or mountain pass.

Angus (m.) Scottish and Irish: Anglicized form of the Gaelic name **Aonghus** or **Aonghas**, composed of Celtic elements meaning 'one' and 'choice'. This is the name of an old Celtic god, and is first recorded as a personal name in Adomnan's 'Life of St Columba', where it occurs in the form *Oinogus(s)ius* as the name of a man for whom the saint prophesied a long life and a peaceful death. This is also almost certainly the name of the

8th-century Pictish king variously recorded as *Onnust* and *Hungus*.

Short form: Gus.

Pet form: Angie.

Feminine form: **Angusina**.

Angustias (f.) Spanish: variant of Angosto, altered by folk etymology as if from the Castilian vocabulary word *angustias*, plural of *angustia* mental or physical anguish or distress. The reference is to a title of the Virgin Mary, *Nuestra Señora de las Angustias*, which enshrines the notion that the Virgin will come to the aid of those who pray to her in their distress.

Aniceto (m.) Italian, Spanish, and Portuguese form of Latin *Anicētus*, a derivative of Greek *Anikētos* 'unconquered' or 'unconquerable', from *a-* not + *nikein* to conquer. This was the name of a 2nd-century pope of Syrian origin; see Nikita.

Aniela (f.) Polish form of Angela. This name is now also occasionally used in the English-speaking world, and is sometimes respelled **Anniela** by association with Anne. There has also been some confusion with Italian Aniella.

Aniella (f.) Italian: feminine form of Aniello, rather more popular than the masculine form.

Aniello (m.) Italian: a vernacular variant of the learned form *Agnello*, from Church Latin *Agnellus*, a diminutive of *agnus* lamb. The Paschal Lamb was a particularly important symbol to the early Christians, and so the medieval Latin name was quite common. St Agnellus (d. *c.*596), abbot of San Gaudioso, is one of the patrons of Naples, and this name has enjoyed some currency there as a result, but it is otherwise not common.

Anioł (m.) Polish form of the male name Angel.

Anisim (m.) Russian: from the Greek name *Onesimos* 'useful' or 'profitable'. This was a fairly common slave name during the classical and post-classical periods, and was borne by a runaway slave who was converted to Christianity by St Paul. Paul says of him in the Epistle to his master Philemon that 'in time past he was to thee unprofitable, but now profitable to thee and to me' (Philemon 11). This early Christian use made it a very acceptable name in the Orthodox Church, quite apart from the connotations that it acquired of 'usefulness to Christ'.

Variant: **Onisim**.

Anita (f.) Originally Spanish: pet form of *Ana*, the Spanish version of Anne. It is now widely used in English-speaking countries with little awareness of its Spanish origin.

Anitra (f.) Apparently a literary coinage by Henrik Ibsen, who used it as the name of an Eastern princess in *Peer Gynt* (1867). No Arabic original is known, however. It is now occasionally used as a given name, not only in Norway, but also elsewhere in Scandinavia, in Germany, and in the English-speaking world.

Anke (f.) Low German: pet form of Anne. The name is now quite extensively used in northern Germany.

Anker (m.) Danish: name that has been used since the Middle Ages. It is of uncertain origin, but may derive from the vocabulary word *annkarl* agricultural labourer (from the elements *ann* harvest, busy season + *karl* man), or else from the elements *arn* eagle + *karl* man.

Ann (f.) English: variant spelling of Anne. *Ann* was the more common of the two spellings in the 19th century, but is now losing ground to the form with final *-e*.

Anna (f.) Latinate variant of Anne, in common use as a given name in English, Gaelic, Italian, German, Dutch, Scandinavian languages, and Slavonic languages. Among people with a classical education, it has from time to time been associated with Virgil's *Aeneid*, where it is borne by the sister of Dido, Queen of Carthage. This Phoenician name may ultimately be of Semitic origin, and thus cognate with the biblical *Anne*. However, the connection, if it exists, is indirect rather than direct.

Cognate: Spanish: **Ana**.

Pet forms: Scottish Gaelic: **Annag**. Swedish: **Annika**. Polish: **Anula, Anusia**. Czech: **Anin(k)a, Andul(k)a, Anuška**. Russian: **Asya**.

Annabel (f.) English: sometimes taken as an elaboration of ANNA, but more probably a dissimilated form of AMABEL. It has been common in Scotland since the 12th century (often being used as an Anglicized form of Gaelic *Barabal*; see BARBARA) and in the rest of the English-speaking world since the 1940s.

Variants: **Annabella** (Latinized); **Annabelle** (Gallicized, under the influence of BELLE).

Anndra (m.) Scottish Gaelic form of ANDREW; see also AINDREA.

Anne (f.) English, French, and German form (via Old French, Latin, and Greek) of the Hebrew female name *Hanna* 'He (God) has favoured me (i.e. with a child)'. This is the name borne in the Bible by the mother of Samuel (see HANNAH), and according to non-biblical tradition also by the mother of the Virgin Mary. It is the widespread folk cult of the latter that has led to the great popularity of the name in various forms throughout Europe. The simplified form ANN was in the 19th century very much more common, but the form with final *-e* has grown in popularity during the 20th century, partly perhaps due to the enormous popularity of L. M. Montgomery's story *Anne of Green Gables* (1908), and partly due to Princess Anne (b. 1950). In Ireland *Anne* has been used as an Anglicized form of ÁINE. See also ANNA.

Pet forms: English: **Annie**. French: **Annette, Ninon**. Breton: **Annick**. Low German: **Anke, Antje**. Dutch: **Anneke**.

Anneka (f.) Latinate variant of the Dutch name **Anneke**, a pet form of ANNE, popularized in Britain in the 1980s by the television personality Anneka Rice.

Anneli (f.) Scandinavian: shortened form of the originally German given name ANNELIESE.

Anneliese (f.) German and Scandinavian: compound name composed of the elements ANNE and LIESE.

Annella (f.) English and Scottish: elaborated form, common particularly in the Highlands, of ANNE.

Annetta (f.) English: Latinate elaboration of ANNETTE, not in very common use.

Annette (f.) French: pet form of ANNE, now also widely used in the English-speaking world.

Annfrid (f.) Norwegian: from the Old Norse female personal name *Arnfríðr*, composed of the elements *arn* eagle + *fríðr* fair, beautiful.

Annibale (m.) Italian: bestowed in honour of the Carthaginian general Hannibal Barca (247–182 BC), who led a Carthaginian army from Spain across the Alps and into Italy to attack the Romans. He was eventually defeated by Scipio at Zama (202 BC), but not until he had shaken the Roman republic to its core. The name is sometimes chosen by Italians with strong regional loyalties, opposed to the centralizing tendencies of the government in Rome. The name is composed of the Phoenician elements *hann* grace, favour (and so distantly related to HANNAH) + the name of the god *Baal*.

Annice (f.) English: variant spelling of ANNIS, based on the numerous women's names ending in the syllable *-ice*.

Annick (f.) Breton: pet form of ANNE.

Annika (f.) Swedish: pet form of ANNA, apparently derived from the German dialect form *Anniken*.

Annis (f.) Scottish and English: a medieval vernacular form of AGNES, which gave rise to a surname. Its modern use as a given name is probably at least in part a transferred use of the surname as well as a revival of the medieval given name.

Variants: **Annys, Annice.**

Annunziata (f.) Italian: one of the many Roman Catholic names in Italy and Spain that are derived from titles of the Virgin Mary. This one refers to the Annunciation to her of God's favour and the impending birth of Christ (Luke 1: 20–38). The festival of the Annunciation has been celebrated since the 5th century. It was at first kept on Ember Wednesday during Lent, but was later moved to 25 March, exactly nine months before Christmas Day, replacing pagan festivals celebrating the vernal equinox.

Short form: **Nunzia.**

Annwyl (f.) Welsh: from the vocabulary word *annwyl* beloved.

Variant: **Anwyl.**

Annys (f.) Scottish and English: variant of ANNIS, in a deliberately archaic spelling.

Anona (f.) English: of uncertain origin, apparently not recorded before the 1920s. It seems most likely that it arose as an artificial combination of elements from existing names, for example ANNE and FIONA. In form it resembles Latin *annona* corn supply, but this is unlikely to have influenced the formation of the name.

Anraí (m.) Irish Gaelic form of HENRY; see also EINRÍ.

Anselmo (m.) Italian: of Germanic origin, composed of the elements *ans* divinity + *helm* helmet. This name seems to have been largely confined to Italy until brought to England by St Anselm, who was archbishop of Canterbury in the late 11th and early 12th centuries, and is regarded as one of the Doctors of the Church. He was born at Aosta in Piedmont.

Cognates: English: **Anselm** (rare, borne mainly by Roman Catholics). Polish: **Anzelm.**

Anshel (m.) Jewish (Yiddish): variant of ANTSHEL.

Antal (m.) Hungarian form of ANTHONY.

Antero (m.) Finnish form of ANDREW.

Pet form: **Antti.**

Anthea (f.) Latinized spelling of Greek *Antheia*, a personal name derived from the feminine of the adjective *antheios* flowery. This was used in the classical period as a byname of the goddess Hera at Argos, but as a modern given name it was reinvented in the 17th century by English pastoral poets such as Robert Herrick.

Anthony (m.) The usual English form of the old Roman family name *Antōnius*, which is of uncertain (probably Etruscan) origin. The spelling with *-th-* (not normally reflected in the pronunciation) represents a learned but erroneous attempt to associate it with Greek *anthos* flower. In the post-classical period it was a common name, borne by various early saints, most notably a 3rd-century Egyptian hermit monk, who is regarded as the founder of Christian monasticism.

Variant: **Antony.**

Cognates: Irish Gaelic: **Antain(e).** French: **Antoine.** Italian, Spanish: **Antonio.** Catalan: **Antoni.** Basque: **Andoni.** German: **Anton.** Polish: **Antoni.** Czech: **Antonín.** Russian: **Anton.** Hungarian: **Antal.**

Short forms: English: **Tony.** Italian: **Tonio.** Spanish: **Toño.** Low German, Frisian: **Tönjes.**

Pet forms: Spanish: **Tonete.**

Antigone (f.) Classical name in occasional modern use. In Greek mythology Antigone was a daughter of Oedipus by his accidental incestuous marriage to his own mother, Jocasta. She tended her father as he wandered through Greece, blinded, disgraced, and suffering mental anguish. After her brothers, Eteocles and Polynices, killed each other, she gave funeral rites to both of them, defying the order of her uncle Creon, King of Thebes, that the rebel Polynices should be left unburied. For this, Creon had her buried alive. Its choice as a modern given name is perhaps made with reference to her strength of character in doing what she perceived as right in terrible circumstances. Her name is composed of the Greek elements *anti* against, contrary + *gen-*, *gon-* born.

Antioco (m.) Italian: a typically Sardinian name, bestowed in honour of a Christian saint who was martyred under the Emperor Hadrian in *c.*110 on the islet of Sulcis near Sardinia, which is now also known as the Isola di Sant'Antioco ('island of St Antiochus'). The name is from Greek *Antiochos*, composed of the elements *anti* against + *ekhein* to have, i.e. to hold out against, denoting stubborn tenacity of character. It was borne in classical times by the father of the Macedonian general Seleucus I, who in *c.*300 BC named the city of Antioch in Asia Minor after him.

Antip (m.) Russian: from the Greek personal name *Antipas*, a short form of *Antipatēr*, which means 'like a father', from the elements *anti-* like + *patēr* father. This name is mentioned in the Book of Revelation (2: 13), where the bearer is the first bishop of Pergamum, who was martyred there *c.*90. He is greatly revered in the Orthodox Church.

Antje (f.) Low German and Dutch: pet form of ANNE.

Antoine (m.) French form of ANTHONY, now also used in the English-speaking world. It was the thirtieth most common male name among American Blacks in 1982.

Antoinette (f.) French: feminine diminutive of ANTOINE, which has become even more popular in the English-speaking world than the masculine form.

Short form: **Toinette**.

Anton (m.) German and Russian form of ANTHONY, now also used in the English-speaking world.

Antoni (m.) Catalan and Polish form of ANTHONY.

Antonia (f.) English, German, Dutch, Scandinavian, Italian, Spanish, and Portuguese: feminine form of ANTHONY and its cognates, unaltered since classical times, when it was a common Roman feminine family name.

Cognates: Czech: **Antonie**. Finnish: **Toini**.
Pet form: English: **Toni**.

Antonín (m.) Czech form of ANTHONY, actually from the Latin derivative *Antonīnus*.

Antonina (f.) Latin derivative of ANTONIA, common in Poland and occasionally used in the English-speaking world.

Cognate: Czech: **Antonína**.

Antonio (m.) Italian and Spanish form of ANTHONY, from Latin *Antōnius*. It is now also used in parts of the English-speaking world.

Antony (m.) English: variant spelling of ANTHONY.

Antshel (m.) Jewish (Yiddish): ultimately from Latin *angelus* angel.

Variants: **Anshel**, **Amshel**.

Antti (m.) Finnish: pet form of ANTERO.

Anula (f.) Polish: pet form of ANNA.

Anunciación (f.) Spanish: one of a whole set of names derived from titles of the Virgin Mary. It commemorates the Annuciation to her of God's favour and the forthcoming birth of Christ (cf. ANNUNZIATA).

Short form: **Anuncia**.

Anusia (f.) Polish: pet form of ANNA.

Anuška (f.) Czech: pet form of ANNA.

Anwyl (f.) Welsh: variant of ANNWYL.

Anzelm (m.) Polish form of ANSELMO.

Aodh (m.) Irish and Scottish Gaelic: name, meaning 'fire', of the old Celtic sun god. This was a very common personal name from the earliest times. From the later Middle Ages it was commonly Anglicized as HUGH and more recently as EUGENE, but the Gaelic form has also survived in common use. It has given the surnames *Magee* (Gaelic *Mac Aodha*) in Ireland and *McKay* (Gaelic *Mac Aoidh*) in Scotland.

Aoibheann (f.) Irish Gaelic: traditional name meaning 'beautiful'. It was borne by a number of women in the early history of the royal family of Ireland.

Variant: **Aoibhinn**.

Anglicized form: **Eavan**.

Aoife (f.) Irish Gaelic: of uncertain origin, probably a derivative of *aoibh* beauty (cf. AOIBHEANN). It was borne by a daughter of King Dermot of Leinster, who married Richard de Clare, Earl of Pembroke, the leader of the Anglo-Norman invasion of 1169. The name has sometimes been Anglicized as EVA.

Aonghas (m.) The modern Gaelic form of ANGUS.

Variant: **Aonghus**.

Aparición (f.) Spanish: religious name, referring to Christ's appearance to the apostles after the Resurrection.

Aphra (f.) English: of uncertain origin, perhaps an Anglicization of an Irish name; see AFRICA, EITHRIG. It could also be a hypercorrected spelling of a Late Latin name, *Afra*. This was originally an ethnic name for a woman from Africa (in Roman times meaning the area around Carthage). It was used in the post-classical period as a nickname for someone with dark colouring, and eventually became a given name, being borne, for example, by saints martyred at Brescia under the Roman emperor Hadrian and at Augsburg under Diocletian. The respelling of the name may have been prompted by Micah 1: 10 'in the house of Aphrah roll thyself in the dust', where *Aphrah* is often taken as a personal name, but is in fact a placename meaning 'dust'. The first name has never been frequently used, but is remembered as the name of the English writer Aphra Behn (1640–89).

Apollinare (m.) Italian: a name characteristic of the Romagna region and in particular of Ravenna, where it is borne in honour of St Apollinaris, a 1st-century bishop of the city who was martyred under the Emperor Vespasian. The name is of classical origin, being taken from an adjectival form of the name of the god Apollo (see APOLLONIA).

Apollinaria (f.) Feminine form of Latin *Apollinaris* (see APOLLINARE), influenced by APOLLONIA. It has been used in Russian and occasionally in English.

Pet form: Russian: **Polina**.

Apollonia (f.) Latin feminine form of the Greek masculine name *Apollonios*, an adjectival derivative of the name of the sun god, *Apollo*. This is of uncertain origin, and may be pre-Greek. St Apollonia was an elderly deaconess martyred at Alexandria under the Emperor Decius in the mid-3rd century. The name in this form has been used in both English and German.

Derivatives: French: **Apolline**. Danish: **Abelone**.

April (f.) English: from the month (Latin (*mensis*) *aprīlis*, probably a derivative of *aperīre* to open, as the month when buds open and flowers appear). It forms a series with the more common names MAY and JUNE, all taken from months associated with the spring, a time of new birth and growth, and may originally have been intended as an English version of the supposedly French name AVRIL.

Aquiles (m.) Portuguese form of ACHILLES.

Arabella (f.) Scottish and English: of uncertain etymology. It probably represents an alteration of *An(n)abella* (see ANNABEL).

Variant: **Arabel** (now rare, but commoner in earlier centuries, when it was also sometimes found as **Orabel**, apparently altered by folk etymology to conform with Latin *orābilis* invokable (from *orāre* to pray to), i.e. a saint who could be invoked).

Araceli (f.) Spanish (mainly Latin American): apparently a modern coinage from Latin *ara* altar + *c(o)eli* of the sky.

Arailt (m.) Scottish Gaelic form of HAROLD.

Aram (m.) Biblical: name (meaning 'height' in Hebrew) borne by a son of Shem and grandson of Noah mentioned in a genealogy (Genesis 10: 22).

Aranka (f.) Hungarian: originally a pet form derived from Hungarian *arany* gold (cf. *Zlata* at ZLATAN). Later, it came to be regarded as a vernacular form of AURELIA.

Aranrhod (f.) Welsh: name borne in the *Mabinogi* by the mother of Dylan and Lleu Llaw Gyffes. It seems to be composed of Old Celtic elements meaning 'huge, round, humped' + 'wheel'; the legendary heroine may originally have been a moon goddess. See also ARIANRHOD.

Aránzazu (f.) Basque: from the name of a place near Oñate in the province of Guipúzcoa, whose name means 'thorn-bush' in Basque. It was adopted as a given name because in 1469 the Virgin Mary appeared in a vision to a shepherd at this place.

Pet form: **Arantxa**.

Archibald (m.) Scottish: of Norman French origin, from Continental Germanic, composed of the elements *ercan* genuine + *bald* bold, brave. It has always been largely associated with Scotland, where it is in regular use as the English equivalent of Scottish Gaelic *Gilleasbaig* (see GILLESPIE).

Pet forms: **Archie**, **Archy** (Gaelic **Eair(r)dsidh**); **Baldie**.

Ardal (m.) Irish: Anglicized form of the traditional Gaelic name *Ard(gh)al*, composed of the elements *ard* high or possibly *art* bear + *gal* valour.

Arduino (m.) Italian form of HARTWIN.

Are (m.) Scandinavian: from the Old Norse personal name *Ari*, originally a byname meaning 'eagle', or else a short form of the compound names containing this first element.

Ariadne (f.) From classical mythology: the name of a daughter of the Cretan king Minos. She gave the Athenian hero Theseus a ball of wool to enable him to find his way out of the Labyrinth after killing the Minotaur. He took her with him when he sailed from Crete, but abandoned her on the island of Naxos on the way back to Athens. Greek lexicographers of the Hellenistic period claimed that the name was composed of the Cretan dialect elements *ari-* an intensive prefix + *adnos* holy. The name survived in the Christian era because of St Ariadne (d. *c.*130), an early Phrygian martyr.

Derivatives: French: **Arianne**. Italian: **Arianna**.

Arianrhod (f.) Welsh: altered form of ARANRHOD, made up of the modern Welsh elements *arian* silver + *rhod* wheel.

Arianwen (f.) Welsh: composed of the elements *arian* silver + *(g)wen*, feminine of *gwyn* white, fair, blessed, holy. The name was borne in the 5th century by one of the daughters of Brychan, a semi-legendary Welsh chieftain.

Ariel (m., f.) Jewish: from the biblical placename *Ariel*, said to mean 'lion of God' in Hebrew. It is mentioned in the prophecies of Ezra (8: 16) and Isaiah (29: 1–2). It has achieved popularity as a modern Hebrew first name, perhaps as an alternative to ARYE.

Arina (f.) Russian: variant of IRINA.

Pet forms: **Arisha, Orya**.

Aristide (m.) French: from the classical Greek name *Aristides*, which is in origin a patronymic from a short form of any of the various compound names having as a first element the word *aristos* best, excellent. In the classical period this was borne by an Athenian statesman known as Aristides the Just, whose probity was such that he helped to vote for his own banishment by writing his own name down when asked to do so by an illiterate citizen. In the Christian era, St Aristides (d. *c.*123) was an Athenian philosopher who presented an *Apologia* for Christianity to the Emperor Hadrian. In recent times, the name is best known as being that of the French socialist statesman Aristide Briand (1862–1932), who advocated the idea of a United States of Europe.

Arkadi (m.) Russian: from Greek *Arkadios*, an adjective referring to the region of Arcadia in the central Peloponnese. This placename was explained in classical mythology as being derived from *Arkas*, the name of a son of Zeus and the nymph Callisto, founder of the Arcadian people. The true origin is unknown. In the later classical period Arcadia became the conventional setting for pastoral idylls, a convention copied in later European literature. The Russian given name owes its existence mainly to St Arkadios, a 4th-century missionary bishop venerated in the Eastern Church.
Cognate: Hungarian: **Árkos**.

Arke (m.) Jewish: Yiddish pet form of AARON.

Arkhip (m.) Russian: from Greek *Arkhippos*, composed of the elements *arkhē* beginning or rule + *hippos* horse. St Arkhippos was one of the earliest Christians, twice mentioned by St Paul in his epistles (Colossians 4: 17; Philemon 2). Tradition has it that he became the first bishop of Colossae in Phrygia.
Pet form: **Khipa**.

Árkos (m.) Hungarian form of ARKADI.

Arlene (f.) English: modern coinage, most common in the United States. It is of unknown origin, probably a fanciful coinage based on MARLENE or CHARLENE or on both.

Arlette (f.) French and English: of ancient but uncertain origin. It seems to represent a Norman French double diminutive form derived from the Germanic name element *arn* eagle. It was the name of the mistress of Duke Robert of Normandy in the 11th century; their son was William the Conqueror.

Armelle (f.) French (of Breton origin): feminine form of the rarer male name *Armel*, originally borne by a Breton saint of the 6th century who founded the abbeys of St-Armel-des-Bascheaux and Plouërmel which still bear his name. According to medieval sources, he was born in Wales and was a cousin of St Samson. His name seems to be composed of the Celtic elements *art* stone + *mael* prince, chief.

Armin (m.) German: a modern revival of an ancient Germanic name, mentioned in the form *Arminius* by the Roman historian Tacitus. Arminius (d. AD 21) was a chief of a Germanic tribe called the Cherusci, who in AD 9 inflicted a tremendous defeat on the Roman armies at the Teutoburgerwald, so that they abandoned any serious further attempts to extend their influence east of the Rhine. The name, which is probably etymologically identical with HERMANN, enjoyed a vogue during the period of National Socialism, with its emphasis on German military achievements.

Armstrong (m.) English and Scottish: transferred use of the surname, which originated in the Borders in the Middle Ages, probably as a nickname for a man with strong arms. Like most given names derived from surnames, it no doubt owes its adoption as a given name to a maternal maiden name, but its choice may also have been influenced by the still transparent etymology.

Arn (m.) 1. Jewish: Yiddish contracted form of AARON.
2. English: short form of ARNOLD, of recent origin.
Pet form: **Arnie**.

Arnaldo (m.) Italian form of ARNOLD.

Arnaud (m.) French form of ARNOLD.

Arnbjörn (m.) Swedish: from an Old Norse personal name composed of the elements *arn* eagle + *björn* bear.
Variant: **Ambjörn**.
Cognate: Norwegian: **Arnbjørn**.

Arndt (m.) German (esp. N. Germany): contracted form of ARNOLD.
Variant: **Arnd.**
Pet form: **Arne.**

Arne (m.) 1. Scandinavian: short form of any of various names derived from Old Norse names containing the first element *arn* eagle, for example ARNBJÖRN, *Arnfinn*, and *Arnsten*. It is now quite widely used as a given name in its own right.
2. German: pet form of ARNDT.

Arno (m.) German: an old Germanic personal name, a short form of the various compound names beginning with the element *arn* eagle, for example ARNOLD and *Arnulf* ('eagle wolf').

Arnold (m.) English and German: of Continental Germanic origin, composed of the elements *arn* eagle + *wald* ruler. It was introduced to Britain by the Normans. An early saint of this name, whose cult contributed to its popularity, was a musician at the court of Charlemagne. He is said to have been a Greek by birth; it is not clear when and how he acquired his Germanic name. It had died out in England by the end of the Middle Ages and was revived in the 19th century, along with a large number of other medieval Germanic names.
Variant: **Arndt** (N. German).
Cognates: French: **Arnaud.** Italian: **Arnaldo.**
Short form: English: ARN.

Arnon (m.) Jewish: modern name taken from that of a river mentioned in the Bible (Numbers 21: 15). The river name means 'swift' in Hebrew.

Arnošt (m.) Czech form of ERNEST.

Aron (m.) Simplified variant of AARON, also the regular Polish form.

Árpád (m.) Hungarian: apparently from a diminutive of the vocabulary word *árpa* seed, barleycorn. It was the name of the Magyar chieftain who first conquered the territory that is modern Hungary, in the late 9th century, and who led his people to settle there. He is regarded as a national hero in Hungary, and many children are named after him.

Arrigo (m.) Italian: vernacular form of the more learned ENRICO, a cognate of English HENRY, German *Heinrich*. *Arrigo* is the older form of the name, and was used throughout the Middle Ages.

Arron (m.) English: altered spelling of ARON.

Arseni (m.) Russian: from the Greek name *Arsenios* 'male, virile'. St Arsenius the Great (d. *c.*449) was a Roman deacon who served as tutor to Arcadius and Honorius, the sons of the Emperor Theodosius, who divided the Roman Empire between them. In later life Arsenius became a hermit.
Pet form: **Senya.**

Art (m.) English, Irish, and Scottish: now generally taken as an informal short form of ARTHUR. There is also a traditional Gaelic name of this form (from the vocabulary word *art* bear) which has generally been Anglicized as *Arthur* although it in fact has no connection with that name. In the diminutive form *Artan* it has given rise to the Skye surname *Mac Artain*, Anglicized as *McCartan*.

Artair (m.) Scottish Gaelic form of ARTHUR.

Artemas (m.) Of New Testament Greek origin, from a name that in fact represents a short form of various compound names containing that of the goddess ARTEMIS (for example, *Artemidoros* 'gift of Artemis' and *Artemisthenes* 'strength of Artemis'). It is borne in the Bible by a character mentioned briefly in St Paul's letter to Titus (3: 12). The name enjoyed some popularity among the Puritans in the 17th century, but fell out of use again.
Variant: **Artemus** (Latinized).

Artemi (m.) Russian: from Greek *Artemios*, a derivative of ARTEMAS. St Artemius (d. 363) was a powerful official under the Emperor Constantine the Great, and was prefect of Egypt under his successor Constantius Chlorus. However, when Julian the Apostate came to the throne, Artemius was beheaded.

Variant: **Artyom.**

Pet form: **Tyoma.**

Artemis (f.) From the name of the Greek goddess of the moon and of hunting, equivalent to the Latin DIANA. It is of uncertain derivation, and may well be pre-Greek. As a given name, it is rare in any country, but is chosen occasionally by parents in search of something distinctive. It is borne by a granddaughter of Lady Diana Cooper, perhaps as an oblique tribute to the grandmother.

Arthur (m.) Of Celtic origin. King Arthur was a British king of the 5th or 6th century, about whom virtually no historical facts are known. He ruled in Britain after the collapse of the Roman Empire and before the coming of the Germanic tribes, and a vast body of legends grew up around him in the literatures of medieval Western Europe. His name is first found in the Latinized form *Artorius* and is of obscure derivation. The spelling with *-th-*, now invariably reflected in the pronunciation of the English name, is not found before the 16th century, and seems to represent no more than an artificial embellishment. The name became particularly popular in Britain in the 19th century, partly as a result of the fame of Arthur Wellesley (1769–1852), Duke of Wellington, partly because of the popularity of Tennyson's *Idylls of the King* (1842–85), and partly because of the enormous Victorian interest in things medieval in general and in Arthurian legend in particular. This interest also accounts for its adoption as a given name in France and elsewhere in Western Europe.

Cognates: Scottish Gaelic: **Artair** (from which derives the surname *Mac Artair*, Anglicized as *McArthur* and *Carter*). Irish Gaelic: **Artúr.** Italian, Spanish: **Arturo.**

Short form: ART.

Artyom (m.) Russian: variant of ARTEMI.

Arvid (m.) Scandinavian: from an Old Norse personal name composed of the elements *arn* eagle + *viðr* wood, tree.

Arye (m.) Jewish: meaning 'lion' in Hebrew. The lion is traditionally associated with the name JUDAH, Hebrew YEHUDA, because of Jacob's words in his dying blessing: 'Judah is a lion's whelp' (Genesis 49: 9). It became common during the Middle Ages when such animal names were popular in Europe and is often used together with the Yiddish name LEIB.

Asa (m.) Biblical: name of one of the early kings of Judah, who reigned for forty years, as recorded in 1 Kings and 2 Chronicles. It was originally a byname meaning 'doctor, healer' in Hebrew, and is still a common Jewish name. It was first used among English-speaking Christians by the Puritans in the 17th century, and although now far from common, it has never completely dropped out of use. In the 20th century it is largely known as the given name of the historian Asa Briggs and of the footballer Asa Hertford. See also ÅSA.

Åsa (f.) Scandinavian: short form of any of various Old Norse female personal names containing the first element *áss* god. In Norway and Denmark the form **Åse** is also common.

Asaph (m.) Biblical: from a Hebrew vocabulary word meaning 'collector'. This is found attached to some of the Psalms (50 and 73–83), and may have been the name of the writer or of a cantor. Asaph is also mentioned at 1 Chronicles 6: 39, 9: 15, and 25: 1; and other, apparently unrelated bearers of the name are mentioned at 2 Kings 18: 37 and Isaiah 36: 3 and 36: 22. In more recent times the name was borne by Asaph Hall (1829–1907), the American astronomer who discovered the two satellites of Mars.

Asdrubale (m.) Italian: from the name of the Carthaginian general *Hasdrubal* Barca

(d. *c.*207 BC), brother of Hannibal (see ANNIBALE). The name is composed of the Phoenician elements *asru* aid (related to EZRA) + the divine name *Baal* 'lord'. As a given name in Italy, this is not as common as ANNIBALE and AMILCARE.

Asenath (f.) Biblical: name borne by Joseph's Egyptian wife (Genesis 41: 45), who became the mother of Manasseh and Ephraim. The name seems to have meant 'she belongs to her father' in ancient Egyptian.

Asher (m.) Jewish: meaning 'fortunate' or 'happy' in Hebrew. This was borne in the Bible by one of the sons of Jacob: 'and Leah said, Happy am I, for the daughters will call me blessed; and she called his name Asher' (Genesis 30: 13).

Variant: **Osher**.

Ashley (m., f.) English: an increasingly popular given name for girls, this is a transferred use of the surname, which comes from any of numerous places in England named in Old English with the elements *æsc* ash + *lēah* wood. Its use as a given name may have been first inspired by admiration for the humanitarian work of Anthony Ashley Cooper (1801–85), Earl of Shaftesbury.

Ashling (f.) Irish: Anglicized form of AISLING.

Aslög (f.) Swedish: from an Old Norse female personal name composed of the elements *áss* god + *laug* consecrated, dedicated. The form **Åslög** is also used.

Cognates: Norwegian: **Aslaug**, **Åslaug**. Danish: **Asløg, Aslaug**.

Åsmund (m.) Scandinavian: from the Old Norse personal name *Ásmundr*, composed of the elements *áss* god + *mundr* protector.

Cognate: English: OSMOND.

Assumpta (f.) Latin form of ASSUNTA, used especially in Ireland among Roman Catholics.

Assunta (f.) Italian: from a title of the Virgin Mary, *Maria Assunta*, referring to her assumption into heaven. Cf. ASUNCIÓN.

Asta (f.) Scandinavian: short form of ASTRID. There has been much confusion with ÅSTA.

Åsta (f.) Scandinavian: from the Old Norse female personal name *Ásta*, derived from the vocabulary element *ást* love.

Aston (m.) English: transferred use of the surname, which originated in the Middle Ages as a local name, from any of the numerous English places so called, most being named with the Old English elements *ēast* east + *tūn* settlement.

Astrid (f.) Scandinavian: composed of the Old Norse elements *áss* god + *fríðr* fair, beautiful. It has become fairly common in the English-speaking world during the 20th century, in part as a result of the fame of the Queen of the Belgians (1905–35) who bore this name.

Short form: **Asta**.

Pet form: Swedish: **Sassa**.

Asunción (f.) Spanish: another of the many female names bestowed in honour of the Virgin Mary. This one commemorates her assumption into heaven, the festival of which has been celebrated on 15 August since at least the 7th century, although this has been a matter of official dogma since only 1950.

Short form: **Asun**.

Asya (f.) Russian: pet form of both ANASTASIA and ANNA.

Atalanta (f.) From classical mythology. Atalanta was a girl who was a swift runner and who took part in the hunt for the Calydonian boar. Meleager, leader of the hunt, gave her its pelt, for he had fallen in love with her. However, he died as a result of quarrels with his brothers. Atalanta undertook to marry only a man who could defeat her in a race; losers were condemned to death. Eventually, Hippomenes defeated her by dropping three golden apples which she stopped to pick up.

Atarah (f.) Biblical: from a Hebrew word meaning 'crown'. Atarah was one of the wives of Jerahmeel (1 Chronicles 2: 26).

Variant: **Atara** (now a common modern Hebrew name, possibly as a translation of Yiddish KREINE).

Athanasius (m.) Latin: the name of an early Christian saint (*c.*297–373), an Alexandrian theologian venerated particularly in the Eastern Church. His name is derived from the Greek vocabulary word *athanatos* immortal, and was popular among early Christians, since it expressed their confidence in eternal life.

Derivatives: French: **Athanase**. Russian: **Afanasi**. Polish: **Atanazy**.

Pet form: Russian: **Afonya**.

Athene (f.) From classical mythology: the name of the Greek goddess of wisdom and patron of Athens. It is used occasionally in the English-speaking world by parents seeking a distinctive name.

Athol (m., f.) Scottish: transferred use of the name of a district of Perthshire, seat of the dukes of Atholl. The placename is thought to derive from Gaelic *ath Fodla* new Ireland.

Variants: **Atholl, Athole**.

Attila (m.) Hungarian: name bestowed occasionally in honour of the great pagan military leader Attila the Hun (d. 453), who struck terror into the hearts of people in the Roman Empire, acquiring the nickname 'the Scourge of God'. The origin of his name is unknown. His exploits were recorded and embroidered in Germanic legend; he lies behind the figure of Etzel in the *Nibelungenlied*, for example. Although the Huns inhabited what is now Hungary, and indeed gave it its modern English name, they were probably a Mongoloid people, and almost certainly unrelated to the Magyars, the modern inhabitants of Hungary.

Attilio (m.) Italian: from the Latin family name *Attilius*, which is generally taken to be of Etruscan origin. The name was taken up in Italy during the Renaissance in honour of the Roman general Marcus Attilius Regulus (d. *c.*250 BC), who fought against Hamilcar during the First Punic War.

Attracta (f.) Irish: Latinized version (as if from *attractus* attracted, drawn) of the Gaelic name **Athracht**. St Athracht or Attracta was a contemporary of St Patrick who lived as a recluse in Sligo.

Auberon (m.) English: of Norman French origin, from Germanic. There is much doubt about the form and meaning of the elements of which it was originally composed; it may be connected with AUBREY, or may derive from the elements *adal* noble + *ber(n)* bear.

Variant: **Oberon**.

Aubrey (m., f.) English: from a Norman French form of the Germanic name *Alberic*, composed of the elements *alb* elf, supernatural being + *ric* power. This was the (appropriate) name, according to Germanic mythology, of the king of the elves. The native Old English cognate, *Ælfric*, borne by a 10th-century archbishop of Canterbury, did not long survive the Conquest. *Aubrey* was a relatively common given name during the Middle Ages, but later fell out of favour. Its occurrence since the 19th century may in part represent a transferred use of the surname derived from the Norman given name, as well as a revival of the latter.

Audrey (f.) English: drastically reduced form of the Old English female name *Æðelþryð*, composed of the elements *æðel* noble + *þryð* strength. This was the name of a 6th-century saint (normally known by the Latinized form of her name, *Etheldreda*), who was a particular favourite in the Middle Ages. According to tradition she died from a tumour of the neck, which she bore stoically as a divine punishment for her youthful delight in fine necklaces. The name went into a decline at the end of the Middle Ages, when it came to be considered vulgar, being associated with *tawdry*, that is, lace and other goods sold at fairs held in her name (the word deriving from a misdivision of *Saint Audrey*). Shakespeare bestowed it on Touchstone's comic sweetheart in *As You Like It*. In the last century such associations have largely been forgotten, and the name has enjoyed some revival of popularity. The form **Audra** is also used, especially in the southern United States in double names such as *Audra Jo* and *Audra Rose*.

Audrina (f.) English: recent fanciful elaboration of AUDREY.

August (m.) German and Polish form of AUGUSTUS.

Augusta (f.) Latinate feminine form of AUGUSTUS, which enjoyed a vogue in Britain towards the end of the 19th century.

Auguste (m.) French form of AUGUSTUS.

Augustine (m.) English form of the Latin name *Augustīnus* (a derivative of AUGUSTUS). Its most famous bearer is St Augustine of Hippo (354–430), perhaps the greatest of the Fathers of the Christian Church. He formulated the principles followed by the numerous medieval communities named after him as *Austin* canons, friars, and nuns. Also important in England was St Augustine of Canterbury, who brought Christianity to Kent in the 6th century. See also AUSTIN.

Cognates: Irish Gaelic: **Ághaistín, Aibhistín**. Italian: **Agostino**. Spanish: **Agustín**. Catalan: **Agustí**. Portuguese: **Agostinho**. Russian: **Avgustin**. Polish: **Augustyn**. Finnish: **Tauno**.

Augustus (m.) Latin name, from the adjective *augustus* great, magnificent (from *augēre* to increase). This word was adopted as a title by the Roman emperors, starting with Octavian (Caius Julius Caesar Octavianus), the adopted son of Julius Caesar, who assumed it in 27 BC and is now generally known as the Emperor Augustus. This name, together with AUGUSTA, was revived in England in the 18th century, but it has now again declined in popularity.

Derivatives: German, Polish: **August**. French: **Auguste**. Italian, Spanish, Portuguese: **Augusto**. Russian: **Avgust**.

Short form: English, Irish: **Gus**.

Aulay (m.) Scottish: Anglicized form of *Amhla(i)dh* (see AMHLAOIBH).

Auliffe (m.) Irish: Anglicized form of AMHLAOIBH.

Aune (f.) Finnish form of AGNES.

Aurèle (m.) French form of the Roman family name *Aurēlius*, which is derived from *aureus* golden. Its most famous bearer was the 2nd-century emperor Marcus Aurelius Antoninus, also noted as a philosophical writer. It was later borne by various saints, including a 5th-century archbishop of Carthage who was a friend of St Augustine. It did not, however, enjoy much popularity in the Middle Ages, nor has it done so since; the modern use of the feminine form since the 17th century seems to be the result of its relatively transparent etymology ('golden').

Cognates: Italian, Spanish, Portuguese: **Aurelio**. German: **Aurel**; **Orell** (Switzerland).

Aurelia (f.) Feminine form of Latin *Aurēlius* (see AURÈLE), used occasionally in the English-speaking world.

Derivative: French: **Aurélie**.

Aurkene (f.) Basque equivalent of PRESENTACIÓN.

Aurora (f.) From Latin *aurōra* dawn, also used in the classical period as the name of the personified goddess of the dawn. It was not used as a given name in the post-classical or medieval period, but is a reinvention of the Renaissance, and has generally been bestowed as a learned equivalent of DAWN by parents conscious of its etymology.

Derivative: French: **Aurore**.

Austin (m.) English: from a medieval contracted form of the Latin name *Augustīnus* (see AUGUSTINE). The present-day use of this form as a given name is probably a reintroduction from its survival as a surname, for the full forms are rare in the English-speaking world.

Variant: **Austen**.

Cognate: Welsh: **Awstin**.

Auxilio (f.) Spanish: religious name meaning 'help', referring to the feast of *Maria Auxiliadora* 'Mary the Helper' celebrated on 24 May.

Ava (f.) English: of uncertain origin, probably Germanic, from a short form of various female compound names containing the element *av* (cf. AVIS). St Ava or Avia was a 9th-century abbess of Dinart in Hainault and a member of the Frankish royal family. However, evidence for its use between the early Middle Ages and the mid-20th century is lacking, and it may be a modern invention. Its recent popularity is largely due to the film actress Ava Gardner (1922–90).

Avdotya (f.) Russian: vernacular form of the learned name *Evdokia*, from the Greek name *Eudokia* (a compound of *eu* well, good + *dokein* to seem). This was Latinized as *Eudocia*. St Eudocia (98–117) was a Samaritan martyr beheaded by Trajan at Heliopolis in Syria.

Pet forms: **Avdunya, Dunya, Dunyasha**.

Aveline (f.) English: of Germanic origin, introduced by the Normans. It seems to represent an Old French diminutive form of the Germanic name AVILA, a derivative of AVIS. See also EILEEN.

Averil (f.) English: variant of AVRIL.

Averill (m.) English (esp. U.S.): transferred use of the surname, which originated during the Middle Ages from the Old English female personal name *Eoforhild* (see AVRIL).

Variant: **Averell**.

Averki (m.) Russian: from the Greek name *Aberkios* (Latin *Abercius*), which is of uncertain, presumably non-classical, origin. It was borne by a 2nd-century bishop of Hieropolis in Phrygia, who is revered as a saint in the Orthodox Church.

Avery (m.) English: transferred use of the surname, which originated in the Middle Ages from a Norman French pronunciation of ALFRED.

Avgust (m.) Russian form of AUGUSTUS.

Avgustin (m.) Russian form of AUGUSTINE.

Avice (f.) English: variant spelling of AVIS.

Avila (f.) English: this occurs in the Middle Ages as a Latinized form of a medieval Germanic name related to AVIS. In modern use, however, it is borne almost exclusively by Roman Catholics, among whom it is bestowed in honour of St Theresa of Avila (1515–82).

Avis (f.) English: from a Norman French form of the Germanic name *Aveza*, derived from a short form of various female compound names containing the first element *av* (of uncertain meaning). The name probably owes its modest popularity in the later Middle Ages and subsequent centuries to its correspondence in form to the Latin feminine noun *avis* bird.

Variant: **Avice**.

Avishag (f.) Jewish: modern Hebrew form of ABISHAG.

Avital (f.) Jewish: modern Hebrew form of the biblical name *Abital*, meaning 'dewy', borne by a wife of King David (2 Samuel 3: 4).

Aviva (f.) Jewish: recent coinage from a modern Hebrew vocabulary word meaning 'spring'.

Avner (m.) Jewish: modern Hebrew form of ABNER.

Avraham (m.) Jewish: modern Hebrew form of ABRAHAM.

Avril (f.) English: although generally taken as the French form of the name of the fourth month (see APRIL), this has also been influenced by the English surname *Everill*, which is from an Old English female personal name composed of the elements *eofor* boar + *hild* battle.

Avrom (m.) Jewish: Yiddish form of ABRAHAM.

Axel (m.) Scandinavian (Danish) form of ABSALOM, sometimes also used in the United States.
Pet form: **Acke**.

Ayala (f.) Jewish: modern Hebrew name meaning 'hind' or 'doe'; cf. HINDE.

Aylwin (m.) English: variant of ALWYN.

Azaria (f.) English: female name apparently created in the 20th century and modelled on the rare male name AZARIAS.

Azarias (m.) Biblical: Greek form of the Hebrew name *Azariah* 'helped by God', the name of a prophet who recalled King Asa to a proper observance of religion (2 Chronicles 15: 1–8).

Azriel (m.) Jewish: name (meaning 'God helps' in Hebrew) borne in the Bible by a character briefly mentioned as a leading member of the tribe of Manasseh (1 Chronicles 5: 24).

Azucena (f.) Spanish: from the vocabulary word *azucena* madonna lily (from Arabic *as-susana* the lily; cf. SUSANNA). The word seems to have been adopted as a given name because of the association of the flower with the Virgin Mary.

B

Babs (f.) English: informal pet form of BARBARA.

Badane (f.) Jewish: Yiddish form of *Bogdana* (see BOGDAN).

Baibín (f.) Irish Gaelic: pet form of BAIRBRE.

Bailey (m.) English: transferred use of the surname, which has various origins. Most commonly it was an occupational name for a bailiff or administrative official; in other cases it apparently originated as a local name for someone who lived near a bailey, i.e. a city fortification, and in others it may be a local name from *Bailey* in Lancashire, which gets its name from Old English *bēg* berry + *lēah* wood, clearing.

Bairbre (f.) Irish Gaelic form of BARBARA.

Pet form: **Baibín**.

Bakarne (f.) Basque equivalent of SOLEDAD.

Balázs (m.) Hungarian form of BLAISE.

Baldassare (m.) Italian cognate of BALTHASAR, occasionally borne in honour of the Blessed Balthasar of Chiavari, venerated in Pavia.

Balder (m.) Swedish: from the name of an Old Norse god, meaning 'prince' or 'ruler', cognate with *bold* brave, strong. According to Norse mythology, this was the name of a son of Odin by his wife Frigg. According to some stories, Balder was the god of light. His mother persuaded everything in the world to swear an oath not to harm him, but she overlooked the mistletoe. The evil and cunning god Loki persuaded the blind god Hoder to aim a dart made of mistletoe at Balder, and it killed him. He is sometimes taken as a personification of doomed purity and beauty.

Cognate: German: **Baldur**.

Baldie (m.) Scottish: pet form of ARCHIBALD.

Baldomero (m.) Spanish: from a Germanic (Frankish) personal name composed of the elements *bald* bold, brave + *mari*, *meri* famous. This name was borne by a 7th-century saint from Lyons, patron of locksmiths.

Cognate: Provençal: **Baldomar**.

Baldur (m.) German cognate of BALDER.

Baldwin (m.) English: Norman name composed of the Germanic elements *bald* bold, brave + *wine* friend. In the Middle Ages this was a comparatively common name, which gave rise to a surname. It was the given name of the Norman crusader (Baldwin of Boulogne) who in 1100 was elected first king of Jerusalem. It was also the name of four further crusader kings of Jerusalem. In modern English use, it normally represents a transferred use of the surname rather than a direct revival of the Norman given name.

Cognate: French (esp. Belgian): **Baudouin**.

Bálint (m.) Hungarian form of VALENTINE.

Balthasar (m.) English: name ascribed in medieval Christian tradition to one of the three wise men of the Orient who brought gifts to the infant Jesus (see also JASPER and MELCHIORRE). The name is a variant of that of the biblical king *Belshazzar* and means 'Baal protect the king'. It has never been a common given name in the English-speaking world.

Variant: **Balthazar**.

Cognates: Italian: **Baldassare**. Spanish: **Baltasar**.

Baptist (m.) English and German form of BAPTISTE. As an English name it is used mainly in the United States by Blacks who are members of evangelical sects.

Baptiste (m.) French: meaning 'baptist' (Late Latin *baptista*, Greek *baptistēs*, from *baphein* to dip), the epithet of the most popular of the numerous saints called JOHN. Although it occurs independently as a given name, it is normally found in combination with *Jean* (see JOHN).

Cognates: German, English: BAPTIST. Italian: **Battista**. Spanish: **Bautista**. Portuguese: **Batista**.

Barbara (f.) English, German, and Polish: from Latin, meaning 'foreign woman' (a feminine form of *barbarus* foreign, from Greek, referring originally to the unintelligible chatter of foreigners, which sounded to the Greek ear like no more than *bar-bar*). St Barbara has always been one of the most popular saints in the calendar, although there is some doubt whether she ever existed. According to legend, she was imprisoned in a tower and later murdered by her father, who was then struck down by a bolt of lightning; accordingly, she is the patron of architects, stonemasons, and fortifications, and of firework makers, artillerymen, and gunpowder magazines. The name is now occasionally modishly spelled **Barbra**, notably in the case of the actress and singer Barbra Streisand (b. 1942).

Cognates: Irish Gaelic: **Bairbre**. Scottish Gaelic: **Barabal**. Swedish: **Barbro**. Czech: **Barbora**. Russian: **Varvara**. Hungarian: **Borbála**.

Short forms: English: **Barb** (mainly U.S. informal). French: **Barbe**.

Pet forms: English: **Barbie, Babs**. Irish Gaelic: **Baibín**. German: **Bärbel**. Polish: **Basia**. Czech: **Bára, Bora, Bar(čin)ka, Barun(k)a, Baruška**.

Barclay (m.) Scottish, English, and Irish: generally a transferred use of the Scottish surname, which was taken to Scotland in the 12th century by Walter de Berchelai, who became chamberlain of Scotland in 1165. His name is almost certainly derived from *Berkeley* in Gloucestershire, which is named with the Old English elements *beorc* birch tree + *lēah* wood or clearing. His descendants became one of the most powerful families in Scotland, and the transferred use as a given name probably originated in Scotland with reference to this family. In Ireland it has been pressed into service as an Anglicized form of PARTHALÁN.

Barnabas (m.) English and German: from the New Testament, where *Barnabas* represents a Greek form of the name of a companion of St Paul. The Aramaic original meant 'son of consolation'.

Variant: English: **Barnaby** (from a medieval vernacular form).

Cognates: French: **Barnabé**. Spanish: **Bernabé**. Polish: **Barnaba**. Czech: **Barnabá**. Hungarian: **Barna**.

Pet forms: English: **Barney, Barny**.

Barrett (m.) English: transferred use of the surname, which is of obscure origin. It is probably a nickname from Middle English *baret* dispute, argument. The transferred use as a given name is recent.

Barry (m.) Irish: Anglicized form of the Gaelic name **Barra** (Old Irish *Bairre*), a short form of *Fionnb(h)arr* (see FINBAR). In the 20th century this name has also become very popular in other areas of the English-speaking world, particularly Australia.

Informal pet forms: **Baz, Bazza** (Australian).

Bart (m.) English: short form of BARTON and BARTHOLOMEW.

Barthold (m.) Low German form of BERTHOLD.

Bartholomew (m.) English: of New Testament origin, the name of an apostle mentioned in all the synoptic gospels (Matthew, Mark, and Luke) and in the Acts of the Apostles. It is an Aramaic formation meaning 'son of Talmai', and has been assumed by many scholars to be a byname of the apostle Nathaniel. *Talmai* is a Hebrew name, said to mean 'abounding in furrows' (Numbers 13: 22).

Cognates: Irish Gaelic: **Bairtliméad**; PARTHALÁN. Scottish Gaelic: **Pàrlan**. French: **Barthélemy**. Provençal: **Barthomieu**. Catalan: **Bartomeu**. Spanish: **Bartolomé**. Portuguese: **Bartolomeu**. Italian: **Bartolo(m)meo**. German: **Bartholomäus**. Dutch: **Bartholomeus** (learned); **Bartel** (vernacular). Polish: **Bartłomiej** (learned); **Bartosz** (vernacular). Czech: **Bartoloměj**. Russian: **Varfolomei**. Hungarian: **Bartal, Bartos, Bartó**. Finnish: **Perttu**.

Short forms: English: **Bart**. Irish: **Bartle, Bartley**. Italian: **Bàrtolo; Meo**.

Barton (m.) English: transferred use of the surname, originally a local name from any of the numerous places in England so called from Old English *bere* barley + *tūn* enclosure, settlement.

Short form: **Bart**.

Baruch (m.) Jewish: biblical name meaning 'blessed' in Hebrew (cf. BENEDICT). It is borne by a character who appears in the Book of Jeremiah.

Baruna (f.) Czech: pet form of *Barbora* (see BARBARA).

Variants: **Barunka, Baruška**.

Bashe (f.) Jewish: Yiddish pet form of BATYAH.

Basia (f.) Polish: pet form of BARBARA.

Basil (m.) English: from the Greek name *Basileios* 'royal' (a derivative of *basileus* king). This name was borne by St Basil the Great (*c.*330–79), bishop of Caesarea, a theologian regarded as one of the Fathers of the Eastern Church. It was also the name of several early saints martyred in the East.

Cognates: Polish: **Bazyli**. Russian: **Vasili**.

Bastien (m.) French: aphetic short from of *Sébastien* (see SEBASTIAN).

Feminine form: **Bastienne**.

Basye (f.) Jewish: Yiddish pet form of BATYAH.

Bathsheba (f.) Biblical name, meaning 'daughter of the oath' in Hebrew. This was the name of the woman who became the wife of King David, after he had disposed of her husband Uriah, and mother of King Solomon (2 Samuel 11–12). It was popular with the Puritans in England, no doubt because of the great beauty attributed to the biblical character.

Variant: Jewish: **Batsheva** (the modern Hebrew form).

Batista (m.) Portuguese form of BAPTISTE.

Battista (m.) Italian form of BAPTISTE.

Batyah (f.) Jewish: modern Hebrew name composed of the elements *bat* daughter + *yah* God. It is also possibly a variant of *Bithiah*, the name of an Egyptian princess mentioned in 1 Chronicles 4: 18. The Hebrew spelling of *Batyah* and *Bithiah* is identical.

Pet forms: **Basye, Bashe**.

Batzion (f.) Jewish: modern Hebrew name meaning 'daughter of Zion'.

Baudouin (m.) French form of BALDWIN, common especially in Belgium, where it is borne by Baudouin I (b. 1930), King of the Belgians since 1951.

Bautista (m.) Spanish form of BAPTISTE.

Baxter (m.) English: transferred use of the surname, which originated in the Middle Ages as an occupational name for a baker, Old English *bæcestre*. The *-estre* suffix was originally feminine, but by the Middle English period the gender difference had been lost; *Baxter* was merely a regional variant of *Baker*.

Baz (m.) English: informal pet form of BARRY.

Variant: **Bazza** (Australian).

Bazyli (m.) Polish form of BASIL.

Bea (f.) English: informal short form of BEATRICE or BEATRIX.

Bean (m.) Scottish: Anglicized form of the Gaelic name BEATHAN.

Bearnard (m.) Irish and Scottish Gaelic form of BERNARD.

Bearnas (f.) Scottish Gaelic form of BERENICE, often considered as a feminine equivalent of BEARNARD.

Beat (m.) Swiss German: name borne in honour of the apostle of Switzerland, a hermit of uncertain date who established himself at the place now called *Beatenberg*, above the lake of Thun. His name derives from Late Latin *Beātus* 'blessed'; cf. BEATA.

Beata (f.) Late Latin feminine form of *Beātus* 'blessed'. St Beata is the name of an early Christian saint martyred at an unknown date in North Africa. The name is widely used among Roman Catholics in Germany, Poland, and elsewhere; it is less common in the English-speaking world.

Beathan (m.) Scottish Gaelic: traditional name, a derivative of *beatha* life.

Anglicized forms: **Bean**; BENJAMIN.

Feminine form: **Beathag** (often Anglicized as SOPHIA or REBECCA).

Beatrice (f.) Italian and French form of BEATRIX, occasionally used in England during the Middle Ages, and strongly revived in the 19th century. It is most famous as the name of Dante's beloved.

Cognates: Scottish Gaelic: **Beitiris**. Welsh: **Betrys** (a modern Welsh spelling of the English given name).

Short form: English: **Bea**.

Pet forms: English: **Beat(t)ie**. Italian: **Bice**.

Beatrix (f.) English and German: from a Late Latin personal name, which was borne by a saint executed in Rome, together with Faustinus and Simplicius, in the early 4th century. The original form of the name seems to have been *Viātrix*, a feminine version of *Viātōr* 'voyager (through life)', which was common among early Christians. This was then altered by association with Latin *Beātus* 'blessed' (*Via-* and *Bea-* being pronounced very similarly in Late Latin).

Cognate: Spanish: **Beatriz**. See also BEATRICE.

Beau (m.) English: recent coinage as a given name, originally a nickname meaning 'handsome', as borne by Beau Brummell (1778–1840), the dandy who was for a time a friend of the Prince Regent. The word was also used in the 19th century with the meaning 'admirer' or 'sweetheart'. Its adoption as a given name seems to have been due to the hero of P. C. Wren's novel *Beau Geste* (1924) or to the character of Beau Wilks in Margaret Mitchell's *Gone with the Wind* (1936), which was made into an exceptionally popular film in 1939.

Bechor (m.) Jewish: Hebrew name meaning 'firstborn'. This given name is borne particularly by Jews of Sephardic descent.

Becky (f.) English: pet form of REBECCA. It has occasionally been used as an independent given name, and was especially popular in the 18th and 19th centuries. The modern short form **Becca** is also occasionally used, and the form **Beca** is well established in Wales.

Bedřich (m.) Czech form of FREDERICK.

Feminine form: **Bedřiška**.

Pet forms: **Béda** (m., f.); **Bedříšek** (m.); **Bed'ka, Beduna, Řiška** (f.).

Begoña (f.) Spanish (largely confined to the Basque country): name bestowed in honour of our Lady of Begoña, venerated as the patron saint of Bilbao. There is no connection with the flower *begonia*, which was so named in the 18th century after Michel Bégon (1630–1710), a French patron of science.

Beile (f.) Jewish (Yiddish): probably derived from the Slavonic element *beli* white (cf. the Czech female name *Běla*). According to others, it is from the Romance element *bella* beautiful (cf. BELLA and SHAYNA).

Variant: **Beyle**.

Pet form: **Beylke**.

Beileag (f.) Scottish Gaelic: pet form of ISEABAIL.

Variants: **Bella(g)** (Anglicized forms).

Beistean (m.) Scottish Gaelic: pet form of *Gille Easbaig* (see GILLESPIE).

Beitidh (f.) Scottish Gaelic form of BETTY.

Beitiris (f.) Scottish Gaelic form of BEATRICE.

Béla (m.) Hungarian: of uncertain origin. There seems to be no linguistic foundation for connecting it with the German name *Albrecht* (see ALBERT). It may be a borrowing from Slavonic, from *belo* white, the first element in such names as *Beloslav*. Alternatively, it may be from the Hungarian vocabulary word *bél* inner part, or from a Turkic byname meaning 'distinguished'.

Belén (f.) Spanish: chosen in commemoration of Jesus's birthplace at *Bethlehem* in Judea, the Spanish form of which is *Belén*. The placename means 'house of bread' in Hebrew.

Belinda (f.) English: of uncertain origin. It was used by Sir John Vanbrugh for a character in his comedy *The Provok'd Wife* (1697), was taken up by Alexander Pope in *The Rape of the Lock* (1712), and has enjoyed a steady popularity ever since. It is not certain where Vanbrugh got the name from. The notion that it is Germanic (with a second element *lind* lime tree) does not seem to be well-founded. In Italian literature it is the name ascribed to the wife of Orlando, vassal of Charlemagne, but this use is not supported in Germanic sources. The name may be an Italian coinage from *bella* beautiful (see BELLA) + the feminine name suffix *-inda* (cf. e.g. LUCINDA).

Bella (f.) Italian, Scottish, and English: aphetic short form of *Isabella*, the Italian form of ISABEL, but also associated with the Italian adjective *bella*, feminine of *bello* handsome, beautiful (Late Latin *bellus*).

Bellarmino (m.) Catholic name given in honour of the Italian saint Roberto Bellarmino (1542–1621), a prominent Jesuit. He was canonized in 1930 and declared a Doctor of the Church in 1931; his surname has occasionally been used as a given name in the 20th century.

Belle (f.) English: variant of BELLA, reflecting the French feminine adjective *belle* beautiful.

Beltrán (m.) Spanish form, by dissimilation, of BERTRAM.

Ben (m.) English: short form of BENJAMIN, or less commonly of BENEDICT or BENNETT.

Pet forms: **Benny, Bennie**.

Benedict (m.) English: from Church Latin *Benedictus* 'blessed'. This was the name of the saint (*c.*480–*c.*550) who composed the Benedictine rule of Christian monastic life that is still followed in essence by all Western orders. He was born near Spoleto in Umbria, central Italy. After studying in Rome, he went to live as a hermit at Subiaco, and later organized groups of followers and imitators into monastic cells. In *c.*529 he moved to Monte Cassino, where he founded the great monastery that is still the centre of the Benedictine order. His rule is simple, restrained, and practical. The name is used mainly by Roman Catholics.

Variant: English: BENNETT.

Cognates: Scottish Gaelic: **Benneit**. French: **Benoît**. Italian: **Benedetto**. Spanish: BENITO. Portuguese: **Bento**. Catalan: **Benet**. Provençal: **Bénézet**. German, Dutch: **Benedikt**. Danish: **Bendt, Bent**. Swedish: **Bengt**. Russian: **Venedikt**. Polish: **Benedykt**. Czech: **Beneš**. Hungarian: **Benedek**. Finnish: **Pentti**.

Feminine forms: Latin: **Benedicta**. French: **Benoîte**. Italian: **Benedetta**. German, Dutch: **Benedikta**.

Benigno (m.) Italian and Spanish: from the Late Latin name *Benignus* 'kind' (a derivative of Latin *bene* well), which was borne by a large number of early saints. One was the 3rd-century martyr to whom Dijon cathedral is dedicated; another was a 5th-century disciple of St Patrick.

Benito (m.) Spanish form of BENEDICT. In the 20th century it has also been used in Italy, most notably by the dictator Benito Mussolini (1883–1945), who was named after the Mexican revolutionary leader Benito Pablo Juarez (1806–72).

Benjamin (m.) English (also French and German): of biblical origin. Benjamin was one of the founders of the twelve tribes of Israel, the youngest of the twelve sons of Jacob. His mother Rachel died in giving birth to him, and in her last moments she named him *Benoni*, meaning 'son of my sorrow'. His father, however, did not wish him to bear such an ill-omened name, and renamed him *Benyamin* (Genesis 35: 16–18; 42: 4). This means either 'son of the right hand' or more likely 'son of the south' (Hebrew *yamin* can also mean 'south'), since Benjamin was the only child of Jacob born in Canaan and not in Mesopotamia to the north. Another tradition is that the second element of the name is a variant of the Hebrew word *yamim* which means 'days' but is used idiomatically to mean 'year' or 'years'. The name would then mean 'son of (my) old age' and refer to the fact that Benjamin was Jacob's youngest child. In the Middle Ages the name was often given to sons whose mothers had died in childbirth. Today it has no such unfortunate associations, but is still mainly a Jewish name. In the Scottish Highlands it has been used as an Anglicized form of the Gaelic name BEATHAN.

Variant: Jewish: **Binyamin** (the modern Hebrew form).

Cognate: Russian: **Venyamin.**

Short form: English: **Ben.**

Pet forms: English: **Benny, Bennie, Benji(e).**

Benneit (m.) Scottish Gaelic form of BENEDICT.

Bennett (m.) English: the normal medieval form of BENEDICT, now sometimes used as an antiquarian revival, but more often it is a transferred use of the surname, which is derived from the medieval given name.

Variants: **Benett, Bennet, Benet.**

Benno (m.) German: from a medieval short form of various compound Germanic names containing the first element *bern* bear. By the later Middle Ages it came to be considered and used as a short form of BENEDICT. St Benno (1010–1106) was a bishop of Meissen, who preached to the Wends in what is now East Germany. He is the patron saint of Munich.

Benoît (m.) French form of BENEDICT.

Feminine form: **Benoîte.**

Benson (m.) English: transferred use of the surname, which originated in part as a patronymic from *Ben(n)*, a short form of BENEDICT, and in part as a local name from *Benson* (formerly *Bensington*) in Oxfordshire.

Bent (m.) Danish: simplified form of *Bendt* (see BENEDICT).

Bentley (m.) English: transferred use of the surname, which originated as a local name from any of the dozen or so places in England so called from Old English *beonet* bent grass + *lēah* wood or clearing.

Bento (m.) Portuguese form of BENEDICT.

Benvenuto (m.) Italian: from a medieval given name meaning 'welcome', composed of the elements *bene* well, good + *venuto*, past participle of *venire* to come, arrive. The Italian metalworker, sculptor, and writer Benvenuto Cellini (1500–71) is one of the most vital and engaging figures of the Renaissance, and the name may in some cases be bestowed in his honour, although parts of his autobiography are far from spiritually uplifting. The meaning of the name has remained transparent, however, and in the majority of cases it has no doubt been bestowed as an expression of the parents' joy in the birth of their child.

Benzion (m.) Jewish: modern Hebrew name meaning 'son of Zion' (cf. BATZION).

Beppe (m.) Italian: pet form of GIUSEPPE.

Variant: **Beppo.**

Ber (m.) Jewish: from the Yiddish vocabulary word *ber* bear (cf. modern German *Bär*), probably influenced by the early medieval European practice of giving animal names to people. It is often paired with Dov in order to provide a Hebrew name in certain rituals.

Berenice (f.) English and Italian: from the Greek personal name *Berenikē*, which seems to have originated in the royal house of Macedon. It is almost certainly a Macedonian dialectal form of the Greek name *Pherenīkē* 'victory bringer'. It was introduced to the Egyptian royal house by the widow of one of Alexander the Great's officers, who married Ptolemy I. It was also borne by an early Christian woman mentioned in Acts 25, for which reason it was felt to be acceptable by the Puritans in the 17th century. It has now fallen out of fashion again.

Variant: **Bernice** (the form used in the Authorized Version).

Cognates: Scottish Gaelic: **Bearnas**. French: **Bérénice**.

Berit (f.) Scandinavian: variant of BIRGIT.

Berkley (m.) English and Irish: variant of BARCLAY.

Bernabé (m.) Spanish form of BARNABAS.

Bernadette (f.) French: feminine diminutive of BERNARD. Its use in Britain and Ireland is almost exclusively confined to Roman Catholics, who take it in honour of St Bernadette Soubirous (1844–79), a French peasant girl who had visions of the Virgin Mary and uncovered a spring near Lourdes where miraculous cures are still sought.

Variant: **Bernardette**.

Cognate: Italian: **Bernardetta**.

Bernard (m.) English and French: from a Germanic personal name composed of the elements *ber(n)* bear + *hard* hardy, brave, strong. This was the name of three famous medieval churchmen: St Bernard of Menthon (923–1008), founder of a hospice on each of the Alpine passes named after him; the monastic reformer St Bernard of Clairvaux (1090–1153); and the scholastic philosopher Bernard of Chartres. In England before the Norman Conquest a native Old English form of the name, *Beornheard*, existed, but it is the Norman form, derived through French from Continental Germanic, that became established as a conventional English given name.

Cognates: Gaelic: **Bearnard**. Italian, Spanish: **Bernardo**. Catalan: **Bernat**. German: **Bernhard(t), Bernd(t)**. Scandinavian: **Bernt**.

Pet form: English: **Bernie**.

Berneen (f.) Irish: diminutive from a shortening of BERNADETTE.

Bernice (f.) French and English: contracted form of BERENICE, now fairly popular in the English-speaking world.

Berry (f.) English: from the vocabulary word (Old English *berie*). This is one of the less common of the names referring to flowers, fruit, and vegetation introduced to the English-speaking world in the 20th century.

Bert (m.) English: short form of any of the various names containing this syllable as a first or second element, for example ALBERT and BERTRAM. See also BURT.

Pet form: **Bertie**.

Bertha (f.) German and English: Latinized version of a Germanic name, a short form of various compound women's personal names containing the element *berht* famous (cognate with Modern English *bright*). It probably existed in England before the Conquest, and was certainly reinforced by Norman use, but fell from currency. It was reintroduced into the English-speaking world from Germany in the 19th century, but has once again fallen out of fashion.

Cognates: French: **Berthe**. Polish, Czech: **Berta**.

Berthold (m.) German: from an old Germanic personal name composed of the elements *berht* bright, famous + *wald* ruler. The second element has been altered by association with German *hold* lovely, splendid.

Cognate: Low German: **Barthold**.

Bertil (m.) Scandinavian: from a Germanic pet form of various compound names containing the first element *berht* bright, famous, with the hypocoristic suffix *-il*. The Blessed Bertilo (d. *c.*878) was an abbot of St Benignus at Dijon in Burgundy, who was murdered by Norman raiders.

Variant: **Bertel**.

Bertram (m.) English: from a Norman French name composed of the Germanic elements *berht* bright, famous + *hramn* raven. Ravens were traditional symbols of wisdom in Germanic mythology; Odin was regularly accompanied by ravens called Hugin and Munin. See also BERTRAND.

Cognate: Spanish: **Beltrán**.

Short form: English: **Bert**.

Pet form: English: **Bertie**.

Bertrand (m.) French and English: variant of BERTRAM, originating in the Middle Ages. In modern times it has been made famous by the English philosopher Bertrand Russell (1872–1970).

Berwyn (m.) Welsh: from an ancient Welsh personal name composed of the elements *barr* head +*(g)wyn* white, fair.

Beryl (f.) English: one of several women's names that are taken from gemstones and which came into fashion at the end of the 19th century. Beryl is a pale green stone (of which emerald is a variety). Other colours are also found. The word is from Greek, and is ultimately of Indian origin.

Bess (f.) English: short form of ELIZABETH, in common use in the days of Queen Elizabeth I, who was known as 'Good Queen Bess'.

Pet forms: **Bessie, Bessy**.

Bet (f.) English: short form of ELIZABETH.

Pet form: **Betty**.

Běta (f.) Czech: short form of ALŽBĚTA.

Pet forms: **Bětka, Bětuška**.

Beth (f.) English: short form of ELIZABETH, not used before the 19th century, when it became popular in America and elsewhere after publication of Louisa M. Alcott's novel *Little Women* (1868), in which Beth March is one of the four sisters who are the central characters.

Pet form: Welsh: **Bethan** (now also popular elsewhere in the English-speaking world).

Bethany (f.) English: of New Testament origin. In the New Testament it is a placename, that of the village just outside Jerusalem where Jesus stayed during Holy Week, before going on to Jerusalem and crucifixion (Matthew 21: 17; Mark 11: 1; Luke 19: 29; John 12: 1). Its Hebrew name may mean 'house of figs' (*beth te'ena* or *beth te'enimf*). The given name is favoured mainly by Roman Catholics, being bestowed in honour of Mary of Bethany, sister of Martha and Lazarus. She is sometimes identified with Mary Magdalene (see MADELEINE), although the grounds for this identification are very poor.

Betrys (f.) Welsh form of BEATRICE.

Betsy (f.) English: pet form of ELIZABETH, a cross between *Betty* (see BET) and *Bessie* (see BESS).

Bettina (f.) 1. English: Latinate elaboration of BETTY.

2. Italian: contracted elaboration of *Benedetta* (see BENEDICT).

Betty (f.) English: pet form of ELIZABETH, dating from the 18th century.

Cognate: Scottish Gaelic: **Beitidh**.

Beulah (f.) Biblical: from the name applied to the land of Israel by the prophet Isaiah (Isaiah 62: 4). It means 'married' in Hebrew, but 'the land of Beulah' has sometimes been taken as a reference to heaven. It was taken up as a given name in England at the time of the Reformation and was popular among the Puritans in the 17th century. It is still occasionally used in the United States, largely among Blacks.

Beverley (f., also m.) English: transferred use of the surname, which comes from a place in Humberside named in Old English with the elements *beofor* beaver + *lēac* stream. The spelling **Beverly** is apparently used exclusively for girls, and is the usual form of the female name in America. It is not clear why it should have become a comparatively popular female name. In America, association with Beverly Hills in Los Angeles, the district where many film stars live, may have been an influencing factor.

Beynish (m.) Jewish (Yiddish): from the Czech given name *Beneš*, a form of BENEDICT. It was no doubt adopted by Jews on account of its auspicious meaning, 'blessed', and as a translation of BARUCH.

Bhàtair (m.) Scottish Gaelic form of WALTER.

Variant: **Bhaltair**.

Bhictoria (f.) Scottish Gaelic form of VICTORIA.

Biagio (m.) Italian form of BLAISE.

Bianca (f.) Italian: from *bianca* white (i.e. 'pure', but cf. BLANCHE). The name was used by Shakespeare for characters in two of his plays that are supposed to take place in an Italian context: the mild-mannered sister of Katharina, the 'shrew' in *The Taming of the Shrew*, and a courtesan in *Othello*. Recently, it has been borne most famously by Bianca Jagger, the Nicaraguan fashion model, peace worker, and diplomat who was for a time married to the rock singer Mick Jagger.

Cognates: French: **Blanche**. Spanish: **Blanca**. Polish, Czech: **Blanka**.

Bice (f.) Italian: contracted pet form of BEATRICE.

Biddy (f.) Irish and English: pet form of BRIDE or BRIDGET. It was formerly quite common, but is now seldom used outside Ireland, partly perhaps because the informal expression 'an old biddy' in English has come to denote a tiresome old woman.

Bigge (m.) Swedish: pet form of BIRGER.

Bill (m.) English: altered short form of WILLIAM, not used before the 19th century. The reason for the change in the initial consonant is not clear, but it conforms to the pattern regularly found when English words beginning with *w*- are borrowed into Gaelic; the nickname 'King Billy' for William of Orange is an early example from Ireland which may have influenced English usage.

Pet forms: English: **Billy**, BILLIE. Gaelic: **Builidh**.

Billie (f., m.) English: variant of *Billy* (see BILL), now mainly used for girls, and sometimes bestowed at baptism as a feminine equivalent of WILLIAM.

Bina (f.) 1. Jewish (Yiddish): from the Yiddish vocabulary word *bin*(*e*) bee. This was used as a translation of the Hebrew name *Devorah* (see DEBORAH), meaning 'bee'. However, it was often taken as being from Hebrew *bina* understanding.

2. Among Gentiles, it occasionally occurs as an aphetic short form of ALBINA.

Variants: **Binah, Bine**.

Pet form: **Binke**.

Binyamin (m.) Jewish: modern Hebrew form of BENJAMIN.

Bionda (f.) Italian: originally a nickname for a woman with fair hair, from the vocabulary word meaning 'blonde' (of Germanic origin).

Birger (m.) Swedish: of Old Norse origin, apparently an agent derivative of the verb *biarga* to help. Earlier forms of the name are *Birghir* and *Byrghir*. It has been in use from the Viking period to the present day, and it may in some cases have been chosen as a masculine form of BIRGIT.

Variant: BÖRJE.

Pet forms: **Bigge, Birre**.

Birgit (f.) Swedish (also used elsewhere in Scandinavia): borrowing of the Irish Gaelic name *Brighid* (see BRIDGET). This name owes its enormous popularity in Scandinavia, especially in Sweden, to St Birgitta (1304–73), patron saint of Sweden. She was a noblewoman who bore her husband eight children. After his death, she founded an order of nuns, the 'Bridgettines' or Order of the Most Holy

Saviour. She also went to Rome, where she attempted to reform religious life.

Variants: **Berit, Britt, Brit(t)a; Birgitta** (now rare). Danish: **Birgitte, Birt(h)e, Gitte.**

Birre (m.) Swedish: pet form of BIRGER.

Björn (m.) Swedish: from an Old Norse byname meaning 'bear'. It is also in part a short form of compound names such as ARNBJÖRN and TORBJÖRN.

Cognates: Norwegian: **Bjørn, Bjarne.**

Blahoslav (m.) Czech: from an old Slavonic personal name composed of the elements *blago* blessed + *slav* glory.

Feminine form: **Blahoslava.**

Pet forms: **Blahoš(ek)** (m.); **Blahuše** (f.).

Blair (m., f.) Scottish: transferred use of the surname, a local name from various places named with Gaelic *blàr* plain, field. In North America, it is now widely used as a female given name.

Blaise (m.) French: the name (Latin *Blasius*, probably from *blaesus* lisping) of a saint popular throughout Europe in the Middle Ages but almost forgotten today. He was a bishop of Sebaste in Armenia, and was martyred in the early years of the 4th century; these bare facts were elaborated in a great number of legends that reached Europe from the East at the time of the Crusades. The name is rare in the English-speaking world; its modern popularity in France is partly due to the 17th-century French philosopher and mathematician Blaise Pascal.

Cognates: Italian: **Biag(g)io.** Spanish: **Blas.** Portuguese: **Bras, Braz.** Catalan: **Blai.** Provençal: **Blasi.** Polish: **Błażej.** Czech: **Blažej.** Russian: **Vlas(i).** Hungarian: **Balázs.**

Blake (m.) English: transferred use of the surname, which has two quite distinct etymologies. It is both from Old English *blæc* black and from Old English *blāc* pale, white; it was thus originally a nickname given to someone with hair or skin that was either remarkably dark or remarkably light. It is now quite popular as a male given name.

Blanche (f.) French and English: originally a nickname for a blonde, from *blanche*, feminine of Old French *blanc* white (of Germanic origin). It came to be associated with the notion of whiteness as indicating purity, and was introduced into England as a given name by the Normans. A pale complexion combined with light hair has long been an ideal of beauty in Europe (cf. modern English *fair*, which at first meant 'beautiful' and then, from the 16th century, 'light in colouring').

Cognates: Italian: BIANCA. Spanish: **Blanca.** Polish, Czech: **Blanka.**

Bláthnaid (f.) Irish Gaelic: originally an affectionate nickname representing a diminutive form of *bláth* flower.

Variants: **Bláithín, Bláthnait.**

Bleddyn (m.) Welsh: ancient byname derived from the vocabulary element *blaidd* wolf + the diminutive suffix *-yn*. *Blaidd* was often used in medieval Welsh as a term for a hero.

Blodwedd (f.) Welsh: name borne by a character in the *Mabinogi*. She was conjured up out of flowers as a bride for Lleu Llaw Gyffes, and was originally called *Blodeuedd*, a derivative of *blawd* flowers. After she had treacherously had her husband killed she was transformed into an owl, and her name was changed to *Blodeuwedd* 'flower face', an allusion to the markings round the eyes of the owl.

Blodwen (f.) Welsh: traditional name composed of the elements *blawd* flowers + *(g)wen* white, feminine of *gwyn* white, fair, blessed, holy. The name was a relatively common one in the Middle Ages and has recently been revived.

Blossom (f.) English: 19th-century coinage, from the vocabulary word for flowers on a fruit-tree or ornamental tree (Old English *blōstm*), used as an affectionate pet name for a young girl.

Blume (f.) Jewish: Yiddish name, originally an affectionate nickname meaning 'flower' (from Middle High German *bluome*).

Pet form: **Blumke**.

Bo (m.) Swedish and Danish: originally a byname for a householder, from a derivative of Old Norse *búa* to live, dwell, have a household.

Pet form: Swedish: **Bosse**.

Boaz (m.) Biblical: Hebrew name of uncertain origin, perhaps meaning 'swiftness'. In the Bible it is borne by a distant kinsman of Ruth who treats her generously and eventually marries her. The given name was in occasional use in England in the 17th and 18th centuries but is now very rare. It is sometimes used in Jewish families.

Variant: **Boas**.

Bob (m.) English: altered short form of ROBERT, a later development than the common medieval forms *Hob*, *Dob*, and *Nob*, all of which, unlike *Bob*, have given rise to English surnames.

Pet forms: **Bobby**, BOBBIE.

Boba (m.) Russian: pet form of BORIS.

Bobbie (f., m.) English: variant of *Bobby* (see BOB), now mainly used as a female name, in part as a pet form of *Roberta* (see ROBERT).

Bodek (m.) Polish: pet form of BOGDAN.

Bodil (f.) Scandinavian (originally Danish): from an Old Norse female personal name composed of the elements *bót* bettering, remedy, compensation + *hildr* battle.

Variants: **Botilda** (Latinized). Swedish: **Bothild**.

Bodo (m.) German: from an old Germanic personal name, originally a short form of various compound names containing the first element *bod* tidings, messenger.

Bódog (m.) Hungarian: originally a nickname meaning 'fortunate', used as a loan translation of FELIX.

Bodzio (m.) Polish: pet form of BOGDAN.

Bogdan (m.) Polish and Ukrainian: from an old Slavonic personal name composed of the elements *bog* god + *dan* gift. It is therefore semantically equivalent to THEODORE and DOROTHY as well as to MATTHEW, NATHANIEL, and JONATHAN.

Cognate: Czech: **Bohdan**.

Pet forms: Polish: **Bodek, Bodzio**.

Feminine forms: Polish: **Bogdana, Bogna, Dana**. Czech: **Bohdana**. Ukrainian: **Bohdanna**. Yiddish: **Badane**.

Boguchwał (m.) Polish: vernacular name originating in the Middle Ages, composed of the elements *Bóg* God + *chwała* praise (cf. GOTTLOB). This is a specifically Christian formation, modelled on already existing names of pagan origin such as BOGUMIERZ.

Variant: **Bogufał**. See also CHWALIBÓG.

Bogumierz (m.) Polish: from an old Slavonic personal name composed of the elements *bog* god + *meri* great, famous (see CASIMIR).

Cognates: Czech: **Bohumír**. Ukrainian: **Bohomir**.

Bogumił (m.) Polish: from an old Slavonic personal name composed of the elements *bog* god + *mil* grace, favour. St Bogumił (d. 1182) was an archbishop of Gniezno (Gnesen) who founded the abbey of Koronowa. His cult was not officially approved by the Church until 1925, but it flourished nevertheless during seven centuries of turbulence and repression, sometimes serving as a symbol of Polish national and spiritual aspirations.

Cognate: Czech: **Bohumil**.

Feminine forms: Polish: **Bogumiła**. Czech: **Bohumila**.

Bogusław (m.) Polish: from an old Slavonic personal name composed of the elements *bog* god + *slav* glory.

Cognate: Czech: **Bohuslav**.

Pet forms: Polish: **Bogusz, Bohusz**.

Feminine forms: Polish: **Bogusława**. Czech: **Bohuslava**.

Bojan (m.) Czech: from an old Slavonic personal name, a derivative of the element *boi* battle.

Feminine form: **Bojana**.

Pet forms: **Bojánek, Bojek, Bojík** (m.); **Bojka** (f.).

Boje (m.) Frisian spelling of BOYE.

Bolesław (m.) Polish: from an old Slavonic personal name composed of the elements *bole* large + *slav* glory.

Cognate: Czech: **Boleslav**.

Feminine forms: Polish: **Bolesława**. Czech: **Boleslava**.

Pet forms: Czech: **Bolek** (m.); **Bolen(k)a** (f.).

Bona (f.) Italian and Polish: from the feminine form of the Late Latin name *Bonus* 'good'. This was a traditional hereditary name in the royal house of Savoy, and in the 16th century it was taken to Poland by Bona Sforza, who married King Sigismund I of Poland. She was noted as a patron of the arts, and was instrumental in bringing the Renaissance to Poland. The name was also borne by a Pisan saint (d. 1207), and also by the first abbess of Rheims (d. *c*.680). In the latter case, however, an alteration by folk etymology from the Germanic name *Bova* may be in question.

Bonaventura (m.) Italian: common medieval vernacular given name, composed of the elements *b(u)ona* good + *ventura* luck, fortune. It was borne by a follower of St Francis of Assisi, who was so called by the saint in exchange for his baptismal name *Giovanni*.

Bonifacio (m.) Italian, Spanish, and Portuguese: from the Late Latin name *Bonifatius*, derived from the elements *bonum* good + *fatum* fate, bestowed on a child as a hopeful omen. In the early Middle Ages the name came to be alternatively written as *Bonifacius* (with the same pronunciation), and reanalysed as a compound of *bonum* + *facere* to do, i.e. 'doer of good deeds'. The name was borne by several early saints, including a 7th-century pope and an Anglo-Saxon missionary who evangelized extensively in Germany in the 8th century. The latter was originally named *Winfrid*, but took the name *Bonifacius* on entering holy orders.

Cognate: German: **Bonifaz**.

Bonita (f.) English: apparently coined in America in the 1940s, probably from the feminine form of Spanish *bonito* pretty, although this is not used as a given name in Spanish-speaking countries. *Bonita* looks like the feminine form of a medieval Latin male name, *Bonītus* (from *bonus* good), which was borne by an Italian saint of the 6th century and a Provençal saint of the 7th. However, the feminine form is not found in medieval records, and this is an unlikely source of the name.

Bonnie (f.) English (esp. U.S.): originally an affectionate nickname from the Scottish word *bonnie* fine, attractive, pretty. However, it is not—or at any rate has not been until recently—used as a given name in Scotland. Its popularity may be attributed to the character of Scarlett O' Hara's infant daughter Bonnie in the film *Gone With the Wind* (1939), based on Margaret Mitchell's novel of the same name. (Bonnie's name was really Eugenie Victoria, but she had 'eyes as blue as the bonnie blue flag'.) A famous American bearer was Bonnie Parker, accomplice of the bank robber Clyde Barrow; their life together was the subject of the film *Bonnie and Clyde* (1967). The name has enjoyed a vogue in the second part of the 20th century, and has also been used as a pet form of BONITA.

Bora (f.) Czech: short form of *Barbora* (see BARBARA), used as a pet name.

Borbála (f.) Hungarian form of BARBARA.

Borghild (f.) Scandinavian (mainly Norwegian): from an Old Norse female personal name composed of the elements *borg* fortification + *hildr* battle. The name is attested from the Viking period, but modern use appears to be the result of a 19th-century revival.

Boris (m.) Russian: apparently in origin not of Slavonic etymology, but from the Tartar nickname *Bogoris* 'small'. It was later, however, taken to be a shortened form of **Borislav**, composed of the elements *bor* battle + *slav* glory. The name was borne in the 9th century by a ruler of Bulgaria who converted his kingdom to Christianity and sheltered disciples of Sts Cyril and Methodius when they were expelled from Moravia. The name was also borne by a 10th-century Russian saint, son of Prince Vladimir of Kiev and brother of St Gleb. It is as a result of his influence that *Boris* is one of the very few non-classical names that the Orthodox Church allows to be taken as baptismal names (although the saint himself bore the baptismal name *Romanus*).

Pet forms: **Borya, Boba.**

Bořivoj (m.) Czech: from an old Slavonic personal name composed of the elements *borit* to fight + *voi* warrior.

Pet forms: **Bořa, Bořek, Bořik.**

Börje (m.) Swedish: variant of BIRGER, first found in the 14th century in the forms *Byrghe* and *Byrie*.

Cognates: Danish: **Børge**. Norwegian: **Børge, Børre.**

Börries (m.) Low German: from the Late Latin personal name *Liborius*. This is of uncertain origin, perhaps an altered form of *Liberius* (see LIBOR), or possibly of Celtic origin. St Liborius was a 4th-century bishop of Le Mans, whose relics were taken to Paderborn in the 9th century.

Borya (m.) Russian: pet form of BORIS.

Bosse (m.) Swedish: pet form of BO.

Bothild (f.) Swedish form of BODIL.

Variant: **Botilda** (Latinized).

Boye (m.) Dutch: of uncertain origin, found in this form from the early Middle Ages onwards. It may derive from the Germanic personal name *Bodo* (a short form of various compound names containing the element *bod* messenger, tidings), with the loss of *d* between vowels typical of Dutch. Alternatively, it may have been originally a byname cognate with modern English *boy* lad, young man.

Cognate: Frisian: **Boje.**

Bożydar (m.) Polish: from a medieval personal name composed of the vocabulary elements *boży* divine + *dar* gift.

Cognate: Czech: **Božidar.**

Feminine form: Czech: **Božidara.**

Pet forms: Czech: **Boža** (m., f.); **Božek** (m.); **Božka, Božena** (f.).

Brad (m.) English (mainly U.S.): short form of BRADFORD and BRADLEY.

Bradford (m.) English (mainly U.S.): transferred use of the surname, in origin a local name from any of the numerous places in England so called from Old English *brād* broad + *ford* ford. The surname was borne most famously by William Bradford (1590–1657), leader of the Pilgrim Fathers from 1621 and governor of Plymouth Colony for some 30 years. It was also the name of another William Bradford (1722–91), a printer who played an important part in the American Revolution.

Bradley (m.) English (mainly U.S.): transferred use of the surname, in origin a local name from any of the numerous places in England so called from Old English *brād* broad + *lēah* wood or clearing. The most famous American bearer of this surname was General Omar N. Bradley (1893–1981).

Brady (m.) Irish and English (mainly U.S.): transferred use of the surname, which is of Irish origin, from Gaelic *Ó Brádaigh* 'descendant of Brádach'. *Brádach* is an old Irish byname, the meaning of which is not clear. It is unlikely to be connected with Gaelic *bradach* thieving, dishonest, which has a short first vowel; it may represent a contracted form of *Brághadach* 'large-chested', a derivative of *brágha* chest, throat.

Brandon (m.) English (mainly U.S.): transferred use of the surname, in origin a local name from any of various places so called, most of which get their name from Old English *brōm* broom, gorse + *dūn* hill. In 1982 this was the seventh commonest male given name among Blacks in the United States, and the twenty-third commonest among Whites. In part it may be regarded as an altered form of BRENDAN. There has probably also been some influence from the surname of the Italian American actor Marlon Brando (b. 1924).

Branislav (m.) Czech: variant of *Bronislav* (see BRONISŁAW).

Feminine form: **Branislava.**

Pet forms: **Branek** (m.); **Braňa, Branka** (f.).

Branton English (mainly U.S.): variant of BRANDON or transferred use of the surname *Branton*. This is a local name from places in Northumbria and West Yorkshire so named from Old English *brōm* broom, gorse + *tūn* enclosure, settlement.

Branwen (f.) Welsh: apparently composed of the elements *brân* raven + *(g)wen*, feminine of *gwyn* white, fair, blessed, holy. Alternatively, it is possible that it is a variant of BRONWEN. The story of Branwen, daughter of Llŷr, forms the second chapter or 'branch' of the *Mabinogi*: it tells of her beauty and of the conflict on her account between her brother Bran, King of the 'Island of the Mighty' (Britain), and her husband Matholwch, King of Ireland.

Bras (m.) Portuguese form of *Blaise*.

Variant: **Braz.**

Bratislav (m.) Czech: from an old Slavonic personal name composed of the elements *brat* brother + *slav* glory.

Feminine form: **Bratislava.**

Bratumił (m.) Polish: from an old Slavonic personal name composed of the elements *brat* brother + *mil* grace, favour.

Brayne (f.) Jewish: Yiddish name, a back-formation from **Brayndel**, itself an affectionate diminutive form of Yiddish *broyn* brown (cf. modern German *braun*).

Breeda (f.) Irish: Anglicized form (with the typical feminine name-suffix *-a*) of Gaelic *Bríd*; see BRIDE.

Brenda (f.) Scottish, Irish, and (in the 20th century) English: of uncertain derivation. It seems to be of Scandinavian rather than Celtic origin (in spite of its similarity to BRENDAN), and may be a short form of various compound names containing the element *brand* (flaming) sword.

Brendan (m.) Irish: from the old Irish personal name *Bréanainn*, derived from a Celtic element meaning 'prince'. This was the name of two 6th-century Irish saints, Brendan the Voyager and Brendan of Birr. According to legend, the former was the first European to set foot on North American soil. The modern Irish Gaelic form **Breandán** and the Anglicized *Brendan* are based on the medieval Latin form *Brendanus*.

Brent (m.) English: transferred use of the surname, which is derived from any of several places in Devon and Somerset which are on or near prominent hills, and seem therefore to have been named with a Celtic or Old English term for a hill. The given name has enjoyed considerable popularity in Britain in the 1970s and 1980s, and may have been influenced by BRETT, which has experienced a similar vogue, starting somewhat earlier.

Břetislav (m.) Czech: from an old Slavonic personal name composed of the elements *brech* noise, din (of battle) + *slav* glory.

Feminine form: **Břetislava.**

Pet forms: **Břetík** (m.); **Břet'ka, Bretička** (f.).

Brett (m.) English: transferred use of the surname, which originated in the Middle Ages as an ethnic name for one of the Bretons who arrived in England in the wake of the Norman Conquest; it is most common in East Anglia, where Breton settlement was particularly concentrated. As a given name, it has enjoyed something of a vogue in the latter half of the 20th century.

Brewster (m.) English (mainly U.S.): transferred use of the surname, in origin an occupational name for a brewer, Middle English *brēowestre*. The *-estre* suffix was originally feminine, but by the Middle English period this grammatical distinction had been lost (cf. BAXTER).

Brian (m.) Irish and English: perhaps from an Old Celtic word meaning 'high' or 'noble'. The name has been perennially popular in Ireland, largely on account of the fame of Brian Boru (Gaelic *Brian Bóroimhe*), a 10th-century high king of Ireland. In the Middle Ages it was relatively common in East Anglia, to which it was introduced by Breton settlers, and in north-west England, to which it was introduced by Scandinavians from Ireland. In Gaelic Scotland it was at first borne exclusively by members of certain professional families of Irish origin.

Variant: **Bryan**.

Brianne (f.) English: recent coinage to create a female equivalent of BRIAN.

Briartach (m.) Irish Gaelic: variant form of MUIRIARTACH, common particularly in Connacht.

Brice (m.) French: from the name of a 5th-century saint who was a disciple and successor of St Martin of Tours. His name is found in the Latinized forms *Bri(c)tius* or *Bricius* and is probably of Gaulish origin, possibly derived from an element meaning 'speckled' (Welsh *brych*).

Cognate: Italian: BRIZIO.

Bride (f.) Irish: Anglicized form of **Bríd**, the modern Gaelic contracted form of *Brighid* (see BRIDGET).

Variant: **Breeda**.

Pet forms: **Bridie** (English); **Brídín** (Gaelic).

Bridget (f.) Irish, Scottish, and English: Anglicized form of the Gaelic name **Brighid**. This was the name of an ancient Celtic goddess, of uncertain origin; it is unlikely to be connected with Gaelic *brígh* strength, force, since this word has a long vowel. St Brigid of Kildare (*c.*450–*c.*525) is one of the patron saints of Ireland. Very few facts are known about her life. She founded a religious house for women at Kildare, and is said to be have been buried at Downpatrick, where St Patrick and St Columba were also buried. Many of the stories of miracles told about St Brigid seem to be Christianized versions of pagan legends concerning the goddess.

Variants: **Brigit**, BRIDE.

Cognates: Welsh: **Ffraid**. German, French: **Brigitte**. Italian: **Brigida**. Scandinavian: BIRGIT. Finnish: **Pirjo, Pirkko**.

Pet form: Irish, English: BIDDY.

Brigham (m.) English (mainly U.S.): name adopted in honour of the early Mormon leader, Brigham Young (1801–77). It was originally a surname, a local name from places in Cumbria and North Yorkshire so called from Old English *brycg* bridge + *hām* homestead, settlement. It is not known why the Mormon leader received this given name; he was the son of John and Abigail Young of Whitingham, Vermont.

Briony (f.) English: variant spelling of BRYONY.

Britt (f.) Swedish: contracted form of BIRGIT, made famous in the English-speaking world by the actress Britt Ekland (b. 1942; her surname was originally Eklund).

Variants: **Britta, Brita**.

Brizio (m.) Italian: 1. From *Brictius*, an ancient name probably of Gaulish origin (see BRICE). St Brizio (d. *c.*312) was bishop of Martola near Spoleto in Umbria, who suffered in the persecutions instituted by the Emperor Diocletian. His cult is still popular in the region.

2. Short form of *Fabrizio* (see FABRICE).

Broder (m.) Swedish, Danish, and Frisian: from the Old Norse vocabulary word *bróðir* brother. This seems to have been bestowed on younger sons.

Variant: Swedish: **Bror**.

Pet form: Swedish: **Brolle**.

Brogio (m.) Italian: short form of *Ambrogio* (see AMBROSE).

Bronisław (m.) Polish: from an old Slavonic personal name composed of the elements *bron* armour, protection + *slav* glory.

Cognates: Czech: **Bronislav, Branislav**.

Pet form: Czech: **Branek**.

Bronisława (f.) Polish: feminine form of BRONISŁAW. The Blessed Bronislava (d. 1259) was a cousin of St Hyacinth of Poland (see JACEK).

Cognates: Czech: **Bronislava, Branislava**.

Pet forms: Czech: **Broňa, Braňa, Bron(ič)ka, Branka**.

Bronwen (f.) Welsh: composed of the elements *bron* breast + *(g)wen*, feminine of *gwyn* white, fair, blessed, holy.

Bronya (f.) Polish: pet form of various old Slavonic compound names containing the element *bron* armour, protection (e.g. BRONISŁAWA).

Bror (m.) Swedish: contracted variant of BRODER.

Pet form: **Brolle**.

Brož (m.) Czech: short form of *Ambroz* (see AMBROSE).

Pet form: **Brožek**.

Bruce (m.) Scottish and English: transferred use of the Scottish surname, now used as a given name throughout the English-speaking world, but in recent years particularly popular in Australia. The surname was originally a Norman baronial name, but a precise identification of the place from which it was derived has not been made (there are a large number of possible candidates). The Bruces were an influential Norman family in Scottish affairs in the early Middle Ages; its most famous member was Robert 'the Bruce' (1274–1329), who is said to have drawn inspiration after his defeat at Methven from the perseverance of a spider in repeatedly climbing up again after being knocked down. He ruled Scotland as King Robert I from 1306 to 1329.

Brunella (f.) Latinate feminine formation from BRUNO. Its formation may have been influenced by the existence of the name PRUNELLA.

Brunhilde (f.) German: from an old Germanic female personal name composed of the elements *brun* armour, protection + *hild* battle. In so far as it is found at all in modern use, it is a literary name. In Germanic legend, Brunhilde is a warrior queen, wife of Gunther, who plays a central role in the *Nibelungenlied*. She appears as *Brynhild* in the Icelandic *Volsungasaga*, where she is the chief of the Valkyries, a group of supernatural warrior maidens who collect the slain after a battle and carry them off to Valhalla. She is also a central figure in Richard Wagner's opera cycle *The Ring of the Nibelungs*. Wagner's Brünnhilde is a Valkyrie, daughter of Wotan, chief of the gods, who defies her father to help the lovers Siegmund and Sieglinde. As a punishment she is immolated on a mountain top, surrounded by a wall of fire. Her rescue by Siegfried, the son of Siegmund and Sieglinde, has a tragic outcome, leading to universal destruction. The character of Brunhilde may have a historical basis in the person of Brunhilda (?534–613), a powerful Frankish queen.

Variants: **Brunhild, Brünhilde, Brünnhilde**.

Cognate: Icelandic: **Brynhildur**.

Bruno (m.) German and English: from the Germanic vocabulary element *brun* brown. This name was in use in many of the ruling families of Germany during the Middle Ages, being borne by a 10th-century saint, son of the Emperor Henry the Fowler, and also by the Saxon duke who gave his name to Brunswick (German *Braunschweig*, i.e. 'Bruno's settlement').

Its use in the English-speaking world, which dates from the end of the 19th century, may have been partly influenced by Lewis Carroll's *Sylvie and Bruno* (1889), but more probably it was first used by settlers of German ancestry in the United States.

Bryan (m.) English: variant of BRIAN, influenced by the usual spelling of the associated surname.

Bryant (m.) English: transferred use of the surname, which is derived from the given name BRIAN. The final *-t* seems to have arisen as a result of association with names such as CONSTANT.

Brychan (m.) Welsh: from an Old Welsh byname meaning 'speckled'. A traditional Welsh figure of this name was the father of ten sons and twenty-four daughters (more in one Cornish list), many of whom came to be venerated as saints.

Bryn (m.) Welsh: 20th-century coinage from the Welsh topographical term *bryn* hill, in part as a short form of BRYNMOR.

Brynmor (m.) Welsh: 20th-century coinage from the name of a place in Gwynedd, composed of the Welsh elements *bryn* hill + *mawr* large.

Bryony (f.) English: from the name of the plant (Greek *bryonia*). This is one of a more recently coined (20th-century) batch of names taken from vocabulary words denoting flowers.

Variant: **Briony**.

Buck (m.) English (U.S.): from the English nickname *Buck*, denoting a robust and spirited young man, from the vocabulary word for a male deer (Old English *bucc*) or a he-goat (Old English *bucca*).

Bud (m.) English (U.S.): originally a short form of the nickname or vocabulary word *buddy* friend, which may be an alteration, perhaps a nursery form, of *brother* or else derive from the Scottish Gaelic vocative case *a bhodaich* 'old man!'. It is now occasionally used as a given name in its own right, especially in America.

Budzisław (m.) Polish: from an old Slavonic personal name composed of the elements *budit* to arouse, stir + *slav* glory.

Cognate: Czech: **Budislav**.

Pet forms: Polish: **Budzyk, Budzisz**. Czech: **Buděk**.

Buffy (f.) English: pet form of ELIZABETH, based on a child's unsuccessful attempts to pronounce the name.

Bunem (m.) Jewish: Yiddish name derived ultimately from the French phrase *bon homme* 'good man' bestowed as an affectionate nickname.

Bunty (f.) English: nickname and occasional baptismal name, relatively popular in the early 20th century, but of uncertain derivation. It seems most likely that it derives from what was originally a dialectal pet name for a lamb, from the verb to *bunt* to butt gently.

Burgess (m.) English: transferred use of the surname, which is derived from the Old French word *burgeis* freeman of a borough (a derivative of *burg* town, of Germanic origin).

Burkhard (m.) German: from an old Germanic personal name composed of the elements *burg* protection + *hard* hardy, brave, strong. St Burkhard (d. *c.*754) was a companion of St Boniface who became the first bishop of Würzburg and founded several Benedictine monasteries in the area. Like Boniface, he seems to have been an Anglo-Saxon by birth, perhaps originally bearing the cognate Old English personal name *Burgheard*.

Burt (m.) English (U.S.): of various origins. In the case of the film actor Burt Lancaster (b. 1913) it is a short form of BURTON, but it has also been used as a variant spelling of BERT. The pianist and composer Burt Bacharach (b. 1928) was the son of a Bert Bacharach, and his given name is presumably simply a variation of his father's.

Burton (m.) English: transferred use of the surname, which is a local name from any of the numerous places in England so called. In most cases the placename is derived from Old English *burh* fortress, fortified place + *tūn* enclosure, settlement.

Buster (m.) English (U.S.): originally a nickname from the slang term of address *buster*, which is apparently a derivative of the verb *bust* to break, smash (an altered form of *burst*). It was the nickname of the silent movie comedian Joseph Francis 'Buster' Keaton (1895–1966).

Byron (m.) English: transferred use of the surname, first bestowed as a given name in honour of the poet Lord Byron (George Gordon, 6th Baron Byron, 1784–1824). The surname derives from the Old English phrase *æt ðǣm bȳrum* 'at the byres or cattlesheds', and was given to someone who lived there because it was his job to look after cattle.

C

Cäcilie (f.) German form of CECILY.

Cade (m.) English: transferred use of the surname, which originated as a nickname from a vocabulary element denoting something round and lumpish. It is one of several given names that owe their origin to their use for a character in Margaret Mitchell's novel *Gone with the Wind* (1936).

Cadell (m.) Welsh: from an Old Welsh personal name composed of the elements *cad* battle + the diminutive suffix *-ell*.

Cadogan (m.) Welsh, Irish, and English: Anglicized form of the Old Welsh personal name **Cadwgan** or **Cadwgawn**, a compound of the elements *cad* battle + *gwogawn* glory, distinction, honour. The name was borne by several Welsh rulers in the early Middle Ages, and is mentioned as the name of two characters in the *Mabinogi*. It has been revived to some extent in the 19th and 20th centuries, probably under the influence of the surname derived from it, which was taken to Ireland in the 17th century.

Cadwalader (m.) Welsh: Anglicized form of **Cadwaladr**, an ancient Celtic name composed of the elements *cad* battle + *gwaladr* leader and commonly given to the sons of kings and princes. St Cadwalader (d. *c.*682) was a British chieftain who died maintaining a stronghold against the pagan Saxon invaders.

Caerwyn (m.) Welsh: altered form of CARWYN, influenced by the many Welsh placenames with the fist element *caer* fort.

Caesar (m.) English (esp. U.S.): Anglicized form of Italian *Cesare* or French CÉSAR, or a direct adoption of the Roman imperial family name *Caesar*; cf. DUKE, EARL, KING, and PRINCE.

Caetano (m.) Portuguese form of GAETANO.

Cahal (m.) Irish: Anglicized spelling of CATHAL.

Cahir (m.) Irish: Anglicized spelling of CATHAOIR.

Cainneach (m.) Irish Gaelic form of COINNEACH, generally Anglicized as KENNY. See also CANICE.

Cairistìona (f.) Scottish Gaelic form of CHRISTINE.

Variant: **Cairistíne**.

Pet form: **Stìneag**.

Cáit (f.) Irish Gaelic form of KATE or short form of CAITRÍONA.

Caitir (f.) Scottish: name derived from Gaelic *Caitrìona* (see CATRIONA), by misanalysis as *Caitir Fhìona*, the second element taken as meaning 'of wine'. This name has sometimes been Anglicized as CLARISSA.

Caitlín (f.) Irish Gaelic form of KATHERINE, derived from the Old French form *Catheline*.

Caitrín (f.) Irish Gaelic form of KATHERINE, derived from the Old French form *Catherine*.

Caitríona (f.) Irish Gaelic: the most usual form of KATHERINE.

Short forms: **Cáit**, **Tríona**. See also RÍONA.

Cajetan (m.) English: Roman Catholic religious name; see GAETANO.

Caleb (m.) Biblical: name borne by an early Israelite, one of only two of those who set out with Moses from Egypt to live long enough to enter the promised land (Numbers 26: 65). The name, which is related to the the word for 'dog' in Hebrew, is said in some traditions to symbolize his rabid devotion to God. It was popular among the Puritans and was introduced by them to America, where it is still in use.

Callisto (m.) Italian: from the Late Latin personal name *Callistus*, which is apparently adopted from the Greek vocabulary word *kallistos*, superlative of *kalos* fair, good. The forms *Callixtus* and *Calixtus* are also found in Late Latin, but seem to be later developments. The name was borne by several early saints, including a 3rd-century pope and a 6th-century bishop of Todi in central Italy.

Cognate: Spanish: **Calisto**.

Calogero (m.) Italian: characteristically southern Italian and especially Sicilian name. St Calogerus the Anchorite (d. *c.*486) lived as a hermit near Grigenti in Sicily, and is the subject of a local cult. The name is composed of the Greek elements *kalos* fair, good + *gēras* old age; in the Late Greek period it was used as a title of respect for anchorites and monks.

Calum (m.) Scottish Gaelic form of the Late Latin personal name *Columba* 'dove'. This was popular among early Christians because the dove was a symbol of gentleness, purity, peace, and the Holy Spirit. St Columba (see also COLM) was one of the most influential of all the early Celtic saints. He was born in Donegal in 521 into a noble family, and was trained for the priesthood from early in life. He founded monastery schools at Durrow, Derry, and Kells, and then, in 563, sailed with twelve companions to Scotland, to convert the people there to Christianity. He established a monastery on the island of Iona, and from there converted the Pictish and Irish inhabitants of Scotland. He died in 597 and was buried at Downpatrick, along with St Patrick and St Brighid. See also COLIN (2).

Pet forms: **Cally, Caley**.

Feminine forms: **Calumina, Calaminag**.

Calvin (m.) English (esp. U.S.): from the French surname, used as a given name among Nonconformists in honour of the French Protestant theologian Jean Calvin (1509–64). It has enjoyed a recent vogue as a given name. The surname meant originally 'little bald one', from a diminutive of *calve*, a Norman and Picard form of French *chauve* bald. (The theologian was born in Noyon, Picardy.)

Short form: **Cal**.

Cameron (m.) Scottish: transferred use of the surname, which is borne by one of the great Highland clans. Their name is derived from an ancestor with a 'crooked nose' (Gaelic *cam shron*). There were also Camerons in the Lowlands, apparently the result of an assimilation to this name of a Norman baronial name derived from *Cambernon* in Normandy.

Camilla (f.) English and Italian: feminine form of the old Roman family name *Camillus*, of obscure and presumably non-Roman origin. According to tradition, recorded by the Roman poet Virgil, Camilla was the name of a warrior maiden, Queen of the Volscians, who fought in the army of Aeneas (*Aeneid* 7. 803–17). The masculine form is much less common, except in Italy, where it is bestowed in honour of St Camillo de Lellis (1550–1614), who founded the nursing order of the Ministers of the Sick.

Cognates: French: **Camille** (also m.). Polish, Czech: **Kamila**.

Short form: English: **Milla**.

Pet form: English: **Millie**.

Masculine forms: Italian: **Camillo**. Spanish, Portuguese: **Camilo**. French: **Camille** (also f.). Polish, Czech: **Kamil**.

Campbell (m.) Scottish: transferred use of the surname, borne by one of the great Highland clans, whose head is the Duke of Argyll. The name is derived from an ancestor with a 'crooked mouth' (Gaelic *cam beul*).

Candace (f.) English: from the hereditary name of a long line of queens of Ethiopia. One of them is mentioned in the Bible, when the apostle Philip baptizes 'a man of Ethiopia, an eunuch of great authority under Candace queen of the Ethiopians, who had the charge of all her treasure' (Acts 8: 27). This name is now much less common than its presumed derivative CANDICE.

Candelaria (f.) Spanish: religious name referring to the feast of Candlemas (a derivative of *candela* candle). This festival, on 2 February, commemorates the Purification of the Virgin Mary (cf. PURIFICACIÓN) and the Presentation of Christ in the temple (cf. PRESENTACIÓN).
Pet form: **Candela**.

Candice (f.) English: apparently a respelling of CANDACE. The spelling may have been influenced by CLARICE; or more probably by a folk etymology deriving the name from Late Latin *canditia* whiteness.

Candida (f.) English: from Late Latin, meaning 'white'. The colour was associated in Christian imagery with purity and salvation (cf. Revelation 3: 4 'thou hast a few names even in Sardis which have not defiled their garments; and they shall walk with me in white: for they are worthy'). This was the name of several early saints, including a woman supposedly cured by St Peter himself.

Candy (f.) English (esp. U.S.): from an affectionate nickname derived from the vocabulary word *candy* confectionery. The word *candy* is from French *sucre candi* 'candied sugar', i.e. sugar boiled to make a crystalline sweet. The French word is derived from Arabic *qandi*, which is in turn of Indian origin. *Candy* could, in theory, also be a short form of CANDICE and of CANDIDA, but there is no evidence that this is so.

Canice (m.) Irish: from the Latinized form, *Canisius*, of the Old Irish personal name *Cainnech* (modern Gaelic **Cainneach**; cf. COINNEACH). It seems to have been originally a byname meaning 'handsome, fair one', and was borne by a large number of early saints. The most important of these is St Cainnech of Aghaboe, patron of Kilkenny. See also KENNY.

Caoilte (m.) Irish Gaelic: name of uncertain derivation, borne by the legendary hero Caoilte Mac Rónáin, famous as a swift runner. It has been revived as a given name in the 20th century.

Caoimhe (f.) Irish Gaelic: modern name representing the abstract noun derived from the vocabulary word *caomh* kind, gentle (earlier 'beloved' or 'beautiful'; cf. KEVIN).

Cara (f.) English: 20th-century coinage, from the Italian term of endearment *cara* 'beloved' or the Irish Gaelic vocabulary word *cara* friend. This is not normally used as a given name in Italy, where such innovations are held in check by the hostility of the Roman Catholic Church to baptismal names that have not been borne by saints.

Caradoc (m.) Welsh: respelling of **Caradog**. This represents an ancient Celtic name apparently derived from the root *cār* love. A form of this name was borne by the British chieftain recorded under the Latinized version *Caratacus*, son of Cunobelinos. He rebelled against Roman rule in the 1st century AD, and although the rebellion was swiftly put down he is recorded by the Roman historian Tacitus as having impressed the Emperor Claudius by his proud bearing in captivity.

Careen (f.) English: of recent origin and uncertain derivation. Its first appearance seems to have been in Margaret Mitchell's novel *Gone with the Wind* (1936), where it is borne by one of the sisters of Scarlett O'Hara (the other being Sue Ellen). The name may represent a combination of CARA with the hypocoristic suffix *-een* (of Irish origin; cf. MAUREEN), or it may be an altered form of CARINA.

Carey (f., m.) 1. Irish: transferred use of the surname *Carey*, which has two origins. It is in part a local name from Carew Castle in Pembrokeshire, and was taken to Ireland in the 12th century by followers of Strongbow, Earl of Pembroke. To this has been assimilated an Irish patronymic, *Ó Ciardha* 'descendant of the dark one'.

2. English: variant spelling of CARY, used mainly as a female name, under the influence of CARRIE.

Caridad (f.) Spanish form of CHARITY.

Cognate: Portuguese: **Caridade**.

Carina (f.) Scandinavian, German, and English: late 19th-century coinage, apparently representing a Latinate elaboration of CARA; in part it may also have been inspired by KARIN.

Carl (m.) German and English: old-fashioned German spelling variant of KARL, the German version of CHARLES. It is now increasingly used in English-speaking countries, and for some reason is particularly popular in Wales.

Carla (f.) Italian, English, and German: feminine form of CARLO, CHARLES, or CARL. See also *Karla* at KARL.

Carlin (f.) English: elaborated from of CARLA, apparently of German origin.

Carlo (m.) Italian form of CHARLES.

Carlos (m.) Spanish and Portuguese form of CHARLES.

Carlotta (f.) Italian form of CHARLOTTE, occasionally used in the English-speaking world.

Carlton (m.) English: transferred use of the surname, which is of the same origin as CHARLTON, being derived from any of various places (in Beds., Cambs., Co. Durham, Leics., Lincs., Northants, Notts., Suffolk, and Yorks.) named with the Old English elements *ceorl* (free) man + *tūn* settlement, i.e. 'settlement of the free peasants'. The initial /k/ sound is the result of Anglo-Scandinavian influence.

Carly (f.) English: pet form or variant of CARLA.

Variants: **Carlie, Carley**.

Carmel (f.) English: of early Christian origin, referring to 'Our Lady of Carmel', a title of the Virgin Mary. *Carmel* is the name (meaning 'garden' or 'orchard' in Hebrew) of a mountain in the Holy Land near modern Haifa, which was populated from very early Christian times by hermits. They were later organized into the Carmelite order of monks. The name is favoured mainly by Roman Catholics.

Cognates: Portuguese: **Carmo**. Spanish: CARMEN; **Carmela** (also S. Italian and Sicilian).

Pet forms: Spanish: **Carmencita, Carmelita; Menchu**.

Masculine forms: Spanish: **Carmelo**. Italian: **Carmine**.

Carmela (f.) 1. Spanish, S. Italian, and Sicilian form of the given name CARMEL.

2. Jewish: modern Hebrew name derived from the placename CARMEL.

Carmen (f.) Spanish form of CARMEL, altered by folk etymology to the form of the Latin word *carmen* song. It is now sometimes found as a given name in the English-speaking world, in spite of, or perhaps because of, its association with the tragic romantic heroine of Bizet's opera *Carmen* (1875), based on a short story by Prosper Mérimée.

Carol (f., originally m.) English: Anglicized form of *Carolus* (see CHARLES), or of its feminine derivative **Carola**. It has never been common as a male name, and has become even less so since its growth in popularity as a female name. This seems to be of relatively recent origin (not being found much before the end of the 19th century) and may have originated as a short form of CAROLINE.

Carole (f.) French form of CAROL, formerly quite commonly used in the English-speaking world in order to make it clear that a female name was in question. Now that *Carol* is used almost exclusively for girls, *Carole* has become slightly less common.

Caroline (f.) English and French: from the French form of Latin or Italian **Carolina**, a feminine derivative of *Carolus* (see CHARLES).

Variant: **Carolyn**. [*cont.*]

Cognates: German, Danish: **Karoline**. Scandinavian, Polish, Czech: **Karolina**.

Short forms: English: **Caro** (not normally used as an independent given name); CARRIE.

Carrie (f.) English: pet form of CAROLINE or occasionally of other girls' names beginning with the syllable *Car-*. It was first used in the 19th century and is now popular in its own right, *Caro* having to some extent taken over the role of the short form.

Carroll (m.) Irish: Anglicized form of CEARBHALL.

Carson (m.) Scottish and Northern Irish: transferred use of the surname, which is of uncertain derivation; in spite of its *-son* ending, it does not seem to be a true patronymic. The first known bearer is a certain Robert *de Carsan* (or *de Acarson*), recorded in 1276; the 'de' in his name suggests derivation from a placename, but no suitable candidates have been identified. Among Protestants in Northern Ireland, it is sometimes bestowed in honour of Edward Carson (1854–1935), the Dublin barrister and politician who was a violent opponent of Home Rule for Ireland. In America the popularity of the name may have been affected by the legendary Missouri frontiersman Kit Carson (1809–68).

Carsten (m.) Low German form of CHRISTIAN.

Carter (m.) English: transferred use of the surname, which for the most part originated as an occupational name for someone who transported goods in a cart. In Scotland the surname also represents an Anglicized form of the Gaelic surname *Mac Artair* 'son of Artair'.

Carwyn (m.) Welsh: modern coinage, composed of the elements *cār* love + *(g)wyn* white, fair, blessed, holy.

Cary (m., sometimes f.) English: transferred use of the surname, which comes from one of the places in Devon or Somerset so called from an old Celtic river name. *Cary* became popular as a given name in the middle of the 20th century, due to the fame of the film actor Cary Grant (1904–89), who was born in Bristol and made his first theatrical appearances under his original name of Archie Leach.

Variant: CAREY.

Caryl (f., occasionally m.) English: of uncertain origin, probably a variant of CAROL, possibly influenced by BERYL. As a male name it is probably an altered spelling of CARROLL.

Carys (f.) Welsh: modern coinage, from the vocabulary element *cār* love + the ending *-ys*, by analogy with names such as BETRYS and GLADYS.

Casey (m., now occasionally also f.) English (esp. U.S.): 1. Bestowed originally in honour of the American engine-driver and folk hero 'Casey' Jones (1863–1900), who saved the lives of passengers on the 'Cannonball Express' at the expense of his own. He was baptized Johnathan Luther Jones in Cayce, Kentucky, and acquired his nickname from his birthplace.

2. From the Irish surname, the Gaelic form of which is *Ó Cathasaigh* 'descendant of *Cathasach*', a byname meaning 'vigilant, wakeful'.

3. As a female name it is probably a variant of *Cassie* (see CASS).

Casilda (f.) Spanish: of uncertain origin. This was the name of an 11th-century saint who was born in Toledo. She was probably of Moorish descent. She lived as an anchorite nun in the province of Burgos, and is particularly venerated in Burgos and Toledo.

Casimir (m.) Anglicized spelling of Polish *Kazimierz*, derived from *kazić* to destroy + the Old Slavonic element *meri* great, famous (later taken as the medieval and modern word *mir* peace or world). This was a traditional name of Polish kings in the Middle Ages. Casimir I succeeded in reuniting Polish lands and restoring Polish power. Casimir III, 'the Great'

(1310–70), king from 1333 to 1370, was an effective and able ruler, and also a just and humane one, who presided over a golden age in Polish history. St Casimir (1458–83) was a son of King Casimir IV; his father wished him to seize the crown of Hungary, but instead he retired from the world, eventually dying of consumption.

Caspar (m.) Dutch form of JASPER, also found as an occasional variant in English. According to legend, this was the name of one of the three Magi or 'wise men' who brought gifts to the infant Christ. The Magi are not named in the Bible, but early Christian tradition assigned them the names *Caspar*, *Balthasar*, and *Melchior*.

Variants: **Casper, Kaspar, Kasper.**

Cognates: German: **Kaspar**. Polish: **Kasper**. Italian: **Gasparo**. French: **Gaspard**. Hungarian: **Gáspár**.

Cass (f.) English: medieval and modern short form of CASSANDRA, now often used as an independent given name.

Pet form: **Cassie** (common in Scotland).

Cassandra (f.) from Greek legend. Cassandra was a Trojan princess blessed with the gift of prophecy but cursed with the fate that nobody would ever believe her. She was brought back to Greece as a captive concubine by Agamemnon, but met her death at the hands of his jealous wife Clytemnestra. This was one of the most popular girls' names in the Middle Ages, and has recently been revived by parents looking to the pages of classical mythology for distinctive girls' names.

Cassia (f.) English: apparently an adoption of the name of the spice (cf. KEZIA). It may also in part have been adopted as a feminine form of CASSIAN.

Cassian (m.) English: from the name (Latin *Cassiānus*) of several early saints, most notably one martyred at Tangier in 298. The name is a derivative of the old Roman family name *Cassius*. It is of uncertain derivation, but may be connected with the Latin vocabulary word *cassus* empty, hollow.

Cassidy (m., f.) English (esp. U.S.): from the Irish surname *Ó Caiside*. Its use as a female name may be due to the *-y* ending, coupled with the fact that it could be taken as an expanded form of CASS.

Catalina (f.) Spanish form of KATHERINE.

Catarina (f.) Portuguese form of KATHERINE.

Caterina (f.) Italian form of KATHERINE.

Cathal (m.) Irish Gaelic: name derived from the Old Celtic vocabulary elements *cath* battle + *val* rule. It was borne by a 7th-century saint who served as head of the monastic school at Lismore, before being appointed bishop of Taranto in south Italy. In Gaelic Scotland the name appears to have been borne only by descendants of the Mac Mhuirichs, a learned family of Irish origin.

Variants: **Cathaldus; Cahal, Catheld, Kathel** (Anglicized forms).

Cathán (m.) Irish Gaelic: traditional name, representing a diminutive form of the element *cath* battle.

Anglicized form: **Kane.**

Cathaoir (m.) Irish Gaelic: from *cathaoir* warrior, a derivative of the Old Celtic vocabulary elements *cath* fight, battle + *vir* man.

Variant: **Cahir** (Anglicized form).

Catherine (f.) English: variant spelling of KATHERINE. This form of the name is also used in France.

Variant: English: **Catharine.**

Short form: English: **Cath.**

Pet form: English: **Cathy.**

Cathleen (f.) Irish: variant spelling of KATHLEEN.

Cathy (f.) English: pet form of CATHERINE.

Catraoine (f.) Irish Gaelic form of KATHERINE, less common than *Caitríona*, *Caitrín*, and *Caitlín*.

Catrin (f.) Welsh form of KATHERINE.

Catriona (f.) Scottish and Irish: Anglicized form of the Gaelic names **Ca(i)trìona** (Scottish) and **Caitríona** (Irish), which are themselves forms of KATHERINE. The name is now also used elsewhere in the English-speaking world, although it is still especially popular among people of Scottish ancestry. It attracted wider attention as the title of Robert Louis Stevenson's novel *Catriona* (1893), sequel to *Kidnapped*.

Variant: **Catrina**.

Cayetano (m.) Spanish form of GAETANO.

Cayo (m.) Spanish: from the classical Latin personal name *Caius*, *Gaius*, which is of extremely ancient origin and uncertain etymology. It was borne, for example, by the dictator Caius Julius Caesar, and in the early Christian period by numerous saints.

Ceallachán (m.) Irish Gaelic: diminutive form of CEALLAGH.

Ceallagh (m.) Irish Gaelic: of uncertain origin; it is probably a derivative of *ceall* monastery, church.

Anglicized form: KELLY.

Cearbhall (m.) Irish Gaelic: name of uncertain derivation; it possibly arose as a nickname for a violent warrior, from *cearbh* hacking. In the Middle Ages it was common among the learned Ó Dálaigh family of traditional poets. In modern times, it has been borne by Cearbhall Ó Dálaigh (1911–78), president of the Irish Republic.

Variant: **Cearúl(l)** (a modern 'reformed' spelling).

Anglicized forms: **Carroll**, CHARLES.

Cebrià (m.) Catalan form of CIPRIANO.

Cebrián (m.) Spanish form of CIPRIANO.

Cecil (m.) English: transferred use of the surname of a great noble family, which rose to prominence in England during the 16th century. The Cecils were of Welsh origin, and their surname represents an Anglicized form of the Welsh given name *Seissylt*, apparently a Brittonic or Old Welsh form of the Latin name *Sextilius*, from *Sextus* 'sixth'. In the Middle Ages *Cecil* was occasionally used as an English form of Latin *Caecilius* (an old Roman family name derived from the byname *Caecus* 'blind'), borne by a minor saint of the 3rd century, a friend of St Cyprian.

Cecily (f.) English: from the Latin name *Caecilia*, feminine of *Caecilius* (see CECIL). This was a good deal more common than the masculine form, largely due to the fame of the 2nd- or 3rd-century virgin martyr whose name is still mentioned daily in the Roman Catholic Canon of the Mass. She is regarded as the patron saint of music and has inspired works such as Purcell's 'Ode on St Cecilia's Day', although the reasons for this association are not clear.

Variants: **Cecilia**, **Cicely**.

Cognates: Irish Gaelic: **Síle**. Scottish Gaelic: **Sìle**, **Sìleas**. French: **Cécile** (sometimes also used in the English-speaking world). German: **Cäcilie**. Finnish: **Silja**.

Pet forms: English: **Sessy**, **Sissy**. Low German, Frisian: **Silke**.

Cedric (m.) English: coined by Sir Walter Scott for the character Cedric of Rotherwood in *Ivanhoe* (1819). It seems to be a metathesized form of *Cerdic*, the name of the traditional founder of the kingdom of Wessex. Cerdic was a Saxon (Scott's novel also has a Saxon setting), and his name is presumably of Germanic origin, but the formation is not clear. The name has acquired something of a 'sissy' image, probably on account of Cedric Errol Fauntleroy, the long-haired, velvet-suited boy hero of Frances Hodgson Burnett's *Little Lord Fauntleroy* (1886).

Cees (m.) Dutch: variant spelling of KEES.

Ceinwen (f.) Welsh: composed of the vocabulary elements *cain* fair, lovely + *(g)wen* white, blessed, holy. The name was borne by a 5th-century saint, daughter of the chieftain Brychan, about whom little is known.

Ceit (f.) Scottish Gaelic spelling of KATE.

Pet form: **Ceiteag.**

Céleste (f.) French, now also quite common in the English-speaking world: from Latin *Caelestis* 'heavenly', a popular name among early Christians.

Variant: English: **Celeste.**

Celia (f.) English and Italian: from Latin *Caelia*, feminine of the old Roman family name *Caelius* (of uncertain origin, probably a derivative of *caelum* heaven). The name was not used in the Middle Ages, but was introduced to the English-speaking world as the name of a character in Shakespeare's *As You Like It.* It is now often regarded as a short form of *Cecilia.*

Cognate: French: **Célie** (not now a common given name).

Pet form: Low German, Frisian: **Silke.**

Céline (f.) French, also found occasionally in the English-speaking world: apparently from Latin *Caelīna*, a feminine form of *Caelīnus*, which is a derivative of *Caelius* (see CELIA). It may alternatively be an aphetic short form of *Marcel(l)ine*, a feminine diminutive of MARCEL.

Celso (m.) Italian and Spanish: from the Latin family name (later a personal name) *Celsus.* This was originally a nickname from the Latin vocabulary word *celsus* tall, high, lofty. The name was borne by various minor early Roman saints, and it has also been used as a Latinized form of several Irish saints called CEALLAGH.

Čenek (m.) Czech: pet form of *Vincenc* (see VINCENT).

Ceri (f.) Welsh: of uncertain origin, probably a short form of CERIDWEN.

Ceridwen (f.) Welsh: name borne in Celtic mythology by the goddess of poetic inspiration. It is apparently composed of the elements *cerdd* poetry + *(g)wen* feminine of *gwyn* white, fair, blessed, holy. This is said to have been the name of the mother of the legendary 6th-century Welsh hero Taliesin, but it is not clear whether in fact it represents a personal name or whether Taliesin is to be regarded as the son of the goddess of poetry.

Césaire (m.) French: from the Late Latin personal name *Caesarius*, a derivative of CAESAR. The name was borne most notably by an early bishop of Arles (470–542). During the siege of that city in 508 he sold the treasures of his church in order to relieve the distress being suffered by the poor.

César (m.) French: from the old Roman family name *Caesar*, of uncertain meaning. It has been connected with Latin *caesaries* head of hair, but this is probably no more than folk etymology; the name may be of Etruscan origin. Its most notable bearer was Gaius Julius Caesar (?102–44 BC) and it also formed part of the full name of his relative Augustus (Gaius Julius Caesar Octavianus Augustus). Subsequently it was used as an imperial title and eventually became a vocabulary word for an emperor (leading to German *Kaiser* and Russian *tsar*).

Cognates: Italian: **Cesare.** English: CAESAR.

Česlav (m.) Czech form of CZESŁAW.

Chad (m.) English: modern spelling of Old English *Ceadda*, name of a 7th-century saint who was for a time archbishop of York. This is of uncertain derivation. The name is comparatively rare, even among Roman Catholics, by whom it is chiefly favoured.

Chaim (m.) Jewish: variant spelling of HYAM.

Chandler (m.) English: transferred use of the surname, which originated in the Middle Ages as an occupational name for someone who made and sold candles (a derivative of Old French *chandele*, Latin *candēla*). The extended sense 'retail dealer' (in various goods) arose in the 16th century.

Chantal (f.) French, also sometimes found in the English-speaking world: bestowed in honour of St Jane Frances (Jeanne Françoise) Frémiot (1572–1641). In 1592 she married the Baron de Chantal (a place in Saône-et-Loire, so called from a dialect form of Old Provençal *cantal* stone, boulder) and adopted his family name. After his death she became an associate of St Francis of Sales and founded a new order of nuns.

Variants: English: **Chantale**; **Chantelle** (influenced by the feminine diminutive suffix *-elle*).

Chapman (m.) English: transferred use of the surname, which originated in the Middle Ages as an occupational name for a merchant or a smaller-scale pedlar, from Old English *cēapmann* (a compound of *cēapan* to buy, sell, trade + *mann* man).

Charis (f.) English: from Greek *kharis* grace. This was a key word in early Christian thought, but was not used as a name in the early centuries after Christ or in the Middle Ages. As a given name it seems to be an innovation of the 17th century, chosen either to express the original idea of charity, or else as a reference to the three Graces (Greek *kharites*) of classical mythology (Aglaia, Euphrosyne, and Thalia, of which the first and third have also been occasionally used as given names).

Charissa (f.) English: apparently a recent elaboration of CHARIS, perhaps as a result of crossing with CLARISSA.

Charity (f.) English: from the vocabulary word, denoting originally the Christian's love for his fellow man (Latin *caritās*, from *carus* dear). In spite of St Paul's words 'and now abideth faith, hope, charity, these three; but the greatest of these is charity' (1 Corinthians 13: 13), *Charity* is now rarely used as a given name in comparison with the shorter FAITH and HOPE.

Cognates: Spanish: **Caridad**. Portuguese: **Caridade**. Finnish: **Karita**.

Charlene (f.) English (chiefly Australian and southern U.S.): 20th-century coinage, from *Charles* + *-ene* taken as a feminine ending. It may have been influenced by the older but much rarer French name **Charline**, a feminine diminutive of CHARLES.

Charles (m.) English and French: originally from a Germanic word meaning 'free man', cognate with Old English *ceorl* man. (The modern English words *churl* and *churlish* are derived from this, and their unpleasant overtones are a much later accretion.) The name originally owed its popularity in Europe to the Frankish leader Charlemagne (?742–814), who in 800 established himself as Holy Roman Emperor. His name (Latin *Carolus Magnus*) means 'Charles the Great'. *Charles* or KARL (the German form) was a common name among Frankish leaders, including Charlemagne's grandfather Charles Martel (688–741). The name was also borne by a succession of Holy Roman Emperors and ten kings of France. It was hardly used at all among the Normans, and was introduced to Britain by Mary Queen of Scots (1542–87), who had been brought up in France. She chose the names *Charles James* for her son (1566–1625), who later became King James VI of Scotland and, from 1603, James I of England. His son and grandson both reigned as King Charles, and the name thus became established in the 17th century both as a name in the Stuart royal house and as a favoured name among English and Scottish supporters of the monarchy. In the 19th century the popularity of the name was further increased by romanticization of the story of 'Bonnie Prince Charlie', Stuart pretender to the throne in the preceding century and leader of the 1745 rebellion. This popularity continued in the 20th century with the baptism in 1948 of the heir to the British throne as Prince Charles.

In Ireland this name has been used as an Anglicized form of CEARBHALL and sometimes of CORMAC; in Scotland it has been used for TEÀRLACH.

Cognates: Irish Gaelic: **Séarlas**. Welsh: **Siarl**. Italian: **Carlo**. Spanish, Portuguese: **Carlos**. German: **Karl**, CARL. Dutch: **Karel**. Scandinavian: **Karl**. Polish: **Karol**. Czech: **Karel**. Hungarian: **Károly**. Finnish: **Kaarle**.

Pet form: English: **Charlie**.

Charlie (m., f.) 1. (m.) English and Scottish: pet form of CHARLES.

2. (f.) English: modern pet form of CHARLOTTE.

Charlotte (f.) English and French: feminine diminutive of CHARLES, used in England since the 17th century, but most popular in the 18th and 19th centuries, in part due to the influence of firstly Queen Charlotte (1744–1818), wife of George III, and secondly the novelist Charlotte Brontë (1816–55). In the Scottish Highlands this name has been used as an Anglicized form of *Teàrlag* (see TEÀRLACH).

Cognates: Irish: **Séarlait**. Italian: **Carlotta**. German: **Karlotte**. Scandinavian: **Charlotta**.

Pet forms: English: **Lottie, Tottie, Charlie**.

Charlton (m.) English: transferred use of the surname, used as a given name largely as a result of the fame of the film actor Charlton Heston (b. 1924; *Charlton* was his mother's maiden name). The surname originally denoted someone who came from one of the numerous places in England named in Old English as the 'settlement of the free peasants', Old English *ceorlatun*. The first element of the place-name is ultimately connected with the source of CHARLES.

Charmaine (f.) English: possibly a variant of CHARMIAN, influenced by names such as GERMAINE, but more probably an invented name based on the vocabulary word *charm* + *-aine* as in LORRAINE. It is not found before 1920, but enjoyed some popularity in the 1960s due to The Bachelors' hit song of this name.

Charmian (f.) English: from the Late Greek name *Kharmion* (a diminutive of *kharma* delight). The name was used by Shakespeare in *Antony and Cleopatra* for one of the attendants of the Egyptian queen; he took it from Sir Thomas North's translation of Plutarch's *Parallel Lives*.

Charna (f.) Jewish: Yiddish name, from a Slavonic element meaning 'dark, black' (cf. Polish *czarny*).

Pet forms: **Charnke, Charnele**.

Charo (f.) Spanish: pet form of ROSARIO.

Chase (m.) English (esp. U.S.): transferred use of the surname, which originated in the Middle Ages as a nickname for a huntsman, from Anglo-Norman *chase* chase, hunt.

Chauncey (m.) English: American coinage from a well-known New England surname. It seems to have been originally chosen as a given name in honour of the Harvard College president Charles Chauncy (1592–1672), the New England clergyman Charles Chauncy (1705–87), or the naval officer Isaac Chauncey (1772–1840). All these men were almost certainly descended from a single family; the surname is found in England in the Middle Ages, and probably has a Norman baronial origin, but now seems to be extinct in Britain.

Chaya (f.) Jewish: feminine counterpart of CHAIM, from Hebrew *Hayya* 'alive' or 'animal'. In the first meaning it corresponds to CHAIM and names such as VIDAL, and in the second meaning it parallels animal names such as ARYE, DOV, and ZVI. See also EVE.

Chelle (f.) English: informal short form of MICHELLE. See also SHELL.

Chelo (f.) Spanish: pet form of CONSUELO.

Cherelle (f.) English: apparently a respelling of CHERYL, influenced by the popular name ending *-elle* (originally a French feminine diminutive suffix).

Cherene (f.) English (esp. U.S.): modern coinage, a combination of the popular element *Cher-* (cf. CHERIDA, CHERYL, and CHERYTH) with the productive feminine suffix *-ene*.

Cherida (f.) English: a modern coinage, apparently the result of crossing CHERYL with PHILLIDA.

Cherish (f.) English: modern coinage, apparently an alteration of CHERYTH to match the vocabulary element *cherish* to treasure, care for (borrowed in the Middle Ages from Old French *cherir*, a derivative of *cher* dear).

Cherna (f.) Jewish: Yiddish name, from a Slavonic element meaning 'dark, black' (cf. Russian *cherny*).

Pet forms: **Chernke, Chernele**.

Cherry (f.) English: now generally regarded as an Anglicized spelling of the French word *chérie* darling (cf. CARA). However, Dickens used it as a pet form of CHARITY: in *Martin Chuzzlewit* (1844) Mr Pecksniff's daughters Charity and Mercy are known as Cherry and Merry. Nowadays the name is sometimes also taken as referring to the fruit.

Cheryl (f.) English: not found before the 1920s, and not common until the 1940s. It seems to be an artificial creation, perhaps the result of a crossing of CHERRY with BERYL.

Cheryth (f.) English: apparently the result of a crossing of CHERRY with GWYNETH.

Cheslav (m.) Russian form of CZESŁAW

Chester (m.) English: transferred use of the surname, which originally denoted someone from the town of *Chester*, so called from an Old English form of Latin *castra* legionary camp. Use as a given name has become quite common in the 20th century.

Chevonne (f.) Anglicized spelling of SIOBHÁN.

Chiara (f.) Italian form of CLARE.

Chirsty (f.) Scottish: usual spelling in the Highlands of KIRSTIE.

Chita (f.) Spanish: short form of *Conchita* (see CONCHA).

Chloe (f.) From the Late Greek name *Khloē*, originally used in the classical period as an epithet of the fertility goddess Demeter. It seems to be connected with CHLORIS. It occurs only fleetingly in the New Testament (1 Corinthians 1: 11), but its use as a given name in the English-speaking world almost certainly derives from this, having been adopted by 17th-century Puritans. It has survived much better than the majority of the minor biblical names taken up in the 17th century.

Chloris (f.) From Greek mythology. *Khlōris* was a minor goddess of vegetation; her name derives from Greek *khlōros* green. It was used by the Roman poet Horace for one of his loves (cf. LALAGE), and was taken up by Augustan poets of the 17th and 18th centuries.

Chole (f.) Spanish: pet form of SOLEDAD.

Chris (m., f.) English: 1. (m.) Short form of CHRISTOPHER.

2. (f.) Short form of CHRISTINE and the group of related female names.

Chrissie (f.) English and Scottish: pet form of CHRISTINE and the group of related women's names. It is especially common in Scotland.

Variants: Scottish: **Criosaidh** (a Gaelic form).

Christa (f.) Latinate short form of CHRISTINE and CHRISTINA. It seems to have originated in Germany, but is now also well established in Scandinavia and the English-speaking world.

Christabel (f.) English: a 19th-century coinage from the first syllable of CHRISTINE, combined with the productive suffix *-bel* (see BELLE). The coinage was apparently made by Samuel Taylor Coleridge (1772–1834) in a poem called *Christabel* (1816). The name was also borne by the suffragette Christabel Pankhurst (1880–

1958), in whose honour it is now sometimes bestowed.

Variants: **Christabelle, Christabella.**

Christelle (f.) French: altered form of CHRISTINE, derived by replacement of the seemingly feminine diminutive suffix *-ine* with the suffix *-elle* of similar function. The name is now also used in the English-speaking world, where its popularity has been enhanced by that of the similar-sounding CRYSTAL.

Christer (m.) Swedish and Danish form of the male name CHRISTIAN. It is first found in the 15th century, when it began to be borne regularly in a few noble families. It came into more general popularity in the 1940s.

Christhard (m.) German: hybrid religious name based on the name *Christ* (see CHRISTIAN) + the Germanic personal name element *-hard* hardy, brave, strong.

Christian (m., occasionally f.) English: from Latin *Christiānus* 'follower of Christ', in use as a given name during the Middle Ages, and sporadically ever since. The name *Christ* itself (Greek *Khristos*) is a translation of the Hebrew term *Messiah* 'anointed'.

Cognates (m.): Low German: **Carsten**. Danish: **Kristen**.

Christiana (f.) English: medieval learned feminine form of CHRISTIAN. As a recent revival it represents an elaborated form of CHRISTINA. It is also sometimes spelled **Christianna** under the influence of the name ANNA.

Christie (m., f.) 1. (m.) Scottish and Irish: pet form of CHRISTOPHER.

2. (f.) English: pet form of CHRISTINE.

Variant: **Christy**.

Christina (f.) English: simplified form of Latin *Christiāna*, feminine of *Christiānus* (see CHRISTIAN), or a Latinized form of Middle English *Christin* 'Christian' (Old English *christen*, from Latin).

Cognates: Scottish Gaelic: **Cairistìona, Cairistìne**. Irish Gaelic: **Crístíona**. Italian, Spanish, Portuguese: **Cristina**. Polish: **Krystyna**.

Christine (f.) English and French: form of CHRISTINA, not much used in Britain until the end of the 19th century. Until fairly recently it was principally associated with Scotland, but now it is very popular in all parts of the English-speaking world.

Short form: English: **Chris**.

Pet forms: Scottish: **Chrissie**; **Chirsty**, KIRSTIE (Gaelic **Ciorstaidh, Curstaidh**; **Ciorstag**; **Ciorsdan**).

Christmas (m.) English: from the festival celebrating the birth of Christ (so called from *Christ* (see CHRISTIAN) + *mass* festival). It is sometimes given to a boy born on Christmas Day. See also NOËL and NATALIE.

Christopher (m.) English: from Greek *Khristophoros*, a name composed of the elements *Khristos* Christ + *pherein* to bear. This was popular among early Christians, conscious of the fact that they were metaphorically bearing Christ in their hearts. A later, over-literal interpretation of the name gave rise to the legend of a saint who actually bore the Christ-child over a stream; he is regarded as the patron of travellers.

Cognates: Irish Gaelic: **Críostóir**. Scottish: **Kester**; see also CRÌSDEAN. French: **Christophe**. Italian: **Cristoforo**. Spanish: **Cristóbal**. Catalan: **Cristòfol**. Portuguese: **Cristovão**. German: **Christoph**. Scandinavian: **Kristoffer**. Polish: **Krzysztof**. Czech: **Kryštof**. Finnish: **Risto**.

Short forms: English: **Chris**. Spanish: **Cristo**.

Pet forms: English: **Kit**. German: **Stoffel**.

Christy (m., f.) Scottish, Irish, and English: variant spelling of CHRISTIE.

Chrystal (f.) English: rare variant spelling of CRYSTAL, apparently influenced by the Greek-origin element *khrysos* gold.

Variant: **Chrystalla** (Latinate).

Chucho (m., f.) Spanish: pet form of JESÚS or *María Jesús*.

Chuck (m.) English (almost exclusively U.S.): nickname occasionally used as a given name in its own right. It derives from the English term of endearment, itself probably from Middle English *chukken* to cluck (of imitative origin). It is now often used as a pet form of CHARLES.
Pet form: **Chuckie**.

Chus (m., f.) Spanish: pet form of JESÚS or *María Jesús*.

Chwalibog (m.) Polish: religious name of medieval origin, composed of the elements *chwała* praise + *bóg* God.
Variant: **Falibog**. See also BOGUCHWAŁ.

Cian (m.) Irish: traditional Gaelic name, from the Irish vocabulary word meaning 'ancient'. It was borne by a son-in-law of Brian Boru who played a leading role in the Battle of Clontarf (1014).
Anglicized forms: **Kean(e)**.

Ciannait (f.) Irish: Gaelic name representing a feminine diminutive form of CIAN.

Ciara (f.) Irish: modern name created as a feminine form of CIARÁN.

Ciarán (m.) Irish: Gaelic name often Anglicized as KIERAN. It was originally a byname, representing a diminutive form of *ciar* black, and was borne by two Irish saints, of the 5th and 6th centuries.

Cibor (m.) Polish: simplified variant of CZCIBOR.

Cicely (f.) English: variant spelling of CECILY. This was a common form of the name in the Middle Ages.
Cognate: Scandinavian: **Sissel**.
Pet form: English: SISSY.

Cillian (m.) Irish: Gaelic name often Anglicized as KILLIAN. It was originally a byname representing a diminutive form of Gaelic *ceallach* strife, or possibly derived from Gaelic *ceall* monastery, church (cf. KELLY), and was borne by various early Irish saints, including the 7th-century author of a life of St Bridget and missionaries to Artois and Franconia.
Variant: **Cillín**.

Cindy (f.) English: pet form of CYNTHIA or, less often, of LUCINDA, now very commonly used as an independent given name, especially in America. It has occasionally also been taken as a short form of the name of the fairy-tale *Cinderella*, which in fact is not related to it (French *Cendrillon*, a derivative of *cendre* cinders).

Cinzia (f.) Italian form of CYNTHIA.

Ciorstaidh (f.) Scottish Gaelic form of KIRSTIE.
Variant: **Ciorstag**.

Cipriano (m.) Italian: from Latin *Cypriānus*, originally an ethnic name for someone from the island of Cyprus. The most famous of several early saints of this name is a 3rd-century bishop of Carthage who was a major theological thinker and writer.
Cognates: Spanish: **Cebrián**. Catalan: **Cebrià**.

Ciriaco (m.) Italian and Spanish (more common in the latter country): from Latin *Cyriācus*, Greek *Kyriakos*, a derivative of *kyrios* lord. This was a very popular name among early Christians, who chose it as a token of their devotion to their Lord, and it was borne by a very large number of minor saints of the first centuries AD.

Ciro (m.) Italian form of CYRUS, commonly used in that country.

Claire (f.) French form of CLARA. It was introduced to Britain by the Normans, but subsequently abandoned. This spelling was revived in the 19th century as a variant of CLARE.
Variant: **Clair**.

Clancy (m.) Irish (esp. U.S.): from the Irish surname, Gaelic *Mac Fhlannchaidh* 'son of *Flannchadh*', a personal name perhaps meaning 'red warrior'.
Variant: **Clancey**.

Clara (f.) English, Italian, and German: post-classical Latin name, from the feminine form of the adjective *clārus* famous. In the modern English-speaking world it represents a re-Latinization of the regular

English form CLARE. In the Scottish Highlands it has been used as a translation equivalent of the Gaelic name SORCHA.

Variant: German: **Klara**.

Pet form: English: **Clarrie**.

Clare (f.) English: the normal vernacular form of CLARA during the Middle Ages and since. The name has always been particularly popular in Italy (in the forms *Chiara* and *Clara*) and has been borne by several Italian saints, notably Clare of Assisi (*c.*1193–1253), an associate of Francis of Assisi and founder of the order of nuns known as the Poor Clares. In Britain the given name was probably reinforced by the Anglo-Irish surname, derived from a place in Suffolk. The surname was taken to Ireland by Richard de Clare, 2nd Earl of Pembroke (d. 1176), known as 'Strongbow'.

Clarence (m.) English: in use from the end of the 19th century, but now rare. It was first used in honour of the popular elder son of Edward VII, who was created Duke of Clarence in 1890, but died in 1892. His title (*Dux Clarentiae* in Latin) originated with a son of Edward III, who in the 14th century was married to the heiress of Clare in Suffolk (which is so called from a Celtic river name and has no connection with the given name CLARE). The title has been held by various British royal princes at different periods in history.

Pet form: **Clarrie**.

Clarette (f.) English: rare extended form of CLARE, with the French feminine diminutive suffix *-ette*. The formation may have been influenced by the wine *claret* (Medieval Latin (*vīnum*) *clārātum* clarified wine).

Clarice (f.) English: medieval English and French form of the Latin name *Claritia*. This seems to have meant 'fame' (an abstract derivative of *clārus* famous), but it may simply have been an arbitrary elaboration of CLARA. It was borne by a character who features in some versions of the medieval romances of Roland and the other paladins of Charlemagne.

Clarinda (f.) English: elaboration of CLARA with the suffix *-inda* (cf. BELINDA and LUCINDA). *Clarinda* first appears in Spenser's *Faerie Queene* (1596). The formation seems to have been influenced by the name *Clorinda*, which occurs in Torquato Tasso's *Gerusalemme Liberata* (1580), and is probably a similarly arbitrary elaboration of CHLORIS. Robert Burns (1759–96) wrote four poems *To Clarinda*.

Clarissa (f.) English: Latinate form of CLARICE occasionally found in medieval documents. It was revived by Samuel Richardson as the name of the central character in his novel *Clarissa* (1748).

Cognate: Spanish: **Clarisa**. See also CAITIR.

Clark (m.) English: transferred use of the surname, originally an occupational name denoting a *clerk* or secretary, in the Middle Ages a man in minor holy orders, who earned his living by his ability to read and write. It is now quite commonly used as a given name, especially in the United States. The word *clerk* derives from Latin *clēricus*, but this more common form of the surname and given name reflects a widespread medieval shift in pronunciation from *-er-* to *-ar-* (preserved in the British but not the American pronunciation of the vocabulary word).

Clarrie (m., f.) English: pet form of CLARENCE, also of CLARA and the various similar womens' names. It is now fairly rare and almost never used as an independent given name.

Claud (m.) English: Anglicized spelling of CLAUDE.

Claude (m.) French and English: from the Latin name *Claudius* (itself occasionally used as a modern given name), which was an old Roman family name derived from the byname *Claudus* 'lame'. It was borne by various early saints, but its popularity in France is largely due to the fame of the 7th-century St Claude of Besançon. In France, *Claude* also occasionally occurs as a female name (cf. CLAUDIA).

Cognates: Italian, Spanish, Portuguese: **Claudio**. Russian: **Klavdii**. Polish: **Klaudiusz**. Hungarian: **Kolos**.

Claudette (f.) French: feminine diminutive form of CLAUDE, now also occasionally used in the English-speaking world.

Claudia (f.) English and German: from the Latin female name, a feminine form of *Claudius* (see CLAUDE). The name receives a fleeting mention in one of St Paul's letters to Timothy (2. 4: 21 'Eubulus greeteth thee, and Pudens, and Linus, and Claudia, and all the brethren'), from which it was taken up in the 16th century (cf. CHLOE).

Cognates: Russian: **Klavdia**. Polish: **Klaudia**.

Claudine (f.) French: feminine diminutive form of CLAUDE. It was made popular at the beginning of the 20th century as the name of the heroine of a series of novels by the French writer Colette (1873–1954), and is now also occasionally used in the English-speaking world.

Claudio (m.) Italian, Spanish, and Portuguese form of CLAUDE.

Claus (m.) German: aphetic form of *Niclaus* or *Niklaus*, representing the usual German form of NICHOLAS. In America this name tends to be associated with the figure of *Santa Claus* (originally *Sankt Niklaus*), which inhibits serious use of it.

Variant: German: **Klaus**.

Cognates: Dutch: **Klaas**. Frisian: **Klaes**. Finnish: **Launo**.

Claver (m.) Catholic name given in honour of the Catalan saint Pere Claver (1581–1654), a Jesuit who worked among Black slaves in Central America. He was canonized in 1888. His surname is a Catalan occupational name for a locksmith.

Clay (m.) English: either a shortened form of CLAYTON or a transferred use of the independent surname, which was originally a local name for someone who lived on a patch of land whose soil was predominantly clay (Old English *clǣg*).

Clayton (m.) English (esp. U.S.): transferred use of the surname, originally a local name from any of the several places in England (for example, in Lancs., Staffs., Sussex, and W. Yorks.) originally named with the Old English elements *clǣg* clay + *tūn* enclosure, settlement.

Cledwyn (m.) Welsh: traditional name, apparently composed of the elements *caled* hard, rough + *(g)wyn* white, fair, blessed, holy.

Clelia (f.) Italian and English: from Latin *Cloelia*, the name borne by a semi-mythological heroine of early Roman history. She was given as a hostage to the Etruscan invader Lars Porsenna, but made an escape back to Rome by swimming the Tiber.

Clem (m.) English: short form of CLEMENT and of women's names such as CLEMENCE. It is occasionally used as an independent given name, especially in the United States.

Clematis (f.) English: from the name of the flower (so named in the 16th century from Greek *klēmatis* climbing plant), perhaps under the influence of names such as CLEMENCE and the ending *-is* found in names such as PHYLLIS.

Clemence (f.) English: medieval French and English form of Latin *Clēmentius* (masculine derivative of *Clēmens*; see CLEMENT) or of *Clēmentia* (feminine version of *Clēmentius* or an abstract noun meaning 'mercy'). It has never been particularly common, but is still occasionally used as a female name.

Short form: **Clem**.

Pet form: **Clemmie**.

Clemency (f.) English: rare variant of CLEMENCE or a direct use of the abstract noun, on the model of CHARITY, FAITH, MERCY, etc.

Clement (m.) English: from the Late Latin name *Clēmens* (genitive *Clēmentis*) meaning 'merciful'. This was borne by several early saints, notably the fourth pope and the early Christian theologian Clement of Alexandria (Titus Flavius Clemens, ?150–?215).

Cognates: Scottish Gaelic: **Cliamain**. French: **Clément**. Italian, Spanish, Portuguese: **Clemente**. German, Danish, Swedish, Polish: **Klemens**. Russian, Czech: **Kliment**. Hungarian: **Kelemen**.

Short form: English: **Clem**.

Pet forms: English: **Clemmie**. Polish: **Klimek**.

Clementine (f.) English: feminine form of CLEMENT, created with the French feminine diminutive suffix *-ine*. The name was first used in the 19th century, and for a time it was very popular. It is now largely associated with the popular song with this title. The Latinate form **Clementina** is also found.

Cognate: Polish: **Klementyna**.

Clemmie (f., m.) English: diminutive form of CLEM, borne more often by girls than by boys.

Cleo (f.) English: short form of CLEOPATRA (see also CLIO).

Cleopatra (f.) From Greek *Kleopatra*, the name (composed of the elements *kleos* glory + *patēr* father) borne by a large number of women in the Ptolemaic royal family of Egypt. The most famous (?69–30 BC) was the lover of Mark Antony, and has always figured largely in both literature and the popular imagination as a model of a passionate woman of unsurpassed beauty, who 'gave all for love' and in the process destroyed the man she loved. She had previously been the mistress of Julius Caesar. The name is occasionally chosen, especially in Black families.

Cleto (m.) Italian, Spanish, and Portuguese: short form of ANACLETO.

Cliamain (m.) Scottish Gaelic form of CLEMENT.

Cliff (m.) English: short form of CLIFFORD (now also sometimes of CLIFTON). It is commonly used as an independent given name, especially since the rise to fame in the 1950s of the pop singer Cliff Richard (real name Harry Webb). It has sometimes also been associated with CLIVE.

Clifford (m.) English: transferred use of the surname, originally a local name from any of several places (Gloucs., Herefords., Yorks.) named in Old English with the elements *clif* cliff, slope, riverbank + *ford* ford.

Clifton (m.) English: transferred use of the surname, originally a local name from any of the numerous places named in Old English with the elements *clif* cliff, slope, riverbank + *tūn* enclosure, settlement. Use of this as a given name is more recent than that of CLIFFORD, and it may in some cases have been adopted as an expanded form of CLIFF.

Clint (m.) English: short form of the surname *Clinton*, made famous by the actor Clint Eastwood (b. 1930). It was apparently originally used as a given name in America in honour of the Clinton family, whose members included the statesman George Clinton (1739–1812), governor of New York, and his nephew De Witt Clinton (1769–1828), who was responsible for overseeing the construction of the Erie Canal. It was also borne by Sir Henry Clinton (1735–95), British commander-in-chief in America during the Revolution.

Clio (f.) English: from Greek *Kleio*, the name borne in classical mythology both by one of the nymphs and by one of the Muses. It is probably ultimately connected with the word *kleos* glory; cf. CLEOPATRA. The name is now sometimes used as a variant of CLEO.

Clíona (f.) Irish: contracted spelling of the Gaelic name **Clíodhna** (Old Irish *Clídna*), borne in Fenian legends by a fairy princess. It has been revived in the 20th century and become a popular given name in Ireland.

Clitus (m.) Mainly U.S.: Latinized form of Greek *Kleitos*, the name of one of Alexander the Great's generals. This name is probably ultimately connected with *Kleio* (see CLIO).

Clive (m.) English: transferred use of the surname, originally a local name from any of the various places (in e.g. Cheshire, Shropshire) so called from Old English *clif* cliff, slope. As a given name it seems to have been originally chosen in honour of 'Clive of India' (Robert Clive, created Baron Clive of Plassey in 1760).

Clodagh (f.) Irish: of recent origin. It is the name of a river in Tipperary, and seems to have been arbitrarily transferred to use as a given name. There may be some association in the minds of givers with the Latin name *Clōdia* (borne by the mistress of the Roman poet Catullus), a variant of CLAUDIA.

Clothilde (f.) French: from a Germanic female personal name, composed of the elements *hlōd* famous + *hild* battle. The most famous bearer of the name (*c.*474–545) was a daughter of the Burgundian king Chilperic who married the Frankish king Clovis and converted him to Christianity.

Clover (f.) English: modern name taken from the flower (Old English *clāfre*). Its popularity may have been influenced by its slight similarity in sound to CHLOE.

Clyde (m.) English (esp. U.S.): apparently from the river in south-west Scotland that runs through Glasgow, perhaps by way of a surname derived from the river name. The name is comparatively popular among West Indian and American Blacks; Dunkling points out that geographical names such as *Aberdeen* and *Glasgow* were bestowed on slaves in the southern United States. A large number of plantation owners were of Scottish origin. *Clyde*, unlike other such names, seems to have survived, and even gained some currency among southern Whites. The bank robber Clyde Barrow became something of a cult figure, especially after the film *Bonnie and Clyde* (1967).

Coinneach (m.) Scottish Gaelic: traditional name, probably originally a byname meaning 'handsome, fair one'. This is one of the two names that have merged in the Anglicized form KENNETH, and it remains in common use in the Highlands. From it is derived the surname *MacKenzie* (Gaelic *Mac Coinnich*).

Cokkie (f.) Dutch: pet form of CORNELIA.

Colbert (m.) English: from a Germanic personal name introduced by the Normans, composed of the element *col* of uncertain meaning + *berht* bright, famous. In modern use it probably represents a transferred use of the surname derived from the given name in the Middle Ages.

Cole (m.) English: transferred use of the surname, itself derived from a medieval given name of uncertain origin. It seems to represent the Old English byname *Cola* 'swarthy, coal-black' (from *col* charcoal). The given name is occasionally used as a short form of NICHOLAS.

Coleman (m.) English and Irish: variant of COLMAN. In part it also represents a transferred use of the surname, which derives in most cases from the Gaelic personal name *Colmán*, but in others may be an occupational term for a charcoal burner.

Colette (f.) French and English: short form of *Nicolette* (pet form of NICOLE) or feminine diminutive of the medieval name *Col(le)* (cf. COLIN). It was given particular currency from the 1920s onwards by the fame of the French novelist Colette (1873–1954).

Colin (m.) 1. English: diminutive form of the medieval name *Col(le)*, a short form of NICHOLAS. It has been enduringly popular and is now normally regarded as an independent name rather than as a pet form of *Nicholas*.

2. Scottish: Anglicized form of the Gaelic name **Cailean**, particularly favoured among the Campbells and the MacKenzies. It relates to St Columba (see CALUM) as *Crìsdean* does to Christ and *Moirean* to Mary.

Coll (m.) Scottish: Anglicized form of the Gaelic name **Colla**, perhaps from an Old Celtic root meaning 'high'.

Colleen (f.) Mainly U.S. and Australian: from the Anglo-Irish vocabulary word *colleen* girl, wench (Gaelic *cailín*). The name arose during the period of enthusiasm for Irish names in the 1940s and became especially popular in America, although it is not in fact used as a given name in Ireland. It is sometimes taken as a feminine of COLIN.

Collette (f.) English: variant spelling of COLETTE.

Colm (m.) Irish Gaelic form of Latin *Columba*; see CALUM.

Variant: **Colom** (an older Gaelic form).

Pet form: **Cóilín**.

Colman (m.) Irish: Anglicized form of the Gaelic name **Colmán**, from Late Latin *Columbānus*, a derivative of *Columba* (see CALUM and COLOMBE). The name was borne by a large number of early Irish saints, including Colman of Armagh, a 5th-century disciple of St Patrick. St Colmán or *Columban* (*c.*540–615) founded the monastery at Bobbio in northern Italy in 614, and became something of a cult figure in central Europe. St Colman of Stockerau (d. 1012) was an Irish pilgrim who was killed at Stockerau near Vienna while on his way to the Holy Land. He is said to have worked numerous miracles after his death, and was particularly venerated in Hungary.

Cognates: Czech: **Kolman**. Hungarian: **Kálmán**. Italian: **Columbano**. French: **Colombain**.

Colombe (f.) French: from the Late Latin name *Columba* 'dove', borne both by men (see CALUM) and by women. In France the name is borne principally in honour of St Colombe of Sens (d. 273), who fled to France from Spain to avoid persecution but was put to death near Meaux.

Columbine (f.) English: from Italian *Colombina*, a diminutive of *Colomba* 'dove'. In the tradition of the *commedia dell'arte* this is the name of Harlequin's sweetheart. The modern name, however, was probably coined independently as one of the class of names taken in the 19th century from flowers. The columbine gets its name from the fact that its petals are supposed to resemble five doves clustered together.

Comgal (m.) Irish: Anglicized form of the Gaelic name **Comhghall**, composed of the elements *comh* together, joint + *gall* pledge. It was borne by a 6th-century saint, founder of Bangor Abbey in Northern Ireland and teacher of Columbanus.

Comgan (m.) Irish: Anglicized form of the Gaelic name **Comhghán**, composed of the elements *comh* together, joint + *gan-*, *gen-* born. It seems originally to have been a byname referring to a twin. The name was borne by an 8th-century Irish prince who lived as a monk in Scotland.

Comyn (m.) Irish: Anglicized form of CUIMÍN.

Conall (m.) Irish and Scottish Gaelic: name composed of Old Celtic elements meaning 'wolf' + 'strong'. This name was borne by many early chieftains and warriors of Ireland, including the Ulster hero Conall Cearnach.

Variant: Scottish: **Comhnall**.

Conan (m.) Irish: Anglicized form of the Gaelic name **Cónán**, originally a byname representing a diminutive of *cú* hound. The name was borne by a 7th-century saint, who probably served as a bishop on the Isle of Man. Sir Arthur Conan Doyle (1859–1930), creator of the fictional detective Sherlock Holmes, was of Irish stock.

Concepción (f.) Spanish: name commemorating the Immaculate Conception of the Virgin Mary. This doctrine was officially proclaimed by the Roman Catholic Church only in 1854, but had been debated since the 12th century and reached a peak of popularity in the late Middle Ages.

Pet forms: **Concha, Conchita.**

Cognate: Portuguese: **Conceição.**

Concepta (f.) Latin form of CONCETTA, used especially in Ireland among Roman Catholics.

Concetta (f.) Italian: name referring to a title of the Virgin Mary, *Maria Concetta*, that alludes to her Immaculate Conception (cf. CONCEPCIÓN).

Concha (f.) Spanish: pet form of CONCEPCIÓN.

Variant: **Conchita.**

Conleth (m.) Irish: Anglicized form of the obsolete Gaelic personal name *Connlaeth*, apparently composed of the elements *conn* chief + *flaith* lord.

Variant: **Conla.**

Conn (m.) Irish Gaelic: name derived from an Old Celtic element meaning 'chief'. It is now also used as a short form of CONNOR and of various non-Irish names beginning with the syllable *Con-*.

Connie (f.) English: pet form of CONSTANCE.

Connor (m.) Irish: Anglicized form of the Gaelic name **Conchobhar**, possibly meaning 'lover of hounds'. Conchobhar was a semi-legendary Irish king who lived shortly after the time of Christ.

Variant: **Cnochúr** (a modern Gaelic form).

Conrad (m.) English and German: variant spelling of KONRAD, a Germanic personal name composed of the elements *kuon* bold + *rad* counsel. It was used occasionally in Britain in the Middle Ages in honour of a 10th-century bishop of Constance in Switzerland, but modern use in the English-speaking world is a reimportation dating mainly from the 19th century.

Variants: German: **Konrad, Kurt.**

Cognates: Dutch: **Koenrad, Kort.** Polish: **Konrad.** Italian: **Corrado.**

Conseja (f.) Spanish: religious name referring to the Marian title, *Nuestra Señora del Buen Consejo* 'Our Lady of Good Counsel'. There is a festival dedicated to this aspect of the Virgin on 26 April.

Cognate: Italian: **Consilia.**

Consolata (f.) Italian: name referring to a title of the Virgin Mary, *Maria Consolata* (cf. CONSUELO).

Constance (f.) English and French: medieval form of the Late Latin name *Constantia*, which is either a feminine form of *Constantius*, a derivative of *Constans* (see CONSTANT), or an abstract noun meaning 'constancy'. This was a popular name among the Normans, and was borne by, amongst others, the formidable Constance of Sicily (1158–98), wife of the Emperor Henry VI.

Pet form: English: **Connie.**

Constant (m.) English and French: medieval form of the Late Latin name *Constans* (genitive *Constantis*) 'steadfast', but not common in the Middle Ages. It was taken up by the Puritans because of its transparent meaning, as an expression of their determination to 'resist stedfast in the faith' (1 Peter 5: 9).

Equivalent: Hungarian: **Szilárd.**

Constantine (m.) English and French: medieval form of the Late Latin name *Constantīnus* (a derivative of *Constans*; see CONSTANT). This was the name of Constantine the Great (?288–337), the first Christian emperor of Rome. It was also born by three kings of Scotland, apparently as an Anglicized form of CONN.

Cognates: Scottish Gaelic: **Còiseam.** Russian, Czech, Hungarian, Scandinavian, German: **Konstantin.** Polish: **Konstantyn.**

Consuelo (m.) Spanish: name referring to a title of the Virgin Mary, *Nuestra Señora del Consuelo* 'Our Lady of Solace' (Spanish *consuelo*, from Latin *consolātus*). Mary is traditionally a comforter of the bereaved and distressed and an intercessor with God.

Cognate: Italian: **Consolata.**

Short form: Spanish: **Suelo.**

Pet form: Spanish: **Chelo.**

Cor (m.) Dutch: short form of CORNELIS.

Cora (f.) English: name apparently coined by James Fenimore Cooper for one of the characters in *The Last of the Mohicans* (1826). It could represent a Latinized form of Greek *Korē* 'maiden'. In classical mythology this was a euphemistic name of the goddess of the underworld, Persephone, and would not have been a well-omened name to take.

Coral (f.) English: late 19th-century coinage. This is one of the group of girls' names taken from the vocabulary of jewellery. Coral is a beautiful pink calcareous material found in warm seas; it actually consists of the skeletons of millions of tiny sea creatures. The word is from Late Latin *corallium* and is probably ultimately of Semitic origin.

Coralie (f.) English: apparently an elaboration of CORA or CORAL on the model of ROSALIE.

Corazón (f.) Spanish: religious name referring to the Sacred Heart of Jesus, from Spanish *corazón* heart (an augmentative formation from Latin *cor*). Devotion to the Sacred Heart is known to some extent from early Christian times, but it became official and public in the 17th century; the feast was formally established in the Roman Catholic Church in 1855.

Cordelia (f.) English: name used by Shakespeare for King Lear's one virtuous daughter. It is not clear where he got it from; it does not seem likely to have a genuine Celtic origin. It may be a fanciful elaboration of Latin *cor* (genitive *cordis*) heart, and certainly this association has been made by many of those who have subsequently chosen it.

Cordula (f.) English and German: apparently a Late Latin diminutive form of *cor* (genitive *cordis*) heart. A saint of this name was, according to legend, one of Ursula's eleven thousand companions.

Coretta (f.) English: elaborated form of CORA, with the addition of the productive feminine suffix *-etta* (originally an Italian diminutive form). This is the name of the widow of the American civil rights campaigner Martin Luther King.

Corey (m.) English (U.S.): a fairly common male name among Blacks in the United States, but the reasons for its popularity are not clear. It is identical in form with the English surname *Corey*, which is derived from the Old Norse personal name *Kori*.

Variant: **Cory.**

Corin (m.) French: from Latin *Quirīnus*, the name of an ancient Roman divinity partly associated with the legendary figure of Romulus. It is of uncertain origin, probably connected with the Sabine word *quiris* or *curis* spear. In the early Christian period the name was borne by several saints martyred for the faith. The name is occasionally also used in the English-speaking world (where it is often regarded as a male equivalent of CORINNA), notably by the actor Corin Redgrave (b. 1939).

Corinna (f.) English and German: from the Greek name *Korinna* (probably a derivative of *Korē*; cf. CORA), borne by a Boeotian poetess of uncertain date, whose works survive in fragmentary form. The name was also used by the Roman poet Ovid for the woman addressed in his love poetry.

Corinne (f.) French form of CORINNA, also used in the English-speaking world.

Cormac (m.) Irish Gaelic: traditional name, apparently composed of the elements *corb* defilement + *mac* son. This has been a very popular name in Ireland from the earliest times. Cormac Ó Cuilleannáin, a 10th-century king and bishop, wrote an important dictionary of the Irish language.

Cognate: Scottish Gaelic: **Cormag.**

Cornelia (f.) English, German, and Dutch: from the Latin feminine form of the old Roman family name CORNELIUS. It was borne most notably in the 2nd century BC by the mother of the revolutionary reformers Tiberius and Gaius Sempronius Gracchus, and is still occasionally bestowed in her honour.

Pet forms: Dutch: **Cokkie, Nelleke**.

Cornelis (m.) Dutch form of CORNELIUS, very common in Holland and South Africa.

Short forms: **Cor, Niels**.

Pet forms: **Kees, Cees**.

Cornelius (m.) From an old Roman family name, *Cornēlius*, which is of uncertain origin, possibly a derivative of Latin *cornu* horn. This was the name of an early Christian who died in Civitavecchia in *c.*253.

Variants: Dutch: CORNELIS. French: **Corneille**. Polish: **Kornel(i), Korneliusz**. Czech: **Kornel**.

Cornell (m.) Medieval vernacular form of CORNELIUS in various languages, including English. In modern use it normally represents a transferred use of the surname, which is of very varied origin.

Corona (f.) German (S. Germany): from a Late Latin name meaning 'crown'. St Corona was a minor saint martyred in Syria in the 2nd century, together with her husband Victor. During the Middle Ages she was venerated in Bavaria, Austria, and Bohemia.

Corrado (m.) Italian form of CONRAD. This was a common name in several of the Italian royal houses during the Middle Ages, and is still used as a result of the fame of St Conrad Confalonieri (1290–1354), a nobleman of Piacenza.

Cosima (f.) English, German, and Italian: feminine form of COSMO, occasionally used in the English-speaking world. The most famous bearer is probably Cosima Wagner (1837–1930), daughter of Franz Liszt and wife of Richard Wagner.

Cosmo (m.) Italian, English, and German: Italian form (also found as **Cosimo**) of the Greek name *Kosmas* (a short form of various names containing the element *kosmos* order, beauty). This was borne by a Christian saint martyred, together with his brother Damian, at Aegea in Cilicia in the early 4th century. It was first brought to Britain in the 18th century by the Scottish dukes of Gordon, who had connections with the ducal house of Tuscany. The name was traditional in that family, having been borne most famously by Cosimo de' Medici (1389–1464), its founder and one of the chief patrons of the Italian Renaissance.

Courtney (m., f.) English (mainly U.S.): transferred use of the surname, originally a Norman baronial name from any of various places in northern France called *Courtenay* ('domain of Curtius'). However, from an early period it was taken as a nickname from Old French *court nez* 'short nose'. It is also used as a female name, especially in America.

Coy (m.) U.S.: of uncertain origin. It is hardly likely to be from the modern English vocabulary word, which has both feminine and pejorative connotations. It probably represents a transferred use of the surname *Coy*, or it may be of Irish origin (from *McCoy*, a variant of *McKay*, meaning 'son of Aodh'; *Aodh* was an old Gaelic name meaning 'fire').

Craig (m.) Scottish and English: transferred use of the surname, originally a local name derived from any of the many places in Scotland named with the Gaelic element *creag* rock. It is now widely fashionable throughout the English-speaking world, and is chosen as a given name by people who have no connection with Scotland.

Creighton (m.) Scottish and English: transferred use of the surname, which is of Scottish origin. It arose as a local name from *Crichton* in Midlothian, so called from Gaelic *crioch* border, boundary +

Middle English *tune* settlement (Old English *tūn*).

Crescentia (f.) German (S. Germany): original Latin form of the vernacular name KRESZENZ.

Cressa (f.) English: modern name, apparently originating as a contracted short form of CRESSIDA.

Cressida (f.) English: from a medieval legend, told by Chaucer and Shakespeare among others, set in ancient Troy. Cressida is a Trojan princess, daughter of Calchas, a priest who has defected to the Greeks. When she is restored to her father, she jilts her Trojan lover Troilus in favour of the Greek Diomedes. The story is not found in classical sources. Chaucer used the name in the form *Criseyde*, getting it from Boccaccio's *Criseida*. This in turn is ultimately based on Greek *Khryseis* (a derivative of *khrysos* gold), the name of a Trojan girl who is mentioned briefly as a prisoner of the Greeks at the beginning of Homer's *Iliad*. Chaucer's version of the name was Latinized by Shakespeare as *Cressida*. In spite of the unhappy associations of the story, the name has enjoyed some popularity in the 20th century.

Críostóir (m.) Irish Gaelic form of CHRISTOPHER.

Crìsdean (m.) Scottish Gaelic: name derived from *Crìosd* Christ, used as an equivalent of CHRISTOPHER.

Crispian (m.) English: medieval variant of CRISPIN, now very rarely used as a given name.

Crispin (m.) English: from Latin *Crispīnus*, a derivative of the old Roman family name *Crispus* 'curly(-headed)'. St Crispin was martyred with his brother Crispinian in *c.*285, and the pair were popular saints in the Middle Ages.

Cristina (f.) Italian, Spanish, and Portuguese form of CHRISTINA.

Crístíona (f.) Irish Gaelic form of CHRISTINA.

Cristo (m.) Spanish: short form of CRISTÓBAL. It is occasionally also used in the English-speaking world as an informal pet form of CHRISTOPHER.

Cristóbal (m.) Spanish form of CHRISTOPHER.

Cristòfol (m.) Catalan form of CHRISTOPHER.

Cristoforo (m.) Italian form of CHRISTOPHER.

Cristovão (m.) Portuguese form of CHRISTOPHER.

Cronan (m.) Irish: Anglicized form of the Gaelic name **Crónán**, originally a byname representing a diminutive form of Gaelic *crón* swarthy.

Variant: **Cronin**.

Cruz (f.) Spanish: religious name referring to the agony of Mary at the foot of the Cross (Spanish *cruz*, from Latin *crux*, genitive *crūcis*).

Pet form: **Crucita**.

Crystal (f.) English: 19th-century coinage. This is one of the group of names taken from or suggestive of gemstones. The word *crystal*, denoting high-quality cut glass, is derived from Greek *krystallos* ice. (As a male name, *Crystal* originated as a Scottish pet form of CHRISTOPHER, but it is hardly, if ever, used today.)

Variant: **Krystle**.

Ctibor (m.) Czech form of CZCIBOR.

Pet form: **Ctík**.

Ctislav (m.) Czech variant of *Česlav* (see CZESŁAW).

Cuán (m.) Irish Gaelic: originally a byname representing a diminutive form of Gaelic *cú* hound; cf. CONAN. This name has been strongly revived in the 20th century.

Cuddy (m.) Lowland Scottish: pet form of CUTHBERT. It has also become established as a conventional byname for a donkey.

Cugat (m.) Catalan: from Latin *Cucuphas* (genitive *Cucuphatis*), a name of Carthaginian origin and unknown derivation. It was borne by a 3rd-century saint who was martyred near Barcelona.

Cuimín (m.) Irish Gaelic: originally a byname representing a diminutive form of Gaelic *cam* bent, twisted.

Anglicized form: **Comyn.**

Cuithbeart (m.) Scottish Gaelic form of CUTHBERT.

Variant: **Cuithbrig.**

Curro (m.) Spanish: pet form of *Francisco* (see FRANCIS).

Curstaidh (f.) Scottish Gaelic spelling of KIRSTIE.

Variant: **Curstag.**

Curt (m.) 1. German: variant spelling of KURT.

2. English: originally an Anglicized spelling of German KURT, but now also used as a short form of CURTIS. Association with the vocabulary word *curt* 'brusque' does not seem to have harmed its popularity.

Curtis (m.) English: transferred use of the surname, which originated in the Middle Ages as a nickname for someone who was 'courteous' (Old French *curteis*). At an early date, however, it came to be associated with Middle English *curt* short + *hose* leggings; cf. COURTNEY.

Cuthbert (m.) English: from an Old English personal name composed (somewhat tautologously) of the elements *cūð* known + *beorht* bright, famous. It was borne by two pre-Conquest English saints: a 7th-century bishop of Lindisfarne and an 8th-century archbishop of Canterbury who corresponded with St Boniface.

Cognates: Scottish Gaelic: **Cuithbeart, Cuithbrig.**

Pet form: Scottish (Lowland): **Cuddy.**

Cy (m.) English: short form of CYRUS, sometimes used in America as an independent given name.

Cynddelw (m.) Welsh: traditional name of uncertain derivation, perhaps from an Old Celtic element meaning 'high, exalted' + Welsh *delw* image, statue, effigy.

Cynthia (f.) English: from Greek *Kynthia*, an epithet applied to the goddess Artemis, who was supposed to have been born on Mount *Kynthos* on the island of Delos. The mountain name is of pre-Greek origin. *Cynthia* was later used by the Roman poet Propertius as the name of the woman to whom he addressed his love poetry. The English given name was not used in the Middle Ages, but dates from the classical revival of the 17th and 18th centuries.

Cognate: Italian: **Cinzia.**

Cyril (m.) English: from the post-classical Greek name *Kyrillos*, a derivative of *kyrios* lord. It was borne by a large number of early saints, most notably the theologians Cyril of Alexandria and Cyril of Jerusalem. It was also the name of one of the Greek evangelists who brought Christianity to the Slavonic regions of Eastern Europe; in order to provide written translations of the gospels for their converts, they devised the alphabet still known as Cyrillic. In Ireland this has been used as an Anglicized form of the Gaelic name **Coireall** or **Caireall** (Old Irish *Cairell*).

Cognate: Russian: **Kirill.**

Cyrille (m., f.) French form of CYRIL, now also occasionally used in the English-speaking world, sometimes as a elaborated spelling variant and sometimes as a feminine form.

Cyrus (m.) U.S.: from the Greek form (*Kyros*) of the name of several kings of Persia, most notably Cyrus the Great (d. 529 BC). The origin of the name is not known, but in the early Christian period it was associated with Greek *kyrios* lord, and borne by various saints, including an Egyptian martyr and a bishop of Carthage.

Cognate: Italian: **Ciro**.

Short form: U.S.: **Cy**.

Czcibor (m.) Polish: from an old Slavonic personal name composed of the elements *chest* honour + *borit* to fight.

Variants: **Ścibor, Cibor**.

Cognate: Czech: **Ctibor**.

Czesław (m.) Polish: from an old Slavonic personal name composed of the elements *chest* honour + *slav* glory.

Cognates: Czech: **Česlav, Ctislav**. Russian: **Cheslav**.

Pet forms: Polish: **Czech, Czesiek**.

D

Daffodil (f.) English: one of the rarer flower names, which perhaps originated as an expanded version of DAFFY. The flower got its name in the 14th century from a run-together form of Dutch *de affodil* 'the asphodel'.

Daffy (f.) English: pet form of DAPHNE, not much used as an independent given name. Its popularity has not been aided by the occurence since the 19th century of the homonymous adjective *daffy* frivolous, absent-minded (from *daff* fool, connected with *daft*).

Dafydd (m.) Welsh form of DAVID; see also DEWI. This form of the name was in widespread use during the Middle Ages. Later it was largely replaced in Wales by the English form *David*, but from the late 19th century it has come into its own again.

Dag (m.) Scandinavian: from the Old Norse vocabulary word *dagr* day.

Dagmar (f.) Scandinavian (now also used in the German-speaking world): of uncertain origin. It would appear to be composed of the Old Scandinavian elements *dag* day + *mār* maid. It is possible that it represents a reworking of the Slavonic name *Dragomira*, composed of the elements *dorog* dear + *meri* great, famous (see CASIMIR). It is now occasionally used also in the English-speaking world.

Dagny (f.) Scandinavian: from an Old Norse female personal name composed of the elements *dag* day + *ný* new. The forms **Dagna** and **Dagne** are also used.

Dahlia (f.) English: from the name of the flower, which was so called in the 19th century in honour of the pioneering Swedish botanist Anders Dahl (1751–89). His surname represents a cognate of English DALE.

Variant: **Dalya**.

Dai (m.) Welsh: now used as a Welsh pet form of DAVID, but originally of distinct origin, probably from an Old Celtic element *dei* to shine.

Dàibhidh (m.) Scottish Gaelic form of DAVID.

Daisy (f.) English: from the name of the flower, Old English *dægesēage*, the 'day's eye', so called because it uncovers the yellow disc of its centre in the morning and closes its petals over it again at the end of the day. The name seems to have been used early on as a punning pet form of MARGARET, by association with French *Marguerite*, which is both a version of that name and the word for the flower. However, it was not widespread until taken up at the end of the 19th century as part of the general vogue for flower names.

Dale (m., f.) English: transferred use of the surname, originally a local name for someone who lived in a *dale* or valley. It is now commonly used as a given name, especially in America, along with other monosyllabic surnames of topographical origin (cf. e.g. DELL and HALE). It is for the most part a male name, but occasionally also given to girls.

Daley (m.) Irish and English: from the Irish surname, the Gaelic form of which is *Ó Dálaigh* 'descendant of *Dálach*', a personal name derived from *dál* assembly, gathering.

Variant: **Daly**.

Dalibor (m.) Czech: from an old Slavonic personal name composed of the elements *dal* afar + *borit* to fight.

Feminine form: **Dalibora**.

Pet forms: **Dal(ek)** (m.); **Dal(en)(k)a** (f.).

Dalmazio (m.) Italian: from the Late Latin personal name *Dalmatius*, originally an ethnic name for someone from Dalmatia, across the Adriatic from Italy. The name was borne by an early bishop of Pavia who was martyred in 304.

Cognate: Spanish: **Dalmacio**.

Daly (m.) English: variant spelling of DALEY.

Dalya (f.) English: variant of DAHLIA.

Damaris (f.) New Testament: name of a woman mentioned as being converted to Christianity by St Paul (Acts 17: 34). Its origin is not clear, but it is probably Greek, perhaps a late form of *Damalis* 'calf'. It was taken up in the 17th century, along with the names of other characters fleetingly mentioned in the New Testament, and has been occasionally used ever since.

Damaso (m.) Spanish: name borne in honour of a 4th-century pope, St *Damasus*, who was a close friend of St Jerome. He was apparently of Spanish descent. The name is of Greek origin and is derived from the element *damān* to tame, subdue, kill (cf. DAMON and DAMIAN).

Damian (m.) English and Polish: from Greek *Damianos*, the name of the brother of Cosmas (see COSMO); the two brothers were martyred together at Aegea in Cilicia in the early 4th century. The origin of the name is not certain, but it is probably akin to DAMON.

Cognates: French: **Damien** (sometimes also used in the English-speaking world). Italian: **Damiano**. Spanish: **Damián**. Portuguese: **Damião**. Russian: **Demyan**.

Damon (m.) English: from a classical Greek name, a derivative of *damān* to tame, subdue (often a euphemism for 'kill'). This was made famous in antiquity by the story of Damon and Pythias. In the early 4th century BC Pythias was condemned to death by Dionysius, ruler of Syracuse. His friend Damon offered to stand surety for him, and took his place in the condemned cell while Pythias put his affairs in order. When Pythias duly returned to be executed, rather than absconding and leaving his friend to his fate, Dionysius was so impressed by the trust and friendship of the two young men that he pardoned both of them. The name was not used in the early centuries of the Christian era or during the Middle Ages. Its modern use seems to date from the 1930s and is probably due to the fame of the American short-story writer Damon Runyon (1884–1946). It is sometimes taken as a variant of DAMIAN.

Dan (m.) 1. Biblical: name (meaning 'he judged' in Hebrew) borne by one of Jacob's twelve sons (Genesis 30: 6). Samson was a member of the tribe which descended from him.

2. English: short form of DANIEL.

Dana (f., m.) 1. (f.) E. European: for the most part a feminine form of DAN (1) or DANIEL. In Poland it is also used as a short form of *Bogdana* (see BOGDAN) and a pet form of DARIA.

2. (f., m.) English (esp. U.S.): from the surname, which is relatively common in the United States, but of uncertain derivation. Use as a given name began in honour of Richard Dana (1815–82), author of *Two Years before the Mast*. A lawyer by profession, he supported the rights of fugitive slaves, and lent his backing to the Union during the Civil War.

Pet forms (of 1): Czech: **Danka, Danuše, Danuška, Danička, Danul(k)a**.

Danaë (f.) Name borne in Greek mythology by the daughter of Acrisius, who was ravished by Zeus in the form of a shower of gold; as a result she gave birth to the hero Perseus. Her name is of uncertain derivation; she was a great-great-granddaughter of *Danaus*, the eponymous founder of the Greek tribe of the *Danai* or Argives.

Dane (m.) English: transferred use of the surname, which was originally a local name representing a dialect variant of

DEAN that was common in south-east England.

Daniel (m.) Jewish, English, French, German, Polish, and Czech: biblical name (meaning 'God is my judge' in Hebrew) borne by the prophet whose story is told in the Book of Daniel. He was an Israelite slave of the Assyrian king Nebuchadnezzar, who obtained great favour through his skill in interpreting dreams and the 'writing on the wall' at the feast held by Nebuchadnezzar's son Belshazzar. His enemies managed to get him cast into a lions' den, but he was saved by God. This was a favourite tale in the Middle Ages, often represented in miracle plays. The name is popular among both Jews and Gentiles; in Ireland it has often been used as an Anglicized form of Gaelic *Domhnall* (see DONALD).

Cognates: Welsh: **Deiniol**. Scottish Gaelic: **Dàniel**. Italian: **Daniele**. Russian: **Daniil**. Ukrainian: **Danilo**. Finnish: **Taneli**.

Short form: English: **Dan**.

Pet forms: English: **Danny**. Czech: **Danek**, **Daneš**, **Danoušek**.

Daniela (f.) Polish and Czech: Latinate feminine form of DANIEL, occasionally used also in the English-speaking world.

Danièle (f.) French: feminine form of DANIEL, occasionally used also in the English-speaking world.

Variant: **Danielle** (rather more commonly used in the English-speaking world).

Pet form: **Dany**.

Danika (f.) Eastern European name, now also in occasional use in the English-speaking world. It is derived from a Slavonic element denoting the morning star.

Danny (m.) English: pet form of DANIEL, with the hypocoristic suffix *-y*.

Dante (m.) Italian: name bestowed in honour of the medieval poet Dante Alighieri (1265–1321). The medieval given name *Dante* represents a contracted form of *Durante* 'steadfast, enduring' (from Latin *dūrans*, genitive *dūrantis*, present participle of *dūrāre* to endure).

Danuta (f.) Polish: of uncertain origin, apparently a derivative of DANA. It is also possible that *Danuta* may derive from Latin *Donāta*, feminine of *Donātus* (see DONATO).

Dany (f.) French: pet form of DANIÈLE and its variant *Danielle*.

Daphne (f.) Name borne in Greek mythology by a nymph who was changed into a laurel by her father, a river god, to enable her to escape the attentions of Apollo, who was pursuing her. The name means 'laurel' in Greek. According to the myth, then, the nymph gave her name to the shrub, but in fact of course it was the other way about: her name was taken from the vocabulary word (which seems to be of pre-Greek origin, and may therefore have been thought to need explaining). The name was not used in England until the end of the 19th century, when it seems to have been adopted as part of the vogue for flower names at that time.

Dara (m.) Irish Gaelic: short form of MAC DARA. This name is common in Connemara and now also elsewhere in Ireland. It was formerly often Anglicized as DUDLEY.

Variant: **Darach**.

Darby (m.) English: transferred use of the surname, which originated in the Middle Ages as a local name for someone from the city of Derby or the district of West Derby near Liverpool. These are so called from Old Norse *diur* deer + *býr* settlement. The Middle English change of *-er-* to *-ar-* is normally reflected in the spelling of the given name as well as most cases of the surname, whereas the placename retains a more conservative orthographic form. In Ireland this name has often been used as an Anglicized form of Gaelic *Diarmait* (see DERMOT).

Darcy (m.) English: transferred use of the surname, originally a Norman baronial name (*d'Arcy*) borne by a family who came from Arcy in northern France. It has always retained a somewhat aristocratic flavour, which has enhanced its popularity as a given name. It is the surname of the hero of Jane Austen's novel *Pride and Prejudice* (1813).

Daria (f.) English, Italian, and Polish: feminine form of the much rarer male name *Darius* (see DARIO). St Daria (d. 283) was a Greek woman married to an Egyptian Christian called Chrysanthus; they lived at Rome and were both martyred under the joint emperors Numerian and Carinus.

Cognates: Russian: **Darya**. Czech: **Darie**.

Pet forms: Polish: **Dana**. Russian: **Dasha**. Czech: **Darka, Darin(k)a, Daruška**.

Dario (m.) Italian: from the Late Latin name *Darius*, Greek *Dareios*, originally a transliterated version of the name of various ancient Persian kings. The original form of the name seems to have been *Darayavahush*, composed of the elements *daraya(miy)* to hold, possess, maintain + *vahu* well, good. A rather obscure saint of this name was martyred at Nicaea with three companions at an uncertain date. The Latin form **Darius** is occasionally used as a given name in the United States.

Darlene (f.) English (esp. Australia and U.S.): modern coinage, apparently representing an alteration of the affectionate nickname *Darling* by fusion with the suffix *-lene*, found as an ending in other female given names.

Darrell (m.) English: transferred use of the surname, originally a Norman baronial name (*d'Airelle*) borne by a family who came from Airelle in Calvados. It was first used as a given name towards the end of the 19th century, and has enjoyed a considerable vogue in the latter part of the 20th century.

Variants: **Darrel, Darell**.

Darren (m.) English: recently coined name of uncertain derivation. It may well have been an arbitrary coinage, or from a surname (of obscure origin). It seems to have been first borne by the American actor Darren McGavin (b. 1922). It came to the attention of the public as the name of a character in the popular American television comedy series *Bewitched* (made in the 1960s). In the spelling **Darin**, it is associated with the singer Bobby Darin (1936–73), who was originally called Walden Robert Cassotto and who chose the name he made famous from a telephone directory.

Darrene (f.) English: feminine form of DARREN, formed by fusion with the productive feminine suffix *-ene*.

Darryl (m., occasionally f.) English: apparently a variant of DARRELL. Together with the variant **Daryl**, it is occasionally borne by women, perhaps under the influence of names such as CHERYL.

Darya (f.) Russian form of DARIA.

Pet form: **Dasha**.

Dassah (f.) Jewish: aphetic short form of HADASSAH. The shortening may have been assisted by the erroneous association of the first syllable with the Hebrew definite article *ha*.

David (m.) Biblical: name of the greatest of the Israelite kings, whose history is recounted in 1 Samuel and elsewhere. As a boy he killed the giant Philistine, Goliath, with his slingshot; as king of Judah, and later of all Israel, he expanded the power of the Israelites and established their security. He was also noted as a poet, with many of the Psalms being attributed to him. He had many sons and, according to the gospels, Jesus was descended from him. The Hebrew derivation of the name is uncertain; it is said by some to represent a nursery word meaning 'darling'. In America this is mainly a Jewish name, but it has no such weighting in Britain, where it is particularly common in Wales and Scotland, having been borne by the patron saint of Wales (see DEWI) and by two medieval kings of Scotland.

Cognates: Scottish Gaelic: **Dàibhidh**. Irish Gaelic: **Dáibhídh**. Welsh: DAFYDD, DEWI. Polish: **Dawid**. Finnish: **Taavi**.

Short form: English: **Dave**. [*cont.*]

Pet forms: English and Scottish: **Davy, Davey, Davie**. Welsh: DAI.

Davina (f.) Scottish and English: Latinate feminine form of DAVID. The name seems to have originated in Scotland, and is occasionally elaborated to **Davinia**, on the model of LAVINIA. The more straightforward feminine **Davida** is considerably less frequent.

Davy (m.) English and Scottish: pet form of DAVID. It is fairly extensively used as an independent given name, particularly in Scotland.

Variants: **Davey, Davie**.

Dawn (f.) English: from the vocabulary word for daybreak, no doubt originally bestowed because of the connotations of freshness and purity of this time of day. It may have originated as a vernacular translation of AURORA. According to Dunkling, it was first used in 1928, after which it quickly became popular. Twin girls are sometimes given the names *Dawn* and EVE, although the latter name does not in fact have anything to do with the time of day.

Dean (m.) English: transferred use of the surname, which has a double origin. In part it is a local name for someone who lived in a valley (Middle English *dene*, Old English *denu*), in part an occupational name for someone who served as a dean, i.e. ecclesiastical supervisor (Latin *decanus*). The given name also sometimes represents Italian DINO, as in the case of the American actor and singer Dean Martin (b. 1917).

Variants: **Deane, Dene**.

Deanna (f.) English: originally a fanciful respelling of DIANA, now often taken as a feminine form of DEAN. It was made popular by the singing actress Deanna Durbin (b. 1922), whose original given name was EDNA; *Deanna* may have been derived as a partial anagram of this.

Deborah (f.) Jewish and English: biblical name (meaning 'bee' in Hebrew) borne by the nurse of Rebecca (Genesis 35: 8) and by a woman judge and prophet (Judges 4–5), who led the Israelites to victory over the Canaanites. The name has always been popular among Jews. It was taken up among Christians by the Puritans in the 17th century, no doubt in part because the bee was a symbol of industriousness. It has steadily increased in popularity ever since and is currently enjoying a great vogue.

Variants: **Debora, Debra**. Jewish: **Devora(h)** (Hebrew); **Dvoire** (Yiddish).

Pet forms: English: **Debbie, Debbi, Debi, Debs**.

Declan (m.) Irish: Anglicized form of Gaelic **Deaglán**, of uncertain derivation. It was borne by a 5th-century disciple of St Colman, who became a bishop in the district of Ardmore. In recent years the name has been strongly revived in Ireland.

Dee (f., m.) English: pet form of any of the given names beginning with the letter *D*- (cf. KAY), especially DOROTHY. It is also used as an independent name, and may in some cases be associated with the River Dee (cf. CLYDE).

Deforest (m.) U.S.: name apparently adopted in honour of John DeForest (1826–1906), the author of several once popular novels, mostly set during the American Civil War.

Variant: **Deforrest**.

Deiniol (m.) Welsh: apparently a form of DANIEL. The name was borne by a 6th-century Welsh saint.

Deirdre (f.) Irish and English: name borne in Celtic legend by a tragic heroine, sometimes referred to as 'Deirdre of the Sorrows'. The story goes that she was betrothed to Conchobhar, King of Ulster, but instead eloped with her beloved Naoise. Eventually, however, the jilted king murdered Naoise and his brothers, and Deirdre herself died of a broken heart. She is sometimes taken as symbolic of the fate of Ireland under English rule, but this has not stopped her name's being used by English parents with no Celtic blood in them. It became popular in Ireland and elsewhere in the Edwardian era, following retellings of the legend by both the poet W. B. Yeats (1907) and the playwright J. M. Synge (1910). The name itself is of uncertain derivation; the earliest Celtic forms are very variable.

Del (m.) English: colloquial pet form of DEREK, with alteration of the exposed *-r* of the short form to *-l* (cf. SAL and TEL).

Delbert (m.) English (borne mainly by Blacks): apparently a modern coinage, composed of the name elements *Del-* (see DELMAR and DELROY) + *-bert*. In the 1980s it was adopted by the comedian Lenny Henry as the name of one of his comic creations, Delbert Wilkins.

Delfina (f.) Italian and Spanish form of DELPHINE, sometimes also used in the English-speaking world.

Delia (f.) English: from a classical Greek epithet of the goddess Artemis, referring to her birth on the island of *Delos* (cf. CYNTHIA). It was taken up by the pastoral poets of the 17th century, and has been moderately popular ever since.

Delice (f.) English: variant of DELICIA, apparently modelled on medieval given names such as AMICE and CLARICE.

Delicia (f.) English: feminine form of the Late Latin name *Delicius*, a derivative of *deliciae* delight. Use as a given name seems to be a modern phenomenon; it is not found in the Middle Ages.

Delilah (f.) Biblical: name (of uncertain origin) of Samson's mistress, who wheedled him into revealing the secret of his strength and then betrayed him to the Philistines (Judges 16: 4–20). Although the biblical Delilah was deceitful and treacherous, the name was taken up quite enthusiastically by the Puritans in the 17th century, perhaps because she was also beautiful and clever. The name fell out of use in the 18th century, but has been occasionally revived as an exotic name.

Variant: **Delila**.

Delite (f.) English: modern coinage, apparently based on the vocabulary word *delight* (from Old French *delit*, cf. DELICIA; the *-gh-* of the modern spelling is not justified by the etymology).

Dell (m.) English: transferred use of the surname, originally a local name for someone who lived in a *dell* or hollow.

Della (f.) English: name which first appeared in the 1870s and has continued to grow steadily in popularity ever since. Its derivation is not clear; if it is not simply an arbitrary creation, it may be an altered form of DELIA or DELILAH, or a short form of ADELA. In modern use it is sometimes taken as a feminine form of DELL.

Delma (f.) Irish: short form of FIDELMA.

Delmar (m.) English: of uncertain derivation, possibly an arbitrary alteration of ELMER (cf. DELROY and ELROY). In form it coincides with Spanish *del mar* 'of the sea', which occurs in various placenames as a distinguishing epithet and also in the Marian title, *Reina del Mar* 'Queen of the Sea'. As a given name, it is popular chiefly among American Blacks.

Delores (f.) English: variant of DOLORES, quite common in the United States.

Variant: **Deloris**.

Delphine (f.) French and English: from Latin *Delphīna* 'woman from Delphi'. The Blessed Delphina (1283–1358) was a Provençal nun, who may herself have been named in honour of the 4th-century St Delphinus of Bordeaux. In modern times the name seems often to have been chosen for its association with the *delphinium* flower.

Cognate: Italian, Spanish: **Delfina**.

Delroy (m.) Apparently an altered form of LEROY, perhaps representing the Old French phrase *del roy* '(son, servant) of the king'. It is used chiefly among West Indians in Britain.

Delwyn (f.) Welsh: modern name composed of the elements *del* pretty, neat + *(g)wyn* white, fair, blessed, holy.

Delyth (f.) Welsh: modern name composed of the vocabulary word *del* pretty, neat + the ending *-yth*, formed on the analogy of names such as GWENYTH.

Demelza (f.) Modern Cornish name that has no history as a Celtic personal name but derives from a place in the parish of St Columb Major. The given name began to be used in the 1950s and was given a boost by the serialization on British television of the 'Poldark' novels by Winston Graham, in which it is the name of the heroine.

Demetrio (m.) Italian and Spanish form of Latin *Dēmētrius* (see DMITRI).

Demid (m.) Russian: from Greek *Diomēdēs*, composed of a byform of the divine name *Zeus* + the element *mēdesthai* to care for, consider. St Diomedes was born at Tarsus in Cilicia and martyred at Nicaea in Bithynia under the Emperor Diocletian.

Demyan (m.) Russian form of DAMIAN.

Den (m.) English: short form of DENNIS.
Pet form: **Denny**.

Dena (f.) English: modern coinage, representing either a respelling of DINA, or else a form created as a feminine version of DEAN.

Dene (m.) English: variant spelling of DEAN.

Dénes (m.) Hungarian form of DENNIS.

Denice (f.) English: altered form of DENISE, based on the alternative pronunciation of that name.

Denis (m.) French and Russian form of DENNIS, and a variant spelling in the English-speaking world.

Denise (f.) French: feminine form of DENIS, now also widely used in the English-speaking world.

Dennis (m.) English and French: medieval vernacular form of the Greek name *Dionysios*, which was borne by several early Christian saints, including St Denis, a 3rd-century evangelist who converted the Gauls and became a patron saint of Paris. It was on his account that the name was popular among the Normans. In classical times, the word originally denoted a devotee of the god Dionysos. This deity was a relatively late introduction to the classical pantheon; his orgiastic cult seems to have originated in Persia or elsewhere in Asia. His name is of uncertain derivation, although the first part seems to be related to the name of the supreme god *Zeus*.
Cognates: French, Russian: **Denis**. Polish: **Dionizy**. Hungarian: **Dénes**.
Short form: English: **Den**.
Pet form: English: **Denny**.

Denton (m.) English: transferred use of the surname, originally a local name from any of the numerous places so called from Old English *denu* valley + *tūn* enclosure, settlement.

Denzil (m.) English: from the Cornish surname, the original spelling of which was *Denzell*, a local name from a place in Cornwall. It came to be used as a given name in the Hollis family in the 16th century, when the Hollis family and the Denzell family became connected by marriage, and spread from there into more general use.

Deòiridh (f.) Scottish Gaelic: from the vocabulary word meaning 'pilgrim'. This name has been Anglicized as DORCAS.

Deònaid (f.) Scottish Gaelic: dialectal variant of SEÒNAID.

Deòrsa (m.) Scottish Gaelic form of GEORGE; see also SEÒRAS.

Derek (m.) English: from a Low German form of *Theodoric* (see TERRY), introduced to Britain during the Middle Ages by Flemish settlers connected with the cloth trades. It is a comparatively rare name in the United States.

Cognates: German: **Dietrich**. Low German: **Diederick**. Flemish, Dutch: **Dirk**. E. Frisian: **Tjark**.

Pet form: English: **Del**.

Derick (m.) 1. English: variant of DEREK. 2. Scottish: short form of RODERICK.

Dermot (m.) Irish: Anglicized form of the Gaelic name **Diarmaid**. An earlier Gaelic form is *Diarm(u)it*. It occurs in the 7th-century Latin *Life of St Columba* as *Diormitius*. The derivation is uncertain, but it has been suggested that it is composed of the elements *dí* without + *airmit* injunction or *airmait* envy.

Cognates: Scottish: **Diarmad** (Gaelic); **Diarmid, Dermid** (Anglicized forms).

Derrick (m.) English: variant spelling of DEREK. This is the usual American spelling of the given name, but in Britain it is more common as a surname than as a given name.

Derry (m.) English: of uncertain origin, perhaps a cross between DEREK and the ultimately cognate TERRY.

Dervla (f.) Irish: Anglicized form of the Gaelic name **Deirbhile**, composed of the elements *der* daughter + *file* poet.

Variant: **Dervila**.

Desdemona (f.) English: name chosen occasionally by parents in search of an unusual name, who are no doubt attracted by the sweet nature and innocence of Shakespeare's character and not deterred by her tragic fate. She was murdered by her husband Othello in an ill-founded jealous rage, and her name is in fact particularly appropriate to her destiny, as it probably represents a Latinized form of Greek *dysdaimōn* ill-starred.

Desiderio (m.) Italian, Spanish, and Portuguese form of *Desiderius* (see DIDIER).

Desirée (f.) French (now also used in the English-speaking world): from Latin *Desiderāta* 'desired'. This name was given by early Christians to a longed-for child, but the French form is now often taken as suggesting that the bearer will grow up into a desirable woman.

Desmond (m.) Irish and English: apparently originally a local name for someone who came from south Munster (Gaelic *Deas-Mhumhan*). The form has been influenced by the Norman (Germanic) name ESMOND.

Short form: **Des**.

Pet form: **Desy**.

Desya (m.) Russian: pet form of MODEST.

Detlev (m.) Low German: from an old Germanic personal name composed of the elements *þeud* people, race + *leib* relic, inheritance, descendant. The High German form, *Dietleib*, is not current as a given name.

Variant: **Detlef**.

Cognates: E. Frisian: **Tjalf**. Swedish: **Detlof**.

Detta (f.) Italian: short form of various given names such as *Benedetta* (see BENEDICT) and *Bernardetta* (see BERNADETTE).

Devereux (m.) English (esp. U.S.): transferred use of a surname, which was originally a Norman baronial name derived (with fused preposition *de*) from *Evreux* in the *département* of Eure. It was the family name of the 16th-century earls of Essex; Robert Devereux, the 2nd earl, was a favourite of Queen Elizabeth I, later disgraced and executed for treason.

Devorah (f.) Jewish: modern Hebrew form of DEBORAH.

Devorgilla (f.) Scottish: Anglicized form of Gaelic **Diorbhail**, earlier *Diorbhorguil*, apparently meaning 'true testimony'. See also DOROTHY.

Dewey (m.) U.S.: of uncertain origin, perhaps a respelling of DEWI.

Dewi (m.) A Welsh form (earlier *Dewydd*) of DAVID, traditionally associated with the patron saint of Wales. This form of the given name was little used during the Middle Ages, but during the 20th century it has become quite common in Wales, but rare elsewhere. St Dewi was born in South Wales in the 5th century and became the first bishop of Menevia, the tiny cathedral city now known as St Davids.

Dex (m.) Mainly U.S.: short form of DEXTER (cf. LEX and TEX).

Dexter (m.) English (mainly U.S.): transferred use of the surname. Although this is now a male given name, the word that gave rise to the surname originally denoted a female dyer, from Old English *dēag* dye + *-estre* feminine suffix of agent nouns. However, the distinction of gender was already lost in Middle English. The name coincides in form with Latin *dexter* right-handed, auspicious, and may sometimes have been chosen because of this.

Dezső (m.) Hungarian form of *Desiderius* (see DIDIER).

Dezydery (m.) Polish form of *Desiderius* (see DIDIER).

Diana (f.) English: name borne in Roman mythology by the goddess of the moon and of hunting, equivalent to the Greek Artemis. In mythology she is characterized as both beautiful and chaste. Her name is of ancient and uncertain derivation. It probably contains a first element that is also found in the name of the supreme god *Jupiter* and in Greek *Dionysios* (see DENNIS). It was adopted in Britain during the Tudor period as a learned name, a borrowing from Latin influenced by the French form DIANE. It was not particularly popular until the end of the 19th century, and its increased frequency at that time has been attributed in part to George Meredith's novel *Diana of the Crossways* (1885). However, Dunkling casts doubt on this suggestion. In earlier centuries, some clergymen were reluctant to baptize girls with this pagan name, remembering the riots against St Paul stirred up by worshippers of Diana of the Ephesians (Acts 19: 24–41).

Short form: **Di**.

Diane (f.) French form of DIANA, now also used in the English-speaking world. It was especially popular among the Renaissance aristocracy, who loved hunting and were therefore proud to name their daughters after the classical goddess of the chase.

Variants: **Dianne** (by association with ANNE); **Dyan** (U.S.).

Short form: **Di**.

Diarmad (m.) Scottish Gaelic form of DERMOT. It has sometimes been Anglicized as JEREMIAH.

Variants: **Diarmid, Dermid** (Anglicized).

Dick (m.) English: short form of RICHARD (cf. *Rick*). The alteration of the initial consonant is supposed to result from the difficulty that English speakers in the Middle Ages had in pronouncing the trilled Norman *R*-.

Dickie (m.) English: pet form of DICK, with the originally Scottish and northern English hypocoristic suffix *-ie*. This has more or less completely replaced the medieval diminutive *Dickon*, with the Old French suffix *-on*.

Didier (m.) French: from Late Latin *Dēsīderius*, a derivative of *dēsīderium* longing. The name was popular among the early Christians, who chose it to give expression to their longing for Christ. Among the saints who bore it are an early bishop of Langres and 7th-century bishops of Auxerre, Cahors, and Vienne, all of whom are subjects of local cults.

Cognates: Italian, Spanish, Portuguese: **Desiderio**. Polish: **Dezydery**. Hungarian: **Dezső**.

Diederik (m.) Dutch form of DIETRICH.

Pet form: **Tiede**.

Diego (m.) Spanish: of uncertain origin. Although it is often claimed to be an aphetic form of SANTIAGO, it is clear that its regular Latin form in the Middle Ages was *Didacus*. This may possibly be a derivative of Greek *didakhē* teaching, but it is more likely that is represents a Latinized form of some native Iberian name.

Cognate: Portuguese: **Diogo**.

Dieter (m.) German: from an old Germanic personal name composed of the elements *þeud* people, race + *hari*, *heri* army, warrior. St Theuderius (d. *c.*575) was a monk of Lérins who founded three monasteries near his native city of Vienne.

Dietfried (m.) German: from an old Germanic personal name composed of the elements *þeud* people, race + *fred, frid* peace.

Dietlinde (f.) German: from an old Germanic female personal name composed of the elements *þeud* people, race + *lind* weak, tender, soft.

Dietmar (m.) German: from an old Germanic personal name composed of the elements *þeud* people, race + *māri, mēri* famous. St Theodemar (d. 1152) was a native of Bremen who became a missionary to the Wends. Another St Theodmarus (d. 1102), also known by the short form *Thieme*, was a member of the Bavarian royal family who became archbishop of Salzburg.

Dietrich (m.) German form of DEREK.

Dieudonné (m.) French: medieval given name meaning 'given by God' in the vernacular, from Old French *Dieu* God (Latin *Deus*) + *donné* given (Latin *donātus*). It is thus an equivalent in meaning of such names as MATTHEW, NATHANIEL, THEODORE, and DOROTHY. The name is occasionally used nowadays in a spirit of self-conscious antiquarianism.

Digby (m.) English: transferred use of the surname, originally a local name for someone from Digby in Lincolnshire, so called from the Old Norse elements *díki* ditch + *býr* settlement.

Digna (f.) Spanish: from the Late Latin name *Digna* 'worthy', which was borne by a martyr beheaded in Spain during the 9th century.

Dillon (m.) English: variant spelling of DYLAN, based on an English surname of different origin. The surname *Dillon* or *Dyllon* derives in part from a now extinct Norman French personal name of Germanic origin; in part it is a local name for someone from *Dilwyn* in Hereford.

Dilly (f.) English: pet form of DILYS, DILWEN, and DAFFODIL, now sometimes used as an independent given name.

Dilwen (f.) Welsh: modern name, composed of the elements *dil* from DILYS + *(g)wen* feminine form of *gwyn* white, fair, blessed, holy.

Dilwyn (m.) Welsh: modern name, composed of the elements *dil* from DILYS + *(g)wyn* white, fair, blessed, holy.

Dilys (f.) Welsh: of modern origin, from the vocabulary word *dilys* genuine, steadfast, true.

Dimitri (m.) Russian: variant of DMITRI.

Dina (f.) 1. English: in part a variant spelling of DINAH, with which it often has the same pronunciation. In part, however, it seems to represent the adoption of a feminine form of DINO.

2. Scottish: short form of *Murdina* (see MURDO).

Dinah (f.) Biblical: name (a feminine form derived from Hebrew *din* judgment) borne by a daughter of Jacob. She was raped by Shechem but avenged by her brothers Simeon and Levi (Genesis 34). In modern times it has often been taken as a variant of the much more common DIANA.

Variant: Yiddish: **Dine**.

Dino (m.) Italian: aphetic short form of any of the various names ending in these syllables, as for example *Bernardino* (see BERNARD) and *Leonardino* (see LEONARD).

Diogo (m.) Portuguese form of DIEGO.

Dion (m.) French: from Latin *Dio* (genitive *Diōnis*), a short form of the various names of Greek origin containing as their first element the divine name *Dio-* Zeus, as, for example, *Diodoros* 'gift of Zeus' and *Diogenēs* 'born of Zeus'. The name is also used in the English-speaking world, where it is particularly common among Blacks.

Dionizy (m.) Polish form of DENNIS.

Dionne (f.) English: feminine form of DION, or an altered form of *Dianne* (see DIANE).

Dirk (m.) Flemish and Dutch form of DEREK. Its use in the English-speaking world since the 1960s is largely due to the fame of the actor Dirk Bogarde (b. 1921; originally Derek Niven van den Bogaerde). He is of Dutch descent, although he was actually born in Scotland. The manly image of the name has been reinforced by its coincidence in form with the Scottish vocabulary word *dirk* dagger (from Gaelic *durc*).

Disa (f.) Scandinavian: Latinized version of an aphetic short form of the various women's names of Old Norse origin containing the final element *dís* goddess (cf. e.g. HJÖRDIS and TORDIS).

Dmitri (m.) Russian: from the Greek name *Dēmētrios*, a derivative of the name of the goddess *Dēmētēr*, which in turn seems to be composed of *dē*, a variant of *gē* earth + *mētēr* mother. The most famous St Demetrius was an early 4th-century martyr executed at Sirmium in Dalmatia under the Emperor Diocletian; many legends have grown up around him in the Eastern Church.

Variant: **Dimitri**.

Cognates: Italian, Spanish: **Demetrio**. Romanian: **Dumitru**. Polish: **Dymitr**. Ukrainian: **Dmitro**.

Pet form: Russian: **Mitya** (see also MITROFAN).

Dobre (f.) Jewish (E. Yiddish): from the Slavonic element *dobro* good, kind.

Variant: **Dobe**.

Pet form: **Dobke**.

Dobrila (f.) Slavonic: derivative of the element *dobro* good, kind. This may in origin be an affectionate nickname, or else a short form of the various compound names with this first element.

Variant: Russian: **Dobryna**.

Dobromierz (m.) Polish: from an old Slavonic personal name composed of the elements *dobro* good, kind + *meri* great, famous (see CASIMIR).

Cognate: Czech: **Dobromír**.

Feminine forms: Polish: **Dobromira**. Czech: **Dobromíra**.

Dobromił (m.) Polish: from an old Slavonic personal name composed of the elements *dobro* good, kind + *mil* grace, favour.

Cognate: Czech: **Dobromil**.

Feminine form: Czech: **Dobromila**.

Dobrosław (m.) Polish: from an old Slavonic personal name composed of the elements *dobro* good, kind + *slav* glory.

Cognate: Czech: **Dobroslav**.

Feminine forms: Polish: **Dobrosława**. Czech: **Dobroslava**.

Dodie (f.) English: unusual pet form of DOROTHY, derived from a child's unsuccessful attempts to pronounce the name.

Dolina (f.) Scottish: Latinate formation based on the Gaelic name *Dolag*, a feminine diminutive form of DONALD.

Variant: **Dolanna**.

Dolly (f., m.) 1. (f.) English: originally (from the 16th century onwards) a pet form of DOROTHY, but now more commonly used as a pet form of DOLORES and as an independent given name (taken as being from the vocabulary word *doll*, although in fact this was derived from the pet name in the 17th century).

2. (m.) Highland Scottish: pet form of DONALD.

Dolores (f.) Spanish (now also borne in the English-speaking world, mainly by Roman Catholics): from the Marian title, *Maria de los Dolores* 'Mary of Sorrows', a reference to the Seven Sorrows of the Virgin in Christian belief. The feast of Our Lady's Dolours was established in 1423.

Variants: English: **Delores, Deloris**.

Cognate: Portuguese: **Dores**.

Pet forms: Spanish: **Lola, Lolita**. English: **Dolly**.

Domicela (f.) Polish form of DOMITILLA.

Dominga (f.) Spanish: feminine form of *Domingo* (see DOMINIC).

Dominic (m.) English and Irish: from the Late Latin name *Dominicus* (a derivative of *dominus* lord; cf. CYRIL). It is used mainly by Roman Catholics, in honour of St Dominic (1170–1221), founder of the Dominican order of monks.

Variant: **Dominick** (an old spelling, still in occasional use).

Cognates: French: DOMINIQUE. Italian: **Domenico.** Spanish: **Domingo.** Catalan: **Domenge.** Basque: **Txomin.** Polish, Czech: **Dominik.** Hungarian: **Domonkos.**

Dominica (f.) Latinate feminine form of DOMINIC. This name was borne by a saint martyred in Campania under the Emperor Diocletian and by a wealthy Roman widow who was an associate of St Laurence.

Dominique (f., m.) French form of DOMINICA and DOMINIC. It is used as both a female and a male name, but is now much more commonly used as a female name, and as such has also become widespread in the English-speaking world. In Britain it is found especially among Roman Catholics.

Domitilla (f.) Italian and English: name used by Roman Catholics in honour of a 2nd-century saint, Flavia Domitilla, who was a member of the Roman imperial family. She was the great-niece of the Emperor Domitian, and her name represents a diminutive form of *Domitius*, the old Roman family name of which *Domitiānus* is a derivative. It is most probably derived from the nickname *Domitus* 'tamed'.

Cognate: Polish: **Domicela.**

Domonkos (m.) Hungarian form of DOMINIC.

Don (m.) English and Scottish: short form of DONALD. It is also a variant of the Irish name DONN.

Pet forms: Scottish: **Donny, Donnie** (Gaelic **Donnaidh**).

Donagh (m.) Irish: Anglicized form of the Gaelic name **Donnchadh**; see DUNCAN.

Variants: **Dono(u)gh.**

Donal (m.) Irish: Anglicized form of the Gaelic name **Dónal**, a simplified form of *Domhnall* (see DONALD). The form **Donall** is also used.

Donald (m.) Scottish and English: Anglicized form of the Gaelic name **Domhnall**, composed of the Old Celtic elements *dubno* world + *val* rule. The final *-d* of the Anglicized form derives partly from misinterpretation by English-speakers of the Gaelic devoiced sound (cf. DUGALD), and partly from association with Germanic-origin names such as RONALD. This name is very much associated with clan Macdonald, the clan of the medieval Lords of the Isles. In the Highlands and Islands it now ranks second only to *Iain* (see IAN). *Donald* is now quite commonly also used in Britain and America by families with no Scottish connections.

Short form: **Don.**

Pet forms: Scottish: **Donny, Donnie** (Gaelic **Donaidh**); **Dolly** (Gaelic **Dolaidh**).

Feminine forms: Scottish Highland: **Donalda, Donella; Donna(g), Dol(l)ag, Doileag, Dolina, Dolanna.**

Donat (m.) French, Provençal, Catalan, and Polish form of DONATO.

Donatella (f.) Italian: feminine diminutive form of DONATO. Half a dozen saints of this name were martyred in the early persecutions of the Christians.

Donatien (m.) French: from Late Latin *Dōnātiānus*, a derivative of *Dōnātus* (see DONATO). The name was borne by various early saints, including a 4th-century bishop of Rheims who became the patron of Bruges when his relics were taken there in the 9th century. This was the given name of the Marquis de Sade (1740–1814).

Donato (m.) Italian, Spanish, and Portuguese: from Late Latin *Dōnātus* 'given (by

God)' (the past participle of *dōnāre* to give, donate). The name was popular among early Christians and was borne by over twenty saints in the first centuries AD. Among the most famous is a bishop of Arezzo in Tuscany who was beheaded under Julian the Apostate.

Cognate: French, Provençal, Catalan, Polish: **Donat**.

Donella (f.) Scottish: name coined as a feminine equivalent of DONALD.

Donla (f.) Irish: modern spelling of a traditional Gaelic name composed of the elements *donn* brown + *flaith* lady, revived in this form in the 20th century.

Donn (m.) Irish Gaelic: ancient byname meaning either 'brown' or 'king', in use from the earliest times until the 19th century. It is borne in Irish mythology by the king of the underworld. In modern use *Donn* normally represents a short form of any of the various Gaelic names containing the first element *donn* brown.

Donna (f.) English and Scottish: of recent origin (not found before the 1920s). It seems to be taken from the Italian word *donna* lady (cf. MADONNA), but it has often been used as a feminine form of DONALD.

Donnchadh (m.) Gaelic form of DUNCAN.

Donny (m.) English: pet form of DON.

Donough (m.) Irish: variant spelling of **Donagh**.

Variant: **Donogh**.

Donovan (m.) Irish and English: from the Irish surname, Gaelic *Ó Donndubháin* 'descendant of *Donndubhán*', a personal name composed of the elements *donn* brown + *dubh* black, dark, with the addition of the diminutive suffix *-án*. Its use as a given name dates from the early 1900s. The folk-rock singer Donovan may have had some influence on its increase in popularity in the 1960s. It is now also used by people with no Irish connections.

Doortje (f.) Dutch: pet form derived from a contracted version of DOROTHEA.

Dora (f.) English and French: 19th-century coinage, representing a short form of ISIDORA, THEODORA, DOROTHY, and any other name containing the Greek element *dōron* gift. In some cases, it seems to have been taken as actually meaning 'gift', presumably as a Latinate version of the Greek word. Wordsworth's daughter (b. 1804), christened Dorothy, was always known in adult life as Dora. The name's popularity was enhanced by the character of Dora Spenlow in Dickens's novel *David Copperfield* (1850).

Pet form: **Dory**.

Doran (m.) Irish and English: from the Irish surname, in Gaelic *Ó Deoradháin* 'descendant of Deoradhán'. *Deoradhán* is an old Irish personal name meaning 'exile, wanderer'.

Dorcas (f.) English: from Greek *dorkas* doe, gazelle. It does not actually seem to have been used as a personal name by the ancient Greeks, but is offered in the Bible as an 'interpretation' of the Aramaic name TABITHA (Acts 9: 36), and was taken up by the early Christians. It was much used among the Puritans in the 16th century, and has remained in occasional use ever since. In Scotland it has been used as an Anglicized form of DEÒIRIDH.

Dorean (f.) Irish: Anglicized form of the Gaelic name **Doireann**, possibly from Gaelic *der* daughter + the name of the legendary hero FINN. This has been revived as a given name in the 20th century, and has become very popular, perhaps in part as a result of the popularity of the similar name DOREEN.

Doreen (f.) English: derivative of DORA, with the addition of the productive suffix *-een* (in origin an Irish diminutive). The name came into use at the beginning of the 20th century, when there was a particular vogue for such names. See also DOREAN.

Variants: **Dorene, Dorine.**

Dores (f.) Portuguese form of DOLORES.

Dorete (f.) Danish form of DOROTHEA.

Doria (f.) English: of uncertain origin, probably a back-formation from DORIAN or else an elaboration of DORA on the model of the numerous women's given names ending in *-ia*.

Dorian (m.) English: early 20th-century coinage, apparently invented by Oscar Wilde, as no evidence has been found of its existence before he used it for the central character in *The Portrait of Dorian Gray* (1891). Dorian Gray is a dissolute rake who retains unblemished youthful good looks; in the attic of his home is a portrait which does his ageing for him, gradually acquiring all the outward marks of his depravity. This macabre background has not deterred parents from occasionally bestowing the name on their children. Wilde probably took the name from Late Latin *Dōriānus*, from Greek *Dōrieus*, member of the Greek-speaking people who settled in the Peloponnese in pre-classical times. *Dorian* would thus be a masculine version of DORIS. It may have been selected occasionally by admirers of ancient Sparta and its militaristic institutions, since the Spartans were of Dorian stock.

Dorinda (f.) English: artificial extension of DORA, with the suffix *-inda* (cf. CLARINDA). The name was coined in the 18th century, and has undergone a modest revival of interest in the 20th.

Doris (f.) English and German: from the classical Greek ethnic name meaning 'Dorian woman'. The Dorians were one of the tribes of Greece; their name was traditionally derived from an ancestor, *Dōros* (son of Hellen, who gave his name to the Hellenes), but it is more likely that Doros (whose name could be from *dōron* gift) was invented to account for a tribal name of obscure origin. In Greek mythology, Doris was a minor goddess of the sea, the consort of Nereus and the mother of his daughters, the Nereids or sea-nymphs, who numbered fifty (in some versions, more). The name was especially popular from about 1880 to about 1930, and was borne by the American film star Doris Day (b. 1924).

Dorofei (m.) Russian: from Greek *Dōrotheus*, composed of the elements *dōron* gift + *theos* god (cf. THEODORE and DOSIFEI). The name was borne by various early saints much venerated in the Eastern Church, including a 4th-century bishop of Tyre and the abbots Dorotheus the Archimandrite (7th century) and Dorotheus the Younger (11th century).

Doron (m.) 1. English: apparently a variant spelling of DORIAN (perhaps influenced by the pair of names DAMIAN and DAMON), although it corresponds in form with the Greek word *dōron* gift.

2. Jewish: modern Hebrew name based on a direct borrowing of the Greek word *doron* gift.

Dorothea (f.) English, German, and Dutch: Latinate form of a post-classical Greek name composed of the elements *dōron* gift + *theos* god (the same elements as in THEODORA, but in reverse order). The masculine form *Dōrotheus* (see DOROFEI) was borne by several early Christian saints, the feminine only by two minor ones, but in Western Europe today it only survives as a female name. In modern use in the English-speaking world it represents a 19th-century Latinization of DOROTHY, or a learned reborrowing.

Cognates: Danish: **Dorete, Dort(h)e.** Polish, Czech: **Dorota.** Hungarian: **Dorottya.**

Pet forms: Dutch: **Doortje.** Polish: **Dosia.**

Dorothy (f.) Usual English form of DOROTHEA. The name was not used in the Middle Ages, but was taken up in the 16th century and became common thereafter. In Scotland it has been used as an Anglicized form of the Gaelic name **Diorbhail**, also Anglicized as DEVORGILLA.

Short form: **Dot**.

Pet forms: **Dottie, Dodie, Dolly**.

Dorte (f.) Danish: contracted variant of DORETE.

Variant: **Dorthe**.

Dory (f.) English: pet form of DORA, now seldom used in that function and even less commonly bestowed as an independent given name.

Dosia (f.) Polish: pet form of *Dorota* (see DOROTHEA).

Dosifei (m.) Russian: from Greek *Dōsitheos*, composed of the elements *dōsis* giving and *theos* god (see also TEODOSIO). St Dositheus (d. *c.*530) was a monk of Gaza who led an unspectacular life but is much venerated in the Eastern Church.

Dot (f.) English: short form of DOROTHY.

Dottie (f.) English: pet form of DOT, with the hypocoristic suffix *-ie*. The form **Dotty** is also used, and its popularity does not seem to have been adversely affected by the fact that it coincides in form with the slang word meaning 'crazy'.

Doug (m.) English: short form of DOUGLAS.

Dougal (m.) Scottish: Anglicized form of the Gaelic name **Dubhghall** or **Dùghall**, composed of the elements *dubh* black, dark + *gall* stranger. This is said to have been a byname applied to Danes, in contrast to the fairer Norwegians and Icelanders (see FINGAL).

Variants: **Dugald, Dugal**.

Pet form: **Dougie**.

Douglas (m.) Scottish and English: transferred use of the surname borne by what was one of the most powerful families in Scotland, the earls of Douglas and of Angus, also notorious in earlier times as Border reivers. Today this name is sometimes assumed to be connected with DOUGAL, but it seems more likely that the surname is derived from the place in the Southern Uplands of Scotland where the family had their stronghold. This is probably named with the Gaelic elements *dubh* black + *glas* stream.

Variant: **Dùbhghlas** (Gaelic).

Short form: **Doug**.

Pet form: **Dougie**.

Dov (m.) Jewish: name meaning 'bear' in Hebrew. There is no biblical character of this name: it represents a translation into Hebrew of an animal name that became popular in European languages in the early Middle Ages. The bear is often associated with the name ISSACHAR, although the reason for this is not clear, for in Jacob's dying blessing (Genesis 49: 14) Issachar is referred to as a 'strong ass couching down between two burdens'. There was a famous rabbi named Issachar Dov, but this may have been simply a fortuitous pairing of the two names. Subsequent bearers may then have been named after him.

Doyle (m.) Irish and English: variant of DOUGAL and DUGALD, in part derived from an Anglicized form of the Gaelic surname *Ó Dubhghaill* 'descendant of Dubhghall'.

Drahomír (m.) Czech form of DROGOMIR.

Feminine: **Drahomíra**.

Pet forms: **Draha** (m., f.); **Drahoš(ek)** (m.); **Drahuše, Drahuška, Dráža** (f.).

Dreda (f.) English: short form of ETHELDREDA, quite commonly used as an independent given name in the 19th century, when the longer form was also in fashion. It has survived slightly better than the more cumbersome quadrisyllabic form, but is nevertheless now rare.

Drew (m.) Scottish short form of ANDREW, often used as an independent name in Scotland, and in recent years increasingly popular elsewhere in the English-speaking world.

Dries (m.) Low German and Dutch short form of ANDRIES.

Drogo (m.) English (Norman): of uncertain etymology. Norman given names are most often of Continental Germanic derivation, and this one is possibly ultimately from the Old Saxon word *drog* ghost, phantom, or perhaps from Old High German *tragan* to carry. However, the most plausible suggestion is that it was brought into Germanic from Slavonic, representing a short form of a name containing the element *dorogo* dear (see DROGOMIR). This particular name was revived in the Montagu family in the 19th century, when a fashion grew up for Norman, Old English, and Celtic names.

Drogomir (m.) Polish: from an old Slavonic personal name composed of the elements *dorogo* dear, beloved + *meri* great, famous (see CASIMIR).
Cognate: Czech: **Drahomír**.

Drusilla (f.) From a Late Latin name, a feminine diminutive of the old Roman family name *Dr(a)usus*, which was first taken by a certain Livius, who had killed in single combat a Gaul of this name and, according to a custom of the time, took his victim's name as a cognomen. Of the several women in the Roman imperial family who were called Livia Drusilla, the most notorious was Caligula's sister and mistress. The name is borne in the Bible by a Jewish woman, wife of the Roman citizen Felix, who was converted to Christianity by St Paul (Acts 24: 24). In England it was taken up as a given name in the 17th century as a result of the biblical mention.

Drystan (m.) Welsh and English: variant of TRISTRAM. Drystan son of Tallwch is fleetingly mentioned in the *Mabinogi* as one of the members of King Arthur's council of advisers.

Duald (m.) Irish: Anglicized form of the Gaelic name **Dubhaltach**, possibly meaning 'black-haired', 'black-jointed', or 'dark-limbed'. This name has also formerly been Anglicized as DUDLEY.

Duane (m.) Irish and English: Anglicized form of the Gaelic name **Dubhán**, originally a byname representing a diminutive form of Gaelic *dubh* dark, black. In modern use it may well represent the surname *Ó Dubháin* 'descendant of Dubhán', derived from the personal name. Its popularity since the mid-1950s was no doubt influenced by the fame of the guitarist and singer Duane Eddy.
Variants: **Dwane, Dwayne**.

Duarte (m.) Portuguese form of EDWARD.

Dubhdara (m.) Irish Gaelic: name composed of the elements *dubh* black + *dara* of oak. This is a common given name in Connemara; cf. DARA and MAC DARA. It was formerly often Anglicized as DUDLEY.

Dud (m.) English: short form of DUDLEY, in fairly common use (although not normally as an independent name) in spite of its coincidence in form with the modern slang term *dud* meaning 'useless'.

Dudley (m.) English: transferred use of the surname of a noble family, who came originally from Dudley in the West Midlands, named in Old English as the 'wood or clearing of Dudda'. Their most famous member was Robert Dudley, Earl of Leicester (?1532–88), who came closer than any other man to marrying Queen Elizabeth I. In America this given name is much less common than in England. In Ireland it was formerly used as an Anglicized form of DUBHDARA and DARA and of *Dubhaltach* (see DUALD).

Duff (m.) Scottish: short form of various Gaelic compound names containing the element *dubh* dark, black. In modern use it is in part a transferred use of the surname *Duff*, originally a nickname for a person with dark hair or a swarthy complexion.

Dugald (m.) Scottish: variant of DOUGAL. The final consonant is explained by the fact that the devoicing of the final *-ll* of the Gaelic form suggested to English ears that a *d* or *t* followed.

Duggie (m.) English: pet form of DOUG.

Duke (m.) English: in modern use this normally represents a coinage parallel to EARL and KING, but it is also a short form of MARMADUKE. It is especially popular in the United States.

Dulcie (f.) English: learned re-creation in the 19th century of the medieval name *Dowse*, *Duce* (forms that have given rise to surnames), from Late Latin *Dulcia*, a derivative of *dulcis* sweet. See also TOLTSE.

Dumitru (m.) Romanian form of DMITRI.

Duncan (m.) Scottish and English: Anglicized form of the Gaelic name **Donnchadh**, composed of Old Celtic elements meaning 'brown' and 'battle'. The name was borne by a 7th-century Scottish saint, abbot of Iona, and a 10th-century Irish saint, abbot of Clonmacnoise. The Anglicized form of the final syllable seems to be the result of confusion with the Gaelic element *ceann* head during Latinization into *Duncanus*. The oblique case *Donnchaidh* is possibly the origin of the English word *donkey* (cf. CUDDY).

Pet form: **Dunky**.

Dunstan (m.) English: from an Old English personal name composed of the elements *dun* dark + *stān* stone, borne most notably by a 10th-century saint who was archbishop of Canterbury. The name is now used mainly by Roman Catholics.

Dunya (f.) Russian: short form of *Avdunya*, itself a pet form of AVDOTYA.

Pet form (a further derivative): **Dunyasha**.

Dušan (m.) Czech: equivalent of the Russian name SPIRIDON, derived from the element *dusha* spirit, soul.

Feminine form: **Dušana**.

Pet forms: **Duša** (m., f.); **Duš(an)ek** (m.); **Duš(an)ka, Dušička** (f.).

Dustin (m.) English: transferred use of the surname, which is of uncertain origin, probably a Norman form of the Old Norse personal name *Þórsteinn*, composed of elements meaning 'Thor's stone'. It is now used fairly commonly as a given name, largely as a result of the fame of the film actor Dustin Hoffman (b. 1937), who is said to have been named in honour of the less well-known silent-film actor Dustin Farman.

Dusty (m., f.) English: apparently a pet form, or in some cases a feminine form, of DUSTIN. As a female name it was made popular in the 1960s by the singer Dusty Springfield.

Dvoire (f.) Jewish: Yiddish form of DEBORAH (Hebrew *Devorah*).

Variant: **Dvoyre**.

Pet form: **Dvosye**.

Dwane (m.) Irish and English: variant of DUANE.

Variant: **Dwayne**.

Dwight (m.) English: transferred use of the surname, which probably comes from the medieval English female name *Diot*, a pet form of *Dionysia* (see DENNIS). It is especially common in America, where its increase in popularity since the Second World War is mainly a result of the fame of the American general and president Dwight D. Eisenhower (1890–1969). He was apparently named in honour of the New England thinker Timothy Dwight (1752–1817) and his brother Theodore Dwight (1764–1846).

Dyan (f.) English: modern variant spelling of DIANE, especially popular in America.

Dylan (m.) Welsh: of uncertain origin, probably connected with a Celtic element meaning 'sea'. In the *Mabinogi* it is the name of the miraculously born son of Arianrhod, who became a minor divinity of the sea. In the second half of the 20th century the name has become fairly popular outside Wales as a result of the fame of the Welsh poet Dylan Thomas (1914–53) and the American singer Bob Dylan (b. 1941), who changed his surname from Zimmerman as a tribute to the poet.

Dymphna (f.) Irish: Anglicized form of the Gaelic name **Damhnait**, apparently a feminine diminutive form of *damh* fawn. Little is known of the saint of this name, who is regarded as the protector of the deranged and lunatic; her relics are preserved at Gheel, near Antwerp in Belgium.

Variant: **Dympna**.

E

Éabha (f.) Irish Gaelic form of *Eve*; see EVA.

Eachann (m.) Scottish Gaelic: name composed of the elements *each* horse + *donn* brown. It has often been Anglicized as HECTOR.

Éadaoin (f.) Irish Gaelic: modern form of the Old Irish name *Étáin*, borne in Irish mythology by a sun goddess. The name seems to be a derivative of Old Irish *ét* jealousy.

Eairdsidh (m.) Scottish Gaelic form of ARCHIE.

Variant: **Eairrsidh.**

Ealasaid (f.) Scottish Gaelic form of ELIZABETH.

Eamon (m.) Irish and English: from the Gaelic form of EDMUND. The normal Gaelic spelling is **Éamon** or **Éamonn.** Éamon de Valera (1882–1973) was president of Ireland 1959–73.

Cognate: Scottish Gaelic: **Eumann.**

Eanraig (m.) Scottish Gaelic form of HENRY.

Earl (m.) English (mainly U.S.): from the English aristocratic title, originally a nickname parallel to DUKE, KING, etc. The title was first used in England in the 12th century, as an equivalent to the French *comte* count; it is from Old English *eorl* warrior, nobleman, prince. In some cases the given name may have been taken from the surname *Earl*, which was given originally to someone who worked in the household of an earl.

Variants: **Earle, Erle.**

Eavan (f.) Irish: Anglicized form of Gaelic AOIBHEANN.

Ebba (f.) 1. German: probably from the various compound Germanic female names containing the first element *eber* wild boar, as for example *Ebergard* and *Eberhild*.

2. English: 19th-century revival of an Old English female name, a contracted form of *Eadburga*, composed of the elements *ēad* prosperity, riches, fortune + *burg* fortress. St Ebba the Elder (d. 638) was a sister of Oswald, King of Northumbria, who founded a Benedictine abbey at Coldingham in Berwickshire; St Ebba the Younger (d. *c.*870) was abbess there and was murdered by marauding Danes.

Ebbe (m.) 1. Scandinavian: pet form of ESBJÖRN.

2. German: pet form of EBERHARD.

Ebenezer (m.) English: originally the name (meaning 'stone of help' in Hebrew) of a place mentioned in the Bible, where the Israelites were defeated by the Philistines (1 Samuel 4: 1). When they took their revenge Samuel set up a memorial stone with this same name (1 Samuel 7: 12). It was taken up as a given name by the Puritans in the 17th century, possibly after being misread in the Bible as a personal name, or else because of its favourable etymological connotations. It now has unfavourable connotations because of the miserly character of Ebenezer Scrooge in Charles Dickens's *A Christmas Carol* (1843).

Eberhard (m.) German: from an old Germanic personal name, composed of the elements *eber* wild boar + *hard* hardy, brave, strong. St Eberhard of Salzburg (1085–1164) was a leading ecclesiastical figure of his day.

Cognate: Low German: **Evert.**

Pet form: German: **Ebbe.**

Ebony (f.) English: from the name of the deeply black wood (Late Latin *ebenius*, from Greek *ebenos*; the word seems to be ultimately of Egyptian origin). The name has been adopted very recently (since the 1970s) by Blacks as a symbol of pride in their colour. This was the third commonest name among Black females in the United States in 1982.

Eckehard (m.) German: from an old Germanic personal name composed of the elements *ek*, *eg* edge, point (of a sword) + *hard* hardy, brave, strong. The Blessed Ekhard (d. 1084) was canon of the cathedral of Magdeburg and first abbot of Huysberg.

Variant: **Eckhard(t)**.

Cognates: Low German: **Eggert**. Frisian: **Edzard**.

Ed (m.) English: short form of the various male names with the first syllable *Ed-*, especially EDWARD. See also TED.

Edan (m.) Scottish and Irish: variant of AIDAN. St Edan was an Irish disciple of St David of Wales who later became bishop of Ferns.

Edda (f.) Italian form of HEDDA.

Eddie (m.) English: pet form of ED, with the addition of the hypocoristic suffix *-ie*.

Edeltraud (f.) German: later form of ADELTRAUD.

Variant: **Edeltrud**.

Eden (m.) English: transferred use of the surname, itself derived in the Middle Ages from a given name *Edun* or *Edon*. This is of Old English origin, composed of the elements *ēad* prosperity, riches, fortune + *hūn* bear cub. Use as a modern given name has probably been encouraged by association with the biblical Garden of Eden, so named from Hebrew *'ēden* place of pleasure.

Edgar (m.) English (also used in France): from an Old English personal name composed of the elements *ēad* prosperity, riches, fortune + *gār* spear. This was the name of an English king and saint, Edgar the Peaceful (d. 975), and of Edgar Atheling (?1060–?1125), the young prince who was chosen to succeed Harold as king in 1066, but who was supplanted by the Normans.

Variant: French: **Edgard** (probably influenced in spelling by the more common ÉDOUARD).

Edith (f.) English (also occasionally used in France, Germany, and Scandinavia): from an Old English female personal name composed of the elements *ēad* prosperity, riches, fortune + *gȳð* strife. This was borne by a daughter (961–84) of Edgar the Peaceful, who was named in accordance with the common Old English practice of repeating name elements within a family. She spent her short life in a convent, and is regarded as a saint.

Variant: **Edythe**.

Cognate: Polish: **Edyta**.

Pet form: English: **Edie**.

Edmé (f.) Scottish: variant of ESMÉ, used as a female name. The reason for the change of *-s-* to *-d-* is not clear, but it may have been due to the influence of the coexisting given names ESMOND and (commoner) EDMUND. In spite of its accent, it is not found as a French name.

Variant: **Edmée**.

Edmund (m.) English (also used in Germany): from an Old English personal name composed of the elements *ēad* prosperity, riches, fortune + *mund* protector. It was borne by several early royal and saintly figures, including a 9th-century king of East Anglia killed by invading Danes, allegedly for his adherence to Christianity. This story earned him a cult that spread throughout Western and Central Europe.

Cognates: Irish: EAMON. Scottish Gaelic: **Eumann**. French, Dutch: **Edmond**. Italian: **Edmondo**. Spanish, Portuguese: **Edmundo**. Hungarian: **Ödön**.

Edna (f.) Irish and English: in Ireland an Anglicized form of EITHNE, and probably of this origin in England too. However, the name also occurs in the Bible, in the apocryphal Book of Tobit, where it is the name of the mother of Sarah and stepmother of Tobias. This is said to be from Hebrew *'ednah* rejuvenation, pleasure, or delight, and if so it is connected with the name of the Garden of EDEN. It does not occur in the Hebrew Bible or Old Testament, although the variants *ʿeden* and *ʿadnah* occur as male names. The earliest known uses of the given name in England are in the 18th century, when it was probably imported from Ireland, rather than taken from the Bible.

Edoardo (m.) Italian form of EDWARD.

Edom (m.) Biblical: byname of Esau, meaning 'red' in Hebrew. The name was given to him because he sold his birthright for a bowl of red lentil soup. It was frequently used in medieval Scotland, where it was taken to represent a variant of ADAM, and is occasionally bestowed in modern times by parents with Scottish connections.

Édouard (m.) French form of EDWARD.

Edsel (m.) In Germanic mythology this name is a variant of ETZEL. In modern times its most famous bearer was Edsel Ford, son of Henry Ford, founder of the Ford Motor Corporation. The family was partly of Dutch or Flemish descent, but the reason for the choice of given name is not known.

Eduard (m.) Czech form of EDWARD.

Eduardo (m.) Spanish form of EDWARD.

Edurne (f.) Basque equivalent of NIEVES.

Edvard (m.) Scandinavian and Czech form of EDWARD.

Edvige (f.) Italian form of HEDWIG.

Edward (m.) English (also Polish in this spelling): from an Old English personal name composed of the elements *ēad* prosperity, riches, fortune + *weard* guard. This has been one of the most successful of all Old English names, surviving from before the Conquest to the present day, and even being exported into other European languages. It was the name of three Anglo-Saxon kings and has been borne by eight kings of England since the Norman Conquest. It is also the name of the youngest son of Queen Elizabeth II. Undoubtedly the most influential bearer was King Edward the Confessor (?1002–66; ruled 1042–66). In a troubled period of English history, he contrived to rule fairly and (for a time at any rate) firmly. But in the latter part of his reign he paid more attention to his religion than to his kingdom. He died childless, and his death sparked off conflicting claims to his throne, which were resolved by the victory of William the Conqueror at the Battle of Hastings. His memory was honoured by Normans and English alike, for his fairness and his piety. Edward's mother was Norman; he had spent part of his youth in Normandy; and William claimed to have been nominated by Edward as his successor. Edward was canonized in the 12th century, and came to be venerated throughout Europe as a model of a Christian king.

Derivatives: Scottish Gaelic: **Eideard**; **Eudard** (a dialectal variant). French: **Édouard**. Italian: **Edoardo**. Spanish: **Eduardo**. Portuguese: **Duarte**. German: **Eduard** (influenced by the French form). Scandinavian: **Edvard**. Finnish: **Eetu**. Czech: **Eduard**, **Edvard**. Russian: **Edvard**.

Short forms: English: **Ed**, **Ned**, **Ted**.

Pet form: English: **Eddie**.

Edwige (f.) French form of HEDWIG.

Edwin (m.) English: 19th-century revival of an Old English personal name composed of the elements *ēad* prosperity, riches, fortune + *wine* friend. It was borne by a 7th-century king of Northumbria, who was converted to Christianity by St Paulinus and was killed in battle against pagan forces, a combination of circumstances which led to his being venerated as a martyr.

Edwina (f.) English: 19th-century coinage, representing a Latinate feminine form of EDWIN or, in at least one case, of EDWARD. Edwina Ashley, a descendant of Lord Shaftesbury who became the wife of Earl Mountbatten, was so named in honour of Edward VII; the king had originally wished her to be called *Edwardina*.

Edyta (f.) Polish form of EDITH.

Edythe (f.) English: fanciful respelling of EDITH, popular in the United States during the early part of the 20th century.

Edzard (m.) Frisian form of ECKEHARD.

Eero (m.) Finnish form of ERIC; see also ERKKI.

Eetu (m.) Finnish form of EDWARD.

Effemy (f.) English and Scottish: older vernacular form of EUPHEMIA.

Effi (f.) German: pet form derived from an assimilated version of **Elfriede**, the German form of ELFREDA.

Effie (f., m.) 1. (f.) English: pet form of EUPHEMIA, now as rarely used as the full form, but popular in the 19th century.

2. (f.) Scottish: Anglicized form of the Gaelic name OIGHRIG.

3. (m.) Jewish: pet form of EPHRAIM.

Efisio (m.) Italian: typically Sardinian name, borne in honour of a martyr allegedly put to death at Cagliari under the Emperor Diocletian in 303. He is greatly venerated on the island and every 1 May a large festival commemorates his intervention in the plague of 1625; nevertheless, there is no mention of him in any sources before the 15th century. The name is from Latin *Ephesius*, originally a local name from the Greek city of Ephesus, where there was a famous temple of Diana in antiquity.

Efraín (m.) Spanish form of EPHRAIM, used mainly in Latin America.

Efric (f.) Scottish: Anglicized form of the Gaelic name OIGHRIG; see also AFRICA.

Egan (m.) Irish: Anglicized form of the Gaelic name **Aogán**, earlier *Aodhagán*, a double diminutive of AODH.

Cognate: Scottish: **Iagan**.

Egbert (m.) English: from an Old English personal name composed of the elements *ecg* edge (of a sword) + *beorht* bright, famous. It was borne by two English saints of the 8th century and by a 9th-century king of Wessex. It survived for a while after the Conquest, but fell out of use by the 14th century. It was briefly revived in the 19th century, but is now again completely out of fashion.

Eggert (m.) Low German form of ECKEHARD.

Egidio (m.) Italian form of GILES.

Egidiusz (m.) Polish: learned form of IDZI, the Polish vernacular form of GILES.

Egil (m.) Scandinavian: from the Old Norse personal name *Egill*, in origin a diminutive of the element *ag*, *eg* edge, point (cf. e.g. EILERT).

Eglantine (f.) English: flower name, used as a nickname by Chaucer, and occasionally as a given name in the 19th century, but not at present in use. It is from an alternative name for the sweetbrier, derived in the 14th century from Old French *aiglent*, ultimately a derivative of Latin *acus* needle, referring to the prickly stem of the plant.

Egon (m.) German: medieval name derived from the Germanic element *ek*, *eg* edge, point (of a sword), an element that is found for example in ECKEHARD. St Egon or Egino (d. 1122) was abbot of the monastery of Ulric and Afra in Augsburg.

Eguzki (f.) Basque equivalent of SOL.

Egyed (m.) Hungarian form of GILES.

Ehrenfried (m.) German: apparently a reworking of the old Germanic personal name *Arnfried*, composed of the elements *arn* eagle + *fred*, *frid* peace. The first element has been assimilated to modern German *Ehre* (combining form *Ehren-*) honour.

Ehud (m.) Jewish: name (probably meaning 'pleasant, sympathetic' in Hebrew) borne in the Bible by a left-handed Benjaminite, who saved the Israelites by stabbing the Moabite king Eglon (Judges 3: 15–26).

Éibhear (m.) Irish Gaelic: of unknown origin. According to legend, this was the name of the son of Míl, leader of the first Gaels to settle in Ireland.

Anglicized forms: HEBER, IVOR.

Eiddwen (f.) Welsh: modern coinage, apparently derived from the element *eidd-un* desirous, fond, with the addition of the common suffix of women's names *(g)wen*, feminine of *gwyn* white, fair, blessed, holy.

Eideard (m.) Scottish Gaelic form of EDWARD.

Eileen (f.) Irish and English: Anglicized form of the Gaelic name **Eibhlín** or *Aibhilín*, derived from Norman-French AVELINE. The combination *bh* is normally pronounced as *v*, but sometimes dropped, as reflected in the Anglicized spelling. This name became tremendously popular in the early part of the 20th century, but the reasons for this sudden rise in favour are not known.

Variant: **Aileen** (esp. Scottish).

Eilert (m.) Frisian and Scandinavian: from an old Germanic personal name composed of the elements *eg(il)* edge, point (of a sword) + *hard* hardy, brave, strong (cf. ECKEHARD). The name is now also quite commonly used in Scandinavia, where it was taken in the 17th century.

Eilidh (f.) Scottish Gaelic form of ELLIE, now normally Anglicized as HELEN.

Variant: **Ailie** (an Anglicized spelling).

Eilif (m.) Norwegian: from an Old Norse personal name composed of the elements *ei* always, ever or *einn* one, alone + *lífr* alive.

Variant: **Eiliv**.

Eilís (f.) Irish Gaelic form of ELIZABETH.

Einar (m.) Scandinavian: from an Old Norse personal name composed of the elements *einn* one, alone + *herr* army, warrior.

Einion (m.) Welsh: traditional name, originally a byname meaning 'anvil'.

Pet form: **Einwys**.

Eino (m.) German: medieval name derived from the Germanic element *eg(in)* edge, point (of a sword), and so a byform of EGON.

Einrí (m.) Irish Gaelic form of HENRY; see also ANRAÍ.

Eira (f.) Welsh: modern name, from the vocabulary word *eira* snow.

Eireen (f.) Irish and English: of recent origin, probably a respelling of IRENE under the influence of EILEEN.

Eiric (f.) Scottish Gaelic: variant of OIGHRIG; see also EITHRIG.

Eirik (m.) Norwegian form of ERIC.

Eirwen (f.) Welsh: modern name, composed of the elements *eira* snow + *(g)wen* feminine form of *gwyn* white, fair, blessed, holy.

Eistir (f.) Irish Gaelic form of ESTHER.

Eitan (m.) Jewish: modern Hebrew form of ETHAN.

Eithne (f.) Irish Gaelic: traditional name, apparently from the vocabulary word *eithne* kernel, which was used as a term of praise in old bardic poetry. The name has been Anglicized variously as EDNA, **Et(h)na**, and ENA. St Ethenia was a daughter of King Laoghaire and one of St Patrick's first converts, together with her sister Fidelmia (see FIDELMA).

Eithrig (f.) Scottish Gaelic: variant of OIGHRIG; see also EIRIC.

Eladio (m.) Spanish: from the Late Latin name *Helladius*, Late Greek *Helladios*, a derivative of *Hellas* (genitive *Hellados*) Greece. St Helladius of Toledo (d. 632) was a minister at the court of the Visigothic kings, who retired from public life to become a monk, and was eventually appointed archbishop of Toledo.

Elaine (f.) English: originally a version of HELEN, but now generally regarded as an independent name. The Greek and Latin forms of the name had a long vowel in the second syllable, which produced this form (as opposed to ELLEN) in Old French. In

Arthurian legend, Elaine is the name of one of the women who fell in love with Lancelot. The name occurs in this form in the 15th-century English *Morte D'Arthur* of Thomas Malory. In the 19th century it was popularized in one of Tennyson's *Idylls of the King* (1859). Most of the characters in Arthurian legend have names that are Celtic in origin, although subjected to heavy French influence, and it has therefore been suggested that *Elaine* may actually be derived from a Welsh element meaning 'hind' or 'fawn'.

Elda (f.) Italian: not in use before the 20th century. It seems to represent an altered form of HILDA.

Eldon (m.) English: transferred use of the surname, which originated in the Middle Ages as a local name from a place in Co. Durham, so called from the Old English male personal name *Ella* + Old English *dūn* hill.

Eleanor (f.) English: from an Old French respelling of the Old Provençal name *Alienor*, which has been taken as a derivative of HELEN, but is probably of Germanic derivation (with a first element *ali* other, foreign). The name was introduced to England by Eleanor of Aquitaine (1122–1204), who came from south-west France to be the wife of King Henry II. It was also borne by Eleanor of Provence, the wife of Henry III, and Eleanor of Castile, the wife of Edward I.

Variants: **Ellenor, Elinor**.

Cognates: Irish Gaelic: **Eileanóra**. French: **Eléonore**. Italian: **Eleonora**. German: **Eleonore**.

Pet forms: English: NELL, **Ellie**.

Eleazar (m.) Biblical: variant of ELIEZER. See also LAZARUS.

Elen (f.) Welsh: probably a Welsh form of HELEN. It is identical with the vocabulary word *elen* nymph, but was used in Welsh texts from an early period as the name of the mother of Constantine, finder of the True Cross.

Variant: **Elin**.

Elena (f.) Italian and Spanish form of HELEN.

Eleonora (f.) Italian form of ELEANOR, now sometimes also used in the English-speaking world.

Eleonore (f.) German form of ELEANOR.

Eléonore (f.) French form of ELEANOR.

Eleri (f.) Welsh: ancient name of uncertain origin. It was borne in the 5th century by a daughter of the semi-legendary chieftain Brychan. *Eleri* is also a Welsh river name; in this case it seems to derive from the element *alar* surfeit.

Elettra (f.) Italian: name of a heroine of classical mythology, in English *Electra*, who, with her brother Orestes, avenged the murder of her father Agamemnon by her stepfather Aegisthus and her mother Clytemnestra. The name is derived from the Greek vocabulary word *ēlektōr* brilliant.

Elfleda (f.) English: Latinized form of the Old English female personal name *Æðelflǣd*, composed of the elements *æðel* noble + *flǣd* beauty. It was revived briefly in the 19th century.

Elfreda (f.) English: 19th-century revival of a Latinized form of the Old English female personal name *Ælfþryð*, composed of the elements *ælf* elf, supernatural being + *þryð* strength. This form may also have absorbed the originally distinct *Æðelþryð* (see AUDREY).

Cognate: German: **Elfriede**.

Short forms: English: **Freda**. German: **Friede**.

Pet forms: German: **Effi, Elfi**.

Eli (m.) 1. Biblical: from a Hebrew word meaning 'height'. *Eli* was the name of the priest and judge who brought up the future prophet Samuel (1 Samuel 3). It was especially popular among Puritans in the 17th century.

2. Jewish: short form of any of numerous names containing the first element *'el* God, such as ELIEZER, ELIJAH, and *Elisha* (see ELISEO).

Éliane (f.) French: from Latin *Aeliāna*, feminine form of the Late Latin family name *Aeliānus*. This name seems to represent a hypercorrected form of *Ēliānus* or *Hēliānus*, from Greek *hēlios* sun. St Eliana was an early martyr of Amasea in Pontus.

Cognate: Italian, Spanish, Portuguese: **Eliana**.

Eliezer (m.) Biblical: name (meaning 'God helps' in Hebrew) borne by one of the sons of Aaron (Exodus 6: 23). In the Authorized Version the name is rendered as ELEAZAR.

Eligio (m.) Italian form of ELOY. This form is also used in Spain as a learned byform.

Elijah (m.) Biblical: name (meaning 'Yahweh is God') of an Israelite prophet whose exploits are recounted in the First and Second Book of Kings. Elijah's victory over the prophets of Baal on Mount Carmel played an important part in maintaining the Jewish monotheistic religion. This story, and the other stories in which he figures, including his conflicts with Ahab's queen, Jezebel, and his prophecies of doom, are among the most vivid in the Bible. For some reason it has not been much used as a given name by Christians, although it was among the names used by the early Puritan settlers in New England, and recently it has also been adopted among Black Muslims. See also ELIYAHU.

Elin (f.) Welsh: variant of ELEN.

Elinor (f.) English: variant spelling of ELEANOR.

Eliot (m.) English: variant spelling of ELLIOT.

Variant: **Eliott**.

Elisabet (f.) The usual Scandinavian form of ELIZABETH.

Elisabeth (f.) The spelling of ELIZABETH used in the Authorized Version of the New Testament, and in most modern European languages. This was the name of the mother of John the Baptist (Luke 1: 60). Etymologically, the name means 'God is my oath', and is therefore identical with *Elisheba*, name of the wife of Aaron, according to the genealogy at Exodus 6: 23. The final element seems to have been altered by association with Hebrew *shabbāth* sabbath.

Elisabetta (f.) Italian form of ELIZABETH.

Élise French: short form of ELISABETH. The name was introduced into the English-speaking world (where it is often written without the accent) in the late 19th century.

Eliseo (m.) Italian and Spanish: name of the biblical prophet normally known in English as *Elisha*, the successor of Elijah. The feast of St *Eliseus*, as he is known in Latin, is liturgically observed (on 14 June) by the Carmelite order of monks, and is also important in the Eastern Church. The Latin form of the name derives from the Greek *Elisaios*, used in the New Testament. The name is composed of the Hebrew elements *'el* God + *sha'* to help, save.

Cognate: Russian: **Yelisei**.

Eliyahu (m.) Jewish: Hebrew name meaning 'Jehovah is God', familiar in the English-speaking world in the form ELIJAH.

Pet form: Elye (Yiddish).

Eliza (f.) English: short form of ELIZABETH, first used in the 16th century. It became popular, sometimes as an independent name, in the 18th and 19th centuries. The name was used by George Bernard Shaw for the main female character, Eliza Dolittle, in his play *Pygmalion* (1913), which was the basis for the musical and film *My Fair Lady*.

Elizabeth (f.) The usual spelling of ELISABETH in English. It was first made popular by being borne by Queen Elizabeth I of England (1533–1603). In the 20th century it became extremely fashionable, partly because it was the name of Elizabeth Bowes-Lyon (b. 1900), who in 1936 became Queen Elizabeth as the wife of King George VI, and, even more influentially, it is the name of her daughter Queen Elizabeth II (b. 1926).

Variant: **Elisabeth.** See also ELSPETH and ISABEL.

Cognates: Irish Gaelic: **Eilís.** Scottish Gaelic: **Ealasaid.** French, German: **Elisabeth.** Italian: **Elisabetta.** Spanish: **Isabel.** Scandinavian: **Elisabet.** Polish: **Elżbieta.** Czech: **Alžběta.** Russian: **Yelizaveta.** Hungarian: **Erzsébet.**

Short forms: English: ELIZA, ELSA; **Liza, Lisa, Liz; Beth, Bet, Bess; Elspeth; Lisbet.** French: **Élise, Lise.** German: **Elsa, Else, Ilse;** LIESE. Scandinavian: **Elsa, Else; Lisa, Lise, Lis.** Polish: **Ela.**

Pet forms: English: **Elsie; Bessie, Bessy, Betty, Betsy; Tetty; Libby; Lizzie, Lizzy.** French: **Lisette.** German: **Lil(l)i; Elli.**

Elkan (m.) Jewish and English: shortened form of the Hebrew name *Elkanah* 'possessed by God', borne in the Bible by several people, including the father of the prophet Samuel (1 Samuel 1: 1).

Elke (f.) 1. Frisian and Dutch: pet form derived from a shortened version of ADELHEID.

2. Jewish: Yiddish name, apparently adopted as a feminine form of ELKAN. The variant **Elkie** is well known as the name of the singer Elkie Brooks.

Ella (f.) English: of Germanic origin, introduced to Britain by the Normans. The name was probably originally a short form of any of various compound names containing the element *ali* other, foreign (cf. ELEANOR and ELVIRA). It is now often taken to be a variant or pet form of ELLEN.

Ellar (m.) Scottish: Anglicized form of the Gaelic name **Eallair**, originally a byname **Ceallair**, referring to someone who was a butler or steward in a monastery (Latin *cellārius*, a derivative of *cella* storeroom, cellar). The initial *C-* was lost through the frequent use of the given name in association with the patronymic surname *Mac Ceallair*.

Ellen (f.) English: originally a variant of HELEN, although now no longer associated with that name. Initial *H-* tended to be added and dropped rather capriciously, leading to many doublets (cf. e.g. ESTHER and *Hester*; ÉLOISE and *Héloïse*).

Pet form: NELL.

Ellenor (f.) English: variant spelling of ELEANOR, the result of blending with ELLEN.

Elli (f.) German: pet form of ELISABETH.

Ellie (f.) English: pet form of any of the numerous female names beginning with the syllable *El-*, in particular ELEANOR.

Cognate: Scottish Gaelic: EILIDH (re-Anglicized as HELEN).

Elliot (m.) English: transferred use of the surname, which is itself derived from a medieval (Norman French) masculine given name. This was a diminutive of *Elie*, the Old French version of *Elias* (see ELLIS).

Variants: **Elliott, Eliot(t).**

Ellis (m.) English: transferred use of the surname, which is derived from *Elias*, the Greek version (used in the New Testament) of the name of the Old Testament prophet ELIJAH. In Wales it is now often taken as an Anglicized form of the Old Welsh name *Elisud*, which is really from *elus* kind, benevolent.

Elmer (m.) English: transferred use of the surname, which is itself derived from an Old English personal name composed of the elements *æðel* noble + *mǣr* famous. This has been used as a given name in America since the 19th century, in honour of the brothers Ebenezer and Jonathan Elmer, leading supporters of the American Revolution.

Elmo (m.) Italian (occasionally used also in the English-speaking world): in origin probably a Germanic name derived from *helm* helmet, protection, either as a byname or else as a short form of any of the various compound names with this first element, as for example HELMUT. Later, however, along with the variant *Ermo*, it came to be used as a pet form of ERASMUS.

Elodia (f.) Spanish: Latinized version of a Visigothic female personal name, composed of the elements *ali* other, foreign + *od* riches, wealth, prosperity. The name was borne by a 9th-century saint, martyred at Huesca together with her sister Nuncilo, at the behest of their Islamic stepfather.
Cognate: French: **Élodie**.

Elof (m.) Swedish: from an Old Norse personal name composed of the elements *ei* ever, always or *einn* one, alone + *lāfr* descendant, heir.
Variant: **Elov**.
Cognate: Danish: **Eluf**.
Pet form: Swedish: **Loffe**.

Eloi (m.) French and Portuguese form of ELOY.

Éloise (f.) French: probably of Germanic origin, although the elements of which it is composed have not been identified. Éloise or Héloïse was the name of the learned and beautiful wife (d. *c.*1164) of the French philosopher and theologian Peter Abelard (1079–1142), whom she married secretly. A misunderstanding with her uncle and guardian, the powerful and violent Canon Fulbert of Notre Dame led to Abelard being set upon, beaten up, and castrated. He became a monk, and Héloïse spent the rest of her days as abbess of a nunnery, but they continued to write to each other. The name has been occasionally revived in modern times in allusion to her fidelity and piety.
Cognate: English: **Eloise**.

Elov (m.) Swedish: variant of ELOF.

Eloy (m.) Spanish: from the Latin name *Eligius*, a derivative of *eligere* to choose, select. St Eligius (588–660) was a bishop of Noyon who evangelized the districts around Antwerp, Ghent, and Courtrai.
Variant: **Eligio**.
Cognates: French, Portuguese: **Eloi**. Italian: **Eligio**.

Elpidio (m.) Italian and Spanish: from the Late Latin name *Elpidius*, Greek *Elpidios*, a derivative of Greek *elpis* (genitive *elpidos*) hope. The name was borne by various early saints, particularly a 4th-century hermit who spent twenty-five years in a cave in Cappadocia. Relics believed to be his were preserved in the Middle Ages at the village of Sant'Elpidio in the marches of Ancona, and the name was most commonly used in that region.

Elroy (m.) English: variant of LEROY. The initial syllable seems to be the result of simple transposition of the first two letters; it may also have been influenced by the Spanish definite article *el* and by the associated name DELROY. This is now a popular name among Blacks.

Elsa (f.) English, German, and Swedish: shortened form of ELISABETH or ELIZABETH. The name was borne by the English-born film actress Elsa Lanchester (1902–86), whose original name was Elizabeth Sullivan. The name is now also associated with the lioness named Elsa featured in the book and film *Born Free*.

Elsdon (m.) English (mainly U.S.): transferred use of the surname, which originated in the Middle Ages as a local name from a place in Northumbria. The place-name is recorded in the 13th century in the forms *Eledene*, *Hellesden*, *Elisden*, and *Ellesden*; it seems to derive from the genitive case of the personal name *Elli* + Old English *denu* valley.

Else (f.) Danish form of ELSA, used also in Germany (particularly in the north of the country).

Elsie (f.) Scottish and English: simplified form of **Elspie**, a pet form of ELSPETH. This came to be used as an independent name, and in the early 20th century proved more popular than *Elspeth*.

Elspeth (f.) Scottish and English: contracted form of ELIZABETH.

Elton (m.) English: transferred use of the surname, which originated in the Middle

Ages as a local name from any of numerous places in England so called (mostly from the Old English masculine personal name *Ella* + Old English *tūn* enclosure, settlement). In England it is largely associated with the singer-songwriter Elton John; born Reginald Dwight, he took his adopted given name in honour of the saxophonist Elton Dean.

Eluf (m.) Danish form of ELOF.

Eluned (f.) Welsh: apparently a reformed version of earlier *Luned, Lunet. Lunete* is the form of the name used by the French writer Chrétien de Troyes; cf LYNETTE.

Elvira (f.) Spanish: of Germanic (Visigothic) origin, very common in the Middle Ages and still in use today. The original form and meaning of the elements of which it is composed are far from certain (probably *ali* other, foreign + *wēr* true). The name was not used in the English-speaking world until the 19th century, when it was made familiar as the name of the long-suffering wife of Don Juan, both in Mozart's opera *Don Giovanni* (1789) and Byron's satirical epic poem *Don Juan* (1819–24).

Elvis (m.) English (esp. U.S.): of obscure derivation, made famous by the American rock singer Elvis Presley (1935–77). It may be derived from the surname of an ancestor, or it may have been made up, but it was certainly not chosen for the singer in anticipation of a career in show business, for his father's name was Vernon Elvis Presley. A St Elvis, apparently an Irishman of the 6th century, is also known as *Elwyn, Elwin, Elian*, and *Allan*.

Elżbieta (f.) Polish form of ELIZABETH.

Emanuel (m.) Scandinavian form of EMMANUEL. This form of the name is also used in Germany, alongside *Emmanuel* and the commoner German form IMMANUEL.

Emanuele (m.) Italian form of EMMANUEL. The name is fairly common in Italy among Gentiles as well as Jews. It was introduced to the royal house of Savoy at the beginning of the 16th century, when a daughter of Manoel I of Portugal married Carlo II of Savoy; the name was given to their son.

Emeny (f.) English: medieval name of uncertain origin. It appears in various forms such as *Emonie* and *Imanie* and seems to be of Germanic origin. It was Latinized as ISMENE.

Emer (f.) Irish Gaelic: traditional name of uncertain derivation. This was the name of Cú Chulainn's beloved, a woman of many talents who was blessed with the gifts of beauty, voice, sweet speech, wisdom, needlework, and chastity. It has been revived as a given name in the 20th century.

Cognates: Scottish Gaelic: **Eamhair, Éimhear.**

Emerald (f.) English: from the name of the gemstone, representing a vernacular form of ESMERALDA.

Emerenzia (f.) Italian: from Latin *Emerentia*, a derivative of *ēmerēri* to earn, merit. The name was borne by a Roman martyr of uncertain date, who has become associated with the legend of St Agnes.

Emeterio (m.) Spanish: from Latin *Emeterius* or *Hemiterius*, a name of uncertain (probably Greek) origin. St Hemiterius was martyred together with a certain Chelidonius at Calahorra in Spain in the 4th century.

Cognate: Catalan: **Medir.**

Emidio (m.) Italian: of uncertain origin. The name is borne in honour of St *Emidius* or *Emygdius* (d. *c.*303), the patron saint of Ascoli Piceno. He is said to have come from a noble Gaulish family and to have been born at Trier.

Emil (m.) German and Scandinavian: from the Latin name *Aemilius* (see EMILY).

Cognates: French: **Émile.** Italian, Spanish, Portuguese: **Emilio.**

Émilie (f.) French form of EMILY. Without the accent this form of the name is also used in Germany.

Émilien (m.) French: from Latin *Aemiliānus*, a family name representing a derivative of *Aemilius* (see EMILY). This was made popular as a Christian name by various minor early saints.

Cognate: Catalan: **Millà**.

Emilio (m.) Italian, Spanish, and Portuguese form of EMIL.

Emily (f.) English: from a medieval form of the Latin name *Aemilia*, the feminine version of the old Roman family name *Aemilius* (probably from *aemulus* rival). It was not common in the Middle Ages, and when it was revived in the 19th century there was much confusion between the originally distinct AMELIA and the Latinate form of this name, *Emilia*.

Cognates: French: **Émilie**. German: **Emilie**.

Emlyn (m.) Welsh: of uncertain origin, possibly from Latin *Aemiliānus* (see ÉMILIEN). On the other hand, it may have a Celtic origin; there are Breton and Irish saints recorded as *Aemilianus*, which may be a Latinized form of a lost Celtic name.

Emma (f.) English: of Germanic origin, introduced to Britain by the Normans. It was the name of the mother of Edward the Confessor. It originated as a short form of the medieval versions of compound names such as ERMINTRUDE and IRMGARD, containing the element *erm*(*en*), *irm*(*en*) entire (cf. IRMA). It is now sometimes used as a pet form of EMILY, but this is etymologically unjustified.

Emmanuel (m.) Biblical: the name (meaning 'God is with us' in Hebrew) of the promised Messiah, as prophesied by Isaiah (7: 14; reported in Matthew 1: 23). The Authorized Version of the Bible uses the Hebrew form IMMANUEL in the Old Testament, *Emmanuel* in the New. Both forms have been used as given names in England. This has always been a comparatively rare name in the English-speaking world, whereas the Hispanic cognate *Manuel* is one of the commonest Spanish given names.

Derivatives: German: **Immanuel**. Scandinavian: **Emanuel**. Italian: **Emanuele**. Spanish: **Manuel**. Portuguese: **Manoel**. Basque: **Imanol**.

Pet forms: Jewish: **Man, Manny**.

Feminine form: Spanish: **Manuela**.

Emmarald (f.) English: variant of EMERALD, influenced by the given name EMMA.

Emmeline (f.) English: of Germanic origin, introduced to Britain by the Normans. Even in the Middle Ages it was not clear whether this name was a derivative of EMMA or of AMALIA (the spellings are very varied), and when it was revived in the 19th century there was further confusion with EMILY. A famous bearer was the suffragette Emmeline Pankhurst (1858–1928), mother of Christabel and Sylvia.

Emmet (m.) English: transferred use of the surname, which itself was derived in the Middle Ages from the female given name *Emmet*, a diminutive form of EMMA. It may sometimes be used by parents with Irish connections, in honour of the rebel Robert Emmet (1778–1803), who led a disastrous attempt at rebellion against the English.

Emmy (f.) English: pet form of EMMA, EMILY, and related names. It is occasionally used as an independent given name, especially in the United States and in combinations such as **Emmy Jane** and **Emmy Jo**.

Emrys (m.) Welsh form of AMBROSE. The name has been very commonly used in families of Welsh origin in the 20th century.

Emyr (m.) Welsh: originally a byname meaning 'ruler, king, lord'. The name was borne by a 6th-century Breton saint who settled in Cornwall.

Ena (f.) Irish and English: one of several Anglicized forms of the Gaelic name EITHNE. However, in the case of Queen Victoria's granddaughter Princess Ena

(Victoria Eugénie Julia Ena, 1887–1969) it had a different origin: it was apparently a misreading by the minister who baptized her of a handwritten note of the originally intended name EVA. In England, the name is currently out of fashion, and is remembered principally as that of the fearsome Ena Sharples in the television soap opera *Coronation Street*.

Encarnación (f.) Spanish: name commemorating the festival of the Incarnation (Spanish *encarnación*, from Late Latin *incarnātio*, a derivative of *caro* flesh), celebrated on Christmas Day.
Short form: **Encarna**.

Enda (m.) Irish: Anglicized form of the Gaelic name **Éanna**, a derivative of *éan* bird. This name was borne by the famous St Éanna of Aran, and it is still a popular given name in the west of Ireland.

Endre (m.) Hungarian form of ANDREW.

Enfys (f.) Welsh: modern name, taken from the vocabulary word meaning 'rainbow'.

Engelbert (m.) German: from an old Germanic personal name, composed of the ethnic term *Angil* Angle + the element *berht* bright, famous. St Engelbert (1186–1255) was an archbishop of Cologne, murdered by a hired assassin.

Engracia (f.) Spanish: from the Latin name *Encratis* or *Encratia*. This is derived from the Greek word *enkratēs* in control, temperate, moderate, but it has been influenced by Latin *grātia* grace. St Encratia (d. *c.*304) was martyred at Saragossa under Diocletian and is commemorated by the poet Prudentius.

Enid (f.) Welsh and English: Celtic name of extemely uncertain derivation, borne by a virtuous character in the Arthurian romances, the long-suffering wife of Geraint. The name was revived in the second half of the 19th century, and enjoyed a great vogue in England in the 1920s.

Ennio (m.) Italian: from Latin *Ennius*, a family name (of uncertain derivation) borne by the early Roman poet Quintus Ennius (239–161 BC).

Enoch (m.) Biblical: name (possibly meaning 'experienced' in Hebrew) of the son of Cain (Genesis 4: 16–22) and father of Methuselah (Genesis 5: 18–24). The latter is said to have lived for 365 years and the apocryphal 'Books of Enoch' are attributed to him.

Enola (f.) English: 20th-century coinage of uncertain derivation. One theory is that it originated as a reversal in spelling of the word *alone*, but this may be no more than coincidental.

Enos (m.) Biblical: name (meaning 'mankind' in Hebrew) borne by a son of Seth and grandson of Adam (Genesis 4: 26) who allegedly lived for nine hundred and five years. In Ireland this name has been used as an Anglicized form of the Gaelic name *Aonghus* (see ANGUS).

Enric (m.) Catalan form of HENRY.

Enrico (m.) Italian form of HENRY (see also AMERIGO and ARRIGO).

Enrique (m.) Spanish form of HENRY.
Pet form: **Quique**.

Enzo (m.) Italian: probably of Germanic origin, but of uncertain derivation. It may have been originally a byname from *ent* giant. Alternatively, it could have originated as a short form of given names such as LORENZO or *Vicenzo* (see VINCENT), or perhaps as an Italianized form of the German name HEINZ.

Eóghan (m.) Irish and Scottish Gaelic: name of great antiquity and disputed derivation. It has been suggested that it may be composed of Old Celtic elements meaning 'yew' and 'born', i.e. 'born of the yew'. It is Anglicized in Ireland as OWEN and EUGENE, in Scotland as EWAN, *Ewen*, *Euan*, EVAN, and sometimes HUGH.
Variant: Scottish Gaelic: **Eòghann**.

Eoin (m.) Gaelic form of JOHN, used especially to designate the saints of that name. It is also in secular use, especially in Ireland, but also in Scotland (**Eòin**), where it tends to be Anglicized as JONATHAN.

Ephraim (m.) Biblical: name of one of the sons of Joseph and of one of the tribes of Israel. The name probably means 'fruitful' in Hebrew; it is so explained in the Bible (Genesis 41: 52 'and the name of the second called he Ephraim: For God hath caused me to be fruitful in the land of my affliction'). Unlike many Old Testament names, this was not particularly popular with the Puritans, and was used more in the 18th and 19th centuries than the 17th. It is still a common Jewish given name.

Derivatives: Spanish: **Efraín**. Russian: **Yefrem**. Yiddish: **Evron, Froim**.

Pet form: Jewish: **Effie**.

Eppie (f.) English: pet form of EUPHEMIA, fairly common in Victorian times. This is the name of the orphan child adopted by the eponymous hero of George Eliot's novel *Silas Marner*; in this case it represents a pet form of HEPHZIBAH.

Erasmus (m.) English: Latinized form of Greek *Erasmos*, a derivative of *erān* to love. St Erasmus (d. 303) was a bishop of Formiae in Campania, martyred under Diocletian; he is numbered among the Fourteen Holy Helpers and is a patron of sailors. This is a fairly rare given name in the English-speaking world, and is borne mainly by Roman Catholics. It is sometimes bestowed in honour of the great Dutch humanist scholar and teacher Erasmus Rotterodamus (?1466–1536).

Ercole (m.) Italian form of HERCULES. The name is particularly common in the region of Emilia.

Erdmann (m.) German: altered form of HARTMANN. This form seems to have come into use during the 17th century, when the first element was associated with modern German *Erde* earth. The meaning 'earth-man' was seen to be an appropriate one for a Christian, since Adam was made by God from earth.

Erdmut (m.) German: altered form of HARTMUT, in use since the 17th century, although never common.

Variant: **Erdmuth**.

Erdmute (f.) German: feminine form of ERDMUT, for some reason rather more popular than the male name. In the 20th century, however, it too has fallen out of fashion.

Variant: **Erdmuthe**.

Erhard (m.) German: from an old Germanic personal name composed of the elements *ēra* honour, respect + *hard* hardy, brave, strong. It was borne by a 7th-century saint, allegedly of Irish origin, who served as a missionary bishop around the area of Regensburg in Bavaria.

Eric (m.) English: of Old Norse origin, composed of the elements *ei* ever, always or *einn* one, alone + *ríkr* ruler. It was introduced into Britain by Scandinavian settlers before the Conquest and was occasionally used during the Middle Ages and later. The surname *Herrick* derives from it. As a modern given name it was revived in the mid-19th century.

Cognates: German: **Erich**. Swedish: **Erik** (the most common male name given in Sweden in 1973); **Jerk(er)**. Norwegian: **Eirik**. Finnish: **Erkki, Eero**.

Erica (f.) English and Scottish: Latinate feminine form of ERIC, coined towards the end of the 18th century. It remains common in Gaelic Scotland as an Anglicized form of OIGHRIG (see also EIRIC and EITHRIG). It has no doubt also been reinforced by the fact that *erica* is the Latin word for 'heather'.

Cognate: German, Scandinavian: **Erika**.

Erin (f.) English and Irish: from Gaelic *Éirinn*, dative case of *Éire* Ireland. *Erin* has been used as a poetic name for Ireland for centuries, and in recent years this has become a very popular given name. It has enjoyed particular popularity in the United States, even among people with no Irish ancestry.

Erkki (m.) Finnish form of ERIC (see also EERO).

Erland (m.) Scandinavian: from an Old Norse personal name, originally a byname from the vocabulary word *örlendr* foreigner, stranger.

Variant: **Erlend**.

Erle (m.) English: variant spelling of EARL.

Erline (f.) English: apparently a feminine derivative of ERLE.

Ermanno (m.) Italian form of HERMANN. This is not one of the Germanic personal names that were in use in Italy in the Middle Ages; it seems to have been introduced from Germany relatively recently.

Ermenegildo (m.) Italian form and Spanish variant of HERMENEGILDO.

Ermentraud (f.) German form of ERMINTRUDE.

Variant: **Ermentrud**.

Ermete (m.) Italian: from Latin *Hermēs*, genitive *Hermētis*, the name of the Greek messenger god (of extremely uncertain derivation, perhaps taken from one of the languages of Asia Minor). In spite of its pagan connotations, the name was common among the early Christians and was borne by more than twenty saints of the early centuries AD, most of them rather minor figures. In modern use the name is mainly found in Tuscany and Emilia.

Ermine (f.) English: in origin perhaps a variant of HERMINE, but strongly influenced in popularity by association with the name of the fur (Old French *ermine*, medieval Latin *armēnius* (*mūs*) Armenian mouse).

Ermintrude (f.) English: of Germanic origin, introduced to Britain by the Normans. It is composed of the elements *erm*(*en*), *irm*(*en*) entire + *traut* beloved. The name did not survive long into the Middle Ages, but was occasionally revived in the 18th and 19th centuries. It is now completely out of fashion.

Cognates: German: **Erm(en)tr(a)ud**. See also IRMTRAUD.

Ern (m.) English: short form of ERNEST.

Pet form: **Ernie**.

Erna (f.) German: simplified form of *Ernesta* (see ERNEST).

Ernan (m.) Irish: Anglicized form of the Gaelic name **Earnán**, possibly a derivative of *iarn* iron. St Earnán is the patron saint of Tory Island.

Ernest (m.) English: of Germanic origin, derived from the Old High German vocabulary word *eornost* seriousness, battle (to the death). The name was introduced into England in the 18th century by followers of the Hanoverian Elector who became George I of England. A variant spelling **Earnest** has arisen from the modern English adjective *earnest*, which is only distantly connected with the name.

Cognates: Italian, Spanish, Portuguese: **Ernesto**. German: **Ernst**. Czech: **Arnošt**. Hungarian: **Ernő**.

Short form: English: **Ern**.

Pet form: English: **Ernie**.

Feminine forms: English: **Ernesta, Ernestine**. German: **Ernsta, Erna**.

Errol (m.) English (borne mainly by Blacks): from the Scottish surname, which derives from a placename. It has been made famous by the film actor Errol Flynn (1909–59), noted for his 'swashbuckling' roles. It is now very popular among Blacks, influenced by such figures as the jazz pianist Errol Garner (1923–77).

Errukiñe (f.) Basque equivalent of PIEDAD.

Erskine (m.) Scottish, Irish, and English: from the Scottish surname, which derives from the name of a place near Glasgow. The surname has also been taken to Ireland by Scottish settlers, and was first brought to public attention as a given name by the half-Irish writer and political activist Erskine Childers (1870–1922).

Erwin (m.) German: from an old Germanic personal name composed of the elements *ēra* honour, respect + *win* friend. During the Middle Ages it was most common in the Rhine region and was borne, for example, by the founder of Strasburg cathedral. In modern times it has been borne most notably by the Second World War field marshal Erwin Rommel (1891–1944). In the United States it is sometimes used as a variant of IRWIN and IRVING.

Erzsébet (f.) Hungarian form of ELIZABETH.

Esa (m.) Finnish form of ISAIAH.

Esau (m.) Biblical: name of the elder twin brother of Jacob, to whom he sold his birthright for a bite to eat when he came home tired and hungry from a hunt. The name seems to have meant 'hairy' in Hebrew (Genesis 25: 25 'and the first came out red, all over like an hairy garment; and they called his name Esau'). It is now rarely used as a given name in the English-speaking world.

Esbjörn (m.) Swedish: from an Old Norse personal name composed of the elements *áss* god, divinity + *björn* bear.

Cognates: Norwegian: **Esbjørn, Asbjørn.** Danish: **Esben, Esbern.**

Pet form: **Ebbe.**

Esdras (m.) Biblical: Greek form of the Hebrew name EZRA, used in the Douay Bible as the title of the Books of Ezra (1 Esdras) and Nehemiah (2 Esdras) and of two further books (3 and 4 Esdras) not included in the Protestant canon.

Eskarne (f.) Basque equivalent of MERCEDES.

Eskil (m.) Scandinavian: from an Old Norse personal name composed of the elements *áss* god, divinity + *ketill* sacrificial cauldron.

Variant: **Eskel.**

Esmé (m.) French: from the past participle of the verb *esmer* to love (Latin *aestimāre* to value, esteem). In French this verb was absorbed by *amer* (see AMY) in the modern French form *aimer*, but has survived in a different sense in English *aim* (originally 'estimate, reckon'). The name was introduced to Scotland in the 16th century, and is still occasionally used as a male given name in the English-speaking world, where it is often spelled without the accent; it is occasionally also used as a female name. See also EDMÉ.

Feminine form: French, English: **Esmée.**

Esmeralda (f.) English: from the Spanish vocabulary word *esmeralda* emerald. Its occasional modern use as a given name seems to date from Victor Hugo's *Notre Dame de Paris* (1831), in which it is the nickname of the gypsy girl loved by the hunchback Quasimodo; she was given the name because she wore an amulet containing an artificial emerald.

Variant: **Esmerelda.**

Esmond (m.) English: from an Old English personal name composed of the elements *ēast* grace, beauty + *mund* protection. This, or a Continental Germanic cognate, was adopted into Norman French but was not used as a given name between the 14th century and the late 19th century, when it was revived.

Esperanza (f.) Spanish: from the Late Latin name *Sperantia* 'hope' (a derivative of *sperans*, present participle of *sperāre* to hope, replacing the classical Latin noun *spēs*).

Esta (f.) English: Latinate respelling of ESTHER.

Estéban (m.) Spanish form of STEPHEN.

Estefanía (f.) Spanish form of STEPHANIE.

Estelle (f.) English: Old French name meaning 'star' (Latin STELLA), comparatively rarely used during the Middle Ages. It was revived in the 19th century, together with the Latinate form **Estella,** which was used by Dickens for the ward of Miss Havisham in *Great Expectations* (1861).

Ester (f.) Scandinavian and Eastern European form of ESTHER.

Estevão (m.) Portuguese form of STEPHEN.

Esteve (m.) Catalan form of STEPHEN.

Estève (m.) Provençal form of STEPHEN.

Esther (f.) Biblical: name borne in the Bible by a Jewish captive who became the wife of the Persian king Ahasuerus. According to the book of the Bible that bears her name, she managed, by her perception and persuasion, to save large numbers of the Jews from the evil machinations of the royal counsellor Haman. Her Hebrew name was *Hadassah* 'myrtle', and the form *Esther* is said to be a Persian translation of this, although others derive it from Persian *stara* star. It may also be a Hebrew form of the name of the Persian goddess *Ishtar*.

Cognates: Scandinavian and E. European: **Ester**. Hungarian: **Eszter**. Irish Gaelic: **Eistir**.

Estrella (f.) Spanish form of STELLA. The prothetic *E-* before the consonant cluster *-st-* is a regular feature of Spanish, and the intrusive *-r-* in this word is found also in Portuguese and some north Italian dialects.

Estrild (f.) English (rare): from an Old English or Continental Germanic female personal name composed of the divine name *Éastre* (a goddess of spring, whose name lies behind modern English *Easter*) + the element *hild* battle. According to a legend narrated by Geoffrey of Monmouth, *Estrildis* was the name of a German princess who was captured and brought to England. She so enchanted King Locrine that he left his wife Gwendolen for her: in revenge, Gwendolen had both Estrildis and her daughter Sabrina thrown into the River Severn and drowned.

Eszter (f.) Hungarian form of ESTHER.

Ethan (m.) Biblical: name (meaning 'firmness' or 'long-lived' in Hebrew) of an obscure figure, Ethan the Ezrahite, mentioned as a wise man whom Solomon surpassed in wisdom (1 Kings 4: 31). The name was sparingly used even among the Puritans, but became famous in the United States since it was borne by Ethan Allen (1738–89), leader of the 'Green Mountain Boys', a group of Vermont patriots who fought in the American Revolution. It has also been revived as a popular modern Hebrew given name and surname.

Variants: Jewish: **E(i)tan** (Hebrew).

Ethel (f.) English: 19th-century revival of an Old English or Continental Germanic short form of the various female personal names beginning with the Germanic element *ethel* noble, including *Ethelburga* 'noble fortress', ETHELDREDA, and *Ethelgiva* 'noble gift'. All of these are now very rare (and were never common), but *Ethel* itself enjoyed great popularity for a period at the beginning of the 20th century, although it is now out of fashion.

Etheldreda (f.) English: Latinized form of the Old English female personal name *Æðelþryð* (see AUDREY). It was taken up as a given name in the 19th century, but is now rare.

Ethna (f.) Irish: Anglicized form of EITHNE.

Étienne (m.) French form of STEPHEN.

Étiennette (f.) French: feminine form of ÉTIENNE, with the diminutive suffix *-ette*.

Etna (f.) Irish: Anglicized form of EITHNE.

Etta (f.) English and Scottish: short form of the various names ending in this element (originally an Italian feminine diminutive suffix), now sometimes used as an independent given name. In Gaelic Scotland it is used as a pet form of MAIREAD (Anglicized as *Mar(i)etta*).

Ettore (m.) Italian form of HECTOR, sometimes deliberately chosen as a non-saint's name by anti-clerical parents.

Etzel (m.) German: medieval name apparently derived from the element *adal* noble, or else from the nickname *Atta* 'father'.

Variant: EDSEL.

Euan (m.) Scottish: Anglicized form of Gaelic ÉOGHAN, currently much in fashion.

Eubh (f.) Scottish Gaelic form of *Eve*; see EVA.

Variant: **Eubha**.

Eudora (f.) English: ostensibly a Greek name, composed of the elements *eu* well, good + a derivative of *dōron* gift. However, there is no saint of this name, and it is more probably a modern combination of elements which are both common in other given names.

Eufemia (f.) Italian, Spanish, and Portuguese form of EUPHEMIA.

Eugene (m.) English: from the Old French form of the Greek name *Eugenios* (from *eugenēs* well-born, noble). This was the name of various early saints, notably a 5th-century bishop of Carthage, a 7th-century bishop of Toledo, and four popes. The popularity of the name in Russia is due to the cult of a 4th-century missionary bishop who preached in the Crimea and southern Russia. In Western Europe, the name owes its popularity at least in part to the fame of Prince Eugene of Savoy (1663–1736), a general in the service of Austria who co-operated with Marlborough in defeating the French forces of Louis XIV. He was noted not only for his brilliance as a commander, but also for his strong moral principles. In Ireland the name has been used as an Anglicized form of ÉOGHAN and AODH.

Cognates: French: **Eugène**. Italian, Spanish: **Eugenio**. Portuguese: **Eugênio**. German: **Eugen**. Polish: **Eugeniusz**. Czech: **Evžen**. Russian: **Yevgeni**. Hungarian: **Jenő**.

Short form: English (esp. U.S.): **Gene**.

Eugenia (f.) English, Italian, and Spanish: feminine form of Greek *Eugenios* or Latin *Eugenius*; see EUGENE.

Eugénie (f.) French form of EUGENIA. The name was introduced to England as the name of the Empress Eugénie (Eugenia María de Montijo de Guzmán, 1826–1920), wife of Napoleon III, and has since been occasionally used (sometimes without the accent) in the English-speaking world.

Eugenio (m.) Italian and Spanish form of EUGENE.

Eugênio (m.) Portuguese form of EUGENE.

Eugeniusz (m.) Polish form of EUGENE.

Eulalia (f.) English, Italian, and Spanish: from a Late Greek personal name composed of the elements *eu* well, good + *lalein* to talk, chatter. It was very common in the Middle Ages, when it was to a large extent confused with HILARY, but is now rare.

Cognates: French: **Eulalie**. Spanish: OLALLA.

Eumann (m.) Scottish Gaelic form of EDMUND (cf. EAMON).

Euna (f.) Scottish: Anglicized form of the Gaelic name *Ùna* (see ÚNA).

Eunan (m.) Irish and Scottish: Anglicized form of the Gaelic name **Ádhamhnán**. This is possibly a diminutive form of *Ádhamh*, the Gaelic version of ADAM, but is now thought more likely to represent a diminutive form of *adomnae* great fear, hence 'Little Horror'. The name was borne by a 7th-century saint, abbot of Iona and biographer of St Columba.

Eunice (f.) English: from a Late Greek name composed of the elements *eu* well, good + *nikē* victory. It is mentioned in the New Testament as the name of the mother of Timothy, who introduced him to Christianity (2 Timothy 1: 5). This reference led to the name being taken up by the Puritans in the 17th century.

Euphemia (f.) Latin form of a Late Greek name composed of the elements *eu* well, good + *phēmi* I speak. This is the name of various early saints, most notably a virgin martyr supposedly burnt at the stake at Chalcedon in 307. It was particularly popular in England in the Victorian period, especially in the pet form EFFIE. See also OIGHRIG.

Derivatives: French: **Euphémie**. Italian, Spanish, Portuguese: **Eufemia**.

Pet forms: English: **Effie, Eppie**.

Masculine form: Russian: **Yefim**.

Eusebio (m.) Spanish, Portuguese, and Italian: from the Late Greek name *Eusebios*, derived from the adjective *eusebēs* respectful, pious (from *eu* well, good + *sebein* to worship, honour). This name was borne by a large number of early saints, including a friend of St Jerome traditionally regarded as the founder of the abbey of Guadalupe in Spain, and a 4th-century bishop of Bologna.

Eustace (m.) English: from the Old French form of the Late Greek names *Eustakhios* and *Eustathios*. These were evidently of separate origin, the former composed of the elements *eu* well, good + *stakhys* grapes, the latter of *eu* + *stēnai* to stand. However, the tradition is very confused. The name was introduced in this form to Britain by the Normans, among whom it was popular as a result of the fame of St Eustace, who was said to have been converted to Christianity by the vision of a crucifix between the antlers of the stag he was hunting. It is at present out of fashion.

Cognates: French: **Eustache**. Italian: **Eustachio**. Spanish: **Eustaquio**.

Eutropio (m.) Spanish: from the Late Greek name *Eutropios*, composed of the elements *eu* well, good + *tropos* way, manner, i.e. 'well-mannered'. Alternatively, it may derive from the classical Greek adjective *eutropos* versatile, in which the second element derives from the root of the verb *trepein* to turn. The name was borne by various minor early saints.

Cognate: French: **Eutrope** (not common).

Eva (f.) Latinate form of EVE, used commonly in English, Italian, Spanish, Portuguese, and Scandinavian languages among others. In Ireland it has sometimes been used as an Anglicized form of AOIFE.

Variants: Polish: **Ewa**. Irish Gaelic: **Éabha**. Scottish Gaelic: **Eubh, Eubha**.

Pet forms: Spanish: **Evita**. Czech: **Evka, Evuška, Evulka, Evinka, Evička**.

Evadne (f.) English: from a Greek personal name composed of the element *eu* well, good + another element that is of uncertain meaning. It was borne by a minor figure in classical legend who threw herself on to the funeral pyre of her husband, and was regarded as an example of wifely piety. The modern spelling and pronunciation is the result of transmission through Latin sources. The name has never been common, and is now completely out of fashion. It is associated with the character of Dr Evadne Hinge in the British comedy television series *Hinge and Bracket*.

Evan (m.) 1. Welsh: Anglicized form of *Iefan*, a later development of IEUAN.

2. Scottish: Anglicized form of EÒGHAN.

Variant (of 1): **Ifan**.

Evander (m.) Scottish (Highland): classical name used as an Anglicized form of Scottish Gaelic *Ìomhair* (see IVOR). This form is peculiar to the MacIver family, apparently coined to differentiate it from the surname. In classical legend, *Evander* is the name of an Arcadian hero who founded a city in Italy where Rome was later built. It is a Latin form of Greek *Euandros*, composed of the elements *eu* well, good + *anēr* man (genitive *andros*).

Evangeline (f.) English: fanciful name derived from Latin *evangelium* gospel (Greek *euangelion*, from *eu* well, good + *angelma* tidings) + the suffix (in origin a French feminine diminutive) *-ine*. *Evangeline* is the title of a narrative poem (1848) by the American poet Henry Wadsworth Longfellow, in which the central character is called Evangeline Bellefontaine.

Evaristo (m.) Italian, Spanish, and Portuguese: from the Late Greek personal name *Euarestos*, derived from the elements *eu* well, good + *areskein* to please, satisfy. The second element has been respelled as if from Greek *aristos* best, excellent. This name was borne by an early pope, said to have been martyred under the Roman emperor Hadrian in about 107.

Cognate: French: **Évariste**.

Eve (f.) English and French form of the name borne in the Bible by the first woman, created from one of Adam's ribs (Genesis 2: 22). It derives, via Latin *Ēva*, from Hebrew *Havva*, which is considered to be a variant of the vocabulary word *hayya* living or animal (see CHAYA). Adam gave names to all the animals (Genesis 2: 19–20) and then to his wife, who was 'the mother of all living' (Genesis 3: 20).

Variant: EVA.

Pet form: **Evie**.

Evelina (f.) English and Irish: apparently a Latinate form of the female name EVELYN, or perhaps a combination of EVE with the suffix *-lina*.

Evelyn (m., f.) English: modern use of this as both a female and a male given name seems to derive from an English surname, which is in turn derived from a Norman female name (see AVELINE).

Variants: **Evelyne, Eveline**.

Everard (m.) English: from an Old English personal name composed of the elements *eofor* boar + *heard* hardy, brave, strong. This was reinforced at the time of the Conquest by a Continental Germanic cognate (see EBERHARD) introduced by the Normans. In modern use this may be a transferred use of the surname, but it was in regular use in the Digby family of Rutland from the 15th to the 17th century, probably as a survival of the Old English or Norman name. It alternated in this family with KENELM.

Cognate: French: **Evrard**.

Everett (m.) English: transferred use of the surname, a variant of EVERARD.

Evert (m.) Low German form of EBERHARD.

Evette (f.) English and French: altered form of YVETTE, influenced by the given name EVE.

Evie (f.) English: pet form of EVE or EVA, occasionally also of EVELYN as a female name.

Evita (f.) Spanish: pet form of EVA. This was the name by which Eva Duarte de Perón (1919–52), wife of the Argentinian dictator Juan Domingo Perón, was affectionately known. Its popularity in the English-speaking world has recently been increased by the musical based on her life.

Evonne (f.) English: altered form of YVONNE, influenced by the given name EVE.

Evrard (m.) French: contracted form of EVERARD.

Evron (m.) Jewish: Yiddish form of EPHRAIM.

Evžen (m.) Czech form of EUGENE.

Feminine form: **Evženie**.

Pet forms: **Evža** (m., f.); **Evženek, Evžík** (m.); **Evženka, Evžička** (f.).

Ewa (f.) Polish form of EVE.

Pet forms: **Ewka, Ewusia**.

Ewald (m.) German: from an old Germanic personal name composed of the elements *ēo* law, right + *wald* rule. This name was borne in the 7th century by a pair of brothers, apparently originally from Northumbria, who evangelized north Germany and Frisia. In order to distinguish them they were known as 'Ewald the Fair' and 'Ewald the Dark'.

Cognate: Dutch: **Ewould**.

Ewan (m.) The usual Anglicized form in Scotland of Gaelic EÓGHAN, also used occasionally in Ireland and elsewhere.

Variant: **Ewen**.

Ewart (m.) Scottish and English: transferred use of the surname, probably first used as a given name in honour of the Victorian statesman William Ewart Gladstone (1809–98). The surname has several possible origins: it may represent a Norman form of EDWARD, or an occupational name for a ewe-herd, or a local name from a place in Northumbria.

Ewould (m.) Dutch form of EWALD.

Eydl (f.) Jewish: Yiddish name, originally an affectionate nickname meaning 'noble' (Yiddish *eydl*, cf. modern German *edel*).

Variant: **Eyde** (a back-formation based on the belief that *Eydl* was a pet form with the hypocoristic suffix -*(e)l*).

Eyolf (m.) Norwegian: of Old Norse origin, composed of the Protoscandinavian elements *anja* luck, gift + *(w)olf*. It was brought to the attention of the public by Henrik Ibsen's play *Little Eyolf* (1894), and has been in occasional use ever since.

Ezekiel (m.) Biblical: name (meaning 'God strengthens' in Hebrew) borne by one of the major prophets. The book of the Bible that bears his name is probably best known for its vision of a field of dry bones, which Ezekiel prophesies will live again (chapter 37). His prophecies were addressed to the Jews in Babylonian exile, after Nebuchadnezzar had seized Jerusalem in 597 BC.

Derivatives: Yiddish: **Heskel**; **Haskel** (U.S.).
Short form: English: **Zeke**.

Ezio (m.) Italian: from the Late Latin personal name *Aetius*. This represents a conflation of two originally distinct names: *Aetius*, an old Roman family name of apparently Etruscan origin and unknown meaning, and *Aëtios*, a Late Greek name derived from Greek *a(i)etos* eagle. The name has been popular in Italy since Verdi's opera *Attila* (1846), in which Ezio (the historical character Flavius Aëtius, general of the Emperor Valentinian in his campaign against the Huns) was seen as a prototype Italian revolutionary hero.

Ezra (m.) Biblical: name (meaning 'help' in Hebrew) of a prophet, author of the book of the Bible that bears his name. It was taken up by the Puritans in the 17th century, and has remained in occasional use ever since, especially in America, where it was borne, for example, by the poet Ezra Pound (1885–1972).

Variant: ESDRAS.

Ezzo (m.) Italian: of uncertain derivation. It seems to be of Germanic origin, and may be derived from the element *adal* noble or the rarer *atta* father (cf. ETZEL).

F

Faas (m.) Dutch and Flemish: from the old Germanic personal name *Fastred*, composed of the elements *fast* firm, resolute + *red* counsel. The Blessed Fastred of Cavamiez (d. 1163) was born in Hainault; he was a disciple of Bernard of Clairvaux.

Fabia (f.) Latin feminine form of the old Roman family name *Fabius* (see FABIO).

Fabian (m.) English and Polish form of the Late Latin name *Fabiānus*, a derivative of the family name *Fabius* (see FABIO). It was borne by an early pope (236–50), who was martyred under the Emperor Decius. The name was introduced into Britain by the Normans, but it has never been much used in the English-speaking world.

Cognates: French: **Fabien**. Italian: **Fabiano**. Spanish: **Fabián**. Portuguese: **Fabião**.

Feminine form: French: **Fabienne**.

Fabio (m.) Italian, Spanish, and Portuguese: from the old Roman family name *Fabius*, said to be a derivative of *faba* bean. Members of this family were prominent in republican Rome. The most famous of them was Quintus Fabius Maximus (d. 203 BC), the Roman general who harassed the invader Hannibal but never joined battle, giving his name to the phrase 'Fabian tactics', implying a policy of gradual attrition as opposed to full-scale confrontation. The name was also used among the early Christians: St Fabius (d. 300) was a Roman soldier beheaded at Caesarea in Mauretania under the Emperor Diocletian.

Fabiola (f.) Late Latin feminine diminutive form of *Fabius* (see FABIO). St Fabiola (d. *c.*400) was a Roman widow who founded the first Western hospital, originally a hostel to accommodate the flood of pilgrims who flocked to Rome, but in which she tended the sick as well as accommodating the healthy.

Fabrice (m.) French: from the old Roman family name *Fabricius*, probably a derivative of *faber* craftsman, smith. There are no saints of this name, but it is permitted as a given name by the Catholic Church in honour of the Roman republican general and statesman Caius Fabricius Luscinus (d. 250 BC), who was noted not only for his skill as a military commander and negotiator of peace treaties, but also for the great simplicity of his lifestyle and for his refusal to take bribes.

Cognates: Italian: **Fabrizio**. Spanish: **Fabricio**.

Short form: Italian: BRIZIO.

Fachtna (m.) Irish Gaelic: traditional name of uncertain origin, possibly meaning 'malicious, hostile'. It has sometimes been Latinized as FESTUS.

Faddei (m.) Russian form of THADDEUS.

Fae (f.) English: variant spelling of FAY.

Faith (f.) English: from the abstract noun denoting the quality of believing and trusting in God. The name began to be used in the 16th century, and was very popular among the Puritans of the 17th.

Faivish (m.) Jewish (Yiddish): probably from Greek *Phoibos*, an epithet of the sun god Apollo. It is said to have been adopted as a learned translation equivalent of Hebrew *Shimshon* (see SAMSON), but it is more likely derived directly from the Greek. The Greeks often named captured slaves after gods, and it would thus have been likely for Jews to come to have this name. It was often paired with the Aramaic name SHRAGA meaning 'fire, lantern' as *Shraga Faivish*, since it was important for Jewish men to be called by a

Hebrew or Aramaic name in certain religious rites.

Pet forms: **Fayvel, Feivel.**

Falibóg (m.) Polish: variant of CHWALIBÓG.

Falk (m.) Jewish: from the Yiddish vocabulary word *falk* falcon (modern German *Falke*). It is sometimes taken as a translation of the Hebrew given name *Yehoshua* (see JOSHUA); there have been many famous rabbis named Joshua Falk. The association between the main Hebrew personal names and various animals is traditional in Jewish culture, and is usually to be explained on the basis of some biblical reference. In this case, however, the connection is far from clear; it has been suggested that Joshua circled the Land of Canaan like a bird of prey before swooping down on it triumphantly.

Fanchon (f.) French: pet form of *Françoise* (see FRANÇOIS).

Fania (f.) Italian: short form of STEFANIA.

Fanny (f.) English: pet form of FRANCES, sometimes used as an independent name in its own right. It was very popular in the 19th century, but is now rarely found, no doubt due to the vulgar sense of the vocabulary word that has been derived from it in the 20th century.

Fardoragh (m.) Irish: Anglicized form of FEARDORCHA.

Farkas (m.) Jewish: name meaning 'wolf' in Hungarian, borne among Hungarian Jews as a translated form of Yiddish VOLF.

Farquhar (m.) Scottish: Anglicized form of the Gaelic name **Fearchar**, composed of Old Celtic elements meaning 'man' + 'dear'.

Farry (m.) Irish: Anglicized form of the Gaelic name FEARADHACH.

Fatima (f.) Usually a Muslim name, given in honour of Muhammad's daughter. However, it is occasionally borne by Roman Catholics in honour of 'Our Lady of Fatima', who in 1917 appeared to three shepherd children from the village of Fatima, near Leiria in western Portugal.

Fay (f.) English: late 19th century coinage, from the archaic word *fay* fairy. It was to some extent influenced by the revival of interest in Arthurian legend, in which Morgan le Fay is King Arthur's half-sister, a mysterious sorceress who both attempts to destroy Arthur and tends his wounds in Avalon after his last battle. She is sometimes identified with the 'Lady of the Lake'.

Variants: **Faye, Fae.**

Fayge (f.) Jewish (Yiddish): variant of FEIGE.

Fayvel (m.) Jewish (Yiddish): variant of FEIVEL.

Fearadhach (m.) Irish Gaelic: from a vocabulary word meaning 'manly' or 'masculine', a derivative of *fear* man.

Anglicized forms: **Farry**; FERDINAND, **Ferdie.**

Feardorcha (m.) Irish Gaelic: name composed of the elements *fear* man + *dorcha* dark.

Anglicized forms: **Fardoragh**, FERDINAND, FREDERICK.

Fearghal (m.) Irish Gaelic: name Anglicized as FERGAL.

Fearghas (m.) Scottish and Irish Gaelic: name Anglicized as FERGUS.

Fedele (m.) Italian form of FIDEL.

Fedelma (f.) Irish: variant of FIDELMA.

Federico (m.) Italian and Spanish form of FREDERICK. This Germanic name was introduced to Sicily by the Normans, where it was borne by, amongst others, the son of the Norman queen Constance and the German emperor Henry VI. At the age of three, in 1197, Federico became King of Sicily; he later went on to become King of the Germans and Holy Roman Emperor. He was a patron of the arts and sciences, and in 1224 founded the University of Naples.

Fedosi (m.) Russian form of TEODOSIO.

Variant: **Feodosi**.

Fedot (m.) Russian: from Greek *Theodotos*, composed of the elements *theos* God + *dotos* given. This name, like the related *Theodoros* and *Theodosius*, was popular among early Christians because of its auspicious sense, and was borne by several saints of the first century AD. The most famous (d. 304) was an innkeeper in Ancyra who was executed under Diocletian for having given Christian burial to the seven virgin martyrs Thecusa, Alexandra, Claudia, Phaina, Euphrasia, Matrona, and Julitta.

Fedya (m.) Russian: pet form of FYODOR and of the rarer FEDOSI and FEDOT.

Feel (m.) Dutch form of FELIX.

Feichín (m.) Irish Gaelic: originally a byname representing a diminutive of Gaelic *fiach* raven. It has sometimes been Latinized as FESTUS.

Feige (f.) Jewish: from Yiddish **Feygl** 'bird' (modern German *Vogel*; cf. ZIPPORAH). The present form of the name was arrived at by back-formation, the final *-l* having been interpreted as a Yiddish hypocoristic suffix rather than an integral part of the word.

Variant: **Fayge**.

Feivel (m.) Jewish (Yiddish): pet form of FAIVISH.

Variant: **Fayvel**.

Felice (m.) Italian form of FELIX.

Felicia (f.) Latinate feminine form of FELIX, of medieval origin.

Derivatives: German: **Felicie**. Hungarian: **Felícia, Lícia**.

Feliciano (m.) Italian, Spanish, and Portuguese: from the Latin personal name *Feliciānus*, a derivative of *Felicius*, itself a derivative of FELIX. The main saint of this name was a 3rd-century bishop of Foligno in Umbria.

Felicity (f.) English: from the abstract noun denoting luck or good fortune (via Old French from Latin *felicitās*; cf. FELIX). The English vocabulary word was first used as a given name in the 17th century. It also represents the English form of the Late Latin personal name *Felicitas*, which was borne by several early saints, notably a slave who was martyred in 203 together with her mistress Perpetua and several other companions.

Cognates: Italian: **Felìcita**. Spanish: **Felicidad**. Portuguese: **Felicidade**.

Pet form: English: **Flick**.

Felip (m.) Catalan form of PHILIP.

Felipe (m.) Spanish form of PHILIP.

Felix (m.) Latin name meaning 'lucky', which has from time to time been popular as a given name in Britain and elsewhere because of its auspicious omen. It was in use as a byname in Latin, being applied for example to the dictator Sulla (138–78 BC). It was very popular among the early Christians, being borne by a large number of early saints.

Derivatives: French: **Félix**. Italian: **Felice**. Dutch: **Feel**. See also SZCZĘSNY.

Fenella (f.) Scottish: Anglicized form of Gaelic **Fionnuala.**

Variants: **Finella, Finola, Fionola**. See also NUALA.

Fenton (m.) English: transferred use of the surname, originally a local name from any of the various places (for example, in Cumbria, Lincs., Northumbria, Notts., Staffs., and W. Yorks.) so called from Old English *fenn* marsh, fen + *tūn* enclosure, settlement.

Feodora (f.) Russian form of THEODORA.

Feodosi (m.) Russian: variant of FEDOSI.

Feofil (m.) Russian form of THEOPHILUS.

Feoras (m.) Irish Gaelic form of PIERS.

Ferapont (m.) Russian: from the Greek name *Therapōn* (genitive *Therapontos*) meaning 'attendant, servant', and hence, among the early Christians, 'worshipper'.

Ferdie (m.) 1. English: pet form of FERDINAND.

2. Irish: Anglicized form of the Gaelic name FEARADHACH.

Ferdinand (m.) English, German, and French: from a Spanish name, originally *Ferdinando*, which is of Germanic (Visigothic) origin, being composed of the elements *farð* journey (or possibly a metathesized form of *frið* peace) and *nand* ready, prepared. The name was hereditary in the royal families of Spain from an early date. It was borne, for example, by Ferdinand I (d. 1065) of Castile and Leon, sometimes called Ferdinand the Great, who conducted successful campaigns against the Moors, and by his descendant Ferdinand V (1452–1516), who finally expelled the Moors from Spain altogether. Ferdinand V was the king who gave financial backing to Columbus. Through the marriage in 1496 of his daughter Joan the Mad of Castile to the Habsburg Archduke Philip, the name Ferdinand also became hereditary in the Austrian imperial family. Their younger son was called Ferdinand; he lived from 1503–64, acquiring the succession to the kingdoms of Hungary and Bohemia by marriage in 1521, and becoming Holy Roman Emperor in 1558. Thus the name Ferdinand is intimately associated, not only with the history of Spain, but also with the origins of the Austro-Hungarian Empire.

The Old French contracted form *Ferrand* was sometimes used in England in the Middle Ages, but has not survived. The current form appeared in Britain in the 16th century, probably introduced by Roman Catholic supporters of Queen Mary I, who married Philip II of Spain in 1554.

In Ireland it has been used as an Anglicized form of the Gaelic names FEARADHACH and FEARDORCHA.

Variant: French: **Fernand**.

Cognates: Spanish: **Fernando**, **Hernando**; **Fernán**, **Hernán**. Portuguese: **Fernando**, **Fernão**, **Ferrão**. Italian: **Ferdinando**. Romanian: **Nandru**. Hungarian: **Nándor**.

Ferenc (m.) Hungarian form of FRANCIS.

Fergal (m.) Irish: Anglicized form of the Gaelic name *Fearghal*, composed of the elements *fear* man + *gal* valour.

Fergus (m.) Scottish and Irish: Anglicized form of the Gaelic name *Fearghas*, composed of the elements *fear* man + *gus* vigour. This was the name of a shadowy hero in Irish mythology, also of the grandfather of St Columba. It is still used mainly by families in Scotland and Ireland, and those who remain conscious of their Gaelic ancestry.

Pet form: Scottish: **Fergie**.

Fermin (m.) Spanish form of FIRMIN.

Fern (f.) English: from the vocabulary word denoting the plant (Old English *fearn*). Use of this word as a given name is of comparatively recent origin: it is one of several words denoting flowers and plants that have been pressed into service during the past hundred years. Its popularity seems to be increasing.

Fernán (m.) Spanish form of FERDINAND, more common in the Middle Ages than today.

Fernand (m.) French form of FERDINAND.

Fernando (m.) Spanish and Portuguese form of FERDINAND, rather more common in modern use than *Hernando*.

Fernão (m.) Portuguese form of FERDINAND.

Variant: **Ferrão**.

Ferrer (m.) Catholic name given in honour of the Valencian saint, Vicente Ferrer (*c.*1350–1418), who travelled throughout Europe seeking to heal the papal schism. His surname is a Catalan occupational name for a blacksmith.

Ferruccio (m.) Italian: from a medieval diminutive form of the byname *Ferro* 'iron', applied either to someone with grey hair or to a person of stalwart temperament and sturdy physique.

Fester (m.) Low German: variant of VESTER.

Festus (m.) 1. Latin name meaning 'firm, steadfast'. This was the name of the Roman procurator of Judea who refused to bow to pressure from the Jews and condemn St Paul to death for his preaching, although he was totally unconvinced by it (Acts 25; 26: 30–2). It was also borne by some early minor saints.

2. Irish: Latinized form of FACHTNA and FEICHÍN.

Ffraid (f.) Welsh cognate of BRIDGET.

Fiachna (m.) Irish Gaelic: apparently a derivative of *fiach* raven (cf. FEICHÍN and FIACHRA). It has been revived as a given name in the 20th century.

Fiachra (m.) Irish Gaelic: apparently a derivative of *fiach* raven (cf. FEICHÍN and FIACHNA). A 7th-century St Fiachra settled at Meaux in France, and his cult became popular in that country, where he came to be regarded as the patron of gardeners. Through the Hôtel de Saint Fiacre in Paris he gave his name to the vocabulary word *fiacre*, since these carriages were originally available for hire outside the building.

Fiammetta (f.) Italian: from a diminutive form of the vocabulary word *fiamma* flame, fire, which is also used as a term of endearment.

Fidel (m.) Spanish: from the Late Latin name *Fidelis* 'faithful'. St Fidelis (d. *c.*570) seems to have come from the East, reaching Mérida in the company of merchants; eventually he became bishop of that city. The name is now chiefly associated with that of the left-wing Cuban leader Fidel Castro (b. 1927).

Cognate: Italian: **Fedele**.

Fidelma (f.) Irish: Anglicized form of Gaelic **Feidhelm**, an ancient personal name of uncertain derivation. It may have some connection with the male name *Feidhlimidh*; see PHELIM. St Fidelmia was a daughter of King Laoghaire and one of St Patrick's first converts.

Variant: **Fedelma**.

Short form: **Delma**.

Fidelis (m.) Original Latin form of FIDEL, occasionally used as a given name in the English-speaking world.

Fieke (f.) Low German: pet form of SOFIE.

Fife (m.) Scottish and English: transferred use of the surname, which originated in the Middle Ages as a local name for someone from the kingdom (now region) of Fife. This is said to get its name from that of the legendary Pictish hero *Fib*, one of the seven sons of Cruithne.

Variant: **Fyfe**.

Fifi (f.) French: nursery form of JOSÉPHINE. It may have been influenced by the term of endearment *ma fille* 'my daughter'. In the English-speaking world it now has definite connotations of frivolity.

Filat (m.) Russian: the usual vernacular contracted form of *Feofilakt*, from the Greek personal name *Theophylaktos* 'guarded by God' (from *theos* god + *phylassein* to guard, protect). This was the name of a 9th-century saint, bishop of Nicomedia, venerated in the Orthodox Church. In the Roman Martyrology he is commemorated under the much more common name *Theophilus*.

Filib (m.) Scottish Gaelic form of PHILIP. From this comes the surname *Mac Fhilib*, Anglicized as *MacKillop*.

Filiberto (m.) Italian: from a Germanic personal name composed of the elements *fil* much + *berht* bright, famous. This was a traditional name, of Frankish origin, in the royal house of Savoy. In the present century it has been moderately popular in many parts of Italy.

Filip (m.) Polish and Czech form of PHILIP.

Pet forms: Polish: **Filipek**. Czech: **Filípek**, **Fil(ouš)ek**.

Filippo (m.) Italian form of PHILIP.

Fima (f.) Russian: short form of *Serafima* (see SERAPHINA).

Pet form: **Fimochka**.

Fina (f.) 1. Irish: Anglicized form of Gaelic FÍONA.

2. English: short form of SERAPHINA.

Finbar (m.) Irish: Anglicized form of the Gaelic name **Fionnb(h)arr**, composed of the elements *fionn* white, fair + *barr* head. This was the name of at least three early Irish saints, one of whom became the first bishop of Cork in the 6th century. He is the subject of many legends, for example that he crossed the Irish Sea on horseback and that he made a pilgrimage to Rome with St David. He gave his name to the Isle of Barra in the Hebrides.

Finella (f.) Scottish: variant of FENELLA.

Fingal (m.) Scottish: Anglicized form of the Gaelic name **Fionnghall**, composed of the elements *fionn* white, fair + *gall* stranger. It was originally a byname applied to Norse settlers (cf. DOUGAL), and was adopted by James Macpherson (1736–96), author of the Ossianic poems, to render the name of the Gaelic hero *Fionn* (see FINN).

Variant: **Fingall**.

Fínín (m.) Irish Gaelic: modern form of the Old Irish name *Fíngin*, composed of elements meaning 'wine' and 'born'. In the Middle Ages it was commonly Anglicized as the male name FLORENCE.

Finlay (m.) Scottish: Anglicized form of the Gaelic name **Fionnlagh** (dialectally **Fionnla**), composed of the elements *fionn* white, fair + *laogh* warrior or calf. The Gaelic surname *Mac Fhionnlaigh* is Anglicized as *MacKinlay*.

Variant: **Finley**.

Finn (m.) 1. Irish Gaelic: traditional name meaning 'white, fair'. The modern Gaelic form is **Fionn**. The mythological Irish hero Finn MacCool (*Finn Mac Cumaill* in Irish) was noted for his wisdom and fairness. He was leader of the Fenians or *Fianna*, a band of warriors about whom many stories are told. There may be a basis of fact behind the legends, in that Finn may be identified with an early Irish leader who defended Ireland against Norse raiders.

2. Scandinavian: from the Old Norse personal name *Finnr*, originally either an ethnic byname for someone from Finland or else a short form of the various compound names containing this element.

Finnian (m.) Irish Gaelic: earlier *Finnén*, a derivative of Old Irish *finn* white, fair. This name was borne by two 6th-century Irish bishops.

Variant: **Finian**.

Finola (f.) Irish and Scottish: Anglicized form of FIONNUALA.

Fio (m.) Italian: short form of FIORENZO.

Fiona (f.) Scottish: Latinate derivative of the Gaelic element *fionn* white, fair. It was first used by James Macpherson (1736–96), author of the Ossianic poems, which were supposedly translations from ancient Gaelic. It was subsequently used as a pen-name by William Sharp (1855–1905), who produced many romantic works under the name of Fiona Macleod. It has since become extremely popular in England as well as Scotland, and is sometimes used as an Anglicized form of the Irish name FÍONA.

Fíona (f.) Irish Gaelic: traditional name meaning 'vine'. In origin this has no connection with the Scottish name FIONA, which, however, is often now used as an Anglicized form of it.

Variant: **Fina** (Anglicized).

Fionnán (m.) Irish Gaelic: originally a byname representing a diminutive of Gaelic *fionn* white, fair.

Fionnuala (f.) Irish Gaelic: modern form of *Fionnguala*, a traditional name composed of the elements *fionn* white, fair + *guala* shoulder.

Cognate: Scottish Gaelic: **Fionn(a)gh(u)al(a)** (Anglicized as FLORA).

Short form: **Nuala**.

Fionola (f.) Scottish: variant of *Finella* and *Finola*. In the English-speaking world it is now sometimes taken as an elaboration of FIONA.

Fiontan (m.) Irish Gaelic: earlier *Fintan*, apparently representing a derivative of Old Irish *finn* white, fair.

Fiorella (f.) Italian: from a diminutive form of the vocabulary word *fiore* flower, used as a term of endearment.

Fiorenzo (m.) Italian form of the male name FLORENCE.

Short form: **Fio**.

Firmin (m.) French: from Late Latin *Firminus*, a derivative of *firmus* firm, steadfast. This was a popular name among early Christians mindful of St Paul's injunction to 'be stedfast in the faith'. It was borne by several early saints, including the first and third bishops of Amiens (2nd and 3rd centuries); the third bishop of Gévaudon; a 5th-century bishop of Metz; and 6th-century bishops of Viviers, Uzès, and Verdun.

Cognates: Italian, Portuguese: **Firmino**. Spanish: **Fermin**.

Firs (m.) Russian: from Greek *Thyrsos* (see TIRSO).

Fisa (f.) Russian: short form of ANFISA.

Fishl (m.) Jewish (Yiddish): diminutive form of the vocabulary word *fish* fish (modern German *Fisch*). It seems to have been adopted as a given name because of the biblical prophecy that the descendants of Ephraim and Manasseh would multiply as the fish in the sea (Genesis 48: 16).

Variant: **Fishke**.

Flann (m.) Irish Gaelic: originally a byname meaning 'red, ruddy'.

Flannan (m.) Irish: Anglicized form of the Gaelic name **Flannán**, originally a byname representing a diminutive of Gaelic *flann* red, ruddy. St Flannan is the patron of the diocese of Killaloe in Co. Clare, and this is still a popular given name in that area.

Flavia (f.) Italian: feminine form of the old Roman family name *Flāvius* (from *flāvus* yellow, yellow-haired, golden). This was the name of at least five saints, most notably Flavia DOMITILLA.

Cognate: French: **Flavie**.

Flemming (m.) Danish: from a medieval byname, originally an ethnic byname for someone from Flanders. This is now one of the most common of all Danish male given names.

Fletcher (m.) English: transferred use of the surname, which originated as an occupational name for a maker of arrows, from Old French *flech(i)er*, an agent derivative of *fleche* (of Germanic origin). An early bearer of this as a given name was Fletcher Christian, leader of the mutiny on the *Bounty* in 1789.

Fleur (f.) English: from an Old French name meaning 'flower', occasionally used in the Middle Ages. Modern use, however, seems to derive mainly from the character of this name in John Galsworthy's *The Forsyte Saga* (1922). The English vocabulary word, **Flower**, is also occasionally found as a given name, probably as a translation equivalent of *Fleur*. The latter is not, however, in general use as a French given name.

Diminutive: **Fleurette**.

Flick (f.) English: pet form based on the given name FELICITY.

Flo (f.) English: short form of FLORENCE and FLORA, common in the early part of the 20th century, but now widely considered somewhat old-fashioned (in contrast to most other short forms in *-o*, e.g. JO).

Floella (f.) English: name of recent origin, used among British Blacks. It presumably originated as a compound of the independent short names FLO and ELLA.

Flora (f.) Scottish, English, and German: name borne in Roman mythology by the goddess of flowers and the spring (a derivative of Latin *flōs* flower, genitive *flōris*). It is also the feminine form of the old Roman family name *Flōrus*, likewise derived from *flōs*. There were medieval given names for both sexes from this root, but they have mostly died out (see FLORIAN, however). *Flora* was little used in England before the 18th century, when it was imported from Scotland. In 1746 Flora Macdonald (1722–90), daughter of Ranald Macdonald of Milton in South Uist, helped Bonnie Prince Charlie to escape from there to the Island of Skye, disguised as a woman, after his defeat at Culloden. In fact, *Flora* was merely an Anglicized form of her Gaelic name, *Fionnaghal*, a variant of *Fionnghuala* (see FENELLA). However, her fame made the name *Flora* popular in the Highlands as well as elsewhere.

Short form: English: **Flo**.

Pet form: English and Scottish: **Florrie** (Gaelic **Flòraidh**).

Florence (f., formerly also m.) English and French: medieval form of the Latin masculine name *Florentius* (a derivative of *florens* blossoming, flourishing) and its feminine form *Florentia*. In the Middle Ages the name was borne by men (for example, the historian Florence of Worcester), but it is now exclusively a female name, except in Ireland, where it has been used as an Anglicized form of *Flaithrí* (see FLORRY) and FÍNÍN. In the second half of the 19th century the female name was revived, being given in honour of Florence Nightingale (1820–1910), the founder of modern nursing, who organized a group of nurses to serve in the Crimean War. She herself received the name because she was born in the Italian city of Florence (Latin *Florentia*, Italian *Firenze*).

Cognates (all m.): Italian: **Fiorenzo**. Spanish, Portuguese: **Florencio**. German: **Florenz**. Dutch: **Floris**. Russian: **Florenti**.

Short form: English: **Flo** (f.).

Pet forms: English: **Florrie, Flossie** (f.).

Florentina (f.) Latin: feminine form of *Florentīnus*, an elaborated form of *Florens* (see FLORENCE). The name was borne by a 7th-century Spanish saint, sister of the other saints Fulgentius, Isidore, and Leander.

Cognate: Polish: **Florentyna**.

Florian (m.) German and Polish: from Latin *Flōriānus*, a derivative of *Flōrus* (see FLORA). St Florian is the patron of Upper Austria and Poland; he was a high-ranking Roman officer who was put to death by drowning in the River Enns during the persecutions under the Emperor Diocletian. A second saint of the same name was martyred in Palestine in the 7th century together with sixty companions.

Floris (m.) Dutch form of the male name FLORENCE.

Florrie (f.) English and Scottish: pet form of FLORA and FLORENCE, now little used except in the Highlands.

Florry (m.) Irish: 1. Anglicized form of the Gaelic name **Flaithrí**, composed of the elements *flaith* prince, leader + *rí* king.

2. Pet form of the male name FLORENCE, itself used as an Anglicized form of the Gaelic names *Flaithrí* and FÍNÍN.

Variant: **Flurry**.

Flossie (f.) English: pet form from a contraction of FLORENCE, common in the 19th century, but now no longer much used. The popularity of the name was no doubt enhanced by association with the soft downy material known as *floss*.

Floyd (m.) English: variant of LLOYD. This form of the name results from an attempt to represent the sound of the Welsh initial *Ll-* using standard English pronunciation and orthography. In the 20th century it has been particularly common in the southern United States and among American Blacks.

Flurry (m.) Irish: variant of FLORRY.

Foka (m.) Russian: from the Late Greek personal name *Phokas* (apparently a derivative of *phokē* seal (the animal)). This name was borne by several early saints venerated in the Orthodox Church, particularly Phocas the Gardener who was martyred under Diocletian. The name is stressed on the second syllable.

Folant (m.) Welsh form of the male name VALENTINE.

Folke (m.) Scandinavian: from the Old Norse personal name *Folki*, a short form of the various compound names containing the element *folk* people, tribe (as for example *Folkvarðr* 'people guard', which has given rise to the modern forms **Folkvar** and **Falkor**.

Cognate: English: FULK.

Foma (m.) Russian form of THOMAS. It is stressed on the second syllable.

Fonsie (m.) Irish: pet form of ALPHONSUS.

Variant: **Fonso**.

Forbes (m.) Scottish: transferred use of the surname, which originated as a local name from the lands of Forbes in Aberdeenshire. These are so called from the Gaelic element *forba* field, district + the locative suffix *-ais*. In Scotland this name was traditionally pronounced in two syllables, but a monosyllabic pronunciation is now the norm.

Ford (m.) English: transferred use of the common surname, originally a local name for someone who lived near a place where a river could be crossed by wading through it (Old English *ford*).

Forrest (m.) English: transferred use of the surname, which originated as a local name for someone who lived in or by an enclosed wood, Old French *forest*.

Fortunato (m.) Italian, Spanish, and Portuguese: from the Late Latin name *Fortūnātus* 'fortunate', a derivative of *fortūna* fortune, fate. This name was popular because of its good omen and was borne by a large number of early saints.

Feminine form: **Fortunata**.

Foster (m.) English: transferred use of the surname, originally an occupational name with at least four possible derivations—from Middle English *foster* foster-parent, *for(e)ster* forester, *fors(e)ter* shearer, or *fu(y)ster* saddle-tree maker.

Fran (f., m.) English: short form of FRANCES, or less commonly (in Britain at least) of FRANCIS.

Franca (f.) Italian: feminine form of FRANCO.

France (m.) English: either from the name of the country or, in some cases, a short form of FRANCIS that is sometimes used in America as an independent given name.

Frances (f.) English: feminine form of FRANCIS. In the 16th century the two spellings were used indiscriminately for both sexes, the distinction in spelling not being established until the 17th century.

Short form: **Fran**.

Pet form: **Fanny**.

Francesca (f.) Italian: feminine form of FRANCESCO. Originally a vocabulary word meaning 'French', it was bestowed from the 13th century onwards in honour of St Francis of Assisi. It has also been used independently as an English name. Probably its most famous bearer was Francesca di Rimini, daughter of Giovanni da Polenta, Count of Ravenna. A legendary beauty, she was betrothed by her father to the misshapen Giovanni Malatesta, Lord of Rimini, in return for military support. However, when Malatesta's good-looking younger brother, Paolo, acted as proxy in the betrothal, Francesca and he fell in love. They were discovered, and put to death by Malatesta in 1289. Their tragedy is enshrined in the Fifth Canto of Dante's *Inferno*, as well as in several other works of literature and in a symphonic fantasy by Tchaikovsky.

Cognates: English: FRANCES. Irish Gaelic: **Proinséas**. Scottish Gaelic: **Frangag**. French: **Françoise**. Spanish, Portuguese: **Francisca**. German: **Franziska**. Polish: **Franciszka**. Czech: **Františka**.

Pet forms: Spanish: **Frascuela, Frasquita**. German: **Zissi**.

Francesco (m.) Italian: originally a vocabulary word meaning 'French' or 'Frenchman' (Late Latin *Franciscus*; cf. FRANK). This was a nickname given to St Francis of Assisi (1181–1226) because of his wealthy father's business connections in France. His baptismal name was GIOVANNI. He had a pleasant, ordinary life as a child and young man, but after two serious illnesses, a period of military service, and a year as a prisoner of war in Perugia, he turned from the world and devoted himself to caring for the poor and the sick. He was joined by groups of disciples, calling themselves 'minor friars' (*friari minores*). The main features of the Franciscan rule are humility, poverty, and love for all living creatures. In his honour the various vernacular forms of *Francesco* came to be commonly used as given names from the 13th century onwards in France, Spain, and elsewhere as well as Italy.

Variant: FRANCO.

Cognates: Irish Gaelic: **Proinsias**. Scottish Gaelic: **Frang**. Spanish, Portuguese: **Francisco**. Catalan: **Francesc**. Basque: **Patxi**. French: FRANÇOIS. English: FRANCIS. German: FRANZ. Polish: **Franciszek**. Czech: **František**. Hungarian: **Ferenc**. Finnish: **Ransu**.

Pet forms: Scottish Gaelic: **Frangan**. Spanish: **Frascuelo, Frasquito, Paco, Pancho, Paquito, Curro**. Basque: **Patxi**.

Feminine forms: See FRANCESCA, FRANCES.

Francine (f.) French and English: diminutive pet form of *Françoise* (see FRANÇOIS).

Variants: English: **Francene, Franceen**.

Francis (m.) English (and Old French) form of Italian FRANCESCO, introduced into England in the early 16th century, when there was a surge of admiration for, and imitation of, Italian Renaissance culture.

Short forms: FRANK, **Fran, France**.

Feminine form: FRANCES.

Franco (m.) Italian: contracted form of FRANCESCO, occasionally taken as an Italian version of FRANK.

Feminine form: **Franca**.

François (m.) French: from the Old French word *françois* 'French' (*français* in modern French; see also FRANK). The use of this word as a given name was inspired by the fame of St Francis of Assisi (see FRANCESCO). The popularity of the name has been further enhanced by its patriotic meaning, and, less recently, by the fact that it was borne by two kings of France: François I, otherwise known as François d'Angoulême, who reigned 1515–47, presiding over a rich period of prosperity and cultural activity, and François II, who died in 1560 at the age of 16, having been King of France for a year and married to Mary Queen of Scots for two years.

Feminine form: **Françoise**.

Frank (m.) English: 1. Of Germanic origin. The name referred originally to a member of the tribe of the Franks, who are said to have got the name from a characteristic type of spear that they used (as the Saxons did from a characteristic knife). When the Franks migrated into Gaul in the 4th century, the country received its modern name of France (Late Latin *Francia*) and the tribal term Frank came to mean 'Frenchman'.

2. Now quite often taken, especially in America, as a short form of FRANCIS.

3. Anglicized form of the Italian name FRANCO. The popularity of *Frank* as a given name was greatly enhanced, especially among Italian Americans, by the fame of the singer Frank Sinatra (b. 1915).

Frankie (m., f.) English: 1. (m.) Pet form of FRANK.

2. (f.) Pet form of FRANCES, FRANCESCA, or FRANCINE. As a female name, it is perhaps most familiar as the name of the heroine of *The Ballad of Frankie and Johnny*, who ended up in the electric chair, 'with the sweat running through her hair'.

Franklin (m.) English: transferred use of the surname, which derives from Middle English *frankeleyn* freeman, which came to denote a member of a class of freeholders who were not of noble birth. This is derived from the Norman French word *frank*, which means both 'free' and 'Frankish'. The connection between freemen and Franks is reflected in the Late Latin term *francālia*, originally denoting lands held by Franks, which came to mean lands that were not subject to taxes. The given name is now quite common, especially in the United States, having been so used at first in honour of the American statesman and scientist Benjamin Franklin (1706–90), and more recently of President Franklin D. Roosevelt (1882–1945).

František (m.) Czech form of FRANCESCO.

Feminine form: **Františka**.

Pet forms: **Franta, Frantík, Franek, Fanoušek** (m.); **Fráňa** (m., f.).

Franz (m.) German form of FRANCESCO. This name was introduced to the Habsburg family in 1736, when Franz, François, or Francesco, Duke of Lorraine and Grand Duke of Tuscany (1708–65), married Maria Theresa of Austria. In 1740, he became Holy Roman Emperor jointly with her. The name was also borne by the Emperor Franz Josef (reigned 1848–1916) and his great-nephew the Archduke Franz Ferdinand, whose assassination in 1914 sparked off the First World War. The name is still popular in German-speaking countries, especially among Roman Catholics.

Feminine form: **Franziska** (rare).

Frascuelo (m.) Spanish: pet form of *Francisco* (see FRANCIS).

Feminine form: **Frascuela**.

Fraser (m.) Scottish: transferred use of the surname of a leading Highland and Lowland family. The surname is undoubtedly of Norman origin, but its exact derivation is uncertain. The earliest forms are *de Frisselle* and *de Fresel*(*iere*), but the name seems to have been altered by association with Old French *fraise* strawberry.

Variant: **Frazer**.

Frasquito (m.) Spanish: pet form of *Francisco* (see FRANCIS).

Feminine form: **Frasquita**.

Frauke (f.) Low German: originally a byname representing a diminutive formation from the vocabulary word *Frau* lady (Middle High German *vrouwe*, Old High German *frouwa*; Old Saxon *frūa*). It has also been used as a pet form of *Veronika* (see VERONICA), because of the similarity in sound. In the 1960s it came to be commonly used as an independent given name in German-speaking countries.

Fred (m.) English: short form of FREDERICK or, occasionally, of ALFRED. It has also been used as an independent given name (cf. BERT).

Pet forms: **Freddie, Freddy**.

Freda (f.) English: short form of various names such as ELFREDA and WINIFRED, also, occasionally, of FREDERICA. The name is sometimes spelled **Frieda**, under the influence of German FRIEDE.

Pet form: **Freddie**.

Freddie (m., f.) English: 1. (m.) Pet form of FRED.

2. (f.) Pet form of FREDA and FREDERICA.

Variant: **Freddy** (m.).

Frédéric (m.) French form of FREDERICK.

Frederica (f.) Latinate feminine form of FREDERICK.

Cognates: French: **Frédérique**. German: **Friederike**. Czech: **Bedřiška**.

Short forms: English: **Freda**. German: **Friede**.

Pet forms: English: **Freddie**. German: **Fritzi**.

Frederick (m.) 1. English: from an old Germanic name, composed of the elements *fred, frid* peace + *rīc* power, ruler. It was first introduced into Britain by the Normans at the time of the Conquest, but did not survive long. However, it continued to be popular as a royal name elsewhere in Europe (see FRIEDRICH). Modern use in Britain dates from its reintroduction in the 18th century by followers of the Elector of Hanover, who in 1714 became George I of England, and was reinforced by the vogue for Germanic names in Victorian times.

2. Irish: used as an Anglicized form of the Gaelic name FEARDORCHA.

Variants (of 1): **Fred(e)ric** (becoming increasingly fashionable, no doubt under the influence of French *Frédéric* and perhaps also of English *Dominic*, where the spelling *Dominick* is perceived as distinctly archaic).

Cognates (of 1): French: **Frédéric**. Italian, Spanish: FEDERICO. German: FRIEDRICH. Low German, Danish: FREDERIK. Swedish: FREDRIK. Dutch: **Frerik, Freek**. Polish: **Fryderyk**. Czech: **Bedřich**. Hungarian: **Frigyes**. Finnish: **Rieti**.

Short form: English: **Fred**.

Pet forms: English: **Freddie, Freddy**. German: **Fritz**.

Frederik (m.) Danish and Low German form of FREDERICK. This has been the name of no less than nine kings of Denmark.

Fredrik (m.) Swedish form of FREDERICK. The name was first used in Sweden in the 14th century, but did not become popular until the 18th century, with the reigns of the kings Fredrik I (1720–51) and Adolf Fredrik (1751–71).

Freja (f.) Swedish form of FREYA, revived in the 19th century.

Frerik (m.) Dutch form of FREDERICK. The omission of dental consonants between vowels is a regular feature of Dutch.

Freya (f.) Scottish: of Old Norse origin. *Freya* or *Fröja* was the goddess of love in Scandinavian mythology, and her name seems to be derived from an element cognate with Old High German *frouwa* lady, mistress. The name was long a traditional one in Shetland, and is still used in Scotland. A notable modern bearer is the explorer and writer Freya Stark.

Cognate: Swedish: **Freja**.

Freyde (f.) Jewish: name meaning 'joy' in Yiddish (modern German *Freude*).

Friede (f.) German form of FREDA.

Friedelinde (f.) German: from an old Germanic female personal name composed of the elements *fred, frid* peace + *lind* weak, tender, soft. The name was revived in the 19th century, but has not become common.

Friedemann (m.) German: from an old Germanic personal name composed of the elements *fred, frid* peace + *man* man. It is to a large extent borne by Jews as a translation of SHLOMO. One notable non-Jewish bearer was Wilhelm Friedemann Bach (1710–84), the eldest son of Johann Sebastian Bach, and himself a composer.

Friederike (f.) German form of FREDERICA.

Pet form: **Fritzi**.

Friedhelm (m.) German: from an old Germanic personal name composed of the elements *fred, frid* peace + *helm* helmet, protection.

Friedrich (m.) German form of FREDERICK. It owes its great popularity in Germany at least in part to having been a royal name from an early date. It was borne by both Hohenstauffens and Habsburgs. Notable bearers include Friedrich Barbarossa (King of Germany 1152–90 and Holy Roman Emperor 1155–90), and Friedrich II (King of Sicily from 1197, when he was three years old, King of Germany 1212–20, and Holy Roman

Emperor 1220–50: he called himself 'lord of the world'). The name was later borne by many German princes and princelings, as well as several kings of Prussia. The most famous of these is undoubtedly Friedrich der Grosse (Frederick the Great, reigned 1740–86), noted as a glorious patron of the arts as well as being a decisive statesman and victorious military commander.
Pet form: **Fritz**.

Frigyes (m.) Hungarian form of FREDERICK.

Fritjof (m.) Scandinavian: from an Old Norse personal name composed of the elements *friðr* peace + *þjófr* thief. The spellings **Fridtjof** and **Fri(d)tjov** are also used. The former was borne, for example, by the Norwegian explorer Fridtjof Nansen (1861–1930), who also served as the League of Nations' high commissioner for refugees and was responsible for the issuing of 'Nansen' passports to stateless persons after the First World War.

Fritz (m.) German: pet form of FRIEDRICH. The name is also sometimes used as a given name or nickname in the English-speaking world.

Fritzi (f.) German: pet form of FRIEDERIKE.

Frode (m.) Danish and Norwegian: from the Old Norse personal name *Fróði*, originally a byname for a wise or prudent person, from *fróðr* knowing, learned, well-informed. The name was revived *c.*1930 and has become increasingly popular since about 1970.

Froim (m.) Jewish: Yiddish form of EPHRAIM.

Frume (f.) Jewish: Yiddish name, originally a nickname meaning 'pious, devout' (modern German *fromm*).
Pet form: **Frumke**.

Fryderyk (m.) Polish form of FREDERICK.

Fucho (f.) Spanish: pet form of REFUGIO.

Fulgencio (m.) Spanish: from the Latin name *Fulgentius*, a derivative of *fulgens* (genitive *fulgentis*) shining. The name was borne by a 7th-century Spanish saint, brother of Isidore of Seville.

Fulgenzio (m.) Italian form of FULGENCIO. The name was borne by a saint (468–533) who served as bishop of Ruspe but was expelled by the Vandals and retired to Sardinia.

Fulk (m.) English: of Germanic origin, introduced to Britain by the Normans. The name originally represented a short form of various compound names containing the element 'people, tribe' (cf. modern English *folk*). It has gradually died out of general use, but is still used in certain families, such as the Grevilles. Fulke Greville, 1st Baron Brooke, was a leading figure at the court of Elizabeth I.
Variant: **Fulke**.

Fülöp (m.) Hungarian form of PHILIP.

Fulton (m.) Scottish: transferred use of the surname, which seems to have been originally a local name from a lost place in Ayrshire. Robert Fulton (1765–1815) was the American engineer who designed the first commercially successful steamboat.

Fulvia (f.) Italian and English: from the feminine form of the old Roman family name *Fulvius*, a derivative of Latin *fulvus* dusky, tawny (ultimately connected with *flāvus*; cf. FLAVIA). The name does not seem to have been much used among early Christians, and there are no saints Fulvia or Fulvius. In classical times its most famous bearer was the wife of Mark Antony, who opposed Octavian by force on her husband's behalf while he was in Egypt.

Fyfe (m.) Scottish: variant spelling of FIFE.

Fyodor (m.) Russian form of THEODORE.
Pet form: **Fedya**.

G

Gabino (m.) Spanish form of GAVINO.

Gábor (m.) Hungarian form of GABRIEL. It is particularly popular in Hungary because of the legend that in the year 1001 the archangel Gabriel advised Pope Sylvester II to send a holy crown to King (later St) Stephen (ISTVÁN), thus recognizing Hungary as a Christian sovereign state.

Gabriel (m.) Biblical: name (meaning 'man of God' in Hebrew) of one of the archangels. Gabriel appeared to Daniel in the Old Testament (Daniel 8: 16; 9: 21), and in the New Testament to Zacharias (Luke 1: 19; 26: 27) and, most famously, to Mary to announce the impending birth of Christ (Luke 1: 2). *Gabriel* has occasionally been used as a given name in the English-speaking world, mainly as a result of Continental European influence (rather more commonly than RAPHAEL, but much less so than MICHAEL, the names of two other chief archangels).

Cognates: Hungarian: GÁBOR. Italian: **Gabriele**. Finnish: **Kaapo**.

Feminine forms: French (now also used in English): **Gabrielle, Gaby**. Italian: **Gabriella**. German: **Gabriele, Gabi**. Polish: **Gabriela**. Czech: **Gabriele**.

Pet forms: Irish: **Gay**. Polish: **Gabryś, Gabrysz** (m.); **Gabrysia** (f.). Czech: **Gába** (m., f.); **Riel, Gabek** (m.); **Gabra, Gabin(k)a** (f.).

Gae (f.) English: variant spelling of GAY.

Gaenor (f.) Welsh: apparently a form of GAYNOR adapted to Welsh orthography. It also may have been influenced by the name of the saint commemorated at *Llangeinwyr* in Glamorgan, known popularly as *Llangeinor*. Her name seems to be composed of the Welsh elements *cain* beautiful + *(g)wyry(f)* maiden.

Gaetano (m.) Italian: from Latin *Caietānus*, originally an ethnic name for someone from *Caieta* (now *Gaeta*) in Latium. According to Roman legend, the town was named in honour of Aeneas' faithful nurse Caieta, who accompanied him from Troy to Italy and died at that spot. St Gaetano (*c.*1480–1547) was a religious reformer who lived in Naples; he is not to be confused with his contemporary Cardinal Gaetano, an active opponent of Martin Luther.

Cognates: French: **Gaétan**. Spanish: **Cayetano**. Portuguese: **Caetano**. German: **Kayetan**. Polish: **Kajetan**. English: **Cajetan** (rarely, if ever, used as a given name, but sometimes adopted as a clerical name by members of Roman Catholic religious orders).

Gaia (f.) From the name borne in classical mythology by the primeval goddess of the earth, who bore Ouranos 'sky' and by him Okeanos 'sea', Kronos 'time', and the Titans. Her name, spelled in Latin *Gaea*, derives from Greek *gē* earth.

Gail (f.) English: aphetic short form of ABIGAIL, now very commonly used as an independent given name, but apparently not in existence before the middle of the 20th century.

Variants: **Gale, Gayle**.

Gaitzka (m.) Basque equivalent of SALVADOR.

Gala (f.) Russian: normally a pet form of GALINA. In the case of the wife (1904–84) of the Catalan painter Salvador Dali, it was a pet name bestowed on her by her first lover Paul Eluard; she was born Yelena Diakonov in Kazan. The name has now also been adopted into English, perhaps influenced by the festive connotations of the vocabulary word.

Gale (f.) English: variant spelling of GAIL.

Galen (m.) English: from the name of the Graeco-Roman medical writer Claudius *Galēnus* (AD ?130–?200). His name appears to represent a Latinized form of a Greek name derived from *galēnē* calm.

Galia (f.) Jewish: modern Hebrew name, meaning 'wave'.

Galina (f.) Russian: of uncertain origin, probably from Greek *galēnē* calm (cf. GALEN). Another possibility is that it may represent a vernacular form of HELEN, beside the more learned YELENA.

Gamaliel (m.) Biblical: name, apparently meaning 'benefit of God' in Hebrew, borne in the New Testament by a wise Pharisee (Acts 5: 34) and by a teacher of St Paul (Acts 22: 3), possibly the same person. In the Old Testament it is the name of the prince of the tribe of Manasseh at the time of the Exodus (Numbers 1: 10).

Garbikunde (f.) Basque equivalent of PURIFICACIÓN.

Garbiñe (f.) Basque equivalent of INMACULADA. This name shares with the previous one a derivation from the Basque element *garbi* clean, pure.

Gärd (f.) Swedish: variant of GERD.

Gareth (m.) Welsh and English: of Celtic origin, but uncertain ultimate derivation. It first occurs in Malory's *Morte D'Arthur*, as the name of the lover of Eluned and seems to have been heavily altered from its original form, whatever that may have been (possibly the same as GERAINT). It is now very common in Wales, partly because GARY, which is actually an independent name, is often taken to be a pet form of it.

Garfield (m.) English: transferred use of the surname, originally a local name for someone who lived near a triangular field, from Old English *gār* triangular piece of land + *feld* open country.

Garret (m.) Irish and English: transferred use of the surname, which is derived from the given names GERALD and GERARD. In Ireland it often represents a direct Anglicization of GEARÓID.

Variant: **Garrett**.

Garrison (m.) English (mainly U.S.): transferred use of the surname, originally a local name from *Garriston* in North Yorkshire or else a patronymic for the son of someone called GARRET. William Lloyd Garrison (1805–79) was a prominent American anti-slavery campaigner: the given name may originally have been bestowed in honour of him. It is now sometimes given to the sons of fathers who are called GARY or GARRY (cf. JEFFERSON).

Garrit (m.) Frisian: variant of GERRIT.

Garry (m.) English: variant spelling of GARY, influenced in spelling by BARRY.

Garsha (m.) Russian: pet form of GERASIM.

Garth (m.) English and Welsh: from a surname, but often taken to be a contracted form of GARETH. As a surname it originated in the north of England, and originally denoted someone who lived beside an enclosure (Old Norse *garðr*). In modern times its popularity has been influenced by the virile superhero of this name, main character in a long-running strip cartoon in the *Daily Mirror* newspaper.

Gary (m.) English: from a surname, which is probably derived from a Norman personal name of Germanic origin, a short form of any of the various compound names with *gar* spear as a first element. One bearer of this surname was the American industrialist Elbert Henry Gary (1846–1927), who gave his name to the steel town of Gary, Indiana (chartered in 1906). In this town was born the theatrical agent Nan Collins, who suggested *Gary* as a stage name for her client Frank Cooper, who thus became Gary Cooper (1901–61). His film career caused the name to become enormously popular from the 1930s to the present day. Its popularity has been maintained by the cricketer

Gary Sobers (b. 1936; in his case it is in fact a pet form of *Garfield*) and the pop singer Gary Glitter (real name Paul Gadd). It is now often taken as a pet form of GARETH. Curiously, in the spelling *Garaidh*, the name is borne by a minor warrior in the Gaelic Finn sagas and hence has been used as a dog's name in the Highlands.

Variant: **Garry**.

Pet form (informal): **Gaz**.

Gáspár (m.) Hungarian form of CASPAR.

Gaspard (m.) French form of CASPAR. The *-d* has been added as a result of association with the many personal names of Germanic origin ending in *-ard* (from the name element *hard* hardy, brave, strong).

Gaspare (m.) Italian form of CASPAR.

Gaston (m.) French: of uncertain derivation. It seems to have originated in the south of France, and in the Middle Ages was a hereditary name among the counts of Foix and viscounts of Béarn. It is probably of Germanic origin, derived from the element *gast* guest, stranger. According to another theory, it was originally an ethnic name for a *Gascon*. There are no grounds for the common association made between this name and *Vedastus* (see VAAST).

Gavin (m.) Scottish and English: of Celtic origin, but uncertain ultimate derivation; it first appears in French sources as *Gauvain*. The name is borne in the Arthurian romances by one of the knights of the Round Table (more familiar in English versions as Sir *Gawain*). It died out in the 16th century except in Scotland, whence it has been reintroduced in the past couple of decades. It is now extremely popular in England, Wales, and elsewhere in the English-speaking world.

Gavino (m.) Italian: characteristically Sardinian name, unrelated to GAVIN. It is probably from Late Latin *Gabīnus*, originally an ethnic name for someone from the city of *Gabium* in Latium. St Gabinus was martyred at Torres in Sardinia, together with his companion Crispulus, under the Roman emperor Hadrian (*c.* 130).

Cognate: Spanish: **Gabino**.

Gaweł (m.) Polish: from the old Roman family name *Gallus*, originally a byname meaning 'cock' but later taken to be an ethnic name meaning 'Gaul'. In the Christian period it was borne by an uncle (*c.*489–*c.*554) of Gregory of Tours, and by a 7th-century Irish saint and missionary to central Europe. The latter founded a monastery to the south of Lake Constance, which later became known as St Gall and gave its name to a Swiss town and canton. His name probably represents a Latinization of an Irish name derived from *gall* stranger. The form of the Polish given name has been altered by association with *Paweł* (from Latin *Paulus*; see PAUL).

Cognate: Czech: **Havel**.

Gay (f., m.) 1. (f., m.) English: from the vocabulary word meaning 'blithe, cheerful' (from Old French, of Germanic origin), chosen as a given name because of its well-omened meaning (cf. HAPPY and MERRY). It was not used before the 20th century, and has fallen out of favour again since the 1960s, since the vocabulary word *gay* has acquired the meaning 'homosexual'. It was generally a female name, but has also been borne by men.

2. (m.) Irish: pet form of GABRIEL.

Variants (of 1): **Gaye**, **Gae** (f.).

Gayle (f.) English: variant spelling of GAIL. Its popularity has no doubt been increased by the fame of the American film actress Gayle Hunnicutt (b. 1942).

Gaylord (m.) English: from a surname, which is a form, altered by folk etymology, of the Old French nickname *Gaillard* 'dandy'. It may sometimes have been chosen as a given name because parents liked the idea of their son's living as a fine lord, but it now seems likely to suffer the same fate as GAY.

Gaynor (f.) English: a medieval form of the name of Arthur's queen, GUINEVERE, recently undergoing a strong revival in popularity.

Gaz (m.) English: informal pet form of GARY (cf. BAZ and LAZ).

Gearóid (m.) Irish Gaelic form of GERALD, from Old French *Geraud*. The name originated in Ireland at the time of Strongbow's invasion (1170): the constable of Strongbow's castle at Pembroke was called *Gerald*, and his son founded a major Irish family, the Fitzgeralds. The Irish form of the name has been revived in modern times.
Variant: **Gearalt**.

Gebhard (m.) German: from an old Germanic personal name composed of the elements *geb*, *gib* gift + *hard* hardy, brave, strong. St Gebhard was bishop of Constance in the late 10th century, and founded the abbey of Petershausen near there.
Cognate: Low German: **Gebbert**.

Ged (m.) English: short form of GERARD or GERALD.

Gedeon (m.) Russian form of GIDEON.

Geert (m.) Low German and Dutch form of GERHARD.

Geerta (f.) Low German and Dutch: Latinate version of a contracted form of GERTRUDE, or occasionally of *Gerharde*, a rare feminine version of GERHARD.
Pet forms: **Geertke, Geertje**.

Gellért (m.) Hungarian form of GERARD. St Gerard Sagredo, born in Venice, was a missionary to Hungary during the 11th century, and became the first bishop of Czanad. He was murdered by being thrown into the Danube by unconverted heathens.

Gemma (f.) English, Irish, and Italian: from a medieval Italian nickname meaning 'gem, jewel'. It has been chosen in modern times mainly because of its transparent etymology. Among Roman Catholics it is sometimes chosen in honour of St Gemma Galgani (1878–1903), who was the subject of many extraordinary signs of grace, such as ecstasies and the appearance of the stigmata.
Variant: English: **Jemma**.

Gene (m.) English: short form of EUGENE, now quite commonly used as an independent given name in America. It has been made familiar especially by film stars such as Gene Autry, Gene Hackman, and Gene Wilder.

Genette (f.) English: variant spelling of JEANNETTE.

Geneva (f.) English: of recent origin and uncertain derivation. In form it coincides with the city in Switzerland (cf. FLORENCE and VENETIA), but it may rather have been intended as a Latinate short form of GENEVIÈVE.

Geneviève (f.) French: the name of the patron saint of Paris, a 5th-century Gallo-Roman nun who encouraged the people of Paris in the face of the occupation of the town by the Franks and threatened attacks by the Huns. Her name seems to have been composed of Celtic elements meaning 'people, tribe' and 'woman', but if so it has been heavily altered by its transmission through French sources. The name was introduced to Britain from France in the 19th century.
Cognates: English: **Genevieve**. Italian: **Genoveffa, Ginevra**.

Genista (f.) English: modern name, a learned coinage taken from the Latin name of the broom plant, *genesta*, *genista*. It is from this word that the English royal dynasty of the Plantagenets took its name: the founder, Geoffrey Plantagenet (d. 1151) wore a sprig of broom (Latin *planta genesta*) to distinguish himself in battle.

Gennadi (m.) Russian: from Greek *Gennadios*, a name of very uncertain origin. It may come from a derivative (originally patronymic in form) of a short form of the various Greek names such as *Diogenes* 'born of Zeus' and *Hermogenes* 'born of Hermes'. St Gennadius has been venerated from ancient times in the Eastern Church, together with his companion Felix, but very little is known about them. Another saint of the same name (d. *c.*936) was a bishop of Astorga.

Gennaro (m.) Italian: from Latin *Januārius*, a derivative of *(mensis) Januārius* January. The name of the month is derived from that of the god *Janus*, who was associated with doors (*januae*) and new beginnings; he was represented in sculpture as having two faces on a single head, one looking forwards and the other backwards. The name *Januarius* was borne by a large number of early saints, but the one most particularly associated with Italy was a bishop of Benevento beheaded at Pozzuoli under Diocletian in 304. His body was enshrined at Naples and he is the patron of that city. Phials of his blood are preserved at both Naples and Pozzuoli and are believed to liquefy regularly to this day.

Cognate: Spanish: **Jenaro**.

Genoveffa (f.) Italian form of GENEVIÈVE.

Gentzane (f.) Basque equivalent of PAZ.

Geoff (m.) English: short form of GEOFFREY. See also JEFF.

Geoffrey (m.) English: of Germanic (Frankish and Lombard) origin, introduced to Britain by the Normans. It was in regular use among the counts of Anjou, ancestors of the English royal house of Plantagenet, who were descended from Geoffrey Plantagenet, Count of Anjou (1113–51). Godefroy de Bouillon, leader of the First Crusade, is commemorated in Torquato Tasso's *Gerusalemme Liberata* (1581). It was a particularly popular name in England and France in the later Middle Ages; notable bearers in England include the poet Geoffrey Chaucer (*c.*1340–1400) and in Wales the chronicler Geoffrey of Monmouth (Gaufridus Monemutensis; d. 1155). The original form and meaning of the elements of which the name is composed are disputed. According to one theory, the name is merely a variant of GODFREY; others derive the first part from the Germanic elements *gawia* territory, *walah* stranger, or *gisil* pledge. Medieval forms can be found to support all these theories, and it is possible that several names have fallen together, or that the name was subjected to reanalysis by folk etymology at an early date.

Variant: JEFFREY.

Cognates: French: **Geoffroi**. Italian: **Goffredo**. Spanish, Portuguese: **Godofredo**. Welsh: **Sieffre**. Irish Gaelic: **Siothrún**.

Geordie (m.) Pet form of GEORGE, still used in Scotland and the north of England. It is from this name that the generic term *Geordie* for a Tynesider derives.

George (m.) English: from Old French, from Latin *Georgius*, from Greek *Georgios* (from *geōrgos* farmer, a compound of *gē* earth + *ergein* to work). This was the name of several early saints, including the shadowy figure who is now the patron of England (as well as of Germany and Portugal). Gibbon identified him with a Cappadocian leader of this name, but this cannot be right. If the saint existed at all, he was perhaps martyred in Palestine in the persecutions instigated by the Emperor Diocletian at the beginning of the 4th century. The popular legend in which the hero slays a dragon is a medieval Italian invention. He was for a long time a more important saint in the Orthodox Church than in the West, and the name was not much used in England during the Middle Ages, even after St George came to be regarded as the patron of England in the 14th century. The real impulse for its popularity was the accession of the first king of England of this name, who came from Germany in 1714 and brought many German retainers with him. It has been one of the most popular English male names ever since.

Cognates: Irish Gaelic: **Seoirse**. Scottish Gaelic: **Seòras, Deòrsa**. Welsh: **Siôr, Sior(y)s**. French: **Georges**. Provençal: **Jori**. Italian: **Giorgio**. Spanish, Portuguese: **Jorge**. Catalan: **Jordi**. Basque: **Gorka**. German: **Georg; Jörg** (dialectal); **Jürgen** (Low German in origin).

Dutch, Frisian: **Joris, Joren, Jurg**. Danish: **Jørgen, Jørn**. Swedish: **Göran, Jöran, Jörgen, Örjan**. Finnish: **Yrjö**. Russian: **Georgi, Yuri, Yegor**. Polish: **Jerzy**. Czech: **Jiří**. Hungarian: **György**. Romanian: **Gheorghe, Iorghu**. See also YORICK.

Pet forms: English: **Georgie, Geordie**. Russian: **Goga, Gora, Gorya**. Polish: **Jurek**.

Feminine forms: English: GEORGIA, GEORGINA, GEORGETTE. Scottish Gaelic: **Seòrdag**.

Georgene (f.) English: altered form of GEORGINE, by association with the productive suffix *-ene*.

Georgette (f.) French: feminine diminutive of *Georges* (see GEORGE), now also used in the English-speaking world. The crêpe material so called derives its name from that of an early 20th-century French dressmaker, Mme Georgette de la Plante.

Georgia (f.) Latinate feminine form of GEORGE. It was borne by a 5th-century saint who became a recluse near Clermont in the Auvergne.

Georgiana (f.) Elaborated Latinate form of GEORGIA or GEORGINA, now sometimes used in the English-speaking world. It seems to take its pattern from Latin names such as JULIANA, a derivative of JULIA. In Latin the suffix *-ānus* was originally a derivative element used in names as a distinguishing feature; for example, on his adoption by Julius Caesar, Caius Octavius (later known as the Emperor Augustus) became Caius Julius Caesar Octavianus.

Georgie (m., f.) English: occasionally used as a pet form of GEORGE, but more commonly as a female name, a pet form of GEORGIA or GEORGINA.

Georgina (f.) Scottish, English, etc.: Latinate feminine derivative of GEORGE. This feminine form originated in Scotland in the 18th century, when *George* itself became common among anti-Jacobites. It has now been borrowed by other European languages, including Dutch, German, Danish, Norwegian, and Swedish.

Cognates: French: **Georgine**. Czech: **Jiřina**.

Georgine (f.) French form of GEORGINA, now also used in the English-speaking world.

Variant: English: **Georgene**.

Geraint (m.) Welsh: of uncertain origin, derived from a British name that first appears in a Greek inscription in the form *Gerontios*, possibly influenced by the Greek vocabulary word *gerōn* (genitive *gerontos*) old man. The story of Geraint (or *Gereint*), son of Erbin of Cornwall, is told in the *Mabinogi*. Geraint is one of the knights of Arthur's Round Table. He wins the love of Enid at a tournament, and marries her. He is infatuated with her to the point of neglecting all else, but comes to suspect her, wrongly, of infidelity. By her submissiveness and loyalty, she regains his trust. The story of Geraint and Enid was used by Tennyson in the *Idylls of the King*. In recent years the name has become extremely popular in Wales.

Gerald (m.) English and Irish: of Germanic origin, composed of the elements *gār*, *gēr* spear + *wald* rule. The name was introduced to Britain by the Normans, but soon became confused with GERARD. It died out in England at the end of the 13th century. However, it continued in Ireland, where it had been brought in the 12th century, at the time of Strongbow's invasion, principally by Maurice *Fitzgerald*, 'son of Gerald'. The name was revived in England in the 19th century, along with several other long-extinct names of Germanic and Celtic origin, and is now more common than GERARD, which survived all along as an English 'gentry' name.

Variant: **Jerrold**.

Cognates: Irish Gaelic: **Gearóid, Gearalt**. Welsh: **Gerallt**. Dutch: **Gerolt**. German: **Gerhold**. Italian: **Giraldo**. French: **Gérald, Géraud**.

Short form: English: **Ged**.

Pet forms: English: **Gerry, Jerry**.

Geraldine (f.) English: feminine derivative of GERALD, invented in the 16th century by the English poet the Earl of

Surrey, in a poem praising Lady Fitzgerald. However, it remained very little used until the 18th century.
Pet form: **Gerry**.

Gerard (m.) English, Irish, and Dutch: of Germanic origin, introduced to Britain by the Normans. It is composed of the elements *gār*, *gēr* spear + *hard* brave, hardy, strong. In the Middle Ages this was a much more common name than GERALD, with which it was sometimes confused, but nowadays is less common. It survives mainly among Roman Catholics.
Variants: **Gerrard, Jerrard**.
Cognates: French: **Gérard**. Italian: **Gerardo**. German: **Gerhard, Gerhar(d)t**. Low German: **Gerrit, Ge(e)rt**. Dutch, Flemish: **Geeraard, Geerd, Ge(e)rt**. Frisian: **Gerrit, Garrit**. Hungarian: **Gellért**.
Short form: English: **Ged**.
Pet forms: English: **Gerry, Jerry**.

Gerasim (m.) Russian: from the Late Greek personal name *Gerasimos*, a derivative of *geras* old age (cf. GERAINT and GEREON), or of the homonymous *geras* honour. The name was borne by a 5th-century saint venerated in the Eastern Church; he lived as a hermit in the Holy Land.
Pet form: **Garsha**.

Gerd (f.) Scandinavian: name borne in Old Norse mythology by a beautiful goddess who was the wife of Frey. The pair seem to have been originally fertility gods, and her name is probably connected with the Old Norse word *garðr* enclosure, stronghold.
Variant: **Gärd**.

Gerda (f.) Scandinavian, German, and Dutch: Latinate form of GERD, revived in Scandinavia in the 19th century. In Germany and the Netherlands, it is sometimes taken as a feminine derivative of GERARD. It is now sometimes also found in the English-speaking world.
Variant: German: **Gerde**.
Pet form: German: **Gerdi**.

Gereon (m.) German: confined almost exclusively to the Cologne area, this represents the name of a saint martyred there at the beginning of the 4th century. He was executed together with a band of companions traditionally said to have numbered 318. The name is apparently a derivative of Greek *gerōn* old man.

Gergely (m.) Hungarian form of GREGORY.

Gerhard (m.) German form of GERARD.
Variants: **Gerhart, Gerhardt**.

Gerlach (m.) German and Dutch: from an old Germanic personal name composed of the elements *geri*, *gari* spear + *laic* play, sport. St Gerlach was a hermit who lived near Valkenberg in the 12th century.

Gerlinde (f.) German: from an old Germanic female personal name composed of the elements *geri*, *gari* spear + *lind* weak, tender, soft. St Gerlinde lived in the 8th century; she was a member of the royal family of Alsace, sister of St Ottilie.

Germaine (f.) French and English: feminine form of the rarer French male name **Germain** (Late Latin *Germānus* 'brother'; the original reference may have been to the concept of Christian brotherhood). Germaine Cousin (*c.*1579–1601) was a Provençal saint, the daughter of a poor farmer. Her canonization in 1867 gave an additional impulse to the use of the name in Europe and the English-speaking world. It is now particularly known as the name of the Australian feminist writer Germaine Greer (b. 1939). See also JERMAINE.

Gernot (m.) German: from an old Germanic personal name composed of the elements *gār*, *gēr* spear + *nōt* need, want or perhaps *hnod-* crush). The same elements are found in reverse order in the name NOTGER.

Geronimo (m.) Italian: learned form of JEROME, much less common than the vernacular GIROLAMO. In the United States it is known as the name of a famous Apache chief (1829–1909), presumably a phonetic approximation to his native name.

Gerrard (m.) English: variant spelling of GERARD, in part from the modern surname.

Gerrit (m.) Low German and Frisian form of GERHARD, current predominantly in the North Rhine area.

Variants: Low German: **Ge(e)rt**. Frisian: **Garrit**; **Gerritt** (E. Frisian).

Gerry (f., m.) English: 1. (f.) Pet form of GERALDINE; it is also sometimes used as an independent female name.

2. (m.) Pet form of GERALD or GERARD; cf. JERRY.

Gershom (m.) Biblical: name borne by a son of Moses (Exodus 2: 22). The name possibly means 'exile' (i.e. a person in exile) in Hebrew, but it is usually interpreted as 'sojourner', from Hebrew *ger sham* meaning 'a stranger there'.

Gershon (m.) Biblical: byform of GERSHOM, borne by a son of Levi (Genesis 46: 11).

Gert (m., f.) 1. (m.) Dutch and Low German: contracted form of GERARD.

2. (f.) English: short form of GERTRUDE.

Variant (of 1): **Geert**.

Pet form (of 2): **Gertie**.

Gertrude (f.) English, Dutch, and German: from a Germanic personal name composed of the elements *gār, gēr* spear + *þrūþ* strength. The name does not appear in England immediately after the Conquest, but only in the later Middle English period: it is probable that it was introduced by migrants from the Low Countries, who came to England in connection with the cloth trade. It was popular in the 19th century, at the time of the revival of many Germanic names, but has now fallen from favour again. In Germany, usually in the form *Gertrud*, it was much more popular than it ever was in England. It was the name of two famous 13th-century nuns of the Cistercian abbey of Helfta near Eisleben, whose spiritual writings had a great influence.

Variants: German: **Gertrud**; **Gertraud**; **Gertraut** (by association with the element *traut* dear, beloved). Dutch: **Ge(e)rtruida**.

Cognates: Spanish: **Gertrudis**. Portuguese: **Gertrudes**. Low German, Dutch: **Geerta**. Finnish: **Kerttu**.

Short form: English: **Gert**.

Pet forms: English: **Gertie**. German: **Gerda**, **Gerdi**, **Trude**, **Trudi**. Dutch: **Geertke**, **Geertje**. Low German, Frisian: **Gesa**.

Gervaise (m.) English: introduced to Britain by the Normans. It is of unknown derivation: it has been suggested that it might be a dithematic Germanic name, with the first element *gār, gēr* spear, but it is difficult to suggest a plausible second element. The use of the name seems to be due entirely to a certain St Gervasius, whose remains, together with those of Protasius, were discovered in Milan in the year 386. Nothing is known about their lives, but St Ambrose, who had ordered the search for their remains, declared that they were martyrs, and a cult soon grew up. Given these circumstances, we might expect their names to be Greek or Latin, but if they are, the elements remain unidentified. The name is in use mainly among Roman Catholics. *Protasius* has not survived as a given name. See also JARVIS.

Variant: **Gervase**.

Cognates: French **Gervais**. Italian, Spanish, Portuguese: **Gervasio**. German: **Gervas**. Dutch: **Gervaas**. Polish: **Gerwazy**. Russian: **Gervasi**.

Gesa (f.) Frisian pet form of GERTRUDE.

Gesualdo (m.) Italian: from a medieval given name of Germanic origin, probably originally composed of the elements *gisil* pledge (see GISELLE) + *wald* ruler. It has been influenced in form by association with *Gesú* Jesus.

Gethin (m.) Welsh: derived from a lenited adjectival form of the byname *Cethin* 'dusky, swarthy'.

Variant: **Gethen**.

Géza (m.) Hungarian: of uncertain derivation, said to be from a medieval honorific title of Turkic origin.

Gheorghe (m.) Romanian form of GEORGE.

Ghislain (f.) English: of recent origin, or at any rate a recent introduction to the English-speaking world. It is apparently a revival of the Old French oblique case of GISELLE. The spelling indicates some Low German influence.

Variant: **Ghislaine**.

Giacobbe (m.) Italian form of JACOB, rather less common than GIACOMO.

Giacomo (m.) Italian form of JAMES.

Giambattista (m.) Italian: contracted form of GIANNI and BATTISTA.

Giammaria (m.) Italian: contracted form of GIANNI and MARIA.

Giampaolo (m.) Italian: contracted form of GIANNI and PAOLO.

Gianni (m.) Italian: contracted form of GIOVANNI, in very common use.

Feminine form: **Gianna**.

Pet forms: **Giannino**, **Nino** (m.); **Giannetta**, **Giannina** (f.).

Gib (m.) English: medieval and modern short form of GILBERT.

Gideon (m.) Biblical name (meaning 'one who cuts down' in Hebrew) borne by an Israelite leader appointed to deliver his people from the Midianites (Judges 6: 14). He did this by getting his army to creep up on them with their torches hidden in pitchers. The name was popular among the 17th-century Puritans, and is still used in America and in modern Hebrew.

Derivatives: Russian: **Gedeon**. Jewish: **Gidon** (Hebrew).

Gigi (f.) French: pet name, originally a nursery reduplication, based on GEORGINE or *Virginie* (see VIRGINIA).

Gil (m.) Spanish and Portuguese form of GILES.

Gilbert (m.) English, French, Flemish, and Dutch: of Germanic origin, introduced to Britain by the Normans. It is composed of the elements *gisil* pledge + *berht* bright, famous. This was the name of the founder of the only native British religious order (abolished at the Dissolution of the Monasteries), St Gilbert of Sempringham (?1083–1189), in whose honour it is still sometimes bestowed, especially among Roman Catholics. It gained a wider currency in the 19th century. In Gaelic Scotland the name was used from an early period to render the name *Gille Brighde* 'servant of St BRIDGET', gradually assuming the form **Gilleabart**.

Short form: English: **Gib**.

Pet forms: Scottish: **Gibby** (Gaelic **Gibidh**).

Gilda (f.) Italian: apparently of Germanic origin, representing a feminine short form of names containing the element *gild* sacrifice (cf. e.g. HERMENEGILDO). Its popularity as a current given name derives in part from its use in Verdi's *Rigoletto*, in which Gilda, the innocent young daughter of the hunchback jester Rigoletto, becomes the object of the Duke of Mantua's affections and is murdered on her father's orders as the result of a series of misunderstandings.

Giles (m.) English: much altered version of the Late Latin name *Aegidius*, from Greek *Aigidios* (a derivative of *aigidion* kid, young goat). The name was very popular in the Middle Ages, as the result of the fame of the 8th-century St Giles. According to tradition, he was an Athenian citizen who fled to Provence because he could not cope with the fame and adulation caused by his power to work miracles, in particular by healing the lame and crippled. He is the patron saint of cripples.

Variant: **Gyles**.

Cognates: French: **Gilles**. Provençal, Spanish, Portuguese: **Gil**. Danish, Dutch: **Gillis**. Italian: **Egidio**. German: **Ägid(ius)**. Polish: **Egidiusz**, **Idzi**. Hungarian: **Egyed**.

Gill (f.) English: short form of GILLIAN, rather less commonly used as an independent given name than JILL.

Gillanders (m.) Scottish: Anglicized form of Gaelic *Gille Ainndreis* or *Gille Anndrais* 'servant of St ANDREW'.

Gilleonan (m.) Scottish: Anglicized form of Gaelic *Gille Àdhamhnain* 'servant of St Adomnan' (see EUNAN).

Gilles (m.) French form of GILES.

Gillespie (m.) Scottish: Anglicized form of Gaelic *Gille Easbaig* 'bishop's servant'. See also ARCHIBALD.
Pet form: **Beistean**.

Gillian (f.) English: variant of JULIAN, from which it was differentiated in spelling in the 17th century.
Variant: **Jillian**.
Short forms: **Gill, Jill**.
Pet form: **Gilly**.

Gillies (m.) Scottish: Anglicized form of Gaelic *Gille Ìosa* 'servant of Jesus'.

Gillis (m.) Danish and Dutch form of GILES.

Gilly (f.) English: pet form of GILL. There may have been some influence from the name of the *gillyflower* (earlier *gilofre, girofle*, from Late Greek *karyophyllon*).

Gilroy (m.) Irish and Scottish: transferred use of the surname, probably influenced to some extent by ELROY, DELROY, and LEROY. The surname is of Gaelic origin (Irish *Mac Giolla Ruaidh*, Scottish *Mac Gille Ruaidh*), meaning 'son of the red-haired lad'.

Gina (f.) Italian and English: short form of GEORGINA and *Giorgina*, now sometimes used as an independent given name. It has been made famous by the Italian actress Gina Lollobrigida (b. 1927). As an Italian name it also represents in part a short form of *Luigina*, a feminine diminutive form of LUIGI.

Ginevra (f.) Italian form of GENEVIÈVE, now also occasionally used in the English-speaking world.

Ginger (m., f.) English: 1. (m., f.) Originally a nickname for someone with red hair (or, occasionally, with a violent temper), sometimes used as a given name in the 20th century, perhaps for a child with ginger hair.

2. (f.) As a female name it may also represent a pet form of VIRGINIA (as in the case of the film actress Ginger Rogers, born in 1911 as Virginia McMath).

Ginny (f.) English: pet form of VIRGINIA, rarely used as an independent given name.

Gino (m.) Italian: short form of any of the many given names ending in *-gino*, for example *Ambrogino* (a diminutive of *Ambrogio*; see AMBROSE), *Biagino* (a diminutive of BIAGIO), *Giorgino* (a diminutive of GIORGIO), and *Luigino* (a diminutive of LUIGI).

Gioacchino (m.) Italian form of JOACHIM, now only fairly rarely used as a given name.
Variant: **Gioachino**.

Gioconda (f.) Italian: name meaning 'happy, jovial' (from Latin *jucunda*). St Jucunda (d. 466) was a virgin of Reggio in Aemilia, associated with St Prosper.

Giorgio (m.) Italian form of GEORGE.

Giosuè (m.) Italian form of JOSHUA.

Giovanni (m.) Most common Italian form of JOHN. There are several others, e.g. *Gianni* and *Vanni*.
Feminine form: **Giovanna**.

Girolamo (m.) Italian: vernacular form of JEROME, much more common than the learned form GERONIMO.

Giselle (f.) French and English: of Germanic origin, derived from the vocabulary element *gisil* pledge. It was a common practice in medieval Europe to leave children as pledges for an alliance, to be brought up at a foreign court, and the name may be derived as a byname from this practice. This was the name by which the wife of Duke Rollo of Normandy (*c.*860–*c.*930) was known. She was a daughter of Charles the Simple of France, and may indeed have been offered to Rollo as a pledge for their truce in 911. On her account the name enjoyed considerable popularity in France from an early period. *Gisela* was also the name of the wife (*c.*995–*c.*1085) of King Stephen I of Hungary. She was a Bavarian princess, noted for her Christian faith and her good works. Use of the name in English-speaking countries is much more recent, and is due mainly to the ballet *Giselle* (first performed in 1841).

Variant: French: **Gisèle**.

Cognate: German, Dutch: **Gisela**.

Short form: German: **Gisa**.

Gislög (f.) Swedish: from an Old Norse female personal name composed of the elements *gisil* hostage + *laug* consecrated.

Cognate: Norwegian: **Gislaug**.

Gitte (f.) 1. German and Danish: short form of *Brigitte* (see BRIDGET) and *Birgitte* (see BIRGIT).

2. Jewish: of Yiddish origin, originally a nickname meaning 'good' (modern German *gut*).

Pet form (of 2): Jewish: **Gittel**.

Giulia (f.) Italian form of JULIA.

Giulietta (f.) Italian: diminutive of GIULIA.

Giulio (m.) Italian form of JULIUS.

Giuseppe (m.) Italian form of JOSEPH.

Pet forms: **Beppe, Beppo**.

Giuseppina (f.) Italian form of JOSEPHINE.

Gixane (f.) Basque equivalent of ENCARNACIÓN.

Gjord (m.) Swedish: contracted form of an (unattested) Old Norse personal name composed of the elements *guð* god + *friðr* peace, or of the German cognate GOTTFRIED.

Cognate: Norwegian: **Gjurd**.

Gladstone (m.) Scottish and English: transferred use of the surname, originally a local name from *Gledstanes* in Biggar, so called from Old English *glæd* kite + *stān* rock (the final *-s* is a later addition). As a given name it has been adopted in honour of the Victorian Liberal statesman William Ewart Gladstone (1809–98). It is now favoured by West Indians: the Warwickshire and England fast bowler Gladstone Small is of West Indian parentage.

Gladwin (m.) English: transferred use of the surname, itself from a medieval given name composed of the Old English elements *glæd* bright + *wine* friend.

Gladys (f.) Welsh and English: from the Welsh name *Gwladus*, which is of uncertain derivation. It has been quite widely used outside Wales in the 20th century.

Gleb (m.) Russian: of Scandinavian origin, from an Old Norse personal name composed of the elements *guð* god + *leifr* life. St Gleb was a son of Prince Vladimir, first Christian ruler of Kiev, and was assassinated in 1015 together with his brother Boris; his name in the Church was *David*.

Glen (m.) Scottish and English: probably a transferred use of the surname, which was originally a topographic name from the Gaelic element *gleann* valley. It is also possible, however, that the given name is derived directly from the topographic term (compare DEAN). In recent years it has been adopted in England as well as Scotland as a given name. There also appears to have been some confusion with the Welsh name GLYN.

Variant: **Glenn** (borne as a female name by the American actress Glenn Close (b.1947)).

Feminine form: **Glenna**.

Glenda (f.) Welsh: modern coinage, composed of the vocabulary words *glân* clean, pure, holy + *da* good.

Glenys (f.) Welsh: modern coinage, probably from *glân* clean, pure, holy + the ending *-ys* by analogy with names such as DILYS and GLADYS.

Gloria (f.) English: from the Latin word meaning 'glory', not used as a given name before the 20th century, but now very popular. It first occurs as the name of a character in George Bernard Shaw's play *You Never Can Tell* (1898).

Glory (f.) English: Anglicized form of GLORIA, now occasionally used as a given name, especially among Blacks.

Glyn (m.) Welsh: from the Welsh placename element *glyn* valley. This seems to have been transferred directly from a placename to a given name in the 20th century, as the result of a desire to bestow on Welsh children specifically Welsh names.

Variant: **Glynn**.

Glyndwr (m.) Welsh: adopted in the 20th century in honour of the medieval Welsh patriot Owain Glyndŵr (*c.*1359–1416; known in English as Owen Glendower). In his case it was a byname referring to the fact that he came from a place named with the Welsh elements *glyn* valley + *dŵr* water.

Glynis (f.) English: apparently an altered form of GLENYS.

Gobnait (f.) Irish Gaelic: traditional name, of uncertain derivation. It seems to represent a feminine diminutive form of *goba* smith, apparently a reference to the Celtic god of craftsmanship, *Gobniu*. This was the name of an important Munster saint, and the name is still in use in west Munster. It was formerly often Anglicized as ABBIE and ABIGAIL.

Variant: **Gobnet** (Anglicized).

Goddard (m.) English: from the Old English personal name *Godeheard*, composed of the elements *god* god + *heard* hardy, brave, strong. Modern use as a given name is probably a transferred use of the surname derived from this given name in the Middle Ages, rather than a revival of the Old English name.

Cognate: German: GOTTHARD.

Godelieve (f.) French (Walloon): from a Germanic personal name composed of the elements *god* god or *gōd* good + *liob* dear. It is thus a feminine equivalent of German GOTTLIEB. St *Godleva* or *Godliva* (Latinized forms of the name) was murdered in the 11th century by her husband, Bertulf of Ghistelles; she has a cult in Flanders as a suffering innocent, and the name is still in use there.

Godfrey (m.) English: of Germanic origin, introduced to Britain by the Normans. It is composed of the elements *god* god (or *gōd* good) + *fred*, *frid* peace. The name was very popular in the Middle Ages. It was borne by, among others, a Norman saint (*c.*1066–1115) who became bishop of Amiens. There has been considerable confusion with GEOFFREY.

Cognates: Scottish Gaelic: **Goiridh**, **Goraidh**. German: **Gottfried**. Dutch: **Godfried**.

Pet form: German: **Götz**.

Godiva (f.) English: Latinized form of an Old English female personal name composed of the elements *god* god + *gyfu* gift. It is thus the equivalent of THEODORA and *Bogdana* (see BOGDAN). The name was borne by an 11th-century Mercian noblewoman who, according to a famous legend, rode naked on horseback through the streets of Coventry to dissuade her husband Earl Leofric from imposing a heavy tax on the townspeople. It is rarely, if ever, used as a modern given name.

Godwin (m.) English: from the Old English personal name *Godwine*, composed of the elements *god* god + *wine* friend. This name was borne in the 11th century by the Earl of Wessex, the most important man in the England after the king. He was an influential adviser to successive kings of England, and father of the King Harold who was defeated at Hastings in 1066. The personal name continued in use after the Norman Conquest long enough to give rise to a surname. Modern use as a given name is probably a transferred use of the surname, rather than a revival of the Old English name.

Goga (m.) Russian: pet form of *Georgi* and *Yegor* (see GEORGE).

Goito (m.) Spanish: variant of GOYO.

Goldie (f.) Jewish: Anglicized form of Yiddish **Golde** or **Golda** (borne, for example, by the former Israeli prime minister, Golda Meir, 1898–1978, who

Hebraicized her name from Golda Meyerson). It was originally a nickname meaning 'gold'. Occasionally it is a non-Jewish name, derived from an English nickname for a fair-haired person.

Gomer (m.) Biblical: name (meaning 'complete' in Hebrew) borne by a son of Japheth and grandson of Noah. It was taken up by the Puritans, and is still in occasional use in America, where it has been reinforced by the homophonous English surname *Gomer*. This is derived from an Old English personal name composed of the elements *gōd* good + *mǣr* famous.

Gonçalvo (m.) Portuguese form of GONZALO.

Gonzague (m.) French: name chosen in honour of St Aloysius Gonzaga (1568–91). He was a Jesuit of noble birth, who died at the age of twenty-three while tending victims of the plague: he is regarded as a special patron of young people.

Gonzalo (m.) Spanish: of Germanic (Visigothic) origin. The name is found in the Middle Ages in the Latin form *Gundisalvus*, composed of the elements *gund* strife + *salv*, of uncertain meaning (it may be a borrowing of Latin *salvus* whole, safe).

Cognate: Portuguese: **Gonçalvo**.

Goodwin (m.) English: tranferred use of the surname, which is derived from the Old English personal name *Gōdwine*. This is composed of the elements *gōd* good + *wine* friend. There has been considerable confusion with GODWIN.

Gora (m.) Russian: pet form of *Georgi* and *Yegor* (see GEORGE).

Göran (m.) Swedish form of GEORGE. The *-n* suggests derivation from a Latinate elaboration *Georgianus* (based on pairs such as *Julius* and *Julianus*), rather than directly from *Georgius*.

Variants: **Jöran, Örjan**.

Gordon (m.) Scottish and English: from the Scottish surname, which is derived from a placename. It is a matter of dispute whether it referred originally to the Gordon in Berwickshire or to a similarly named place in Normandy. As a given name it seems to have been taken up in honour of Charles George Gordon (1833–85), the British general who died at Khartoum.

Goretti (f.) English and Irish (borne by Roman Catholics): name bestowed in honour of the 20th-century Italian saint, Maria Goretti. In 1902, at the age of eleven, she was savagely assaulted by a neighbour in an attempted rape. She forgave her attacker before expiring in hospital, and was canonized in 1950 as an example to children of a saintly life at an early age.

Gorka (m.) Basque form of GEORGE.

Gormlaith (f.) Irish and Scottish Gaelic: traditional name composed of the elements *gorm* illustrious, splendid + *flaith* lady, princess. This name was borne by the wife of Brian Boru and mother of Sitric, King of Dublin (d. 1030).

Variants: **Gormla** (modern Gaelic spelling); **Gormelia** (an Anglicized form used in Scotland).

Goronwy (m.) Welsh: of uncertain derivation, borne in the *Mabinogi* by Goronwy the Staunch, Lord of Penllyn. He became the lover of the flower-maiden Blodeuedd and murdered her husband Lleu Llaw Gyffes, but Lleu was later restored to life and definitively dispatched Goronwy.

Gorya (m.) Russian: pet form of *Georgi* and *Yegor* (see GEORGE).

Gosia (f.) Polish: short form of *Małgosia*, a pet form of MAŁGORZATA.

Gösta (m.) Swedish: vernacular form of GUSTAV, used in its own right as a baptismal name, but also as a pet form of the learned version.

Gottfried (m.) German form of GODFREY. This was a common name in medieval Germany, and has been ever since. A famous early bearer was the 13th-century poet Gottfried von Strassburg.

Pet form: **Götz**.

Gotthard (m.) German form of GODDARD. St Gotthard was an 11th-century bishop of Hildesheim in Bavaria.

Gotthelf (m.) German: religious name, dating from the 17th century, composed of the elements *Gott* God + the verbal stem *helf, hilf* help.

Variants: **Gotthilf, Helfgott**.

Gotthold (m.) German: religious name, dating from the 17th century, composed of the elements *Gott* God + *hold* lovely, splendid. -(*h*)*old* is a common second element in Germanic personal names, but in most cases it derives from *-wald* rule. This given name was borne, for example, by the dramatist and critic Gotthold Lessing (1729–81).

Gottlieb (m.) German: religious name, dating from the 17th century, composed of the elements *Gott* God + the verbal stem *lieb* love (and so an equivalent of THEOPHILUS).

Cognate: Dutch: **Godlef**.

Gottlob (m.) German: religious name, dating from the 17th century, composed of the elements *Gott* God + the verbal stem *lob* praise.

Gottschalk (m.) German: religious name, dating from the early Middle Ages, composed of the elements *god, got* God + *scalc* servant. St Gotteschalk (d. 1066) was a Wendish prince who was married to a grand-niece of King Canute of England. An earlier Gotteschalk (d. *c.*868) preached total predestination. In the later Middle Ages the name was for a time characteristically Jewish, used as a translation of the Hebrew names *Abdiel* or OBADIAH. It is now little used by any group.

Götz (m.) German: pet form of GOTTFRIED.

Gotzon (m.) Basque: vernacular equivalent of ANGEL; see also AINGERU.

Feminine form: **Gotzone**.

Goyo (m.) Spanish: pet form of *Gregorio* (see GREGORY).

Variant: **Goito**.

Grace (f.) English, Irish, and Scottish: from the abstract noun (from Latin *grātia*), first used as a given name by the Puritans in the 17th century, and still moderately popular (and to a large extent dissociated from the vocabulary word). Its popularity has increased in the 20th century owing to the fame of the late wife of Prince Rainier of Monaco, the actress Grace Kelly (1928–82). It has always been a popular name in Scotland and northern England (borne, for example, by Grace Darling, the lighthouse keeper's daughter whose heroism in 1838, saving sailors in a storm, caught popular imagination). In Ireland it has often been used as an Anglicized form of GRÁINNE, for example in the case of the famous 16th-century female sea captain Gráinne Ní Mháille, known in English as Grace O'Malley.

Cognates: Italian: **Grazia**. Spanish: **Gracia**. German, Dutch: **Gratia**.

Pet form: English, Scottish: **Gracie**.

Graciano (m.) Spanish and Portuguese form of GRATIEN.

Gracie (f.) English and Scottish: pet form of GRACE. It was made famous by the Lancashire singer and comedienne Gracie Fields (1898–1979), whose original name was Grace Stansfield.

Graham (m.) Scottish and English: from a Scottish surname, which derives from a place that is in neither Scotland nor Normandy, but Lincolnshire. *Grantham*, near the border with Leicestershire and Nottinghamshire, is recorded in Domesday Book not only in its current form but also as *Grandham*, *Granham*, and *Graham*; it seems to have been originally named as the 'gravelly place', from Old English *grand* gravel (unattested) + *hām* home-

stead. The surname was taken to Scotland in the 12th century by Sir William de Graham, founder of a famous clan. The earls of Montrose were among his descendants.
Variants: **Grahame, Graeme.**

Gráinne (f.) Irish Gaelic: of uncertain origin, possibly a derivative of *grán* grain or *gráin* disgust. In Irish legend Gráinne was the daughter of King Cormac; she was beloved by the hero Finn, but eloped with Finn's nephew Diarmait. Finn pursued them over great distances, and eventually brought about the death of Diarmait, after which Gráinne killed herself. The name has sometimes been Anglicized as GRACE.

Grania (f.) English and Irish: Latinized form of GRÁINNE.
Variant: **Granya.**

Grant (m.) Scottish and English: from the Scottish surname, the name of a famous clan, which is nevertheless probably derived from a Norman nickname meaning 'large' (Anglo-Norman *grand*). In America the name is sometimes bestowed in honour of the Civil War general and 18th president, Ulysses S. Grant (1822–85).

Granville (m.) English: from one of the Norman baronial names that subsequently became aristocratic English surnames and are now used intermittently as male given names. This one derives from any of several places in Normandy named with the Old French elements *grand* large + *ville* settlement.

Granya (f.) English and Irish: variant spelling of GRANIA.

Gratia (f.) Latinate form of GRACE, used in Germany and Holland.

Gratien (m.) French: from Latin *Gratiānus*, a derivative of *Gratius*, itself a derivative of *gratus* pleasing, lovely. St Gratian (d. ?*c.*337) was a disciple of St Denis of Paris; he became the first bishop of Tours.
Cognates: Italian: **Graziano.** Spanish, Portuguese: **Graciano.**

Grazia (f.) Italian form of GRACE.

Graziano (m.) Italian form of GRATIEN.

Graziella (f.) Italian: diminutive form of GRAZIA.

Greer (f.) Scottish and English: from the Scottish surname, which originated in the Middle Ages from a contracted form of GREGOR. It has become known as a female name in the English-speaking world through the fame of the actress Greer Garson (b. 1908), whose mother's maiden name it was.
Variant: **Grier.**

Greg (m.) English and Scottish: short form of GREGORY or GREGOR.
Variants: **Gregg, Greig** (chiefly Scottish, and generally a transferred use of the surname so spelled, which is itself a derivative of the given name).

Greger (m.) Swedish form of GREGORY.

Gregers (m.) Danish and Norwegian form of GREGORY (from Latin *Gregorius*).

Grégoire (m.) Traditional French form of GREGORY.

Gregor (m.) Scottish form of GREGORY, currently undergoing a revival in popularity. In part it represents an Anglicized form of Gaelic **Griogair**, which gave rise to the Highland surname *MacGregor*. This is derived in turn from the Norman French form of *Gregory* (see GRÉGOIRE).

Gregory (m.) English and Scottish: via Latin *Gregorius* from the post-classical Greek name *Gregōrios* 'watchful' (a derivative of *gregōrein* to watch, be vigilant). The name was an extremely popular one with the early Christians, who were mindful of the instruction 'be sober, be vigilant' (1 Peter 5: 8): it was borne by a number of early saints. The most important, in honour of whom the name was often bestowed from medieval times onwards, were Gregory of Nazianzen (*c.*329–90), Gregory of Nyssa (d. *c.*395), Gregory of Tours (538–94), and Pope Gregory the

Great (*c.*540–604). The name has traditionally been particularly popular in Scotland, where it often took the form GREGOR.

Cognates: Irish Gaelic: **Gréagóir**. Scottish Gaelic: **Griogair**. Welsh: **Grigor**. French: **Grégoire**; **Grégory** (Provençal in origin, now more fashionable than the traditional form). Italian, Spanish, Portuguese: **Gregorio**. Dutch, Frisian: **Joris**. Swedish: **Greger**. Danish, Norwegian: **Gregers**. Polish: **Grzegorz**. Czech: **Řehoř**. Russian: **Grigori**. Hungarian: **Gergely**. Finnish: **Reijo**.

Short forms: English: **Greg**. Scottish: **Greg(g)**, **Greig**.

Pet forms: Spanish: **Goyo, Goito**. Russian: **Grisha**.

Greville (m.) English: transferred use of the surname, which is a Norman baronial name from *Gréville* in La Manche. The Greville family were earls of Warwick, and held Warwick Castle from the time of Queen Elizabeth I, who granted it to her favourite Fulke Greville (1554–1628).

Greta (f.) Short form of *Margareta* (see MARGARET), used particularly in Sweden, Germany, and Ireland. It became fairly popular in the English-speaking world as a result of the fame of the Swedish-born film actress Greta Garbo (1905–92; b. Greta Louisa Gustafsson).

Grete (f.) German and Danish: short form of *Margarete* (see MARGARET), now also occasionally used as an independent given name in the English-speaking world.

Pet form: German: **Gretel** (made famous by the story of Hansel and Gretel, the 'babes in the wood' in *Grimm's Fairy Tales*).

Gretta (f.) English: variant spelling of GRETA.

Griet (f.) Low German, Dutch, and Frisian: short form of *Margriet* (see MARGARET), now used as an independent given name.

Variants: **Greet, Gret**.

Pet forms: **Grietje, Greetje, Gretje**.

Griff (m.) Welsh: informal short form of GRIFFITH.

Griffin (m.) Welsh: from a medieval Latinized form, *Griffinus*, of GRIFFITH.

Griffith (m.) Welsh: Anglicized form of **Gruffudd** or **Griffudd**, Old Welsh *Grip(p)iud*. The second element of this means 'lord, prince', but the first is extremely uncertain. Gruffydd ap Llewellyn (d. 1063) was one of the most able rulers of Wales in the Middle Ages, scoring some notable victories over the English until he was eventually defeated by King Harold in 1063.

Short form: **Griff**.

Pet forms: **Guto; Gutun, Gutyn**.

Grigori (m.) Russian form of GREGORY.

Pet form: **Grisha**.

Griogair (m.) Scottish Gaelic form of GREGOR.

Variant: **Griogal** (a dialectal form).

Griselda (f.) Scottish and English: of uncertain origin, possibly from a Germanic name composed of the elements *gris* grey + *hild* battle. It became popular in the Middle Ages with reference to the tale of 'patient Griselda' (told by Boccaccio and Chaucer), who was taken as a model of the patient, long-suffering wife.

Variant: Scottish: **Grizel**.

Grisha (m.) Russian: pet form of GRIGORI.

Grit (f.) German: short form of *Margrit* (see MARGARET).

Variants: **Gritt, Gritta**.

Grizel (f.) Scottish: vernacular form of GRISELDA. The name has now almost or completely died out, no doubt in part because of its similarity to the vocabulary word *grizzle* meaning 'to grumble or whine'.

Gro (f.) Scandinavian (esp. Norwegian): from an Old Norse female personal name of uncertain derivation. It may derive from the Norse verb *gróa* to grow, increase, or possibly be related to the Celtic element *gruach* woman.

Grover (m.) English: transferred use of the surname, which originated as a local name for someone who lived near a grove of trees (Old English *grāf*). Use as a given name may be partly due to the American president Stephen Grover Cleveland (1837–1908), who was generally known as 'Grover Cleveland'.

Grunya (f.) Russian: pet form of AGRAFENA.

Grusha (f.) Russian: pet form of AGRAFENA.

Grzegorz (m.) Polish form of GREGORY.

Guadalupe (f.) Spanish: name reflecting a title of the Blessed Virgin Mary, Our Lady of Guadalupe. Guadalupe is a place in the province of Cáceres, so called from Arabic *wādī al-lubb* river of the wolf; it was the site of a famous Hieronymite convent, founded in the 14th century, which possesses a celebrated image of the Virgin. In 1531 a Mexican peasant saw a vision of the Virgin Mary, in which she allegedly declared herself to be the 'Lady of Guadalupe'; it has been suggested that this choice of title was inspired by the name of a native Mexican goddess, derived from Nahuatl *coatl* serpent.
Pet form: **Lupita**,

Gudrun (f.) Scandinavian: from an Old Norse female personal name composed of the elements *guð* god + *rūn* secret lore. In Norse legend this was the name borne by the heroine of the *Volsungasaga*, sister of Gunnar and wife of Sigurd, whose destruction she brought about. The name was revived in the second part of the 19th century, and is now also used in Germany and to some extent in the English-speaking world, probably under the influence of Wagner, although the character of Gutrune in Wagner's *Götterdämmerung* does not correspond to the Gudrun of the *Volsungasaga*.
Pet form: Norwegian: **Guro** (informal).

Guglielmo (m.) Italian form of WILLIAM.

Guido (m.) Italian form of GUY. Two important saints of this name lived in the 11th century: an abbot of Pomposa, near Ferrara, and a bishop of Acqui in Monferrato, Piedmont.

Guilherme (m.) Portuguese form of WILLIAM.

Guillaume (m.) French form of WILLIAM.

Guillem (m.) Catalan form of WILLIAM.

Guillermo (m.) Spanish form of WILLIAM.

Guinevere (f.) English: from the Old French form of the Welsh name *Gwenhwyfar*, composed of the elements *gwen* white, fair, blessed, holy + *hwyfar* smooth, soft. It is famous as the name of King Arthur's beautiful wife, who in most versions of the Arthurian legends is unfaithful to him, having fallen in love with Sir Lancelot. See also GAYNOR and JENNIFER.

Gull (f.) Scandinavian: pet form of the various women's names of Old Norse origin containing the first element *guð* god. It has also been associated with *gull* gold, and is now much used in Swedish compound names such as **Gull-Britt**, **Gull-Lis**, and **Gull-Maj**.

Gumersinda (f.) Spanish: from a Germanic (Visigothic) personal name composed of the elements *guma* man + *sind* path.
Short form: **Sinda**.

Gunder (m.) Danish: variant of GUNNAR.

Guni (m.) Jewish: name (meaning 'painted, coloured' in Hebrew) borne in the Bible by a son of Naphtali and grandson of Jacob (Genesis 46: 24).

Gunilla (f.) Swedish: Latinized form of GUNNHILD, in use from the 16th century to the present day. It enjoyed a vogue of particular popularity in Sweden during the 1940s.

Gunn (f.) Scandinavian: short form of the various women's names of Old Norse origin containing the first element *gunnr* strife, such as GUNNBORG, GUNNHILD, and GUNNVOR.

Variant: **Gun**.

Gunnar (m.) Scandinavian form of GÜNTHER. The name is of West Germanic, not Old Norse, origin but has been used in Scandinavia since the time of the sagas at least.

Variant: Danish: **Gunder**.

Gunnborg (f.) Scandinavian: from an Old Norse female personal name composed of the elements *gunnr* strife + *borg* fortification.

Variant: **Gunborg**.

Gunne (m.) Scandinavian: from Old Norse *Gunni*, a short form of GUNNAR and of the various rarer male names of Old Norse origin containing the first element *gunnr* strife, such as **Gunnbjörn** ('strife + bear') and **Gunnleif** ('strife + descendant'). In Norway it is occasionally used as a female name, from Old Norse *Gunna*, a short form of the various female names containing this same element.

Gunnhild (f.) Scandinavian: from an Old Norse female personal name composed of the nearly synonymous elements *gunnr* strife + *hildr* battle. The name has been in common use since the Viking period. It lies behind the English surnames *Gunnell* and *Cunnell*.

Variant: **Gunhild**.

Gunnvor (f.) Scandinavian: from an Old Norse female personal name composed of the elements *gunnr* strife + *vor* cautious, wary.

Variants: **Gunvor**; **Gunver** (chiefly Danish).

Günther (m.) German: from an old Germanic personal name composed of the elements *gund* strife + *heri*, *hari* army, warrior. According to Germanic legend, as recounted in the *Nibelungenlied*, Günther was the name of a king of Burgundy, brother-in-law of the warrior hero Siegfried. Siegfried obtains the beautiful Brunhild as wife for Günther, but the outcome is tragedy and destruction: Brunhild contrives Siegfried's death; Siegfried's widow Kriemhild, Günther's sister, takes her revenge by destroying Günther, Brunhild, and all their house. This grisly story was taken up by Richard Wagner and adapted for his opera *Götterdämmerung* (1876), and the revival of popularity of the name probably owes something to Wagner. The name has long been popular in German-speaking countries, in spite of the tragic story with which it is associated. On a more historical level, its currency in the Middle Ages probably owed something to the Blessed Günther (955–1045), a Bavarian monk, who was a cousin of St Stephen of Hungary.

Variants: **Gunt(h)er**, **Günter**.

Cognates: Scandinavian: **Gunnar**; **Gunder** (Danish).

Guro (f.) Norwegian: informal pet form of GUDRUN.

Gurutz (m.) Basque: name expressing devotion to the Cross. The vocabulary word *gurutz* is a borrowing from Latin (cf. CRUZ), but in Basque the name is a male one, not female.

Gus (m.) English, Scottish, and Irish: short form of AUGUSTUS, ANGUS, or *Gustave* (see GUSTAV). In the case of Gus the Theatre Cat, a character in T. S. Eliot's *Old Possum's Book of Practical Cats* (1939), it is a short form of *Asparagus*!

Gustav (m.) Scandinavian: from an Old Norse personal name composed of the tribal name *Gautr* + the element *stafr* staff. According to some scholars this name is of Slavonic origin (cf. DAGMAR), and originally had the form *Gostislav* or *Goslav*. It has been borne by various kings of Sweden, beginning with Gustav Vasa (?1496–1560), who was elected king in 1523 after freeing Sweden from Danish rule.

Variants: **Gustavus** (Latinized). Swedish: **Gustaf**, **Gösta**.

Cognates: French: **Gustave** (used also occasionally in the English-speaking world). Finnish: **Kustaa**, **Kyösti**. Dutch: **Gustaaf**, **Staaf**.

Guto (m.) Welsh: pet form of *Gruffudd* (see GRIFFITH).

Variants: **Gutun, Gutyn.**

Guy (m.) English and French (of Norman origin): from a short form of a compound Germanic name having as its first element *witu* wood or *wīt* wide. In Norman French initial *w-* regularly became *gu-*, and the usual Norman forms of the name were *Gy* or *Guido*. In medieval Latin the same name occurs as *Wido*. It was a popular name among the Normans, enhanced no doubt by the romance of *Guy of Warwick*, recounting the exploits of a folk hero of the Crusades.

Cognates: Italian: **Guido**. Dutch: **Veit**.

Gwalchmai (m.) Welsh: traditional name composed of the elements *gwalch* hawk + *mai* plain. In the *Mabinogi*, Gwalchmai (or *Gwalchmei*) is the name of one of King Arthur's nine captains, 'the most distinguished for his fighting ability and his noble bearing'.

Gwallter (m.) Welsh form of WALTER.

Gwatcyn (m.) Welsh form of WATKIN.

Gwen (f.) Welsh and English: short form of GWENDOLEN or GWENLLIAN, or an independent name from Welsh *gwen*, the feminine form of *gwyn* white, fair, blessed, holy (see GWYN). It was borne by a 5th-century saint, aunt of St David and mother of the minor saints Cybi and Cadfan, and by a reputed daughter of Brychan.

Gwenda (f.) Welsh and English: of modern origin, composed of the vocabulary words *gwen* white, fair, blessed, holy (see GWEN) + *da* good.

Gwendolen (f.) Welsh and English: apparently composed of the elements *gwen* white, fair, blessed, holy + *dolen* ring, bow. According to Geoffrey of Monmouth, this was the name of the wife of the mythical Welsh king Locrine, who, however, left her for a German princess called Estrildis. Gwendolen in revenge had Estrildis and her daughter Sabrina drowned in the River Severn. The name is borne by one of the principal characters in Oscar Wilde's play *The Importance of Being Earnest* (first performed in 1895).

Variants: **Gwendolin, Gwendolyn; Gwendoline** (formed under the influence of the many female given names ending in *-line*).

Gwenfrewi (f.) Welsh: from *gwen* white, fair, blessed, holy + *frewi* reconciliation. This was borne by a 7th-century Welsh saint around whom a large body of legends grew up. It has been Anglicized as WINIFRED.

Gwenhwyfar (f.) Welsh form of GUINEVERE.

Gwenllian (f.) Welsh: traditional name composed of the elements *gwen*, feminine form of *gwyn* white, fair, blessed, holy + *lliant* flood, flow (probably in the transferred sense 'foamy, white', referring to a pale complexion).

Gwenyth (f.) Welsh and English: variant of GWYNETH. It may alternatively be based on Welsh *gwenith* wheat, a word used in poetry to mean 'the favourite' or 'the pick of the bunch'.

Gwerful (f.) Welsh: traditional name composed of *gwair* bend, ring, circle + the mutated form of *mul* shy, modest.

Variants: **Gweirful, Gwerfyl.**

Gwilym (m.) Welsh form of WILLIAM, in use since the Middle Ages, and currently undergoing a revival in popularity.

Gwladus (f.) The original Welsh spelling of GLADYS, occasionally revived in recent years.

Variant: **Gwladys.**

Gwyn (m.). Welsh: originally a byname from Welsh *gwyn* white, fair, blessed, holy. See also WYN.

Gwynedd (m.) Welsh: name taken from a region of medieval North Wales (now resurrected as the name of a new composite county in Wales).

Gwyneth (f.) Welsh: altered form of GWYNEDD, used as a female name. Its popularity from the late 19th century, at first in Wales and then more widely in the English-speaking world, seems to have been due originally to the influence of Annie Harriet Hughes (1852–1910), who adopted the pen-name Gwyneth Vaughan.

Gwynfor (m.) Welsh: coined in the 20th century, apparently from the elements *gwyn* white, fair, blessed, holy + the mutated unaccented form of *mawr* great, large, found in this form in a number of placenames.

Gwythyr (m.) Welsh: traditional name derived in sub-Roman times from the Latin name VICTOR. A character with this name appears in the *Mabinogi*.
Variant: **Gwydyr**.

Gyles (m.) English: variant spelling of GILES.

György (m.) Hungarian form of GEORGE.

Győző (m.) Hungarian: name meaning 'conqueror', used as a loan translation of VICTOR.

Gytha (f.) English: from an Old English female personal name, a short form of various compound names containing the element *gyð* strife. This name was born in the 11th century by the wife of Godwin, Earl of Wessex. It was revived in Victorian times and has been occasionally used since then.

Gyula (m.) Hungarian form of JULIUS.

H

Habacuc (m.) Biblical name, meaning 'embrace' in Hebrew, borne by one of the twelve minor prophets, author of the book of the Bible that bears his name. The name is hardly, if ever, used in modern times, but was occasionally used by Puritans and Dissenters from the 17th century to the 19th.

Variant: **Habakkuk** (spelling used in the Authorized Version of the Bible).

Hadassah (f.) Jewish: Hebrew name (Esther 2: 7) of the biblical queen more commonly known by her Persian name ESTHER. It is sometimes used as a modern given name by Jews.

Short form: **Dassah**.

Hagen (m.) Danish form of HÅKAN.

Hagar (f.) Biblical name (meaning 'flight' in Hebrew, although the biblical character so called was Egyptian) borne by a handmaid of Abraham's wife Sarah. Sarah let Hagar conceive a child by Abraham since she herself was barren, but she later resented her and treated her so harshly that she fled. Hagar was sent back by an angel, and her son Ishmael became Abraham's first child.

Haidee (f.) English: as the name of a character in Byron's poem *Don Juan* (1819–24), this may have been intended to be connected with the classical Greek adjective *aidoios* modest. In modern use it is taken as a variant of HEIDI.

Håkan (m.) Swedish: from the Old Norse personal name *Hákon*, composed of the elements *hā* horse or high + *konr* son, descendant.

Variant: **Hakon** (an older form).

Cognates: Danish: **Hagen**. Norwegian: **Håkon**.

Hal (m.) English: short form of HARRY, of medieval origin. It was used by Shakespeare in *King Henry IV* as the name of the king's son, the future Henry V. Substitution of *-l* for *-r* has also occurred in derivatives of *Terry* (*Tel*), *Derek* (*Del*), and in girls' names such as *Sally* (from *Sarah*).

Haldor (m.) Scandinavian: from an Old Norse personal name composed of the element *hallr* rock + a derivative of the divine name *Þórr* Thor, the god of thunder.

Variant: **Halldor** (chiefly Norwegian).

Hale (m.) English: transferred use of the surname, originally a local name for someone living in a nook or recess (Old English *halh*).

Haley (f.) English: variant spelling of HAYLEY.

Halina (f.) Polish: of uncertain derivation. It seems to be a form of either GALINA or HELEN.

Hall (m.) English: transferred use of the surname, originally a local name for someone, usually a servant or retainer, who lived at a manor house (Old English *heall*).

Halle (m.) Scandinavian: short form of the names HALSTEN and HALVARD, or a pet form of HARALD.

Halsten (m.) Swedish: from an Old Norse personal name composed of the nearly synonymous elements *hallr* rock + *steinn* stone.

Variant: **Hallsten**.

Cognate: Norwegian: **Hallstein**.

Halvard (m.) Scandinavian: from an Old Norse personal name composed of the elements *hallr* rock + *varðr* guardian, watcher, defender.

Variants: **Halvor**; **Hallvard**, **Hallvor** (chiefly Norwegian); **Halvar** (Swedish).

Halvdan (m.) Scandinavian: from an Old Norse personal name, originally a byname for someone who was of partly Danish stock (from Old Norse *hálfr* half + the ethnic name *Danr*). The personal name was a relatively common one in the Viking period and lies behind the English surname *Haldane*.

Hamilton (m.) English (mainly U.S.) and Scottish: transferred use of the Scottish and American surname. Use as a given name seems to have begun in America in honour of Alexander Hamilton (?1757–1804), who was Secretary of the Treasury under George Washington and did much to establish the political and financial system on which the industrial growth and prosperity of the United States came to be founded. He was killed in a duel with the irascible Aaron Burr. The surname was brought to Scotland in or before the 13th century from a village (now deserted) called *Hamilton* or *Hameldune*, near Barkby in Leicestershire (named with the Old English elements *hamel* blunt, flat-topped, or crooked + *dun* hill). It became the surname of an enormously widespread and influential family, who acquired many titles, including the dukedom of Hamilton. The town near Glasgow so called is named after the family, not vice versa.

Hamish (m.) Scottish: Anglicized spelling of the vocative case, *Sheumais*, of the Gaelic version of JAMES; see SEUMAS.

Hana (f.) Czech: short form of JOHANA.

Handel (m.) From the surname of the composer, adopted as a given name particularly by the music-loving Welsh (cf. HAYDN). Georg Friedrich Handel (1685–1759), who came to England with George I when he succeeded to the English throne in 1714, is regarded as one of the greatest exponents of the baroque. His surname is derived from a diminutive form of the given name HANS.

Hank (m.) English: originally a medieval back-formation from *Hankin*, which is composed of *Han* (a short form of *Jehan* JOHN) + the Middle English diminutive suffix *-kin*. However, the suffix was mistaken for the Anglo-Norman diminutive *-in*, hence the form *Hank*. *Hank* is now sometimes used as an independent given name in America, where it is usually taken as a pet form of HENRY. It has more or less died out in Britain.

Hanke (m.) Low German: pet form from a short form of JOHAN.

Hannah (f.) Biblical: name of the mother of the prophet Samuel (1 Samuel 1: 2), Hebrew *Hanna*, from a Hebrew word meaning 'He (God) has favoured me (i.e. with a child)' (see ANNE). This form of the name was taken up as a given name by the Puritans in the 16th and 17th centuries, and has always been a common Jewish name.

Derivative: Polish: **Hania**.

Hanne (f.) German: short form of JOHANNA. The name is often used in combinations such as **Hannelore**.

Hannes (m.) Short form of *Johannes*, the Latin form of JOHN. It is found in Dutch, and is a common name in South Africa, where the Latin forms of names (such as *Jacobus*, *Petrus*, and *Stephanus*) are still very much in current use among Afrikaners.

Hanni (f.) Swiss: pet form of HANNE.

Hannibal (m.) English form of ANNIBALE, extremely rarely used as a given name.

Hannu (m.) A Finnish form of JOHN.

Hans (m.) German form of JOHN, derived from a shortened and contracted form of Latin *Johannes*.

Hansi (m., f.) German: 1. (m.) Pet form of HANS.

2. (f.) Less commonly, a pet form of JOHANNA, occasionally used as an independent given name, in line with other pet forms such as MAXI and MITZI.

Hansine (f.) German and Danish: feminine form of HANS, formed with the suffix seen in names such as *Wilhelmine* (see WILHELMINA).

Hanuš (m.) Czech: pet form of JOHAN.

Variants: **Hanušek, Hanek, Nušek.**

Happy (f.) English: from the English vocabulary word, occasionally used in the 20th century for the sake of the good omen of its meaning; cf. MERRY and GAY.

Harald (m.) Scandinavian form of HAROLD. It has been popular in Norway, Sweden, and Denmark uninterruptedly from the time of the very earliest records, and was borne by several medieval kings of Norway and Denmark. Harald Fairhair (?850–933) was the first proper king of Norway, and presided over a remarkable period of Viking civilization. During his reign the first substantial wave of Scandinavian settlers migrated to Iceland.

Pet form: **Halle.**

Harbert (m.) Dutch form of HERBERT.

Variant: **Harbrecht.**

Harding (m.) English: transferred use of the surname, which is derived from a medieval English given name. The Old English form was *Hearding*, a derivative (originally patronymic in form) of *Heard* 'hardy, brave, strong', a byname or short form of the various compound personal names containing this element.

Harlan (m.) English (esp. U.S.): transferred use of the surname, originally a local name from any of various places in England, mostly named with the Old English elements *hara* hare + *land*. Use as a given name honours the American judge John Marshall Harlan (1833–1911), a conservative Republican who was nevertheless a pioneering supporter of civil rights in the Supreme Court.

Variant: **Harland.**

Harold (m.) English: from an Old English personal name composed of the elements *here* army + *weald* ruler, reinforced before the Norman Conquest by the Scandinavian cognate *Haraldr*, introduced by Norse settlers. The name was not common in the later Middle Ages, perhaps because it was associated with King Harold, the loser at the Battle of Hastings in 1066. It was revived in the 19th century, along with a number of other Old English names.

Cognates: Scandinavian: **Harald.** Scottish Gaelic: **Arailt, Haral.**

Harper (m., f.) English (mainly U.S.): transferred use of the surname, originally an occupational name for someone who played the harp. As a female name it has been borne in particular by the southern American writer Harper Lee, author of *To Kill a Mockingbird* (1960).

Harriet (f.) English: Anglicized form of French *Henriette*, a feminine diminutive of HENRY (French *Henri*) coined in the 17th century. It was quite common in England in the 18th and early 19th centuries. In Scotland it has been used as an Anglicized form of OIGHRIG.

Pet form: **Hattie.**

Harriette (f.) English: variant of HARRIET, probably coined to look more 'feminine', but it could be a reconstructed form, blending HARRIET with its source *Henriette*.

Harrison (m.) English: transferred use of the surname, which originated as a patronymic, meaning 'son of HARRY'.

Harry (m.) English: pet form of HENRY, sometimes used as an independent name. This was the usual English form of HENRY in the Middle Ages and later, and was the form used by Shakespeare as the familiar name of the mature King Henry V (compare HAL). The intermediate form *Herry* probably arose from the French pronunciation with a nasalized vowel, or it may be the result of straightforward assimilation; the change of *-er-* to *-ar-* was a regular feature of late Middle English.

Pet form: **Hal.**

Hartley (m.) English: transferred use of the surname, originally a local name from any of the numerous places so called. Most (for example, those in Berkshire, Dorset, Hampshire, and Kent) are so called from Old English *heorot* hart, male deer + *lēah* wood or clearing. One in Northumbria is from *heorot* + *hlāw* hill, and one in Cumbria is probably from *harað* wood + *clā* claw, i.e. river-fork.

Hartmann (m.) German: from an old Germanic personal name composed of the elements *hard* hardy, brave, strong + *man* man. The Blessed Hartmann (d. 1164) enjoyed a cult in Austria. Hartmann von Aue (*c.*1170–*c.*1220) was an influential writer of chivalric romances. See also ERDMANN.

Hartmut (m.) German: from an old Germanic personal name composed of the elements *hard* hardy, brave, strong + *muot* spirit, courage. See also ERDMUT.

Hartwig (m.) German: from an old Germanic personal name composed of the elements *hard* hardy, brave, strong + *wīg* battle. The Blessed Hartwig was archbishop of Salzburg 991–1023.

Hartwin (m.) German: from an old Germanic personal name composed of the elements *hard* hardy, brave, strong + *wine* friend.

Cognate: Italian: **Arduino.**

Harvey (m.) English: transferred use of the surname, which is of Breton origin, from a personal name composed of the elements *haer* battle + *vy* worthy. It was introduced to Britain by the Bretons who settled in East Anglia and elsewhere in the wake of the Norman Conquest.

Cognate: French: **Hervé** (a direct borrowing of the Breton personal name).

Short form: English: **Harv(e).**

Haskel (m.) Jewish (U.S.): altered form of HESKEL, made to correspond with the non-Jewish surname *Haskel*, which is a medieval English derivative of the Old Norse personal name *Áskell*, composed of the elements *ás* god, divinity + *ketill* sacrificial cauldron.

Hattie (f.) English: pet form of HARRIET, now rarely used.

Hava (f.) Jewish: modern Hebrew form of EVE.

Havel (m.) Czech form of GAWEŁ.

Pet forms: **Háva, Havelek, Havlík.**

Haya (f.) Jewish: name meaning 'life' in Hebrew. It represents a feminine form of HYAM.

Haydn (m.) From the surname of the composer, adopted in his honour particularly by the music-loving Welsh (cf. HANDEL). Josef Haydn (1732–1809) was court composer and kapellmeister to the powerful Count Nicholas Esterhazy, and spent most of his working life at the Esterhazy palace near Vienna. His surname is a respelling of the nickname *Heiden* 'heathen' (Middle High German *heiden*, Old High German *heidano*).

Hayley (f.) English: transferred use of the surname, which derives from a placename, probably *Hailey* in Oxfordshire, which was originally named from Old English *hēg* hay + *lēah* clearing. Its use as a given name began only in the 1960s, inspired by the actress Hayley Mills, daughter of Sir John Mills and Mary Hayley Bell, but it has enjoyed great popularity since then.

Variant: **Haley.**

Hazel (f.) English: from the vocabulary word denoting the tree (Old English *hæsel*), or its light reddish-brown nuts. This is one of the most successful of the names coined in the 19th century from words denoting plants, and it has enjoyed continuous popularity. The fact that it also denotes an eye colour may have influenced its continuing choice.

Heather (f.) English: from the word denoting the hardy, brightly coloured plant (Middle English *hather*; the spelling was altered in the 18th century as a result of folk etymological association with *heath*). The name was first used in the late

19th century; it has been particularly popular since about 1950.

Hebe (f.) English (pronounced as two syllables): from a Greek name, a feminine form of the adjective *hēbos* young. This was borne in Greek mythology by a minor goddess who was a personification of youth. She was a daughter of Zeus and the wife of Hephaistos; it was her duty to act as cup-bearer to the gods. The name was taken up in England in the late 19th century, but it has fallen out of fashion again.

Heber (m.) 1. Biblical: name, meaning 'enclave' in Hebrew, borne by various minor characters. This name has only occasionally been used outside Ireland (see below).

2. Irish: from the Gaelic name **Éibhear**, assimilated in form to the biblical name. *Éibhir* was the name of the son of Míl, leader of the Gaelic race that, according to legend, first conquered Ireland. This is still a common given name among the McMahon families.

Hector (m.) 1. English and Scottish (also French and Spanish): name borne in classical legend by the Trojan champion, who was killed by the Greek Achilles. His name (Greek *Hektōr*) seems to be an agent derivative of Greek *ekhein* to check, restrain.

2. Scottish: Anglicized form of the Gaelic name EACHANN.

Cognates: Italian: **Ettore**. Portuguese: **Heitor**.
Pet form: Scottish: **Heckie**.
Feminine form: Scottish: **Hectorina**.

Hedda (f.) Scandinavian: pet form of HEDVIG. It is widely known in the English-speaking world as the name of the eponymous heroine of Henrik Ibsen's play *Hedda Gabler* (1890).

Cognate: Italian: **Edda**.

Heddwyn (m.) Welsh: modern coinage, composed of the elements *hedd* peace + *(g)wyn* white, fair, blessed, holy. Use as a given name was popularized by the fame of the young poet Ellis Humphrey Evans who posthumously won the bardic chair at the National Eisteddfod in 1917, having been killed in the First World War; his bardic name was *Hedd Wyn*.

Hedley (m.) English: transferred use of the surname, originally a local name from any of various places in Durham and Northumbria so called from Old English *hǣþ* heather + *lēah* wood or clearing.

Hedvig (f.) Scandinavian form of HEDWIG, popular in Denmark, Norway, and Sweden. It is borne by the young girl who is the central character in Henrik Ibsen's play *The Wild Duck* (1886).

Hedwig (f.) German: from an old Germanic female personal name composed of the elements *hadu* contention + *wīg* war. The Blessed Hedwig or Hadwigis (d. *c.*887) was the Benedictine abbess of Herford in Westphalia.

Cognates: French: **Edwige**. Italian: **Edvige**. Scandinavian: **Hedvig**. Polish: JADWIGA. Czech: **Hedvika**.
Pet form: Scandinavian: **Hedda**.

Heidi (f.) Swiss: pet form of ADELHEID, now also popular in the English-speaking world, as a result of the cult of Johanna Spyri's popular children's classic *Heidi* (1881).

Heike (f.) Low German: contracted pet form of HENRIKE. It has now attained a wider popularity in the German-speaking world as an independent given name.

Heikki (m.) Finnish form of HENRY.

Heiko (m.) Low German and Frisian: pet form of HENRIK.

Heilyn (m.) Welsh: traditional name, originally an occupational byname for a steward or wine-pourer, composed of the stem of the verb *heilio* to prepare, wait on + the diminutive suffix *-yn*. The name is borne in the *Mabinogi* by two characters: Heilyn the son of Gwynn the Old, and Heilyn the Red, son of Cadwgawn.

Heino (m.) German: from an old Germanic personal name, a short form of various names containing the element *heim* home, as for example *Heimbert* ('home famous') and *Heinrad* ('home counsel'). It has been revived in modern times as a pet form of HEINRICH.

Heinrich (m.) German form of HENRY.

Feminine form: **Heinrike**.

Heinz (m.) German: pet form of HEINRICH, used as such since the Middle Ages, and now extremely popular as a given name in its own right.

Heitor (m.) Portuguese form of HECTOR, which enjoys considerable popularity. It was borne, for example, by the Brazilian composer Heitor Villa-Lobos (1887–1959).

Heledd (f.) Welsh: traditional name of uncertain derivation. It was borne by a semi-legendary princess of the 7th century, in whose name a lament for her brother's death was composed in the 9th century.

Variant: **Hyledd**.

Helen (f.) English form of the name (Greek *Hēlēnē*) borne in classical legend by the famous beauty, wife of Menelaus, whose seizure by the Trojan prince Paris sparked off the Trojan War. Her name is of uncertain origin; it may be connected with an element meaning 'ray, beam of the sun'; cf. Greek *hēlios* sun. It has sometimes been taken as connected with the Greek word for 'Greek', *Hellēn*, but this is doubtful speculation. In the early Christian period the name was borne by the mother of the Emperor Constantine, who is usually known by the Latin version of her name, *Helena*. She is credited with having found the True Cross in Jerusalem. She was born in about 248, probably in Bithynia. However, in medieval England it was thought that she had been born in Britain, which greatly increased the popularity of the name there.

Variant: **Helena** (Latinate form, used also in Germany, the Netherlands, Scandinavia, and E. Europe).

Cognates: Irish Gaelic: **Léan**. Scottish Gaelic: **Eilidh**. French: **Hélène**. Italian, Spanish, Portuguese: **Elena**. German: **Helene**. Romanian: **Ileana**. Russian: **Yelena**. Ukrainian: **Olena**. Hungarian: **Ilona**. See also ELLEN and ELEN.

Short forms: German, Dutch, Scandinavian: **Lena**. German, Dutch: **Lene**.

Helfgott (m.) German: reversed variant of GOTTHELF. Among Jews this given name has been popular as a translation of the Hebrew names AZRIEL or ELIEZER.

Helga (f.) German and Scandinavian: feminine form of HELGE. It was introduced to England before the Conquest, but did not survive long. It has been reintroduced to the English-speaking world in the 20th century from Scandinavia and Germany.

Variant: **Hella**.

Helge (m.) Scandinavian: from an early medieval personal name, a derivative of the adjective *heilagr* prosperous, successful (from Old Norse *heill* hale, hearty, happy). The word later developed the meaning 'blessed, holy', with the result that the name seemed a particularly suitable choice to give expression to pious hopes.

Variant: **Helje** (Danish).

Hella (f.) German and Scandinavian: assimilated variant of HELGA.

Helma (f.) German: short form of HELMINE, or an independently formed Latinate feminine derivative of WILHELM.

Helmfried (m.) German: from an old Germanic personal name composed of the elements *helm* helmet, protection + *fred*, *frid* peace.

Variants: **Helmfrid, Helfried**.

Helmine (f.) German: short form of WILHELMINA.

Helmut (m.) German: from an old Germanic personal name composed of the elements *helm* helmet, protection + *muot* spirit, courage. Although both these elements are well attested in other names from the earliest times, this particular combination does not seem to occur before the late Middle Ages. It continues to be an extremely popular and widespread German given name.

Variant: **Helmuth**.

Héloïse (f.) French: variant of ÉLOISE, which enjoyed a revival of popularity in the 18th century after publication of Rousseau's philosophical novel *La Nouvelle Héloïse* (1761).

Hemming (m.) Scandinavian: of disputed origin, probably a derivative of Old Norse *hamr* shape, in which case it could have been a byname for a 'shape changer' or werewolf.

Hendrik (m.) Dutch and Scandinavian form of HENRY.

Henning (m.) Low German and Danish: derivative (originally patronymic in form) of a short form of HENRIK and also of *Johannes* (see JOHN).

Henri (m.) French form of HENRY.

Henrietta (f.) English: Latinate form of French *Henriette*, a feminine diminutive of HENRI. This form of the name enjoyed a vogue from the late 19th century until well into the 20th century. In Scotland it has been used as an Anglicized form of OIGHRIG. See also HARRIET.

Pet forms: **Hettie, Hattie**.

Henrik (m.) Low German, Scandinavian, and Hungarian form of HENRY. It has enjoyed great popularity in recent years, especially in Denmark.

Pet forms: Low German: **Heiko, Henning**. Danish: **Henning**.

Henrike (f.) German: feminine form of HEINRICH.

Pet form: Low German: **Heike**.

Henry (m.) English: a perennially enduring given name, of Continental Germanic origin, composed of the elements *haim* home + *rīc* power, ruler. It was introduced to Britain by the Normans, and has been borne by eight kings of England. In its various European cognate forms and in the Latin form *Henricus*, it has been borne by kings and princes in many countries of Europe. Henry the Fowler (*c.*876–936), Duke of Saxony, was elected King of the Germans and became the first of a long succession of bearers of the name to rule in central Europe. It was also borne by six kings of France and four kings of Castile and Leon. In England it was not until the 17th century that the form *Henry* (rather than HARRY) became the standard vernacular form, mainly as a result of the influence of Latin *Henricus* and French *Henri*.

Cognates: Irish Gaelic: **Anraí, Éinrí**. Scottish Gaelic: **Eanraig**. French: **Henri**. Italian: **Enrico**. Spanish: **Enrique**. Catalan: **Enric**. Portuguese: **Henrique**. Romanian: **Henric**. German: **Heinrich**. Low German: **Henrik, Hinrich**. Dutch: **Hendrik**. Scandinavian: **Hen(d)rik**. Polish: **Henryk**. Czech: **Jindřich**. Finnish: **Heikki**. Hungarian: **Henrik**; see also IMRE.

Pet forms: English: HAL, HANK, HARRY. Spanish: **Quique**. German: **Heino, Heinz**. Low German: **Heiko, Henning**. Danish: **Henning**.

Hephzibah (f.) Biblical name meaning 'my delight is in her (i.e. a new-born daughter)'. This was borne by the wife of Hezekiah, King of Judah; she was the mother of Manasseh (2 Kings 21). It is also used in the prophecies of Isaiah as an allusive name for the land of Israel (cf. BEULAH).

Variant: **Hepzibah**.

Herb (m.) English: short form of HERBERT, used especially in the United States.

Pet form: **Herbie**.

Herbert (m.) English, German, and French: of Continental Germanic origin, introduced to Britain by the Normans. It is composed of the elements *heri*, *hari* army + *berht* bright, famous. A form of this name (*Herebeorht*) existed in England before the Conquest, at which time it was replaced by the Continental form introduced by the Normans. This gave rise to an important surname. The family were earls of Pembroke in the 16th and 17th centuries, and the poet George Herbert was a member of the family. By the end of the Middle Ages *Herbert* was little used as a given name, and its greater frequency in Britain from the 19th century onwards owes something to the trend for the revival of medieval names of Germanic origin and something to the trend for the transferred use of surnames.

Variant: German: **Heribert**.

Cognate: Dutch: **Harbert**.

Short form: English: **Herb**.

Pet form: English: **Herbie**.

Hercules (m.) Latin form of the name of the Greek mythological hero *Herakles*, whose name means 'glory of Hera'. He was the son of Zeus, king of the gods, by Alcmene, a mortal woman. In many versions of the legend, despite the meaning of the name, Hera, chief goddess in the Greek pantheon and wife of Zeus, is portrayed as the implacable enemy of Hercules, the child of her unfaithful husband. Hercules was noted for his exceptional physical strength; according to the myth, he was set a daunting series of twelve labours, and after successfully completing them he was made a god. The name has occasionally been used in the English-speaking world, under European influence. In the Highlands of Scotland it has been used as an Anglicized form of the rare Gaelic name **Athairne**.

Derivatives: French: **Hercule**. Italian: **Ercole**.

Heribert (m.) German: historical form of HERBERT, currently undergoing a modest revival.

Herleif (m.) Scandinavian: from an Old Norse personal name composed of the elements *herr* army + *leifr* heir, descendant.

Variants: **Härlief**, **Herlof**; **Herluf** (Danish form).

Herlindis (f.) Dutch: of Germanic origin, composed of the elements *heri*, *hari* army + *lind* weak, tender, soft. St Herlindis (d. *c.*745) was the first abbess of Aldeneyck on the Meuse; she was succeeded by her sister Relindis.

Cognates: German: **Herlinde** (not a common given name). Spanish: **Herlinda**.

Herman (m.) English form of HERMANN. The name was in use among the Normans, and enjoyed a limited revival in Britain in the 19th century, when it also became common in America, most probably as a result of the influence of German settlers.

Hermann (m.) German: from an old Germanic personal name composed of the elements *heri*, *hari* army + *man* man. The given name was popular in the 19th century, when it was widely believed to have been borne by the early Teutonic national leader *Arminius* the Cheruscan, mentioned by Tacitus (see ARMIN).

Cognate: Italian: **Ermanno**.

Hermenegildo (m.) Spanish and Portuguese: of Germanic (Visigothic) origin, composed of the elements *ermen*, *irmen* whole, entire + *gild* sacrifice. St Hermenigild (d. 585) was a son of the Visigothic king Leovigild; he is considered a martyr, though the reasons behind the revolt against his father which led to his death were at least as much political as religious.

Variant: **Ermenegildo**.

Cognates: Italian: **Ermenegildo**. French: **Ermenegilde**.

Hermia (f.) Latinate derivative of the name of the Greek god *Hermes* (cf. HERMIONE). This was used by Shakespeare for the name of a character in *A Midsummer Night's Dream* (1595). The name is occasionally also used in Germany, where it is taken as a Latinate version of HERMINE.

Hermine (f.) German: feminine form of HERMANN, formed on the lines of *Wilhelmine* (see WILHELMINA). The name is now also used in France.

Hermione (f.) Name borne in classical mythology by a daughter of Helen and Menelaus, who grew up to marry her cousin Orestes. It is evidently a derivative of *Hermes*, name of the messenger god, but the formation is not clear. The name was used by Shakespeare for one of the main characters in *A Winter's Tale*, and is still occasionally used in the 20th century.

Hernán (m.) Spanish form of FERDINAND, a variant of FERNÁN.

Hernando (m.) Spanish form of FERDINAND, regular in the Middle Ages, but now much less common than FERNANDO.

Hershel (m.) Jewish (Yiddish): pet form of HIRSH, derived from a dialect variant.

Variants: **Herschel, Heshel, Heshi.**

Hertha (f.) German: apparently the result of a misreading of the name of the Germanic goddess *Nertha* (cf. NJORD), mentioned by the Roman historian Tacitus. For a similar 'accidental' coining, cf. IMOGEN.

Variant: **Herta.**

Hervé (m.) French (originally Breton) form of HARVEY.

Heshel (m.) Jewish (Yiddish): variant of HERSHEL. The form **Heshi** is also found.

Heskel (m.) Jewish: Yiddish form of EZEKIEL. See also HASKEL.

Hesketh (m.) English: transferred use of the surname, originally a local name from any of the various places in northern England named with the Old Norse elements *hestr* horse + *skeiðr* racecourse. Horse racing and horse fighting were favourite sports among the Scandinavian settlers in England.

Hester (f.) English: variant of ESTHER, of medieval origin. For a long while the two forms were interchangeable, the addition or dropping of *h-* being commonplace in a whole range of words, but now they are generally regarded as two distinct names.

Hettie (f.) English: pet form of HENRIETTA and occasionally also of HESTER, now rarely used either as such or as an independent name.

Hewie (m.) Scottish and N. English: variant spelling of HUGHIE.

Hieronymus (m.) Latinate form of JEROME, still used in Germany, especially in Catholic Bavaria and in the north German Rhineland.

Hilary (m., f.) English: from the medieval form of the (post-classical) Latin masculine name *Hilarius* (a derivative of *hilaris* cheerful) and its feminine form *Hilaria.* From the Middle Ages onwards, the name was borne principally by men (in honour of the 4th-century theologian St Hilarius of Poitiers). Now, however, it is more commonly given to girls.

Variant: **Hillary.**

Cognates (all masculine): Welsh: **Ilar**. French: **Hilaire**. Italian: **Ilario**. Spanish, Portuguese: **Hilario**. Russian: **Ilari**. See also VIDOR.

Hilda (f.) English, German, Dutch, and Scandinavian: of Germanic origin, a Latinized short form of any of several female names containing the element *hild* battle (e.g. HILDEGARD). Many of these are found in both Continental Germanic and Old English forms. St Hilda (614–80) was a Northumbrian princess who founded the abbey at Whitby and became its abbess. *Hilda* was a popular name in England both before and after the Norman Conquest. Its popularity waned in Tudor times, but it never quite died out, and was strongly revived in the 19th century.

Variants: English: **Hylda**. German: **Hilde**.

Cognate: Hungarian: **Ildikó**.

Masculine forms: Dutch: **Hild, Hildo**.

Hildebrand (m.) German: from an old Germanic personal name composed of the elements *hild* battle + *brand* (flaming) sword. The name was borne by a saint (*c.* 1020–85) who became pope under the name of Gregory VII.

Hildegard (f.) German, Scandinavian, and English: from an old Germanic female personal name composed of the elements *hild* battle + *gard* enclosure. It was borne by the second wife of Charlemagne and by the mystical writer Hildegard of Bingen (1098–1179).

Hillel (m.) Jewish: Hebrew name (apparently derived from the Hebrew word meaning 'praise') borne in the Bible by the father of one of the Judges of Israel (Judges 12: 13). It was also the name of an outstanding 1st-century rabbi and has been a popular Jewish name as a result of his fame.

Hillevi (f.) Danish: reworking of the rare German name **Heilwig**, which is composed of the Germanic elements *heil* whole, safe + *wīg* war. The name is now also more widely used in Scandinavia.

Hilppa (f.) Finnish form of PHILIPPA.

Hiltraud (f.) German: from an old Germanic female personal name composed of the elements *hild* battle + *trūd* strength. St Hiltrude (d. *c.*790) was a Benedictine nun who lived as a recluse near Liesses.

Variant: **Hiltrud**.

Hinde (f.) Jewish: from Yiddish *hinde* hind, female deer (modern German *Hinde*), originally an affectionate pet name or female equivalent of HIRSH.

Hinrich (m.) Low German form of HEINRICH.

Hippolyte (m.) French: from Greek *Hippolytos*, composed of the elements *hippos* horse + *lyein* to loose, free. The name was borne by several early saints, including an important 3rd-century ecclesiastical writer. In classical legend it had been borne by an unfortunate youth who was the object of his stepmother's love and met his death in a chariot accident. The popularity of the name in France was increased by the use of the legend as the subject of a tragedy by Racine (1677).

Cognates: Italian: **Ippolito**. Spanish, Portuguese: **Hipolito**. Catalan: **Hipòlit, Pòlit**.

Hiram (m.) Biblical name, borne by a king of Tyre who is repeatedly mentioned in the Bible (2 Samuel 2: 11; 1 Kings 5; 9: 11; 10: 11; 1 Chronicles 14: 1; 2 Chronicles 2: 11) as supplying wood, craftsmen, and money to enable David and Solomon to construct various buildings. It was also the name of a craftsman of Tyre who worked in brass for Solomon (1 Kings 7: 13). The name is presumably of Semitic origin, but is probably a Phoenician name; if it is Hebrew, it may be an aphetic form of *Ahiram* 'brother of the exalted'. In England, the name was taken up by the Puritans in the 17th century, but soon dropped out of use again. It is still used in America.

Hirsh (m.) Jewish: from a Yiddish vocabulary word meaning 'hart, deer' (modern German *Hirsch*). See also ZVI.

Variant: **Hirsch**.

Hjalmar (m.) Scandinavian: from an Old Norse personal name composed of the elements *hjálmr* helmet, protection + *herr* army, warrior. The name was revived towards the end of the 18th century, and for this reason it did not undergo the usual Swedish development, which would yield **Hjälmar** (a form which, however, now also occurs).

Hjördis (f.) Scandinavian: from an Old Norse female personal name composed of the elements *hjǫrr* sword + *dís* goddess.

Holger (m.) Scandinavian: from an Old Norse personal name composed of the elements *hólmr* island + *geirr* spear. The name was borne by a character of medieval romance, one of Charlemagne's generals, known in English as *Ogier* the Dane. One tale about him is that he quarrelled with the emperor after Charlemagne's son Charlot had killed his own son. He was flung into prison, but agreed to lead an army against the attacking Saracens on condition that Charlot was handed over to him. When this request was granted he spared his life, won a great victory, and was reconciled with Charlemagne and richly rewarded by him. This form of the name results from mediation through Old French sources, where it fell together with a different Germanic name having the first element *odal* riches, prosperity, fortune.

Pet form: **Hogge**.

Hollie (f.) English: variant spelling of HOLLY, altered in accordance with the vague convention that spellings in *-ie* are more appropriate for girls.

Holly (f.) English: from the vocabulary word denoting the evergreen shrub or tree (Middle English *holi(n)*, Old English *holegn*). The name was first used at the beginning of the 20th century, and has been particularly popular since about 1960. It is bestowed especially on girls born around Christmas, when sprigs of holly are traditionally taken indoors to decorate rooms.
Variant: HOLLIE.

Homer (m.) English (esp. U.S.): the usual English form of the name of the Greek epic poet *Homēros*, now regularly used as a given name in America (cf. VIRGIL). Many theories have been put forward to explain the ancient Greek name of the poet, but none is conclusive. It is identical in form with the Greek vocabulary word *homēros* hostage.

Honey (f.) English: from the vocabulary word, Old English *huneg*. Honey was used throughout the Middle Ages in place of sugar (which was only introduced from the New World in the 16th century), and the word has long been used as an expression of endearment. Its modern life as a given name was prompted by use as such in Margaret Mitchell's novel *Gone with the Wind*, which was made into a film in 1939, the enormous popularity of which yielded several other modern given names, such as SCARLETT and RHETT.

Honore (f.) French form of HONORIA, also used occasionally in the English-speaking world.

Honoré (m.) French: from the Late Latin name *Honorātus* meaning 'honoured', borne by various early saints, including Honoratus of Toulouse (3rd century), Honoratus of Arles (d. 429), and Honoratus of Amiens (d. *c.*600).

Honoria (f.) Feminine form of the Late Latin male name *Honorius* (a derivative of *honor* honour), which was borne by various early saints, including a 7th-century archbishop of Canterbury. It is occasionally used in the English-speaking world as an elaborated form of HONOUR.

Honorine (f.) French: from the Late Latin name *Honorina*, a derivative of HONORIA. St Honorina was one of the early martyrs of Gaul, but nothing is known of her life.

Honour (f.) English: from the vocabulary word *honour* (via Old French from Latin *honor*). The name was popular with the Puritans in the 17th century and has survived to the present day.
Variants: **Honor** (esp. U.S.); **Honora** (esp. Ireland; cf. NORA).

Hope (f.) English: from the vocabulary word *hope* (Old English *hopa*), denoting the quality, in particular the Christian quality of expectation in the resurrection and in eternal life. The name was created by the Puritans and has been one of their most successful coinages. The given name is still fairly common, and has its existence independently of the vocabulary word. It has probably been reinforced by transferred use of the surname *Hope*, which is derived from the dialect term *hope* meaning 'enclosed valley' (Old English *hop*).

Hopkin (m.) English and Welsh: transferred use of the surname, now found mainly in Wales. It is derived from a medieval given name, a pet form (with the hypocoristic suffix *-kin*) of *Hob*, which is a short form of ROBERT that probably had its origin through English mishearing of the Norman pronunciation of *R-*.
Variant: **Hopcyn** (a Welsh spelling).

Horace (m.) English and French: from the old Roman family name HORATIUS. The name was once widely used among admirers of the Roman poet Horace (Quintus Horatius Flaccus), but it is at present out of fashion. See also HORATIO.
Cognate: Italian: **Orazio**.

Horatia (f.) Feminine form of Latin HORATIUS. It has never been common in the English-speaking world, but was borne, for example, by the daughter of Horatio, Lord Nelson.

Horatio (m.) English: variant of HORACE, influenced by the Latin form HORATIUS and the Italian form *Orazio*. *Horatio* has occasionally been used in the English-speaking world; for example, it was borne by the admiral Horatio Nelson (1758–1805).

Horatius (m.) Latin: an old Roman family name, which is of obscure, possibly Etruscan, origin. Its most famous bearer by far was the Roman poet Quintus Horatius Flaccus (65–8 BC), generally known in English as HORACE. From the mid-19th century, the name has occasionally been used by English speakers in its original Latin form. This probably owes more to the *Lays of Ancient Rome* (1842) by Thomas Babbington Macaulay than to the poet Horace. Macaulay relates, in verse that was once popular, the exploit of an early Roman hero, recounting 'How Horatius kept the bridge'.

Hořek (m.) Czech: pet form of *Řehoř*, the Czech form of GREGORY.

Variant: **Hořík**.

Horst (m.) Low German: apparently from the vocabulary word *horst* wood, wooded hill (cf. Old English *hyrst*, which lies behind the many English placenames in *-hurst*). It is not clear why this should have given rise to a given name; an alternative suggestion is that it may derive from the Old Saxon personal name *Horsa* 'horse', altered by association with the related *Hengist* 'stallion'. (Hengist and Horsa were 5th-century leaders of the first Germanic settlers in England.) The name *Horst* is first recorded in the 15th century; it is now quite common throughout the German-speaking world.

Hortense (f.) French form of Latin *Hortensia*, the feminine version of the old Roman family name *Hortensius*. This is of uncertain origin, but may be derived from Latin *hortus* garden. The given name began to be used in the English-speaking world in the 19th century, but is not common today.

Howard (m.) English: transferred use of the surname of an English noble family. The surname has a large number of possible origins, but in the case of the noble family early forms often have the spelling *Haward*, and so it is probably from a Scandinavian personal name composed of the elements *hā* high + *ward* guardian. (The traditional derivation from the Old English name *Hereweard* 'army guardian' is untenable.)

Howell (m.) English and Welsh: Anglicized form of the Welsh name HYWEL, or a transferred use of the surname derived from that name.

Hrothgar (m.) Old English cognate form of ROGER. The name is borne in the Old English narrative poem *Beowulf* by the Danish king who suffered the depradations of the monster Grendel for twelve years. In modern times it has been borne by Hrothgar J. Habakkuk (b. 1915), a former vice-chancellor of Oxford University.

Hubert (m.) English, French, German, and Dutch: of Germanic origin, composed of the elements *hug* heart, mind, spirit + *berht* bright, famous. It was popular among the Normans, who introduced it to Britain, where it was later reinforced by settlers from the Low Countries. An 8th-century St Hubert succeeded St Lambert as bishop of Maastricht and is regarded as the patron of hunters, since, like St Eustace, he is supposed to have seen a vision of Christ crucified between the antlers of a stag; he is sometimes called 'the apostle of the Ardennes'. The name is at present somewhat out of fashion.

Variants: German: **Huppert, Hupprecht**. Dutch: **Hubrecht, Hubertus**.

Short forms: Dutch: **Huub, Huib**.

Hugh (m.) English: of Germanic origin, brought to Britain by the Normans. It is derived from the element *hug* heart, mind, spirit. Originally, the name was a short form of various compound names containing this element. Little Hugh of Lincoln was a child supposed in the Middle Ages to have been murdered by Jews in about 1255, a legend responsible for several outbursts of anti-Semitism at various times. The story is referred to by Chaucer in *The Prioress's Tale*. He is not to be confused with St Hugh of Lincoln (1140–1200), bishop of Lincoln (1186–1200), who was noted for his charity and good works, his piety, and his defence of the Church against the State.

In Scotland and Ireland this has been used as an Anglicized form of the Gaelic names AODH, ÙISDEAN, and sometimes EÓGHAN.

Variant: **Hugo** (Latinized; also used in Dutch and German).

Cognates: French: HUGUES. Italian: **Ugo**. Welsh: **Huw**.

Feminine form: Scottish: **Hughina**.

Hughie (m.) 1. English: pet form of HUGH.

2. Scottish: Anglicized form of the Gaelic name **Eódhnag**, a derivative of *Àdhamhnan* (see EUNAN).

Variant: **Hewie**.

Hugues (m.) French form of HUGH. This name was borne by Hugues Capet (?938–96), ruler of France (987–96) and founder of the Capetian dynasty.

Huguette (f.) French: feminine diminutive form of HUGUES.

Variant: **Huette**.

Hùisdean (m.) Scottish Gaelic: variant of ÙISDEAN.

Hulda (f.) 1. Biblical name (meaning 'weasel' in Hebrew) borne by a prophetess who foretold to Josiah the destruction of Jerusalem (2 Kings 22).

2. Swedish: 18th-century derivation from the adjective *huld* sweet, lovable. The name has also been adopted in Denmark, Norway, and Germany.

Variant (of 1): **Huldah**.

Humbert (m.) English, French, and German: of Germanic origin, introduced to Britain by the Normans. It is composed of the elements *hun* bear-cub, warrior + *berht* bright, famous. It was not common in Britain in the Middle Ages, and has always had a Continental flavour. It was used by Vladimir Nabokov for the name of the demented pederast, Humbert Humbert, who is the narrator in his novel *Lolita* (1955). This has no doubt contributed to its demise as a given name in the English-speaking world.

Cognate: Italian: UMBERTO.

Humphrey (m.) English: of Germanic origin, introduced to Britain by the Normans. It is composed of the elements *hun* bear-cub, warrior + *fred*, *frid* peace. A form of this name (*Hunfrith*) existed in England before the Conquest, but it was replaced by the Norman Continental version *Hunfrid*. The spelling with *-ph-* reflects classicizing influence. It has always enjoyed a modest popularity in England. Perhaps its best known bearer was the Duke of Gloucester (1391–1447), youngest son of King Henry IV, known as 'Duke Humphrey'. He was noted as a patron of literature, and founded what is now part of the Bodleian Library at Oxford. In Ireland this has been used as an Anglicized form of Gaelic AMHLAOIBH.

Variant: **Humphry**.

Cognate: Welsh: **Wmffre**.

Pet form: English: **Huffie**.

Huub (m.) Dutch: short form of HUBERT.

Huw (m.) Welsh form of HUGH, now sometimes also used in other parts of the English-speaking world.

Hyacinth (f.) English form of the name borne in classical mythology by a beautiful youth (*Hyakinthos* in Greek, *Hyacinthus* in Latin) who was accidentally killed by Apollo and from whose blood sprang a flower bearing his name (not the modern hyacinth, but a type of dark lily). The name was later borne by various early saints, principally one martyred in the 3rd century with his brother Protus. This gave encouragement to its use as a male name in Christian Europe, including, occasionally, Britain. However, in Britain at the end of the 19th century there was a vogue for coining new female names from vocabulary words denoting plants and flowers (e.g. DAISY, IVY). *Hyacinth* accordingly came to be regarded as an exclusively female name. It has never been common. However, the Spanish, Portuguese, and Polish cognates given below are still used as male names.

Cognates (masculine): Spanish, Portuguese: **Jacinto**. Polish: JACENTY.

Pet form: Polish: JACEK.

Hyam (m.) Jewish: from the Hebrew word *hayyim* life. Several different transliterations are in use; another common one is CHAIM. This name is sometimes added to the existing name of a seriously ill person during prayers for his recovery.

Hylda (f.) English: variant spelling of HILDA.

Hyledd (f.) Welsh: variant of HELEDD.

Hyman (m.) Jewish: altered form of HYAM, influenced by the common Yiddish name element *man* man.

Variant: **Hymen** (altered form, perhaps under the influence of *Hymen* in Latin and Greek, which was the name of the god of marriage).

Hymie (m.) Jewish: pet form of HYMAN or HYAM.

Hywel (m.) Welsh: traditional name, originally a byname from a vocabulary word meaning 'eminent, conspicuous'. This name was common in the Middle Ages and lies behind the Anglicized surname *Howell*. In the 20th century it has been revived and now enjoys great popularity.

Variants: **Hywell**; **Howell** (Anglicized).

I

Iagan (m.) Scottish Gaelic: modern spelling of *Aodhagán*, a diminutive form of AODH (cf. EGAN). From this given name is derived the surname *Mac Iagain*, Anglicized as *MacKeegan*.

Iaione (f.) Basque equivalent of NATIVIDAD.

Ian (m.) Scottish version of JOHN, now very widely used as an independent given name in the broader English-speaking world, where it has largely lost its connection both with Scotland and with *John*. The Gaelic form **Iain** is popular in Scotland.

Iarlaith (m.) Irish Gaelic: name composed of the elements *ior*, of uncertain meaning, + *flaith* prince, leader.
Anglicized form: JARLATH.

Ib (m.) Danish: relatively common name, attested since the Middle Ages, probably a vernacular development of JACOB (via *Jep*).

Ida (f.) English: originally a Norman name, of Germanic origin, derived from the element *īd* work. This died out during the later Middle Ages. It was revived in the 19th century, mainly as a result of its use in Tennyson's *The Princess* (1847) as the name of the central character, who devotes herself to the cause of women's rights and women's education in a thoroughly Victorian way. The name is also associated with Mount Ida in Crete, which was connected in classical times with the worship of Zeus, king of the gods, who was supposed to have been brought up in a cave on the mountainside.

Idony (f.) English: medieval name derived from the Old Norse female personal name *Iðunnr*, which is also the name of a goddess in Old Norse mythology. It is probably a derivative of the element *ið* again: Iðunnr was in charge of the gods' apples of eternal youth. The name has sometimes been Latinized as **Idonea**, as if from the feminine form of the Latin adjective *idoneus* suitable.

Idoya (f.) Spanish: name assumed in honour of the Virgin of *Idoia*, a place in the Basque country so called from an element meaning 'pool' or 'pond'.

Idris (m.) Welsh: traditional name composed of the elements *iud* lord + *rīs* ardent, impulsive. It was common in the Middle Ages and earlier, and has been strongly revived since the late 19th century.

Idwal (m.) Welsh: traditional name composed of the elements *iud* lord, master + *(g)wal* wall, rampart.

Idzi (m.) Polish form of GILES.

Iestyn (m.) Welsh form of JUSTIN, occasionally used in modern times.

Ieuan (m.) The original Welsh form of JOHN, from Latin *Johannes*. Later forms are **Iefan** (Anglicized as EVAN) and **Ifan**.

Ifor (m.) Welsh: traditional name of uncertain derivation. It has sometimes been Anglicized as IVOR, but there is in origin no connection between the two names.

Ignatius (m.) Late Latin name, derived from the old Roman family name *Egnatius* (of uncertain origin, possibly Etruscan). This was altered in the early Christian period by association with Latin *ignis* fire. It was borne by various early saints, and more recently by St Ignatius Loyola (1491–1556), who founded the Society of Jesus (the Jesuits). In the modern English-speaking world it seems to be used exclusively by Roman Catholics. In Ireland it has been used as an Anglicized form of the Gaelic name *Eighneachán* (see AENEAS).

Derivatives: French: **Ignace**. Italian: **Ignazio**. Spanish: **Ignacio**. German: **Ignatz**. Dutch: **Ignaas**. Polish: **Ignacy**. Czech: **Ignác**. Basque: **Iñaki**. See also INIGO.

Short form: Spanish: **Nacio**.

Pet forms: Spanish: **Nacho**. Polish: **Ignacek**, **Nacek**. Czech: **Ignácek**, **Nác(ič)ek**.

Igor (m.) Russian: variant form of IVOR, one of the names taken to Russia at the time of the first Scandinavian settlement of Kiev in the 9th century (cf. OLEG, OLGA, and RURIK).

Ike (m.) English: pet form of ISAAC. However, it was made famous in the 20th century as the nickname of the American general and president Dwight D. Eisenhower (1890–1969), in whose case it was based on the surname.

Ikerne (f.) Basque equivalent of VISITACIÓN.

Ilana (f.) Modern Jewish name, meaning 'tree' in Hebrew.

Masculine form: **Ilan**.

Ilar (m.) Welsh form of the male name HILARY.

Ilari (m.) Russian form of the male name HILARY.

Ilario (m.) Italian form of the male name HILARY.

Ilayne (f.) English: apparently a fanciful respelling of ELAINE.

Ildikó (f.) Hungarian: a derivative of German *Hilde* (see HILDA).

Ileana (f.) Romanian form of HELEN.

Ilene (f.) English: apparently a fanciful respelling of EILEEN.

Ilie (m.) Romanian form of *Elias* (see ELLIS).

Feminine form: **Ilinca**.

Ilka (f.) Hungarian: pet form of ILONA.

Illarion (m.) Russian: from Greek *Hilarion*, a derivative of *Hilarios* (see HILARY). St Hilarion (*c.*291–*c.*371) was a famous hermit born at Gaza in Palestine; he desired to live a solitary, contemplative life, but was continually forced to move on by the crowds that flocked to follow him.

Illtud (m.) Welsh: traditional name composed of the elements *il*, *el* multitude + *tud* land, people. The name was borne by a famous Welsh saint (d. *c.*505) who founded the abbey of Llantwit (originally *Llan-Illtut* 'church of Illtud').

Variant: **Illtyd** (a modern spelling).

Ilona (f.) Hungarian form of HELEN, now also sometimes used in the English-speaking world.

Pet form: **Ilka**.

Ilse (f.) German: short form of ELIZABETH.

Ilya (m.) Russian form of *Elias* (see ELLIS).

Imanol (m.) Basque form of EMMANUEL.

Imelda (f.) Italian and Spanish: of Germanic origin. It seems to be composed of the elements *irm(en)*, *erm(en)* whole, entire + *hild* battle.

Imke (f.) Low German: pet form of **Imma**, an assimilated byform of IRMA. *Imke* is now quite widely used as an independent given name in northern Germany.

Immacolata (f.) Italian: name reflecting a title of the Blessed Virgin Mary, *Maria Immacolata*, referring to the doctrine of her Immaculate Conception; cf. CONCEPCIÓN. The name is also sometimes used by Roman Catholics in the English-speaking world.

Immaculata (f.) Latin form of IMMACOLATA, used in Ireland by Roman Catholics.

Immanuel (m.) Variant of EMMANUEL, used in the Old Testament. This is the usual German form of the name, and was borne, for example, by the philosopher Immanuel Kant (1724–1804). In the

English-speaking world this spelling in particular is generally a Jewish name.

Imogen (f.) English: the name owes its existence to a character in Shakespeare's *Cymbeline* (1609), but in earlier accounts of the events on which the play is based this character is named as *Innogen*. The modern form of the name is thus due to a misreading of these sources by Shakespeare, or of the play's text by his printer. The name *Innogen* is of Celtic origin, probably connected with Gaelic *inghean* girl, maiden.

Imre (m.) Hungarian form of the Germanic name *Emeric* or *Emmerich*. This seems to be a byform of HENRY, but it has possibly also absorbed a rarer name composed of the elements *amal* work + *rīc* rule. St Emeric (1007–31) was the son and heir of St Stephen of Hungary. In spite of his comparatively short life, he was canonized together with his father in 1063.

Ina (f.) English and Scottish: short form of any of the various female names ending in this syllable (often a Latinate feminine suffix), for example CHRISTINA, GEORGINA, KATRINA. Scottish examples include DOLINA and *Murdina* (see MURDO); the pronunciation is usually /-aɪnə/ rather than /-iːnə/ as in England.

Iñaki (m.) Basque form of IGNATIUS.

Indalecio (m.) Spanish: from Latin *Indaletius*, a name of obscure derivation. St Indaletius was a 1st-century evangelist of Spain who worked principally at Urci in Almería and is believed to have died a martyr.

India (f.) English: presumably from the name of the subcontinent, and apparently taken into regular use as a result of its occurence in Margaret Mitchell's novel *Gone with the Wind* (1936), which contributed a remarkable number of given names to the English language. In the case of India Hicks, Lord Mountbatten's granddaughter, the name was chosen because of her family's association with, and affection for, India.

Inés (f.) Spanish form of AGNES. The name is now also used, without the accent, in the English-speaking world.

Inês (f.) Portuguese form of AGNES; cf. INÉS.

Inga (f.) Swedish: short form of the various female names of Old Norse origin containing as their first element the name of the fertility god *Ing*, as, for example, INGEBORG, INGEGERD, and INGRID. It is now widely used as an independent given name.

Inge (f., m.) 1. (f.) German and Danish: short form of INGEBORG or, in the case of Danish, of any of the other female Scandinavian names with *Ing*(*e*)- as a first element.

2. (m.) Swedish: short form of various male names, such as INGEMAR and INGVAR, with *Ing*(*e*)- as a first element.

Ingeborg (f.) Scandinavian and German: from an Old Norse female personal name composed of the name of the fertility god *Ing* + *borg* fortification.

Ingegerd (f.) Scandinavian: from an Old Norse female personal name composed of the name of the fertility god *Ing* + *garðr* enclosure, stronghold.

Variant: Swedish: **Ingegärd**.

Ingemar (m.) Scandinavian: from an Old Norse personal name composed of the name of the fertility god *Ing* + the element *mærr* famous. The contracted form **Ingmar** is also used, notably as the name of the Swedish film director, Ingmar Bergman (b. 1918).

Inger (f.) Swedish: variant form of both INGEGERD and INGRID, attested from the 16th century.

Ingram (m.) English: transferred use of the surname, which is derived from a medieval given name. This was probably a contracted form of the Norman name *Engelram*, composed of the Germanic ethnic name *Engel* Angle + *hramn* raven. It is also possible that in some cases the first element was the name of the Old Norse fertility god, *Ing*.

Ingrid (f.) Scandinavian and German: from an Old Norse female personal name composed of the name of the fertility god *Ing* + *fríðr* fair, beautiful. It was introduced into the English-speaking world in the 20th century and became extremely popular, largely because of the fame of the Swedish film actress Ingrid Bergman (1915–82).

Ingvar (m.) Scandinavian: from an Old Norse personal name composed of the name of the fertility god *Ing(w)*- + *arr* warrior.

Variant: **Yngvar**.

Inigo (m.) English: from the medieval Spanish given name *Íñigo*, a vernacular derivative of IGNATIUS, apparently the result of crossing with a name recorded in the Middle Ages as *Ennecus*. This is of uncertain, possibly Basque, origin. *Íñigo* is now rarely used as a given name in Spain. In the English-speaking world it is mainly associated with the architect and stage designer Inigo Jones (1573–1652). The name had previously been borne by his father, a London clothmaker, who may well have received it at around the time of Queen Mary's marriage to Philip of Spain, when Spanish ways and Spanish names were fashionable, especially among devout Roman Catholics. The architect passed it on to his son, but later occurrences are rare.

Inmaculada (f.) Spanish: name corresponding to Italian IMMACOLATA.

Innes (m., f.) Scottish: Anglicized form based on the pronunciation of the Gaelic name *Aonghas* (see ANGUS). It is also a surname, and use as a female name is in part the result of a regular trend (cf. e.g. LESLEY), but may have been influenced by adoption in the English-speaking world of the Spanish name INÉS.

Innokenti (m.) Russian: from Late Latin *Innocentius*, a derivative of *innocens* innocent, harmless. The name was borne by various early saints venerated in the Eastern Church, including the leader of a group of thirty-two martyrs who were killed at Sirmium, now Mitrovica, in the Balkans.

Cognates: Italian: **Innocenzo**. Spanish: **Inocencio**.

Pet form: Russian: **Kenya**.

Iolanthe (f.) English: modern coinage based on the Greek elements *iolē* violet + *anthos* flower, possibly also influenced by the name YOLANDE. The name is chiefly known as the title of a Gilbert and Sullivan opera.

Iole (f.) English: from the name borne in classical mythology by a daughter of Eurytus of Oechalia. Herakles' infatuation with her led to his murder by his wife Deianeira. It represents the classical Greek vocabulary word meaning 'violet', and may in part have been chosen as a learned response to the 19th-century vogue for given names derived from vocabulary words denoting flowers and plants.

Iolo (m.) Welsh: pet form of IORWERTH.

Variant: **Iolyn**.

Ion (m.) Romanian and Basque form of JOHN.

Iona (f.) Scottish and English: from the name of the tiny island in the Hebrides, off the west coast of Mull, where in 563 St Columba founded a monastery that became an important early centre of Christianity. It is said to result from a misreading of the Latin form of the island's name, *Ioua*, as *Iona*. Its Gaelic name is *Ì*, from Old Norse *ey* island. The given name is most common in Scotland, but is also used elsewhere in the English-speaking world.

Ione (f.) English: 19th-century coinage, apparently with reference to the glories of Ionian Greece in the 5th century BC. No such name exists in classical Greek.

Iorgu (m.) Romanian form of GEORGE.

Iorwerth (m.) Welsh: traditional name composed of the elements *iōr* lord + a mutated form of *berth* handsome. It is borne in the *Mabinogi* by the jealous brother of Madawg, son of Maredudd. *Iorwerth* came to be regarded as a Welsh form of EDWARD, but in origin it had no connection with that name.

Variant: **Yorath**.

Pet forms: IOLO, **Iolyn**.

Iosif (m.) Russian form of JOSEPH (see also OSIP).

Ipati (m.) Russian: from the Late Greek personal name *Hypatios*, a derivative of *hypatos* highest, best, adopted by early Christians because of its symbolic significance. The name was borne by several early saints venerated in the Eastern Church, notably a bishop of Ganyra in Paphlagonia who played a prominent part at the Council of Nicaea.

Pet form: **Patya**.

Ippolito (m.) Italian form of HIPPOLYTE.

Ira (m.) Biblical: name (meaning 'watchful' in Hebrew) borne by a character mentioned very briefly in the Bible, one of the chief officers of King David (2 Samuel 20: 26). In England it was taken up by the Puritans in the 17th century, and is still occasionally used, mainly in America.

Iragarte (f.) Basque equivalent of ANUNCIACIÓN.

Irena (f.) Latinate form of IRENE, used as a female given name in several languages, including Dutch, Polish, and Czech.

Irene (f.) English: name (from Greek *eirēnē* peace) borne in Greek mythology by a minor goddess who personified peace, and by a Byzantine empress (752–803). The name was taken up in the English-speaking world at the end of the 19th century, and became popular in the 20th, partly as a result of being used as the name of a character in John Galsworthy's *The Forsyte Saga* (1922). It was formerly pronounced in three syllables, as in Greek, but is now thoroughly naturalized as an English name and usually pronounced as two syllables.

Cognates: IRENA. French: **Irène**. Russian: IRINA.

Iréné (m.) French: from *Iren(a)eus*, Latin form of Greek *Eirēnaios* 'peaceable' (see IRENE). This was favoured as a given name by the early Christians. St Irenaeus (*c.*125–*c.*202) was bishop of Lyons and a major early father of the Church.

Cognates: Dutch: **Ireneus**. Polish: **Ireneusz**. Russian: IRINEI.

Irial (m.) Irish Gaelic: name of obscure derivation. It was borne by a son of the Ulster hero Conall Cearnach, and has been revived as a given name in the 20th century.

Irina (f.) Russian form of IRENE, one of the commonest of all female names in the Soviet Union.

Variant: **Arina** (much less common).

Pet form: **Orya**.

Irinei (m.) Russian: from Greek *Eirēnaios*, a derivative of *eirēnē* peace (cf. IRENE). The name was borne by several early saints venerated in the Eastern Church. The form **Irenei** is also used; cf. IRÉNÉ.

Iris (f.) English, German, and Dutch: name (from Greek *iris* rainbow) borne in Greek mythology by a minor goddess, one of the messengers of the gods, who was so named because the rainbow was thought to be a sign from the gods to men. In English her name was used in the 16th century to denote both the flower and the coloured part of the eye, on account of their varied colours. In modern English use the name is often taken as being from the word for the flower, but it is also in use in Germany, where there is no such pattern of flower names.

Irma (f.) German: pet form of various female names beginning with the element *irm(en)*, *erm(en)* whole, entire, such as IRMGARD and IRMTRAUD. Its origins are thus the same as those of EMMA. It was introduced to the English-speaking world at the end of the 19th century.

Irmgard (f.) German: from an old Germanic female personal name composed of the elements *irm(en)*, *erm(en)* whole, entire + *gard* enclosure. The Blessed Irmgard (d. 866), a great-granddaughter of Charlemagne, was abbess of Buchau and later of Chiemsee.

Irmtraud (f.) German: variant of *Ermtraud* (see ERMINTRUDE).

Variant: **Irmtrud**.

Irune (f.) Basque equivalent of TRINIDAD.

Irving (m.) Scottish and English (chiefly U.S.): transferred use of the Scottish surname, which originated as a local name from a place in the former county of Dumfriesshire. The surname variant **Irvine** (which in most cases comes from a place in Ayrshire) is also used as a given name. One of the most famous of modern bearers was the lyricist Irving Berlin (b. 1888), but in his case the name was adopted: he was of Jewish origin, and was originally called Israel Baline.

Irwin (m.) English: transferred use of the surname, which is derived from the medieval given name *Erwin*, composed of the Old English elements *eofor* boar + *wine* friend. There has also been some confusion with IRVING. See also ERWIN.

Isaac (m.) Biblical name, borne by the son of Abraham, who was about to be sacrificed by his father according to a command of God which was changed at the last moment. A ram, caught in a nearby thicket, was sacrificed instead (Genesis 22: 1–13). Isaac lived on to marry Rebecca and become the father of Esau and Jacob. The derivation of the name is not certain; it has traditionally been connected with the Hebrew verb meaning 'to laugh'. In the Middle Ages it seems to have been borne only by Jews, but it was taken up by the Puritans in the 17th century and has continued in use since then among Christians in the English-speaking world, although it is still more common among Jews.

Cognates: Hebrew: **Yitzhak**. Yiddish: **Aizik**. German: **Izaak**. Swedish: **Isak**.

Pet form: English (esp. U.S.): **Ike**.

Isabel (f.) Spanish, French, and English: originally a Spanish version of ELIZABETH, which was coined by deletion of the first syllable and alteration of the final consonant sound to one that can normally end a word in Spanish. The name was imported into France in the early Middle Ages, and thence into England. It was a royal name, and its popularity may have been enhanced by the fact that it was borne by a queen of England—Isabella (1296–1358), daughter of Philip IV of France—even though she led a turbulent life and eventually had her husband, Edward II, murdered.

Variants: English: **Isobel**, **Isbel**; **Isabella** (Latinate form, which became popular in England in the 18th century).

Cognates: Scottish: **Iseabail** (Gaelic), **Ishbel** (Anglicized). Irish Gaelic: **Isibéal**, **Sibéal**.

Short form: English: **Sabella**.

Pet forms: English: **Izzy**, **Izzie**. Scottish Gaelic: **Beileag**.

Isaiah (m.) English form of a biblical name (meaning 'God is salvation' in Hebrew) borne by the most important of the major prophets. Rather surprisingly perhaps, the name has never been common in the English-speaking world, apart from a brief flicker among the Puritans in the 17th century. In modern use it is either a Jewish name or an Anglicized version of one of the forms in other languages listed below.

Cognates: Italian: **Isaia**. French: **Isaïe**. Finnish: **Esa**.

Isaura (f.) Spanish: from the Late Latin personal name *Isaura*, originally an ethnic byname denoting a woman from *Isauria* in Asia Minor.

Isbel (f.) English and Scottish: contracted form of ISABEL and ISOBEL.

Iseabail (f.) Scottish Gaelic form of ISABEL. The Anglicized spelling **Ishbel**, which is occasionally used, is based on the Gaelic pronunciation.

Pet form: **Beileag**.

Iser (m.) Jewish: back-formation from Yiddish **Iserl** (a metathesized form of ISRAEL), the final *-l* having been taken as a hypocoristic element.

Variant: **Issur**.

Iseult (f.) English: variant of ISOLDE, from the medieval French form of the name.

Ishbel (f.) Scottish: Anglicized form of Gaelic ISEABAIL.

Ishmael (m.) Biblical name borne by Abraham's first son, the offspring of his barren wife's maidservant Hagar. It is composed of Hebrew elements meaning 'to hearken' and 'God'; an angel told Hagar 'Behold, thou art with child, and shalt bear a son, and shalt call his name Ishmael; because the Lord hath heard thy affliction' (Genesis 16: 11). The name is hardly ever used in the English-speaking world. In Islamic tradition, Ishmael or *Ismail* is believed to have been the ancestor of the Arabs.

Isidora (f.) Feminine form of ISIDORE. This name was little used in the Middle Ages, but has recently become more popular as a result of the fame of the American dancer Isadora Duncan (1878–1927).

Variant: **Isadora**.

Isidore (m.) English form (via Old French and Latin) of the Greek name *Isidōros*, composed of the name of the goddess *Isis* (who was Egyptian in origin) + the Greek element *dōron* gift. In spite of its pagan connotations the name was a common one among early Christians, and was borne, for example, by the great encyclopaedist St Isidore of Seville (*c.*560–636). By the late Middle Ages, however, it had come to be considered a typically Jewish name (although originally adopted as a Christianized version of ISAIAH).

Cognates: German: **Isidor**. Polish: **Izydor**.

Isla (f.) Scottish: of recent origin, apparently taken from the usual pronunciation, /ˈaɪlə/, of the island-name *Islay*.

Masculine form: **Islay** (less common).

Islwyn (m.) Welsh: taken from the name of a mountain in the county of Gwent, the name of which is composed of the elements *is* below + *llwyn* grove.

Ismene (f.) Name borne in classical mythology by a daughter of Oedipus. Like the names of her mother *Jocasta* and her sister *Antigone*, it has been used occasionally in modern times by parents looking for an unusual name, in spite of the grim fate of the house of Oedipus. After Oedipus has blinded himself on discovering that he has killed his father and that Jocasta is not only his wife but also his mother, Ismene deserts her father, while Antigone stays with him and supports him.

Isobel (f.) Variant of ISABEL, found mainly in Scotland. The contracted form **Isbel** also occurs.

Isolde (f.) English: the name of the tragic mistress of Tristram in the Arthurian romances. There are several different versions of the story. The main features are that the beautiful Isolde, an Irish princess, is betrothed to the aged King Mark of Cornwall. However, through accidentally drinking a magic potion, she and the young Cornish knight Tristram fall in love, with tragic consequences. The story has exercised a powerful hold on the European imagination. The name was relatively common in Britain in the Middle Ages, but is much rarer today. The Welsh form **Esyllt** probably originally meant 'of fair aspect'.

Variant: **Iseult**.

Israel (m.) Biblical: the byname (meaning 'he who strives with God' in Hebrew) given to Jacob after he had wrestled with an angel: 'Thy name shall be called no more Jacob, but Israel: for as a prince hast thou power with God and with men, and hast prevailed' (Genesis 32: 28). The name was later applied to his descendants, the Children of Israel, and was chosen as the name of the modern Jewish state. The given name was used by the Puritans in the 17th century, but is now once again almost exclusively a Jewish name.

Derivatives: Yiddish: **Sroel**, **Iser**, **Issur**.

Issachar (m.) Biblical: name, probably meaning 'hireling' in Hebrew, borne by one of the sons of Jacob: 'And Leah said, God hath given me my hire, because I have given my maiden to my husband: and she called his name Issachar' (Genesis 30: 18). The name is still borne by Jews, but is rare or unused among Gentiles.

Issur (m.) Jewish: variant of ISER.

István (m.) Hungarian form of STEPHEN. St Stephen of Hungary (975–1038), Duke of Hungary (997–1001) and first King of the Magyars (1001–1038), is the patron saint of Hungary. He continued the Christianization of the country begun by his father Géza, and is remembered as an effective ruler who created a strong and united nation.

Ita (f.) English and Irish: Anglicized form of the Gaelic name **Íde**, of uncertain origin (possibly connected with Old Irish *ítu* thirst). This name was borne by a 6th-century saint who founded a convent in Limerick.

Italo (m.) Italian: from Latin *Italus*, the name borne, according to Roman legend, by the father of the twins Romulus and Remus, founders of Rome. Italy (Latin *Italia*) is said to have got its name from him, but in fact the character was invented to explain the name of the country, which is of very uncertain derivation.

Feminine form: **Itala**.

Itamar (m.) Jewish: Hebrew name (meaning 'palm island') borne in the Bible by a son of Aaron and brother of Eleazar (Exodus 6: 23; Leviticus 10: 1–7).

Itzal (f.) Basque equivalent of AMPARO.

Ivan (m.) Russian, Belorussian, Ukrainian and Czech form of JOHN, sometimes used in the English-speaking world in the 20th century.

Pet form: Russian: **Vanya**.

Feminine forms: Ukrainian: **Ivanna**. Czech: **Ivana**.

Ivo (m.) Form of YVES used in Germany and occasionally in other countries. It represents the nominative case of the Latinized form of the name.

Variant: **Ivon** (derived from the oblique case of the name).

Ivor (m.) 1. English: of Scandinavian origin, from an Old Norse personal name composed of the elements *ýr* yew, bow + *herr* army, warrior.

2. Scottish: Anglicized form of the ancient Gaelic name *Éibhear*.

Cognates (of 1): Scandinavian: **Ivar**; **Iver** (Danish). Scottish Gaelic: **Ìomhar**, **Ìmhear**.

Ivy (f.) English: from the vocabulary word denoting the plant (Old English *īfig*). This given name was coined at the end of the 19th century together with a large number of other female given names derived from words denoting flowers and plants. It is currently somewhat out of fashion.

Iwo (m.) Polish form of YVES (cf. IVO).

Izydor (m.) Polish form of ISIDORE.

Izzy (f.) English: pet form of ISABEL.

Variant: **Izzie**.

J

Jaakko (m.) Finnish form of JACOB.

Jaap (m.) Dutch: pet form of JACOB.

Jabez (m.) Biblical name, possibly meaning 'sorrowful' in Hebrew, borne by a descendant of Judah: 'and his mother called his name Jabez, saying, Because I bare him with sorrow' (1 Chronicles 4: 9). The name is thus metathesized from Hebrew *ya'zeb*, but there are other cases of metathesis in biblical names. His name occurs in a long list of genealogies, and is memorable because of the characterizations given: he was 'more honourable than his brethren', and he called on God for material success and protection: 'Oh that thou wouldest bless me indeed and enlarge my coast, and that thine hand might be with me.' The Puritans found great support for their beliefs in this, especially since the Bible says explicitly that God granted his request. Consequently the name was particularly popular among Puritans and Dissenters from the 17th century onwards. It is out of fashion now.

Jacek (m.) Polish: pet form of JACENTY, now more common than the original from which it is derived.

Short form: JACH.

Jacenty (m.) Polish form of the male name HYACINTH. This was popular in Poland in earlier centuries, and is the source of the modern Polish given name JACEK. It owes less to the early Christian saints called *Hyacinthus* than to the Polish missionary St Jacenty (1185–1257). He was a canon of Cracow and was initiated into the Dominican order by St Dominic himself. He is said to have undertaken missionary journeys to Pomerania, Russia, Denmark, Norway, Sweden, and even China and Tibet.

Jach (m.) Polish and Czech: short form of any of several names beginning with *Ja-*, principally JAN, JAKUB, JOACHIM or JÁCHYM, and JACEK.

Jáchym (m.) Czech form of JOACHIM.

Jacinta (f.) Spanish: feminine form of JACINTO.

Cognate: French: **Jacinthe**.

Jacinto (m.) Spanish form of the male name HYACINTH.

Jack (m.) English: originally a pet form of JOHN, but now well established as a given name in its own right. It is derived from Middle English *Jankin*, later altered to *Jackin*, from *Jan* (a contracted form of *Jehan* John) + the hypocoristic suffix *-kin*. This led to the back-formation *Jack*, as if the name had contained the Old French diminutive suffix *-in*. It is sometimes also taken to be an informal pet form of JAMES, influenced no doubt by French JACQUES. See also JOCK and JAKE.

Jackie (m., f.) English: originally a male name, a pet form of JACK, but now also found as a female name, a pet form of JACQUELINE.

Variant: **Jacky**.

Jackson (m.) English: transferred use of the surname, meaning originally 'son of JACK' and in modern times sometimes bestowed with precisely this meaning. In the United States it has also been used in honour of President Andrew Jackson (1767–1845) and of the Confederate general Thomas 'Stonewall' Jackson (1824–63).

Jacob (m.) English (and Dutch) form of the biblical Hebrew name *Yaakov*. This was borne by perhaps the most important of all the patriarchs in the Book of Genesis. Jacob was the father of twelve sons, who gave their names to the twelve tribes of Israel. He was the son of Isaac and Rebecca. According to the story in Genesis, he was the cunning younger twin, who persuaded his fractionally older brother Esau to part with his right to his inheritance in exchange for a bowl of soup ('a mess of pottage'). Later, he tricked his blind and dying father into blessing him in place of Esau. The derivation of the name has been much discussed. It is traditionally explained as being derived from Hebrew *akev* heel and to have meant 'heel grabber', because when Jacob was born 'his hand took hold of Esau's heel' (Genesis 25: 26). This is interpreted later in the Bible as 'supplanter'; Esau himself remarks, 'Is he not rightly named Jacob? for he has supplanted me these two times' (Genesis 27: 36).

As a given name, *Jacob* is especially common among Jews, although it has also been used by Christians. The usual Christian form *James* and its cognates in other languages arose from a Late Latin byform, *Iacomus*, of the Latin form *Iacobus*.

Cognates: Italian: **Giacobbe**. German, Scandinavian: **Jakob**. French: JACQUES. Polish, Czech: **Jakub**. Russian: **Yakov**. Finnish: **Jaako**. Hebrew: **Yakov**. See also at JAMES.

Pet forms: Dutch: **Jaap, Cobus, Coos**. Polish: **Kuba**. Yiddish: **Koppel**.

Jacqueline (f.) English and French: feminine diminutive of the French male name JACQUES. In the 1960s it became very popular in America and elsewhere, no doubt strongly influenced by the fame and stylish image of Jacqueline Kennedy, wife of President John F. Kennedy. She is herself of French extraction.

Variants: English: **Jacquelyn** (influenced by the productive suffix *-lyn*; see LYNN); **Jacklyn** (influenced by the male name JACK).

Pet forms: English: **Jackie, Jacky, Jacqui** (all now very common).

Jacques (m.) French form of JAMES and JACOB. In French there is no distinction between a form corresponding to *Jacob* and a form corresponding to *James*. This is a perennially popular French given name, and *Jacques* or *Jacques Bonhomme* has been used (like *John Bull* in English) as a typification of the ordinary citizen.

Jacquetta (f.) English: respelling (influenced by JACQUELINE) of the Italian name *Giachetta*, a feminine diminutive of *Gia-c(om)o*, the Italian version of JAMES.

Jacqui (f.) English: variant spelling of JACKIE, reflecting the influence of the full form JACQUELINE and the increasing tendency to use *-i* as a distinctively feminine suffix (cf. e.g. TONI).

Jade (f.) English: from the name of the precious stone, a word that reached English from Spanish (*piedra de*) *ijada*, which literally means '(stone of the) bowels'. It was so called because it was believed to have the magical power of providing protection against disorders of the intestines. The vogue for this word as a given name developed later than that for other gemstone names, possibly because of the unfortunate etymological associations, or more probably because it sounds the same as the vocabulary word denoting a broken-down old horse or a nagging woman. Its popular appeal received a considerable boost in the early 1970s when the daughter of the English rock singer Mick Jagger was so named.

Jadwiga (f.) Polish form of HEDWIG. St Jadwiga (*c.*1174–1243) was born in Bavaria of Moravian descent, the daughter of the Duke of Croatia and Dalmatia. St Elizabeth of Hungary was her niece. When she was twelve she was married to the Duke of Silesia, head of the Polish royal family. She did much to foster Christianity in Poland. The Blessed Jadwiga (1371–99) was a later queen of Poland who converted many Lithuanians to Christianity, starting with her husband, Władysław Jagiełło, Grand Duke of Lithuania.

Short form: **Wiga**.

Pet form: **Wisia**.

Jael (f.) Jewish: variant of YAEL.

Jaffe (f.) Jewish: Polish and German spelling of a modern Hebrew name from the Hebrew vocabulary word *yafe* lovely, beautiful.

Variant: **Yaffa**.

Jago (m.) Cornish form of JAMES. It has increased in popularity recently, perhaps as a transferred use of the surname *Jago*, which itself derives from the Cornish given name.

Jaime (m., f.) 1. (m.) Spanish form of JAMES.

2. (f.) English (esp. Canadian): apparently a respelling of the female name JAMIE.

Jake (m.) Variant of JACK, of Middle English origin, which has now come back into fashion as an independent name. It is also sometimes used as a short form of JACOB.

Jakob (m.) German, Dutch, and Scandinavian form of JACOB.

Jakub (m.) Polish and Czech form of JACOB.

Pet forms: Polish: **Kuba**. Czech: **Jakoubek; Kuba, Kubiček, Kubeš**.

James (m.) English and Scottish form of the name borne in the New Testament by two of Christ's disciples, James son of Zebedee and James son of Alphaeus. This form comes from Late Latin *Iacomus*, a variant of *Iacobus*, Latin form of the New Testament Greek name *Iakobos*. This is the same name as Old Testament JACOB (Hebrew *Yaakov*). For many centuries now it has been thought of in the English-speaking world and elsewhere as a distinct name, but in some other cultures, e.g. French, no distinction is made.

In Britain, *James* is a royal name that from the beginning of the 15th century onwards has been associated particularly with the Scottish house of Stewart: James I of Scotland (1394–1437; ruled 1424–37) was a patron of the arts and a noted poet, as well as an energetic monarch. King James VI of Scotland (1566–1625; reigned 1567–1625) succeeded to the throne of England in 1603. His grandson, James II of England (1633–1701; reigned 1685–8) was a Roman Catholic, deposed in 1688 in favour of his Protestant daughter Mary and her husband William of Orange. From then on he, his son (also called James), and his grandson Charles ('Bonnie Prince Charlie') made various unsuccessful attempts to recover the English throne. Their supporters were known as Jacobites (from *Jacobus*, Latin form of *James*), and the name James became for a while particularly associated with Roman Catholicism on the one hand, and Highland opposition to the English government on the other. It is now widely used by people of many different creeds and nationalities.

Cognates: French: JACQUES. Italian: **Giacomo**. Spanish: **Jaime**. Catalan: **Jaume**. Galician: **Xaime**. Irish: **Séamas, Séamus, Seumas, Seumus** (Gaelic); **Shamus** (Anglicized). Scottish: **Seumas** (Gaelic); HAMISH (Anglicized). Cornish: **Jago**. See also JEM.

Short form: English: **Jim**.

Pet form: English, Scottish: **Jimmy, Jimmie**.

Feminine form: Scottish: **Jamesina**. See also JAMIE.

Jamie (m., occasionally f.) 1. (m.) Scottish: pet form of JAMES, used especially among Lowland Scots, in contrast to the Highland form HAMISH, which is derived from a Gaelic form.

2. (f.) English (esp. U.S.): recent adoption as a feminine equivalent of *James*, influenced by the fact that *-ie* has come to be regarded as a characteristically feminine ending, except in Scotland.

Jan (m., f.) 1. (m.; pronounced /jan/) Dutch, Low German, Scandinavian, Polish, and Czech form of JOHN.

2. (m.; pronounced /dʒæn/) English: a revival of Middle English *Jan*, a byform of JOHN. The forms *Johan* and *Jehan* are found in Old French and Early Middle English, but in Middle English the name was generally shortened to a monosyllable, spelled variously *Jon*, *John*, and *Jan*. It has sometimes been suggested that the

latter is an importation from Low German or Dutch, but this seems unnecessary.

3. (f.; pronounced /dʒæn/) English: an increasingly popular female given name, formed either as an independent feminine form of JOHN (alongside JOAN, JEAN, JANE, etc.) or as a shortened form of names beginning with *Jan-*, principally JANET and JANICE.

Pet forms (of 1): Polish: **Janek, Janik, Janko, Janusz**. Czech: **Janek, Janík, Janeček**.

Jana (f.) Polish and Czech: feminine form of JAN (1).

Jancis (f.) English: modern blend of JAN (3) and FRANCES, apparently first used in the novel *Precious Bane* (1924) by Mary Webb, for the character of Jancis Beguildy, daughter of Felix and Hephzibah.

Jane (f.) English: originally a feminine form of JOHN, from the Old French form *Je(h)anne*. Since the 17th century it has proved the most common of the feminine forms of *John*, ahead of JOAN and JEAN. It now also commonly occurs as the second element in combinations such as *Sarah-Jane*.

It is not a royal name: the nearest it ever came was as the name of the tragic Lady Jane Grey (1537–54), who was unwillingly proclaimed queen in 1553, deposed nine days later, and executed the following year. Seventy years earlier, the name had come into prominence as that of Jane Shore, mistress of King Edward IV and subsequently of Thomas Grey, 1st Marquess of Dorset, Lady Jane's grandfather. Jane Shore's tribulations in 1483 at the hands of Richard III, Edward's brother and successor, became the subject of popular ballads and plays, which may well have increased the currency of the name in the 16th century. A 19th-century influence was its use as the name of the central character in Charlotte Brontë's novel *Jane Eyre* (1847). In the 20th century it has been used intermittently since the 1940s as the name of a cheerful and scantily clad beauty whose adventures are chronicled in a strip cartoon in the *Daily Mirror*.

Variant: **Jayne**. See also JEAN, JOAN, and JOANNA.

Pet forms: English: **Janey, Janie, Jaynie**.

Cognates: Irish Gaelic: **Síne, Siobhán**. Scottish Gaelic: **Sìne, Siubhan**. Welsh: **Siân**. French: **Jeanne**. Spanish: **Juana**. Italian: **Giovanna, Gianna**. German: **Johanna, Hanne, Hansine**. Dutch: **Johanna**. Scandinavian: **Johanna; Jensine** (Danish, Norwegian); **Jonna** (Danish). Polish: **Jana**. Czech: **Johana, Hana, Jana**.

Janelle (f.) English: modern elaborated form of JANE, with the feminine ending *-elle* abstracted from names such as *Danielle*.

Variant: **Janella** (a Latinate form; for the ending, cf. PRUNELLA).

Janet (f.) English: diminutive of JANE, already in common use in the Middle English period. Towards the end of the Middle Ages the name largely died out except in Scotland. It was revived at the end of the 19th century to much more widespread use, but still retains its popularity in Scotland. See also SEÒNAID, SINÉAD, and SIONED.

Short form: JAN.

Janette (f.) English: either an elaborated version of JANET, emphasizing the feminine form of the suffix, or a simplified form of JEANNETTE.

Janey (f.) English: pet form of JANE.

Variants: **Janie, Jaynie**.

Janice (f.) English: derivative of JANE, with the addition of the suffix *-ice*, abstracted from female names such as CANDICE and BERNICE. It seems to have been first used as the name of the heroine of the novel *Janice Meredith* by Paul Leicester Ford, published in 1899.

Variant: **Janis**.

Short form: **Jan**.

Janine (f.) English: simplified form of French JEANNINE.

Variant: **Janina** (Latinate form).

Janis (f.) English: variant spelling of JANICE, made popular in the 1960s and 1970s by the American rock singer Janis Joplin (1943–70).

Janna (f.) English: Latinate elaboration of the female name JAN.

Janne (m., f.) 1. (m.) Swedish: pet form of the male name JAN (1).
2. (f.) Danish, Norwegian: contracted form of JOHANNA.

Jannike (f.) Scandinavian: apparently derived from French JEANNE, via the diminutive *Jeannique*.

János (m.) Hungarian form of JOHN.

Janusz (m.) Polish: pet form of JAN (1), now also used as an independent given name.

Jared (m.) Biblical name, probably meaning 'descent' in Hebrew, borne by a descendant of Adam (Genesis 5: 15). According to the Book of Genesis, he became the father of Enoch at the age of 162, and lived for a further eight hundred years. This name was occasionally used by the Puritans; Dunkling records that it was briefly revived in the 1960s, for reasons that are not clear.

Variant: **Yered** (Hebrew).

Jarek (m.) Polish and Czech: pet form of various names of Slavonic origin containing the element *jaro* spring (cf. JAROGNIEW, JAROMIERZ, JAROMIŁ, JAROPEŁK, and JAROSŁAW).

Feminine form: Czech: **Jarka**.

Pet forms: Czech: **Jaroušek** (m.); **Jaruše**, **Jaruška** (f.).

Jarlath (m.) Irish: Anglicized form of Gaelic IARLAITH. St Jarlath is the patron of the diocese of Tuam in Co. Galway, and *Jarlath* is still a popular given name in that area.

Jarogniew (m.) Polish: from an old Slavonic personal name composed of the elements *jaro* spring + *gniew* anger.

Jaromierz (m.) Polish: from an old Slavonic personal name composed of the elements *jaro* spring + *meri* great, famous (see CASIMIR).

Cognate: Czech: **Jaromír**.

Jaromił (m.) Polish: from an old Slavonic personal name composed of the elements *jaro* spring + *milo* grace, favour.

Cognates: Czech: **Jar(o)mil**.

Feminine form: Czech: **Jarmila**.

Jaropełk (m.) Polish: from an old Slavonic personal name composed of the elements *jaro* spring + *polk* people, tribe.

Cognates: Czech: **Jaropluk**. Russian: **Yaropolk**.

Jarosław (m.) Polish: from an old Slavonic personal name composed of the elements *jaro* spring + *slav* glory.

Cognates: Czech: **Jaroslav**. Russian: **Yaroslav**.

Feminine forms: Polish: **Jarosława**. Czech: **Jaroslava**.

Jarvis (m.) English: transferred use of the surname, which is from a Middle English form of the Norman given name GERVAISE. Modern use may in part represent an antiquarian revival of the medieval given name.

Jasmine (f.) English: from the vocabulary word denoting the climbing plant with its delicate, fragrant flowers (from Old French, ultimately from Persian *yasmin*).

Variants: **Jasmin**, YASMIN.

Jason (m.) English form of the name (Greek *Iasōn*) borne in classical mythology by a hero, leader of the Argonauts, who sailed to Colchis in search of the Golden Fleece, enduring many hardships and adventures. The sorceress Medea fell in love with him and helped him to obtain the Fleece; they escaped together and should have lived happily ever after. However, Jason fell in love with another woman (either Creusa or Glauce, daughter of King Creon), and deserted Medea. Medea took her revenge by killing her rival, but Jason himself survived to be killed in old age by one of the rotting timbers of his ship, the *Argo*, falling on his head.

The classical Greek name *Iasōn* probably derives from the Greek vocabulary word *iasthai* to heal. *Iasō* (f.) was the name of a minor goddess of healing. In New Testament Greek, the name probably represents a classicized form of JOSHUA. It was borne by an early Christian in Thessalonica, at whose house St Paul stayed (Acts 17: 5–9; Romans 16: 21). Probably for this reason, it enjoyed some popularity among the Puritans in the 17th century. In the mid-20th century it has enjoyed a considerable increase in its popularity, although, as Dunkling comments, it has also been the subject of some rather surprising hostility. A 20th-century influence has been the film actor Jason Robards (b. 1920); his father, also a film actor, was likewise called Jason Robards. The name has been used for numerous characters in films and television series.

Jasper (m.) English: the usual English form of the name assigned in Christian folklore to one of the three Magi or 'wise men', who brought gifts to the infant Christ at his birth (Matthew 2: 1). The name does not appear in the Bible, and is first found in medieval tradition. It seems to be ultimately of Persian origin, from a word meaning 'treasurer'. There is probably no connection with the English vocabulary word *jasper* denoting a gemstone, which is of Semitic origin. The names assigned by the same folklore tradition to the other Magi, BALTHAZAR and *Melchior* (see MELCHIORRE), have also been used as given names in Europe, but only very rarely in the English-speaking world.

Cognates: Danish: **Jesper**. Dutch: CASPAR. German: **Kaspar**. Polish: **Kasper**. Hungarian: **Gáspár**. French: GASPARD. Italian: **Gaspare**.

Jaume (m.) Catalan form of JAMES.

Javier (m.) Portuguese form (and Spanish variant) of XAVIER.

Jay (m., f.) English: pet form of any of the given names beginning with the letter *J*- (cf. DEE and KAY). It is now also used as an independent name in its own right.

Jayne (f.) English: variant spelling of JANE.

Jean (f., m.) 1. (f.) English and Scottish: like JANE and JOAN, a medieval variant of Old French *Je(h)anne*. Towards the end of the Middle Ages this form became largely confined to Scotland. In the 20th century it has been more widely used in the English-speaking world, but still retains a Scottish flavour.

2. (m.) French form of JOHN.

Cognate (of 1): Scottish Gaelic: SÌNE.

Jeane (f.) English: variant spelling of the female name JEAN, common especially in the United States.

Variant: **Jeana**.

Jeanie (f.) Scottish and English: pet form of the female name JEAN, which is more strongly associated with Scotland than *Jean* itself. It is occasionally used as an independent given name.

Variants: **Jeannie**; **Sìneag, Sìonag** (Gaelic).

Jeanne (f.) French: feminine form of the male name JEAN.

Jeannette (f.) French: diminutive form of JEANNE, now also commonly used in the English-speaking world.

Variants: English: **Jeanette**; **Genette** (rare).

Jeannine (f.) French: diminutive form of JEANNE, now also sometimes used in the English-speaking world.

Jed (m.) English (mainly U.S.): now frequently used as an independent name, although originally a short form of the biblical name **Jedidiah**, which was an alternative name of King Solomon (2 Samuel 12: 25), meaning 'beloved of God'. This was a favourite with the Puritans, who considered themselves, too, to be loved by God, but the full form fell out of favour along with other rare or unwieldy Old Testament names.

Jędrej (m.) Polish form of ANDREW.

Jeff (m.) English: short form of JEFFREY, now commonly used as an independent given name, especially in America.

Jefferson (m.) English: transferred use of the surname, originally meaning 'son of JEFFREY', and now occasionally selected by fathers themselves named JEFFREY or GEOFFREY. It has sometimes been used in honour of the American president Thomas Jefferson (1743–1826; president 1801–9), who was principally responsible for the text of the Declaration of Independence, and who is admired as a scientist, architect, and thinker as well as a statesman.

Jeffrey (m.) English: variant spelling of GEOFFREY, common in the Middle Ages (as reflected in surnames such as *Jefferson*). This is the usual spelling of the name in the United States.
Variant: **Jeffery**.
Short form: **Jeff**.

Jem (m.) English: from a medieval vernacular form of JAMES. In modern use, however, it is often taken as a pet form of JEREMY.

Jemima (f.) Biblical name (meaning 'dove' or 'bright as day' in Hebrew) of the eldest of the daughters of Job, born to him towards the end of his life when his prosperity had been restored (Job 42: 14). The name was common in the first part of the 19th century, and has continued in modest use since then. Recently the name of Job's second daughter, KEZIA, has been taken up by parents looking for an unusual name, but that of the youngest, *Keren-happuch*, meaning 'horn of eyepaint', has remained intractable (see KERENA).

Jemma (f.) English: variant spelling of GEMMA.

Jenaro (m.) Spanish form of GENNARO.

Jenkin (m.) English and Welsh: transferred use of the surname, which is derived from the medieval given name *Jankin*. This was a pet form of JAN (2), with the hypocoristic suffix *-kin* (cf. JACK). The modern given name is comparatively popular in Wales, where the surname *Jenkins* also predominates.
Variant: **Siencyn** (a Welsh spelling).

Jenna (f.) English: fanciful alteration of JENNY, with the Latinate feminine ending *-a*.

Jennet (f.) English: variant spelling of JEANNETTE, or a revival of a medieval diminutive form of the female name JEAN.

Jenni (f.) English: variant spelling of JENNY, now commonly used for the sake of variety or stylishness (*-i* as an ending of female names being in vogue; cf. JACQUI, TONI).

Jennifer (f.) English: of Celtic (Arthurian) origin. This represents a Cornish form of the name of King Arthur's unfaithful wife (see GUINEVERE). At the beginning of the 20th century, the name was merely a Cornish curiosity, but since then it has become enormously popular all over the English-speaking world. One factor in its rise was probably Bernard Shaw's use of it for the character of Jennifer Dubedat in *The Doctor's Dilemma* (1905). See also GAYNOR.

Jenny (f.) English: now universally taken as a short form of JENNIFER, but in fact this name existed during the Middle Ages as a pet form of JEAN.
Variants: **Jenni, Jenna**.

Jenő (m.) Hungarian form of EUGENE.

Jens (m.) Scandinavian (mainly Danish) form of JOHN.
Feminine form: **Jensine**.

Jeremiah (m.) Biblical name (meaning 'appointed by God' in Hebrew) borne by the great Hebrew prophet of the 7th–6th centuries BC, whose story, prophecies of judgement, and lamentations are recorded in the book of the Bible that bears his name. The Book of Lamentations is also attributed to him; in this he bewails the destruction of Jerusalem and the temple by the Babylonians in 587 BC.

Despite the gloomy subject-matter of these texts, the name enjoyed some popularity among Puritans and Christian fundamentalists, partly perhaps because Jeremiah also preached reconciliation with God after his wrath was assuaged. In Ireland and Scotland it has been used as an Anglicized form of *Diarmaid* and *Diarmad* (see DERMOT).

Jeremy (m.) English: Anglicized form, used in the Authorized Version of the New Testament (Matthew 2: 17; 27: 9), of the biblical name JEREMIAH. It is a vernacular derivative of the Latin (Vulgate) form of the name, *Jeremias*, which in turn is from Greek *Iēremaias*.

Cognate: Finnish: **Jorma**.

Pet forms: English: **Jerry, Jem**.

Jerker (m.) Swedish: dialectal form of *Erik* (see ERIC), formerly found mainly in the Uppland region.

Variant: **Jerk**.

Jermaine (m.) English: variant spelling of GERMAINE, popular in particular as a male name among Blacks in the United States.

Jerome (m.) English: Anglicized form of the Greek name *Hieronymos*, composed of the elements *hieros* holy + *onoma* name. St Jerome (*c*.342–420) was a citizen of the Eastern Roman Empire, who bore the Greek names Eusebios Hieronymos Sophronios; he was chiefly responsible for the translation into Latin of the Bible, the Vulgate. He also wrote many works of commentary and exposition on the Bible, and is regarded as one of the Doctors of the Church.

Cognates: French: **Jérôme**. Italian: **Geronimo, Girolamo**. Spanish: **Jerónimo**. Dutch: **Jeroen** (the most popular male name of all in Holland in 1981).

Pet form: English: **Jerry**.

Jerrard (m.) English: rare variant of GERARD, probably influenced by the form of the modern surname, if not a transferred use.

Jerrold (m.) English: rare variant of GERALD, probably a transferred use of the modern surname.

Jerry (m., f.) English: 1. (m.) Pet form of JEREMY or GERALD, or occasionally of GERARD and JEROME.

2. (f.) A comparatively rare variant of GERRY.

Jerzy (m.) Polish form of GEORGE.

Pet form: **Jurek**.

Jesper (m.) Danish form of JASPER, still a very popular name in Denmark.

Jess (f., m.) English: usually a female name, a short form of JESSIE or JESSICA. As a male name, it is a simplified form of JESSE.

Jesse (m.) English: name (apparently meaning 'gift' in Hebrew) borne in the Bible by the father of King David (1 Samuel 16), from whose line (according to the New Testament) Jesus was ultimately descended. It was popular among the Puritans, and is still used fairly frequently in the United States, more rarely in Britain.

Variant: JESS.

Jessica (f.) English: apparently of Shakespearian origin. This was the name of the daughter of Shylock in *The Merchant of Venice* (1596). Shakespeare's source has not been discovered, but he presumably intended it to seem like a typically Jewish name. It may be from a biblical name that appeared, in the translations available in Shakespeare's day, as *Jesca* (Genesis 11: 29; *Iscah* in the Authorized Version). This appears in a somewhat obscure genealogical passage; Iscah appears to have been Abraham's niece.

Short form: **Jess**.

Jessie (f.) Scottish and English: apparently originally a Scottish pet form of JEAN, although the derivation is not clear; the Gaelic form is **Teasag**. It is now sometimes used as a given name in its own right, or as a short form of JESSICA.

Short form: **Jess**.

Jesús (m.) Spanish and Portuguese: name taken in honour of Christ. The name *Jesus* is an Aramaic byform (meaning 'saviour') of the earlier Hebrew name JOSHUA. It was suggested to Mary's husband Joseph by the angel of the Lord at the Annunciation: 'she shall bring forth a son, and thou shalt call his name JESUS: for he shall save his people from their sins' (Matthew 1: 21). In many European countries it has been felt impious to give this name to mere mortal children, but there are no such inhibitions in the Hispanic world, where it is regularly bestowed as a token of Christian faith.

Feminine form: **Jesusa**.

Pet forms: **Chus, Chucho** (m., f.).

Jethro (m.) English: name borne in the Bible by the father of Moses's wife Zipporah (Exodus 3: 1; 4: 18). It seems to be a variant of the Hebrew name *Ithra*, said to mean 'excellence', which is found at 2 Samuel 17: 25. It was popular among the Puritans, but then fell out of general use. It was borne by the agricultural reformer Jethro Tull (1674–1741). In 1968 a 'progressive rock' group in Britain adopted the name 'Jethro Tull', and shortly afterwards the given name *Jethro* enjoyed a revival of popularity.

Jetta (f.) English: a comparatively recent coinage, a Latinate derivative of the vocabulary word denoting the mineral *jet*. This is in turn derived from Old French *jaiet*, from Latin (*lapis*) *gagātēs* 'stone from *Gagai*', a town in Lycia, Asia Minor.

Jewel (f.) English: modern coinage from the vocabulary word meaning 'gemstone' (from Old French *jouel*, apparently a diminutive form of *jou* plaything, delight, Latin *iocus*). Use as a given name may derive from its use as a term of affection, or may have been suggested by the vogue in the 19th century for using words denoting particular gemstones as given names, e.g. BERYL, RUBY.

Jill (f.) English: short form (respelled) of GILLIAN, now often used as an independent name in its own right. It was already used as a prototypical female name in the phrase 'Jack and Jill' by the 15th century.

Jim (m.) English and Irish: short form of JAMES, already common in the Middle Ages.

Jimmy (m.) English, Scottish, and Irish: pet form of JIM.

Variant: **Jimmie**.

Jindřich (m.) Czech form of HENRY.

Feminine form: **Jindřiška**.

Pet forms: **Jindra** (m., f.); **Jindřík, Jindříšek, Jindroušek** (m.); **Jindruška, Jindřina** (f.).

Jiří (m.) Czech form of GEORGE.

Pet forms: **Jíra, Jirka, Jiřík, Jiříček, Jiroušek, Jiran, Jiránek**.

Feminine form: **Jiřina**.

Jitka (f.) Czech: pet form of *Judita* (see JUDITH).

Jo (f., m.) English: usually a female name, a short form of JOANNA, JOANNE, JODY, or JOSEPHINE, sometimes used in combination with other names, for example *Nancy Jo* and *Jo Anne* (see JOANNE). Its popularity as a female name was influenced by the character of Jo March in Louisa M. Alcott's *Little Women* (1868). Occasionally it is a male name, a variant of JOE.

Elaborated female form: Scottish (Highland): **Joina** (three syllables).

Joachim (m.) English, French, German, Polish, etc.: from the biblical Hebrew name *Johoiachin*, meaning 'established by God', borne by a king of Judah who was defeated by Nebuchadnezzar and carried off into Babylonian exile (2 Kings 24). Alternatively, it may be a derivative of the name of the father of this king, *Jehoiakim*. The reason for the great popularity of the name in Christian Europe is that in medieval Christian tradition it was the name commonly ascribed to the father of the Virgin Mary. (Other names assigned to him include *Cleopas*, *Eliachim*, *Heli*, *Jonahir*, and *Sadoc*.) He is not named at all in the Bible, but with the growth of the cult of Mary many legends grew up about her early life, and her parents came to be venerated as saints under the names *Joachim* and ANNE.

Cognates: Italian: **Gioac(c)hino**. Spanish: **Joaquin**. Portuguese: **Joaquim**. German: **Jochim, Jochem, Jochen**; **Achim**. Scandinavian: **Joakim**; **Jokum** (Danish, Norwegian); **Jockum** (Danish). Czech: **Jáchym**. Russian: **Yackim, Akim**.

Pet form: Russian: **Kima**.

Joan (f., m.) 1. (f.) English: contracted form of Old French *Jo(h)anne*, from Latin *Jo(h)anna* (see JOANNA). In England this was the usual feminine form of JOHN from the Middle English period onwards, but in the 16th and 17th centuries it was largely superseded by JANE. It was strongly revived in the first part of the 20th century, partly under the influence of George Bernard Shaw's play *St Joan* (1923), based on the life of Joan of Arc (1412–31). In French, her name is *Jeanne D'Arc*; Schiller knew her as *Johanna*. She is also sometimes called 'the maid of Orléans'. Claiming to be guided by the voices of the saints, she persuaded the French dauphin to defy the occupying English forces and have himself crowned, and she led the French army that raised the siege of Orléans in 1429. The following year she was captured by the Burgundians and sold to the English, and a year later she was burned at the stake for witchcraft at the age of 18 or 19. Her story has captured the imagination of many writers, and she is variously portrayed as a national and political hero, a model of apolitical straightforwardness and honesty, and a religious heroine. She was canonized in 1920.

2. (m.) Catalan form of JOHN.

Cognate (of 1): Scottish Gaelic: SEONAG.

Pet forms (of 1): English: **Joanie, Joni**.

Joanna (f.) Latin form of Greek *Iōanna*, the feminine equivalent of *Iōannēs* (see JOHN). In the New Testament, this name is borne by a woman who was one of Jesus's followers (Luke 8: 3; 24: 10). She was the wife of the steward of the household of King Herod Antipas. The name was regularly used throughout the Middle Ages in most parts of Europe as a feminine equivalent of JOHN, but in England it has only been in common use as a vernacular given name since the 19th century.

Short form: **Jo**.

Joanne (f.) English: from an Old French feminine form of JOHN, *Jo(h)anne*, and so a doublet of JOAN. This too was revived as a given name in its own right in the first half of the 20th century. It has to some extent been influenced by the independently formed combination *Jo Anne*.

Short form: **Jo**.

João (m.) Portuguese form of JOHN.

Joaquim (m.) Portuguese form of JOACHIM.

Joaquin (m.) Spanish form of JOACHIM.

Job (m.) Biblical name, borne by the eponymous hero of the Book of Job, a man of exemplary patience, whose faith was severely tested by God's apparently motiveless maltreatment of him. His name, appropriately enough, means 'persecuted' in Hebrew. His story was a favourite one in the Middle Ages and formed the subject of miracle plays. The name was used among Puritans and Christian fundamentalists, but is currently out of favour.

Jobst (m.) Low German form of *Jodocus*, Latinized form of the Breton name *Iodoc*, meaning 'lord' (cf. JOYCE, JOOST). The Low German form was altered under the influence of the biblical name JOB.

Jocasta (f.) English: name borne in classical legend by the mother of Oedipus, King of Thebes. As the result of a series of misunderstandings, she also became his wife and the mother of his children. The derivation of her name is not known. In spite of its tragic associations, the name has enjoyed a certain vogue in recent years. The names of her daughters, *Antigone* and *Ismene*, have been occasionally used since the Middle Ages, but there has been no move to take up those of her sons, *Eteocles* and *Polynices*.

Jocelyn (f., m.) English: now normally a female name, but in earlier times more often given to boys. It represents a transferred use of the English surname, which in turn is derived from a masculine personal name introduced to Britain by the Normans in the form *Joscelin*. This was originally a derivative, *Gautzelin*, of the name of a Germanic tribe, the *Gauts* (cf. WENDELIN). The spelling of the first syllable was altered because the name was taken as a double diminutive (with the Old French suffixes *-el* and *-in*) of *Josce* (see JOYCE).

Variant: **Josceline** (f. only).

Short form: **Joss**.

Jochen (m.) German: variant of JOACHIM.

Variants: **Jochim, Jochem**.

Jock (m.) Scottish: variant of JACK, sometimes used as an archetypal nickname for a Scotsman.

Variant: **Seoc** (Gaelic).

Pet forms: **Jockie, Jockey, Jockan**; **Seocan** (Gaelic).

Jockum (m.) Danish: variant of JOKUM.

Jodene (f.) English: a recent fanciful coinage, formed from JODY plus the productive suffix *-ene*.

Jody (f., m.) English: of uncertain origin. It may be a pet form of JUDITH and JUDE, but if so the reason for the change in the vowel is not clear. Alternatively, it may be a playful elaboration of JO and JOE, with *-d-* introduced for euphony before the hypocoristic suffix *-y*.

Variants: **Jodie, Jodi**.

Joe (m.) English: short form of JOSEPH.

Variant: **Jo**.

Pet form: **Joey**.

Joel (m.) Biblical name, composed of two different Hebrew elements, *Yah*(*weh*) and *El*, both of which mean 'God'; the implication of the name is that the Hebrew God, *Yahweh*, is the only true god. This is a common name in the Bible, being borne by, among others, one of King David's 'mighty men' (1 Chronicles 11: 38), and by a minor prophet who lived in the 8th century BC. The book of the Bible of which the latter was author interprets a plague of locusts as a punishment from God and uses it as an occasion for a call to repentance. The name has been perennially popular among Jews, and was also very popular among the Puritans and other Christian fundamentalists. It is still used in America, where it seems to be enjoying a modest revival of popularity. In Britain, however, it is not common.

Cognate: French: **Joël** (currently a fashionable given name).

Joelle (f.) English borrowing of the fashionable French name **Joëlle**, a feminine form of JOEL. Its selection as a given name may also have been influenced by the fact that it can be taken as a combination of Jo and the productive suffix *-elle* (originally a French feminine diminutive ending).

Joey (m.) English: pet form of JOE.

Johan (m., f.) 1. (m.) Scandinavian and Low German form of JOHN. It is also used as a more learned Czech form of the name, a doublet of JAN.

2. (f.) Older Scottish spelling of JOAN, which was traditionally pronounced as two syllables.

Pet forms (of 1): Low German: **Hanke**. Czech: **Hanuš**.

Johana (f.) Czech form of JOANNA.

Johann (m.) Common German form of JOHN, representing a more learned form than HANS.

Johanna (f.) Latinate feminine form of *Johannes* (see JOHN), used in Germany, Holland, and Scandinavia.

John (m.) English form of Latin *Johannes*, New Testament Greek *Iōannēs*, a contracted form of the Hebrew name *Johanan* 'God is gracious' (the name of several different characters in the Old Testament, including one of King David's 'mighty men'). *John* is the spelling used in the Authorized Version of the New Testament. The name is of great importance in early Christianity: it was borne by John the Baptist (the precursor of Christ himself, who baptized sinners in the River Jordan), by one of Christ's disciples (John the Apostle, a fisherman, brother of James), and by the author of the fourth gospel (John the Evangelist, identified in Christian tradition with the apostle, but more probably a Greek-speaking Jewish Christian living over half a century later). The name was also borne by many subsequent Christian saints and by twenty-three popes, including John XXIII (Giuseppe Roncalli, 1881–1963), whose popularity was yet another factor influencing people to choose this given name. It was also a royal name, being born by eight Byzantine emperors and by kings of Hungary, Poland, Portugal, France, and elsewhere. In its various forms in different languages, it has been the most perennially popular of all Christian names.

Cognates: Irish: EOIN, SEÁN. Scottish: IAN, **Iain, Eòin, Seathan**. Welsh: IEUAN, SIÔN. French: **Jean**. Breton: **Yann**. Italian: **Giovanni, Gianni**. Spanish: **Juan**. Catalan: **Joan**. Galician: **Xoán**. Portuguese: **João**. Basque: **Ion, Yon**. Romanian: **Ion**. German: **Johann, Johannes, Hans**. Low German: **Johan**. Dutch: **Jan**. Danish, Norwegian: **Jens, Johan, Jan**. Swedish: **Johan, Jöns, Jon, Jan**. Polish: **Jan**; **Iwan** (an E. Polish, Belorussian, or Ukrainian form). Czech: **Johan, Jan**. Russian: **Ivan**. Hungarian: **János**. Finnish: **Juhani, Jussi, Hannu**.

Pet forms: English: **Johnny, Johnnie**; JACK; HANK. Scottish Gaelic: **Seonaidh**. Spanish: **Juanito**. Breton: **Yannic(k)**. German: **Hansi**. Low German: **Hanke, Henning**. Dutch: **Joop**. Danish: **Henning**. Swedish: **Jösse**. Polish: **Janusz**. Czech: **Hanuš**.

Johnathon (m.) English: respelled form of JONATHAN, influenced by JOHN.

Johnny (m., f.) English and Scottish: pet form of JOHN. In America it is occasionally also used as a female name.

Variant: **Johnnie**.

Jokum (m.) Danish and Norwegian form of JOACHIM.

Jolanda (f.) Italian form of YOLANDE. The name was a traditional one in the royal house of Savoy, and was revived in Italy in 1901, when it was given by King Victor Emmanuel III to his first child. This spelling is also commonly used in Holland.

Cognates: Polish: **Jolanta**. Czech: **Jolan(t)a**. Hungarian: **Jolán**.

Pet form: Polish: **Jola**.

Jolene (f.) English: a recent coinage, combining the short form Jo with the productive suffix *-lene*, extracted from names such as MARLENE. It seems to have originated in America in the 1940s. It was made famous by a hit song with this title, recorded by Dolly Parton in 1979.

Jolyon (m.) English: medieval variant spelling of JULIAN. Its occasional use in modern Britain derives from the name of a character in John Galsworthy's sequence of novels *The Forsyte Saga* (1922), which was serialized on British television in the late 1960s.

Jon (m.) Swedish form of JOHN. This form of the name is also used in the English-speaking world as a variant spelling of JOHN or short form of JONATHAN.

Jonah (m.) Biblical name (meaning 'dove' in Hebrew) borne by a prophet whose adventures are the subject of one of the shorter books of the Bible. God appeared to Jonah and ordered him to go and preach in Nineveh. When Jonah disobeyed, God caused a storm to threaten the ship in which Jonah was travelling. His shipmates, realizing that Jonah was the cause of their peril, threw him overboard, whereupon the storm subsided. A 'great fish' swallowed Jonah and delivered him, willy-nilly, to the coasts of Nineveh. This story was immensely popular in the Middle Ages, and a favourite subject of miracle plays.

Variant: **Jonas** (from the New Testament Greek form, *Iōnas*).

Jonathan (m.) Biblical name, meaning 'God has given', composed of the same elements as those of MATTHEW, but in reverse order. This is the name of several characters in the Bible, most notably a son of King Saul, who was a devoted friend and supporter of the young David, even when David and Saul were themselves at loggerheads (1 Samuel 31; 2 Samuel 1: 19–26). The name is often taken as symbolic of steadfast friendship and loyalty. See also EOIN.

Variants: English: **Jonathon, Johnathan.**

Cognate: Irish Gaelic: **Seonac.**

Short form: English: **Jon.**

Joni (f.) English: modern respelling of *Joanie*, pet form of JOAN. It is particularly associated with the Canadian folk singer Joni Mitchell (b. 1943).

Jonna (f.) Danish: contracted form of JOHANNA.

Jonquil (f.) English: from the name of the flower, which was taken into English from French *jonquille* (a diminutive of Spanish *junco*, Latin *juncus* reed). This is one of the latest and rarest of the flower names, which enjoyed a brief vogue during the 1940s and 1950s.

Jöns (m.) Swedish: variant of JOHAN, from a contracted form of Latin *Johannes*.

Pet form: **Jösse.**

Joop (m.) Dutch: pet form of *Josef* (see JOSEPH) and of *Johannes* (see JOHN).

Joord (m.) Dutch: pet form of *Jordaan* (see JORDAN).

Joost (m.) Dutch form of the Latin name JUSTUS or of *Jodocus*, a Latinized form of the Breton name *Iodoc* (see JOYCE).

Jöran (m.) Swedish: variant of GÖRAN.

Jordan (m.) English and German: originally a name given to a child (of either sex) baptized in holy water that was, purportedly at least, brought from the River Jordan, whose Hebrew name, *ha-yarden*, means 'flowing down'. It was in this river that Christ was baptized by John the Baptist, and medieval pilgrims to the Holy Land usually tried to bring back a flask of its water with them. The modern given name is either a revival of this, or else a transferred use of the surname that was derived from the medieval given name.

Cognates: French: **Jourdain.** Italian: **Giordano.** Dutch: **Jordaan.**

Pet forms: English: **Judd** (rare). Dutch: **Joord.**

Jordi (m.) Catalan form of GEORGE, the patron saint of Catalonia.

Jörg (m.) German: dialectal form of GEORGE, characteristic of the Alemannic and Swabian dialects.

Jorge (m.) Spanish and Portuguese form of GEORGE.

Jørgen (m.) Danish form of GEORGE (cf. GÖRAN).

Variant: **Jørn.**

Cognate: Swedish: **Jörgen.**

Jori (m.) Provençal form of GEORGE.

Joris (m.) Dutch and Frisian form of both *Georgius* (see GEORGE) and *Gregorius* (see GREGORY).

Jorma (m.) Finnish form of JEREMY.

Jørn (m.) Danish: contracted form of JØRGEN.

Josceline (f.) English: variant of JOCELYN as a female name.

José (m.) Spanish form of JOSEPH, also borne by women as the second part of the compound name *María José*. As a male name, it is now also occasionally used in the English-speaking world.

Josée (f.) French: feminine form of JOSEPH, at one time commonly used in the combination **Marie-Josée.**

Joseba (m.) Basque form of JOSEPH.

Josef (m.) German, Dutch, Scandinavian, and Czech form of JOSEPH.

Pet forms: Czech: **Józa, Joska, Jož(k)a, Jožánek.**

Josefa (f.) Feminine form of JOSEPH, used in Spanish, Portuguese, the Scandinavian languages, and Czech.

Pet forms: Spanish: **Pepa, Pepita.**

Joseph (m.) English and French form of the biblical Hebrew name *Yosef*, meaning

'(God) shall add (another son)'. This was borne by the favourite son of Jacob, whose brothers became jealous of him and sold him into slavery (Genesis 37). He was taken to Egypt, where he rose to become chief steward to Pharaoh, and was eventually reconciled to his brothers when they came to buy corn during a seven-year famine (Genesis 43–7).

In the New Testament *Joseph* is the name of the husband of the Virgin Mary. It is also borne by a rich Jew, Joseph of Arimathea (Matthew 27: 57; Mark 15: 43; Luke 23: 50; John 19: 38), who took Jesus down from the Cross, wrapped him in a shroud, and buried him in a rock tomb. According to medieval legend, Joseph of Arimathea brought the Holy Grail to Britain.

Cognates: Irish Gaelic: **Seosamh**. Scottish Gaelic: **Iòseph**. Italian: **Giuseppe**. Spanish: **José**. Catalan: **Josep**. Galician: **Xosé**. Basque: **Joseba**. German, Dutch, Scandinavian, Czech: **Josef**. Polish: **Józef**. Hungarian: **József**. Russian: **Iosif, Osip**. Hebrew: **Yosef**.

Short forms: English, Irish: **Jo(e)**. German: **Sepp**.

Pet forms: Scottish: **Josie**; **Seòsaidh** (Gaelic). Spanish: **Pepe, Pepito**. Dutch: **Joop**.

Josèphe (f.) French: feminine form of JOSEPH, now much less common than JOSÉPHINE.

Josephine (f.) English form of JOSÉPHINE, now widely adopted in the English-speaking world.

Cognates: Irish Gaelic: **Seosaimhín**. Italian: **Giuseppina**.

Short form: English: **Jo**.

Pet forms: English: **Josie, Josette**, FIFI, POSY.

Joséphine (f.) French: feminine form of JOSEPH, formed with the addition of the productive hypocoristic suffix *-ine*. The name owes much of its popularity in France to the Empress Joséphine (1763–1814), first wife of Napoleon Bonaparte, a charming if somewhat frivolous woman. She presided over a brilliant court until 1809, when Napoleon had the marriage annulled on the grounds that she had not borne him a child. Her original name was Marie Josèphe Rose Tascher de la Pagerie; she had been born in Martinique and, before meeting Napoleon, had been married to Alexandre de Beauharnais, an aristocrat who was guillotined in 1794.

Pet forms: **Josette**, FIFI.

Josette (f.) French: modern pet form of JOSÉPHINE, sometimes also used in the English-speaking world in the 20th century.

Josh (m.) English: short form of JOSHUA, occasionally used as an independent given name.

Joshua (m.) Biblical name (meaning 'God is salvation' in Hebrew) borne by the Israelite leader who took command of the children of Israel after the death of Moses and led them, after many battles, to take possession of the promised land. Other forms of his name include Hebrew *Yehoshua(h)*, *Yeshua*, *Hosea*, *Oshea*, and Greek *Iēsos* (*Jesus*). The name is very popular among Jews, and was also favoured by the Puritans and Nonconformists.

Cognates: Dutch: **Jozua**. Italian: **Giosuè**.

Josiah (m.) Biblical name (meaning 'God heals' in Hebrew) borne by a king of Judah, whose story is recounted in 2 Kings 22–3. This was fairly frequently used as a given name in the English-speaking world, especially among Dissenters, from the 18th to the early 20th century. The most famous English bearer is the potter Josiah Wedgwood (1730–95). In North America this was a recurrent name in the Quincy family of Massachusetts; the best-known Josiah Quincy (1744–75) was a pre-Revolutionary patriot, who died at the age of thirty-one while returning from arguing the cause of the American colonists in London.

Josiane (f.) French: elaborated form of JOSÉE, now occasionally also used in the English-speaking world.

Josie (f., m.) 1. (f.) English: pet form of JOSEPHINE, occasionally used as an independent given name in the 20th century.

2. (m.) Scottish: pet form of JOSEPH, in Gaelic **Seòsaidh**.

Joss (m., f.) English: short form of JOCELYN, occasionally used as an independent given name. In part it may also represent a revival of a medieval spelling of the male name JOYCE.

Jösse (m.) Swedish: pet form of JÖNS.

Josune (f.) Basque form of *Jesusa* (see JESÚS).

Joy (f.) English: from the vocabulary word (from Old French *joie*, Late Latin *gaudia*). Being 'joyful in the Lord' was a duty that the Puritans took seriously, so the name became popular in the 17th century under their influence. In modern times, it is generally used as an omen name, with the intention of wishing the child a happy life (cf. HAPPY and MERRY).

Joyce (f., formerly m.) English: apparently from the Norman male name *Josce* (Middle English *Josse*), which in turn is from *Jodocus*, a Latinized form of a Breton name, *Iodoc*, meaning 'lord', borne by a 7th-century Breton saint. The name was in use among Breton followers of William the Conqueror. However, although this was fairly common as a male given name in the Middle Ages, it had virtually died out by the 14th century. There is some evidence of its use as a female name in the 17th and 18th centuries, perhaps as a variant of JOY. It was strongly revived in the 19th century under the influence of popular fiction. It is borne by characters in Mrs Henry Wood's *East Lynne* (1861) and Edna Lyall's *In the Golden Days* (1885). Modern use may well have been influenced also by the common Irish surname derived from the medieval Norman male name. See also JOSS.

Cognates: Low German: JOBST. Dutch: JOOST, **Joos**.

Jozafat (m.) Polish: from *Josaphat*, a Greek form (used in the New Testament) of Hebrew *Jehoshaphat* 'God has judged'. This was the name in the Bible of a virtuous king of Judah. It owes its popularity as a Polish name to having been borne as a name in religion by a Polish saint (1584–1623), archbishop of Polotsk in Lithuania; his baptismal name was John.

Józef (m.) Polish form of JOSEPH.

Feminine form: **Józefa**.

József (m.) Hungarian form of JOSEPH.

Juan (m.) Spanish form of JOHN, now occasionally used as a given name in English-speaking countries, in spite of the unfavourable associations with *Don Juan*, the heartless seducer of Mozart's opera (1788) and libertine hero of Byron's satirical epic (1819–24).

Juana (f.) Spanish: feminine form of JUAN.

Juanita (f.) Spanish: feminine pet form of JUAN. It is now also occasionally used in the English-speaking world, to which it was introduced mainly by Hispanic settlers in the United States.

Juanito (m.) Spanish: pet form of JUAN.

Judah (m.) Biblical name, possibly meaning 'praised' in Hebrew, borne by the fourth son of Jacob (Genesis 29: 35), who gave his name to one of the twelve tribes of Israel and to one of its two kingdoms.

Cognate: Hebrew: **Yehuda**.

Judas (m.) New Testament: Greek form of JUDAH. This is borne in the New Testament by several characters, but most notably by Judas Iscariot, the apostle who betrayed Christ in the Garden of Gethsemane. There was another apostle called *Judas* (see JUDE), and the name was also borne by Judas Maccabbaeus, who liberated Judea briefly from the Syrians in 165 BC, but was killed in battle (161). His story was very popular in the Middle Ages. However, the association with Iscariot has ensured that this name has hardly ever been used as a Christian name, and that *Jude* has always been much rarer than other apostles' names.

Judd (m.) English: medieval pet form of JORDAN, now restored to use as a given name from the derived surname.

Jude (m.) English: short form of JUDAS, occasionally adopted in the New Testament and elsewhere in an attempt to distinguish the apostle Jude (Judas Thaddaeus), to whom one of the epistles in the New Testament is attributed, from the traitor Judas Iscariot. The name is also borne by the central character in Thomas Hardy's gloomy novel *Jude the Obscure* (1895). More recently it received some support from the Lennon and McCartney song 'Hey Jude' (1968).

Judith (f.) Biblical name, meaning 'Jewess' or 'woman from Judea', borne by a Jewish heroine whose story is recorded in the Book of Judith in the Apocrypha. Judith is portrayed as a beautiful widow who delivers her people from the invading Assyrians by gaining the confidence of their commander, Holofernes, and cutting off his head while he is asleep; without their commander, the Assyrians are duly routed. The name is also borne by one of the Hittite wives of Esau (Genesis 26: 34). This has been a perennially popular Jewish name. In the English-speaking world it was taken up among Nonconformists in the 18th century, and has enjoyed great popularity in the 20th century. It was in occasional use among Gentiles before this: for example, it was borne by a niece of William the Conqueror. Elsewhere in Europe, it has usually been regarded as a characteristically Jewish name. In Ireland and Scotland it has been used as an Anglicized form of the Gaelic names SIOBHÁN and SIUBHAN.

Cognates: Hebrew: **Yehudit**. Latinized: **Juditha**. Polish: **Judyta**. Czech: **Judita**.

Pet forms: English: **Judy, Judi, Judie**. German: **Jutta, Jutte**. Dutch: **Jutka, Jutte, Juut**. Danish: **Jytte**. Czech: **Jitka**.

Judy (f.) English: pet form of JUDITH, now sometimes taken as an independent name in its own right.

Variants: **Judi, Judie**.

Juhani (m.) Finnish form of JOHN.

Juià (m.) Catalan form of JULIAN.

Jules (m., now sometimes also f.) 1. (m.) French form of JULIUS. It is a very common given name in France and is occasionally also found in the English-speaking world.

2. (m.) English: pet form of JULIAN.

3. (f.) English: informal pet form of JULIE.

Julia (f.) Feminine form of the Roman family name JULIUS. A woman called Julia is mentioned in Paul's Epistle to the Romans (Romans 16: 15), and the name was borne by numerous early saints. Its frequency increased with the vogue for classical names in the 18th century, and it continues to enjoy considerable popularity, although the recent introduction of JULIE to the English-speaking world has reduced its popularity somewhat.

Cognates: Italian: **Giulia**. French: JULIE.

Julian (m.; occasionally f.) English: from the common Late Latin given name *Juliānus*, a derivative of JULIUS. In classical times *Juliānus* was a name borne not only by various minor early saints, but also by the Roman emperor Julian 'the Apostate', who attempted to return the Roman Empire from institutionalized Christianity to paganism. For many centuries the English name *Julian* was borne by women as well as men, for example by the Blessed Julian of Norwich (*c.*1342–after 1413). The differentiation in form of *Julian* and GILLIAN did not occur until the 16th century. *Julian* is still occasionally used as a female name.

Variant: JOLYON (m.).

Cognates: French: **Julien**. Spanish: **Julián**. Catalan: **Juià**.

Juliana (f.) Latin feminine form of *Juliānus* (see JULIAN), which was revived in England in the 18th century and has been used occasionally ever since. The name in this form is also used in Germany, the Netherlands, Scandinavia, Spain, and Portugal.

Variant: German: **Juliane**.

Julianne (f.) English: modern combination of the given names JULIE and ANNE, perhaps sometimes intended as a form of JULIANA.

Julie (f.) French form of JULIA. This was imported to the English-speaking world in the 1920s, and for some reason has become enormously popular. Its popularity was increased in the 1960s by the fame of the actresses Julie Harris (b. 1925) and Julie Andrews (b. 1935 as Julia Wells).

Julien (m.) French form of the male name JULIAN.

Feminine form: **Julienne**.

Juliet (f.) English: Anglicized form of French JULIETTE or Italian GIULIETTA. The name is most famous as that of the 'star-crossed' heroine of Shakespeare's tragedy *Romeo and Juliet*.

Juliette (f.) French: diminutive of JULIE, used also in the English-speaking world.

Cognate: Italian: **Giulietta**.

Julio (m.) Spanish form of JULIUS.

Julitta (f.) Italian and English: of uncertain origin, probably a Late Latin form of JUDITH, influenced by JULIA. This was the name borne by the mother of the infant saint, Quiricus (see QUIRCE); she was martyred with him at Tarsus in 304.

Julius (m.) Roman family name, of obscure derivation, borne most notably by Gaius Julius Caesar (?102–44 BC). It was in use among the early Christians, and was the name of an early and influential pope (337–52), as well as of a later pope (1443–1513) who attempted to combat the corruption of the Renaissance papacy. *Julius* is now sometimes found as a Jewish name, having on occasions been chosen as a substitute for any of the numerous Hebrew names normally transliterated with an initial *J*-.

Cognates: Italian: **Giulio**. Spanish: **Julio**. Polish: **Juliusz**. Hungarian: **Gyula**. See also IOLO.

June (f.) English: the most successful and enduring of the names coined in the early 20th century from the names of months of the year (cf. APRIL and MAY).

Juniper (f.) English: from the name of the plant (derived in the Middle Ages from Late Latin *junipērus*, of uncertain origin). The term is also used in the Authorized Version of the Old Testament as a translation of Hebrew *rothem*, a substantial desert shrub whose wood was used in the building of the temple of Solomon. This is not a particularly common given name; there may have been some influence from JENNIFER (the surname *Juniper* is in part derived from *Jennifer*).

Junita (f.) English: variant of JUANITA, perhaps influenced by the name of the Roman goddess *Juno* or by the given name JUNE, or by both.

Juno (f.) Irish: Anglicized form of ÚNA, assimilated to the name of the Roman goddess *Juno*, consort of Jupiter.

Jurek (m.) Polish: pet form of JERZY.

Jürgen (m.) Low German form of GEORGE.

Jussi (m.) A Finnish form of JOHN.

Justin (m.) English: Anglicized form of the Latin given name *Justīnus*, a derivative of JUSTUS. *Justīnus* was the name borne by various early saints, notably a 2nd-century Christian apologist and a (possibly spurious) boy martyr of the 3rd century. As an English name, *Justin* has enjoyed considerable popularity in the second part of the 20th century.

Cognate: Welsh: **Iestyn**.

Justine (f.) English: feminine form of JUSTIN. Its popularity in Britain since the

1960s is no doubt partly due to the influence of Lawrence Durrell's novel of this name.

Variant: **Justina** (Latin form).

Justus (m.) Latin name meaning 'just' or 'fair'. Because of its transparently well-omened meaning, it has been used occasionally as a given name in several countries, including Germany and the Netherlands.

Cognates: French: **Just(e)**. Dutch: JOOST.

Jutte (f.) German: vernacular form of JUDITH, now well established as an independent given name in its own right.

Variant: **Jutta**.

Jytte (f.) Danish form of JUTTE.

K

Kaapo (m.) Finnish form of GABRIEL.

Kaarle (m.) Finnish form of CHARLES.

Kai (m.) Scandinavian (mainly Danish), N. German, and Frisian: a popular name of uncertain origin. It may be connected with the Old Norse vocabulary word *kaða* hen, chicken. Alternatively, it may come from the Roman name *Gaius* (see CAYO). See also KAY (2).

Variant: **Kaj**.

Cognate: Czech: **Kája, Kájin**.

Pet forms: Czech: **Kajík, Kajíček, Kajínek**.

Kajetan (m.) German and Polish form of GAETANO.

Kajsa (f.) Swedish: pet form of KATARINA.

Kaley (f.) English: variant spelling of KAYLEY.

Variant: **Kaleigh**.

Kalle (m.) Swedish: pet form of KARL. The name is now also used to some extent in Germany.

Kálmán (m.) Hungarian form of COLMAN. It is a common name as a result of the fame of St Colman of Stockerau (d. 1012), an Irish pilgrim who was killed at Stockerau near Vienna while on his way to the Holy Land, and who worked numerous miracles after his death. It was also the name of an early king of Hungary (ruled 1095–1116), remembered as a lawgiver.

Kamil (m.) Polish and Czech form of the Latin name *Camillus* (see CAMILLA).

Feminine form: **Kamila**.

Kane (m.) Irish: Anglicized form of the Gaelic name CATHÁN.

Kapiton (m.) Russian: from the Late Latin name *Capito* (genitive *Capitōnis*), originally a nickname meaning 'bigheaded', from *caput* (genitive *capitis*) head. St Capiton was a 4th-century missionary bishop who preached in the Crimea and south Russia.

Kåre (m.) Scandinavian: from the Old Norse personal name *Kári*, originally a byname meaning 'curly-haired'.

Karel (m.) Dutch and Czech form of CHARLES.

Pet forms: Czech: **Karlí(če)k, Karloušek**.

Karen (f.) Danish form of KATHERINE, first introduced to the English-speaking world by Scandinavian settlers in America. It has been used in Britain only since the 1950s, but has become very popular.

Kari (f.) Norwegian (or dialectal Swedish) form of KATHERINE; cf. KARIN and KAREN.

Karin (f.) Swedish form of KATHERINE, found as a less common variant of KAREN in America and Britain.

Karita (f.) Scandinavian form of CHARITY, from the Late Latin name *Caritas*.

Karl (m.) German and Scandinavian form of CHARLES, now also used to some extent in the English-speaking world. The perennial popularity of this name in the German-speaking world was reinforced by the fact that it was an aristocratic and royal name from an early date, being borne, for example, by no less than seven Austrian emperors. Its status as an imperial name is reflected in the fact that the Polish, Czech, and Hungarian vocabulary words for 'emperor' are derived from the personal name: *król*, *král*, and *király* respectively. See also CARL.

Pet form: **Kalle**.

Cognates: Dutch, Czech: **Karel**. Polish: **Karol**. Hungarian: **Károly**. See also CHARLES.

Feminine forms: German, Scandinavian: **Karla**. See also CARLA.

Karlmann (m.) German: from an old Germanic personal name, an elaboration of KARL with the Old High German element *man* man. The Blessed Carloman (707–55) was a member of the Frankish royal family, being the eldest son of Charles Martel, brother of Pepin the Short, and uncle of Charlemagne.

Karlotte (f.) German form of CHARLOTTE.

Karol (m.) Polish form of CHARLES.

Karolina (f.) Scandinavian, Polish, and Czech form of CAROLINE.

Karoline (f.) German and Danish form of CAROLINE.

Károly (m.) Hungarian form of CHARLES.

Karp (m.) Russian: from the Late Greek personal name *Karpos*, from *karpos* fruit, produce, result. This seems to have been a short form of the name *Karpophoros* 'fruit-bearing', i.e. fruitful, productive. The name is found in the New Testament, when St Paul refers in passing to 'the cloak that I left at Troas with Carpus' (2 Timothy 4: 13); in the Eastern Church this person is believed to have been an early bishop.

Karsten (m.) Low German: variant spelling of CARSTEN.

Kasia (f.) Polish: pet form of *Katarzyna* (see KATHERINE).

Kaspar (m.) The principal German and Scandinavian form of CASPAR.

Kasper (m.) Polish form of CASPAR, also used in Scandinavia.

Katarina (f.) Swedish form of KATHERINE.

Pet forms: **Kata, Kajsa.**

Katarzyna (f.) Polish form of KATHERINE.

Kate (f.) English: short form of KATHERINE (or any of its variant spellings), reflecting the French pronunciation with *-t-* for *-th-*, which was also usual in medieval England. This short form has been continuously popular since the Middle Ages. It was used by Shakespeare for two important characters: the daughter of the King of France who is wooed and won by King Henry V, and the 'shrew' in *The Taming of the Shrew*.

Cognates: Irish Gaelic: **Cáit**. Scottish Gaelic: **Ceit**.

Katerina (f.) Russian: popular form of KATHERINE.

Kateřina (f.) Czech form of KATHERINE.

Kath (f.) English: modern short form of KATHERINE and its variants.

Katha (f.) English: altered form of *Kathy* or name formed directly from KATHERINE.

Katharine (f.) Variant of KATHERINE, the preferred form in America. The spelling has been affected by folk-etymological association with Greek *katharos* pure.

Käthe (f.) German: pet form of KATHARINE.

Katherine (f.) English form of the name of a saint martyred at Alexandria in 307. The story has it that she was a brilliant and learned young woman who was condemned to be broken on the wheel for her Christian belief and opposition to paganism. However, the wheel miraculously fell apart, so she was beheaded instead. There were innumerable elaborations on this story, which was one of the most popular in early Christian mythology, and she has been the object of a vast popular cult. The earliest sources that mention her are in Greek and give the name in the form *Aikaterinē* (still the modern Greek form, reflected also in the Russian form, *Yekaterina*). The name is of unknown etymology; the suggestion that it may be derived from *Hecate*, the pagan goddess of magic and enchantment, is not convincing. From an early date, it was associated with the Greek adjective *katharos* pure. This led to spellings with *-th-* and to a change in the middle vowel (see KATHAR-

INE). Several later saints also bore the name, including the mystic St Katherine of Siena (1347–80), who both led a contemplative life and played a role in the affairs of state of her day.

Katherine is also a royal name: in England it was borne by the formidable and popular Katherine of Aragon (1485–1536), first wife of Henry VIII, as well as by the wives of Henry V and Charles II. In France, it was borne by Catherine de' Medici (1519–89), wife of King Henry II and regent (1560–74). Probably the most famous royal bearer of all was the Russian empress Catherine the Great (1729–96; reigned 1762–96).

Variants: **Katharine, Catherine, Catharine, Kathryn, Cathryn.**

Cognates: Irish Gaelic: **Caitríona, Caitrín, Catraoine, Caitlín.** Scottish: CATRIONA, **Ca(i)trìona.** Welsh: **Catrin.** French: **Catherine.** Italian: **Caterina.** Spanish: **Catalina.** Portuguese: **Catarina.** German: **Kat(h)arine, Katrine.** Dutch: **Katrien, Katrijn.** Polish: **Katarzyna.** Czech: **Kateřina.** Russian: **Yekaterina; Katerina** (popular form). See also KAREN, KARIN, KARI.

Short forms: English: KATE; **Kath, Cath.**

Pet forms: English: **Kathy, Cathy; Katie, Katy, Kit(ty).** German: **Käthe.** Polish: **Kasia.** Russian: **Katya, Katinka.**

Kathleen (f.) Irish and English: Anglicized form of Gaelic CAITLÍN.

Variant: **Cathleen.**

Kathryn (f.) American form of KATHERINE, now the most common spelling in the United States. It seems to have originated as a deliberate alteration for the sake of distinction, perhaps influenced by the suffix *-lyn* (see LYNN).

Katie English: pet form of KATE, with the hypocoristic suffix *-ie.*

Variant: **Katy.**

Cognate: Scottish Gaelic: **Ceiteag.**

Katinka (f.) Russian: pet form derived from an extended version of KATYA.

Katrien (f.) Dutch form of KATHERINE.

Variant: **Katrijn.**

Katriona (f.) English: variant spelling of CATRIONA.

Katrine (f.) German and Danish: contracted form of KATHARINE, now used occasionally in the English-speaking world, in part as an Anglicized form of Irish Gaelic *Caitrín.*

Katy (f.) English: variant spelling of KATIE.

Katya (f.) Russian: pet form of YEKATARINA, now sometimes used as an independent given name in the English-speaking world.

Kay (f., m.) English: 1. (f.) Pet form of any of the various female names beginning with the letter *K*- (cf. DEE and JAY), most notably KATHERINE and its variants.

2. (m.) Comparatively rare male name, which presumably originated in honour of the Arthurian knight so called, although Sir Kay is not a particularly attractive character. His name seems to be a Celticized form of Latin *Gaius*, an old Roman given name of uncertain derivation (cf. CAYO).

Kayla (f.) English: recently coined altered form of KAYLEY.

Kayley (f.) Irish and English: of recent origin and uncertain derivation. *Kayley* is an Irish surname, an Anglicized form of Gaelic *Ó Caollaidhe* 'descendant of *Caolladhe*', an old male personal name derived from the element *caol* slender. Its adoption as a modern given name has probably also been influenced by the popularity of the names KELLY and KYLIE.

Variants: **Kayly, Kaley, Ka(y)leigh.**

Kazimierz (m.) Polish form of CASIMIR.

Kean (m.) Irish: Anglicized form of the Gaelic name CIAN.

Variant: **Keane.**

Keeley (f.) English and Irish: of recent origin and uncertain etymology, possibly an alteration of KEELIN to fit in with the pattern of female names ending in -*(e)y* or

-*ie*. The Irish surname *Keeley* is a variant of KAYLEY.

Variants: **Keely, Keeleigh,** KEIGHLEY.

Keelin (f.) Irish: Anglicized form of the Gaelic name **Caoilfhionn**, composed of the elements *caol* slender + *fionn* white.

Kees (m.) Dutch: pet form of CORNELIS, now also used as an independent given name.

Variant: **Cees**.

Keighley (f.) English: fanciful respelling of KEELEY, inspired by the Yorkshire town of *Keighley*, which is, however, pronounced /ki:θlɪ/.

Keir (m.) Scottish: transferred use of the surname, in origin a variant of KERR. In some cases, the name may be chosen in honour of the trade unionist and first Labour MP, James Keir Hardie (1856–1915), whose mother's maiden name was Keir.

Keith (m.) English and Scottish: from a Scottish surname, originally a local name derived from lands so called in East Lothian, probably from a Celtic (Brythonic) word meaning 'wood'. The principal family bearing this surname were hereditary Earls Marischal of Scotland from 1455 to 1715. This is one of a number of Scottish aristocratic surnames that have become well established since the 19th century as male names throughout the English-speaking world, not just in Scotland. Others include BRUCE, GRAHAM, DOUGLAS, and LESLIE.

Feminine form: **Keitha**.

Kelan (m.) Irish: Anglicized form of Gaelic **Caolán**, originally a byname representing a diminutive form of *caol* slender.

Keld (m.) Danish form of KETTIL.

Kelemen (m.) Hungarian form of CLEMENT.

Kelly (m., f.) English: As a male name, an Anglicized form of Irish Gaelic CEALLAGH. In Australia and elsewhere in the English-speaking world it is now more commonly used as a female given name. This use probably derives from the Irish surname (Gaelic *Ó Ceallaigh* 'descendant of Ceallagh'); cf. the similar recent use of CASEY and CASSIDY as female given names.

Variants: **Kelley, Kellie** (f.).

Kelsey (m., f.) English: transferred use of the surname, which is derived from the Old English masculine personal name *Cēolsige*, composed of the elements *cēol* ship + *sige* victory.

Variant: **Kelsie**.

Kelvin (m.) English: modern given name, first used in the 1920s. It is taken from a Scottish river which runs through Glasgow into the Clyde (cf. CLYDE). Its choice as a given name may also have been influenced by the form of such names as MELVIN and CALVIN and the fame of the scientist Lord Kelvin.

Kemp (m.) English: transferred use of the surname, which originated in the Middle Ages as an occupational name or nickname from Middle English *kempe* athlete, wrestler (from Old English *kempa* warrior, champion).

Ken (m.) English: short form of KENNETH, or occasionally of various other male names with this first syllable.

Kendall (m., f.) English, Cornish, and Welsh: transferred use of the surname, which is at least in part a local name, either from *Kendal* in Cumbria (formerly the county town of Westmorland, so named because it stands in the valley of the river *Kent*), or from *Kendale* in Driffield, Humberside, where the first element is Old Norse *keld* spring. The distribution of the surname makes it seem likely that it is also partly derived from the Welsh given name CYNDDELW, or from a Cornish cognate.

Variant: **Kendal**.

Kendra (f.) English: recently coined feminine form of KENDRICK.

Kendrick (m.) English: in modern use a transferred use of the surname, the origins of which are confused. Given its distribution, the most likely source in the majority of cases is the Old Welsh personal name *Cynwrig*. This is of uncertain derivation, but may be composed of Old Celtic elements meaning 'high, exalted' + 'hill, summit'.

The Scottish surname *Ken(d)rick* is a shortened form of *MacKen(d)rick* (Gaelic *Mac Eanraig* 'son of Henry'); Scottish bearers are descended from a certain Henry MacNaughton, and therefore the (Mac)Ken(d)ricks are a sept of Clan MacNaughton.

It is also possible that, as an English surname, *Ken(d)rick* is derived in part from the Old English personal names *Cēnrīc* and *Cynrīc*. The first of these is composed of the elements *cēne* keen or bold + *rīc* power; the second is from *cyne* royal + *rīc* power. Withycombe says that 'the Christian name *Cynric* survived into the 17th century,' but unfortunately does not give any evidence. Without information about the location it is impossible to decide whether it is a survival (and, if so, of what), a revival, or a transferred use.

Variant: **Kenrick.**

Kenelm (m.) English: from an Old English personal name composed of the elements *cēne* keen, bold + *helm* helmet, protection. The name was popular in England during the Middle Ages, when a shadowy 9th-century Mercian prince of this name was widely revered as a saint and martyr, although his death seems to have been rather the result of personal and political motives. It has remained in occasional use ever since, especially in the Digby family, where it tended to alternate with EVERARD. The most famous Sir Kenelm Digby (1603–65) was notable as a writer, scientist, adventurer, diplomat, and lover.

Kennard (m.) English: ultimately from an Old English personal name in which several earlier names have fallen together. The first element is either *cēne* keen, bold, or *cyne* royal; the second is either *weard* guard or *heard* brave, hardy. This name seems to have died out during the Middle Ages, and in modern times *Kennard* probably represents a transferred use of the surname derived from it.

Kennedy (m.) Irish, Scottish, and English: Anglicized form of Irish Gaelic *Cinnéidigh*, a traditional name composed of the elements *ceann* head + *éidigh* ugly. In the Scottish Highlands this form has also been used as an Anglicized equivalent of the Scottish Gaelic name UARRAIG, apparently because that given name was common in kindreds surnamed *Kennedy* (Irish *Ó Cinnéidigh*). In recent years it has sometimes been chosen in the English-speaking world in honour of the assassinated American president John F. Kennedy (1917–63) and his brother Robert (1925–68).

Kenneth (m.) Scottish and English: Anglicized form of two different Gaelic names, **Cinaed** and **Cainnech**. The former seems to have been originally a personal name meaning 'born of fire', the latter a byname meaning 'handsome, fair one'. *Cinaed* was the Gaelic name of Kenneth Mac Alpin, first king of the Picts and Scots; *Cainnech* survives today in Scotland as the common Gaelic name **Coinneach**. In the 20th century *Kenneth* has enjoyed great popularity well beyond the boundaries of Scotland.

Derivatives: Scandinavian: **Kennet, Kent.**

Short form: English: **Ken.**

Pet form: Scottish, English: KENNY.

Feminine forms: Scottish: **Kenna, Kenina.**

Kenny (m.) 1. Characteristically Scottish pet form of KENNETH; one of the best-known bearers in modern times is the footballer Kenny Dalglish.

2. Anglicized form of Irish Gaelic CAINNEACH.

Kent (m.) 1. English: transferred use of the surname, which originally denoted someone from the county of Kent. This is probably named with a Celtic element meaning 'border'. Its use as a given name is of recent origin, but is now quite popular.

2. Scandinavian: contracted form of *Kennet*, the Scandinavian form of KENNETH.

Kenton (m.) English: transferred use of the surname, originally a local name from any of various places so called. The one in Devon gets its name from the British river name *Kenn* + Old English *tūn* enclosure, settlement; the one in north-west London is from the Old English personal name *Cēna* 'keen' + *tūn*; the one in Northumberland is from Old English *cyne-* royal + *tūn*; and that in Staffordshire probably from the personal name *Cēna* 'keen' or *Cyna* 'royal' + *tūn*.

Kenya (m.) Russian: pet form of INNOKENTI.

Kepa (m.) Basque equivalent of PETER, taken directly from the Aramaic form *Kephas*.

Kerena (f.) English: Latinate elaboration of **Keren**, itself a version shortened to manageable proportions of the biblical name *Keren-happuch* (meaning 'horn of eye-paint' in Hebrew) borne by the third of Job's daughters (Job 42: 14).

Kermit (m.) English: of Irish and Manx origin, from the Gaelic surname form *Mac Dhiarmaid* 'son of *Diarmad*' (see DERMOT). The name was borne by a son of the American president Theodore Roosevelt, and more recently by a frog puppet on Jim Henson's *Muppet Show*.

Kerr (m.) English: transferred use of the surname, which is a northern English local name for someone who lived by a patch of wet ground overgrown with brushwood (Old Norse *kjarr*).

Kerry (f., m.) English: of recent, Australian, origin, probably from the name of the Irish county. It is now becoming relatively common in Britain as well as Australia, especially as a female name.

Kerstin (f.) Swedish: variant of KRISTINA.

Kerttu (f.) Finnish form of GERTRUDE.

Kester (m.) Medieval Scottish form of CHRISTOPHER, occasionally revived as a modern given name.

Kestrel (f.) English: one of the rarer female names derived from vocabulary words denoting birds that have come into use in the 20th century. The word itself derives from Old French *cresserelle*, apparently a derivative of *cressele* rattle.

Kettil (m.) Swedish: from the Old Norse name *Ketill*, a short form of various compound names containing the second element *ketill* sacrificial cauldron, for example *Thorketill* (see TORKEL) and *Arnketill*.

Variant: **Kjell**.

Cognates: Norwegian: **Kjetil**. Danish: **Kjeld**, **Keld**.

Keturah (f.) Biblical: name (meaning 'incense' in Hebrew) borne by the wife Abraham married after Sarah's death (Genesis 25: 1). The name is occasionally chosen in the English-speaking world by parents in search of an unusual name.

Kevin (m.) Irish and English: Anglicized form of the Gaelic name **Caoimhín**, originally a byname representing a diminutive of Gaelic *caomh* comely, beloved. This was the name of a 7th-century saint who is one of the patrons of Dublin.

Variant: **Kevan** (from Gaelic **Caoimheán**, with a different diminutive suffix).

Kezia (f.) Biblical: name of one of Job's daughters, born to him towards the end of his life, after his prosperity had been restored (Job 42: 14). It represents the Hebrew word for the *cassia* tree (named in English, via Latin and Greek, from a similar Semitic source). The name is used in the English-speaking world rather less frequently than JEMIMA, but considerably more so than *Keren-happuch*, the name of Job's third daughter (see KERENA).

Pet forms: **Kizzie**, **Kizzy**.

Khipa (m.) Russian: pet form of ARKHIP.

Kicki (f.) Swedish: pet form of KRISTINA. Derived apparently from a childish pronunciation of the name, this form is found from the late 19th century onwards.

Kiera (f.) Irish and English: recently coined feminine form of KIERAN; cf. CIARA.

Kieran (m.) Irish: Anglicized form of Gaelic CIARÁN.

Variant: **Kyran**.

Kilina (f.) Ukrainian form of AKILINA.

Killian (m.) Irish: Anglicized form of Gaelic CILLIAN. This name was borne by various early Irish saints, including the 7th-century author of a 'Life of St Bridget', and missionaries to Artois and Franconia.

Variant: **Kilian**.

Kilya (f.) Russian: pet form of AKILINA.

Kim (f., m.) 1. (f., m.) English: originally a male name, a short form of KIMBERLEY, but now much more common than the latter and nearly always a female name. It has become established as an independent name in its own right. The hero of Rudyard Kipling's novel *Kim* (1901) bore the name as a short form of *Kimball* (a surname used as a given name).

2. (m.) Scandinavian: aphetic short form of *Joakim* (see JOACHIM).

Kima (m.) Russian: pet form of AKIM or YAKIM.

Kimberley (f., m.) English: becoming increasingly common as a female name, being regarded, probably rightly, as the full form of KIM. Its history is complicated, in that it is from a placename, from a surname, from a placename. The immediate source is the town in South Africa, the scene of fighting during the Boer War, which brought it to public notice at the end of the 19th century. The town was named after a certain Lord Kimberley, whose ancestors derived their surname from one of the places in England called Kimberley. The first part of the placename derives from various Old English personal names; the second (from Old English *lēah*) means 'wood' or 'clearing'.

Variants: **Kimberly** (the more common U.S. spelling); **Kimberleigh**.

Kina (f.) Scottish (Highland): short form of *Alickina* (see ALICK).

King (m.) English: from the vocabulary word for a monarch, bestowed, especially in America, with a hint of the notion that the bearer would have kingly qualities; cf. DUKE and EARL. In some cases it may be a transferred use of the surname (originally a nickname or an occupational name given to someone who was employed in a royal household). Its frequency has increased recently among American Blacks, no doubt partly as a result of its being bestowed in honour of the civil rights leader Martin Luther King (1929–68).

Kinge (f.) German: pet form of KUNIGUNDE.

Variant: **Kinga**.

Kingsley (m., f.) English: transferred use of the surname, originally a local name derived from various places (in Cheshire, Hampshire, Staffordshire) named in Old English as *Cyningeslēah* 'king's wood'. It is not clear what was the initial impulse towards use as a given name; the usual pattern in such cases is for a mother's maiden name to be chosen as a given name, but in this case the choice may have been made in honour of the author Charles Kingsley (1819–75).

Kirill (m.) Russian form of CYRIL.

Kirk (m.) Scottish and English: transferred use of the surname, originally a northern English and Scottish local name for someone who lived near a church (from Old Norse *kirkja*). Recent use has probably been influenced to some extent by the film actor Kirk Douglas, who was born in 1916 as Issur Danielovich Demsky.

Kirsten (f.) Danish and Norwegian form of CHRISTINE, now well established in English-speaking countries.

Kirstie (f.) Scottish: pet form of KIRSTIN, now quite commonly used as an independent given name in the rest of the English-speaking world as well as in Scotland.
Variants: **Kirsty**; **Chirsty** (the usual spelling in the Highlands); **Curstaidh, Ciorstiadh, Curstag, Ciorstag** (Gaelic).

Kirstin (f.) Scottish: vernacular form of CHRISTINE, now quite widely used in the English-speaking world.

Kit (m., f.) English: 1. (m.) Pet form of CHRISTOPHER.
2. (f.) Pet form of KATHERINE, an altered form of *Kat*.

Kitty (f.) English: pet form of KATHERINE, derived from the pet form KIT + the hypocoristic suffix *-y*.

Kizzie (f.) English: pet form of KEZIA, now sometimes used as an independent name.
Variant: **Kizzy**.

Kjell (m.) Swedish: contracted form of KETTIL.
Cognates: Norwegian: **Kjetil**. Danish: **Kjeld, Keld**.

Klaartje (f.) Dutch: pet form of KLARA.

Klaas (m.) Dutch form of CLAUS.

Klaes (m.) Frisian form of CLAUS.

Klara (f.) German, Dutch, Russian, Polish, and Scandinavian form of CLARA.
Pet form: Dutch: **Klaartje**.

Klaudia (f.) Polish form of CLAUDIA.

Klaudiusz (m.) Polish form of CLAUDE.

Klaus (m.) German: variant spelling of CLAUS.

Klavdia (f.) Russian form of CLAUDIA.

Klavdii (m.) Russian form of CLAUDE.

Klemens (m.) German, Danish, Swedish, and Polish form of CLEMENT.
Pet form: Polish: **Klimek**.

Klementyna (f.) Polish form of *Clementina* (see CLEMENTINE).

Klimek (m.) Polish: diminutive pet form of KLEMENS, now used as an independent given name.

Kliment (m.) Russian and Czech form of CLEMENT.

Knut (m.) Scandinavian: from Old Norse *Knútr* 'knot', originally a byname given to a short, squat man. King Knut (d. 1035) ruled over Denmark, Norway, and England in the 11th century. His great-nephew Knut (d. 1086) was another king of Denmark, who founded churches throughout his realm. He was canonized as a martyr, the main reason apparently being that he was murdered by opponents of the laws enforcing payment of tithes to the Church. The latter's nephew, also Knut (d. 1131), was Duke of Schleswig and is also venerated as a martyr, although the justification for this is not clear. It is still a popular Danish and Norwegian given name.
Variant: Danish: **Knud**.
Anglicized form: **Canute**.

Koenraad (m.) Dutch form of CONRAD.

Koldo (m.) Basque: shortened form of *Koldobika*, a derivative of an Ostrogothic form of the Germanic name *Chlodovik*, and so an equivalent of Spanish *Luis* (see LOUIS).

Kolos (m.) Hungarian form of CLAUDE.

Kolya (m.) Russian: aphetic pet form of NIKOLAI.

Kondrat (m.) Polish form of CONRAD, but there has been considerable confusion between this and the Russian name **Kondrati**, which is officially derived from the Late Greek name *Kodratos*, from the Latin byname *Quadrātus*, meaning 'square', i.e. squat, portly. This was borne by various early saints venerated in the Eastern Church, most notably by the writer of the first apologia for Christianity, addressed to the Emperor Hadrian, and by the leader of a group of forty-three martyrs executed in Anatolia under the Emperor Decius.

Konrad (m.) The usual German and Polish spelling of CONRAD.

Variant: KURT.

Konstantin (m.) German, Scandinavian, Hungarian, Czech, and Russian form of CONSTANTINE.

Pet form: Russian: **Kostya**.

Konstantyn (m.) Polish form of CONSTANTINE.

Koppel (m.) Jewish: Yiddish aphetic pet form of JAKOB.

Korbinian (m.) German (S. Germany): given name bestowed in honour of a Frankish saint (?670–770), who evangelized Bavaria from a base at Freising, near Munich. His name was presumably originally Frankish, but in the form in which it has been handed down it appears to be an adjectival derivative of Latin *corvus* raven, which has a Late Latin variant *corbus*. This may represent a translation of the Germanic personal name *Hraban*.

Pet form: **Körbl**.

Kornel (m.) Polish and Czech form of CORNELIUS.

Variants: Polish: **Korneli, Korneliusz**.

Kort (m.) Dutch form of KURT.

Kostya (m.) Russian: pet form of KONSTANTIN, which is often pronounced as *Kostatin* in the vernacular.

Kreine (f.) Jewish: from a dialect form of Yiddish *kroine* crown (equivalent to modern German *Krone*, from Latin *corōna*). See also ATARAH.

Kreszenz (f.) German (S. Germany): from the Late Latin pesonal name *Crescentia*, a feminine form of the male name *Crescens*, genitive *Crescentis*. This represents a participial form of Latin *crescere* to grow. It seems originally to have been used as a name of good omen, in the hope that the child bearing it would grow up strong and healthy.

Variant: **Crescentia**.

Pet form: **Zenzi**.

Kriemhild (f.) German: from an old Germanic female personal name composed of the elements *grim* mask + *hild* battle. In the *Nibelungenlied* this is the name of the sister of Gunther; she marries Siegfried, and later takes vengeance on her brother for her husband's murder.

Variants: **Kriemhilde, Krimhilde**.

Kristeen (f.) English: fanciful respelling of CHRISTINE, influenced by the Danish forms KRISTEN and KIRSTEN.

Variants: **Kristene, Kristine**.

Kristen (m.) Danish form of CHRISTIAN.

Kristie (f.) English: fanciful respelling of the female name CHRISTIE, under the influence of the Scottish form KIRSTIE.

Variant: **Kristy**.

Kristina (f.) Swedish and Czech form of CHRISTINA. The name is very popular in Sweden. Queen Kristina of Sweden (1626–89) succeeded her father Gustavus Adolphus in 1632. Growing to adulthood, she presided over a glittering court, but in 1654 she abdicated, left Sweden dressed as a man, converted to Roman Catholicism, and lived for most of the rest of her life in Rome. Her character was the subject of a famous but largely fictitious film (1933), in which the part of the queen was played by Greta Garbo.

Variant: Swedish: **Kerstin**.

Pet form: Swedish: **Kicki**.

Kristoffer (m.) Scandinavian form of CHRISTOPHER.

Krystle (f.) English: fanciful respelling of CRYSTAL.

Kryštof (m.) Czech form of CHRISTOPHER.

Pet forms: **Kryša, Kryšek**.

Krystyna (f.) Polish form of CHRISTINA.

Krzysztof (m.) Polish form of CHRISTOPHER.

Ksawery (m.) Polish form of XAVIER.

Kuba (m.) Polish and Czech: pet form of JAKUB. [*cont.*]

Variants: Polish: **Kubú**. Czech: **Kubeš, Kubiček**.

Kukka (f.) Finnish: originally an affectionate nickname meaning 'flower'.

Kulya (f.) Russian: pet form of AKILINA.

Kunigunde (f.) German: from an old Germanic female personal name composed of the elements *kuoni* brave + *gund* strife. St Cunegund (d. 1039) was the wife of the Holy Roman Emperor Henry II, with whom she is said to have lived in 'conjugal virginity'.

Cognates: Dutch: **Kunigonde, Cunegonde**.

Pet forms: German: **Kinge, Kinga**.

Kurt (m.) German: in origin a contracted form of KONRAD, but now well established as a given name in its own right.

Variant: **Curt**.

Cognate: Dutch: **Kort**.

Kustaa (m.) Finnish form of GUSTAV; see also KYÖSTI.

Květa (f.) Czech: originally an affectionate nickname derived from the vocabulary word *květ* flower, which came to be adopted as a given name.

Pet forms: **Květka, Květuše, Květuška**.

Kwiatosław (m.) Polish: from an old Slavonic personal name composed of the elements *kviat* flower + *slav* glory.

Cognate: Czech: **Květoslav**.

Kyla (f.) English: recently coined name, created as a feminine form of KYLE or else a variant of KYLIE.

Kyle (m., f.) English: transferred use of a Scottish surname, which originated as a local name from the region so called in the former county of Ayrshire. *Kyle* is a topographic term referring to a narrow strait or channel, from Gaelic *caol* narrow.

Kylie (f.) English: of Australian origin, said to represent an Aboriginal term for the boomerang. However, in view of the inappropriateness of this meaning, it seems more likely that the name is an artificial invention influenced by KYLE and KELLY. It is extremely popular in Australia and, in part due to the fame of the Australian actress and singer Kylie Minogue (b. 1968), it is gradually coming into use in the rest of the English-speaking world.

Variant: **Kyleigh**.

Kynaston (m.) English: transferred use of the surname, which originated in the Middle Ages as a local name from places in Hereford and Shropshire so called from Old English *Cynefriþestūn* 'settlement of *Cynefriþ*', a male personal name composed of the elements *cyne* royal + *friþ* peace.

Kyösti (m.) Finnish form of GUSTAV; see also KUSTAA.

Kyra (f.) English: apparently a variant spelling of *Cyra*, feminine form of CYRUS, or else a feminine name formed directly from KYRAN.

Kyran (m.) English and Irish: variant spelling of KIERAN.

L

Labhrás (m.) Irish Gaelic form of LAURENCE.

Labhrainn (m.) Scottish Gaelic form of LAURENCE.

Lacey (m., f.) English: transferred use of the surname, originally a Norman baronial name signifying origin in *Lassy*, Calvados. The Lacey family was important in Ireland during the early Middle Ages. As a female name this seems to have been influenced by association with the vocabulary word *lace*, denoting an ornamental trimming (Old French *laz* braid, from Latin *laqueus* noose).

Variant: **Lacy** (mainly m.).

Lachlan (m.) Scottish (Gaelic **Lachlann**, dialectally **Lachann**; earlier *Lochlann*): said to refer originally to a migrant from Norway, the 'land of the lochs'. It is normally used only in families that have some connection with Scotland.

Pet forms: Scottish: **Lachie**. Canadian: **Lockie**.

Feminine form: Scottish (Highland): **Lachina**.

Lachtna (m.) Irish Gaelic: originally a byname meaning 'milk-coloured'. It was borne, according to tradition, by the great-great-grandfather of the legendary king, Brian Boru. It is sometimes found in a Latinized form as LUCIUS.

Ladislao (m.) Italian equivalent of LÁSZLÓ, used mainly in the town of Fiume, which for a long time was under Hungarian control (though since 1947 it has formed part of Yugoslavia, under the name Rijeka).

Ladislas (m.) Latinate form of Polish WŁADISŁAW, Czech VLADISLAV, or Hungarian LÁSZLÓ, occasionally used in Britain, the Netherlands, and elsewhere, but mainly as a translation name.

Variant: **Ladislaus**.

Ladislav (m.) Czech: variant of VLADISLAV.

Feminine form: **Ladislava**.

Laetitia (f.) Original Latin form of LETTICE. This is currently a moderately fashionable name in France.

Laila (f.) 1. English: variant spelling of LEILA.

2. Scandinavian: ancient name of Saami origin, not uncommon in modern Denmark, Norway, and Sweden.

Lajos (m.) Hungarian form of LOUIS.

Lalage (f.) Classical name, pronounced /ˈlæləd͡ʒɪ/ or /ˈlæləgɪ/. It was used by Horace in one of his *Odes* as the name of his beloved of the moment; without doubt it was not her real name, but a literary pseudonym derived from Greek *lalagein* to chatter or babble. It has enjoyed a modest popularity among classically educated parents since the 19th century. It was the name of the central character in E. Arnot Robertson's *Ordinary Families* (1933) and it also occurs in John Fowles's *The French Lieutenant's Woman* (1969).

Lally (f.) English: pet form of LALAGE.

Variants: **Lallie, Lalla, Lala**.

Lambert (m.) English, French, German, and Dutch: of Germanic origin, composed of the elements *land* land, territory + *beorht* famous. It was introduced to Britain by the Normans. Its frequency in Britain in the later Middle Ages, however, was mainly due to its popularity among immigrants from the Low Countries (who came to England in connection with the cloth trade). St Lambert of Maastricht was a 7th-century saint who aided St Willibrord in his evangelical work.

Variants: Dutch and Low German: **Lammert**. German: **Lamprecht**.

Lana (f.) 1. English (esp. U.S.): of uncertain origin. If not simply an invention, it may have been devised as a feminine equivalent of ALAN (of which it is an anagram), or an aphetic form of ALANA. It seems to have been first used by the film actress Lana Turner (b. 1920), whose original name was *Julia*.

2. Russian: aphetic short form of SVETLANA.

Lance (m.) English: from Old French *Lance*, from the Germanic name *Lanzo*, a pet form of various compound names with the first element *land* land, territory (cf. e.g. LAMBERT), but associated from an early date with Old French *lance*, the weapon (from Latin *lancea*). In modern use the given name seems to have originated as a transferred use of the surname derived from the medieval given name, although it is also commonly taken to be a short form of LANCELOT.

Lancelot (m.) English: the name borne by one of King Arthur's best and most valued knights, who eventually betrayed his trust by becoming the lover of Queen Guinevere. The name is of uncertain origin. It is probably, like other Arthurian names, of Celtic derivation, but has been heavily distorted by mediation through French sources.

Laocadia (f.) Portuguese form of LEOCADIA.

Laoiseach (m.) Irish Gaelic: originally an ethnic name for someone from the region of *Laois* in Leinster (the modern county of Leix).

Anglicized forms: LOUIS, LEWIS.

Lara (f.) Russian: short form of LARISSA, introduced in the early 20th century to the English-speaking world. Here it became popular in particular as the name of one of the principal characters in Boris Pasternak's novel *Dr Zhivago* (1957), which was made into a popular Hollywood film in 1965. The name is associated with 'Lara's theme', from the film score by Maurice Jarre. Occasionally the name also represents a short form of KLARA.

Laraine (f.) English (mainly U.S.): of uncertain origin, perhaps a variant spelling of LORRAINE or derived from the French vocabulary word *la reine* meaning 'the queen' (cf. RAINE). The prefix *La-* has become a popular one in female names in America since the 1970s, particularly among Blacks; the forms **Lakisha**, **Latoya**, LATASHA, and LATISHA were among the top one hundred Black female names in 1982.

Variant: **Lareine**.

Larissa (f.) Russian: of uncertain origin. It is the name of a Greek martyr venerated in the Eastern Church, and may perhaps be derived from the ancient Thessalian town of Larissa.

Variant: **Larisa**.

Lark (f.) English: one of a small set of female names derived from vocabulary words denoting birds, which have achieved some currency during the 20th century. The associations of the lark (Old English *lāwerce*) with early rising, cheerfulness, and sweet song have no doubt contributed to its occasional choice as a given name.

Larry (m.) English: pet form of LAURENCE or LAWRENCE.

Informal modern variant: **Laz**.

Lars (m.) Scandinavian form of LAURENCE. This was the second commonest male name in Denmark in 1965 and the third commonest in Sweden in 1973.

Lassarina (m.) Irish: Anglicized form of the Gaelic name **Lasairíona**, composed of the elements *lasair* flame + *fíon* wine.

Lasse (m.) Finnish form of LAURENCE, derived from a Scandinavian pet form of the name. It has been borne, for example, by the Finnish runner Lasse Viren (b. 1949).

Variant: **Lassi**.

László (m.) Hungarian form of WŁADYSŁAW. The name is still very popular in Hungary: its popularity was originally due to St László (1040–95), King of Hungary (1077–95), who is honoured by the Hungarians as a model of chivalry, courage, and Christian virtue, as well as a patriot and lawgiver.

Latasha (f.) English (esp. U.S.): a recent coinage, possibly representing a cross between LATISHA and NATASHA. It was the twenty-second most common female name among American Blacks in 1982.

Latisha (f.) English (esp. U.S.): a recent coinage, probably a respelling of LAETITIA. It enjoys considerable popularity among American Blacks.

Pet form: **Tisha**.

Laughlin (m.) Irish: Anglicized form of Gaelic LOCHLAINN.

Launo (m.) Finnish form of CLAUS.

Laura (f.) Italian, Spanish, and English: feminine form of the Late Latin male name *Laurus* 'Laurel'. St Laura was a 9th-century Spanish nun who met her death in a cauldron of molten lead. Laura is also the name of the woman addressed in the love poetry of the Italian poet Petrarch (Francesco Petrarca, 1304–74), and it owes much of its subsequent popularity to this. There have been various speculations about her identity, but it has not been established with any certainty. He first met her in 1327 while living in Avignon, and she died of the plague in 1348. The current popularity of the given name in the English-speaking world dates from the 19th century, when it was probably imported from Italy.

Cognates: French: **Laure**. Catalan: **Llora**. German: **Lora, Lore**.

Pet form: English: **Laurie**.

Laurel (f.) English: 19th-century adoption of the English vocabulary word denoting the tree (Middle English *lorel*, a dissimilated form of Old French *lorer*), probably influenced by LAURA. It may have been taken as a pet form of LAURA.

Variant (elaborated form): **Laurelle**.

Pet form: **Laurie**.

Lauren (f.) English: apparently modelled on LAURENCE, this was first used, or at any rate first brought to public attention, by the film actress Lauren Bacall (born Betty Jean Perske in 1924). She was famous for her partnership with Humphrey Bogart, especially in *To Have and Have Not* (1943) and *The Big Sleep* (1946).

Variant: **Loren** (occasionally used as a male name).

Laurence (m., f.) 1. (m.) English: from a French form of Latin *Laurentius* 'man from Laurentum'. *Laurentum* was a town in Latium, which may have got its name from Latin *laurus* laurel, or may alternatively be of pre-Roman origin. The given name was popular in the Middle Ages as a result of the fame of a 3rd-century saint who was one of the seven deacons of Rome. He was martyred in 258. The legend is that, having been required to hand over the Church's treasures to the civil authorities, he assembled the poor and sick and presented them. For this, he was supposedly roasted to death on a gridiron. In England the name is also associated with St Laurence of Canterbury (d. 619), the second bishop of Canterbury, who fought against pagan backsliding among his flock. See also LAWRENCE.

2. (f.) French: feminine form of *Laurent*.

Cognates: Irish Gaelic: **Labhrás**. Scottish Gaelic: **Labhrainn**. French: **Laurent**. Italian: **Lorenzo**. Spanish: **Lorencio**. Catalan: **Llorenç**. Portuguese: **Laurenço**. German: **Lorenz**. Dutch: **Laurens**. Scandinavian: **Lars**. Finnish: **Lauri, Lasse, Lassi**. Russian: **Lavrenti**. Polish: **Laurencjusz** (vernacular spelling of Latin *Laurentius*); **Lawrenty; Wawrzyniec** (vernacular form). Czech: **Vavřinec**.

Pet forms: English: **Larry, Laurie**. German: **Lenz**.

Laurent (m.) French form of LAURENCE.

Lauretta (f.) Italian: diminutive form of LAURA; cf. LORETTA.
Cognate: French: **Laurette**.

Lauri (m.) Finnish: learned form of LAURENCE; see also LASSE.

Laurie (f., m.) English: pet form of LAURA, LAUREL, and LAURENCE.

Lavender (f.) English (rare): from the vocabulary word denoting the herb with sweet-smelling flowers (Old French *lavendre*, from Late Latin *lavendula*).

Lavinia (f.) Name, according to Roman mythology, of the wife of Aeneas, and thus the mother of the Roman people. Legend had it that she gave her name to the Latin town of *Lavinium*, but in fact she was almost certainly invented to explain the placename, which is of pre-Roman origin. She was said to be the daughter of King Latinus, who was similarly invented, to account for the name of *Latium*.

Lavrenti (m.) Russian form of LAURENCE.

Lawrence (m.) English: Anglicized spelling of LAURENCE. This is the usual spelling of the surname, and is now becoming increasingly common as a given name, especially in America.
Pet forms: **Larry, Lawrie**.

Laz (m.) English: modern informal pet form of LARRY (cf. *Baz* from *Barry* and *Gaz* from *Gary*).

Lazarus (m.) Name borne in the New Testament by two different characters: the brother of Martha and Mary, who was raised from the dead by Jesus (John 11: 1–44), and the beggar who appears in the parable of Dives and Lazarus narrated by Jesus (Luke 16: 19–31). The form *Lazarus*, used in the Authorized Version, is a Latinate version of Greek *Lazaros*, itself a transliteration of Aramaic *Lazar*, an aphetic short form of Hebrew *Eleazar* 'God is my help'. Because the beggar Lazarus was 'full of sores' the name was often used in the Middle Ages as a generic term for a leper, and so came to be avoided as a given name. It is still not common.
Cognates: French: **Lazare**. Catalan: **Llàtzer**. Italian: **Lazzaro**. Polish: **Łazarz**.

Leagsaidh (f.) Scottish Gaelic form of LEXY.

Leah (f.) Biblical name (meaning 'languid' in Hebrew) borne by the elder sister of Rachel (Genesis 29: 23). Jacob served her father Laban for seven years in return for the hand of Rachel, but was deceived into marrying Leah first. He was then given Rachel as well, but had to labour seven more years afterwards. The name is common mainly among Jews, although it also enjoyed some popularity among the Puritans in the 17th century.
Variant: **Lea**. See also LIA.
Cognate: French: **Léa**.

Léan (f.) Irish Gaelic form of HELEN.

Leander (m.) Latin form of the Greek name *Leandros*, which is composed of the elements *leōn* lion + *anēr* (genitive *andros*) man. In Greek legend, Leander is the name of a hero who swam across the Hellespont every night to visit his beloved, Hero, and back again in the morning, but was eventually drowned during a violent storm. In Christian times, the name was borne by a 6th-century saint, the brother of Sts Fulgentius, Isidore, and Florentina. He was a leading ecclesiastical figure of his day, a friend of Gregory the Great, and became archbishop of Seville. In modern times, the name has occasionally been used as an elaboration of LEE (as a male name). In addition, Dunkling has recorded at least one instance of its use as a female name.
Cognates: French: **Léandre**. Italian, Spanish, Portuguese: **Leandro**.

Leanne (f.) English: modern combination of LEE and ANNE, or else a respelling of LIANE.

Leão (m.) Portuguese form of LEO.

Leberecht (m.) German: religious name, meaning 'live rightly', coined in the 17th century. It was borne, for example, by the Prussian field marshal, Gebhard Lebe-recht von Blücher (1742–1819).

Lech (m.) Polish: name of the legendary founder of the Polish race, brother of the *Czech* and *Rus* who gave their names to the Czechs and Russians respectively. All three of these names are of very ancient origin and uncertain derivation.
Pet form: **Leszek**.

Lechosław (m.) Polish: from an old Slavonic personal name composed of the ethnic term *lech* Pole (see LECH) + *slav* glory.
Variant: **Lesław**.

Leda (f.) Name borne in classical mythology by a queen of Sparta, who was ravished by Zeus in the shape of a swan. She gave birth to two eggs which, when hatched, revealed the two sets of twins: Castor and Pollux, and Helen and Hermione.

Lee (m., f.) English: transferred use of the surname, originally a local name from any of numerous places so called from Old English *lēah* wood or clearing. It is especially popular now in America, where it has sometimes been bestowed in honour of the Confederate general, Robert E. Lee (1807–70). As a female name, it may also be a variant of *Lea* (see LEAH).

Leesa (f.) English: fanciful modern variant spelling of LISA, influenced by the female name LEE.

Léger (m.) French form of LUITGER. This name was borne by a 7th-century bishop of Autun.

Leib (m.) Jewish: Yiddish name, meaning 'lion' (cf. modern German *Löwe*). See also ARYE.

Leif (m.) Scandinavian: from Old Norse *Leifr*, a short form of various compound names containing the second element *leifr* heir, descendant. Leif Ericsson was a Norse navigator who, in around 1000, discovered the New World.
Variant: Norwegian: **Leiv**.

Leighton (m.) English: transferred use of the surname, which originated as a local name from any of several places named with the Old English elements *lēac* leek + *tūn* enclosure, settlement; of these the best known is Leighton Buzzard in Bedfordshire.
Variant: **Layton** (a variant spelling of the surname, reflecting the pronunciation).

Leila (f.) Of Arabic origin, now fairly common in the English-speaking world, having been used as a name for an oriental beauty by both Byron, in *The Giaour* (1813) and *Don Juan* (1819–24), and by Lord Lytton for the heroine of his novel *Leila* (1838). In Arabic it means 'night', apparently alluding to a dark complexion.
Variants: **Laila, Lila**.

Leland (m.) English (esp. U.S.): transferred use of the surname, which originated as a local name for someone who lived by a patch of fallow land, from Middle English *lay*, *ley* fallow (Old English *lǣge*) + *land* land (Old English *land*). The surname is not a particularly common or famous one, and it is not clear why it should have been adopted as a given name. In America it is the name of a town in Mississippi, and it was also the surname borne by the humorous writer Charles Leland (1824–1903), author of *The Breitmann Ballads*.

Lelle (m.) Scandinavian: pet form of LENNART.

Lempi (f.) Finnish: meaning 'love', this is a loan translation of the Latin name *Charitas* or the Greek *Agapē*.

Lemuel (m.) Biblical name (possibly meaning 'devoted to God' in Hebrew) borne by an obscure king who was lectured by his mother on the perils of strong drink and the virtues of a dutiful wife (Proverbs 31). He is mentioned by Chaucer in *The Canterbury Tales*, where his name is carefully distinguished from the more familiar SAMUEL. Lemuel Gulliver was the unusual name of the hero of Jonathan Swift's *Gulliver's Travels* (1726).

Len (m.) English: short form of LEONARD, and possibly also of the rarer given name LENNOX. In the case of the British trade-union leader Len Murray (b. 1922) it represents a short form of LIONEL.

Pet form: LENNY.

Lena (f.) English, Scottish, Dutch, German, and Scandinavian: abstracted from various names ending in *-lena* or *-lina*, such as *Helena* (from HELEN) and *Magdalena* (from MAGDALENE), or, in the Scottish Highlands, *Dolina* (from DONALD). In America it is famous as the name of the singer Lena Horne.

Variant: German and Danish: **Lene**.

Lenda (f.) English: apparently an arbitrary alteration of LINDA, originating in the 20th century.

Lene (f.) German and Danish: aphetic short form of both *Helene* (see HELEN) and MAGDALENE. It is very frequently used as an independent given name, not directly connected with either of these full forms, and was the third commonest female name in use in Denmark in 1965.

Leni (f.) German: pet form of LENA and LENE.

Lennard (m.) English: assimilated spelling of LEONARD, perhaps in part representing a transferred use of the surname derived from this given name in the Middle Ages.

Lennart (m.) Scandinavian form of LEONARD.

Pet forms: **Lenne, Lelle**.

Lennox (m.) Scottish and English: from the Scottish surname and earldom, originally a local name from a district north of Glasgow formerly known as *The Levenach*. This was the first name borne by the composer Sir Lennox Berkeley (1903–89).

Lenny (m.) English: normally a pet form of LEN, to some extent used as an independent given name.

Lenora (f.) English: originally a contracted form of LEONORA, although sometimes chosen as an expanded version of LENA.

Variants: **Lennora, Len(n)orah**.

Lenz (m.) German: contracted short form of LORENZ. This form of the name was formerly common in south and southwest Germany, but is now rare.

Leo (m.) English: from a Late Latin personal name, meaning 'lion', which was borne by a large number of early Christian saints, most notably Pope Leo the Great (?390–461). It is also found as a Jewish name (see LEON). In modern use it seems also to have been given as an omen name by parents who wished for a 'lion-hearted' son.

Cognates: French: LÉON. Italian: **Leone**. Spanish: **León**. Portuguese: **Leão**. Catalan: **Lleó**. Czech: **Leoš**.

Leocadia (f.) Spanish: probably a Latinate derivative of Greek *leukas* (genitive *leukados*), a poetic feminine form of *leukos* light, bright, clear. The first part of the name has subsequently been altered by association with Latin *leo* lion. St Leocadia (d. *c.*303) was a virgin martyr of Toledo, of whose life little is known, but who nevertheless enjoys a considerable cult.

Cognates: Catalan: **Llogaia**. Portuguese: **Laocadia**.

Masculine form: Spanish: **Leocadio**.

Leodegar (m.) French and German: learned form (influenced by the Latin word *leo* lion) of the names found in the vernaculars as LÉGER and LUITGER.

Leon (m.) English, German, and Irish Gaelic form of LEO. This form is common as a Jewish name. The lion is an important symbol among Jews because of Jacob's dying pronouncement that 'Judah is a lion's whelp' (Genesis 49: 9). See also LEIB, ARYE.

Léon (m.) French form of LEO.

Leona (f.) English and German: Latinate feminine form of LEON.

Leonard (m.) English: from an Old French personal name of Germanic origin, composed of the elements *leon* lion (a late borrowing from Romance) + *hard* hardy, brave, strong. This was the name of a 5th-century Frankish saint, who became the patron of peasants and horses. Although it was introduced into Britain by the Normans, *Leonard* was not a particularly common name there during the Middle Ages. It was revived during the 19th century and became very popular. It is now also common as a Jewish name (cf. LEON).

Variant: **Lennard**.

Cognates: French: **Léonard**. Italian, Spanish, Portuguese: LEONARDO. Catalan: **Lleonard**. German: **Leonhard(t)**. Scandinavian: **Lennart**.

Short form: English: **Len**.

Pet forms: English: **Lenny**. Scandinavian: **Lenne, Lelle, Nenne**.

Leonardo (m.) Italian, Spanish, and Portuguese form of LEONARD. Its most famous bearer was the Renaissance genius Leonardo da Vinci (1452–1519), remembered principally as a painter and sculptor, but also as an architect, engineer, and scientist.

Léonce (m.) French form of LEONZIO.

Leoncio (m. Spanish form of LEONZIO.

Leone (m.) Italian form of LEO.

Leonid (m.) Russian: from the Greek name *Leonidas*, a Spartan dialectal form of *Leonidēs*, borne by a king of Sparta who, with seven hundred followers, was killed by the invading Persians at the heroic defence of the pass at Thermopylae (480 BC). This action gave the rest of Greece time to arm and prepare to meet the invaders. He was named from his grandfather *Leōn*, the name being a patronymic derivative of *Leōn* 'lion'. Later the name was borne by two early saints venerated especially in the Eastern Church: an Alexandrian, the father of Origen, martyred in 202, and an Egyptian martyred with several companions in 304.

Léonie (f.) French: from Latin *Leonia*, feminine form of *Leonius*, derived from *leo* lion. It is most common among Jews as a feminine equivalent of LEON, but is now also widely used (normally without the accent, **Leoni(e)**) in the English-speaking world among non-Jews.

Léonne (f.) French: feminine form of LÉON, occasionally also used (normally without the accent) in the English-speaking world.

Leonora (f.) English: aphetic form of ELEONORA.

Cognate: German: **Leonore**.

Leonti (m.) Russian form of the Byzantine Greek name *Leont(e)ios*, Greek equivalent of Latin *Leontius* (see LEONZIO). This was borne by several minor figures venerated in the Eastern Church, including Leontios of Neopolis (d. *c.*630).

Leontina (f.) Italian, from Latin: a feminine derivative of *Leontius* (see LEONZIO).

Léontine (f.) French form of LEONTINA, occasionally also used (normally without the accent) in the English-speaking world.

Leonzio (m.) Italian: from the Late Latin personal name *Leontius*, a derivative of LEO. The name was borne by several early saints, including Leontius the Elder (d. *c.*541) and Leontius the Younger (*c.*510–*c.*565), successive bishops of Bordeaux.

Cognates: French: **Léonce**. Spanish: **Leoncio**. Russian: LEONTI.

Leopold (m.) English: of Germanic origin, composed of the elements *liut* people + *bold* bold, brave. The first element was altered by association with Latin *leo* lion. A name of this origin may have been introduced into Britain by the Normans, but if so it did not survive long. It was reintroduced from the Continent towards the end of the 19th century, partly in honour of King Leopold of the Belgians (1790–1865), the uncle of Queen Victoria, who was an influential adviser to her in her youth, and after whom she named one of her sons. In the 17th and 18th centuries it was also the name of two Austro-Hungarian emperors, who were also kings of Bohemia.

Cognates: French: **Léopold**. Italian, Spanish, Portuguese: **Leopoldo**. German: **Luitpold**.

Leoš (m.) Czech form of LEO. This was the given name borne by the Czech composer Leoš Janaček (1854–1928).

Leroy (m.) English: now considered a typical Black American given name, but formerly also extensively borne by White Americans. It is from a French nickname meaning 'the king', but it is not entirely clear why this particular form should have become such a popular given name in English. See also DELROY.

Les (m.) English: short form of LESLIE.

Lesław (m.) Polish: contracted form of LECHOSŁAW.

Lesley (f., m.) Scottish and English: originally simply a variant of LESLIE, but now specialized in Britain as the female form. Its first recorded use as a female name is in a poem by Robert Burns.

Leslie (m., occasionally f., esp. in the U.S.) Scottish and English: transferred use of the Scottish surname derived from the lands of Lesslyn in Aberdeenshire (a placename perhaps from Gaelic *leas cuilinn* meaning 'garden of hollies'). Surnames and clan names have been used as given names more readily and from an earlier date in Scotland than elsewhere, and this is the name of an ancient clan, who in the 14th and 15th centuries were close associates of the Scottish royal house of Stewart. However, in the 17th century their most famous member, the general David Leslie (d. 1682), was a Covenanter who in the Civil War played a major role in defeating the royalists (including James Graham, Earl of Montrose, in 1645). But by 1650 he had switched sides and was the commander of the Scottish royalists who defeated Cromwell at Dunbar. The Leslies have held the earldom of Rothes since 1457.

The British film actor Leslie Howard (1890–1943), who was of Hungarian origin, had a considerable influence on the popularity of the name, especially in the United States, where he appeared in *Gone with the Wind* (1939), the film that has probably had more influence on naming than any other.

Short form: **Les** (m.).

Lester (m.) English: transferred use of the surname, which is a local name from the city of *Leicester*. The placename is recorded in the 10th century as *Ligora cæster*, representing a British name of obscure origin + the Old English term *cæster* 'Roman fort'.

Leszek (m.) Polish: pet form of LECH.

Letizia (f.) Italian form of LETTICE. This was the given name of Napoleon's mother.

Lettice (f.) English: from the medieval English form of the Latin name *Laetitia* 'happiness'. It was popular among the Victorians, but is now regarded as faintly risible (perhaps because of its similarity to the vocabulary word *lettuce*).

Pet forms: **Letty, Lettie**.

Lev (m.) Russian: from the Russian vocabulary word *lev* lion, representing an early vernacular calque of LEO.

Variant (informal): **Lyov**.

Cognate: Polish: **Lew**.

Levi (m.) Biblical name (meaning 'associated' in Hebrew) given by Jacob's wife Leah to her third son as an expression of her hope, 'Now this time will my husband be joined unto me, because I have born him three sons: therefore was his name called Levi' (Genesis 29: 34). The priestly caste of the Levites are descended from Levi. In the New Testament, Levi is a byname of the apostle and evangelist Matthew. In modern times the name is borne mostly by Jews, but occasionally also by Black revivalist Christians.

Lew (m.) 1. Polish spelling of LEV. The name is common among Jews; cf. LEIB.

2. English: short form of LEWIS.

Lewie (m.) 1. English: respelling of LOUIS or pet form of LEWIS.

2. Irish: Anglicized form of the Gaelic name LUGHAIDH.

Lewis (m.) 1. Common English form, since the Middle Ages, of the Norman and French name LOUIS. In modern use it is also in part a transferred use of the surname derived from this given name.

2. In Wales, an Anglicized form of LLEWELLYN.

3. In Scotland, a variant of LUDOVIC, or, among families connected with the Isle of Lewis, a transferred use of the place-name.

4. In Ireland, an Anglicized form of Gaelic LAOISEACH and LUGHAIDH.

Short form: **Lew**.

Pet forms: **Lewie, Louie**.

Lex (m.) English: short form of ALEX. The minor vogue for this name, and the rhyming DEX and TEX, may have been inspired by the now distinctly old-fashioned REX.

Lexine (f.) English and Scottish: apparently an elaboration of LEXY with the addition of the originally French feminine diminutive suffix *-ine*, which has long been productive in forming English female names.

Lexy (f.) English and Scottish: pet form of ALEXANDRA.

Lia (f.) Italian: of uncertain derivation. It is probably either a form of LEAH or, especially in Sicily, a shortened form of *Rosalia* (see ROSALIE).

Liam (m.) Irish: short form of **Uilliam**, Gaelic form of WILLIAM.

Liane (f.) French and English: short form of ÉLIANE.

Variant: **Lianne**.

Libby (f.) English: pet form of ELIZABETH, based originally on a child's unsuccessful attempts to pronounce the name. It is now also occasionally used as an independent name.

Libe (f.) Jewish: Yiddish name, meaning 'love' (cf. modern German *Liebe*).

Liběna (f.) Czech: equivalent of the Russian name LYUBOV, derived from the element *lib* love.

Pet forms: **Líba, Liběnka, Libuše, Libuška**.

Libor (m.) Czech: from the Latin name *Liberius*, a derivative of *liber* free. St Liberius was a 2nd-century bishop of Ravenna.

Pet forms: **Liborek, Libek**.

Licerio (m.) Spanish: from the Late Latin personal name *Lycerius*, a derivative of either Greek *lykē* light or *lykos* wolf. St Licerius was born in Lérida, and became bishop of Conserans in France (506–*c.*548). The French form of his name is *Lizier*, but this is not regularly used as a given name.

Lícia (f.) Hungarian: shortened form of *Felícia* (see FELICIA).

Licio (m.) Italian: from the Late Latin personal name *Lycius*, originally an ethnic derivative of the region of *Lycia* in Asia Minor. The name was borne principally by slaves, some of whom may have come from this region.

Lida (f.) Czech form of LYDIA.

Lidia (f.) Polish form of LYDIA.

Lidmila (f.) The usual Czech form of LUDMILA.

Pet forms: **Lída; Lidka, Lidun(k)a, Liduše, Liduška**.

Liduina (f.) Italian form of LIDWINA, used in particular in the Emilian region.

Lidwina (f.) Dutch: name borne in honour of the Blessed *Lidwina* or *Lydwina* of Schiedam (1380–1433), a lifelong invalid and mystic. The name is a feminine form of the Germanic name *Lidwin*, composed of the elements *liut* people, race + *win* friend.

Liese (f.) German: a popular pet form of ELISABETH. It is now also quite widely used as an independent given name in both the German-speaking and the English-speaking world.

Lieselotte (f.) German: 19th-century coinage composed of the elements LIESE + *-lotte*, abstracted from KARLOTTE and treated as a feminine diminutive suffix.

Pet form: **Lilo**.

Life (f.) Irish Gaelic: traditional name, borne, according to legend, by a figure who gave her name to the River *Liffey*.

Ligia (f.) Spanish and Portuguese: of uncertain origin, apparently a shortened form of *Eligia*, the feminine version of ELIGIO (see also ELOY and ELOI).

Lila (f.) English: apparently a variant spelling of LEILA or LAILA.

Lilac (f.) English: a modern adoption of the vocabulary word denoting the shrub with large sprays of heavily scented purple or white flowers. The word is from French, which derived it via Spanish from Arabic *līlak*, from Persian *nīlak* bluish, a derivative of *nīl* blue.

Lili (f.) German: pet form, originally a reduplicated nursery form, of ELISABETH. This form is associated in particular with the Second World War popular song *Lili Marlene*.

Variant: **Lilli**.

Lilian (f.) English: of uncertain origin, first recorded in the late 16th century, and probably derived from a nursery form of ELIZABETH. It is now sometimes regarded as a derivative of the flower name LILY, but this was not used as a given name in England until the 19th century.

Variant: **Lillian**.

Lilith (f.) The name borne, according to medieval tradition, by a wife of Adam prior to Eve. She is said to have been turned into an ugly demon for refusing to obey him. *Lilith* occurs in the Bible as a vocabulary word meaning 'night monster' or 'screech owl' (Isaiah 34: 14), and in Jewish folklore is the name of an ugly demon. In spite of its unpleasant connotations, it has occasionally been used as a given name in the 20th century, perhaps in part being taken as an elaborated form of LILY.

Lillian (f.) English: variant spelling of LILIAN, common especially in America.

Lilo (f.) German: pet form of LIESELOTTE.

Lily (f.) English: from the vocabulary word denoting the flower (Latin *lilium*), regarded in Christian imagery as a symbol of purity.

Lincoln (m.) English: transferred use of the surname, a local name derived from the name of the city of Lincoln. This is found in the 7th century as *Lindum colonia*, representing a British name probably meaning 'lake' (cf. Welsh *llyn*) + the Latin defining term *colonia* colony, settlement. As a given name it has sometimes been bestowed in honour of Abraham Lincoln (1809–65), 16th president of the United States, who led the Union to victory in the Civil War and enforced the emancipation of slaves.

Linda (f.) English: of recent and somewhat uncertain origin. It is first recorded in the 19th century, perhaps either as a shortening of BELINDA or as an adoption of the Spanish vocabulary word *linda* pretty (masculine *lindo*). Alternatively, it may be derived from the Latinate form of any of various other Germanic female names ending in the element *-lind* meaning 'weak, tender, soft'. It has become very popular in the 20th century.

Pet form: **Lindie, Lindy**.

Linden (f.) English: ostensibly from the vocabulary word denoting the lime tree (originally the adjectival form, derived from Old English *linde*). However, the given name is of recent, probably 20th-century, origin and it is more likely that this is simply an elaboration of LINDA, along the lines of LAUREN from LAURA.

Lindon (m.) English: variant spelling of LYNDON.

Lindsay (f., m.) Scottish and English: from the Scottish surname, originally borne by Sir Walter de Lindesay, one of the retainers of King David I of Scotland (1084–1153), who took the name to Scotland from Lindsey in Lincolnshire. This place was named in Old English as the 'wetland (Old English *ey*) belonging to Lincoln'. It was at first used as a male name, and this is still the case in Scotland, but elsewhere it is now nearly always used for girls.

Variants: **Lindsey, Lynsey, Linzi.**

Lindy (f.) English: apparently an altered form or pet form of LINDA, by a reversal of the process that derived e.g. JENNA from JENNY.

Linford (m.) English: transferred use of the surname, which originated as a local name from any of various places named with the Old English elements *līn* flax or *lind* lime tree + *ford* ford. In the case of Great and Little Linford in Berkshire, however, the first element seems to have been originally Old English *hlyn* maple. The given name is associated in particular with the athlete Linford Christie.

Linnéa (f.) Swedish: a popular given name first bestowed in honour of the Swedish botanist Carl von *Linné* (1707–70; Latinized as *Linnaeus*). He gave his name to the now internationally recognized *Linnaean* system of taxonomic classification, and to a type of flower known as *Linnaea*. The female given name was first used in the mid-19th century in the form *Linnaea*, and is now sometimes spelled **Linnea** (without the accent).

Short form: **Nea.**

Linnet (f.) English: simplified spelling of LINNETTE, strongly influenced in popularity by the vocabulary word denoting a small bird (Old French *linotte*, a derivative of *lin* flax, on the seeds of which it feeds).

Linnette (f.) English: variant spelling of LYNETTE.

Linton (m.) English: from a local surname, now also quite commonly used as a given name, especially among British Blacks. The surname derives from any of numerous places in England so called; most get the name from Old English *līn* flax, cotton or *lind* lime tree + *tūn* enclosure, settlement.

Linus (m.) Latin form of the Greek name *Linos*, which is of uncertain origin. In Greek mythology, Linus is both a famous musician who taught music to Hercules and an infant son of Apollo who had been exposed to die on a mountainside in Argos. The name may have been invented to explain the obscure refrain, '*ailinon*', of the so-called 'Linus song', a lament sung at harvest time in Argos. In the Christian era, *Linus* is the name of the second pope, St Peter's successor, who was martyred in *c.*76. He has been tentatively identified with the Linus to whom Paul sends greetings in 2 Timothy 4: 21. The given name has occasionally been used in America. It is now associated with a character in the extremely popular *Peanuts* strip cartoon series, a little boy inseparable from his security blanket.

Linzi (f.) English: fanciful respelling of LINDSAY.

Liona (f.) English: apparently an altered form of LEONA, influenced by LIONEL.

Lionel (m.) English: from a medieval diminutive of the Old French name LÉON or the Middle English nickname *Lion*.

Lipa (f.) Romanian: short form of *Filipa* (see PHILIPPA).

Lis (f.) 1. Scandinavian: dramatically shortened form of ELISABET, first used in the early years of the 20th century. It occurs as the second element of numerous compound names, such as *Anne-Lis*, *Ing-Lis*, and *Maj-Lis*.

2. English: variant spelling of LIZ.

Lisa (f.) English: variant of LIZA, influenced by French *Lise* and German *Liese*.

Lisbet (f.) English and Scandinavian: shortened form of ELIZABETH or *Elisabet*, now in fairly wide use as an independent given name.

Lisette (f.) French: diminutive form of *Lise*, which is itself a shortened form of ELISABETH.
Variant: **Lysette**.

Lisha (f.) English: modern coinage, apparently a respelled shortened form of names such as DELICIA and FELICIA, on the model of TRISHA from PATRICIA.

Lissa (f.) English: short form of MELISSA. See also LYSSA.

Liùsaidh (f.) Scottish Gaelic form of LOUISA or LUCY.

Liv (f.) Scandinavian: from an Old Norse female personal name identical in form with the vocabulary word *hlíf* defence, protection. In modern use it is often associated with the Norwegian vocabulary word *liv* life. The name is borne by a character in Nordic legend, and was revived in the late 19th century. It is now sometimes taken as a short form of ELISABET.

Livia (f.) English: in modern use often taken as a short form of OLIVIA, but originally a distinct name, a feminine form of the Roman family name *Livius*. This is of uncertain derivation, perhaps connected with *lividus* bluish.

Liz (f.) English: the most common of all the various short forms of ELIZABETH.

Liza (f.) English: short form of ELIZA.
Variant: **Lisa**.

Lizzie (f.) English: pet form of LIZ, with the hypocoristic suffix *-ie*.
Variant: **Lizzy**.

Llàtzer (m.) Catalan form of LAZARUS.

Lleó (m.) Catalan form of LEO.

Lleonard (m.) Catalan form of LEONARD.

Lleu (m.) Welsh: traditional name, meaning 'bright, shining', cognate with the name of the Celtic god known in Old Irish as *Lugh*, in Gaulish as *Lugus*. This name was borne in the *Mabinogi* by Lleu Llaw Gyffes 'Lleu Skilful Hand', the son of Aranrhod. It has been revived in modern times.

Llew (m.) Welsh: traditional name meaning 'lion'. It is also used as a short form of LLEWELYN.

Llewelyn (m.) Welsh: altered form (influenced by the vocabulary word *llew* lion) of **Llywelyn**, an ancient name of uncertain derivation. It goes back to an Old Celtic form *Lugobelinos*; the first element seems to be the divine name *Lugu-* (see LLEU), the second is found also in names such as *Cunobelinus* or *Cymbeline*. In historical times the name was borne in particular by Llywelyn ap Iorwerth (1173–1240) and his grandson Llywelyn ap Gruffydd (d. 1282), Welsh princes who for a time united their countrymen in North Wales and led opposition to the power of the Norman barons in South Wales and the borders. It has sometimes been Anglicized as LEWIS.
Short forms: LLEW, LYN.
Pet form: **Llelo**.

Llogaia (f.) Catalan form of LEOCADIA.

Llora (f.) Catalan form of LAURA.

Llorenç (m.) Catalan form of LAURENCE.

Lloyd (m.) English: from the Welsh surname, originally a nickname meaning 'grey(-haired)' (Welsh *llwyd*); cf. FLOYD.

Lluch (m.) Catalan form of LUKE.
Variant: **Lluc**.

Lluis (m.) Catalan form of LOUIS.

Llywarch (m.) Welsh: traditional name, now only occasionally used, composed of the god's name *Lugu-* (see LLEU) + Old Celtic *marcos* horse.

Lochlainn (m.) Irish Gaelic: a cognate of Scottish *Lachlann*; see LACHLAN.
Anglicized forms: **Loughlin, Laughlin**.

Lockie (m.) Canadian: pet form of LACHLAN.

Lodewijk (m.) Dutch form of LOUIS.

Lodovico (m.) Italian: learned form of LOUIS, much rarer than the vernacular LUIGI.

Loffe (m.) Scandinavian: pet form of ELOF.

Logan (m.) Scottish: transferred use of the Scottish surname, a local name derived from a place so called in Ayrshire.

Lois (f.) New Testament: name, of unknown origin, borne by the grandmother of the Timothy to whom St Paul wrote two epistles (see 2 Timothy 1: 5). Both Timothy and his mother Eunice bore common Greek names, but *Lois* is hard to explain. It certainly has no connection with either LOUISE or ELOISE (which are both of Germanic origin), although it has often been taken to be associated with them in modern times.

Lola (f.) Spanish and English: originally a nursery form of DOLORES, now established as a popular name in its own right. It owes some of its popularity to the fame of Lola Montez (1818–61), stage name adopted by Marie Gilbert, an Irish dancer and courtesan who had affairs with Liszt, Dumas, and others. From 1846–8 she so captivated the elderly Ludwig I of Bavaria that she became the virtual ruler of the country, precipitating riots, a constitutional crisis, and the abdication of the king. She arrived in New York in 1851, and spent the last years of her life working to help prostitutes.

Lolicia (f.) English (esp. U.S.): elaborated form of LOLA, with the addition of a suffix derived from names such as DELICIA.

Lolita (f.) Spanish: pet form of LOLA. This was once relatively common as a given name in its own right in America, with its large Hispanic population, but has since been completely overshadowed by its association with Vladimir Nabokov's novel *Lolita* (1955). The Lolita of the title is the pubescent object of the narrator's desires, and the name is now used as a generic term for any under-age sex kitten.

Loman (m.) Irish: Anglicized form of Gaelic **Lomán**, originally a diminutive of the vocabulary word *lomm* bare, used as a byname. The name was borne by various early Irish saints, including one who was a nephew of St Patrick, and who became first bishop of Trim in Meath in the early 5th century.

Lonan (m.) Irish: Anglicized form of Gaelic **Lonán**, originally a diminutive of the vocabulary word *lon* blackbird, used as a byname. This name was borne by several minor early Irish saints.

Lone (f.) Danish: shortened form of ABELONE and *Magdelone* (see MAGDALENE). It is now very commonly used as an independent name.

Lonnie (m.) English: of uncertain origin, possibly an Anglicized or pet form of the Spanish name ALONSO, but just as likely a variant of LENNY. It is chiefly associated in Britain with the skiffle singer Lonnie Donegan, famous in the 1950s and 1960s.

Lope (m.) Spanish: name derived in the Middle Ages from the Late Latin personal name *Lupus*, probably adopted as a calque of the Germanic name WOLF. *Lupus* was the name borne by various early but obscure saints, including bishops of Bayeux, Châlons-sur-Saône, Lyons, Sens, Soissons, Troyes, and Verona, between the 4th and 7th centuries.

Lora (f.) German form of LAURA, occasionally also used in the English-speaking world.
Variant: **Lore**.

Lorane (f.) English: variant spelling of LORRAINE.

Lóránt (m.) Hungarian form of ROLAND.

Lorcan (m.) Irish: Anglicized form of the Gaelic name **Lorcán**, originally a byname representing a diminutive of Gaelic *lorc* fierce (or possibly 'dumb'). This name was borne by St Lorcán Ó Tuathail (1128–80), archbishop of Dublin, known in English as Laurence O'Toole.

Lore (f.) German: of two possible origins. In most cases it represents a dramatically contracted form of *Leonore* (see LEONORA), but it is also sometimes also a variant of LORA.

Loredana (f.) Italian: name apparently invented by Luciano Zuccoli for the heroine of his novel *L'amore de Loredana* (1908). It seems to represent a feminine form of the famous Venetian surname *Loredan*, in origin a dialectal derivative of the placename *Loreo* in Rovigo (earlier *Loredo*, from Latin *laurētum* laurel grove).

Loreen (f.) English: elaboration of LORA, with the addition of the suffix *-een* (originally an Irish diminutive, Gaelic *-ín*).
Variant: **Lorene**.

Lorelle (f.) English: elaboration of LORA, with the addition of the suffix *-elle* (originally a French feminine diminutive).

Loren (f., occasionally m.) English: variant spelling of LAUREN.

Lorena (f.) Latinate elaboration of LOREN.

Lorene (f.) English: variant spelling of LOREEN.

Lorenz (m.) German form of LAURENCE.
Short form: **Lenz**.

Lorenzo (m.) Italian form of LAURENCE.

Loreto (f.) English and Irish (borne by Roman Catholics): religious name referring to the town in central Italy to which in the 13th century the Holy House of the Virgin is supposed to have been miraculously transported from Nazareth by angels.

Loretta (f.) English: variant of LAURETTA, normally borne by Catholics, among whom it is associated with LORETO.

Lori (f.) English: pet form of LORRAINE or variant of LAURIE.

Lorin (m.) English (esp. U.S.): variant spelling of the male name LOREN.

Lorinda (f.) English: elaboration of LORA, with the addition of the productive feminine suffix *-inda* (cf. e.g. BELINDA, CLARINDA, LUCINDA).

Lorna (f.) English and Scottish: invented by R. D. Blackmore for the heroine of his novel *Lorna Doone* (1869), child captive of the outlawed Doones on Exmoor, who is eventually discovered to be in reality Lady Lorna Dugal, daughter of the Earl of Dugal. Blackmore seems to have derived the name from the Scottish placename *Lorn(e)* (Gaelic *Latharna*), a territory in Argyll. The given name is now popular in Scotland.

Lorne (m.) English (esp. Canadian): of uncertain derivation, presumably from the territory of *Lorne* in Argyll (cf. LORNA). One of the earliest bearers was the Canadian actor Lorne Greene (b. 1915), and the given name is now also fairly common in Scotland.

Lorraine (f.) English and Scottish: transferred use of the surname, denoting a migrant from the province of Lorraine in eastern France. This derives its name from Latin *Lotharingia* 'territory of the people of Lothar' (see LOTHAR). *Lorraine* began to be used as a female given name in the 19th century, and has recently become enormously popular, for reasons which are not clear.
Variant: **Lorane**.
Pet forms: **Lor(r)i**.

Lorri (f.) English: variant spelling of LORI.

Lorrin (m.) English (esp. U.S.): variant spelling of the male name LOREN.

Lothar (m.) German: from an old Germanic personal name composed of the elements *hlud* fame + *heri*, *hari* army, warrior. St *Lotharius* was an 8th-century bishop of Séez in Orne, founder of the monastery of Saint-Loyer-des-Champs. *Lothar* was also a Frankish royal name in the Middle Ages, and was borne by two Holy Roman Emperors. Lothar I (795–855) gave his name to the province of LORRAINE, which was all he was able to bequeath to his son (also called Lothar), after his quarrels with his brothers

Charles the Bald and Louis the German. Lorraine (Latin *Lotharingia*, German *Lothringen*) was originally a much larger region than the present province.
Anglicized form: **Lothair.**

Lottelore (f.) German: double name composed of the elements *Lotte* (a shortened form of KARLOTTE) and LORE.

Lottie (f.) English: pet form of CHARLOTTE. It was common in the 19th century, but is much less used at the present time.
Variant: **Lotty.**

Lou (m., f.) English: short form of LOUIS or, less commonly, LOUISE.

Louella (f.) English: modern coinage from the first syllable of LOUISE + the productive suffix *-ella* (an Italian or Latinate feminine diminutive; cf. ELLA). It is particularly associated with the Hollywood gossip columnist Louella Parsons (1880–1972).
Variant: **Luella.**

Loughlin (m.) Irish: Anglicized form of Gaelic LOCHLAINN.

Louie (m.) English: Variant spelling of LEWIE.

Louis (m.) French: an extremely common French name, of Germanic origin. It is composed of the elements *hlud* fame + *wīg* warrior, and is thus etymologically the same name as German LUDWIG. From the early Middle Ages onwards, it was very frequently used in French royal and noble families. An archaic Latinized form of the name is *Clovis*, and this is the form generally used for the Frankish leader (?466–511) who ended the Roman domination over Gaul: Clovis defeated rival Germanic tribes, married the Burgundian princess Clothilde, and founded the Frankish monarchy in what is now France. In 496 he and his followers were converted to Christianity. Louis I (778–840) was the son of Charlemagne, who ruled both as King of France and Holy Roman Emperor. Altogether, the name was borne by sixteen kings of France up to the French Revolution, in which Louis XVI perished. Louis XIV, 'the Sun King' (1638–1715), reigned for seventy-two years (1643–1715), presiding in the middle part of his reign over a period of unparalleled French power and prosperity. See also LUDWIG.

In modern times, *Louis* is occasionally used in the English-speaking world (usually pronounced /'lu:i:/). In Britain the Anglicized form LEWIS is rather more common, whereas in America the reverse is true. Both forms have been used as Anglicized versions of Gaelic LAOISEACH and LUGHAIDH.
Cognates: Scottish Gaelic: **Luthais.** Italian: **Luigi, Lodovico.** Spanish, Portuguese: **Luis.** Catalan: **Lluis.** Basque: **Koldo.** German: LUDWIG.
Short form: English: **Lou.**

Louisa (f.) Latinate feminine form of LOUIS, commonly used as an English given name since the 18th century.
Cognates: French: LOUISE (also used in English). German: **Luise.** Swedish: **Lovisa.** Danish, Norwegian: **Lovise.**
Pet form: German: **Lulu.**

Louise (f.) French and English: feminine form of LOUIS, introduced to England in the 17th century.
Short form: English: **Lou.**

Lourdes (f.) English and Spanish (borne almost exclusively by Roman Catholics): from the name of the place in southern France where a shrine was established after a young peasant girl, Bernadette Soubirous, had visions of the Virgin Mary and uncovered a healing spring in 1858. In recent times, Lourdes has become a major centre for pilgrimage, especially by people suffering from various illnesses or physical handicaps.
Variant: Spanish: **Lurdes.**

Lova (f.) Swedish: pet form of LOVISA.

Lovell (m.) English: transferred use of the surname, which originated in the Middle Ages from the Old (Norman) French nickname *Louvel* 'wolf-cub', a diminutive of *lou* wolf.

Lovisa (f.) Latinate form of LOUISE, much used in Sweden.

Pet form: **Lova.**

Lowell (m.) English (mainly U.S.): transferred use of the surname of a well-known New England family, whose members included the poet Robert Lowell (1917–77). The surname is a variant of LOVELL.

Loyal (m.) English (mainly U.S.): a comparatively recent adoption of the vocabulary word (which is from Old French *leial*, from Latin *legalis* legal).

Luana (f.) English and Italian: first used in King Vidor's 1932 film *The Bird of Paradise* as the name of a Polynesian maiden, and taken up since. It is apparently an arbitrary combination of the syllables *Lu-* and *-ana*. The Vidor film achieved considerable popularity in Italy under the title *Luana, la vergine sacra*, and the name is now also relatively common there.

Variants: English: **Luanna, Luanne.**

Lubomierz (m.) Polish: from an old Slavonic personal name composed of the elements *lub* love + *meri* great, famous (see CASIMIR).

Cognates: Czech: **Lubomír, Lubor, Lumír.**

Feminine form: Czech: **Lubomíra.**

Pet forms: Czech: **Luba** (m., f.); **Lubomírek, Lub(or)ek, Luboš(ek)** (m.); **Lubka, Luběna, Lubin(k)a, Luboška** (f.).

Lubomił (m.) Polish: from an old Slavonic personal name composed of the elements *lub* love + *mil* grace, favour.

Luc (m.) French form of LUKE.

Luca (m.) Italian form of LUKE.

Lucas (m.) 1. English: in part a learned form of LUKE, in part a transferred use of the surname derived from it. The Latin form *Lucas* was often used in the Middle Ages in written documents in place of the spoken vernacular form *Luke*, hence the common surname. It is also the spelling preferred in the Authorized Version of the New Testament, which has had some influence on its selection as a given name. *Lucas* is now also used as an Anglicized form of various Eastern European equivalents (see the cognates listed at LUKE).

2. Usual Dutch form of *Luke*.

Lucetta (f.) English: fanciful elaboration of LUCIA or LUCY, formed with the productive suffix *-etta*, originally an Italian feminine diminutive suffix. The name is found in Shakespeare, where it is borne by Julia's waiting woman in *Two Gentlemen of Verona*, but it is not much used in Italy and was unusual in England before the 19th century.

Lucia (f.) Feminine form of the old Roman given name LUCIUS, which is probably a derivative of Latin *lux* light. The female name is common in Italy and elsewhere. It is found as a learned, Latinate doublet of *Lucy* in England, where it is much more frequent than its masculine counterpart. St Lucia of Syracuse, who was martyred in 304, was a very popular saint in the Middle Ages; she is often represented in medieval art as blinded and with her eyes on a platter, but the tradition that she had her eyes put out is probably based on nothing more than the association between light and eyes. She still enjoys a considerable cult in southern Italy and Sicily.

Derivatives: Spanish: **Lucía.** English: LUCY.

Pet forms: Italian: **Luciella.** English: **Lucilla.**

Luciano (m.) Italian, Spanish, and Portuguese form of LUCIEN. The feminine form, *Luciana*, is the name of one of the principal characters in Shakespeare's *Comedy of Errors*.

Feminine form: **Luciana.**

Luciella (f.) Italian: diminutive form of LUCIA.

Lucien (m.) French: from Latin *Luciānus*, a derivative of LUCIUS. Saints Lucian, Maximian, and Julian were three missionaries to Gaul martyred at Beauvais at the end of the 3rd century.

Cognate: Italian, Spanish, Portuguese: **Luciano**.

Feminine form: French: **Lucienne**.

Lucilla (f.) Latin pet form of LUCIA, with the diminutive feminine suffix *-illa*. This name was borne by various minor early saints, including one martyred at Rome in *c.*258.

Lucille (f.) French form of LUCILLA, used also in the English-speaking world, especially in the southern United States.

Lucinda (f.) Derivative of LUCIA, with the addition of the productive suffix *-inda*. The formation is first found in Cervantes's *Don Quixote* (1605), but does not seem to have been much in use in the 17th century except as a literary name. *Lucinde* was used by both Molière (in *Le Médecin malgré lui*, 1665) and Friedrich von Schlegel (in his novel *Lucinde*, 1799). It enjoyed considerable popularity in England in the 18th century, and has been in use ever since.

Cognate: French: **Lucinde**.

Pet forms: **Sinda, Sindy, Cindy**; LUCY.

Lucio (m.) Italian, Spanish, and Portuguese form of LUCIUS.

Lucius (m.) Old Roman given name, probably ultimately a derivative of Latin *lux* light. This is occasionally used as a given name in the English-speaking world, especially in America, but it is not as common as its feminine counterpart, LUCIA. Lucius was the name of two early Christians mentioned in the New Testament (Acts 13: 1; Romans 16: 21), and it was also borne by three popes.

Lucrece (f.) English: vernacular form of LUCRETIA, used, for example, in Shakespeare's narrative poem *The Rape of Lucrece*.

Lucretia (f.) Feminine form of the Roman family name *Lucretius*, which is of unknown derivation. In Roman legend, this is the name of a Roman maiden of the 5th century BC who killed herself after being raped by the King of Rome; the resulting scandal led to the end of the monarchy. It was also borne by a Spanish martyr who perished under Diocletian, but is now chiefly remembered as the name of Lucretia Borgia (1480–1519), regarded in legend as a demon poisoner who had incestuous relations with her father, Pope Alexander VI, and her brother Cesare. Although these allegations cannot now be disproved, history records her, after her marriage in 1501 to Alfonso d'Este, Duke of Ferrara, as being in reality a beautiful, intelligent, and fair-minded woman, and a generous patron of the arts. In spite of its unfortunate associations, the name is still occasionally used, especially in the United States.

Derivatives: Italian: **Lucrezia**. English: LUCRECE.

Lucy (f.) 1. English: from Old French *Lucie*, the vernacular form of LUCIA. It is sometimes assumed that *Lucy* is a pet form of LUCINDA, but there is no etymological justification for this assumption. It was in fairly widespread use in the Middle Ages, and increased greatly in popularity in the 18th century.

2. Irish: Anglicized form of Gaelic LUÍSEACH.

Ludger (m.) Low German and Dutch form of LUITGER. St Ludger (*c.*744–809) was a Frisian who studied at Utrecht and in England, before becoming a missionary in Westphalia and later first bishop of Münster, where he founded a monastery that gave the place its name.

Ludmila (f.) Russian and Czech: from an old Slavonic personal name composed of the elements *lud* people, tribe (apparently a borrowing from Germanic *liut*) + *mil* grace, favour. St Ludmila (d. 921) was a duchess of Bohemia and grandmother of St Wenceslas; she was murdered on the orders of her mother-in-law and came to be regarded as a martyr. The name is now also occasionally used in the English-speaking world, where it is usually spelled **Ludmilla**.

Variant: Czech: **Lidmila**.

Cognate: Polish: **Ludmiła**.

Ludo (m.) English and Scottish: short form of LUDOVIC.

Ludomierz (m.) Polish: from an old Slavonic personal name composed of the elements *lud* people, tribe (cf. LUDMILA) + *meri* great, famous (see CASIMIR).

Cognate: Czech: **Ludomír**.

Pet form: Czech: **Luděk** (see also next entry).

Ludosław (m.) Polish: from an old Slavonic personal name composed of the elements *lud* people, tribe (cf. LUDMILA) + *slav* glory.

Cognate: Czech: **Ludoslav**.

Pet form: Czech: **Luděk** (see also previous entry).

Ludovic (m.) English and Scottish: from Latin *Ludovicus*, the form used in medieval documents to represent the Germanic name *Hludwig* (see LUDWIG, LOUIS). In the Highlands it came to be used as an Anglicized form of the Gaelic name *Maol Dòmhnaich* 'devotee of the Lord', probably because both contained the same succession of sounds: *l-d-o-v-c(h)*. It has survived as a traditional given name in the Grant family, sometimes taking the form LEWIS or *Louis*.

Short form: **Ludo**.

Ludovica (f.) German, Dutch, and occasionally English: Latinate feminine form of LUDOVIC.

Ludvík (m.) Czech form of LUDWIG.

Ludwig (m.) German: from an old Germanic personal name composed of the elements *hlud* fame + *wīg* warrior. It is thus etymologically the same as French LOUIS. *Ludwig* was a royal and imperial name, especially in Bavaria, which Louis the German (Ludwig der Deutsche) had received as his portion of his father's empire when the latter divided it in 817. See also LOUIS, LUDOVIC.

Cognates: Scandinavian: **Ludvig**. Dutch: **Lodewijk**. Polish: **Ludwik**. Czech: **Ludvík**. Hungarian: **Lajos**. French: LOUIS.

Pet form: German: **Lutz**.

Ludwik (m.) Polish form of LUDWIG.

Luella (f.) English: variant spelling of LOUELLA.

Lughaidh (m.) Irish Gaelic: a derivative of the divine name *Lugh* (see LLEU).

Anglicized forms: LEWIE, LEWIS, LOUIS.

Luigi (m.) Italian: vernacular form of LOUIS; cf. LODOVICO.

Luis (m.) Spanish form of LOUIS.

Feminine form: **Luisa**.

Luise (f.) German form of LOUISE, now also sometimes used in the English-speaking world as a spelling variant.

Pet form: **Lulu**.

Luíseach (f.) Irish Gaelic: a feminine derivative of the divine name *Lugh*.

Anglicized form: LUCY.

Luitgard (m.) German: from an old Germanic personal name composed of the elements *liut* people + *gard* protection. It was fairly common in the Middle Ages, and is occasionally revived today.

Luitger (m.) German: from an old Germanic personal name composed of the elements *liut* people + *gari*, *geri* spear. See also LÉGER, LEODEGAR, and LUDGER.

Luitpold (m.) German form of LEOPOLD, rather closer to the original form of the name. This version was common in the Middle Ages, but is now little used except in a few particular families in which its use is traditional. It was associated particularly with the royal house of Bavaria.

Pet form: **Poldi** (chiefly Bavarian).

Luke (m.) English: Middle English form of *Lucas*, Latin form of the post-classical Greek name *Loukas* 'man from Lucania'. This owes its perennial popularity throughout Christian Europe to the fact that, from the 2nd century onwards, the third gospel in the New Testament has been ascribed to the Lucas or Luke mentioned at various places in Acts and in the Epistles. He was a doctor, a Gentile, and a friend and convert of St Paul.

Cognates: Scottish Gaelic: **Lùcas**. Irish Gaelic: **Lúcás**. French: **Luc**. Italian: **Luca**. Catalan:

Lluc(h). German: **Lukas**. Dutch: **Lucas**. Polish: **Łukasz**. Czech: **Lukáš**. Hungarian: **Lukács**. Russian: **Luka**.

Lulu (f.) German: pet form of LUISE, originally a reduplicated nursery form. It is now also used in the English-speaking world, both as a pet form of LOUISE and as an independent given name.

Lupita (f.) Spanish: pet form of GUADALUPE.

Lurdes (f.) Spanish: variant of LOURDES.

Luthais (m.) Scottish Gaelic form of LOUIS.

Luther (m.) English (esp. U.S.): from the German surname, which is derived from a Germanic personal name composed of the elements *liut* people + *heri* army, warrior. It is most commonly bestowed among evangelical Protestants, in honour of the ecclesiastical reformer and theologian Martin Luther (1483–1546). In recent times it has also become especially popular among American Blacks, partly in honour of the assassinated civil rights leader Martin Luther King (1929–68).

Lutz (m.) German: pet form of LUDWIG.

Luvenia (f.) English: apparently an arbitrary coinage originating in the southern United States

Luz (f.) Spanish: name reflecting a title of the Virgin Mary, 'Our Lady of Light' (Spanish *luz*, from Latin *lux*).

Luzdivina (f.) Spanish: apparently derived from LIDWINA, but altered by popular etymology to mean 'divine light' (cf. LUZ).

Lyall (m.) Scottish: transferred use of the surname, which is probably derived from the Old Norse personal name *Liulfr*, of which the first element is obscure. The second is clearly Old Norse *úlfr* wolf. See also LYLE.

Lydia (f.) English: of Greek origin, meaning 'woman from Lydia', an area of Asia Minor. It is borne in the Bible by a woman of Thyatira who was converted by St Paul and who entertained him in her house (Acts 16: 14–15, 40). It has enjoyed steady popularity in the English-speaking world since the 17th century.

Cognates: French: **Lydie**. Polish: **Lidia**. Czech: **Lida**.

Lyle (m.) English and Scottish: transferred use of the surname, which originated as a local name for someone who came 'from the island' (Anglo-Norman *de l'isle*). The island in question would in many cases have been an area of higher, dry ground in a marsh or fen, rather than in a sea or river. There may have been some confusion with LYALL.

Lyn (m., f.) 1. (m.) Welsh: short form of LLEWELLYN.

2. (f.) English: variant of LYNN.

Lyndon (m.) English: transferred use of the surname, derived from the place known as Lyndon in the former county of Rutland (now part of Leicestershire), so called from Old English *lind* linden, lime tree + *dūn* hill. Its modern use as a male given name owes something to the American president Lyndon Baines Johnson (1908–73).

Variant: **Lindon**.

Lynette (f.) English: in modern use a derivative of LYNN, formed with the French feminine diminutive suffix *-ette*. However, this is not the origin for the name as used in Tennyson's *Idylls of the King* (1859–85), through which it first came to public attention. There, it represents an altered form of some Celtic original; cf. Welsh ELUNED.

Variants: **Lynnette**, **Lin(n)ette**.

Lynn (f.) English: apparently a modern short form of LINDA with the spelling arbitrarily altered. There may also be some connection with the French name *Line*, which originated as a short form of various female names ending in this syllable, notably CAROLINE. The element *-lyn(n)* has also been used as a productive suffix in female names since around the middle of the 20th century.

Lynsey (f.) English: variant spelling of LINDSAY.

Lyov (m.) Russian: colloquial variant of LEV.

Lys (f.) English: variant spelling of LIS or LIZ, apparently inspired by medieval French (*fleur de*) *lys* lily.

Lysette (f.) English: variant spelling of LISETTE.

Lyssa (f.) English: short form of ALYSSA. In form it coincides with the name, in Greek mythology, of the personification of madness or frenzy. See also LISSA.

Lyubov (f.) Russian: from the vocabulary word meaning 'love'. It was originally adopted as a vernacular loan translation of Greek *Agapē* (see AGAFYA). See also LIBĚNA.
Pet form: **Lyuba**.

M

Maarten (m.) Dutch form of MARTIN, now rather less common than *Martijn*.

Maartje (f.) Dutch: feminine form of MAARTEN.

Maas (m.) Dutch: short form of THOMAS.

Mabel (f.) 1. English: originally a nickname from the Old French vocabulary word *amabel*, *amable* lovely (related to modern English *amiable* friendly, good-humoured). The initial vowel began to be lost as early as the 12th century (the same woman is referred to as both *Mabilia* and *Amabilia* in a document of 1185), but a short vowel in the resulting first syllable was standard, giving a rhyme with *babble*, until the 19th century, when people began to pronounce the name to rhyme with *table*.

2. Spanish: contracted short form of *Maria Isabel* (cf. MARIBEL).

Variant: English: **Mable**.

Cognate (of 1): Irish Gaelic : **Máible**.

Mabelle (f.) English: altered spelling of MABEL, based on French *ma belle* 'my beautiful one'.

Mabon (m.) Welsh: 20th-century revival of an Old Welsh personal name derived from the Old Celtic element *mab* son. This seems to have been originally the name of a divinity; it is also borne by a character in the tale of 'Culhwch and Olwen'.

Mac Dara (m.) Irish Gaelic: name meaning 'son of oak'. This is the name of the patron saint of a parish in Connemara in which is situated Mac Dara's island, goal of an annual pilgrimage on 16 July. The given name is still common in the surrounding region.

Maciej (m.) Polish form of MATTHEW.

Pet form: **Maciek**.

Madeleine (f.) French and English: the French form of the byname of a character in the New Testament, Mary *Magdalene* 'Mary of Magdala'. Magdala was a village on Lake Galilee, a few miles north of Tiberias. The woman 'which had been healed of evil spirits and infirmities' (Luke 8: 2) was given this name in the Bible to distinguish her from other bearers of the very common name MARY. It was widely accepted in Christian folk belief that she was the same person as the repentant sinner who washed Christ's feet with her tears in the previous chapter (Luke 7), but there is no support in the text for this identification.

Variants: English: **Madeline** (common esp. in Ireland), **Madoline**; **Madelaine**, **Madlyn**; MAGDALENE.

Cognate: Irish Gaelic: **Madailéin**.

Pet forms: English: **Maddie**, **Maddy**. French: **Madelon**.

Madge (f.) English: pet form of MARGARET, representing a palatalized version of *Mag(g)* (see MAGGIE).

Madonna (f.) English (esp. U.S.): from an Italian title of the Virgin Mary (literally 'my lady'), applied to countless Renaissance paintings of beautiful young women (with and without infants), representing the mother of Christ. Its use as a given name seems to be a fairly recent phenomenon, arising among Americans of Italian descent. In the 1980s, the name became particularly well known as a result of the fame of the American pop star Madonna Ciccone (b. 1958).

Madrona (f.) Jewish: from the Romance name MATRONA. The name was apparently chosen in the hope that the baby would live to become a mother herself.

Masculine form: **Madron**.

Mads (m.) Danish form of MATTHEW.

Madzia (f.) Polish: pet form of *Magdalena* (see MAGDALENE).

Mae (f.) English: variant spelling of MAY, possibly influenced by MAEVE. It has been most notably borne by the American film actress Mae West (1892–1980), whose prominent bust led to her name being given, by members of the RAF, to a type of inflatable life-jacket used in the Second World War. This spelling is now no longer much used.

Maeve (f.) Irish: Anglicized form of Gaelic **Meadhbh**, an ancient Celtic name meaning 'intoxicating, she who makes drunk'. It is borne by the Queen of Connacht in the Irish epic *Táin Bó Cuailgne*, 'the Cattle Raid of Cooley'. In this, Meadhbh leads a raid on Ulster in order to seize the Brown Bull of Cooley, but she is repulsed single-handed by the hero Cuchulain. The historical events underlying the epic probably took place in about the 1st century AD. Shakespeare's Queen Mab, 'the fairy's midwife' (*Romeo and Juliet* I. iv. 53), may owe her name, if nothing else, to the legendary Queen of Connacht.

Variants: **Mave** (also an informal short form of MAVIS), **Meave**.

Mafalda (f.) Portuguese and Italian: variant of MATILDA, used especially in Portugal. The name was taken there by a princess from the royal house of Savoy, who in 1146 went to marry the Portuguese king. St Mafalda (1203–52) was a daughter of King Sancho II of Portugal. King Victor Emmanuel III of Italy, a member of the house of Savoy, gave it to a daughter of his in 1902.

Magali (f.) French (of Provençal origin): name of uncertain derivation, possibly a form of MARGARET. It has become widely known as a result of its occurrence in a popular Provençal folk song.

Variant: **Magalie**.

Magdalene (f.) Learned form of MADELEINE, used especially in Germany.

Variants: English: **Magdalen**. Latinate: **Magdalena** (used in Spain, Portugal, Germany, Holland, Norway, Sweden, Poland, and Czechoslovakia).

Cognates: Italian: **Maddalena**. Russian: **Magdalina**. Hungarian: **Magdolna**. Danish: **Magdalone, Malene**.

Short forms: German, Scandinavian, and E. European: **Magda**. German and Czech: **Alena**.

Pet form: Polish: **Madzia**.

Maggie (f.) English: pet form of MARGARET. In the Middle Ages the short form *Mag(g)* was common, as a result of the early loss in pronunciation of the English preconsonantal *r*. This is not now used as a given name, but has given rise to the surname *Maggs*; *Maggie* is also a derivative of *Mag(g)* formed with the characteristically Scottish hypocoristic suffix *-ie*. Until recently it was most common in Scotland. It is now fashionable elsewhere as well.

Cognate: Scottish Gaelic: **Magaidh**.

Magnus (m.) Scandinavian, Scottish, and English: originally a Latin byname meaning 'great', this was first extracted from the name of *Charlemagne* (recorded in Latin chronicles as *Carolus Magnus* 'Charles the Great') and used as a given name by the Scandinavians. It was borne by seven medieval kings of Norway, including Magnus I (1024–47), known as Magnus the Good, and Magnus VI (1238–80), known as Magnus the Law Mender. There are several early Scandinavian saints called Magnus, including an earl of Orkney (d. 1116), to whom Kirkwall cathedral is dedicated. The name was imported to Scotland and Ireland during the Middle Ages.

Vernacular forms: Danish: **Mogens**. Swedish: **Måns**. Scottish Gaelic: **Mànas**. Irish Gaelic: **Maghnus** (Anglicized as MANUS). Finnish: **Mauno**.

Mahalia (f.) English: apparently a cross between the two biblical masculine personal names *Mahali* (Exodus 6: 19) and *Mahalah* (1 Chronicles 7: 18), both fleetingly mentioned in genealogies.

Mahon (m.) Irish: Anglicized form of Gaelic MATHÚIN.

Mai (f.) Swedish: pet form of MARIA and *Margit* (see MARGARET). It is now used as an independent given name and is common as both the first and the second element of compound names such as *Mai-Britt*, *Mai-Lis*, *Anne-Mai*, and *Britt-Mai*.

Maica (f.) Spanish: contracted pet form of *María Carmen*; cf. MAITE.

Maidie (f.) Scottish and Irish: apparently a pet form of modern English *maid* young woman (Old English *mæg(den)*), originally given as an affectionate nickname. However, it may also be an altered form of MAISIE.

Maike (f.) Frisian: pet form of MARIA. The name now also has a wider currency as an independent given name in the Dutch- and German-speaking world.

Variant: **Maiken** (esp. common in Scandinavia).

Màili (f.) Scottish Gaelic: variant of MÀIRI.

Mainchín (m.) Irish Gaelic: originally a byname representing a diminutive of *manach* monk.

Anglicized form: **Mannix**.

Mair (f.) Welsh form of MARY, derived from Latin *Maria* via Old Welsh *Meir*.

Máire (f.) Irish Gaelic form of MARY, derived from Old French *Marie*.

Mairéad (f.) Irish Gaelic form of MARGARET. The name is also used in Scotland, where it is spelled **Mairead** or **Maighread**.

Màiri (f.) Scottish Gaelic form of MARY.

Máirín (f.) Irish Gaelic: name Anglicized as MAUREEN.

Mairtin (m.) Irish Gaelic form of MARTIN.

Maisie (f.) Scottish: pet form derived from *Mairead*, the Gaelic form of MARGARET, with the Scottish and northern English hypocoristic suffix *-ie*. Gaelic palatalized *-r-* sounds to English ears like /z/. The name occurs in Scottish border ballads in the form *Masery*.

Maite (f.) Spanish: contracted pet form of *María Teresa*; cf. MAICA. Coincidentally, the vocabulary word *maite* means 'beloved, dear' in the Basque language.

Maj (f.) Swedish: variant spelling of MAI.

Maja (f.) German and Scandianvian: pet form of MARIA, or else from Latin *Maia* (see MAYA).

Majella (f.) English and Irish (borne by Roman Catholics): name given in honour of St Gerard Majella (1725–55), an Italian Redemptorist monk who was the focus of a number of miraculous phenomena and who was canonized in 1904.

Makari (m.) Russian: from the Late Greek name *Makarios*, a derivative of *makaros* blessed. This was a very popular name among early Christians, and was borne by a large number of saints, among them Macarius the Elder (*c.*300–90) and Macarius the Younger (d. *c.*408), both of whom lived in Egypt, and a 4th-century bishop of Jerusalem who identified the True Cross found by St Helena. Another St Macarius (d. *c.*350) was originally name *Arius*, but has been renamed in order to distinguish him from the founder of the Arian heresy, which he strongly opposed.

Variant: **Makar**.

Cognates: Italian, Spanish, Portuguese: **Macario**. French: **Macaire**. Polish: **Makary**.

Malachy (m.) Irish: name of an Irish king who defeated the Norse invaders in an important battle. His baptismal name was *Maoileachlainn* 'devotee of St Seachnall' or Secundinus, but in medieval sources telling of his life this has already been altered to coincide with that of the biblical prophet generally known in English as **Malachi**. Malachi was the last of the twelve minor prophets of the Old Testament; he foretold the coming of Christ and his name means, appropriately, 'my messenger' in Hebrew.

Malcolm (m.) Scottish and English: Anglicized form of the Gaelic name *Mael Coluim* 'devotee of St Columba'. Columba, whose name means 'dove' in Latin, was a 6th-century monk of Irish origin who played a leading part in the conversion to Christianity of Scotland and northern England; see also CALUM and COLM. He has always been one of the most popular saints in Scotland, but in the Middle Ages it was felt to be presumptuous to give the names of saints directly to children; instead their blessing was invoked by prefixing the name with *mael* 'devotee of' (cf. MARMADUKE) or *gille* 'servant of'. In the Highlands *Malcolm* is still used as an Anglicized form of *Calum*.

Feminine forms: **Malcolmina, Malina.**

Malene (f.) Danish: contracted form of MAGDALENE.

Małgorzata (f.) Polish form of MARGARET.

Pet form: **Małgosia.**

Malkah (f.) Jewish: from Hebrew *malkah* queen. This name does not appear in the Hebrew Scriptures, but represents an affectionate nickname used from the Middle Ages onwards.

Mallory (m., occasionally f.) English (esp. U.S.): transferred use of the surname, which originated as a Norman French nickname for an unfortunate person, from Old French *malheure* unhappy or unlucky.

Mallt (f.) Welsh form of MAUD, a common name in the Middle Ages.

Malvina (f.) Scottish, English, and Scandinavian (esp. Danish): apparently a factitious name, based on Gaelic *mala mhìn* smoothbrow, invented by James Macpherson (1736–96), the Scottish antiquarian poet who published works allegedly translated from the ancient Gaelic bard Ossian. The name became popular in Scandinavia because of the admiration of the Emperor Napoleon for the Ossianic poems: he was godfather to several of the children of his marshal Jean Baptiste Bernadotte (who ruled Norway and Sweden (1818–44) as Karl XIV Johan) and imposed his own taste in naming practices on them, hence the frequency of 'Ossianic' given names in Scandinavia. *Las Malvinas* is the Argentinian name for the Falkland Islands; the origin of this is disputed, but it appears to have no connection with the Ossianic name.

Cognate: German: **Malwine** (now rare).

Mamie (f.) English: short form of MARGARET or MARY, which has been used occasionally as an independent given name, especially in America, where it was the name by which the wife of President Eisenhower was usually known. It seems to have originated as a nursery form.

Mànas (m.) Scottish Gaelic form of MAGNUS.

Manda (f.) English: short form of AMANDA.

Mandel (m.) Jewish: back-formation from MENDEL, assumed by folk etymology to be from German *Männl*, a diminutive of *Mann* man. It probably has no connection with the Yiddish vocabulary word *mandel* almond.

Mandy (f., m.) English: 1. (f.) Pet form of AMANDA, now sometimes used as a given name in its own right.

2. (m.) Occasionally it is also found as a Jewish male name, an Anglicized form of MANDEL.

Manfred (m.) German, Dutch, and English: from an old Germanic personal name, usually said to be composed of the elements *man* man + *fred, frid* peace. However, it is more likely that the first element was *magin* strength (the Norman form being normally *Mainfred*; cf. modern English 'might and *main*') or *manag* much (cf. modern English *many*). This was in use among the Normans, who introduced it to Britain, but it did not become part of the common stock of English given names, and was reintroduced from Germany in the 19th century. It was a traditional name among the Hohenstaufens, and was borne by the last Hohenstaufen king of Sicily (1258–66), who died in battle against papal forces at Benevento. The name was also used by Byron for the central character in his poetic drama *Manfred* (1817), a brooding outcast, tormented by incestuous love for his half-sister.

Variants: German: **Manfried, Manfrid.**

Cognate: Italian: **Manfredo.**

Mania (f.) Polish: pet form of MARIA.

Variant: **Maniuta.**

Manley (m.) English: transferred use of the surname, which in most cases originated as a local name from places in Devon and Cheshire, so called from Old English *(ge)mǣne* common, shared + *lēah* wood or clearing. Its choice as a first name may well have been influenced by association with the vocabulary word *manly* and the hope that the qualities denoted by the adjective would be attributes of the bearer. The vocabulary word may also lie behind some cases of the surname, as a nickname for a 'manly' person.

Manlio (m.) Italian: from the Latin name, *Manlius*, of a famous Roman family of staunch republican virtues and heroism. An earlier form of the name was *Manilius*. It appears to be a derivative of the old Roman given name *Manius*, which is probably derived either from *māne* morning or from the archaic root *mān-* good. Marcus Manlius Capitolinus (d. ?384 BC), who saved Rome from the besieging Gauls in 389 BC, is said to have defended plebeian debtors from their patrician creditors, and the following year to have been impeached and executed by being thrown from the Tarpeian Rock. The Italian form of the name was bestowed by Garibaldi on one of his sons.

Mannix (m.) Irish: Anglicized form of Gaelic MAINCHÍN.

Manny (m.) English: aphetic pet form of EMMANUEL, in use mainly among British Jews.

Manoel (m.) Portuguese form of EMMANUEL. The Portuguese king Manoel I (1469–1521; reigned 1495–1521) presided over a glittering period in Portuguese history, at a time when wealth was flowing in from Portugal's new conquests in both the East Indies and South America.

Manon (f.) French: pet form of MARIE, common in the 18th and 19th centuries. For the formation, cf. MANIA and *Madelon* (from MADELEINE). The name is familiar in the English-speaking world through the Abbé Prévost's story *Manon Lescaut* (1731), which was given operatic treatment by both Puccini and Massenet. In it the young Chevalier des Grieux elopes with the heroine, who supports them by becoming a courtesan, and is eventually deported to Louisiana, where she dies.

Mans (m.) Catalan: variant of AMANS.

Måns (m.) Swedish: vernacular form of MAGNUS.

Manuel (m.) Spanish form of EMMANUEL.

Feminine form: **Manuela.**

Pet forms: **Manolo, Manolito, Manolete** (m.); **Manola, Manolita** (f.).

Manus (m.) Irish: Anglicized form of Gaelic *Maghnus* and *Mánus*, forms of MAGNUS.

Manya (f.) Russian: pet form of MARIA.

Maoilíosa (originally m., now also f.) Irish Gaelic: name meaning 'devotee of Jesus'.

Anglicized form: MELISSA (a modern development).

Cognate (m. only): Scottish Gaelic: **Maoilios** (Anglicized as MYLES).

Maolra (m.) Irish Gaelic: modern spelling, common particularly in the west of Ireland, of earlier *Maoil-Mhuire* 'devotee of Mary'.

Anglicized form: MYLES.

Mara (f.) English: of biblical origin, from Hebrew *Mara* 'bitter', a name referred to by Naomi when she went back to Bethlehem because of the famine in the land of Moab and the deaths of her husband and two sons: 'call me not Naomi, call me Mara: for the Almighty hath dealt very bitterly with me' (Ruth 1: 20).

Marc (m.) French form of MARK, now also quite popular in the English-speaking world. It was given some currency in England in the 1960s by the pop singer Marc Bolan.

Marcel (m.) French: from the Latin name *Marcellus*, originally a diminutive of MARCUS. The name has always been popular in France as it was borne by a 3rd-century missionary to Gaul, martyred at Bourges with his companion Anastasius.

Cognates: Italian: **Marcello**. Spanish, Portuguese: **Marcelo**.

Feminine forms: Irish Gaelic: **Mairsile**. Scottish Gaelic: **Marsaili**. Latin: **Marcella** (used to some extent in the English-speaking world, esp. Ireland, and also in Italy). French: **Marcelle**. Spanish, Polish, Czech: **Marcela**.

Marcellin (m.) French: from the Latin name *Marcellīnus*, a double derivative of MARCUS borne by a dozen early saints, including a pope who died in the persecutions instigated by the Roman emperor Diocletian.

Cognates: Italian: **Marcellino**. Spanish, Portuguese: **Marcelino**.

Marcia (f.) English: often used as a feminine equivalent of MARK, but in fact a feminine form of *Marcius*, itself a derivative of MARCUS. One St Marcia is commemorated in a group with Felix, Luciolus, Fortunatus, and others; another with Zenais, Cyria, and Valeria; and a third with Ariston, Crescentian, Eutychian, Urban, Vitalis, Justus, Felicissimus, Felix, and Symphorosa. None is individually very famous.

Variant: **Marsha**.

Pet forms: **Marcie, Marcy** (chiefly U.S.).

Marcin (m.) Polish form of MARTIN.

Marco (m.) Italian and usual Spanish form of MARK.

Marcos (m.) Portuguese form of MARK. It is also used in Spain as a variant form of the more common MARCO.

Marcus (m.) The original Latin form of MARK, of unknown derivation; it may possibly be connected with MARIUS. This is also the form of the name in Scottish Gaelic, whence the surname *Mac Mharcuis*, Anglicized as *Marquis*. *Marcus* was rarely used as a given name in the English-speaking world until recent years, when it has been seized on by parents seeking to give a distinctive form to a common and popular name. Among American Blacks it is sometimes bestowed in honour of the Black Consciousness leader Marcus Garvey (1887–1940).

Marea (f.) English: apparently an altered spelling of MARIA.

Mared (f.) Welsh form of MARGARET, a simplified version of *Marged*.

Marek (m.) Polish and Czech form of MARK.

Pet forms: Polish: **Mareczek, Maruś**. Czech: **Mareček, Maroušek, Mareš, Mařík**.

Maretta (f.) Scottish: Anglicized form of MAIREAD; see also MARIETTA.

Marga (f.) English: short form of MARGARET or any of the large number of related names beginning with these two syllables.

Margaret (f.) English and Scottish: an extremely common medieval given name, derived via Old French *Marguerite* and Latin *Margarīta* from Greek *Margarītēs*, from *margaron* pearl, a word ultimately of Hebrew origin. The name was always understood to mean 'pearl' throughout the Middle Ages. The first St Margaret was martyred at Antioch in Pisidia during the persecution instigated by the Emperor Diocletian in the early 4th century. However, there seems to be some doubt about her name, as the same saint is venerated in the Orthodox Church as MARINA. There were several other saintly bearers of the name, including St Margaret of

Scotland (d. 1093), wife of King Malcolm Canmore and daughter of Edmund Ironside of England. It was also the name of the wife of Henry VI of England, Margaret of Anjou (1430–82), and of Margaret Tudor (1489–1541), sister of Henry VIII, who married James IV of Scotland and ruled as regent there after his death. In Scandinavia, the name was borne by one of the most powerful rulers in Scandinavian history, Queen Margareta (1353–1412), daughter of the Danish king Waldemar IV, wife of Haakon VI of Norway, and mother of Olaf V of both kingdoms. She effectively ruled Denmark and Norway as regent for her son Olaf and, after his death in 1387, for her great-nephew, Eric of Pomerania, adding Sweden to her empire in 1389. *Margaret* was also well established as a royal name in the Holy Roman Empire, France, Navarre, and Italy. In Britain in 1930 it was selected by the future King George VI and his wife for their second daughter, Princess Margaret Rose. See also MARGERY, MARJORIE.

Cognates: Latinate: **Margaret(t)a**. Irish Gaelic: **Mairéad**. Scottish Gaelic: **Mair(gh)ead**. Welsh: **Mar(g)ed**, **Mererid**. French: MARGUERITE. Italian: **Margherita**. Spanish: **Margarita**. Portuguese: **Margarida**. German and Scandinavian: **Margaret(h)a**. German, Danish: **Margaret(h)e**, **Margrethe**. German (vernacular): **Margrit**, **Margret**; **Meta**. Dutch, Low German: **Margriet**. Scandinavian (vernacular): **Margit**; **Marit** (Norwegian, Swedish); **Merete** (Danish). Polish: **Małgorzata**. Czech: **Markéta**. Hungarian: **Margit**. Finnish: **Marketta**. Jewish (modern Hebrew): **Margalit**, **Marganit**, **Marganita**.

Short forms: English: **Meg**, **Peg**; **Madge**; **Gretta**. Spanish: **Rita**. German: **Greta**, **Grete**, **Gritt(a)**, **Grit**. Low German, Dutch, Frisian: **Griet**, **Gre(e)t**. Swedish: **Maj**, **Greta**. Danish: **Grete**.

Pet forms: English: MAGGIE, **Meggie**, PEGGY; **Marge**, **Margie** (informal); MAY; see also DAISY. Scottish Gaelic: **Magaidh**, **Peigi**. Welsh: MEGAN. French: **Margot**. German, Danish, Swedish: **Meta**. Low German, Dutch, Frisian: **Grietje**, **Gre(e)tje**. Polish: **Małgosia**, **Gosia**, **Gośka**.

Margery (f.) English: the usual medieval vernacular form of MARGARET (now also commonly spelled MARJORIE). This form of the name is preserved in the nursery rhyme 'See-saw, Margery Daw'.

Margot (f.) French, English, German, and E. European: pet form of MARGUERITE, now used as an independent name. In England it is still usually pronounced in the French way, but in Eastern Europe the final consonant is sounded, and this has had some influence in America. The name of the American actress **Margaux** Hemingway (b. 1955) represents a fanciful respelling of this name inspired by a village near Bordeaux noted for its red wine.

Marguerite (f.) French form of MARGARET, also used in the English-speaking world, where its use has been reinforced by the fact that the name was adopted in the 19th century for a garden flower, a large cultivated variety of daisy. *Margaret* was earlier used in English as a dialect word denoting the ox-eye daisy, and the French equivalent was borrowed into English just in time to catch the vogue for deriving female given names from vocabulary words denoting flowers. See also DAISY.

Mari (f.) Welsh form of MARY.

Maria (f.) Latin form of MARY, still used in most European languages, either as the main local form of the name, as in Italian, Spanish (**María**), Portuguese, German, Dutch, Scandinavian, Polish, and Czech, or as a learned doublet of a vernacular form. In English it is a learned revival dating from the 18th century, pronounced both /mə'riːə/ and, more traditionally, /mə'raɪə/. The original Latin name *Maria* arose as a back-formation from the early Christian female name *Mariam*. This was taken as an accusative case, with the usual Latin feminine accusative ending *-am*. In fact, however, it is an indeclinable Aramaic alternative form of the Hebrew name MIRIAM. [*cont.*]

This form of the name is in common use in most European languages; for example, it was the most common of all female names in Sweden in 1973. In Spain not only is the name *María* itself enormously common, but a large number of Marian epithets and words associated with the cult of the Virgin are also used as female given names. *Maria* is also used as a male name in combinations such as *Giammaria* (Italian) and *José María* (Spanish).

Short form: **Ria**.

Cognates and pet forms: see MARY.

Masculine forms: MARIUS. Italian, Spanish, Portuguese: MARIO.

Mariamne (f.) The form of MIRIAM used by the Jewish historian Flavius Josephus, writing in Latin in the 1st century BC, as the name of the wife of King Herod. On the basis of this evidence, it has been thought by some to be closer to the original form of the name actually borne by the Virgin MARY, and has therefore been bestowed in her honour.

Marian (f., m.) 1. (f.) English: originally a medieval variant spelling of MARION. However, in the 18th century, when combined names began to come into fashion, it was sometimes understood as a combination of MARY and ANN.

2. (m.) Polish: from the Latin name *Mariānus* (see MARIANO), often bestowed among Roman Catholics in honour of the Virgin Mary.

Marianne (f.) 1. English: extended spelling of MARIAN, reinforcing the association of the second element with ANN(E).

2. French: assimilated form of MARIAMNE. *Marianne* is the name used for the symbolic figure of the French Republic.

Variant: English: **Marianna** (a Latinate form).

Mariano (m.) Italian, Spanish, and Portuguese: from the Latin name *Mariānus*, a derivative of MARIUS. In the early Christian era it came to be taken as an adjective derived from MARIA, and was associated with the cult of the Virgin Mary. It was borne by various early saints, including a 3rd-century martyr of Lambesa in Numidia and a 5th-century hermit of Berry, France.

Cognate: Polish, Czech: **Marian**.

Feminine form: **Mariana**.

Maribel (f.) Spanish: contracted short form of *Maria Isabel* (see also MABEL). The name is also occasionally used in the English-speaking world, where it may represent a simplified form of MARIBELLA.

Maribella (f.) English: Latinate combination of MARIA with the name BELLA or the productive suffix *-bella* (cf. ANNABEL and CHRISTABEL). The name is also occasionally used in Italy.

Marica (f.) Hungarian pet form of MARIA.

Marice (f.) English: respelling of MARIS, or else a combination ot the first syllable of MARY or MARGARET with the name suffix *-ice* (cf. e.g. JANICE).

Marie (f.) French form of MARIA. When first introduced to England in the Middle Ages, it was Anglicized in pronunciation and respelled MARY. This French form was reintroduced into the English-speaking world as a separate name in the 19th century, and is still pronounced more or less in the French manner, although sometimes with the stress on the first syllable. The French name is also commonly used as a male name in the combination *Jean-Marie*.

Pet form: MANON.

Marie-Ange (f.) French equivalent of ÁNGELES. The name *Ange* is not used on its own in French.

Marie-France (f.) French: combination of MARIE with the national name *France*, invoking the protection of the Virgin Mary as the special guardian of France.

Mariel (f.) English: 1. Shortened form of MARIELLA.

2. Altered form of MURIEL or MERIEL.

Mariella (f.) Italian: diminutive form of MARIA.

Marielle (f.) French: diminutive form of MARIE, now fairly commonly used as an independent given name in the English-speaking world.

Marietta (f.) Italian: diminutive form of MARIA, now sometimes used as an independent name in the English-speaking world. In Gaelic Scotland *Mar(i)etta* is quite commonly used as an Anglicized form of MAIREAD, and abbreviated to ETTA.

Cognate: Spanish: **Marieta**.

Marigold (f.) English: one of the older of the group of names that were adopted from words for flowers in the late 19th and early 20th centuries. The Old English name of the flower was *golde*, presumably from *gold* (the precious metal), in reference to its colour. At some time before the 14th century the flower became associated with the Virgin Mary, and its name was extended accordingly to *marigold*. Not until the 19th century was this used as a female given name.

Marika (f.) Slavonic: pet form of MARIA, sometimes used as an independent given name in the English-speaking world.

Marilee (f.) English: modern coinage, a combination of MARY and LEE.

Marilene (f.) English: modern coinage, a combination of the name MARY with the productive suffix *-lene*, or else a variant of MARILYN.

Marilyn (f.) English: 20th-century elaboration of MARY, with the addition of the productive suffix *-lyn* (see LYNN).

Variant: **Marylyn**, MARILENE.

Marina (f.) Italian, Spanish, English, Scottish, and German: from a Late Latin name, a feminine form of the family name *Marīnus*. This was in fact a derivative of MARIUS, but even during the early centuries AD it was widely assumed to be identical with the Latin adjective *marīnus* 'of the sea'. The early saints of this name are all of extremely shaky historical identification. In Scotland the name has been used as an Anglicized form of MÀIRI, in place of plain MARY, following the pattern of feminine derivatives in *-ina* (cf. e.g. *Angusina* and *Calumina*).

Mario (m.) Italian, Spanish, and Portuguese form of *Marius*, a very common male name in these languages.

Marion (f., m.) English: 1. (f.) Originally a medieval French diminutive form of MARIE, introduced to Britain in the Middle Ages, and now completely Anglicized in pronunciation.

2. (m.) Altered form of the Continental male name MARIAN.

Elaborated form (of 1): **Marionne**.

Maripepa (f.) Spanish: pet form of the compound name *María Josefa*.

Mariquita (f.) Spanish: pet form of MARIA.

Marirrosa (f.) Spanish: compound name made up of the elements MARIA and ROSA.

Maris (f.) English: modern name of uncertain origin. It may derive from the second word of the Marian epithet *stella maris* 'star of the sea'.

Marisa (f.) Italian, Spanish, and English: 20th-century elaboration of MARIA, the suffix *-isa* apparently being abstracted from such names as LISA and *Luisa* (see LUIS).

Cognate: Dutch: **Marijse**.

Marisol (f.) Spanish: compound name made up of the elements MARIA and SOL.

Marit (f.) Norwegian and Swedish: vernacular form of MARGARET.

Marita (f.) Spanish: pet form of MARIA.

Marius (m.) Latin name, used in English, German, French, and other European languages: from a Roman family name of uncertain derivation. It is probably from *Mars*, the name of the Roman god of war, or from the adjective *mas* (genitive *maris*) male, virile. A derivation from *mare* sea has been proposed by some writers, but seems unlikely (cf. MARINA). This name and in particular its southern European form *Mario* owe their popularity to having been pressed into service as masculine equivalents of MARY in countries where the cult of the Virgin Mary is strong.

Cognate: Italian, Spanish, Portuguese: **Mario**. See also MARIAN (2).

Marji (f.) English: modern respelling of *Margie* (see MARGARET).

Variant: **Marjie**.

Marjolaine (f.) French: from the French name of the herb *marjoram*; cf. MARJORIE.

Marjorie (f.) English: usual modern spelling of MARGERY. It seems to have arisen as the result of popular etymological association of the name with that of the herb *marjoram* (cf. ROSEMARY). This word is of uncertain origin; its Middle English and Old French form was *majorane*, without the first *-r-*.

Variant: **Marjory** (the usual spelling in Scotland; see also MARSAILI).

Mark (m.) English: from the Latin name *Marcus*, borne by the evangelist, author of the second gospel in the New Testament, and by several other early and medieval saints. St Mark became the patron saint of Venice, and the Italian name *Marco* has long been especially popular in that city. This was one of the extremely limited number of Roman given names in use in the classical period. There were only about a dozen of these in general use, with perhaps another dozen confined to particular families. In Arthurian legend, King Mark is the aged ruler of Cornwall to whom Isolde is brought as a bride by Tristan. *Mark* was not notably borne by royalty and was not a particularly common name in the Middle Ages outside a few centres such as Venice.

Variant: MARCUS.

Cognates: Irish and Scottish Gaelic: **Marcas**. French: **Marc**. Italian, Spanish: **Marco**. Portuguese (also Spanish): **Marcos**. Romanian: **Marku**. German: **Markus**. Polish, Czech: **Marek**. Ukrainian: **Marko**. Finnish: **Markku**.

Markéta (f.) Czech form of MARGARET.

Marketta (f.) Finnish form of MARGARET.

Marla (f.) English: modern creation, representing an altered form of MARLENE, or else a name invented as a feminine equivalent of MARLON.

Marlene (f.) German, now also widely used in the English-speaking world: contracted form of *Maria Magdalene* (see MADELEINE). Probably the first, and certainly the most famous, bearer of the name is Marlene Dietrich, born in 1902 as Maria Magdalene von Losch. The name was further popularized in the 1940s by the wartime German song 'Lili Marlene', which was immensely popular among both German and British troops in North Africa.

Marlon (m.) English: name apparently first brought to public attention by the American actor Marlon Brando (b. 1924) and now sometimes used more widely as a result of his fame. The name was borne also by his father, and is of uncertain origin, possibly derived from MARC with the addition of the French diminutive suffix *-lon* (originally a combination of two separate suffixes, *-el* and *-on*); the family is said to have been of French origin. In America the name is used fairly regularly among Blacks, but in Britain the most notable bearer is the young go-karting enthusiast in the *Perishers* cartoon strip.

Marmaduke (m.) English: of uncertain derivation. It is generally held to be an Anglicized form of the Old Irish name *Mael-Maedóc* 'devotee of Maedóc'. The name *Maedóc* was borne by various early Irish saints, most notably a 6th-century abbot of Clonmore and a 7th-century bishop of Ferns. Mael-Maedóc Ó Morgair (1095–1148) was a reformer of the Church in Ireland and a friend of Bernard of Clairvaux. However, the modern Gaelic form (from *c.*1200) is *Maol-Maodhóg* (pronounced /mʌl'məʊg/), so that the name would have had to have been borrowed into English before this loss of the *d*. *Marmaduke* has never been common except in a small area of North Yorkshire, and is at present almost completely out of fashion.

Short form: DUKE.

Marna (f.) Swedish: vernacular form of MARINA.

Marnie (f.) English (mainly U.S.): Anglicized form of MARNA.

Marsaili (f.) Scottish Gaelic form of MARGERY and of *Marcella* (see MARCEL).

Marsh (m.) English: 1. Transferred use of the surname, which originated as a local name for someone who lived on a patch of marshy ground, from Middle English *mersche* (Old English *mersc*).

2. Informal short form of MARSHALL.

Marsha (f.) Phonetic spelling of MARCIA, popular especially among American Blacks.

Marshall (m.) English: transferred use of the surname, derived from a Norman French occupational term that originally denoted someone who looked after horses, ultimately from the Germanic elements *marah* horse + *scalc* servant. By the time it became fixed as a surname it had the meaning 'shoeing smith'; later it came to denote an official whose duties were to a large extent ceremonial. The surname is phonetically identical with the English pronunciation of the name of the Roman poet *Martial* (from Latin *Mars*, genitive *Martis*; cf. MARTIN), and this may possibly have contributed something to its use as a given name.

Märta (f.) Danish: contracted form of *Märeta*, an obsolete variant of MERETE. The name is now also very popular in Sweden, where it was the thirty-sixth most common female name in 1973.

Martha (f.) New Testament name, of Aramaic rather than Hebrew origin, meaning 'lady'. It was borne by the sister of Lazarus and Mary of Bethany (John 11: 1). According to Luke 10: 38, when Jesus visited the house of Mary and Martha, Mary sat at his feet, listening to him, while Martha 'was cumbered about much serving', so that she complained to Jesus, 'Lord, dost thou not care that my sister hath left me to serve alone?' For this reason, the name *Martha* has always been associated with hard domestic work, as opposed to the contemplative life.

Other forms: French, German: **Marthe**. Scandinavian: **Mart(h)a, Mart(h)e**. Spanish, Italian, Polish, and Czech: **Marta**. Hungarian: **Márta**.

Pet form: Spanish: **Martita**.

Marti (f.) English: short form of MARTINA (or its French equivalent *Martine*). Its best-known bearer in Britain is the English comedienne Marti Caine (b. 1945).

Variants: **Martie, Marty**.

Martin (m.) English, French, and German form of the Latin name *Martīnus*. This was probably originally derived from *Mars* (genitive *Martis*), the name of the Roman god of war (and earlier of fertility). *Martin* became very popular in the Middle Ages, especially on the Continent, as a result of the fame of St Martin of Tours. He was born the son of a Roman officer in Upper Pannonia (an outpost of the Roman Empire, now part of Hungary), and although he became a leading figure in the 4th-century Church, he is chiefly remembered now for having divided his cloak in two and given half to a beggar. The name was also borne by five popes, including one who defended Roman Catholic dogma against Eastern Orthodox theology. He died after suffering imprisonment and privations in Naxos and public humiliation in Constantinople, and was promptly acclaimed a martyr by supporters of the Roman Church. Among Protestants, the name is sometimes bestowed in honour of the German theologian Martin Luther (1483–1546); *Martin* was used as a symbolic name for the Protestant Church in satires by both Dryden and Swift. A further influence, especially among American Blacks, may be its use as the given name of the civil-rights leader Martin Luther King (1929–68).

Variant: English: **Martyn**.

Cognates: Irish Gaelic: **Máirtín, Mártan**. Scottish Gaelic: **Màrtainn**. Italian: **Martino**. Spanish: **Martín**. Portuguese: **Martinho**. Catalan: **Martí**. Low German: **Merten**. Dutch: **Maarten, Martijn**. Danish, Norwegian: **Morten**. Swedish: **Mårten**. Polish: **Marcin**. Hungarian: **Márton**. Finnish: **Martti**.

Pet form: English: **Marty**.

Feminine forms: MARTINA, **Martine**.

Martina (f.) Feminine form of the Latin name *Martīnus* (see MARTIN). This form is in use in almost all the major languages of Europe, although it is not common in France. It was in use from an early period, being borne by a notorious poisoner mentioned by the historian Tacitus. The 3rd-century saint of the same name is of doubtful authenticity. Modern use of the name in the English-speaking world seems to be the result of German or Eastern European influence, as in the case of the tennis player Martina Navratilova (b. 1956), who was born in Czechoslovakia.

Cognates: French, German, and English: **Martine**. Polish: **Martyna**.

Martirio (f.) Spanish: religious name alluding to the spiritual quality of martyrdom (Spanish *martirio*, from Late Latin *martyrium*, a derivative of Greek *martyr* witness) or suffering for the sake of one's faith.

Martita (f.) Spanish: pet form of *Marta* (see MARTHA), now also sometimes used in the English-speaking world.

Short form: **Tita**.

Marty (m.) English: short form of MARTIN that has come into favour in the latter part of the 20th century, being associated particularly with the comedian Marty Feldman (1933–83), the 1960s pop singer Marty Wilde (b. 1938 as Reginald Smith), and the country-and-western singer Marty Robbins (b. 1926). It occurs occasionally as a female name, a variant of MARTI.

Marva (f.) English: modern creation, apparently invented as a feminine form of MARVIN. The fanciful name **Marvalee** represents an elaboration of this.

Marvin (m.) English: from a medieval variant of MERVYN, resulting from the regular Middle English change of *-er-* to *-ar-*. Modern use may represent a transferred use of the surname derived from this in the Middle Ages. It is very popular in the United States, where it is often borne by Blacks and is associated in particular with the American singer Marvin Gaye (1939–84).

Mary (f.) English: originally a Middle English Anglicized form of French MARIE, from Latin MARIA. This is a New Testament form of MIRIAM, which St Jerome derives from elements meaning 'drop of the sea' (Latin *stilla maris*, later altered to *stella maris* 'star of the sea'). *Mary* is the most popular and enduring of all female Christian names, being the name of the Virgin Mary, mother of Jesus Christ, who has been the subject of a cult from earliest times. Consequently, the name was extremely common among early Christians, several saints among them, and by the Middle Ages was well established in every country in Europe at every level of society. It has been enduringly popular ever since, its popularity having been almost completely undisturbed by the vagaries of fashion that affect other names. In Spain and Portugal, the cult of the Virgin is so widespread and important that vocabulary words and placenames associated with aspects of her cult have been pressed into service as female given names, even when the gender of the vocabulary word is actually masculine: see, e.g., DOLORES, MERCEDES, PILAR, and ROSARIO. The Gaels, reluctant as always to put their saints' names to profane use, keep *Muire* (Irish) and *Moire* (Scottish) for the Virgin herself, and use late derivations of *Maria* (cited below) for secular naming purposes.

In the New Testament, *Mary* is also the name of several other women: Mary Magdalene (see MADELEINE); Mary the sister of Martha, who sat at Jesus's feet while Martha served (Luke 10: 38–42; John 11: 1–46; 12: 1–9) and who came to be taken in Christian tradition as symbolizing the value of a contemplative life; the mother of St Mark (Colossians 4: 10); and a Roman matron mentioned by St Paul (Romans 16: 6).

Cognates: In most European languages, including English: MARIA. Irish Gaelic: **Máire** (see also MOIRA, MAURA); **Máiria** (a learned form). Scottish Gaelic: **Màiri, Màili**. Welsh: **Mair, Mari**. French: MARIE. Basque: **Miren**. Russian: **Marya**.

Pet forms: English: MAY, MOLLY. Irish Gaelic: **Máirín**. Scottish Gaelic: **Màireag**. Italian: **Marietta, Mariella**. Spanish: **Mari(qui)ta, Maruja**. S. German and Swiss: **Mitzi**. Dutch: **Marieke, Mieke, Miep**. Frisian: **Maike**. Danish: **Mia**. Swedish: MAJ, **Maja, Mia**. Russian: **Masha, Manya**. Polish: **Marika** (also found in other Slavonic languages); **Marusia; Marzena; Mania**.

Marylyn (f.) English: variant spelling of MARILYN.

Maryvonne (f.) French: combination of the names MARIE and YVONNE. This has recently become a fashionable given name.

Masha (f.) Russian: pet form of *Marya* (see MARY).

Masław (m.) Polish: vernacular contracted form of MIECZYSŁAW.

Maso (m.) Italian: short form of TOMMASO.

Mason (m.) English (esp. U.S.): transferred use of the surname, which originated in the early Middle Ages as an occupational name for a worker in stone, Old French *maçon* (of Germanic origin, connected with Old English *macian* to make).

Massimo (m.) Italian form of MAXIM.

Masterman (m.) Scottish and English: transferred use of the surname, which originated in Scotland as a term denoting a retainer or servant: the 'man' of the 'master'. This was used in particular for the eldest sons of barons and the uncles of lords. As a given name it is principally known from the central character of Captain Frederick Marryat's novel *Masterman Ready* (1841).

Matěj (m.) Czech form of MATTHEW.

Pet forms: **Máta, Matejek, Matějí(če)k, Matoušek, Matys, Matýsek**.

Mateusz (m.) Polish form of MATTHEW.

Pet forms: **Matus(ek), Matuszek, Matys(ek)**.

Mathúin (m.) Irish Gaelic: modern name meaning 'bear'. It represents a simplified form of the earlier *Mathghamhain*, borne by a brother of Brian Boru, High King of Ireland in the early 11th century.

Anglicized form: **Mahon**.

Matilda (f.) Latinized form of a Germanic personal name composed of the elements *maht, meht* might + *hild* battle. This was the name of an early German queen (895–968), wife of Henry the Fowler, who was noted for her piety and generosity. It was also the name of the wife of William the Conqueror and of the daughter of Henry I of England (see MAUD). The name was introduced into England by the Normans, and this Latinized form is the one that normally occurs in medieval records, although the vernacular form MAUD seems to have been the one in everyday use. *Matilda* was revived in England as a learned form in the 18th century.

Variant: **Mathilda**.

Cognates: French: **Mathilde**. Spanish, Portuguese: **Matilde**. Portuguese, Italian: **Mafalda**. German: **Mechtilde**. Low German: **Mette**. Polish, Czech: **Matylda**.

Short forms: English: **Tilda**. Swedish: **Tilda**. Danish: **Tilde**.

Pet forms: English: **Mattie; Tilly, Tillie**.

Matrona (f.) Russian: from the Late Latin name *Mātrōna* 'lady' (earlier 'married, respectable, noble woman', a derivative of *māter* mother). This name was borne by various early saints martyred for their faith.

Variant: **Matryona** (popular form).

Cognate: Jewish: **Madrona**.

Pet forms: Russian: **Matryosh(k)a**, **Matyush(k)a**, MOTYA.

Matthew (m.) English form of the name of the Christian evangelist, author of the first gospel in the New Testament. His name is a form of the Hebrew name *Mattathia*, meaning 'gift of God', which is fairly common in the Old Testament, being rendered in the Authorized Version in a number of different forms: *Mattan(i)ah*, *Mattatha(h)*, *Mattithiah*, *Mattathias*, and so on. In the Authorized Version, the evangelist is regularly referred to as *Matthew*, while the apostle chosen to replace Judas Iscariot is distinguished as MATTHIAS. A related name from the same Hebrew roots, but reversed, is JONATHAN.

Cognates (also of MATTHIAS): Irish Gaelic: **Maitiú**, **Maitias**. Scottish Gaelic: **Mata**; **Matha** (a dialectal variant). French: **Mathieu**. Italian: **Matteo**, **Mattia**. Spanish: **Mateo**. Portuguese: **Mateus**. Catalan: **Mateu**. German: **Mattäus**. Dutch: **Matthijs**. Swedish, Norwegian: **Mats**. Danish: **Mads**, **Mathies**. Polish: **Mateusz**, **Maciej**. Czech: **Matěj**, **Matyáš**. Russian: **Matvei**. Ukrainian: **Matvi**. Hungarian: **Mátyás**, **Máté**. Finnish: **Matti**.

Short forms: English: **Matt**. Dutch: **Thijs**.

Pet forms: English: **Mattie**. Polish: **Maciek**. Russian: MOTYA.

Matthias (m.) New Testament Greek form of the Hebrew name *Mattathia* (see MATTHEW), or rather of an Aramaic derivative. The Latin form of the name is *Matthaeus*. In English the form *Matthias* is used in the Authorized Version of the New Testament to distinguish the disciple who was chosen after the treachery of Judas to make up the twelve (Acts 1: 23–26) from the evangelist *Matthew*. However, this distinction is not observed in other languages, where *Matthias* (or a version of it) is often a learned doublet existing alongside a vernacular derivative.

Variant: **Mathias**.

Cognates: See MATTHEW.

Mattie (m., occasionally f.) English: 1. (m.) Pet form of MATTHEW.

2. (f.) Pet form of MATILDA.

Matyáš (m.) Czech form of MATTHEW.

Matyusha (f.) Russian: pet form of *Matryona* (see MATRONA).

Variant: **Matyushka**.

Maud (f.) English: a medieval vernacular form of MATILDA. This form was characteristically Low German (i.e. including medieval Dutch and Flemish). The wife of William the Conqueror, who bore this name, was the daughter of Baldwin, Count of Flanders. In Flemish and Dutch the letter *-t-* was generally lost when it occurred between vowels, giving forms such as *Ma(h)auld*. *Maud* or *Matilda* was also the name of the daughter (1102–67) of Henry I of England; she was married early in life to the Holy Roman Emperor Henry V, and later disputed the throne of England with her cousin Stephen. In 1128 she married Geoffrey, Count of Anjou. A medieval chronicler commented, 'she was a good woman, but she had little bliss with him.' The name *Maud* became quite common in England in the 19th century, when its popularity was influenced in part by Tennyson's poem *Maud*, published in 1855.

Mauno (m.) Finnish form of MAGNUS.

Maura (f.) 1. English, Scottish, and Irish: of Celtic origin. St Maura was a 5th-century martyr, of whom very little is known; her companion is variously named as *Britta* (of Celtic origin) and *Baya* (of Latin origin). In Ireland *Maura* is now commonly regarded as a form of MARY (cf. MOIRA and MAUREEN).

2. Italian and Spanish: feminine form of MAURO.

Cognate (of 2): Russian: **Mavra**.

Maureen (f.) English and Irish: Anglicized form of Irish Gaelic **Máirín**, a pet form of *Máire*. See also MOREEN.

Variants: **Maurene**, **Maurine**.

Short form: **Mo**.

Maurice (m.) 1. English and French: from the Late Latin name *Mauricius*, a derivative of *Maurus* (see MAURO), borne by, among others, an early Byzantine emperor (*c.*539–602). It was introduced to Britain by the Normans, and was popular in the Middle English period, but was not widely adopted by the nobility, and became rare in the 17th century. In Germany it became established as a traditional name among the dukes of Saxony in the 16th century. It is now sometimes believed in Britain and America to be a mainly French name, perhaps because of the enormous popular influence of the French singer and film actor Maurice Chevalier (1888–1972), who, in his public image at least, was the very epitome of Gallic charm. See also MORRIS.

2. Irish: Anglicized form of the Gaelic name **Muirgheas,** which is composed of the elements *muir* sea + *gus* choice.

Cognates (of 1): Irish Gaelic: **Muiris**. Welsh: **Meurig**. Italian: **Maurizio**. Spanish, Portuguese: **Mauricio**. German and Jewish: **Moritz**. Scandinavian: **Maurits**. Russian: **Mavriki**.

Short form: English: **Mo**.

Mauro (m.) Italian: from Latin *Maurus*, a byname meaning 'Moor', i.e. 'dark, swarthy', borne by a dozen early saints. In the 6th century it was the name of one of the earliest followers of St Benedict, placed in the care of the monk at an early age by his father Eutychius.

Mave (f.) 1. Irish: variant of MAEVE.

2. English: informal short form of MAVIS.

Mavis (f.) English: not found before the last decade of the 19th century, and apparently one of the small class of female given names taken from vocabulary words denoting birds. *Mavis* is another word for the song-thrush, first attested in Chaucer. It is from Old French, and probably ultimately of Breton origin.

Short form (informal): **Mave**.

Mavra (f.) Russian form of MAURA (2).

Max (m.) English and German: short form of MAXIMILIAN and, perhaps now more commonly in the English-speaking world, of MAXWELL. It is also used as an independent given name.

Maxi (m., f.) German: short form of MAXIMILIAN or its feminine equivalent **Maximiliane**. It is now sometimes also used as an independent female given name in the English-speaking world.

Variant: English: **Maxie** (f.).

Maxim (m.) Russian: from the Latin cognomen *Maximus* 'greatest', later used as a given name. This was the name of a very large number of early saints, including a Byzantine theologian and mystic (*c.*580–662) who was persecuted under the Emperor Constans. *Maxim* Gorki was the pseudonym adopted by the Russian writer Alexei Maximovich Peshkov (1868–1936).

Cognates: Italian: **Massimo**. Spanish, Portuguese: **Máximo**. French: **Maxime**.

Maximilian (m.) German and English: from the Latin name *Maximiliānus* (a diminutive of *Maximus*; see MAXIM). This was borne by a 3rd-century saint numbered among the 'Fourteen Holy Helpers'. Although already existing, the name was reanalysed in the 15th century by the Emperor Friedrich III, who bestowed it upon his first-born son (1459–1519), as a blend of the names *Maximus* and *Aemiliānus*, intending thereby to pay homage to the two classical Roman generals Q. Fabius Maximus 'Cunctator' and P. Cornelius Scipio Aemilianus. The name became traditional in the Habsburg family in Austria-Hungary and also in the royal house of Bavaria. It was borne by an ill-fated Austrian archduke (1832–67) who was set up as emperor of Mexico but later overthrown and shot.

Maxine (f.) English: modern coinage, first recorded around 1930; a derivative of MAX by addition of the feminine ending *-ine*.

Maxwell (m.) Scottish and English: from the Scottish surname, which is derived from a placename, *Maxwell*, originally 'the stream (Old English *well(a)*) of *Mack* (a form of MAGNUS)', a minor place on the River Tweed. It was the middle name of the newspaper tycoon William Maxwell Aitken, Lord Beaverbrook (1879–1964), who was born in Canada, and has been used as a given name among his descendants. It is now also frequently taken as an expansion of MAX.

May (f.) English: pet form of both MARGARET and MARY. The popularity of this name, which was at its height in the early 20th century, has been reinforced by the fact that it fits into the series of month names with APRIL and JUNE, and also belongs to the group of flower names, being another word for the hawthorn, whose white flowers blossom in May. It has been out of fashion for a time.

Maya (f.) English: Latinate version of MAY or a respelled form of the name of the Roman goddess *Māia*, influenced by the common English name MAY. The goddess Maia was one of the Pleiades, the daughters of Atlas and Pleione; she was the mother by Jupiter of Mercury. Her name seems to be derived from the root *māi-* great, seen also in Latin *māior* larger. In the case of the Black American writer Maya Angelou (b. 1928), *Maya* is a nickname acquired in early childhood as a result of her younger brother's reference to her as 'mya sista'.

Maybelle (f.) English: alteration of MABEL, influenced by the independent names MAY and BELLE.

Maynard (m.) English: transferred use of the surname, which is derived from a Norman given name of Germanic origin, composed of the elements *magin* strength + *hard* hardy, brave, strong.

Cognate: German: **Mein(h)ard**.

Meave (f.) Irish: variant of MAEVE.

Mecheslav (m.) Russian form of MIECZYSŁAW.

Mechtilde (f.) German form of MATILDA.

Medardo (m.) Italian, Spanish, and Portuguese: from an old Germanic personal name composed of a first element of uncertain origin + *hard* hardy, brave, strong. It is borne in honour of St Medard (*c.*470–*c.*558), bishop of Noyon and Tournai. His brother, St Gildard, served as archbishop of Rouen.

Medea (f.) Name borne in classical mythology by a Colchian princess who helped Jason to steal the Golden Fleece from her father. Later, however, she was abandoned by Jason in favour of Creusa (or, in some versions, Glauce). She took her revenge by killing the two children previously born to Jason and herself. The name may derive from the Greek verb *mēdesthai* to reflect, meditate, or ponder.

Medir (m.) Catalan form of EMETERIO.

Mefodi (m.) Russian: from the Late Greek personal name *Methodios* 'fellow traveller' (from *meta* with + *hodos* road, path). St Methodius (d. 885) and his brother Cyril (d. 869) together evangelized the Slavonic region of Moravia in present-day Czechoslovakia. It was Methodius who first translated the Bible into Slavonic, although the cyrillic alphabet devised for this purpose bears his brother's name.

Cognates: Polish: **Metody**. Czech: **Metoděj**.

Pet forms: Russian: **Mefodya, Modya**.

Meg (f.) English: short form of MARGARET, an alteration of the obsolete short form *Mag(g)* (as in MAGGIE). Until recently *Meg* was a characteristically Scottish pet form, but it is now used more widely. Its popularity no doubt owes something to Meg March, one of the four sisters who are the main characters in Louisa M. Alcott's novel *Little Women* (1855).

Megan (f.) Welsh: pet form of MEG, nowadays generally used as an independent first name both within and beyond Wales, but nevertheless retaining a strong Welsh flavour.

Variants: **Meghan, Meaghan** (pseudo-Irish spellings much used in Australia and Canada).

Meggie (f.) 1. English: obsolete pet form of MEG.

2. Australian: pet form of MEGAN, as in the case of the central character of Colleen McCullough's novel *The Thorn Birds* (1977).

Mehalia (f.) English: apparently an altered form of MAHALIA.

Mehitabel (f.) Biblical: from the Hebrew name **Mehetabel** 'God makes happy'. Mehetabel 'the daughter of Matred, the daughter of Mezahab' is mentioned in passing in a biblical genealogy (Genesis 36: 39), and the name achieved some currency among the Puritans in the 17th century. Nowadays, however, the name is chiefly associated with the companion (a cat) of Archy, the cockroach in the poems of Don Marquis (1927).

Meical (m.) Welsh form of MICHAEL.

Short form: **Meic.**

Meilyr (m.) Welsh: traditional name derived from an Old Celtic form *Maglorīx*, composed of the elements *maglos* chief + *rīx* ruler.

Meinard (m.) German form of MAYNARD.

Variant: **Meinhard.**

Meinwen (f.) Welsh: modern coinage composed of the elements *main* slender + *(g)wen*, feminine form of *gwyn* white, fair, blessed, holy.

Meinrad (m.) German: from an old Germanic personal name composed of the elements *magin* strength + *rād* counsel. St Meinrad (d. 861) was a member of the Hohenzollern royal family who became a hermit in Switzerland, at the place where the monastery of Einsiedeln was later built.

Meir (m.) Jewish: traditional name, meaning 'giving light' in Hebrew.

Variants: **Meier, Meyer, Myer, Maier, Mayr** (generally assimilations to German surname forms).

Meirion (m.) Welsh: traditional name, derived in the sub-Roman period from Latin *Mariānus* (see MARIANO and MARIAN (2)).

Feminine forms: **Meiriona, Meirionwen** (modern creations).

Mel (m., f.) English: short form of MELVIN or MELVILLE, or, in the case of the female name, of MELANIE or the several other female names beginning with this syllable.

Melanie (f.) English and Dutch: from an Old French form of Latin *Melania*, a derivative of the feminine form, *melaina*, of the Greek adjective *melas* black, dark. This was the name of two Roman saints of the 5th century, a grandmother and granddaughter. St Melania the Younger was a member of an extremely rich patrician family. She led an austere and devout Christian life and, on inheriting her father's wealth, she emancipated her slaves, sold her property, and gave the proceeds to the poor. She also established several contemplative houses, including one on the Mount of Olives to which she eventually retired. The name *Melanie* was introduced to England from France in the Middle Ages, but died out again. It has been reintroduced and has become popular in the late 20th century.

Variants: **Melany,** MELONY.

Cognate: French: **Mélanie.**

Melchiorre (m.) Italian: from the name assigned by medieval tradition to one of the three Magi. It is said to be of Persian origin, composed of the elements *melk* king (cf. MELEK) + *quart* city.

Melek (m.) Jewish: from a vocabulary element meaning 'king' in Hebrew. It originated in part as a nickname, in part as a short form of various compound names containing this element, for example *Elimelek* 'God is king'.

Melinda (f.) English: derived from the first syllable of names such as MELANIE and MELISSA, with the addition of the productive suffix *-inda* (cf. e.g. LUCINDA).

Melissa (f.) 1. English: from the Greek word *melissa* bee. It is the name of the good witch who releases Rogero from the power of the bad witch Alcina in Ariosto's narrative poem *Orlando Furioso* (1532). The name has recently increased considerably in popularity, together with other female names sharing the same first syllable.

2. Irish: recently adopted as an Anglicized form of the Gaelic female name MAOILÍOSA.

Variant (of 1): **Melitta** (from an ancient Greek dialectal variant of the same word).

Melody (f.) English: modern transferred use of the vocabulary word (Greek *melōdia* singing of songs, from *melos* song + *aeidein* to sing), chosen partly because of its pleasant associations and partly under the influence of other female names with the same first syllable.

Melony (f.) Variant of MELANIE, perhaps influenced by MELODY.

Variants: **Mellony, Mel(l)oney.**

Melor (m.) Russian: modern name composed of the initial letters of the words *Marx*, *Engels*, *Lenin*, *October*, *Revolution*. The name has been created by Communist parents spurning the traditional stock of Russian names derived from the names of saints (see also NINEL and VLADILEN).

Melville (m.) English (esp. U.S.): transferred use of the Scottish surname, which originated as a Norman baronial name borne by the lords of a place in northern France called *Malleville* 'bad settlement', i.e. settlement on infertile land. The name was taken to Scotland as early as the 12th century and became an important surname there; use as a given name seems also to have originated in Scotland.

Melvin (m.) English: a very popular modern name of uncertain origin, probably a variant of the less common MELVILLE.

Variant: **Melvyn.**

Menahem (m.) Jewish: name meaning 'comforter' in Hebrew. It was borne in the Scriptures by an evil king of Israel who massacred pregnant women (2 Kings 15: 14–18), but the name has nevertheless always been a popular one among Jews; in earlier times it was given particularly to a child born after the death of a sibling and seen as a comfort to his parents. See also MENDEL.

Variant: **Menachem.**

Menchu (f.) Spanish: pet form of CARMEN.

Mendel (m.) Jewish: Yiddish form of Hebrew MENAHEM. It seems to have originated as a result of substitution of the Yiddish diminutive suffix *-l* (plus an intrusive *-d-*) for *-hem*, which was taken erroneously as the German diminutive suffix *-chen.*

Menuha (f.) Jewish: name meaning 'peace, stillness, tranquillity' in Hebrew.

Variant: **Menuhah.**

Meo (m.) Italian: short form of *Bartolomeo* (see BARTHOLOMEW).

Mercedes (f.) Spanish: Marian name, from the liturgical title *Maria de las Mercedes* (literally, 'Mary of Mercies'; in English, 'Our Lady of Ransom'). Latin *mercēdes* originally meant 'wages' or 'ransom'; in Christian theology, Christ's sacrifice is regarded as a 'ransom for the sins of mankind', and hence an 'act of ransom' was seen as identical with an 'act of mercy'. There are special feasts in the Catholic calendar on 10 August and 24 September to commemorate the Virgin under this name. The name is now occasionally used in England, and more commonly in America, but normally only by Roman Catholics.

Pet form: **Merche.**

Mercia (f.) English: Latinate elaboration of MERCY, coinciding in form with the name of the Anglo-Saxon kingdom of Mercia, which dominated England during the 8th century under its king, Offa.

Mercy (f.) English: 1. From the vocabulary word denoting the quality of magnanimity, and in particular God's forgiveness of sinners, a quality much prized in Christian tradition. The word is derived from Latin *mercēs*, which originally meant 'wages' or 'reward' (see MERCEDES). The name was much favoured by the Puritans; Mercy is the companion of Christiana in the second part of John Bunyan's *Pilgrim's Progress* (1684). Subsequently, it fell out of use as a given name.

2. In modern use, this is often an Anglicized form of *Mercedes*.

Meredith (m., f.) English: from the Old Welsh personal name *Maredudd*, later *Meredudd*. This is of uncertain origin; the second element is Welsh *iudd* lord. In recent years the name has sometimes been given to girls, presumably being thought of as the formal form of MERRY.

Mererid (f.) Welsh form of MARGARET (see also MARED).

Merete (f.) Danish: vernacular form of MARGARET.

Variants: **Mereta; Märta; Mette.**

Merfyn (m.) Welsh: traditional name composed of the Old Welsh elements *mer*, probably meaning 'marrow' + *myn* eminent. This name was borne by a shadowy 9th-century Welsh king.

Meriel (f.) English: variant of MURIEL; both forms are 19th-century revivals of an older Celtic name. Of the two forms, *Meriel* was never as popular as *Muriel*, but for that reason seems to have escaped the current somewhat old-fashioned image of the latter name.

Merle (f., m.) English: probably a contracted form of MERIEL, but also associated with the small class of female names derived from birds, since it is identical in form with Old French *merle* blackbird (Latin *merula*). The name came to public notice in the 1930s with the actress Merle Oberon (1911–79); she was born Estelle Merle O'Brien Thompson. In Britain this is still normally a female name; in the United States it is more commonly borne by males.

Merlin (m.) Usual English form of the Welsh name *Myrddin*. The name is most famous as that of the legendary magician who guides the destiny of King Arthur. It seems to have originally been composed of Old Celtic elements meaning 'sea' and 'hill, fort', but it has been distorted by mediation through Old French sources, which associated the second element with the diminutive suffix *-lin*.

Variant: **Merlyn** (occasionally given to girls, as if containing the productive suffix of female names *-lyn*).

Merrill (m.) English: transferred use of the surname, which is derived from the female name MERIEL or MURIEL.

Merrily (f.) English (U.S.): apparently a respelling of MARILEE, reshaped to coincide with the adverb derived from the adjective *merry*.

Merry (f.) English: originally apparently an assimilated form of MERCY. In Dickens's novel *Martin Chuzzlewit* (1844), Mr Pecksniff's daughters CHARITY and *Mercy* are known as *Cherry* and *Merry*. Nowadays the name is usually bestowed because of its association with the adjective denoting a cheerful and jolly temperament (cf. HAPPY). In the accent of the central and northern United States there is no difference in pronunciation between MERRY and MARY.

Merten (m.) Low German form of MARTIN.

Mertice (f.) English: recent coinage, popular in the southern United States. It seems to be an entirely arbitrary invention.

Mervyn (m.) Anglicized form of Welsh MERFYN, now widely popular both in and beyond Wales.

Variant: **Mervin.**

Meryl (f.) English: a recent coinage, owing its current popularity to the fame of the American actress Meryl Streep (b. Mary Louise Streep in 1949). It has also been influenced in part by the ending *-yl* in names such as CHERYL.

Meshulam (m.) Jewish: Hebrew name, apparently meaning either 'paid for' or 'friend'. It is borne by a minor character in the Old Testament (2 Kings 22: 3); the spelling *Meshullam* is used in the Authorized Version.

Meta (f.) German, Danish, and Swedish: contracted pet form of *Margareta* (see MARGARET). It was very popular in the 19th and early 20th centuries, but is now perceived as old-fashioned.

Metoděj (m.) Czech form of MEFODI.

Pet forms: **Metodek, Metoušek**.

Metody (m.) Polish form of MEFODI.

Mette (f.) 1. Danish: contracted form of MERETE.

2. Low German: contracted form of *Mechtilde* (see MATILDA).

Meurig (m.) Welsh form of MAURICE, derived from Latin *Mauricius* via Old Welsh *Mouric*.

Mia (f.) Danish and Swedish: pet form of MARIA. It is now also used in the English-speaking world, largely as a result of the fame of the actress Mia Farrow (b. 1945).

Micah (m.) Biblical: Hebrew name meaning 'who is like (Yahweh)?', and thus a doublet of MICHAEL. This was the name of a prophet, author of the book of the Bible that bears his name, and which dates from the late 8th century BC.

Michael (m.) English and German form of a common biblical name (meaning 'who is like God?') borne by one of the archangels, who is also regarded as a saint of the Catholic Church (cf. GABRIEL and RAPHAEL). In the Middle Ages, Michael was regarded as captain of the heavenly host (see Revelation 12: 7–9), symbol of the Church Militant, and patron of soldiers. He was often depicted bearing a flaming sword. Because of its sanctified warlike connotations, *Michael* was a popular name among early Christian military leaders, and was borne by eight Byzantine emperors, as well as by the founder (1596–1645) of the Romanov dynasty in Russia. The name is also borne by a Persian prince and ally of Belshazzar mentioned in the Book of Daniel. See also MICHAL.

Cognates: Irish Gaelic: **Mícheál**. Scottish Gaelic: **Mìcheal**. Welsh: **Meical**, MIHANGEL. French: **Michel**. Italian: **Michele**. Spanish, Portuguese: **Miguel**. Catalan: **Miquel**. Basque: **Mikel**. Romanian: **Mihai**. Swedish: **Mikael**. Danish, Norwegian: **Mikkel, Mikael**. Polish: **Michał**. Czech: **Mich(a)el**. Russian: **Mikhail**. Ukrainian: **Mikhailo**. Finnish: **Mikko**. Hungarian: **Mihály**.

Short forms: English: **Mike**, MICK.

Pet forms: English: **Micky**. Russian: **Misha**.

Feminine forms: Latinate: **Michaela** (used in England and Germany); **Micaela** (used in Italy and Spain). French: **Michèle, Michelle**. Polish: **Michalina**.

Michal (f.) Biblical name (meaning 'brook' in Hebrew) borne by a daughter of Saul who married King David. It is probably through confusion with this name that MICHAEL has occasionally been used as a female given name in the English-speaking world.

Michelangelo (m.) Italian: compound made up of *Michele* MICHAEL + *angelo* angel. Its best-known bearer was the Florentine painter, sculptor, architect, and poet Michelangelo Buonarroti (1475–1564).

Michèle (f.) French: feminine form of *Michel* (see MICHAEL).

Micheline (f.) French: diminutive form of MICHÈLE, now used as an independent given name, to some extent also in the English-speaking world.

Michelle (f.) French: variant of MICHÈLE. This name is now also used extensively in the English-speaking world (partly influenced by a Beatles song with this name as its title).

Short forms: English: **Chelle**, SHELL.

Mick (m.) English: short form of MICHAEL; now common as a generic, and often derogatory, term for a Catholic Irishman.

Pet form: **Micky**. See also MIKKI.

Micolau (m.) Catalan: variant of *Nicolau* (see NICHOLAS).

Mieczysław (m.) Polish: from an old Slavonic personal name, in which a first element of uncertain form, probably derived from Old Polish *miecz* man or *mieszka* bear, is combined with the regular name-forming element *slav* glory. It was borne by two early rulers of Poland, the first of whom, Mieczysław I (*c.*922–92), played an important role in opposing Teutonic incursions and securing papal support for the Poles.

Variant: **Masław**.

Cognates: Czech: **Mečislav**. Russian: **Mecheslav**.

Feminine form: Czech: **Mečislava**.

Pet forms: Polish: **Mietek, Mieszko** (m.). Czech: **Mečislavek, Meček, Mečík** (m.); **Mečka, Mečina** (f.).

Mieke (f.) Dutch: pet form of MARIA.

Variant: **Miep**.

Mignonette (f.) English: probably a direct use of the French nickname *mignonette* 'little darling', a feminine diminutive of *mignon* sweet, cute, dainty. Alternatively, it may belong to the class of names derived from vocabulary words denoting flowers (the word in English denotes a species of *Reseda*).

Miguel (m.) Spanish and Portuguese form of MICHAEL.

Mihai (m.) Romanian form of MICHAEL.

Mihály (m.) Hungarian form of MICHAEL.

Mihangel (m.) Older Welsh form of MICHAEL, representing a contraction of the phrase 'Michael the Archangel'.

Mikael (m.) Scandinavian form of MICHAEL.

Mike (m.) English: usual short form of MICHAEL in the English-speaking world. It is also used as an independent given name, particularly in America.

Pet form: **Mikey**.

Mikkel (m.) Danish and Norwegian form of MICHAEL.

Mikki (f.) English: feminine variant of *Micky* (see MICK) or pet form of *Michaela* (see MICHAEL), now sometimes used as an independent given name.

Variants: **Micki, Mickie, Mickey**.

Mikko (m.) Finnish form of MICHAEL.

Miklós (m.) Hungarian form of NICHOLAS.

Mikołaj (m.) Polish form of NICHOLAS.

Pet forms: **Mikulášek, Mikuš**.

Mikoláš (m.) Czech form of NICHOLAS.

Variant: **Mikuláš**.

Milagros (f.) Spanish: from a title of the Virgin Mary, *Nuestra Señora de los Milagros* 'Our Lady of Miracles'. Mary is regarded as the dispenser of miracles above all other saints.

Milan (m.) Czech: masculine equivalent of MILENA.

Mildred (f.) English: 19th-century revival of the Old English female name *Mildþryð*, composed of the elements *mild* gentle + *þrȳð* strength. This was the name of a 7th-century abbess, who had a less famous but equally saintly elder sister called *Mildburh* and a younger sister called *Mildgyð*; all were daughters of a certain Queen Ermenburh. Their names illustrate clearly the Old English pattern of combining and recombining the same small group of name elements within a single family.

Milena (f.) Czech: from a short form of various compound names containing the element *mil* grace, favour (cf. MILES). The name is now fairly common in

Italy, where it is often assumed to be a contraction of *Maria* + *Elena*. In fact it was little known before 1900, when King Victor Emmanuel III married Elena of Montenegro, whose mother was called Milena.

Variants: **Milana, Milada, Mlad(en)a.**

Pet forms: **Milenka, Milanka, Miládka, Milka, Miluše, Miluška, Mlad(uš)ka.**

Miles (m.) English: of Norman origin but uncertain derivation. Unlike most Norman names, it is, as far as can be ascertained, not derived from any known Germanic name element. It may be a greatly altered pet form of MICHAEL, which came to be associated with the Latin word *miles* soldier because of the military attributes of the archangel Michael. However, the usual Latin form of the name in the Middle Ages was *Milo*. There is a common Slavonic name element *mil* grace, favour, with which it may possibly have some ultimate connection. The name has been modestly popular in England ever since the Conquest. See also MYLES.

Milla (f.) English: short form of CAMILLA.

Millà (m.) Catalan form of ÉMILIEN.

Millicent (f.) English: Norman name of Germanic origin, composed of the elements *amal* labour + *swinth* strength. This was the name of a daughter of Charlemagne. It was first introduced to Britain by the Normans in the form *Melisende*.

Pet form: **Millie** (see also CAMILLA).

Milo (m.) 1. English: Latinized form of MILES, regularly used in documents of the Middle Ages, and revived as a given name in the 19th century.

2. Irish: used as a pet form of MYLES.

Milosław (m.) Polish: from an old Slavonic personal name composed of the elements *mil* grace, favour + *slav* glory.

Cognate: Czech: **Miloslav.**

Feminine forms: Polish: **Milosława.** Czech: **Miloslava.**

Miłosz (m.) Polish: pet name derived from a short form of various compound names containing the old Slavonic element *mil* grace, favour, e.g. MIŁOSŁAW.

Variant: **Miłuś.**

Cognates: Czech: **Miloš, Miloň.**

Milton (m.) English: transferred use of the surname, itself derived from any of the numerous places so called, a large number of which get their name from Old English *mylentūn* 'settlement with a mill'. Others were originally named as 'the middle (of three) settlements', from Old English *middel* middle + *tūn* settlement. The surname is most famous as that of the poet John Milton (1608–74), and the given name is sometimes bestowed in his honour.

Miluše (f.) Czech: pet form of MILENA.

Variant: **Miluška.**

Mimi (f.) Italian: pet form of MARIA, originally a nursery name. The heroine of Puccini's opera *La Bohème* (1896) announces 'They call me Mimi', and the name has occasionally been used in the English-speaking world.

Mina (f.) Scottish (Highland): short form of *Calumina* (see CALUM) and *Normina* (see NORMAN).

Mine (f.) 1. German and Danish: short form of WILHELMINA and *Vilhelmina* respectively.

2. Jewish: Yiddish spelling of MINNE.

Minette (f.) English: of uncertain origin. Although ostensibly a French name, it is not in fact used in France. It is possibly a contracted form of MIGNONETTE.

Minne (f.) German: originally an affectionate nickname from Middle High German *minne* love (as celebrated by the medieval German lyric poets and musicians known as the minnesingers). It is now also used as a pet form of WILHELMINA.

Variant: **Minna.**

Minnie (f.) English: pet form of WILHELMINA, at its peak of popularity in the latter half of the 19th century, when several names were introduced into Britain from Germany in the wake of Queen Victoria's consort, Prince Albert of Saxe-Coburg-Gotha, whom she married in 1840. It has now largely fallen out of use, partly because German names in general became unacceptable in Britain during the First World War, partly perhaps also because of association with cartoon characters such as Minnie Mouse (in Walt Disney's animations) and Minnie the Minx (in the *Beano* children's comic).

Miquel (m.) Catalan form of MICHAEL.

Mira (f.) Slavonic: short form of the various Slavonic female names (e.g. *Miroslava*; see MIROSŁAW) containing the element *meri* great, famous (see CASIMIR). It is now also occasionally used in the English-speaking world, probably as a result of association with the feminine form of the Latin adjective *mīrus* wonderful, astonishing (cf. MIRANDA).
Pet form: **Mirka.**

Mirabelle (f.) French and English: apparently coined from the Latin word *mīrābilis* wondrous, lovely (a derivative of *mīrāri* to wonder at, admire; cf. MIRANDA). It was quite common in the late Middle Ages, and occasionally the form **Mirabel** was used for boys as well as girls, but by the 17th century both forms were rare.
Variant: Latinate, Italian: **Mirabella.**

Miranda (f.) English: invented by Shakespeare for the heroine of *The Tempest* (1611). It represents the feminine form of the Latin gerundive *mīrandus* admirable, lovely, from *mīrāri* to wonder at, admire; cf. AMANDA.
Short form: **Randa.**
Pet forms: **Randy, Randie.**

Mireille (f.) French: apparently first used, in the Provençal form **Mireio**, as the title of a verse romance by the poet Frédéric Mistral (1830–1914). The name is probably a derivative of Provençal *mirar* to admire (cf. MIRANDA), but the poet himself declared it to be a form of MIRIAM; this was in order to overcome the objections of a priest to so baptizing his goddaughter with a non-liturgical name.

Mirek (m.) Polish and Czech: pet form of the various old Slavonic personal names (e.g. MIROSŁAW, *Miroslav*) containing the element *meri* great, famous (see CASIMIR).

Mirella (f.) Italian form of MIREILLE or a contracted form of *Mirabella* (see MIRABELLE).

Miren (f.) Basque form of MARY.
Pet form: **Mirentxu.**

Miriam (f.) Biblical: the Old Testament form of the Hebrew name *Maryam* (see MARY). Of uncertain ultimate origin, this is first recorded as being borne by the elder sister of Moses (Exodus 15: 20). Since the names of both Moses and his brother Aaron are probably of Egyptian origin, it is possible that this feminine name is too. It was enthusiastically taken up as a given name by the Israelites, and is still borne mainly, but by no means exclusively, by Jews.
Variant: MARIAMNE.

Mirka (f.) Slavonic: pet form of MIRA.

Mirosław (m.) Polish: from an old Slavonic personal name composed of the elements *meri* great, famous (see CASIMIR) + *slav* glory.
Cognate: Czech, Russian: **Miroslav.**
Feminine forms: Polish: **Mirosława.** Czech: **Miroslava.**

Misha (m.) Russian: pet form of *Mikhail* (see MICHAEL).

Misia (f.) Polish: pet form of *Michalina* (see MICHAEL).

Misty (f.) English: modern name, apparently from the vocabulary word, a derivative of *mist* thin fog (Old English *mist*).

Mitchell (m.) English: transferred use of the surname, itself derived from a common medieval form of MICHAEL, representing an Anglicized pronunciation of Norman French *Michel.*
Short form: **Mitch** (informal).

Mitrofan (m.) Russian: from Greek *Mētrophanēs*, a derivative of *mētēr* (genitive *mētros*) mother (sc. of God) + *phainein* to show, appear. The name was borne by the first bishop of Byzantium.

Pet forms: **Mitroshka**; **Mitya** (see also DMITRI).

Mitzi (f.) S. German and Swiss: pet form of MARIA.

Mladka (f.) Czech: pet form derived from a contracted version of *Milada* (see MILENA).

Variant: **Mladuška**.

Mo (f., m.) English: short form of MAUREEN and, less commonly, of MAURICE.

Modest (f.) Russian: from the Late Latin personal name *Modestus*, originally a byname from a vocabulary word meaning 'moderate, restrained, obedient, modest' (a derivative of *modus* (due) measure, moderation). The name was borne by half a dozen early saints, including a child martyred at Alexandria in Egypt together with his brother Ammonius, and an 8th-century evangelist of Carinthia.

Cognates: Spanish, Portuguese, Italian: **Modesto**. See also SZERÉNY.

Pet form: Russian: **Desya**.

Modya (m.) Russian: pet form of MEFODI.

Mogens (m.) Danish form of MAGNUS.

Moira (f.) Irish, Scottish and English: Anglicized form of Irish Gaelic *Máire* (a form of MARY). This is now an extremely popular name in its own right throughout the English-speaking world.

Variant: **Moyra**.

Moirean (m.) Scottish Gaelic: derivative of *Moire*, the name of the Virgin Mary, just as *Cailean* is based on the name of St Columba and *Crìsdean* on that of Christ.

Molly (f.) English and Irish: long-established pet form of MARY, representing an altered version of the earlier pet form *Mally*. The name is chiefly associated with Ireland, although it is not Gaelic. It is at present somewhat out of fashion.

Mona (f.) 1. Irish and English: Anglicized form of the Gaelic name **Muadhnait**, a feminine diminutive of *muadh* noble. It is no longer restricted to people with Irish connections, and has sometimes been taken as connected with Greek *monos* single, only. In Gaelic Scotland it may represent a feminine form of TORMOD, since the latter was used as a Gaelic form of NORMAN.

2. Scandinavian: short form of *Monika* (see MONICA).

Mona is also found as a female name in Arabic.

Moncho (m.) Spanish: pet form of RAMÓN.

Monica (f.) English: of uncertain ultimate origin. This was the name of the mother of St Augustine, as transmitted to us by her famous son. She was a citizen of Carthage, so her name may well be of Phoenician origin, but in the early Middle Ages it was taken to be a derivative of Latin *monēre* to warn, counsel, or advise, since it was as a result of her guidance that her son was converted to Christianity.

Cognates: French: **Monique**. German, Scandinavian, Slavonic: **Monika**.

Monroe (m.) Scottish and English: transferred use of the Scottish surname, usually spelled *Munro*. The ancestors of the Scottish Munros are said to have originally come from Ireland, apparently from a settlement by the River Roe in County Derry; their name is therefore supposed to be derived from Gaelic *bun Rotha* 'mouth of the Roe'. In America the popularity of the given name may have been influenced by the fame of James Monroe (1758–1831), fifth president of the United States and propounder (in 1823) of the Monroe Doctrine, asserting that European powers should not seek to colonize in North or South America and that the United States would not intervene in European affairs. A more recent influence could have been the film star Marilyn Monroe (1926–62), whose original name was Norma-Jean Baker; however, the

name is not bestowed on female children, so the influence of her adopted surname does not appear to have been significant.
Variants: **Monro, Munro(e)**.

Montague (m.) English: 19th-century transferred use of the English surname. This was originally a Norman baronial name borne by the lords of Montaigu in La Manche. (The placename is composed of the Old French elements *mont* hill (Latin *mons*, genitive *montis*) + *aigu* pointed (Latin *acūtus*).) A certain Drogo of Montaigu is known to have accompanied William the Conqueror in his invasion of England in 1066, and *Montague* thus became established as an aristocratic British family name.

Montgomery (m.) English: transferred use of the surname, originally a Norman baronial name from various places in Calvados. The placename is derived from Old French *mont* hill + the Germanic personal name *Gomeric* 'man power'. It has never been common as a given name, although it was given additional currency by the actor Montgomery Clift (1920–66), and during and after the Second World War by the British field marshal, Bernard Montgomery (1887–1976).

Montmorency (m.) English: transferred use of the surname, originally a Norman baronial name derived from a place in Seine-et-Oise (so called from Old French *mont* hill + the Gallo-Roman personal name *Maurentius*). The given name enjoyed a brief vogue in the 19th century, but is now regarded as affected and so hardly ever used.

Montserrat (f.) Catalan: Marian name, referring to the famous Benedictine monastery of the Virgin Mary founded in 976 on the mountain of Montserrat near Barcelona. The mountain gets its name from Latin *mons serrātus* jagged hill.
Short forms: **Montse, Monse**.

Monty (m.) English: short form of MONTAGUE or of the much rarer MONTGOMERY and MONTMORENCY, all of which have gone through the cycle of transformation from French placename to Norman baronial name to noble British surname to modern given name. The full forms of all these names are now rare. *Monty* is now often used as an independent name, especially among Jews.

Mór (f.) Scottish and Irish Gaelic: originally a byname meaning 'large, great'. This was the commonest of all female given names in late medieval Ireland, and has continued in frequent use in both Scotland and Ireland to the present day. In Scotland it has sometimes been Anglicized as SARAH.
Pet forms: MORAG, MOREEN.

Morag (f.) Scottish: Anglicized spelling of Gaelic **Mórag**, a pet form of MÓR. In the 20th century this name has become hugely popular in its own right in Scotland, and is also used elsewhere in the English-speaking world.

Moray (m.) Scottish: variant of MURRAY, and the more usual spelling of the placename from which the surname is derived.

Mordecai (m.) Biblical: the name of Esther's cousin and foster-father, who secured her introduction to King Ahasuerus (Esther 2–9). The name is of Persian origin and seems to have meant 'devotee of the god Marduk'. It had some currency among English Puritans in the 17th century and Nonconformists in the 18th and 19th centuries, but has always been, and still is, mainly Jewish.
Pet forms: Yiddish: **Motke, Motl**.

Moreen (f.) Irish: Anglicized form of Gaelic **Móirín**, a pet form of MÓR. It has now been to a large extent confused with MAUREEN.

Morgan (m., f.) Welsh: traditional name derived from Old Welsh *Morcant*. The first element is of uncertain derivation, the second represents the Old Celtic element *cant* circle, completion. In recent years it has occasionally been used outside Wales as a female name, perhaps with conscious reference to King Arthur's jealous stepsister Morgan le Fay.

Moritz (m.) German and Jewish form of MAURICE.

Morley (m.) English: transferred use of the surname, which originated as a local name from any of the numerous places in Britain named with the Old English elements *mōr* moor, marsh + *lēah* wood or clearing.

Morna (f.) Irish and Scottish: variant of MYRNA. This is the name borne by Fingal's mother in the Ossianic poems of James Macpherson (cf. MALVINA).

Morris (m.) 1. English: variant of MAURICE. The spelling *Morris* was quite common as a given name in the Middle Ages, but it fell out of use and was readopted in modern times, in part from the surname earlier derived from the given name.

2. Jewish: adopted as an Anglicized form of MOSES, like several other English surnames beginning with *M-*, such as MORTIMER and MORTON.

Morten (m.) Danish form of MARTIN.

Mortimer (m.) 1. English: transferred use of the surname, which is derived from a Norman baronial name, originally borne by the lords of *Mortemer* in Normandy. The placename meant 'dead sea' in Old French, and probably referred to a stagnant marsh. It was not used as a given name until the 19th century.

2. Irish: Anglicized form of MUIRIARTACH.

3. Jewish: Anglicized form of MOSES.

Morton (m.) 1. English: transferred use of the surname, originally a local name derived from any of the numerous places so called from Old English *mōrtūn* 'settlement by or on a moor'.

2. Jewish: adopted as an Anglicized form of MOSES (cf. MORRIS).

Short form (mainly U.S.): **Mort**.

Morven (f.) English: this was the name of Fingal's kingdom in the Ossianic poems of James Macpherson. In reality it is a district in north Argyll, Scotland, properly *Morvern*, known in Gaelic as *a' Mhorbhairne* 'the big gap'. *Morven* could alternatively be held to represent Gaelic *mór bheinn* big peak. It has occasionally been used in modern times as a female given name (cf. SELMA).

Morwenna (f.) Cornish and Welsh: from an Old Celtic personal name derived from an element cognate with Welsh *morwyn* maiden. It was borne by a somewhat obscure Cornish saint of the 5th century; churches in her honour have named several places in Cornwall. The name was revived in Wales in the mid-20th century as a result of nationalistic sentiment.

Moses (m.) Biblical: English form of the name of the patriarch (**Moshe** in Hebrew) who led the Israelites out of Egypt (Exodus 4). His name is thought to be of Egyptian origin, most probably from the same root as that found in the second element of names such as *Tutmosis* and *Rameses*, where it means 'born of (a certain god)'. Various Hebrew etymologies have been proposed, beginning with the biblical 'saved (from the water)' (Exodus 2: 10), but none is convincing. It is now mainly Jewish, and has always been tremendously popular among Jews. Up until the 20th century, however, it also enjoyed some popularity among Christians in England, especially among Puritans and Nonconformists.

Cognates: Irish Gaelic: **Maois**. French: **Moïse**. Jewish (Yiddish): **Moishe**.

Moss (m.) 1. English (also Jewish): from the usual medieval form of MOSES or, among Gentiles, transferred use of the English surname derived from *Moses*.

2. Welsh: in recent years it has also been used as a short form of MOSTYN.

Mostyn (m.) Welsh: from the name of a place in Clwyd, on the Dee estuary. The place in fact derives its name from Old English rather than Welsh elements: it appears in the Domesday Book as *Mos-*

tone, from Old English *mos* moss + *tūn* enclosure, settlement.

Motke (m.) Jewish: Yiddish pet form of MORDECAI.
Variant: **Motl**.

Motya (m., f.) Russian: pet form of both *Matvei* (see MATTHEW) and MATRONA.

Mroż (m.) Polish: short form of *Ambroży* (see AMBROSE).
Pet form: **Mrożek**.

Mścisław (m.) Polish: from an old Slavonic personal name composed of the elements *mshcha* vengeance + *slav* glory.
Cognate: Czech and Russian: **Mstislav**.
Pet form: Czech: **Mstík**.

Muir (m.) Scottish: transferred use of the surname, in origin a local name representing a Scottish dialect variant of *moor* rough grazing.

Muireall (f.) Scottish Gaelic: traditional name, apparently composed of Old Celtic elements meaning 'sea' + 'bright'. It is often Anglicized as MURIEL.
Cognates: Irish Gaelic: **Muirgheal, Muiríol**.

Muireann (f.) Irish Gaelic: traditional name, apparently composed of the elements *muir* sea + *fionn* white, fair. The spelling **Muirinn** is also used, and there has been considerable confusion with both MAUREEN and MOREEN.
Cognate: Scottish Gaelic: **Mora(i)nn**.

Muiriartach (m.) Irish Gaelic: a modern form of earlier *Muicheachtach*, originally a byname meaning 'seaman, mariner'.
Variant: **Briartach**.
Anglicized form: MORTIMER.
Pet form: **Murty**.

Muiris (m.) Irish form of MAURICE. In part it also represents a contracted form of Gaelic **Muirgheas**, composed of the elements *muir* sea + *gus* choice.

Muirne (f.) Irish Gaelic: traditional name, originally a byname meaning 'beloved'.
Anglicized forms: **Myrna, Morna**,

Mungo (m.) Scottish: of uncertain derivation. It is recorded as the byname of St Kentigern, the 6th-century apostle of south-west Scotland and north-west England, and glossed in Latin by his biographer as *carissimus amicus* 'dearest friend', although it does not correspond to any Gaelic elements with this meaning.
Variant: **Munga** (Gaelic).

Murdo (m.) Scottish (Highland): Anglicized spelling of the Gaelic name *Muireadhach* (now **Murchadh**), apparently a derivative of *muir* sea.
Variant: **Murdoch**.
Pet forms: **Murdy, Murdie, Murdanie**.
Feminine forms: **Murdag, Murdann, Murdina, Dina**.

Murgatroyd (m.) English: from the Yorkshire surname, in origin a local name from an unidentified place named as 'the clearing (Yorkshire dialect *royd*) belonging to (a certain) *Margaret*'.

Muriel (f.) English: of Celtic origin; see MUIREALL. Forms of the name are found in Breton as well as in Scottish and Irish Gaelic, and in the Middle Ages it was in use even in the heart of England, having been introduced from various sources; the surname *Merrill* is derived from it. See also MERIEL.

Murray (m.) Scottish (now also used in England, America, and elsewhere): 1. Transferred use of the Scottish surname, originally a local name derived from the region now called *Moray*.

2. Anglicized form of the Gaelic name **Muireach**, a contracted form of *Muireadhach* (see MURDO).
Variant (of 2): **Moray**.

Murty (m.) Irish: pet form of MUIRIARTACH.

Myfanwy (f.) Welsh: name composed of the Welsh affectionate prefix *my-* + *banwy*, a variant form of *banw*, related to *benyw* or *menyw* woman. Its popularity dates only from relatively recent times, when specifically Welsh names have been sought as tokens of Welsh national identity.

Short forms: **Myf(f)** (in English use); **Myf**.

Myles (m.) 1. English: variant spelling of MILES.

2. Irish: Anglicized form of Gaelic MAOLRA.

3. Scottish: Anglicized form of Gaelic *Maoilios* (see MAOILÍOSA).

Myra (f.) English: invented in the 17th century by the poet Fulke Greville (1554–1628). It is impossible to guess what models he had consciously or unconsciously in mind, but it has been variously conjectured that the name is an anagram of MARY; that it is a simplified spelling of Latin *myrrha* myrrh, unguent; and that it is connected with Latin *mīrāri* to admire or wonder at (cf. MIRANDA). In the Highlands of Scotland this name is now sometimes used as an Anglicized form of *Mairead* (see MAIRÉAD), being almost identical in pronunciation with it.

Myriam (f.) French and English: variant of MIRIAM. This is the usual spelling of the name in France.

Myrna (f.) Irish and English: Anglicized form of Gaelic MUIRNE, now also used elsewhere in the English-speaking world.

Variant: **Morna**.

Myron (m.) English: from a classical Greek name, derived from Greek *myron* myrrh. The name was borne by a famous sculptor of the 5th century BC. It was taken up with particular enthusiasm by the early Christians because they associated it with the gift of myrrh made by the three kings to the infant Christ, and because of the association of myrrh (as an embalming spice) with death and eternal life. The name was borne by various early saints, notably a 3rd-century martyr of Cyzicus and a 4th-century bishop of Crete. Their cult is greater in the Eastern Church than the Western.

Myrtle (f.) English: from the word denoting the plant (Old French *myrtille*, Late Latin *myrtilla*, a diminutive of classical Latin *myrta*). This is one of the group of plant names that became popular as female names in the late 19th century.

Myslík (m.) Czech: pet form of *Přemysl* (see PRZEMYSŁ).

N

Nacek (m.) Polish: pet form of *Ignacy* (see IGNATIUS).

Nácek (m.) Czech: pet form of *Ignác* (see IGNATIUS).

Nacho (m.) Spanish: pet form of *Ignacio* (see IGNATIUS).

Nacio (m.) Spanish: short form of *Ignacio* (see IGNATIUS).

Nadezhda (f.) Russian: from the vocabulary word meaning 'hope', an important theological virtue.

Cognates: Polish: **Nadzieja**. Czech: **Naděžda**. See also REMÉNYKE

Pet forms: Russian: **Nadya**. Czech: **Naděja**.

Nadia (f.) French and English spelling of Russian *Nadya* (see NADEZHDA). This name has enjoyed a considerable vogue in the English-speaking world in the 20th century.

Variant: **Nadja** (German).

Nadine (f.) French: elaboration of NADIA. Many names of Russian origin became established in France and elsewhere in the early 20th century as a result of the popularity of the Ballet Russe, established in Paris by Diaghilev in 1909.

Nahman (m.) Jewish: an Aramaic-influenced form of NAHUM 'comforter', from the same root as MENAHEM. This name has been in use from the Middle Ages to the present day.

Nahum (m.) Biblical name, meaning 'comforter' in Hebrew, borne by a prophet of the 7th century BC. He was the author of the book of the Bible that bears his name, in which he prophesies the downfall of Nineveh, which fell in 612 BC. This is a well-established Jewish name, which was also popular among 17th-century Puritans in England. It was borne by the minor Restoration dramatist Nahum Tate (1652–1715), who rewrote Shakespeare's *King Lear* with a happy ending. See also NAHMAN and MENAHEM.

Derivative: Russian: **Naum**.

Naldo (m.) Italian: short form of various given names ending in these syllables, as, for example, RINALDO.

Nan (f.) English: originally a pet form of ANN (for the initial *N*-, cf. NED). It is now generally used as a short form of NANCY.

Pet forms: Scottish: **Nanny** (Gaelic **Nandag**).

Nancy (f.) English: of uncertain origin. From the 18th century it was used as a pet form of ANN (cf. NAN), but it may originally have been a similar formation deriving from the common medieval given name ANNIS. Nowadays it is an independent name, and was especially popular in America between about 1920 and 1960. In the 1980s it came to prominence as the name of President Reagan's wife.

Nando (m.) Italian: short form of various given names ending in these syllables, as, for example, *Ferdinando* (see FERDINAND).

Nándor (m.) Hungarian form of FERDINAND.

Nandru (m.) Romanian form of FERDINAND.

Nanette (f.) English: elaboration of NAN, with the addition of the French feminine diminutive suffix *-ette*.

Nanna (f.) Scandinavian: from the Old Norse mythological woman's name *Nanna*, a derivative of the element *nanþ* daring.

Nanne (m.) Swedish: originally a short form of the Old Norse personal name *Nannulf*, composed of the elements *nanþ* daring + *ulfr* wolf. Nowadays it is used as a pet form of ANDERS.

Naoise (m.) Irish Gaelic: name of uncertain derivation, borne, according to legend, by the lover of Deirdre, who was pursued and murdered by Conchobhar, King of Ulster. The story goes that after Naoise's death, Deirdre died of a broken heart.

Naomi (f.) Biblical name (meaning 'pleasantness' in Hebrew) of the wise mother-in-law of Ruth. The name has long been regarded as typically Jewish, but recently has begun to come into more general use.

Derivatives: French: **Noémie**. Italian: NOEMI.

Naphtali (m.) Biblical: name, probably meaning 'wrestling' in Hebrew, borne by one of the sons of Jacob. The traditional explanation is given in the following quotation: 'and Rachel said, with great wrestlings have I wrestled with my sister, and I have prevailed: and she called his name Naphtali' (Genesis 30: 8). See also ZVI.

Nápla (f.) Irish Gaelic: name derived in the early Middle Ages from Anglo-Norman *Anable*, *Anaple* (see ANNABEL).

Napoleon (m.) Occasionally bestowed in modern times in honour of the French emperor Napoleon Bonaparte (1769–1821), who was born in Corsica into a family that was ultimately of Italian origin. **Napoleone** is a rare Italian given name, used in the Abruzzo, Latium, Umbria, and Tuscany. It is probably of Germanic origin, perhaps connected with the name of the elvish *Nibelungen* 'sons of the mist' (cf. modern German *Nebel*). It was later altered by association with Italian *Napoli* Naples (Greek *nea polis* new city) and *leone* lion.

Narcissus (m.) Latin form of the Greek name *Narkissos*. In classical mythology, Narcissus was a beautiful youth who fell in love with his own reflection in a pool of water and remained there transfixed until he faded away and turned into a flower. The legend purports to account for the name of the flower, a kind of lily, known in Greek as *narkissos*. The name is almost certainly of pre-Greek origin, but attempts have been made to link it with Greek *narkē* numbness. The vocabulary word in English and horticultural Latin denotes the genus of flowers that includes the daffodil. The name was common among slaves and freedmen in the early Christian era, and a Roman citizen bearing this name is mentioned in St Paul's Epistle to the Romans (16: 11). One St Narcissus was bishop of Jerusalem in 195; another was a Spanish bishop put to death at Gerona under Diocletian in *c.*307.

Derivatives: Italian, Spanish, Portuguese: **Narciso**. Catalan: **Narcis**. French: **Narcisse**. Polish: **Narcyz**.

Feminine form (rare): **Narcissa**.

Nastasia (f.) Eastern European: short form of ANASTASIA.

Nastya (f.) Russian: pet form of ANASTASIA.

Cognates: Polish: **Nastka**, **Nastusia**. Czech: **Nast'a**.

Nat (m.) English: short form of NATHAN and NATHANIEL.

Natalie (f.) French form of NATALYA, adopted from Russian in the early 20th century, probably, like NADINE, under the influence of Diaghilev's Ballet Russe, which was established in Paris in 1909. The name is now very common in France and in the English-speaking world, where it was borne by the actress Natalie Wood (1938–82). She was born Natasha Gurdin, in San Francisco. Her father was of Russian descent, her mother of French extraction.

Variant: **Nathalie**.

Natalya (f.) Russian: from the Late Latin name *Natālia*, a derivative of Latin *natālis* (*diēs*) birthday, especially Christ's birthday, i.e. Christmas; cf. NOËL. St Natalia was a Christian inhabitant of Nicomedia who is said to have given succour to the martyrs, including her husband Adrian, who suffered there in persecutions under Diocletian in 303. She is regarded as a

Christian saint, although she was not herself martyred.

Pet forms: **Talya**, NATASHA.

Natasha (f.) Russian: pet form of NATALYA, now widely adopted as an independent name in the English-speaking world and elsewhere. Like *Noëlle* (see NOËL), it is sometimes given to girls born on or about Christmas Day.

Short form (in the English-speaking world): **Tasha**.

Nathan (m.) Biblical name, meaning 'he (God) has given' in Hebrew (cf. NATHANIEL). This was the name of a prophet who had the courage to reproach King David for arranging the death in battle of Uriah the Hittite in order to get possession of the latter's wife Bathsheba (2 Samuel 12: 1–15). It was also the name of one of David's own sons. In modern times this name has often been taken as a short form of *Nathaniel* or of JONATHAN.

Nathaniel (m.) English form of a New Testament name, which is derived from the Greek form of a Hebrew name meaning 'God has given' (cf. NATHAN, which is sometimes taken as a short form of this name). It was borne by one of the less prominent of Christ's apostles (John 1: 45; 21: 2), who in fact is probably identical with BARTHOLOMEW. The spelling used in the Authorized Version of the New Testament is **Nathanael**, but this has never been common as a given name in the English-speaking world. The biblical form of the Old Testament name is *Nethaneel*; it was the name of the prince of the tribe of Issachar at the time of the Exodus (Numbers 1: 8). The name is little used in other European languages.

Cognate: Italian: **Natanaele**.

Natividad (f.) Spanish: religious name name referring to the festival of the Nativity (Spanish *natividad*, from Late Latin *nativitās*, a derivative of *nasci* to be born) of the Virgin Mary. This has been celebrated (on 5 September) since the 5th century in the Eastern Church, since the 7th century in the Western.

Short form: **Nati**.

Naughton (m.) Scottish: Anglicized form of the Gaelic name **Neachdann**, a derivative of *necht* pure. From this personal name comes the surname *Mac Neachdainn*, Anglicized as *MacNaughton*.

Naum (m.) Russian form of NAHUM. Its popularity has been influenced by popular etymological analysis as a compound of the Russian prefix *na* + the adjective *umny* clever, intelligent.

Nazaret (f.) Spanish: religious name, referring to Christ's native village, *Nazareth*. The placename seems to have been derived from a word meaning 'branch' in Hebrew.

Nazario (m.) Italian, Spanish, and Portuguese: from the Late Latin name *Nazarius*, a derivative of *Nazareth* (cf. NAZARET). The name was a relatively common one among early Christians and was borne by several saints, most notably one martyred with Celsus at Milan in the 1st century.

Cognate: French: **Nazaire**.

Nea (f.) Swedish: short form of LINNÉA.

Neacal (m.) Scottish Gaelic form of NICHOLAS.

Neal (m.) English: variant of NEIL, influenced by the surname in this spelling.

Neassa (f.) Irish Gaelic: traditional name of uncertain derivation. In ancient Irish legend, it was borne by the mother of Conchobhar Mac Neassa, King of Ulster.

Ned (m.) English: short form of EDWARD, originating in the misdivision of phrases such as *mine Ed* (cf. NAN). It was common in the Middle Ages and up to the 18th century, but in the 19th was almost entirely superseded in the role of short form by TED. It is now, however, enjoying a modest revival.

Neil (m.) Irish, Scottish, and English: Anglicized form of the enduringly popular

Gaelic name **Niall**. Its derivation is disputed, and it may mean 'cloud', 'passionate', or perhaps 'champion'. It was adopted by the Scandinavians in the form *Njal* and soon became very popular among them. From the Middle Ages onwards, this name was found mainly in Ireland and the English-Scottish Border region. However, in the 20th century it has spread to enjoy great popularity in all parts of the English-speaking world.

Variant: **Neal**. See also NIGEL.

Pet form: Scottish (Highland): **Neillie**.

Feminine form: Scottish (Highland): **Neilina**.

Nekane (f.) Basque equivalent of DOLORES.

Nell (f.) English: short form of ELEANOR, ELLEN, and HELEN; of medieval origin, but now also established as a given name in its own right. For an explanation of the initial *N*-, cf. NED. It was the name by which Charles II's mistress Eleanor Gwyn (1650–87) was universally known to her contemporaries, and at about that time it also became established as an independent name.

Cognate: Irish Gaelic: **Neile**.

Pet forms: English: **Nellie, Nelly**.

Nelleke (f.) Dutch: pet form derived from a short form of CORNELIA.

Nels (m.) S. Swedish: dialectal form of NILS.

Nelson (m.) English: transferred use of the surname, which originated as a patronymic from either NEIL or NELL. Use as a given name probably began as a tribute to the British admiral Lord Nelson (1758–1805), the victor of the Battle of Trafalgar; cf. HORATIO. It is, however, now much more common in America than in Britain.

Nelya (f.) Russian: pet form of both YELENA and NINEL.

Nena (f.) English: variant spelling of NINA.

Nepomuk (m.) Czech: name bestowed in honour of St John of Nepomuk (*c.*1345–93). Born at Nepomuk in Bohemia, he became chaplain at the court of King Wenceslas IV, and was killed by the king, allegedly for refusing to disclose what the queen had revealed in confession. The given name is also used to some extent among Catholics in Germany and Austria.

Short form: **Pomuk**.

Pet form: **Nepomuček**.

Nereida (f.) Latinate name derived from Greek *nērēis* (genitive *nērēidos*) nymph, sea sprite (in origin a patronymic from *Nēreus* god of the ocean).

Nerina (f.) Italian: of uncertain origin. It seems to have arisen as a feminine form of the obsolete *Nerino*, a diminutive of NERO or possibly of NERIO. Alternatively, it may represent a Latinized form of Greek *Nērinē*, derived from the name of the sea god *Nēreus* (cf. NEREIDA and NERISSA).

Nerio (m.) Italian: from Greek *Nēreus*, the name (of uncertain derivation) of a divinity of the sea. This was the name in the 1st century of a Roman soldier who was baptized by St Paul and exiled with Sts Achilleus and Flavia.

Nerissa (f.) English: of Shakespearian origin. It is the name of a minor character in *The Merchant of Venice*, Portia's waiting woman, who marries Gratiano. The name seems to represent a Latinate elaboration of Greek *nērēis* nymph, sea sprite (see NEREIDA).

Nero (m.) Tuscan: short form of RANIERO, not connected with the name of the Roman emperor Nero.

Nerys (f.) Welsh: of uncertain derivation, perhaps intended to be from Welsh *nêr* lord, with the suffix *-ys* by analogy with other female names such as DILYS and GLADYS. This was not used as a given name in the Middle Ages, and dates only from the recent Welsh cultural revival; this has been accompanied by a spate of modern coinages of Welsh names, enabling Welsh parents to give their children names reflecting their national identity.

Neša (f.) Czech: pet form of ANEŽKA.
Variant: **Neška**.

Nessa (f.) 1 English: originally a short form of *Agnessa*, a Latinate form of AGNES. In modern use in the English-speaking world it is more often a short form of VANESSA, and is also used as an independent given name.

2. Irish Gaelic: older form of NEASSA.

3. Jewish: apparently from Hebrew *nes* banner, miracle.
Pet form: **Nessie**.

Nesta (f.) Welsh: Latinized version of **Nest**, a Welsh pet form of AGNES. Nesta was the name of the grandmother of the 12th-century chronicler Giraldus Cambrensis ('Gerald the Welshman').

Nestore (m.) Italian: from the Greek personal name *Nestōr*, possibly a derivative of *nostos* homecoming. In Homer's *Iliad*, Nestor is one of the leaders of the Greeks at Troy, the aged but still vigorous king of Pylos. The name had some currency among early Christians and was borne by several early martyrs.

Neta (f.) Swedish: short form of *Agneta* (see AGNETHE).

Netta (f.) English: apparently a Latinate variant of NETTIE, though in Gaelic Scotland it is more likely to represent a feminine form of NEIL.

Nettie (f.) English: pet form derived from various female names ending in the syllable *-nette*, for example ANNETTE and JEANNETTE, with the hypocoristic suffix *-ie*. It had a brief vogue in the late 19th and early 20th centuries.

Neves (f.) Portuguese form of NIEVES.

Neville (m.) English: transferred use of the surname, which is derived from a Norman baronial name from any of several places in Normandy called *Néville* or *Neuville* 'new settlement'. First used as a given name in the early 17th century, and with increasing regularity from the second half of the 19th, it is now so firmly established as a given name that it has lost touch with its origin as a surname.

Ngaio (f.) New Zealand: from the name of a type of tree cultivated for its wood, originally named in Maori.

Niall (m.) Irish and Scottish Gaelic: original spelling of NEIL. It has been strongly revived among non-Gaelic speakers in the 20th century.

Niallghus (m.) Scottish Gaelic: a compound of NIALL + *gus* strength. From this derives the surname *Mac Niallghuis*, Anglicized as *MacNeillage*.

Niamh (f.) Irish Gaelic: name meaning 'brightness, beauty'. It was borne in Irish mythology by the daughter of the sea god, who fell in love with the youthful Oisín, son of Finn MacCool, and carried him off over the sea to the land of perpetual youth, Tír na nÓg. It is now a very popular given name in Ireland.

Nicanor (m.) Spanish: from the Late Greek name *Nikanōr*. This is probably a byform of the earlier name *Nikandēr*, which is composed of the elements *nikē* victory + *anēr* man (genitive *andros*). It was the name of one of the Hellenized Jews chosen as deacons by the apostles (Acts 6: 5). One of the gates of the temple in Jesusalem was known as 'Nicanor's Gate', apparently after an official who was governor of Jerusalem in the 2nd century AD.

Nicasio (m.) Spanish: from the Late Greek personal name *Nikasios*. This seems to be a derivative of *Nikasia*, the name of a tiny island near Naxos. St Nicasius was a bishop of Rheims who was martyred either by the Vandals in 407 or by the Huns in 451.
Cognate: Catalan: **Nicasi**.

Nicholas (m.) English and French: from the post-classical Greek personal name *Nikolaos*, composed of the elements *nikē* victory + *laos* people. The spelling with *-ch-* first occurred as early as the 12th century, and became firmly established at the time of the Reformation, although *Nicolas* is still occasionally found. St Nicholas was a 4th-century bishop of Myra in Lycia, about whom virtually nothing factual is known, although a vast body of legend grew up around him, and he became the patron saint of Greece and Russia, as well as of children, sailors, merchants, and pawnbrokers. His feast-day is 6 December, and among the many roles which legend has assigned to him is that of bringer of Christmas presents, in the guise of 'Santa Claus' (an alteration of the Dutch form of his name, *Sinterklaas*).

Variant: **Nicolas**.

Cognates: Scottish: NICOL; **Neacal** (Gaelic). Irish Gaelic: **Nioclas**. Italian: **Nicola, Nic(c)olò**. Spanish: **Nicolás, Nicolao**. Catalan: **Nicolau, Micolau**. Portuguese: **Nicolau**. German: **Nikolaus, Niklaus**. Scandinavian: **Niklas**; **Nils** (Swedish, Norwegian); **Niels** (Danish). Finnish: **Launo**. Russian: **Nikolai**. Polish: **Mikołaj**. Czech: **Mikoláš**. Romanian: **Nicolae**. Hungarian: **Miklós**. Finnish: **Niilo**.

Short forms: English: **Nick**. German: **Klaus, Claus**. Dutch: **Claus**.

Pet forms: English: **Nicky**. Swedish: **Nisse**. Russian: **Kolya**.

Feminine forms: English (Latinate): NICOLA. French, English: NICOLE. Spanish: **Nicolasa**.

Nicky (m., f.) English: 1. (m.) Pet form of *Nick* (see NICHOLAS).

2. (f.) Variant of NIKKI.

Nico (m., f.) 1. (m.) Italian: short form of *Nicolò* (see NICHOLAS) or of the rarer *Nicodemo* (see NICODÈME), NICOMEDO, or NICOSTRATO.

2. (m., f.) English: short form of both NICHOLAS and NICOLA (cf. e.g. *Ludo* and *Caro*).

Nicodème (m.) French: from Greek *Nikodēmos*, composed of the elements *nikē* victory + *dēmos* people, population. This is the name borne in the New Testament by one of the leading Greek Jews who spoke up for Jesus at his trial (John 7: 50) and was present at his burial (John 19: 39).

Cognate: Italian, Spanish, Portuguese: **Nicodemo**.

Nicol (m.) Scottish and English: common medieval form of NICHOLAS, current until a relatively late period in Scotland, and now being revived in more general use. Modern use as a given name may owe something to the character Bailie Nicol Jarvie in Sir Walter Scott's novel *Rob Roy*.

Variants: **Nichol, Nic(h)oll**.

Nicola (f., m.) 1. (f.) English: Latinate feminine form of NICHOLAS.

2. (m.) Italian form of NICHOLAS; see also NICOLÒ.

Nicole (f.) French: feminine form of NICHOLAS, now increasingly common in the English-speaking world.

Pet form: **Nicolette** (also used as a given name in its own right in both France and the English-speaking world).

Nicolò (m.) Italian: variant form of the male name *Nicola* (see NICHOLAS).

Variant: **Niccolò**.

Nicomedo (m.) Italian: from Greek *Nikomēdēs*, composed of the elements *nikē* victory + *mēdesthai* to ponder, scheme. St Nicomedes was a Roman priest martyred during the 1st century.

Nicostrato (m.) Italian: from Greek *Nikostratos*, composed of the elements *nikē* victory + *stratos* army. St Nicostratos was the leader of a group of Roman soldiers martyred in Palestine under the Emperor Diocletian (*c.*303).

Niels (m.) 1. Danish form of NICHOLAS (cf. NILS).

2. Dutch: short form of CORNELIS.

Nieves (f.) Spanish: from a title of the Virgin Mary, *Nuestra Señora de las Nieves* 'Our Lady of the Snows'. The name refers to a miracle alleged to have taken place in the 4th century, when Mary caused it to snow in Rome during August.

Cognate: Portuguese: **Neves**.

Nigel (m.) English: Anglicized form of the medieval name *Nigellus*, a Latinized version (ostensibly representing a diminutive

of Latin *niger* black) of the vernacular *Ni(h)el*, i.e. NEIL. Although it is frequently found in medieval records, this form was probably not used in everyday life before its revival by antiquarians such as Sir Walter Scott in the 19th century.
Feminine: **Nigella**.

Niilo (m.) Finnish form of NICHOLAS.

Nikita (m.) Russian: from the Greek name *Anikētos* 'unconquered, unconquerable' (from the negative prefix *a-* + *nikān* to conquer). This was the name of an early pope (*c.*152–60); he was a Syrian by descent and is particularly honoured in the Eastern Church.

Nikki (f.) English: pet form of NICOLA, now sometimes used as an independent given name.
Variants: **Nicki, Nickie, Nicky**.

Nikolai (m.) Russian form of NICHOLAS.
Pet form: **Kolya**.

Nikolaus (m.) German form of NICHOLAS.
Variant: **Niklaus**.

Nille (f.) Scandinavian (esp. Danish): short form of *Pernille* (see PERNILLA).

Nils (m.) Swedish form of NICHOLAS.
Variant: S. Swedish: **Nels**.
Feminine form: **Nilsine**.

Nina (f.) Russian: short form of ANTONINA, now commonly used as an independent name in the French- and English-speaking worlds, as well as in Russia.
Variant: English: **Nena**.

Ninel (f.) Russian: modern coinage adopted by patriotic Soviet citizens, representing *Lenin* spelled backwards (cf. VLADILEN).
Pet form: **Nelya**.

Ninette (f.) French: diminutive form of NINA. Like NADINE, this was one of the names brought to the English-speaking world from Russian via French in the early 20th century.

Ninian (m.) Scottish and Irish: of uncertain origin. This was the name of a 5th-century British saint who was responsible for evangelizing the northern Britons and the Picts. His name first appears in the Latinized form *Ninianus* in the 8th century; this appears to be the same as the *Nynnyaw* recorded in the *Mabinogi*. The given name was used in his honour until at least the 16th century in Scotland and has recently been revived.

Nino (m.) Italian: short form of *Giannino*, a pet form of GIANNI.

Ninon (f.) French: 1. Pet form of ANNE. The most famous bearer of this name was the celebrated Parisian beauty Ninon de Lenclos (1620–1705).
2. Pet form of NINA.

Nioclás (m.) Irish Gaelic form of NICHOLAS.

Nisse (m.) Swedish: pet form of NILS.

Nita (f.) English: short form of various names that end in these syllables, as for example ANITA and *Marganita* (see MARGARET).

Niven (m.) Scottish: Anglicized form of the Gaelic name **Naoimhean** or *Gille Naomh*, a borrowing of Irish *Gille na Naomh* 'servant of the saint'.

Njord (m.) Scandinavian: from the name of a minor Norse divinity, recorded in the form *Nerthus* by the Roman historian Tacitus in the 1st century AD. It is of uncertain derivation, but was revived as a given name in the early 19th century.

Noah (m.) English form of the name of the biblical character whose family was the only one saved from the great Flood ordained by God to destroy mankind because of its wickedness. The origin of the name is far from certain; in the Bible it is implied that it means 'rest' (Genesis 5: 29, 'and he called his name Noah, saying, This same shall comfort us concerning our work and the toil of our hands, because of the ground which the Lord hath cursed'). One tradition indeed explains it as derived from the Hebrew root meaning 'to comfort' (see NAHUM) with the final consonant dropped.

Cognate: French: **Noë**.

Noam (m.) Jewish: modern name, from a Hebrew vocabulary word meaning 'delight, joy, pleasantness' (cf. NAOMI, from the same Hebrew root). Its most famous bearer is the American linguist Noam Chomsky (b. 1928).

Noble (m.) English (esp. U.S.): name derived from the modern English adjective (via Old French from Latin *nobilis*). The idea behind it may have been to hint at high-born origin (cf. DUKE, EARL, KING, and PRINCE) or to suggest qualities of character. In part there may be some influence from the surname, which arose in the Middle Ages as a descriptive nickname in the first sense.

Noël (m.) French: from Old French *noel*, *nael* Christmas, from Latin *natālis diēs* (*Domini*) birthday (of the Lord). The meaning is still relatively transparent, partly because the term occurs as a synonym for 'Christmas' in the refrain of well-known carols. The name is often given to children born at Christmas time. It is also used in the English-speaking world, normally without the diaeresis, **Noel**.

Feminine forms: **Noëlle, Noelle**.

Noemi (f.) Italian form of NAOMI, derived from the representation of the Hebrew name used in the Latin translation of the Vulgate.

Cognate: French: **Noémie**.

Noga (f.) Jewish: modern Israeli female name. In the Authorized Version the form *Nogah* occurs as the name of a man, one of David's sons born in Jerusalem (1 Chronicles 3: 7). The name derives from a Hebrew word meaning 'brightness'.

Nola (f.) Irish and Australian: probably a name created as a feminine form of NOLAN. It may also represent a short form of Gaelic *Fionn*(*gh*)*uala*; see FENELLA and FINOLA.

Nolan (m.) Australian, Irish, and English: from the Irish surname, Gaelic *Ó Nualláin* 'descendant of Nuallán'. *Nuallán* is an old Gaelic personal name, apparently originally a byname representing a diminutive of *nuall* chariot-fighter, champion.

Nolasco (m.) Italian: name adopted in honour of St Peter Nolasco (*c.*1189–1258), who founded the order of Our Lady of Ransom with the purpose of obtaining the release of Christians captured by the Moors during the Crusades.

Nolene (f.) Mainly Australian: name created as a feminine form of NOLAN.

Variant: **Noleen**.

Noll (m.) English: pet form of OLIVER, frequent in the Middle Ages and occasionally revived in modern times. The initial consonant seems to derive from a misdivision of a vocative phrase; cf. NED.

Nona (f.) English: from the feminine form of the Latin ordinal *nonus* ninth, sometimes used as a given name in Victorian times for the ninth-born child in a family if it was a girl, or even for the ninth-born girl. At the present day, when few people have nine children, let alone nine girls, it has passed into more general, if only occasional, use.

Nonie (f.) English: pet form of IONE or of NORA, also used to a limited extent as an independent given name.

Variant: **Noni**.

Nora (f.) English, Irish, Scottish and Scandinavian: short form of names such as *Eleonara* (see ELEANOR), *Honora* (see HONOUR), and LEONORA. Although these are not Gaelic in origin, *Nora* (Gaelic **Nóra**) was particularly associated with Ireland at one time. In the Scottish Highlands it is used as a feminine form of NORMAN. In Scandinavia the name is known particularly as that borne by the heroine of Henrik Ibsen's play *A Doll's House*.

Variant: **Norah**.

Norbert (m.) English: of Norman origin, and so ultimately Germanic, composed of the elements *nord* north + *berht* bright, famous. Its best-known bearer was an 11th-century saint who founded an order of monks known as Norbertians (also called Premonstratensians from their first home at Premontré near Laon). *Norbert* was one of several names of Germanic origin that were revived in Britain in the late 19th century, but it is now rather more common in America than Britain.

Noreen (f.) Irish and English: originally an Anglicized form of the Gaelic name **Nóirín**, a diminutive of *Nóra* (see NORA). It is now used as an independent given name in the English-speaking world.

Variants: **Norene, Norine**.

Norma (f.) Italian and English: apparently invented by Felice Romani in his libretto for Bellini's opera of this name (first performed in 1832). It is identical in form with Latin *norma* rule, standard, but there is no evidence that this word was the actual source of the name. In recent times, it has come to be taken in England and the Scottish Highlands as a feminine equivalent of NORMAN.

Norman (m.) English: of Germanic origin, composed of the elements *nord* north + *man* man, i.e. 'Norseman'. This name was found in England before the Conquest, and was reinforced by its use among the Norman invaders themselves. In the Scottish Highlands it is used as the Anglicized equivalent of TORMOD.

Pet form: Scottish: **Norrie**.

Feminine forms: Scottish (Highland): **Normanna, Normina, Norma, Nora, Mona**.

Norris (m.) English: transferred use of the surname, which is derived from Old Norman French *norreis* (in which the stem represents the Germanic element *nord*), originally a local designation for someone who had migrated from the north.

Notger (m.) German: from an old Germanic personal name composed of the elements *nōt* need, want + *gār, gēr* spear. The form **Notker** is a variant of this. The Blessed Notker Balbulus ('the Stammerer') was a Benedictine monk at the abbey of St Gall in Switzerland in the 10th century; he composed a biography of Charlemagne.

Nuala (f.) Irish: short form of the Gaelic name FIONNUALA. It is now in general use as an independent given name.

Nunzia (f.) Italian: short form of ANNUNZIATA.

Pet forms: **Nunziatella, Nunziatina**.

Masculine form: Italian (characteristic of S. Italy): **Nunzio**.

Nuria (f.) Catalan: from a title of the Virgin Mary, *Nuestra Señora de Nuria* 'Our Lady of Nuria'. Nuria is a place in the province of Gerona, where there is a famous image of the Virgin. This was long venerated as a 'black madonna', but cleaning in the 1940s removed the grime that had come from centuries of smoking candles, and restored the original bright colours.

Nušek (m.) Czech: pet form of HANUŠ, preserving only a single letter of the base form *Jan*.

Nye (m.) Pet form of the Welsh name ANEIRIN, representing the middle syllable of that name as commonly pronounced. The name is particularly associated with the Welsh Labour statesman Aneurin Bevan (1897–1960).

Nyree (f.) English spelling of a Maori name usually transcribed as **Ngaire**, the origin of which is obscure. It is relatively common in New Zealand and has been taken up to some extent in Britain due to the fame of the New Zealand-born actress Nyree Dawn Porter (b. 1940).

O

Obadiah (m.) English: from a biblical name meaning 'servant of God' in Hebrew (cf. Arabic *Abdullah*, which has the same meaning). This was the name of a prophet who gave his name to one of the shorter books of the Bible, and of two other minor biblical characters: a porter in the temple (Nehemiah 12: 25), and the man who introduced King Ahab to the prophet Elijah (1 Kings 18).

Variant: Modern Hebrew: **Ovadia**.

Oberon (m.) English: variant spelling of AUBERON.

Octavia (f.) English: of Latin origin, representing a feminine form of OCTAVIUS. It was borne by various female members of the Roman imperial family.

Cognate: Italian: **Ottavia**.

Octavian (m.) Usual English form of the Latin name *Octāviānus*, a derivative of OCTAVIUS. The first Roman emperor, now generally known by the imperial title *Augustus*, was born Caius Octavius; when he was adopted by Julius Caesar he became Caius Julius Caesar Octavianus. Another Octavianus was a 5th-century Carthaginian saint who was put to death with several thousand companions by the Asiatic Vandal king Hunneric.

Octavius (m.) English: from the Roman family name, derived from Latin *octāvus* eighth. The name was fairly frequently given to a male eighth child (or eighth son) in large Victorian families. It is much less common these days, when families rarely extend to eight children, but is occasionally selected for reasons of family tradition or for some other reason without regard to its original meaning.

Cognate: Italian: **Ottavio**.

Odd (m.) Scandinavian: from an Old Norse personal name, originally perhaps a byname, derived from the vocabulary word *oddr* point (of a weapon).

Oded (m.) Jewish: Hebrew name, meaning 'upholder, encourager', borne in the Bible by a prophet who persuaded the Israelites to release the captives that they had taken from the kingdom of Judah (2 Chronicles 28: 9–15). It is a popular modern Hebrew name.

Odette (f.) French: feminine diminutive form of the Old French masculine name *Oda*, which is of Germanic origin (cf. OTTO). Although the original male name has dropped out of use, this feminine derivative has survived and is now used as a given name in its own right.

Odile (f.) French: from the medieval Germanic name *Odila* (a derivative of the vocabulary element *od* riches, prosperity, fortune; cf. OTTO). This was the name of an 8th-century saint who founded a Benedictine convent at what is now Odilienburg in Alsace. She is the patron saint of Alsace. See also OTTILIE.

Ödön (m.) Hungarian form of EDMUND. The infant Anglo-Saxon princes Edward and Edmund, sons of Edmund Ironside, were sent away from England by the usurping Canute. They eventually settled in Hungary, where they were granted large estates by King Andrew I.

Ofra (f.) Jewish: variant spelling of OPHRAH.

Oighrig (f.) Scottish Gaelic: name of uncertain derivation, apparently from an earlier form *Aithbhreac* meaning 'new speckled one'. It has commonly been Anglicized as ERICA, EFRIC, EFFIE and EUPHEMIA, formerly also as AFRICA. See also EITHRIG and EIRIC.

Okko (m.) Finnish: pet form of *Oskari* (see OSCAR).

Oktyabrina (f.) Russian: name adopted in the Soviet period, in commemoration of the October Revolution of 1917 which brought the Bolsheviks to power.

Olaf (m.) Scandinavian: from an Old Norse personal name composed of the elements *anu* ancestor + *leifr* heir, descendant. St Olaf, King of Norway (995–1030), aided the spread of Christianity in his kingdom. The name was introduced to Britain before the Norman Conquest, but modern use as a given name in the English-speaking world originated in America, where it was taken by recent Scandinavian immigrants.

Variants: Swedish: OLOF, **Olov**, **Oluf**. Norwegian and SW Swedish: **Ola**. Norwegian and Danish: **Olav**, **Ole**. Finnish: **Olavi**. See also AMHLAOIBH.

Olalla (f.) Spanish form of EULALIA. The name was borne by two famous Spanish martyrs, Eulalia of Barcelona (d. 304) and Eulalia of Mérida (d. 364); it is possible that they were identical.

Oldřich (m.) Czech form of ULRICH.

Feminine form: **Oldriška**.

Pet forms: **Oldra**, **Olda** (m., f.); **Oldřišek**, **Oleček**, **Olík**, **Oloušek**, **Olin** (m.); **Oldřina**, **Olina**, **Oluše**, **Riška** (f.).

Oleg (m.) Russian form of HELGE. This name was introduced to Russia by the earliest Scandinavian settlers, and was borne by Prince Oleg of Kiev (d. 912), the Varangian leader who established Kiev as his capital in place of Novgorod and set up trading links with Byzantium. Since he was not a Christian, the name has never been sanctioned by the Russian Orthodox Church, unlike its feminine equivalent, OLGA.

Oleksander (m.) Ukrainian form of ALEXANDER.

Olena (f.) Ukrainian form of HELEN.

Oleś (m.) Polish: pet form of ALEXANDER.

Variants: **Olech**, **Olek**.

Cognate: Czech: **Olexa**.

Olga (f.) Russian: feminine form of OLEG, and equivalent of HELGA, taken to Russia by the Scandinavian settlers who founded the first Russian state in the 9th century. St Olga of Kiev (d. 969) was a Varangian noblewoman who was baptized at Byzantium in about 957 and set about converting her people. The name was introduced to the English-speaking world in the late 19th century, but retains a distinctively Russian flavour. It is also much in use in Scandinavia.

Pet form: **Olya**.

Olive (f.) English: one of the earliest and most successful of the names coined during the 19th century from vocabulary words denoting plants, no doubt partly because an olive branch has been a symbol of peace since biblical times. The Latinate form **Oliva** was used as a given name in medieval times, but dropped out of use in the English-speaking world after its pronunciation became indistinguishable from that of the male name OLIVER. See also OLIVIA.

Oliver (m.) English: of Norman, and hence ultimately Germanic, origin. It was first used as the name (French *Olivier*) of one of Charlemagne's paladins or retainers, the close companion in arms of Roland in the *Chanson de Roland*. Where Roland is headstrong and rash, Oliver is thoughtful and cautious. Ostensibly this name derives from Late Latin *olivārius* olive tree (cf. OLIVE), but Charlemagne's other paladins all bear solidly Germanic names, so it is more probably an altered form of a Germanic name, perhaps a version of OLAF.

Cognates: French: **Olivier**. Scottish Gaelic: **Olghar**, **Oilbhreis**.

Pet forms: English: **Ollie**, NOLL.

Olivia (f.) English: Latinate name, first used by Shakespeare as the name of the rich heiress wooed by the duke in *Twelfth Night* (1599). Shakespeare may have taken it as a feminine form of OLIVER or he may have derived it from Latin *oliva* olive; it may also have been influenced by the medieval female given name *Oliva*, although this had dropped out of use by the 16th century.

Ollie (m.) English: pet form of OLIVER, associated particularly with the comic film actor Oliver Hardy (1892–1957), the rotund partner of Stan Laurel.

Olof (m.) Swedish form of OLAF. St Olof, King of Sweden (d. *c.*950) was murdered by his rebellious heathen subjects for refusing to sacrifice to idols.

Variants: **Olov**, **Oluf**.

Olwen (f.) Welsh: composed of the elements *ôl* footprint, track + *(g)wen* white, fair, blessed, holy. A character of this name in Welsh legend had the magical property of causing flowers to spring up behind her wherever she went.

Olya (f.) Russian: pet form of OLGA.

Olympe (f.) French: from the Latin name *Olympia*, a feminine form of *Olympius*, from Greek *Olympos*, the home, according to classical mythology, of the gods.

Omar (m.) English: biblical name borne by a character mentioned in a genealogy (Genesis 36: 11). It has been occasionally used from Puritan times down to the present day in America. More often, however, it is of Arabic origin, as in the case of the film actor and international bridge player Omar Sharif (b. 1932 in Egypt).

Omri (m.) Jewish: Hebrew name, possibly derived from an element meaning 'sheaf of grain'. It is borne in the Bible by a king of Israel who built the city of Samaria, but who also 'wrought evil in the eyes of the Lord' (1 Kings 16: 23–8). This has not prevented *Omri* from being used as a modern given name.

Ona (f.) English: apparently an aphetic short form of any of the given names ending in these letters, for example FIONA and ANONA.

Ondřej (m.) Czech form of ANDREW.

Pet forms: **Ondra**, **Ondřejek**, **Ondrášek**, **Ondroušek**.

Onisim (m.) Russian: less common form of ANISIM.

Onóra (f.) Irish Gaelic: name derived in the early Middle Ages from Anglo-Norman HONORE.

Oona (f.) Irish: Anglicized form of the Gaelic name ÚNA.

Variant: **Oonagh**.

Opal (f.) English: one of the rarer female names taken in the late 19th century from vocabulary words for gemstones. This is ultimately derived (via Latin and Greek) from an Indian language (cf. Sanskrit *upala* precious stone).

Opaline (f.) English: a comparatively recent coinage; an elaboration of OPAL with the addition of *-ine*, a productive suffix of feminine names.

Ophelia (f.) English: name of a character in Shakespeare's *Hamlet*, the beautiful daughter of Polonius; she loves Hamlet, and eventually goes mad and drowns herself. In spite of the ill omen of this literary association, the name has enjoyed moderate popularity since the 19th century. Apparently it was first used by the Italian pastoralist Jacopo Sannazzaro (1458–1530), who presumably intended it as a feminine form of the Greek name *Ōphelos* 'help'. Shakespeare seems to have borrowed the name from Sannazzaro, without considering whether it was an appropriate name for a play set in medieval Denmark.

Ophrah (f., m.) Jewish: Hebrew name meaning 'fawn'. It is borne in the Old Testament by a man (1 Chronicles 4: 14), but it is now more commonly given to girls. The spellings **Ophra** and **Ofra** are also used.

Oralie (f.) English: of uncertain origin, possibly an altered form of *Aurélie* (see AURELIA).

Variant: **Oralee**.

Oran (m.) Irish: Anglicized form of Gaelic **Odhrán**, originally a byname representing a diminutive of *odhar* dun, sallow.

The name was borne by various early saints, most notably a 6th-century abbot of Meath who accompanied Columba to Scotland.

Orazio (m.) Italian form of HORACE.

Orbán (m.) Hungarian form of URBAN.

Orell (m.) Swiss form of *Aurelius* (see AURÈLE).

Orfeo (m.) Italian: from Greek *Orpheus*, the name in classical mythology of a Thracian musician whose playing on the lyre was so beautiful that he charmed Nature itself. After his wife Eurydice died, he descended in search of her to the underworld, and charmed Hades, the king of the underworld, into allowing him to take her back to the world of the living, on condition that he should not look at her until they had regained the sunlight. He lost her again, because he looked back to check that she was behind him. The name is of very uncertain derivation, and it seems likely that the legend originally concerned a pre-Greek divinity of the natural world.

Oriana (f.) Latinate name first found in the medieval tale of *Amadis of Gaul* as the name of the daughter of Lisuarte, King of England, courted and eventually won by the model knight Amadis. It may be a derivative of Old French *or*, Spanish *oro* gold (Latin *aurum*).

Variant: French: **Oriane**.

Örjan (m.) Swedish: older form of GÖRAN, still in use as a given name.

Orla (f.) Irish: Anglicized form of the Gaelic name **Órla**, earlier *Ór (fh)laith*, composed of the elements *ór* gold + *flaith* lady, princess.

Orlando (m.) Italian form of ROLAND, occasionally used as a given name in the English-speaking world. It is the name of the hero in Shakespeare's comedy *As You Like It*.

Orna (f.) Irish: Anglicized form of the Gaelic name **Odharnait**, a feminine diminutive form of *Odhar* 'dun, sallow' (cf. ORAN). The loss of the final consonant is due to the influence of ORLA.

Ornella (f.) Italian: apparently originated by Gabriele d'Annunzio, who gave the name to one of the characters in his novel *Figlia de Iorio* (1904). It seems to represent a feminine form of the Tuscan dialect word *ornello* flowering ash tree.

Ornetta (f.) Italian: apparently an altered form of ORNELLA, with the substitution of the Italian feminine diminutive suffix *-etta* for the similarly functioning *-ella*. The name is also used in the English-speaking world.

Cognate: French: **Ornette**.

Orson (m.) English: from an Old Norman French nickname meaning 'bear-cub' (a diminutive of *ors* bear, Latin *ursus*), used occasionally in medieval times, but in modern times probably always a transferred use of the associated surname. In the 20th century it has come to public notice as a result of the fame of the American actor Orson Welles (1915–85), who dropped his more prosaic given name, George, in favour of his middle name before embarking on his acting career.

Orville (m.) English: though in appearance a surname of Norman baronial origin, this name seems to have been invented (with the intention of evoking such associations) by the novelist Fanny Burney for the hero, Lord Orville, of her novel *Evelina* (1778).

Orya (f.) Russian: pet form of IRINA and its variant ARINA.

Osane (f.) Basque equivalent of REMEDIOS.

Osbert (m.) English: from an Old English personal name composed of the elements *ōs* god + *beorht* bright, famous. It is not now common in the English-speaking world, but has been borne, for example, by the British cartoonist Osbert Lancaster and the writer Osbert Sitwell.

Osborn (m.) English: from a Late Old English personal name composed of the elements *ōs* god + *beorn* bear, warrior (both of Scandinavian origin). As a modern given name it generally represents a transferred use of the surname that was derived from this name during the Middle Ages.

Variants: **Osborne, Osbourne.**

Oscar (m.) English and Irish: name, apparently composed of the Irish Gaelic elements *os* deer + *cara* friend, borne in the Fenian sagas by a grandson of Finn McCool. It was resuscitated by the antiquarian and poet James Macpherson (1736–96). This is now also a characteristically Scandinavian name; it was introduced there because Napoleon, being an admirer of the works of Macpherson, imposed the name on his godson Oscar Bernadotte, who became King Oscar I of Sweden in 1844. In more recent times it has been associated particularly with the Irish writer and wit Oscar Wilde (1854–1900).

Cognates: Scottish Gaelic: **Osgar**. German, Scandinavian, E. European: **Oskar**. Finnish: **Oskari**.

Osheen (m.) Irish: Anglicized form of the Gaelic name **Oisín**, in origin a byname representing a diminutive form of *os* deer. This is the name altered by James Macpherson, author of the 'Ossianic' poems, to *Ossian*.

Cognate: Scottish Gaelic: **Oisein**.

Osher (m.) Jewish: variant of ASHER, representing an alternative Hebrew pronunciation of the name.

Osip (m.) Russian: vernacular form of JOSEPH.

Osmond (m.) English: 19th-century revival of an Old English personal name composed of the elements *ōs* god + *mund* protector. The name was also in use among the Normans and was borne by an 11th-century saint who was appointed to the see of Salisbury by William the Conqueror. As a modern given name it may be in part a transferred use of the surname derived from this name.

Variant: **Osmund**.

Cognate: Scandinavian: **Åsmund**.

Oswald (m.) English: 19th-century revival of an Old English personal name composed of the elements *ōs* god + *weald* rule. This was the name of two English saints. The first was a 7th-century king of Northumbria, who was killed in battle in 641. He was a Christian, a convert of St Aidan's, and his opponent, Penda, was a heathen, so his death was counted as a martyrdom by the Christian Church. The second St Oswald was a 10th-century bishop of Worcester and archbishop of York, of Danish parentage, who effected reforms in the English Church. The name more or less died out after the Middle Ages, but underwent a modest revival in the 19th century as part of the vogue for pre-Conquest English names.

Oswin (m.) English: 19th-century revival of an Old English personal name composed of the elements *ōs* god + *wine* friend. St Oswin was a 7th-century king of Northumbria, a cousin of King Oswald, who is likewise venerated as a martyr. However, the reasons for his death at the hand of his brother Oswy seem to have been political and personal rather than religious.

Otilie (f.) Czech form of OTTILIE.

Otis (m.) English (esp. U.S.): transferred use of the surname, derived from the genitive case of the medieval given name *Ote* or *Ode* (of Norman, and ultimately Germanic, origin; cf. OTTO). This originally denoted a man who was the 'son of Ote'. It came to be used as a given name in America in honour of the Revolutionary hero James Otis (1725–83); in modern times it has been bestowed in honour of the American soul singer Otis Redding (1941–67).

Otmar (m.) German: from an old Germanic personal name composed of the elements *od*, *ot* prosperity, fortune, riches

+ *meri, mari* famous. This name was borne by an 8th-century saint who refounded the monastery of St Gall in Switzerland.

Pet form: **Otli** (Swiss).

Otokar (m.) Czech form of OTTOKAR.

Ottavia (m.) Italian form of OCTAVIA.

Ottavio (m.) Italian form of OCTAVIUS.

Ottilie (f.) French and German: from the medieval female given name *Odila* (see ODILE), a feminine version of OTTO.

Cognates: Polish: **Otylia**. Czech: **Otilie**.

Otto (m.) German: originally a short form of the various Germanic compound personal names containing the element *od, ot* prosperity, fortune, riches (cf. the corresponding Old English *ēad* in names such as EDWARD and EDWIN). St Otto of Bamberg (d. 1139) was a missionary to the Pomeranians. Otto the Great (912–73) is generally regarded as the founder of the Holy Roman Empire, and the name has been borne by several members of German and Austrian royal houses.

Ottokar (m.) German: from an old Germanic personal name composed of the elements *od, ot* prosperity, fortune, riches + *wacar* watchful, vigilant. A version of this name was borne by the Gothic king *Odo(v)acar* (?434–93), who ruled most of Italy from 476 to 493, in which year he was assassinated by his rival Theodoric. The name was also borne by two 13th-century kings of Bohemia.

Cognate: Czech: **Otokar**.

Ottoline (f.) French and English: originally a diminutive of OTTILIE. It now has independent status in the English-speaking world, partly due to the influence of the literary hostess Lady Ottoline Morrell (1873–1938).

Otylia (f.) Polish form of OTTILIE.

Ovadia (m.) Jewish: modern Hebrew form of OBADIAH.

Ove (m.) Scandinavian: originally a Danish vernacular form of *Aghi*, short form of the various names of Old Norse origin containing the element *ag* edge (of a weapon) or awe, terror. It has long been used as an independent name.

Owen (m.) 1. Welsh: of uncertain origin. It may have derived in the sub-Roman period from the Latin name *Eugenius* (see EUGENE). Alternatively, it may represent an Old Celtic name meaning 'born of Esos'. *Esos* or *Aesos* was a god with a cult in Gaul.

2. Irish: Anglicized form of the Gaelic name EÓGHAN.

Oz (m.) English: short form of OSWALD or any of the various other names beginning with *Os-*.

Pet forms: **Ozzy, Ozzie**.

P

Paavo (m.) Finnish form of PAUL.

Pablo (m.) Spanish form of PAUL.

Paco (m.) Spanish: pet form of *Francisco* (see FRANCIS).

Variant: **Paquito**.

Paddy (m.) English and Irish: pet form of PATRICK. The formation in *-y* is in origin characteristic of Lowland Scots, and this pet form seems to have arisen in Ulster in the 17th century. Since the 19th century it has come to function in English as a generic nickname for an Irishman.

Pádraig (m.) Irish Gaelic form of PATRICK.

Variant: **Páraic** (found in Connacht).

Cognates: Scottish Gaelic: **Pàdraig** (used as a secular form of PETER); **Pàra, Pàdair** (dialectal forms).

Pet forms: Irish Gaelic: **Páidín** (Anglicized as **Paudeen**). Scottish Gaelic: **Pàidean** (from which comes the surname *Mac Phàidein*, Anglicized as *MacFadyen*).

Paige (f.) A modern female given name used regularly in America, but seldom elsewhere. It is evidently a transferred use of the surname *Paige*, a less common variant of *Page*, originally an occupational name given to someone who served as a page to a great lord. It is not clear why this should have been taken up in the 20th century as a female given name. The American film actress Janis Paige (born in 1920 under the name Donna Mae Jaden) may have something to do with it. There are a number of actresses and singers who spell their surname *Page*, but they are unlikely to have directly influenced the choice of the given name in this spelling.

Pál (m.) Hungarian form of PAUL.

Pàl (m.) Scottish Gaelic form of PAUL.

Pål (m.) Swedish form of PAUL.

Palasha (f.) Russian: pet form of *Pelageya*, derived from the older form *Palageya* (see PELAGIA).

Palmiro (m.) Italian: name derived in the Middle Ages from the vocabulary word *palmiere* palmer, pilgrim who had visited the Holy Land (from Latin *palmārius*, a derivative of *palma* palm). The name has been altered by association with the ancient city of *Palmyra* in Syria. In modern times it is sometimes given to boys born on Palm Sunday.

Paloma (f.) Spanish: from the vocabulary word meaning 'dove' (Latin *palumba*, earlier *palumbes*). The given name has originated because of the attractive gentle qualities of the bird; it may in part have a religious significance, as the dove is the symbol of the Holy Spirit.

Pamela (f.) English: invented by the Elizabethan pastoral poet Sir Philip Sidney (1554–86), in whose verse it is stressed on the second syllable. There is no clue to the sources that influenced Sidney in this coinage. It was later taken up by Samuel Richardson for the name of the heroine of his novel *Pamela* (1740). In Henry Fielding's *Joseph Andrews* (1742), which started out as a parody of *Pamela*, Fielding comments that the name is 'very strange'.

Variant: **Pamella** (a modern spelling).

Pancho (m.) Spanish: pet form of *Francisco* (see FRANCIS).

Pancras (m.) English: Middle English form of Greek *Pankratios* (see PANCRAZIO), popular in England during the early Middle Ages because in the 7th century the Pope had sent to an Anglo-Saxon king relics of a saint so called (an obscure 3rd-century martyr, not the more famous Sicilian saint mentioned at *Pancrazio*). It is now very rare, and modern instances are probably adaptations of the Italian name.

Pancrazio (m.) Italian: from the Greek epithet *pankratios* 'all-powerful' (from *pan* all, every + *kratein* to rule). This was a major title of Christ in Byzantine Greek, and was used as a personal name among early Christians. It was borne by a saint of the 1st century, who was stoned to death at Tauromenium (now Taormina) in Sicily, and who is still venerated on the island.

Cognates: Russian: **Pankrati**. German: **Pankraz** (S. Germany). English: PANCRAS.

Pandora (f.) English: name borne in classical mythology by the first woman on earth, created by the fire god Hephaistos as a scourge for men in general, in revenge for Prometheus' act of stealing fire on behalf of mankind. Pandora was given as a wife to Prometheus' foolish brother Epimetheus, along with a box which she was forbidden to open. Being endowed with great curiosity, she nevertheless did open it, and unleashed every type of hardship and suffering on the world, hope alone being left inside the box. The name itself is ironically composed of the Greek elements *pan* all, every + *dōron* gift.

Pansy (f.) English: 19th-century flower name, from the garden flower that got its name from Old French *pensee* thought. This was never especially popular, and is seldom chosen at all now that the word *pansy* has acquired a derogatory slang sense denoting an effeminate man.

Paolino (m.) Italian: a form of PAULINO or a diminutive of PAOLO. It is not a common given name.

Paolo (m.) Italian form of PAUL.

Feminine form: **Paola**.

Paquito (m.) Spanish: diminutive form of PACO.

Páraic (m.) Irish Gaelic: variant of PÁDRAIG, current in Connacht.

Paris (m.) English: apparently an adoption of the name of the character from Greek mythology, the son of Priam who carried off Helen from Sparta to Troy and so caused the Trojan War. The name was borne in the 4th century by a Greek-born bishop of Teano, near Naples, who is venerated as a saint.

Pàrlan (m.) Scottish Gaelic form of PARTHALÁN. From this name derive the surname *Mac Phàrlain*, Anglicized as *MacFarlane*, and the placename *Dùn Phàrlain*, Anglicized as *Dunfermline*.

Parthalán (m.) Irish Gaelic: name of uncertain derivation, possibly from Latin *Bartholomaeus* (see BARTHOLOMEW). It was borne, according to Celtic legend, by an early invader of Ireland, the first to come to those shores after the biblical Flood. It has often been Anglicized as *Bartholomew*, and also as BARCLAY and BERKLEY, but is now being revived in its own right.

Variants: **Párt(h)lán, Partnán**.

Cognate: Scottish Gaelic: PÀRLAN.

Parthenope (f.) Name borne in classical mythology by one of the Sirens, who drowned herself in frustration when Odysseus managed to avoid her lures by having himself tied to the mast and ordering his companions to block their ears with wax. Her name seems to be a derivative of Greek *parthenos* maiden (an epithet of Athena) + *ōps* face, form. This name was borne by a sister of Florence Nightingale who was born at Naples, where the body of the Siren is said to have been washed ashore.

Pascal (m.) French: from Late Latin *Paschālis* 'relating to Easter' (Latin *Pascha*, from Hebrew *pesach* Passover). This was taken up by the early Christians as a personal name, partly in honour of the great Christian festival, but mainly as a name for sons born at this time of the year. It was borne by two medieval popes, neither of whom achieved anything particularly notable. Its popularity may have been influenced by the fame of the French philosopher Blaise Pascal (1623–62), whose *Pensées* ('Thoughts') were published posthumously in 1670. The name is now occasionally used in the English-speaking world, mainly by Roman Catholics.

Variant: **Paschal**.

Cognates: Italian: **Pasquale**. Spanish: **Pascual**. Portuguese: **Pascoal**.

Feminine forms: French, also occasionally English: **Pascale**. Spanish: **Pascuala**.

Pasha (m., f.) Russian: pet form of both *Pavel* (see PAUL) and PRASKOVYA.

Pastor (m.) Spanish: from the Late Latin name *Pastōr* 'shepherd', adopted by early Christians because of the parable of the Good Shepherd caring for his flock. St Pastor was a nine-year-old boy martyred at Alcalá at the beginning of the 4th century, together with his thirteen-year-old brother Justus.

Feminine form: **Pastora**.

Pat (f., m.) English: short form of both PATRICIA and PATRICK.

Pet forms: **Patty, Pattie, Patti** (f.).

Patience (f.) English: from the vocabulary word denoting one of the Seven Christian Virtues. This name was a favourite with the Puritans, and survived better than many similar names, but now seems somewhat old-fashioned. The word is derived from Latin *pati* to suffer, and was associated by the early Christians with those who endured persecution and misfortune without complaint or loss of faith.

Patricia (f.) English: feminine form of PATRICK, also found in Spanish and Portuguese as a feminine of *Patricio*.

Cognate: Italian: **Patrizia**.

Short forms: English: PAT, **Tricia, Trisha**.

Patrick (m.) English and Irish, also very popular in France: name of the apostle and patron saint of Ireland (*c*.389–461). He was a Christian Briton and a Roman citizen, who as a young man was captured and enslaved by raiders from Ireland. He escaped and went to Gaul before returning home to Britain. However, in about 419 he felt a call to do missionary work in Ireland. He studied for twelve years at Auxerre, and in 432 returned to Ireland, where he went to the court of the high kings at Tara, and made some converts. He then travelled about Ireland making further converts until about 445, when he established his archiepiscopal see at Armagh. By the time of his death almost the whole of Ireland was Christian. He codified the laws of Ireland, preserving the social structure of pagan Ireland and grafting Christianity on to it. In his Latin autobiography, as well as in later tradition, his name appears as *Patricius* 'patrician' (i.e. belonging to the Roman senatorial or noble class), but this may actually represent a Latinized form of some lost Celtic (British) name.

Variant: French: **Patrice**.

Cognates: Irish Gaelic: **Pádraig, Páraic**. Scottish Gaelic: **Pàdraig** (usually Anglicized as PETER). Italian: **Patrizio**. Spanish, Portuguese: **Patricio**.

Short form: PAT.

Pet form: PADDY.

Patsy (f., m.) Irish and English: pet form of PATRICIA or PATRICK. It is generally a female name; as a male name it is almost completely restricted to Irish communities. Its popularity does not seem to have been seriously affected by its use in derogatory senses in the general vocabulary, in America meaning 'a dupe' and in Australia 'a homosexual'.

Patxi (m.) Basque form of FRANCIS, representing a shortened version of the full form *Pantzeska*.

Patya (m.) Russian: pet form of IPATI.

Paudeen (f.) Irish: Anglicized form of Gaelic *Páidín*, pet form of PÁDRAIG.

Paul (m.) English, French, and German form of *Paulus*, a Latin family name, originally a nickname meaning 'small', used in the post-classical period as a given name. Pre-eminently this is the name of the saint who is generally regarded, with St Peter, as co-founder of the Christian Church. Born in Tarsus, and originally named SAUL, he was both a Roman citizen and a Jew, and at first found employment as a minor official persecuting Christians. He was converted to Christianity by a vision of Christ while on the road to Damascus, and thereafter undertook extensive missionary journeys, converting people, especially Gentiles, to Christianity all over the eastern Mediterranean. His preaching aroused considerable official hostility, and eventually he was beheaded at Rome in about AD 65. He is the author of the fourteen epistles to churches and individuals which form part of the New Testament.

Cognates: Irish Gaelic: **Pól**. Scottish Gaelic: **Pàl** (in secular use, the form *Pòl* being reserved for the name of the saint). Italian: **Paolo**. Spanish: **Pablo**. Catalan: **Pau**. Portuguese: **Paulo**. Danish: **Poul**. Swedish: **Pål, Påvel**. Russian, Czech: **Pavel**. Polish: **Paweł**. Ukrainian: **Pavlo**. Hungarian: **Pál**. Finnish: **Paavo**.

Pet forms: Russian: **Pava, Pasha, Pusha**. Czech: **Pavlík, Pavliček, Pavloušek**.

Feminine forms: English: **Paula**, PAULINE, PAULETTE. German: **Paula**. French: **Paule**. Czech: **Pavla**.

Paula (f.) English and German: Latinate feminine form of PAUL, borne by various minor early saints and martyrs.

Paulette (f.) French: diminutive feminine form of PAUL. It is widely used in the English-speaking world, where, however, it is a more recent importation than PAULINE.

Paulina (f.) Latin feminine form of *Paulinus* (see PAULINO), borne by several minor early martyrs.

Pauline (f.) French form of PAULINA that has long been common also in the English-speaking world, where it is now established as the most common feminine equivalent of PAUL.

Variants: English: **Paulyne, Paulene, Pauleen**.

Paulino (m.) Spanish and Portuguese: from the Late Latin name *Paulīnus*, a derivative of *Paulus* (see PAUL). St Paulinus of Nola (Pontius Meropius Anicius Paulinus) was a 5th-century bishop and early Christian poet.

Paz (f.) Spanish: name derived from a title of the Virgin Mary, *Nuestra Señora de la Paz* 'Our Lady of Peace'.

Peadar (m.) Irish Gaelic form of PETER. In Scotland this form is reserved to refer to the saint; in secular use *Pàdraig* (see PÁDRAIG) is used instead.

Pearce (m.) English and Irish: variant of PIERCE. It normally represents a transferred use of the English surname derived from the given name in the Middle Ages. It has been a popular name among Irish nationalists since the rising of 1916, led by the writer and educationist Patrick Henry Pearce; he was executed by the British and is regarded as a martyr to the nationalist cause.

Pearl (f.) English: one of the group of names coined in the 19th century from words for precious and semi-precious stones. It has a longer history as a Jewish name, representing an Anglicized form of Yiddish *Perle*, an affectionate nickname or vernacular equivalent of MARGARET.

Cognates: Italian, Spanish: **Perla**.

Pet form: Spanish: **Perlita**.

Pedr (m.) Welsh form of PETER.

Pedro (m.) Spanish form of PETER.

Peggy (f.) English: variant of MAGGIE, or of the obsolete *Meggie*, both pet forms of MARGARET. The reason for the alternation of *M*- and *P*-, which occurs also in *Molly/Polly*, is not known; it has been ascribed to Celtic influence, but this particular alternation does not correspond to any of the usual mutational patterns in Celtic languages.

Short form: **Peg**.

Peig (f.) Irish Gaelic form of *Peg* (see PEGGY).

Pet form: **Peigín** (Anglicized as **Pegeen**).

Peigi (f.) Scottish Gaelic form of PEGGY.

Pekka (m.) Finnish: vernacular form of PETER (cf. PIETARI).

Pelagia (f.) Polish: from the feminine form of the Greek name *Pelagios* (Latin *Pelagius*), a derivative of Greek *pelagos* open sea. The name was borne by various early saints, including a fifteen-year-old virgin martyr of the 4th century who died by throwing herself from the top of a building to preserve her chastity.

Derivatives: Russian: **Pelageya**. French: **Pélagie**.

Pelayo (m.) Spanish form of *Pelagius*; see PELAGIA. The name was borne by a 10th-century saint who was martyred at the hands of the Moors in Cordoba, and who is still venerated in Spain.

Peleg (m.) Biblical name, meaning 'division' in Hebrew, borne by a minor figure mentioned in a genealogy (Genesis 10: 25). The name was in use among the Puritans, but has become very rare in the modern English-speaking world. In Israel, however, it has been taken up, and is now both a given name and a surname.

Pelham (m.) English: transferred use of the surname, which originated as a local name from a place in Hertfordshire, so called from the Old English personal name *Pēo(t)la* + *hām* homestead. From 1715 this was the surname of the dukes of Newcastle.

Pella (f.) Swedish: pet form of PERNILLA, representing a dramatically contracted form of the name.

Pelle (m.) Swedish: pet form of *Per*, the Scandinavian form of PETER.

Pellegrino (m.) Italian form of PEREGRINE.

Penelope (f.) English: name borne in Greek mythology by the wife of Odysseus who sat patiently awaiting his return for twenty years, meanwhile, as a supposed widow, fending off by persuasion and guile a pressing horde of suitors for her hand in marriage. Her name would seem to derive from Greek *pēnelops* duck, and play is made with this word in the *Odyssey*, but this may obscure a more complex origin, now no longer known.

Short form: **Pen**.

Pet form: **Penny** (commonly used as a given name in its own right).

Peninnah (f.) Jewish: traditional name meaning 'coral' in Hebrew. It was borne in the Scriptures by the co-wife (with Hannah) of Elkanah, the father of Samuel. In modern Hebrew it means 'pearl' and has become a popular name, substituting for the foreign forms *Perle* and PEARL.

Variants: **Peninna, Penina**.

Pentti (m.) Finnish form of BENEDICT.

Pepa (f.) Spanish: pet form of JOSEFA.

Variant: **Pepita**.

Pepe (m.) Spanish: pet form of JOSÉ.

Variant: **Pepito**.

Per (m.) Scandinavian: vernacular form of PETER.

Perce (m.) 1. English: informal short form of PERCY.

2. Irish: variant of PIERCE.

Variant (of 2): **Perse**.

Percival (m.) English: from Arthurian legend in its Old French versions, where the name is spelled *Perceval*. According to Chrétien de Troyes (12th century) and Wolfram von Eschenbach (*c.*1170–1220), Perceval (German *Parzifal*) was the perfectly pure and innocent knight who alone could succeed in the quest for the Holy Grail (a cup or bowl with supernatural powers, which in medieval legend was identified with the chalice that had received Christ's blood at the Crucifixion). Later versions of the Grail legend assign this role to Sir Galahad. The name *Perceval* probably represents a drastic remodelling of the Celtic name *Peredur*, as if from Old French *perce(r)* to pierce + *val* valley. This may well have been influenced by PERCY, which was similarly analysed as a compound of *perce(r)* + *haie* hedge.

Percy (m.) English: originally a transferred use of a famous surname, but long established as a given name, and now often erroneously taken as a pet or informal form of PERCIVAL. The surname originated as a Norman territorial name, borne by a baronial family who had held a fief in Normandy called *Perci* (from Late Latin *Persiācum*, composed of the Gallo-Roman personal name *Persius* and the local suffix *-ācum*). As a given name it was taken up in the early 18th century in the Seymour family, which had intermarried with the Percy family. The poet Percy Bysshe Shelley (1792–1822) was also distantly connected with this family, and it was partly due to his influence that the given name became more widespread. It is at present out of fashion.

Perdita (f.) English: Shakespearian coinage, borne by a character in *The Winter's Tale* (1610). The feminine form of Latin *perditus* lost, it has a clear reference to the events of the play, and this is explicitly commented on in the text. The name is now more closely associated in some people's minds with a (canine) character in Dodie Smith's *One Hundred and One Dalmatians* (1956), made into a film by Walt Disney.

Pere (m.) Catalan form of PETER.

Peregrine (m.) English: from Latin *Peregrīnus* 'foreigner, stranger', a name borne by various early Christian saints, perhaps referring to the belief that men and women are merely sojourners upon the earth, their true home being in heaven. In modern times the name is rare, borne mostly by Roman Catholics, who choose it in honour of those saints.

Cognate: Italian: **Pellegrino**.

Perico (m.) Spanish: pet form of PEDRO, derived from the archaic variant *Pero*.

Perla (f.) Italian and Spanish form of PEARL.

Pet form: Spanish: **Perlita**.

Pernilla (f.) Swedish form of Latin *Petronilla* (see PETRONEL).

Cognate: **Pernille** (Danish).

Peronel (f.) English: common medieval simplified form of PETRONEL, occasionally revived in modern times as a given name.

Perrine (f.) French: feminine form of *Perrin*, an obsolete diminutive of PIERRE.

Perry (m.) English: pet form of PEREGRINE, or transferred use of the surname *Perry*, which was originally a local name for someone who lived by a pear tree (Old English *pirige*). In modern times, it has been borne by the American singer Perry Como (b. 1912), whose name was originally Nick Perido.

Persis (f.) English: of New Testament origin, from Greek *Persis*, originally an ethnic name meaning 'Persian woman'. This name is borne by a woman mentioned fleetingly by St Paul—'the beloved Persis, which laboured much in the Lord' (Romans 16: 12)—and was taken up from there at the time of the Reformation.

Perttu (m.) Finnish form of BARTHOLOMEW.

Pesah (m.) Jewish: Hebrew name meaning 'Passover' (cf. PASCAL). It has traditionally been given to boys born during this period.

Variant: **Pesach**.

Pet (f.) English: short form of PETULA, in part influenced by the common affectionate term of address 'pet', derived from the vocabulary word for a tame animal kept for companionship.

Peta (f.) English: modern feminine form of PETER, not used before the 1930s.

Peter (m.) English, German, and Scandinavian (learned form): name of the best-known of all Christ's apostles, traditionally regarded as the founder of the Christian Church. The name derives, via Latin, from Greek *petros* stone or rock. This is used as a translation of the Aramaic byname *Cephas*, given to the apostle

Simon son of Jona, to distinguish him from another of the same name (Simon Zelotes). 'When Jesus beheld him, he said, Thou art Simon the son of Jona: thou shalt be called Cephas, which is by interpretation, A stone' (John 1: 42). According to Matthew 16: 17–18, Christ says more explicitly, 'Blessed art thou, Simon Bar-jona . . . thou art Peter, and upon this rock I will build my church'. In Scotland this is used as an Anglicized form of the Scottish Gaelic names listed at PÁDRAIG.

Cognates: Gaelic: **Peadar**. Welsh: **Pedr**. French: **Pierre**. Italian: **Pietro, Piero**. Spanish: **Pedro**. Catalan: **Pere**. Dutch, Flemish, and Low German: **Piet**. Danish, Norwegian: **Per**. Swedish: **Petter; Per, Pär** (vernacular forms). Russian: **Pyotr**. Ukrainian: **Petro**. Polish: **Piotr**. Czech: **Petr**. Hungarian: **Péter**. See also KEPA.

Short form (informal): English: **Pete**.

Pet forms: Scottish Gaelic: **Peidearan**. Russian: **Petya**. Czech: **Péťa, Peťka, Petulka, Petunka, Petrí(če)k, Petroušek**.

Feminine forms: Latinate: **Petra**. English (modern): **Peta**. French: **Pierrette**. Italian: **Piera**. Norwegian, Danish: **Petrine**.

Petra (f.) English: modern feminine form of PETER, representing a hypothetical Latin name *Petra*; *petra* is in fact the regular Late Latin word for 'stone' (Greek *petra*), of which *petrus* (see PETER) is a byform.

Petronel (f.) English: from Latin *Petronilla*, originally a feminine diminutive of the Roman family name *Petrōnius* (of uncertain derivation). The name *Petronilla* was borne by a 1st-century martyr, and early in the Christian era came to be connected with PETER, so that in many legends surrounding her she is described as a companion or even the daughter of St Peter.

Variant (Latinate): **Petronella**.

Petula (f.) English: of uncertain origin, not used before the 20th century It is possibly a coinage intended to mean 'supplicant, postulant', from Late Latin *petulāre* to ask, or there may be some connection with the flower name *petunia*. Alternatively, it may be an elaboration of the vocabulary word *pet* used as a term of endearment, with the suffix *-ula* abstracted from names such as *Ursula*.

Short form: **Pet**.

Phelim (m.) Irish: Anglicized form of the old Gaelic name **Feidhlim**, of obscure derivation. St Phelim or Fidelminus was a 6th-century disciple of St Columba.

Phil (m., f.) English: short form of PHILIP, PHYLLIS, or of any of the various other male and female names beginning with the syllable *Phil-*.

Philbert (m.) English and French (rare): from a Germanic personal name composed of the elements *fila* much + *berht* bright, famous. The first element has later been associated with the Greek name element *phil-* love. St Philibert (*c.*608–84) was a Frankish monk who founded several abbeys.

Philip (m.) English: from the Greek name *Philippos*, composed of the elements *philein* to love + *hippos* horse, which was popular in the classical period and after. It was the name of the father of Alexander the Great. It was also the name of one of Christ's apostles, of a deacon ordained by the apostles after the death of Christ, and of several other early saints. The spelling **Phillip** is sometimes used, although not etymologically justified; it is in part a result of the influence of the English surname *Phillips*, which is generally spelt with *-ll-*.

Cognates: Irish Gaelic: **Pilib**. Scottish Gaelic: **Filib**. French: **Philippe**. Italian: **Filippo**. Spanish: **Felipe**. Catalan: **Felip**. German: **Philipp**. Polish, Czech, Scandinavian: **Filip**. Hungarian: **Fülöp**. Finnish: **Vilppu**.

Short forms: English: **Phil, Pip**.

Feminine form: PHILIPPA.

Philippa (f.) English and German: Latinate feminine form of PHILIP. In England during the Middle Ages the vernacular name *Philip* was borne by women as well as men, but female bearers were distinguished in Latin records by this form. It was not, however, used as a regular given name until the 19th century.

Variants: **Philipa, Phillip(p)a.**

Cognates: Russian: **Filipa.** Finnish: **Hilppa.**

Pet forms: English: **Pippa.** Romanian: **Lipa.**

Philippina (f.) English and German: Latinate elaboration of PHILIPPA. In the Middle Ages it was sometimes interpreted as a compound of Greek *philein* to love + *poinē* pain, punishment, since Christians were supposed to rejoice in purging themselves of their sins by pain and punishment, such as flagellation and the wearing of hairshirts.

Variants: **Philipina, Phillip(p)ina.**

Cognate: French: **Philippine** (common as a feminine form of *Philippe* in the Middle Ages, and still occasionally used).

Phillida (f.) English: variant of PHYLLIS, derived from the genitive case (Greek *Phyllidos*, Latin *Phyllidis*) with the addition of the Latin feminine ending *-a*.

Variant: **Phyllida.**

Philo (m.) English and German: from the Late Greek personal name *Philōn*, a derivative of the element *phil-* love, in part as a short form of the various compound names containing this element. The name was borne by a 2nd-century saint, a deacon of St Ignatius.

Philomena (f.) English and German: from the name of an obscure saint (probably of the 3rd century) with a local cult in Italy. In 1527 the bones of a young woman were discovered under the church altar at San Severino near Ancona, together with a Latin inscription declaring them to be the body of St Filomena. Her name seems to be a feminine form of Latin *Philomenus*, from Greek *Philomenēs*, composed of the elements *philein* to love + *menos* strength. The name became popular in the 19th century, as a result of the supposed discovery in 1802 of the relics of another St Philomena in the catacombs at Rome. All the excitement, however, resulted from the misinterpretation of the Latin inscription *Filumena pax tecum* 'peace be with you, beloved' (from Greek *philoumena* beloved).

Phineas (m.) Biblical: name borne by two minor characters. One was a grandson of Aaron, who preserved the purity of the race of Israel and deflected God's wrath by killing an Israelite who had taken a Midianite woman to wife (Numbers 25: 6–15); the other, a son of the priest Eli, was killed in combat with the Philistines over the Ark of the Covenant (1 Samuel 1: 3; 4: 6–11). The name is spelled *Phinehas* in the Authorized Version, and has been taken to mean 'serpent's mouth' (i.e. 'oracle') in Hebrew, but this is an incorrect popular etymology. It is in fact derived from the Egyptian name *Panḥsj*, originally a byname meaning 'the Nubian' and used as a personal name in ancient Egypt. *Phineas* was popular among the Puritans in the 17th century, and has been occasionally used since, especially in America. Its variants have long been popular Jewish names.

Variants: Yiddish: **Pinhas, Pinchas.**

Phoebe (f.) English: Latinized form of the name of a Greek deity, *Phoibē* (from *phoibos* bright), partially identified with Artemis, goddess of the moon and of hunting, sister of the sun god Apollo, who was also known as *Phoibos* (Latin *Phoebus*).

Phyllis (f.) English and German: name of a minor character in Greek mythology who killed herself for love and was transformed into an almond tree; the Greek word *phyllis* means 'foliage', so clearly her name doomed her from the start.

Pia (f.) English, Italian, Scandinavian and Polish: from the feminine form of Latin *pius* pious, respectful, honourable. The name is common in Italy, and is also regularly used in Eastern Europe and Scandinavia, but is a recent introduction to the English-speaking world.

Piaras (m.) Irish Gaelic: name derived in the early Middle Ages from Anglo-Norman PIERS. Piaras Feiritéar (1600–53) was a Kerry chieftain and poet. In the 20th century *Piaras* has been used as a Gaelic form of the popular nationalist name PEARCE.

Piedad (f.) Spanish: religious name celebrating the quality of piety (Latin *pietās*, a derivative of *pius*; see PIA). The Virgin Mary is honoured under the title *Nuestra Señora de la Piedad* on 5 November.

Pierce (f.) English and Irish: variant of PIERS, in use in Ireland from the time of the Norman Conquest up to the present day. In many cases it may represent a transferred use of the English surname derived from the given name in the Middle Ages.

Pierluigi (m.) Italian: compound name made up of the elements *Piero* (see PIETRO) + LUIGI.

Pierre (m.) French form of PETER.

Pierrette (f.) French: feminine diminutive form of PIERRE, used as a female equivalent of that name.

Piers (m.) English: regular Middle English form of PETER (from the Old French nominative case, as against the oblique *Pier*). In the form PIERCE it survived into the 18th century, although in part this may be a transferred use of the surname derived from the medieval given name. *Piers* was revived in the mid-20th century, perhaps partly under the influence of William Langland's great rambling medieval poem *Piers Plowman* (1367–86), in which the character of Piers symbolizes the virtues of hard work, honesty, and fairness.

Piet (m.) Low German, Dutch, and Flemish form of PETER.

Variant: Dutch: **Pieter**.

Pietari (m.) Finnish: learned form of PETER (cf. PEKKA).

Pietro (m.) Italian form of PETER. The simplified form **Piero** was formerly more common, but has declined in frequency during the present century. The feminine form is **Piera**.

Pilar (f.) Spanish: name referring to a title of the Virgin Mary, *Nuestra Señora del Pilar* 'Our Lady of the Pillar'. The story is that in AD 40 the Virgin appeared, standing on a pillar, to St James the Greater at Saragossa. The vocabulary word *pilar* is masculine, but this has not inhibited its use as a feminine given name.

Pet forms: **Pili** (most commonly found in the combination **Maripili**); **Pilita, Piluca**.

Pimen (m.) Russian: from the Greek name *Poimēn* 'shepherd'. The name was a popular one among early Christians because of the New Testament parable of the Good Shepherd and his flock (cf. PASTOR). It was borne in the 5th century by a hermit who lived in the Egyptian desert; he is a saint still greatly venerated in the Eastern Church.

Pet form: **Pima**.

Pinchas (m.) Yiddish form of PHINEAS, still in regular use as a Jewish name.

Variant: **Pinhas**.

Pino (m.) Italian: short form of any of various diminutive given names such as *Filippino*, *Giacoppino*, and *Giuseppino*, derived from *Filippo* (PHILIP), *Giacobbe* (JACOB/JAMES), and *Giuseppe* (JOSEPH) respectively.

Pio (m.) Italian, Spanish, and Portuguese: from Latin *Pius* (see PIA).

Piotr (m.) Polish form of PETER.

Pip (m.) English: contracted short form of PHILIP, best known as the name of the main character in Charles Dickens's *Great Expectations* (1861), whose full name was Philip Pirrip.

Pippa (f.) English: contracted pet form of PHILIPPA, now quite commonly used as an independent given name. It was popularized in the 19th century by Browning's narrative poem *Pippa Passes* (1841), in which the heroine is a child worker in an Italian silk-mill, whose innocent admiration of 'great' people is ironically juxtaposed with their sordid lives. The name is presumably supposed to be Italian, but is not in fact used in Italy.

Pirjo (f.) Finnish form of BRIDGET.
Variant: **Pirkko**.

Pirmin (m.) S. German, Austrian, and Swiss (Romansch): name borne by an 8th-century saint who founded numerous Benedictine monasteries, for example at Amorbach, Murbach, and Reichenau. It seems to be an altered form of FIRMIN.

Placido (m.) Italian, Spanish, and Portuguese: from the Late Latin name *Placidus* 'untroubled'. This name was commonly borne by early Christians, to express their serenity in the faith, and there are several minor saints so called.

Poldi (m.) German (esp. Bavarian): pet form of LUITPOLD.

Polina (f.) Russian: pet form of APOLLINARIA.

Pòlit (m.) Catalan: variant form of *Hipòlit* (see HIPPOLYTE).

Polly (f.) English: variant of MOLLY, now established as a given name in its own right. The reason for the interchange of *M-* and *P-* is not clear; cf. PEGGY.
Short form: **Poll**.

Pompeo (m.) Italian: from the old Roman family name *Pompeius*, of uncertain origin. It is probably derived from an Italic dialectal word for 'five', and so is ultimately a doublet of QUINTUS and PONS. The name was borne by a few early saints, but owes its modern use to revival during the Renaissance, in tribute to the Roman general and statesman Pompey the Great (Gnaeus Pompeius Magnus, 106–48 BC).

Pomuk (m.) Czech: short form of NEPOMUK.

Pons (m.) French: from Latin *Pontius*, originally a family name of uncertain origin. It is probably derived from an Italic dialectal word for 'five', and so is ultimately a doublet of QUINTUS and POMPEO. In spite of its unfortunate association with Pontius Pilate, the Roman procurator of Judea who ordered the crucifixion of Jesus, it came to be used occasionally as a given name in honour of the cult of St Pons of Cimiez (d. 258).
Cognates: Italian: **Ponzio**. Spanish: **Poncio**. Catalan: **Ponç**.

Poppy (f.) English: from the name of the flower, Old English *popæg* (ultimately from Latin *papāver*). It has been used as a given name since the latter years of the 19th century, and reached a peak of popularity in the 1920s.

Porfirio (m.) Italian and Spanish: from Late Latin *Porphyrius*, Greek *Porphyrios*, a derivative of *porphyra* purple dye (apparently of oriental origin). This name was borne by some half dozen saints of the first centuries AD.

Porick (m.) Irish: Anglicized spelling of Gaelic PÁDRAIG, representing a common pronunciation of that name.

Portia (f.) English: name that occurs twice in the works of Shakespeare, once as the name of the wife of Brutus in *Julius Caesar*. The historical Brutus' wife was called *Porcia*, feminine form of the Roman family name *Porcius*, which is apparently a derivative of Latin *porcus* pig. The main influence on the choice of this given name, however, is undoubtedly the other Shakespearian character of this name, an heiress in *The Merchant of Venice* who, disguised as a man, shows herself to be a brilliant advocate.

Posy (f.) English: pet form (originally a nursery version) of JOSEPHINE. It has also been associated with the vocabulary word *posy* bunch of flowers (originally a collection of verses, from *poesy* poetry), and is occasionally used as an independent given name, fitting into the series of names associated with flowers.

Poul (m.) Danish form of PAUL.

Praskovya (f.) Russian: vernacular form of learned *Paraskeva*, from Late Greek (*megalē*) *paraskeuē* (Good) Friday (from classical Greek *paraskeuē* preparation). A saint of this name is venerated in the Eastern Church as having been martyred in the 1st century, together with Photina, Joseph, Victor, Sebastian, Anatolius, Photius, Photis, and Cyriaca.

Pet form: **Pasha**.

Preben (m.) Danish: from medieval *Pridbjørn*, a reworking (with assimilation to the Scandinavian element *bjørn* bear) of the Slavonic personal name *Pritbor*, composed of the elements *prid* foremost, leading + *bor* battle.

Presentación (f.) Spanish: religious name referring to the feast of the Presentation (Spanish *presentación*, from Late Latin *praesentātio*, a derivative of *praesens* present), commemorating the presentation of the Virgin Mary in the temple at Jerusalem after the birth of Christ. This has been celebrated (on 21 November) since the 5th century in the Eastern Church and since the 7th century in the Western. However, since it is largely based on incidents in the apocryphal 'Book of James', its significance has been played down in modern times.

Short form: **Presen**.

Preston (m.) English: transferred use of the surname, which originated as a local name from any of the numerous places in England named with the Old English elements *prēost* priest + *tūn* enclosure, settlement.

Pribislav (m.) Russian form of PRZYBYSŁAW.

Primitivo (m.) Spanish: from the Late Latin name *Prīmitīvus* 'earliest' (a derivative of *prīmus* first; see PRIMO). The name was borne by various early martyrs, most notably one born at León in Spain and beheaded *c.*300 together with his companion St Facundus.

Primo (m.) Italian, Spanish, and Portuguese: from the Late Latin name *Prīmus* 'first', borne by four minor early saints.

Cognate: Polish: **Prym**.

Primrose (f.) English: one of the several female names taken from words for flowers in the late 19th century. The word is from Latin *prima rosa* first rose, although it does not in fact have any connection with the rose family and does not bloom particularly early.

Prince (m.) English: originally a nickname from the royal title. The Old French title *prince* (Latin *princeps*, from *prīmus* first + *capere* to take, i.e. one who took the first place) was introduced to Britain by the Normans; before the Conquest young members of the royal house had been known as *æðelingas* (from Old English *æðel* noble). As a given name, *Prince* is common among Blacks in America; it was often bestowed on slaves with cruel irony, but has been perpetuated by their descendants with pride.

Prisca (f.) Of New Testament origin: feminine form of the Roman family name *Priscus* (originally a nickname meaning 'ancient'). Prisca (2 Timothy 4: 19) and Priscilla (Acts 18: 3) are apparently the same person, but it is the diminutive form which became established as a common given name.

Priscilla (f.) Of New Testament origin: from a post-classical Latin personal name, a feminine diminutive of the Roman family name *Priscus* (see PRISCA). *Priscilla* was the name of a woman with whom St Paul stayed at Corinth (Acts 18: 3), referred to elsewhere as *Prisca*. The name was popular among the Puritans in the 17th century and again enjoyed a vogue in the 19th century.

Proinséas (f.) Irish Gaelic form of FRANCES.

Proinsias (m.) Irish Gaelic form of FRANCIS.

Prokhor (m.) Russian: from Greek *Prokhoros*, originally a name given to the leader of a troupe of singers and dancers (from *pro* before, ahead + *khorein* to sing, dance). St Prochorus was one of the seven deacons ordained by the apostles (Acts 6: 5); according to tradition, he later went on to become bishop of Nicomedia and was martyred at Antioch.

Pet forms: **Pronya, Prosha.**

Prokopi (m.) Russian: from Greek *Prokopios*, a derivative of *prokopē* success, progress, prosperity (from *pro* before, ahead + *koptein* to cut, hit). The name was borne by the first victim of the Diocletianic persecution in Palestine (beheaded at Caesarea Maritima in 303), and later by the founder (*c.*980–1053) of the Sabaza abbey in Prague.

Variant: **Prokofi** (vernacular form).

Cognate: Polish, Czech: **Prokop.**

Pet forms: Russian: **Pronya, Prosha.**

Prosper (m.) French and English: from the Latin name *Prosperus*, derived from the adjective *prosper* fortunate, prosperous (originally 'according to one's wishes', Latin *pro spe*). This was the name of various early saints, including a 5th-century theologian and contemporaneous bishops of Orléans and Reggio. It was a favourite among the English Puritans, partly because of its association with the English vocabulary word *prosper*, but is now rare. In France it is best known as the given name of the writer Prosper Mérimée (1803–70).

Cognate: Italian, Spanish, and Portuguese: PROSPERO.

Prospero (m.) Italian, Spanish, and Portuguese form of PROSPER. This form of the name was used by Shakespeare for the central figure of the magician and Duke of Milan in *The Tempest*, and for this reason it has very occasionally been adopted in the English-speaking world.

Prudence (f.) English: originally a medieval form of the Latin name *Prūdentia*, a feminine form of *Prūdentius*, from *prūdens* provident. The Blessed Prudentia was a 15th-century abbess who founded a new convent at Como in Italy. Later, among the Puritans in 17th-century England, *Prudence* was used as a quality name, taken from the vocabulary word.

Short forms: **Prue, Pru.**

Prudencio (m.) Spanish and Portuguese: from Late Latin *Prūdentius*, a derivative of *prūdens* provident, prudent. *Prudentius* was the name of two Spanish saints. One, who lived in the 8th century, was born at Armentia in the province of Álava and became bishop of Tarazona in Aragon. The second (d. 861) was originally called Galindo, but changed his name to Prudentius when he moved to France to escape the Moors; he eventually became bishop of Troyes.

Cognate: Italian: **Prudenzio.**

Prunella (f.) English: Latinate name, probably one of the names coined in the 19th century from vocabulary words for plants and flowers, in this case from a diminutive derived from Late Latin *pruna* plum. The name has enjoyed a minor vogue in the latter part of the 20th century, and is borne by two well-known English actresses, Prunella Scales and Prunella Gee.

Short forms: **Prue, Pru.**

Pryderi (m.) Welsh: traditional name meaning 'caring for' (later 'anxiety'). It is borne in the *Mabinogi* by Pryderi, son of Pwyll, who makes several appearances in the narrative.

Prym (m.) Polish form of PRIMO.

Przemysł (m.) Polish: originally a byname from an Old Polish noun meaning 'trick, stratagem', given to a cunning person. This name was borne by two Polish kings of the Middle Ages, Przemysł I (?1220–57) and Przemysł II (1257–96).

Cognate: Czech: **Přemysl.**

Pet forms: Polish: **Przemko.** Czech: **Přem(ouš)ek, Myslík.**

Przybysław (m.) Polish: from an old Slavonic personal name composed of the elements *pribit* to be present, help + *slav* glory.

[*cont.*]

Cognates: Czech: **Přibislav**. Russian: **Pribislav**.

Feminine form: Czech: **Přibislava**.

Pet forms: Czech: **Přiba, Přibík, Přibišek** (m.); **Přibka, Přiběna, Přibuška** (f.).

Purificación (f.) Spanish: Marian name, taken in honour of the feast of the Purification (Spanish *purificación*, from Late Latin *purificātio*, a derivative of *purus* pure + *facere* to make). This feast is celebrated on 2 February, and commemorates the day when, in accordance with Jewish law, the Virgin Mary took her son Jesus to the temple for the first time to present him to God and be herself purged of the uncleanliness associated with childbirth.

Short form: **Pura**.

Pet form: **Purita**.

Pusha (m.) Russian: pet form of *Pavel* (see PAUL).

Pyotr (m.) Russian form of PETER.

Q

Queenie (f.) English: from the affectionate nickname *Queen* (going back to Old English *cwēn*, related to *cwene* woman, respelled as if derived from Latin), with the addition of the hypocoristic suffix *-ie* (originally characteristic of northern England and Scotland). In the Victorian era it was sometimes used as an allusive pet form for VICTORIA. As a Jewish name it represents an Anglicized form of MALKAH.

Quentin (m.) English and French: from the Old French form of the Latin name *Quintīnus*, a derivative of the given name QUINTUS. The name was borne by a 3rd-century saint who worked as a missionary in Gaul.

Variants: English: **Quintin**, QUINTON.

Cognates: Scottish Gaelic: **Caointean**, **Caoidhean**.

Quincy (m.) English (chiefly U.S.): transferred use of the surname, originally a Norman baronial name borne by the family that held lands at *Cuinchy* in Pas-de-Calais, Normandy, so called from the Gallo-Roman personal name QUINTUS and the local suffix *-ācum*. This was the surname of a prominent New England family in the colonial era. Josiah Quincy (1744–75) was a lawyer and Revolutionary patriot, a close friend of John Adams (1735–1826), who became second president of the United States (1797–1801). The latter's son, John Quincy Adams (1767–1848), also served as president (1825–9). He may have received his middle name in honour of his father's friend Josiah Quincy, or it may have been taken from the township of Quincy, Massachusetts, where he was born and where the Adams family had their seat.

Variant: **Quincey**.

Quinton (m.) English: variant of QUENTIN, influenced by the surname of this form, which originated in the Middle Ages as a local name from any of several places named with the Old English vocabulary elements *cwēn* queen + *tūn* enclosure, settlement.

Quintus (m.) English: an old Roman given name meaning 'fifth'. It has been used in the English-speaking world, mainly in the 19th century, for the fifth-born son or male fifth-born child in a family (cf. SEXTUS, SEPTIMUS, OCTAVIUS, and NONA).

Quique (m.) Spanish: pet form of ENRIQUE.

Quirce (m.) Spanish: from Latin *Quiricus*, which apparently represents a variant of *Cyriācus* (see CIRIACO), crossed with *Quirīnus* (see CORIN). The name was borne by a three-year-old boy martyred at Tarsus in 304 together with his mother Julitta.

Cognate: Catalan: **Quirc**.

Quirino (m.) Italian: from Latin *Quirīnus* (see CORIN).

R

Rabbie (m.) Scottish: pet form of ROBERT, from the short form *Rab*, *Rob*. It is now often associated with the poet Robert Burns (1759–96).

Rachel (f.) English, French, and German: biblical name meaning 'ewe' in Hebrew. This was borne by the beloved wife of Jacob and mother (after long barrenness) of Joseph (Genesis 28–35) and of Benjamin, at whose birth she died. In the Middle Ages and later this was a characteristically Jewish name. It is still extremely popular among Jews, but is now widely used among Gentiles as well. In Scotland it has long been used as an Anglicized form of *Raghnaid* (see RAGHNAILT).

Variants: English: RACHELLE; **Rachael** (apparently by association with MICHAEL).

Cognates: Spanish: RAQUEL. Italian: **Rachele**. Scandinavian: **Rakel**.

Rachelle (f.) English: elaborated form of RACHEL, as if from French, but actually a recent coinage in English. The French form of the name is also *Rachel*, but this is not very common.

Racław (m.) Polish: contracted form of RADOSŁAW.

Rada (f.) Slavonic: short form of various female compound names containing the vocabulary element *rad* glad, as for example *Radosława* (see RADOSŁAW).

Radek (m.) Czech: pet form (with the diminutive suffix *-ek*) derived from a short form of any of the various Slavonic compound names containing the element *rad* glad, as for example *Radimír* (see RADZIMIERZ) and *Radoslav* (see RADOSŁAW).

Variants: **Radík**, **Radko**, **Radoš**, **Radan**, **Radeček**, **Radoušek**.

Radosław (m.) Polish: from an old Slavonic personal name composed of the vocabulary elements *rad* glad + *slav* glory.

Cognate: Czech, Russian: **Radoslav**.

Feminine forms: Polish: **Radosława**. Czech: **Radoslava**.

Radu (m.) Romanian: short form of the various male names of Slavonic origin containing the element *rad* glad (cf. e.g. RADZIMIERZ and RADOSŁAW).

Radzimierz (m.) Polish: from an old Slavonic personal name composed of the elements *rad* glad + *meri* great, famous (see CASIMIR).

Variant: **Radzim**.

Cognates: Czech: **Radimír**, **Radomír**, **Radim**. Russian: **Radimir**.

Feminine form: Czech: **Radomíra**.

Rae (f.) Australian and English: probably originally a short form of RACHEL, but now generally taken as a feminine form of RAY or RAYMOND. It is also possible that in some cases it represents a transferred use of the Scottish surname *Rae*, originally either a short form of *MacRae* (from a Gaelic personal name meaning 'son of grace') or a nickname from the roebuck. It is often used in combinations such as *Rae Ellen* and *Mary Rae*.

Raelene (f.) Australian: fanciful coinage of recent origin, from RAE + the productive feminine suffix *-lene*.

Rafael (m.) Spanish and Portuguese form (also a German variant) of RAPHAEL.

Pet form: Spanish: **Rafa**.

Rafał (m.) Polish form of RAPHAEL.

Rafe (m.) English: spelling representation of the traditional pronunciation of the name RALPH, a pronunciation now largely restricted to the upper classes in England.

Rafel (m.) Catalan form of RAPHAEL.

Raffaele (m.) Italian form of RAPHAEL.
Variant: **Raffaello.**

Raghnailt (f.) Irish Gaelic: from Norse RAGNHILD. This was a very common woman's given name in medieval Ireland, often rendered in Latin documents as REGINA.
Cognate: Scottish Gaelic: **Raghnaid.**

Raghnall (m.) Irish and Scottish Gaelic: name borrowed from Old Norse *Rögnvaldr* (see RAGNVALD). It is usually Anglicized as *Ronald*, *Ranald*, or *Randal*.
Variant: **Raonull.**

Ragna (f.) Scandinavian: from the Old Norse female personal name *Ragna*, a short form of the various compound names containing the element *regin* advice, decision (also, the gods), as, for example, RAGNBORG and RAGNHILD. The name was used in the Viking period and revived in the late 19th century. In modern use it is to a large extent taken as a feminine form of RAGNAR.

Ragnar (m.) Scandinavian: from an Old Norse personal name cognate with RAYNER.

Ragnborg (f.) Scandinavian: from an Old Norse female personal name composed of the elements *regin* advice, decision (also, the gods) + *borg* fortification. The name was used in the Viking period and revived in the 19th century.
Variant: **Ramborg** (Swedish).

Ragnhild (f.) Scandinavian: from an Old Norse female personal name composed of the elements *regin* advice, decision (also, the gods) + *hildr* battle.
Variant: **Ragnild.**
Cognates: Irish Gaelic: **Raghnailt.** Scottish Gaelic: **Raghnaid.**

Ragnvald (m.) Scandinavian: from the Old Norse personal name *Rögnvaldr*, composed of the elements *regin* advice, decision (also, the gods) + *valdr* ruler. This name is cognate with the West Germanic form REYNOLD. See also RONALD.

Raibeart (m.) Scottish Gaelic form of ROBERT.

Raimondo (m.) Italian form of RAYMOND.

Raimundo (m.) Spanish and Portuguese form of RAYMOND.

Raina (f.) Polish and Czech form of REGINA, also sometimes used in the English-speaking world, to which it was introduced by George Bernard Shaw, as the name of a character in *Arms and the Man* (1894).

Raine (f.) English: of modern origin and uncertain derivation. It is possibly a respelling of the French vocabulary word *reine* queen (cf. REGINA and RAINA), or a transferred use of the surname *Raine* or *Rayne*. The surname is derived from various medieval given names beginning with the Germanic element *ra(g)in* advice, decision. In modern times, this given name is borne by the Countess Spencer, daughter of the romantic novelist Barbara Cartland and step-mother of the Princess of Wales.

Rainer (m.) German form of RAYNER.

Rainerio (m.) Spanish form of RAYNER.

Rainier (m.) French form of RAYNER.

Raisa (f.) Russian: from the Late Greek name *Raisa*, of uncertain derivation. It may be a derivative of *rhaiōn*, comparative of *rhadios* easy-going, adaptable. The name was borne by a Christian martyr executed in 308. It has recently come to prominence as the name of the wife of the Soviet leader Mikhail Gorbachev.
Pet form: **Raya.**

Rakel (f.) Scandinavian form of RACHEL.

Ralph (m.) English: of Norman origin, representing a contracted form of the Germanic name *Radulf*, composed of the elements *rād* counsel + *wulf* wolf. The spelling with *-ph* is the result of classically influenced 'improvement' in the 18th century.

Variants: **Ralf**, RAFE.

Cognates: French: **Raoul**. Italian: **Raul**. Spanish: **Raúl**.

Ramborg (f.) Swedish: assimilated variant of RAGNBORG.

Ramiro (m.) Spanish: of Germanic (Visigothic) origin. It is probably composed of the elements *ragin* advice, decision + *māri*, *mēri* famous. St Ramirus was a 5th- or 6th-century prior who was martyred at León by the Visigoths, who subscribed to the Arian heresy, which he opposed.

Ramón (m.) Spanish form of RAYMOND. This name is in frequent use in America among people of Hispanic descent, but has not been taken up outside such communities to anything like the same extent as the feminine form RAMONA.

Pet form: **Moncho**.

Ramona (f.) Spanish: feminine form of RAMÓN. This has achieved some popularity in recent decades with non-Hispanic parents in America and, to a lesser extent, in Britain, partly due to the influence of a popular song about a girl called Ramona.

Ramsay (m.) Scottish: transferred use of the Scottish surname, which was originally a local name imported to Scotland from *Ramsey* in Huntingdonshire (so called from Old English *hramsa* wild garlic + *ēg* island). In the 12th century David, brother of King Alexander I of Scotland, was brought up at the English court, and acquired the earldoms of Huntingdon and Northampton. When he succeeded his brother as king, he took many of his retainers and associates with him to Scotland, and some of them took their surnames with them from places in eastern England. This explains why some famous Scottish surnames, such as *Ramsay*, *Lindsay*, *Graham*, etc., are derived from placenames in that part of England. Some of these surnames have in turn gone on to be used as given names.

Variant: **Ramsey**.

Ran (m.) English and Scottish: short form of the various names beginning with this syllable, as, for example, RANDOLF, RANALD, and RANULF.

Ranald (m.) Scottish: Anglicized form of the Gaelic name *Raghnall*, which itself is borrowed from Old Norse *Rögnvaldr* (see RAGNVALD).

Randa (f.) English: short form of MIRANDA. See also RANDY.

Randall (m.) English: a regular medieval form of RANDOLF. This fell out of use, but before it did so gave rise to a surname. Modern use of the given name represents a transferred use of this surname.

Variants: **Randal, Randel(l), Randle**.

Randolf (m.) English: of Norman origin, derived from a Germanic personal name composed of the elements *rand* rim, edge (of a shield) + *wulf* wolf.

Variant: **Randolph**.

Randy (m., f.) English (esp. U.S. and Australian): as a male name this originated as a pet form of RANDALL, RANDOLF, or, in some cases, ANDREW. As a female name it may have originated either as a transferred use of the male name or else as a pet form of MIRANDA (cf. RANDA). It is now fairly commonly used as an independent name, mainly by men, in spite of the unfortunate connotations of the slang term *randy* meaning 'lustful'.

Variants: **Randi, Randie** (f.).

Raniero (m.) Italian form of RAYNER, a relatively late coinage under French influence.

Short form: NERO.

Ransu (m.) Finnish form of FRANCIS.

Ranulf (m.) Scottish: from an Old Norse personal name, *Reginulfr*, composed of the elements *regin* advice, decision (also, the gods) + *úlfr* wolf. The name was introduced into Scotland by Scandinavian settlers in the early Middle Ages.

Raoul (m.) French form of RALPH, occasionally used in the English-speaking world. The form **Raul** (sometimes pronounced as a single syllable) is either a simplified spelling, or a use of the Italian or Spanish form.

Raphael (m.) English, French, and German: from early Christian tradition, in which it is the name of one of the archangels (see also GABRIEL and MICHAEL). It is composed of Hebrew vocabulary elements meaning 'to heal' and 'God'. Raphael is not named in the canonical text of the Bible, but plays a part in the apocryphal tale of Tobias. The shorter form *Rapha* 'he (God) heals' (cf. NATHANIEL and NATHAN) is borne by several characters in the Old Testament. The name has always been much more common in southern Europe than in Britain, and use in the English-speaking world today generally reflects southern European influence. It has also become a popular modern Hebrew name.

Variant: German: **Rafael**.

Cognates: Italian: **Raffaele, Raffaello**. Spanish, Portuguese: **Rafael**. Catalan: **Rafel**. Polish: **Rafał**.

Pet form: Spanish: **Rafa**.

Raquel (f.) Spanish form of RACHEL, brought to public attention by the fame and good looks of the film actress Raquel Welch (b. 1940 as Raquel Tejada, in Chicago). Her father was Bolivian, her mother of English parentage.

Rastus (m.) English: of New Testament origin, where it is a short form of the Latin name *Erastus* (Greek *Erastos*, from *erān* to love). This was the name of the treasurer of Corinth converted to Christianity by St Paul (Romans 16: 23). In the early 20th century *Rastus* came to be regarded as a typically Black name, for reasons which are unclear.

Rathnait (f.) Irish Gaelic: name representing a feminine diminutive form of *rath* grace, prosperity.

Anglicized form: RONIT.

Raúl (m.) Spanish form of RALPH.

Ray (m.) English: short form of RAYMOND, now often used as an independent name. In a few instances it may represent a transferred use of the surname *Ray*, which was normally first acquired as a nickname, from Old French *rei, roi* king (cf. ROY and LEROY).

Raya (f.) Russian: pet form of RAISA.

Raymond (m.) English and French: of Norman origin, derived from a Germanic personal name composed of the elements *ragin* advice, decision + *mund* protector. It dropped out of use, but was revived in the middle of the 19th century, together with several other given names of Anglo-Saxon and Norman Germanic origin.

Cognates: Irish: **Réamann** (Gaelic); **Redmond** (Anglicized). German: **Rei(n)mund, Raimund**. Italian: **Raimondo**. Spanish: RAMÓN, **Raimundo**. Portuguese: **Raimundo**.

Short form: English: RAY.

Feminine forms: French, English: **Raymonde** (rare). German: **Raimunde**. Italian: **Raimonda**. Spanish: RAMONA, **Raimunda**.

Rayner (m.) English: of Norman origin, derived from a Germanic personal name composed of the elements *ragin* advice, decision + *heri, hari* army, warrior. As a modern given name it in part represents a transferred use of the surname derived from this given name in the Middle Ages.

Cognates: German: **Rainer**. Scandinavian: **Ragnar**. Danish: **Regner**. French: **Rainier**. Italian: **Raniero**. Spanish: **Rainerio**.

Read (m.) American, Scottish, and English: transferred use of the English surname. In most cases, this originated as a nickname for someone with red hair or a ruddy complexion (from Old English *rēad* red; cf. REID). In other cases, it may have arisen as a local name, from Old English *hrēod* reeds or *rēod* cleared land.

Reanna (f.) English: modern name, apparently an altered form of DEANNA, influenced by the Welsh name RHIANNON. The form **Reanne** is also used.

Rearden (m.) Irish: variant of RIORDAN.

Rebecca (f.) Biblical: from the Latin form of the Hebrew name *Rebekah*, borne by the wife of Isaac, who was the mother of

Esau and Jacob (Genesis 24–7). The Hebrew root occurs in the Bible only in the vocabulary word *marbek* cattle stall, and its connection with the name is doubtful. In any case, Rebecca was Aramean, and the name probably has a source in Aramaic. It has always been common among Jews; in England and elsewhere it began to be used also by Christians at the time of the Reformation, when Old Testament names became popular. It was very common among the Puritans in the 17th century, and has enjoyed a further vogue in England in the latter part of the 20th century, among people of many different creeds. In the Scottish Highlands it has been used as an Anglicized form of the Gaelic name *Beathag* (see BEATHAN).

Variants: French: **Rébecca**. Spanish, Portuguese: **Rebeca**. German, Danish, Norwegian: **Rebekka**. Swedish: **Rebecka**. Hebrew: **Rivka**.

Short form: English: **Becca**.

Pet form: English: **Becky**.

Redmond (m.) Irish: apparently an Anglicized form of the Gaelic name **Réamann**, itself a form of RAYMOND. An alternative explanation, which better accounts for the form of the name, derives it from an Old English personal name composed of the elements *rǣd* counsel + *mund* protector.

Reenie (f.) English: respelling of *Renée* (see RENÉ), representing the Anglicized pronunciation of the name. It may also occasionally represent a pet form of various names ending in the syllable *-reen*, such as DOREEN and MAUREEN.

Rees (m.) Welsh and English: Anglicized spelling of the Welsh name RHYS, in some cases representing a transferred use of the surname so spelled, which is derived from the Welsh given name.

Refugio (f.) Spanish: religious name referring to the Marian title, *Nuestra Señora de Refugio* 'Our Lady of Refuge'.

Pet form: **Fucho**.

Reg (m.) English: short form of REGINALD, often preferred by bearers of that name for use in almost all situations, but rarely actually bestowed as a baptismal name.

Regan (f.) English: apparently of Shakespearian origin. This is the name of one of the three daughters in *King Lear* (1605), a most unattractive character, who flatters her father into giving her half his kingdom and then turns him out into a raging storm at night. It is not known where Shakespeare got the name; he presumably believed it to be of Celtic origin. Modern use has been reinforced by the Irish surname *Re(a)gan* (Gaelic *Ó Riagáin*).

Reggie (m.) English: pet form of REG, common in the 19th and early 20th century, but now less so.

Regina (f.) English: from the Latin nickname meaning 'queen'. It seems to have been occasionally used among early Christians; a St Regina, probably of the 3rd century, was venerated as a virgin martyr at Autun from an early date. In modern use it is normally borne by Roman Catholics in allusion to the Marian epithet *Regina Coeli* 'Queen of Heaven', a cult title since the 8th century. In Ireland it has sometimes also been used as a Latinized form of RAGHNAILT and RIONA.

Reginald (m.) English: of Norman origin, derived from *Reginaldus*, a Latinized form of REYNOLD influenced by Latin *regina* queen. It is now regarded as very formal, and bearers generally shorten it to REG in ordinary usage.

Régine (f.) French form of REGINA.

Régis (m.) French: name given in honour of St Jean-François Régis (d. 1640) of Narbonne, who strove to reform prostitutes. His surname derives from an Old Provençal word meaning 'ruler'.

Regner (m.) Danish: variant of RAGNAR.

Regula (f.) Mainly Swiss: from Latin *rēgula* rule (of conduct), adopted as a name by early Christians in their zeal for following the precepts laid down by Christ. It was borne by a 3rd-century saint who was martyred near Zurich, together with her brother Felix. She is the patron saint of Zurich.

Řehoř (m.) Czech form of GREGORY.

Pet forms: **Řehořek, Řehůrek, Řehák; Hořek, Hořík.**

Reid (m.) Scottish and N. English: transferred use of the surname, which originated as a nickname for someone with red hair or a ruddy complexion (from Old English *rēad* red; cf. READ).

Reijo (m.) Finnish form of GREGORY.

Reine (f., m.) 1. (f.) French: vernacular descendant of Latin *rēgina* queen (cf. RÉGINE), probably arising for the most part from a medieval affectionate nickname.

2. (m.) Swedish: short form of the (originally German) given names REINHARD and REINHOLD.

Reinhard (m.) German form of REYNARD.

Reinhold (m.) German form of REYNOLD.

Reinmund (m.) German form of RAYMOND.

Variants: **Reimund, Raimund.**

Reisel (f.) Jewish: Yiddish pet form of **Reise**, itself a Yiddish form of ROSE.

Variant: **Reisl.**

Rella (f.) Jewish: from Yiddish **Rele**, originally a pet form of either RACHEL, REBECCA, or REISEL, but now used as an independent given name.

Rema (m.) Russian: pet form of YEFREM.

Remedios (f.) Spanish: religious name from a title of the Virgin Mary, *Nuestra Señora de los Remedios*, referring to her promised intervention to relieve the suffering of those who pray to her (from Spanish *remedio* remedy, relief, help, from Latin *remedium* cure, remedy, a derivative of *(re)medēre* to cure, restore to health).

Reményke (f.) Hungarian: loan translation of the Russian name NADEZHDA, from Hungarian *remény* hope.

Remus (m.) English: the name, according to ancient Roman tradition, of the brother of Romulus, co-founder with him of the city of Rome. In America this rare given name is associated particularly with the 'Uncle Remus' stories of Joel Chandler Harris (1848–1908), Uncle Remus being a Black who is the narrator of the stories.

Italian form: **Remo** (much less common than ROMOLO).

Rémy (m.) French: from Latin *Rēmigius*, a derivative of *rēmex* (genitive *rēmigis*) oarsman (from *rēmus* oar + *agere* to ply, work). The name was borne by a 6th-century bishop of Rheims who was responsible for the conversion and baptism of Clovis, king of the Franks, and also by an 8th-century bishop of Rouen, the latter being an illegitimate son of King Charles Martel (grandfather of Charlemagne). There has been some confusion with the name *Remedius* (from Latin *(re)medēre* to heal; cf. REMEDIOS), borne by an early bishop of Gap in the French Alps.

Cognates: Italian, Spanish, Portuguese: **Remigio.**

Rena (f.) English: of recent origin, either an altered form of *Renée* (see RENÉ) or else a variant spelling of RINA.

Renata (f.) The original Latin form of *Renée* (see RENÉ). This form of the name is now common in Italy (although it was seldom used there until the mid-19th century), and it is also used in Germany (beside *Renate*), Poland, and Czechoslovakia.

René (m.) French: from the Late Latin name *Renātus* 'reborn', used by early Christians as a baptismal name celebrating spiritual rebirth in Christ. The feminine form is generally commoner than the masculine, especially in Britain.

Cognates: Italian, Spanish, Portuguese: **Renato.** Catalan: **Renat.** *[cont.]*

Feminine forms: French and English: **Renée**. Italian, English, German, Polish, and Czech: RENATA. German: **Renate**.

Resi (f.) German: pet form of *Theresia*; see THERESA.

Variants: **Reserl** (S. Germany); **Resli** (Switzerland).

Reto (m.) Swiss: originally an ethnic name for someone from the region of *R(h)aetia* in east Switzerland, so called from its original occupaton by a Celtic tribe called the *R(h)aeti*.

Reuben (m.) Biblical: Hebrew name borne by one of the twelve sons of Jacob, and so the name of one of the twelve tribes of Israel. It is said to mean 'behold, a son' in Hebrew. Genesis 29: 32 explains it as follows: 'and Leah conceived, and bare a son, and she called his name Reuben: for she said, Surely the Lord hath looked upon my affliction: now therefore my husband will love me'. In Genesis 30: 14–15, Reuben is depicted as a devoted son to his mother, but he incurred his father's wrath for seducing his concubine Bilhah and on his deathbed Jacob, rather than blessing him, cursed Reuben because of this incident (Genesis 49: 4). Despite this, the name has enjoyed popularity among Jews. Among Christians the name experienced something of a vogue at the Reformation, and again in the 19th century, but it is out of fashion at present.

Variant (esp. Jewish): **Reuven**.

Cognates: Spanish: **Rubén**. Scandinavian: **Ruben**. Finnish: **Ruupeni, Ruuppo**.

Short form (informal): U.S.: **Rube**.

Reuel (m.) Biblical: name (meaning 'friend of God' in Hebrew) borne by a character mentioned in a genealogy (2 Chronicles 9: 8).

Rex (m.) English: from Latin *rex* king. This was not used as a personal name in Latin of the classical or Christian periods, and its adoption as a given name seems to have been a 19th-century innovation.

Rexanne (f.) English: apparently an altered form of ROXANE, based on the male given name REX.

Reynard (m.) English: of Norman origin, derived from a Germanic personal name composed of the elements *ragin* advice, decision + *hard* hardy, brave, strong. In French, *renard* (derived from this name) has become the generic name for a fox, as a result of the popularity of medieval beast tales featuring *Re(y)nard le goupil* 'Reynard the fox'.

Cognate: German: **Reinhard**.

Reynold (m.) English: of Norman origin, derived from a Germanic personal name composed of the elements *ragin* advice, decision + *wald* ruler.

Variant: REGINALD. See also RONALD.

Cognates: Welsh: **Rheinallt**. French: **Reynaud**. Italian: **Rinaldo**. German: **Reinhold**. See also RAGNVALD.

Rezső (m.) Hungarian form of RUDOLF.

Rhea (f.) The name borne, according to ancient Roman tradition, by the mother (Rhea Silvia) of Romulus and Remus, who grew up to be the founders of the city of Rome. It was also a title of the goddess Cybele, introduced to Rome from Phrygia, and its meaning is quite obscure. It is comparatively rarely used as a given name in the modern world.

Rheanna (f.) English: apparently an elaboration of RHEA, perhaps influenced by the names DEANNA and RHIANNON.

Rheinallt (m.) Welsh form of REYNOLD.

Rhett (m.) American English: transferred use of an American surname derived from Dutch *de Raedt*, from Middle Dutch *raet* advice. It was invented for the character of Rhett Butler in Margaret Mitchell's *Gone with the Wind* (1936). Like some of the other names in that novel (cf. ASHLEY, CAREEN, and SCARLETT), it has attained a modest currency in the real world.

Feminine: **Rhetta** (a recent coinage).

Rhiannon (f.) Welsh: name borne in Celtic mythology by a minor deity associated with the moon, and in the *Mabinogi* by a daughter of Hyfeidd the Old. It is probably derived from the Old Celtic title *Rigantona* 'great queen'; it was not used as a given name before the 20th century.

Rhisiart (m.) Welsh form of RICHARD.

Rhoda (f.) English: from the post-classical Greek name *Rhoda*, derived either directly from *rhodon* rose, or else indirectly as an ethnic name meaning 'woman from Rhodes', an island which possibly originally got its name from the same word *rhodon*. In the New Testament Rhoda was a servant in the house of Mary the mother of John, where Peter went after his release from prison by an angel (Acts 12: 13). In the Scottish Highlands *Rhoda* appears to be used as a feminine form of RODERICK.

Rhodri (m.) Welsh: from an Old Welsh personal name composed of the elements *rhod* wheel + *rhi* ruler, borne by a 9th-century Welsh king.

Rhona (f.) Scottish and English: of uncertain derivation, apparently originating in Scotland sometime around 1870. The spelling **Rona** is also found, and it is probable that the name was devised as a feminine form of RONALD or an Anglicized form of *Raghnaid* (see RAGNHILD). It has also been suggested that it may be associated with the Hebridean island name *Rona* (cf. AILSA, IONA, ISLA); the spelling would then have been altered by association with RHODA.

Rhonda (f.) English: of recent origin, apparently a blend of RHODA and RHONA. It is now generally taken to be a Welsh name composed of the elements *rhon* pike, lance, as in RHONWEN, + *-da* good, as in GLENDA. The *Rhondda* valley in South Wales was probably also a factor in making this connection, although it derives from a river name of completely different etymology.

Rhonwen (f.) Welsh: traditional name composed either of the elements *rhon* lance + *(g)wen* white, fair, blessed, holy or of *rhawn* hair + *(g)wen*. It was used by medieval Welsh poets as a form of ROWENA, regarded as the progenitrix of the English nation, and is now fairly common in Wales.

Rhydderch (m.) Welsh: traditional name, originally a byname meaning 'reddish-brown'. This was a relatively common name in the Middle Ages and in Tudor times, when it gave rise to the surname *Prothero(e)* (Welsh *ap Rhydderch* 'son of Rhydderch'). It has recently been revived by parents proudly conscious of their Welsh roots and culture.

Anglicized form: RODERICK.

Rhys (m.) Welsh: traditional name meaning 'ardour'. The name was borne in the early Middle Ages by various rulers in south-west Wales, such as Rhys ap Tewdur (d. 1093) and Rhys ap Gruffudd (1132–97).

Anglicized form: REES.

Ria (f.) Short form of MARIA, of German origin but now also used occasionally in the English-speaking world.

Rich (m.) English: short form of RICHARD. There was a medieval name *Rich(e)*, but it is connected only indirectly with the modern form: it represents a short form of several medieval names, including not only *Richard* but also other, rarer names of Norman (Germanic) origin with the same first element, as, for example, *Rich(i)er* 'power army' and *Richaud* 'power rule'. It also came to be used as an independent baptismal name in the 15th century.

Richard (m.) English, French, German, and Czech: one of the most enduringly successful of the Germanic personal names introduced into Britain by the Normans. It is composed of the elements *rīc* power + *hard* hardy, brave, strong. It has enjoyed continuous popularity in England from the Conquest to the present day, strongly influenced by the fact that it was borne by three kings of England, in particular Richard I (1157–99). He was king for only ten years (1189–99), most of which he spent in warfare abroad, costing the people of England considerable sums in taxes. Nevertheless, he achieved the status of a folk hero, and was never in England long enough to disappoint popular faith in his goodness and justice. He was also Duke of Aquitaine and Normandy and Count of Anjou, fiefs which he held at a time of maximum English expansion in France. His exploits as a leader of the Third Crusade earned him the nickname 'Cœur de Lion' or 'Lionheart' and a permanent place in popular imagination, in which he was even more firmly enshrined by Sir Walter Scott's novel *Ivanhoe* (1820).

Cognates: Irish Gaelic: **Ristéard**. Scottish Gaelic: **Ruiseart**. Welsh: **Rhisiart**. Italian: **Riccardo**. Spanish: **Ricardo**. Low German: **Ri(c)kert**. Scandinavian: **Rikard**. Polish: **Ryszard**.

Short forms: English: **Rick**, DICK, RICH.

Pet forms: English: **Ricky**, **Rickie**; **Dicky**, **Dickie**; RICHIE.

Feminine form: **Ricarda** (Latinate, used mainly in Germany).

Richie (m.) Scottish, English, and Australian: pet form of RICHARD. The suffix *-ie* was originally characteristic of Scotland and northern England, but the name is now found elsewhere. In some cases it represents a transferred use of the surname derived from the Scottish pet name.

Variant: **Ritchie** (probably also a transferred use of the surname spelled thus).

Ridley (m.) English: transferred use of the surname, originally a local name from any of various places, in Essex, Kent, Cheshire, Northumbria, and elsewhere. The first two are so called from Old English *hrēod* reeds + *lēah* wood or clearing, the latter two from *rydde* cleared land + *lēah*. The given name may have been chosen in some cases by ardent Protestants to express admiration for Bishop Nicholas Ridley (?1500–55), burnt at the stake for his Protestantism under Mary Tudor.

Riel (m.) Czech: short form of GABRIEL.

Rieti (m.) Finnish form of FREDERICK.

Rigborg (f.) Danish: from an Old High German female personal name composed of the elements *rīc* power + *burg* fortification.

Rigmor (f.) Scandinavian (Danish): from an Old High German female personal name composed of the elements *rīc* power + *muot* spirit, courage. The second element has been replaced by the Scandinavian form *mār* maid.

Rikard (m.) Scandinavian form of RICHARD.

Rike (f.) German: short form of any of the various female names ending thus, for example FRIEDERIKE, *Heinrike* (see HEINRICH), and ULRIKE.

Rikki (f.) English: feminine form of *Ricky* or *Rickie* (pet forms of *Rick*, a short form of RICHARD), modelled on NIKKI and *Vikki* (see VICKY).

Riley (m.) English: in some cases a transferred use of the English surname, originally a local name from a place named with the Old English elements *ryge* rye + *lēah* clearing, meadow. There is one such place in Devon and another in Lancashire. In other cases it probably represents a respelling of the Irish surname *Reilly*, which is from an old Irish personal name, *Raghallach*, of unknown origin.

Rina (f.) English: short form of any of the various female names ending in these syllables or Anglicized form of Irish RÍONA.

Rinaldo (m.) Italian form of REYNOLD.

Ríona (f.) Irish Gaelic: a simplified form of **Ríonach**, earlier *Ríoghnach*, which is probably a derivative of *rioghan* queen (cf. RHIANNON). It is now also commonly used as a short form of CAITRÍONA.

Riordan (m.) Irish: Anglicized form of the Gaelic name **Rórdán**, earlier *Ríogh-*

bhardán, composed of the elements *riogh* king + a diminutive form of *bard* poet.

Variant: **Rearden**.

Riška (f.) Czech: short form of *Bedřiška* (see BEDŘICH) and *Oldřiška* (see OLDŘICH), used as a pet name.

Ristéard (m.) Irish Gaelic form of RICHARD.

Risto (m.) Finnish form of CHRISTOPHER.

Rita (f.) English and Scandinavian: originally a short form of *Margarita*, the Spanish form of MARGARET, or of *Margherita*, the Italian form. This short form is much more common in England and America than either of the full versions.

Rivka (f.) Jewish: Hebrew form of REBECCA.

Roald (m.) Norwegian: from an Old Norse personal name composed of the elements *hróðr* fame + *valdr* ruler.

Roar (m.) Scandinavian form of ROGER.

Robert (m.) English, Scottish, and French (also Scandinavian): one of the many French names of Germanic origin that were introduced into Britain by the Normans. This one is composed of the nearly synonymous elements *hrod* fame + *berht* bright, famous. It had a native Old English predecessor of similar form (*Hreodbeorht*), which was supplanted by the Norman name. It was the name of two dukes of Normandy in the 11th century: the father of William the Conqueror (sometimes identified with the legendary Robert the Devil), and his eldest son. It was borne by three kings of Scotland, notably Robert the Bruce (1274–1329), who freed Scotland from English domination. The altered short form *Bob* is very common, but *Hob* and *Dob*, which were common in the Middle Ages and gave rise to surnames, are extinct. See also RUPERT.

Cognates: Scottish Gaelic: **Raibeart**. Irish Gaelic **Roibéard**. Italian, Spanish, Portuguese: **Roberto**. German: **Rupprecht**. Low German (also English): RUPERT.

Short forms: English: **Bob**, **Rob**. Scottish: **Rob, Rab**.

Pet forms: English: **Bobby**, **Robbie**, ROBIN. Scottish: **Robbie, Rabbie**; **Roban** (Gaelic).

Feminine form: English: **Roberta**.

Robin (m., f.) English: originally a pet form of ROBERT, from the short form *Rob* and the diminutive suffix *-in* (of Old French origin), but now nearly always used as an independent name. In recent years it has been increasingly used as a female name, no doubt partly influenced by the vocabulary word for the bird.

Variant: **Robyn** (f.).

Rocco (m.) Italian: of Germanic origin, derived from the element *hrok* rest. The name was borne by a 14th-century saint, a Frenchman from Montpelier who was on a pilgrimage to Rome when he encountered plague victims in north Italy. He stopped to nurse them, and went from place to place ministering to these unfortunates in many cities. Eventually, at Piacenza, he too was stricken. In his extremity he was comforted by the companionship of a dog (hence his representation in paintings as accompanied by a dog). He is said to have recovered and returned home, but was not recognized by his family and died in prison. He is a patron saint of the sick and his aid is invoked by Roman Catholics against illness.

Cognates: French: **Roch**. Spanish and Portuguese: **Roque**. Catalan: **Roc**.

Rochelle (f.) U.S., French, and English: either a feminine diminutive form of *Roch* (see ROCCO), or else derived from the French fishing port of La Rochelle on the Atlantic coast, which was a stronghold of Protestantism in the 16th and 17th centuries. The given name is little used in France but common in the United States, especially among Blacks. The American name may in part represent a respelling of RACHELLE.

Rocío (f.) Spanish: from a title of the Virgin Mary, *Maria de la Rocío* 'Mary of the Dew' (Spanish *rocío*, from Late Latin *ros-*

cidum, an adjectival derivative of *ros* dew). Dew is closely associated with Mary, and is sometimes symbolically connected in Roman Catholic hagiography with the tears which she sheds for the wickedness of the world.

Rocky (m.) English: of recent American origin, originally a nickname for a tough individual. The name came to public notice through the American heavyweight boxing champion Rocky Marciano (1923–69). He was of Italian extraction, and Anglicized his original name, ROCCO, into a form that seems particularly appropriate for a fighter. It was later taken up in a film as the name of a boxer played by the muscular actor Sylvester Stallone, and it has also been adopted as a nickname among devotees of body-building.

Rod (m.) English: short form of RODERICK and RODNEY.

Pet form: **Roddy**.

Roderick (m.) English: of Germanic origin, composed of the elements *hrōd* fame + *rīc* power. This name was introduced into England, in slightly different forms, first by Scandinavian settlers in the Danelaw and later by the Normans. However, it did not survive beyond the Middle English period. It owes its modern use to a poem by Sir Walter Scott, *The Vision of Don Roderick* (1811), where it is an Anglicized form of the cognate Spanish name RODRIGO, borne by the last Visigothic king of Spain, whose vision is the subject of the poem. It is now also very commonly used as an Anglicized form of two unrelated Celtic names: Scottish Gaelic *Ruairidh* (see RUAIDHRÍ) and Welsh RHYDDERCH. See also RURIK.

Pet form: Scottish: **Roddy**.

Feminine forms: Scottish (Highland): **Rodina**, **Rhoda**.

Rodion (m.) Russian: from a short form of the Greek name *Hērōdion*, a diminutive form of *Hērōdēs*, itself a derivative (originally patronymic in form) of *Hēra*, the name of a Greek goddess, wife of Zeus. The name *Herodion* was borne by a kinsman of St Paul mentioned in the New Testament (Romans 16: 11). According to post-biblical tradition he became bishop of Patras and met a martyr's death.

Pet form: **Rodya**.

Rodney (m.) English: originally a transferred use of the surname, but in independent use as a given name since the 18th century, when it was bestowed in honour of Admiral Lord Rodney (1719–92), who soundly defeated the French navy in 1759–60. The surname probably derives ultimately from a placename, but the location and etymology of this are uncertain. Stoke Rodney in Somerset is probably named from the surname: the manor was held by one Richard de *Rodene* in the early 14th century.

Rodolf (m.) German and Dutch: variant of RUDOLF.

Rodolfo (m.) Italian and Spanish form of RUDOLF.

Rodolphe (m.) French form of RUDOLF.

Rodrigo (m.) Spanish: of Germanic (Visigothic) origin, composed of the elements *hrōd* fame and *rīc* power, and so a cognate of RODERICK, which represents an Anglicized form of it. It was the name of the last king of the Visigoths, who was defeated by the Moors in 711, and of a saint martyred under the Moors at Cordoba in 857. It is now sometimes used in the English-speaking world, but mainly in families of Hispanic descent.

Pet form: **Ruy**.

Rodya (m.) Russian: pet form of RODION.

Roelof (m.) Dutch: vernacular form of RODOLF.

Rogelio (m.) Spanish: from Late Latin *Rogelius* (or *Rogellus*), a name of uncertain derivation. It may be a diminutive form of *Rogātus* 'requested, prayed for'. Sts Rogellus and Servus-Dei were martyred at Cordoba under the Moors in 852.

Roger (m.) English and French: of Germanic origin, composed of the elements *hrōd* fame + *gār, gēr* spear. This, the Continental Germanic form, was introduced to Britain by the Normans, replacing the native Old English cognate *Hrōðgār* (see HROTHGAR). Roger, Count of Sicily (*c.* 1031–1101), son of Tancred, recovered Sicily from the Arabs. His son, also called Roger, ruled Sicily as king, presiding over a court noted for its splendour and patronage of the arts.

In modern English usage, the informal short form **Rodge** is occasionally encountered, but the medieval short forms *Hodge* and *Dodge* are extinct.

Variant: English: **Rodger**.

Cognates: Italian: **Rugg(i)ero**. Spanish: **Rogerio**. German: **Rüdiger**. Low German: **Rötger**. Dutch: **Rutger**. Scandinavian: **Roar**.

Roibéard (m.) Irish Gaelic form of ROBERT.

Róisín (f.) Irish Gaelic: pet form of **Róis**, itself the Gaelic form of ROSE.

Variant: **Rosheen** (Anglicized).

Roland (m.) English and French, also German and Scandinavian: derived from a Germanic personal name composed of the elements *hrōd* fame + *land* land, territory. The name was introduced to Britain by the Normans. It was borne by a legendary Frankish hero, a vassal of Charlemagne, whose exploits are related in the *Chanson de Roland*. The subject of the poem is Roland's death at the Battle of Roncesvalles in the Pyrenees in 778, while protecting the rearguard of the Frankish army on its retreat from Spain. Roland is depicted in literature and legend as headstrong and impulsive. His devoted friendship with the prudent Oliver is also legendary. In Italian literature he appears as ORLANDO.

Variant: English: **Rowland**.

Cognates: Welsh: **Rolant**. Italian: ORLANDO. Spanish: **Roldán**. Portuguese: **Roldão**. Hungarian: **Loránd**.

Feminine form: French and English: **Rolande** (rare).

Rolf (m.) English, German, and Scandinavian: a contracted version of an old Germanic personal name composed of the elements *hrōd* fame + *wulf* wolf. This is found in Old Norse as *Hrólfr*. As an English name, it represents in part a Norman importation of a Continental Germanic form, in part a much more recent (19th-century) importation of the modern German name. See also RUDOLF.

Rollo (m.) Latinized form of *Roul*, the Old French version of ROLF (cf. *Raoul* for *Ralph*). This form appears regularly in Latin documents of the Middle Ages, but does not seem to have been used in everyday vernacular contexts. It is the form by which the first Duke of Normandy (*c.*860–932) is generally known. He was a Viking who, with his followers, settled at the mouth of the Seine and raided Paris, Chartres, and elsewhere. By the treaty of St Clair he received the duchy of Normandy from Charles III, on condition that he should receive Christian baptism. Use of this name in English families in modern times seems to be a consciously archaistic revival.

Roly (m.) English: pet form of ROLAND. See also ROWLEY.

Roman (m.) Russian, Polish, and Czech: from the Late Latin personal name *Rōmānus*, originally an ethnic name meaning 'Roman' (a derivative of *Rōma*; cf. ROMOLO). This name was borne by a large number of early saints, and in the 10th century was given as a baptismal name to Boris, son of Vladimir, the ruler who Christianized Kievan Russia. Boris and his brother Gleb were murdered by their brother Svyatopolk and canonized as martyrs.

Cognates: French: **Romain**. Italian: **Romano**. Spanish: **Román**. Portuguese: **Romão**.

Feminine forms: Latinate: **Romana**. French: **Romaine** (also used in the English-speaking world).

Romeo (m.) Italian: from the medieval religious name *Romeo* 'pilgrim to Rome' (Late Latin *Rōmaeus*, a derivative of *Rōma*;

cf. ROMOLO). For his romantic tragedy, Shakespeare derived the name of the hero, the lover of Juliet, from a poem by Arthur Brooke, *The Tragicall Historye of Romeus and Juliet*. This is ultimately derived from a story by the Italian writer Matteo Bandello (1485–1561), whose works are the source of the plots of several Elizabethan and Jacobean plays.

Romilda (f.) N. Italian: from an old Germanic female personal name composed of the elements *hrōm* fame + *hild* battle.

Romolo (m.) Italian (characteristic of the region around Rome): from the Latin name *Rōmulus*, borne by one of the legendary founders of the Roman state. According to the legend, Romulus won a competition with his twin brother Remus to name and rule over the city which they had founded. In fact the derivation is the other way about, and *Rōmulus* comes from *Rōma* Rome, itself of uncertain origin. The Romans themselves often connected it with Greek *rhōmē* strength, but this is no more than a folk etymology.

Feminine form: **Romola** (the name of the heroine of a novel by George Eliot, set in 15th-century Florence).

Romy (f.) German and English: pet form of *Rosemarie* (see ROSEMARY), made famous by the Austrian film actress Romy Schneider (1938–82).

Variant: English: **Romey**.

Rona (f.) English: variant of RHONA.

Ronald (m.) English and Scottish: from the Old Norse personal name *Rögnvaldr*; see RAGNVALD. This name was regularly used in the Middle Ages in northern England and Scotland, where Scandinavian influence was strong. It is now widespread throughout the English-speaking world. See also RANALD and RAGHNALL.

Short form: **Ron**.

Pet form: **Ronnie**.

Feminine form: **Ronalda** (Scottish).

Ronan (m.) Irish: from Gaelic **Rónán**, originally a byname representing a diminutive form of *rón* seal (the animal). The name is recorded as borne by various early Celtic saints, but there has been much confusion in the transmission of their names and most of them are also reliably named as *Ruadhán* (see ROWAN). The most famous is a 5th-century Irish saint who was consecrated as a bishop by St Patrick and subsequently worked as a missionary in Cornwall and Brittany.

Ronit (f.) 1. Irish: Anglicized form of Gaelic RATHNAIT.

2. Jewish: modern Hebrew name meaning 'song'.

Ronnie (m., f.) English: 1. (m.) Pet form of RONALD.

2. (f.) Pet form of VERONICA.

Roque (m.) Spanish and Portuguese form of ROCCO.

Rory (m.) Irish and Scottish: Anglicized form of the Gaelic name RUAIDHRÍ (Irish) or *Ruairidh*, *Ruaraidh* (Scottish). In Scotland this is further Anglicized to RODERICK.

Ros (f.) English: short form of ROSALIND and ROSAMUND.

Rosa (f.) Spanish, Italian, and Latinate form of ROSE, also in use in Scandinavia.

Pet forms: Spanish: **Rosita**. Italian: **Rosetta**. English: **Rosie**.

Rosalba (f.) Italian: from the Latinate elements *rosa* rose + *alba* (feminine) white. This was apparently originally coined as an ornamental name.

Rosaleen (f.) English: variant of ROSALYN, influenced by the suffix *-een* (in origin the Irish Gaelic diminutive *-ín*). 'Dark Rosaleen' was the title of a poem by James Clarence Mangan (1803–49), based on the Gaelic poem *Róisín Dubh*; in it the name is used as a figurative allusion to the Irish nation.

Rosalie (f.) French form of the Latin name *Rosalia* (from *rosa* rose), introduced to the English-speaking world in the latter part of the 19th century. St Rosalia was a

12th-century Sicilian virgin, and is the patron of Palermo.

Cognate: Italian: **Rosalia.**

Rosalind (f.) English: originally an old Germanic female name composed of the elements *hros* horse + *lind* weak, tender, soft, which was introduced to Britain by the Normans. In the Middle Ages it was reanalysed by folk etymology as if from Latin *rosa linda* 'lovely rose'. Its popularity as a given name owes much to its use by Edmund Spenser for the character of a shepherdess in his pastoral poetry, and by Shakespeare as the name of the heroine in *As You Like It* (1599).

Rosaline (f.) English: originally a variant of ROSALIND; cf. ROSALYN and ROSALEEN. It is the name of a minor character in Shakespeare's *Love's Labour's Lost* and is used for another, who does not appear but is merely mentioned, in *Romeo and Juliet*.

Rosalyn (f.) English: altered form of ROSALIND. **Rosalin** was a common medieval form, since the letter *-d* tended to occur variably with final *-n*. The name has been further influenced by the productive suffix *-lyn* (see LYNN).

Variants: **Rosalynn(e).**

Rosamund (f.) English: from an old Germanic female personal name composed of the elements *hros* horse + *mund* protection. In the Middle Ages it was reanalysed as Latin *rosa munda* 'pure rose' or *rosa mundi* 'rose of the world', titles given to the Virgin Mary. The spelling **Rosamond** has been common since the Middle Ages, when scribes sometimes used *o* for *u*, to distinguish it from *n* and *m*, all of which consisted of very similar downstrokes of the pen. 'Fair Rosamond' (Rosamond Clifford) was a legendary beauty who lived at Woodstock in Oxfordshire in the 12th century. She is said to have been the mistress of King Henry II, and to have been murdered by the queen, Eleanor of Aquitaine, in 1176.

Rosangela (f.) Italian: combination of the names ROSA and ANGELA.

Rosanne (f.) English: modern coinage from a combination of the names ROSE and ANNE, probably influenced by the popularity of the given name ROXANE.

Variants: **Roseanne, Rosanna; Rosannagh** (a fanciful respelling).

Rosario (f.) Spanish: from a title of the Virgin Mary, *Nuestra Señora del Rosario* 'Our Lady of the Rosary'. The rosary (from Latin *rosārium*, originally 'rose bower') became an important symbol in Catholic life during the 15th century; the feast of Our Lady of the Rosary was established in 1573 and extended to the whole Church in 1716. In southern Italy and in Sicily this is occasionally used as a male name, influenced no doubt by the fact that the ending *-o* is characteristically masculine.

Pet form: **Charo.**

Rościsław (m.) Polish: from an old Slavonic personal name composed of the elements *rosts* usurp, arrogate + *slav* glory (cf. SOBIESŁAW).

Cognate: Russian, Czech: **Rostislav.**

Feminine forms: Polish: **Rościsława.** Czech: **Rostislava.**

Pet forms: Russian: **Rostya** (m.). Czech: **Rost'a** (m., f.); **Rostek, Rostí(če)k** (m.); **Rostin(k)a, Rostuška** (f.).

Roscoe (m.) English: transferred use of the surname, which originated as a local name from a place in northern England named with the Old Norse elements *rá* roe-deer + *skógr* wood, copse.

Rose (f.) English: ostensibly from the name of the flower (Latin *rosa*). However, the name was in use throughout the Middle Ages, long before any of the other female names derived from flowers, which are generally of 19th-century origin. In part it may refer to the flower as a symbol of the Virgin Mary, but it seems likely that it also has a Germanic origin, probably as a short form of various female names with the first element *hros* horse or *hrod* fame.

The Latinate form *Rohesia* is commonly found in documents of the Middle Ages. As well as being a name in its own right, it is currently used as a short form of ROSEMARY and, less often (because of their different pronunciation), of other names beginning *Ros-*, such as ROSALIND and ROSAMUND.

Cognates: Spanish, Italian, and Latinate: **Rosa**. Irish Gaelic: **Róis**. Yiddish: **Reise**. Polish: **Róża**. Czech: **Růžena**. Hungarian: **Rózsa**.

Pet form: English: **Rosie**.

Roselle (f.) English: combination of the given name ROSE with the productive suffix *-elle* (originally a French feminine diminutive suffix).

Rosemary (f.) English: a 19th-century coinage, from the name of the herb (which is from Latin *ros marīnus* sea dew). It is often also assumed to be a combination of the names ROSE and MARY.

Cognate: German, Scandinavian: **Rosemarie**.

Pet forms: English: **Rosie**. German: **Röschen**, **Romy**.

Rosendo (m.) Spanish: of Germanic (Visigothic) origin, composed of the elements *hrōd* fame + *sinþs* path. St *Rudesind* or Rosendo (907–77) was born in Galicia of a noble family, and served as bishop of Mondoñedo.

Rosetta (f.) Italian: pet form of ROSA, sometimes also used in the English-speaking world.

Rosie (f.) English: pet form of ROSE, ROSA, or ROSEMARY. It was first used in the 1860s and is now well established as an independent given name, particularly in America.

Rosita (f.) Spanish: pet form of ROSA, sometimes also used in the English-speaking world and in Scandinavia.

Ross (m.) Scottish and English: transferred use of the Scottish surname, which is the name of a large kindred that has played a major role in Scottish history. The kindred name appears to be derived ultimately from the Gaelic word *ros* headland.

Rostislav (m.) Russian and Czech form of ROŚCISŁAW.

Feminine form: **Rostislava**.

Pet form: Russian: **Rostya**.

Roswitha (f.) German: Latinate form of an old Germanic female personal name composed of the elements *hrōd* fame + *swinþ* strength. The name was borne by a 10th-century nun, Roswitha of Gandersheim, who wrote Latin verse and plays in the manner of Terence.

Variant: **Roswithe**.

Rötger (m.) Low German form of ROGER.

Rowan (m., f.) English: 1. (m.) Transferred use of the surname, which is of Irish origin, being an Anglicized form of the Gaelic byname *Ruadhán* 'little red one' (a diminutive of *ruadh* red; cf. ROY). It was borne by a 6th-century saint who founded the monastery of Lothra, and it is an alternative name of the 5th-century saint also known as RONAN.

2. (f.) From the English vocabulary word (of Scandinavian origin) for the tree, an attractive sight with its clusters of bright red berries.

Rowena (f.) English: apparently a Latinized form of a Saxon name (of uncertain original form and derivation, perhaps composed of the Germanic elements *hrōd* fame + *wynn* joy). It first occurs in the Latin chronicles of Geoffrey of Monmouth (12th century) as the name of a daughter of the Saxon invader Hengist, and was taken up by Sir Walter Scott as the name of a Saxon woman, Lady Rowena of Hargottstanstede, who marries the eponymous hero of his novel *Ivanhoe* (1819).

Rowland (m.) English: variant of ROLAND, or a transferred use of the surname derived from that name in the Middle Ages.

Rowley (m.) English: variant of ROLY, or a transferred use of the local surname, which originated in the Middle Ages from any of the various places named with the

Old English elements *rūh* rough, overgrown + *lēah* wood or clearing.

Roxane (f.) English and French: from Latin *Roxana*, Greek *Roxanē*, recorded as the name of the wife of Alexander the Great. She was the daughter of Oxyartes the Bactrian, and her name is presumably of Persian origin; it is said to mean 'dawn'. In English literature it is the name of the heroine of a novel by Defoe (1724), a beautiful adventuress who, deserted by her husband, enjoys a glittering career as a courtesan, but eventually dies in a state of penitence, having been thrown into prison for debt.

Variant: **Roxanne**.

Cognate: Russian: **Roksana**.

Roy (m.) Originally a Scottish name, representing an Anglicized spelling of the Gaelic nickname *Ruadh* 'red' (cf. ROWAN). It has since spread to other parts of the English-speaking world, where it is often reanalysed as Old French *roy* king (cf. LEROY).

Royle (m.) English: transferred use of the surname, which originated as a local name from a place in Lancashire, so called from Old English *ryge* rye + *hyll* hill. It may have become popular as a given name because of association with the vocabulary word *royal* (cf. KING) or because of similarity in sound to the name DOYLE.

Royston (m.) English: transferred use of the surname, derived from the name of a place in Hertfordshire, known in the Middle Ages as the 'settlement of *Royce*' (which name is an obsolete variant of ROSE, from its Germanic form). It is now used as a given name especially among British West Indians, although the reasons for its popularity among them are not clear. It may, in some cases, be taken as a version of 'Roy's son'.

Roz (f.) English: variant spelling of ROS, with the final consonant altered to represent the voiced sound of the names from which it derives.

Róża (f.) Polish form of ROSE.

Rozanne (f.) English: variant spelling of ROSANNE or ROXANE.

Rózsa (f.) Hungarian form of ROSE.

Ruaidhrí (m.) Irish Gaelic: traditional name composed of Old Celtic elements meaning 'red' and 'king'. This was the name of the last high king of Ireland, Rory O'Conor, who reigned 1166–70.

Variant: **Ruairí**.

Cognates: Scottish Gaelic: **Ruairi(dh)**, **Ruaraidh**.

Rube (m., f.) English: informal short form of REUBEN and of RUBY.

Ruby (f.) English: from the vocabulary word for the gemstone (Latin *rubīnus*, from *rubeus* red). The name was chiefly common in the late 19th century and up to the middle of the 20th. It is now out of fashion.

Rudi (m.) German: short form of RUDOLF and, occasionally, of RÜDIGER.

Rüdiger (m.) German cognate of ROGER. It was borne by a hero of the medieval *Nibelungenlied*, but is not now a common name.

Rudolf (m.) German, Dutch, Scandinavian, Polish, Czech, and English: from a Latinized version, *Rudolphus*, of the Germanic name *Hrōdwulf* (see ROLF). It was introduced to the English-speaking world from Germany in the 19th century. *Rudolf* was a hereditary name among the Habsburgs, the Holy Roman Emperors and rulers of Austria, from the Emperor Rudolf I (1218–91) to the Archduke Rudolf, Crown Prince of Austria-Hungary, who died in mysterious circumstances at his country house at Meyerling in 1889.

Rudolf Rassendyll was the central character of Anthony Hope's immensely popular adventure stories *The Prisoner of Zenda* (1894) and *Rupert of Hentzau* (1898), in which he is an English gentleman who turns out to be the half-brother of the King of Ruritania, to whom he bears a great physical resemblance and whom he successfully impersonates for reasons of state. In the 20th century the popularity of this name was further enhanced by the American silent-film actor Rudolph Valentino (1895–1926), born in Italy as Rodolpho di Valentina d'Antonguolla. However, it is at present out of fashion.

Variants: German, Dutch: **Rodolf**. Dutch: **Roelof** (vernacular). English: **Rudolph**.

Cognates: French: **Rodolphe**. Italian, Spanish: **Rodolfo**.

Short forms: German: **Rudi**. Dutch: **Ruud**. English: **Rudy**.

Rufino (m.) Italian, Spanish, and Portuguese: from Latin *Rufinus*, a derivative of RUFUS used originally as a Roman family name. The numerous early saints so called include a 5th-century bishop of Capua.

Variant: **Ruffino**.

Cognate: Catalan: **Rufí**.

Rufus (m.) English: from a Latin nickname meaning 'red(-haired)', sometimes used in medieval documents as a translation of various surnames with the same sense. It began to be used as a given name in the 19th century.

Ruggiero (m.) Italian form of ROGER.

Variant: **Ruggero**.

Ruiseart (m.) Scottish Gaelic form of RICHARD.

Runa (f.) Scandinavian: from the Old Norse female personal name *Rúna*, a short form of various female compound names containing the element *rún* secret lore.

Rune (m.) Scandinavian: from the rare Old Norse male personal name *Rúni*, a short form of various male compound names containing the element *rún* secret lore, as, for example, *Rúnólfr*. Its revival in the late 19th century is probably due to the influence of the more frequent female name RUNA. It has become very popular in the 20th century.

Rupert (m.) English, Low German, and Dutch: Low German form of ROBERT, first brought to England by Prince Rupert of the Rhine (1618–92), a dashing military leader who came to help his uncle, Charles I, in the Civil War.

Cognate: German: **Rupprecht**.

Rurik (m.) Russian: from a Scandinavian cognate of RODERICK. This form of the name was borne by a 9th-century Varangian leader who founded the principality of Novgorod and established the Russian monarchy. His descendants held the throne until the 16th century, and the name *Rurik* is still sometimes used in the Soviet Union. This form is also used to some extent in Finland and Sweden.

Russ (m.) English: short form of RUSSELL, now also used as an independent given name. In some cases it may represent a transferred use of the surname *Russ*, from Old French *rous* red.

Russell (m.) English: transferred use of the common surname, itself originally from the Old French nickname *Rousel* 'little red one' (a diminutive of *rous* red, from Latin *russus*). It is now widely used as a given name in its own right and may in some cases have been bestowed in honour of the philosopher Bertrand Russell (1872–1970), who was noted for his liberal agnostic views and his passionate championship of causes such as pacifism (in the First World War), free love, and nuclear disarmament. He was the grandson of the Victorian statesman Lord John Russell (1792–1878).

Rusty (m., f.) English: nickname for someone with reddish-brown hair, from modern English *rust* (Old English *rust*).

Rut (f.) Form of RUTH used in Italy, Spain, Germany, the Netherlands, Scandinavia, and Poland. Only in Sweden is it really common; there it was the twenty-fourth most frequent female name in 1973.

Rutger (m.) Dutch form of ROGER.

Ruth (f.) Biblical: name (of uncertain derivation) of a Moabite woman who left her own people to remain with her mother-in-law Naomi, and afterwards became the wife of Boaz and an ancestress of David. Her story is told in the book of the Bible that bears her name. It was popular among the Puritans, partly because of its association with the term *ruth* meaning 'compassion'. It is now as common among Gentiles as among Jews.

Cognate: Gaelic, Italian, Spanish, German, Dutch, Scandinavian, and Polish: **Rut**.

Ruud (m.) Dutch: short form of RUDOLF.

Ruy (m.) Spanish: pet form of RODRIGO. This form was common in the Middle Ages, being borne, for example, by El Cid, Ruy Diaz de Vivar (?1043–99).

Růžena (f.) Czech form of ROSE.

Ryan (m.) U.S., Australian, Irish, and English: from the Irish Gaelic surname *Ó Riain* 'descendant of Rian'. *Rian* is an old Gaelic personal name of uncertain origin, probably a derivative of *rí* king.

Ryszard (m.) Polish form of RICHARD.

S

Sabella (f.) English: modern name, apparently derived from *Isabella* by the dropping of the initial vowel (see ISABEL).

Sabia (f.) Irish: Latinized form of Gaelic SADHBH, in use during the Middle Ages and occasionally at the present day.

Sabine (f.) French (two syllables) or German (three syllables): from the Latin name *Sabīna* 'Sabine woman'. The Sabines were an ancient Italic race whose territory was early taken over by the Romans. According to tradition, the Romans made a raid on the Sabines and carried off a number of their women, but when the Sabines came for revenge the women succeeded in making peace between the two groups. The name *Sabina* was borne by three minor early Christian saints, in particular a Roman maiden martyred in about 127.

Variant: **Sabina** (used in Ireland as an Anglicized form of Gaelic SADHBH).

Sabrina (f.) English: from the name of a character in Celtic legend, who supposedly gave her name to the River Severn. In fact this is one of the most ancient of all British river names, and its true origins are obscure. Legend, as preserved by Geoffrey of Monmouth, had it that Sabrina was the illegitimate daughter of a Welsh king called Locrine, and was drowned in the river on the orders of the king's wife Gwendolen. The river name is found in the form *Sabrina* in the Latin writings of Tacitus, Gildas, and Bede. Geoffrey of Monmouth comments that in Welsh the name is *Habren* (modern Welsh *Hafren*). The name of the legendary character is almost certainly derived from that of the river, rather than vice versa.

Sacha (m.) French version of SASHA. Many names of Russian origin were introduced to the English-speaking world, via French, at the time when Diaghilev's Ballet Russe made its great impact in Paris (1909–20).

Sachairi (m.) Scottish Gaelic form of ZACHARY.

Sacheverell (m.) English: transferred use of the surname, apparently originally a baronial name of Norman origin (from an unidentified place in Normandy believed to have been called *Saute-Chevreuil*, meaning 'roebuck leap'). It was made familiar as a given name by the writer Sacheverell Sitwell (1897–1985), who was named in honour of his ancestor William Sacheverell (1638–91), a minor Whig statesman.

Pet form: **Sachie**.

Sadhbh (f.) Irish Gaelic: traditional name, said to mean 'sweet'. This was a very common female given name during the Middle Ages.

Anglicized forms: **Sabia, Sabina, Sive**.

Sadie (f.) English: originally a pet form of SARAH, but now generally treated as an independent name. The exact formation is not clear.

Sal (f., m.) 1. (f.) English: short form of SALLY.

2. (m.) U.S.: short form of Spanish SALVADOR or its Italian cognate, *Salvatore*.

Sally (f.) English: in origin a pet form of SARAH, but in the 20th century normally treated as a name in its own right. It is frequently used as the first element in combinations such as *Sally-Anne* and *Sally-Jane*.

Short form: **Sal**.

Salome (f.) English, German, etc.: Greek form of an unrecorded Aramaic name, related to the Hebrew word *shalom* peace.

It was common at the time of Christ, and was borne by one of the women who were at his tomb at the time of the Resurrection (Mark 16: 1–8). This would normally have led to its common use as a Christian name, and it is indeed found as such in medieval times. However, according to the Jewish historian Josephus, it was also the name of King Herod's stepdaughter, the daughter of Queen Herodias. In the Bible, a daughter of Herodias, generally identified as this Salome, danced for Herod and so pleased him that he offered to give her anything she wanted. Prompted by her mother, she asked for (and got) the head of John the Baptist, who was in one of Herod's prisons (Mark 6: 17–28). This story so gripped medieval imagination that the name Salome became more or less taboo until the end of the 19th century, when Oscar Wilde wrote a play about her and some unconventional souls began to choose the name for their daughters.

Cognates: French: **Salomé**. Polish: **Salomea**.

Salud (f.) Spanish: religious name referring to the Marian title, *Nuestra Señora de la Salud* 'Our Lady of Salvation' (from Latin *salus*, genitive *salūtis*). The Virgin is venerated under this name in several places, especially in Catalonia and Valencia.

Salvador (m.) Spanish: from the Late Latin word *salvātor* saviour; this is a common epithet of Christ, and the name is borne in his honour.

Cognate: Italian: **Salvatore** (common in the south of Italy, where there has been considerable Spanish influence).

Short form: **Sal** (U.S.).

Sam (m., f.) English: 1. (m.) Long-established short form of SAMUEL or, less frequently, of SAMSON.

2. (f.) Short form, which has recently become fashionable, of SAMANTHA.

Pet forms (of 1): **Sammy**. (Of 2): **Sammie**.

Samantha (f.) English: of problematic and much debated origin. It seems to have originated in the southern states of America in the 18th century, possibly as a combination of SAM (from SAMUEL) + a newly coined feminine suffix *-antha* (perhaps suggested by ANTHEA).

Samoyla (m.) Russian: popular form of SAMUEL.

Samson (m.) English form of a biblical name (Hebrew **Shimshon**, probably derived from *shemesh* sun) borne by a Jewish champion and judge famous for his prodigious strength. He was betrayed by his mistress, Delilah, and enslaved and blinded by the Philistines; nevertheless, he was able to bring the pillars of the temple of the Philistines crashing down in a final suicidal act of strength (Judges 13–16). This famous story provided the theme for Milton's poetic drama *Samson Agonistes* (1671), which is modelled on ancient Greek tragedy. In the Middle Ages the popularity of the given name was increased in Celtic areas by the fame of a 6th-century Celtic saint who bore it, probably as a classicized form of some Old Celtic name. He was a Welsh monk who did missionary work in Cornwall and afterwards established a monastery at Dol in Brittany.

Variant: **Sampson** (usually a transferred use of the surname).

Cognate: Italian: **Sansone**.

Samuel (m.) Biblical name (Hebrew **Shemuel**), possibly meaning 'He (God) has hearkened' (presumably to the prayers of a mother for a son). It may also be understood as a contracted form of Hebrew *sha'ul me'el* meaning 'asked of God'. In the case of Samuel the son of Hannah, this would be more in keeping with his mother's statement 'Because I have asked him of the Lord' (1 Samuel 1: 20). Living in the 11th century BC, Samuel was a Hebrew judge and prophet of the greatest historical importance, who established the Hebrew monarchy, anointing as king both Saul and, later, David. In the Authorized Version two books of the Old Testament are named after him, although in

Roman Catholic and Orthodox versions of the Bible they are known as the first and second Book of Kings. The story of Samuel being called by God while still a child serving in the house of Eli the priest (1 Samuel 3) is of great vividness and has moved countless generations.

In England and America the name was particularly popular among the 17th-century Puritans and among Nonconformists from the 17th to the 19th century. It has always been a common Jewish name, and in Gaelic Scotland it has sometimes been used as an Anglicized form of Gaelic *Somhairle* (see SOMERLED).

Cognates: Welsh: **Sawyl**. Hebrew: **Shmuel**. Russian: **Samuil**; **Samoyla** (vernacular form).

Short form: English: SAM.

Pet form: English: **Sammy**.

Sancho (m.) Spanish: of uncertain origin. The vernacular form *Sancho* and the Latin *Sanctius* are used interchangeably in medieval documents, and it is possible that *Sancho* is derived from *Sanctius*, a derivative of *sanctus* holy. On the other hand, the phonetic development is not regular, and it is possible that *Sanctius* is a Latinized form of a name of different origin. St Sancho or Sanctius was martyred at Cordoba by the Moors in 851, but the name is inescapably associated now with Sancho Panza, the dumpy, long-suffering, commonsensical squire of Don Quixote in Cervantes' novel (1605–15).

Feminine forms: **Sanch(i)a**.

Sandalio (m.) Spanish: from Latin *Sandal(i)us*. This seems to be a Latinized form of a Germanic (Visigothic) name composed of the elements *sand* true + *ulf* wolf. A saint of this name was martyred at Cordoba by the Moors in *c.*855.

Sandford (m.) English (U.S.): variant of SANFORD.

Sándor (m.) Hungarian form of ALEXANDER.

Sandra (f.) Italian and English: short form of *Alessandra*, the Italian form of ALEXANDRA. A major influence on its use in English was George Meredith's novel *Sandra Belloni* (1886), originally published as *Emilia in England* (1864); the heroine, Emilia Sandra Belloni, is a beautiful, passionate young singer.

Variant: Scottish: **Saundra**.

Sandro (m.) Italian: short form of *Alessandro* (see ALEXANDER), now common in Italy as a given name in its own right.

Sandy (m., f.) 1. (m.) Scottish and English: pet form, originally Scottish, of ALEXANDER.

2. (f.) English: pet form of ALEXANDRA or SANDRA, now sometimes used as an independent given name.

3. (m., f.) English: nickname for someone with a crop of 'sandy' (light reddish-brown) hair.

Variants: **Sandie** (f.). (Of 1 only): Scottish: **Sandaidh** (Gaelic).

Sanford (m.) English (U.S.): transferred use of the surname, which originated as a local name from any of numerous places in England called *Sandford*, from Old English *sand* sand + *ford* ford. Use as a given name in America honours Peleg Sanford, an early governor (1680–3) of Rhode Island.

Variant: **Sandford**.

Sanna (f.) Scandinavian: short form of SUSANNA. It may be favoured by association with the Swedish and Norwegian adjective *sann* true.

Sansone (m.) Italian form of SAMSON.

Santiago (m.) Spanish: name chosen to invoke the protection of St James on a son. *Iago* is an obsolete Spanish form of JAMES. St James the Greater is the patron saint of Spain; he was one of the twelve disciples of Christ, the brother of John the Baptist, and was martyred under Herod Agrippa. The legend that he visited Spain before his death does not seem to have arisen before the 9th century, but by the 11th century the site of his alleged relics at Compostela in Galicia was a place of pilgrimage from all over Europe. See also DIEGO.

Santos (m.) Spanish and Portuguese: name chosen by parents who wish to invoke the protection of all the saints, without further specification, for their son. It is also often given to a boy born on the feast of All Saints; cf. TOUSSAINT.

Santuzza (f.) Italian: diminutive form, originating in Sicily, of the name *Santa*, a feminine version of *Santo*, from Latin *sanctus* holy. This form of the name has become known through being borne by a character in the opera *Cavalleria Rusticana* (1890) by Mascagni.

Sanya (m.) Russian: pet form of ALEXANDER and ALEXANDRA.

Saoirse (f.) Irish Gaelic: modern name from the vocabulary word meaning 'freedom'.

Sara (f.) Variant of SARAH. This is the form used in the Greek of the New Testament (Hebrews 11: 11).

Sarah (f.) Biblical: name of the wife of Abraham and mother of Isaac. According to the Book of Genesis, she was originally called *Sarai* (possibly meaning 'contentious' in Hebrew), but had her name changed by God to the more auspicious *Sarah* 'princess' in token of a greater blessing (Genesis 17: 15, 'And God said unto Abraham, As for Sarai thy wife, thou shalt not call her name Sarai, but Sarah shall her name be'). In Ireland this has been used as an Anglicized form of SORCHA, in Scotland of MÓR.

Variants: **Sara**, ZARA.

Cognate: Hungarian: **Sára**.

Pet forms: English: SALLY, SADIE. Spanish: **Sarita**. Swedish: **Sassa**. Hungarian: **Sári**.

Sasha (m., f.) English spelling of a Russian pet form of ALEXANDER and ALEXANDRA. It has been used in the English-speaking world as an independent name, introduced in the 20th century via France. Use as a female name in the English-speaking world is encouraged by the characteristically feminine *-a* ending.

Variants: French spelling: **Sacha**. German spelling: **Sascha**.

Saskia (f.) Dutch: of uncertain derivation. The name has been in use since the Middle Ages, and was borne, for example, by the wife of the artist Rembrandt. It may derive by metathesis and Latinization from the Germanic ethnic name element *sachs* Saxon.

Sassa (f.) Swedish: pet form of both ASTRID and SARA.

Saturnino (m.) Italian, Spanish, and Portuguese: from Latin *Saturnīnus*, a derivative of *Saturnus*, the name of the Roman god of agriculture and vegetation. The divine name was connected by the Romans themselves with Latin *satur* full, but this may be no more than folk etymology. There was a very large number of early saints named Saturninus; the most famous is probably the 3rd-century apostle of Navarre and first bishop of Toulouse.

Saul (m.) Biblical: name (from a Hebrew word meaning 'asked for' or 'prayed for') of one of the first kings of Israel, and also, before his conversion, of St Paul. It was popular among the Puritans, but is now once again mainly a Jewish name.

Saundra (f.) Scottish: variant of SANDRA, reflecting the same development in pronunciation as is shown by surnames such as *Saunders* and *Saunderson*, originally from short forms of ALEXANDER.

Sava (m.) Russian: from Late Greek *Sab(b)as*, a derivative of Hebrew *saba* old man. Two early saints of this name are venerated in the Eastern Church. The first was martyred *c.*372 near Tirgovist in Romania; he seems to have been a Goth in origin. The second (439–532) was a Cappadocian who is regarded as one of the founders of Eastern monasticism.

Saveli (m.) Russian: from the Late Latin personal name *Sabellius*, originally an ethnic name denoting a member of the Italian tribe of the Sabelli, displaced by the Romans. The saint venerated under this name, executed under Julian the Apostate in 362, was Persian, and his original name may have been cognate with that discussed at SAVA.

Saverio (m.) Italian form of XAVIER.

Sawney (m.) Scottish: variant of SANDY, resulting from a pronunciation reflected also in the surname *Saunders*. The name declined in popularity in the 19th and 20th centuries, perhaps as a result of its use as a vocabulary word for a fool.

Sawyl (m.) Welsh form of SAMUEL, a reduced version of earlier *Safwyl*.

Scarlett (f.) English: name popularized by the central character in the novel *Gone With the Wind* (1936) by Margaret Mitchell, later made into a famous film. The characters in the novel bear a variety of unusual given names, which had a remarkable influence on naming practices throughout the English-speaking world in the 20th century. According to the novel, the name of the central character was Katie Scarlett O'Hara (the middle name representing her grandmother's maiden surname), but she was always known as Scarlett.

Variant: **Scarlet**.

Scevola (m.) Italian: name chosen out of admiration for the Roman semi-legendary hero of the 6th century BC, Gaius Mucius Scaevola. He is said to have burnt off his own right hand in an altar fire in order to demonstrate to the Etruscan king, Lars Porsenna, the strength of his willpower. Allegedly as a result of this exploit he received the cognomen *Scaevola*, a derivative of *scaevus* left-handed. This was borne in turn by his descendants, several of whom rose to prominent positions in the Roman republic.

Ścibor (m.) Polish: variant of CZCIBOR.

Scott (m.) Scottish and English: although this was in use as a personal name both before and after the Norman Conquest, modern use in most cases almost certainly represents a transferred use of the surname. This originated as a byname for someone from Scotland or, within Scotland itself, a member of the Gaelic-speaking people who originally came from Ireland. The given name is now often chosen by parents conscious of their Scottish ancestry and heritage, but it is also used more widely.

Seaghdh (m.) Scottish Gaelic: traditional name of uncertain derivation, perhaps meaning 'hawk-like, fine, goodly'. It has been Anglicized as SHAW and SETH.

Cognate: Irish Gaelic: **Séaghdha**.

Séamas (m.) Irish Gaelic: modern form of JAMES. Earlier Gaelic spellings are **Séamus, Seumus**, and **Seumas**.

Seán (m.) Irish Gaelic form of JOHN, derived in the early Middle Ages from Anglo-Norman *Jehan*. The name has always been common in Ireland, but is now being increasingly chosen also by parents who have no Irish connections (usually without the accent, **Sean**).

Séarlait (f.) Irish Gaelic form of CHARLOTTE.

Séarlas (m.) Irish Gaelic form of CHARLES.

Seathan (m.) Scottish Gaelic form of JOHN, derived from Old French *Je(h)an*.

Sebastian (m.) English: name of early Christian origin, borne by a 3rd-century saint who was a Roman soldier martyred by the arrows of his fellow officers; his sufferings were a favourite subject for medieval artists. The name means 'man from Sebasta', a town in Asia Minor so called from Greek *Sebastos*, a translation of the Latin imperial title *Augustus*.

Cognates: French: **Sébastien**. Spanish: **Sebastián**. Italian: **Sebastiano**. Dutch: **Sebastiaan**. Russian: **Sevastian**.

Short forms: English: **Seb**. French: **Bastien**. Russian: **Seva**.

Séimí (m.) Irish Gaelic form of the Scottish male name JAMIE, in use in Northern Ireland.

Selig (m.) Jewish: from the Yiddish vocabulary word *selig* happy, fortunate (modern German *selig*), used as a vernacular translation of the Hebrew name ASHER.

Variant: **Zelig.**

Selima (f.) English: of uncertain origin. The name seems to have been first recorded by the poet Thomas Gray (1716–71) as that of Horace Walpole's cat, 'drowned in a tub of gold fishes'. The metre shows that the name was stressed on the first syllable, but there is no clue as to its derivation. Gray was possibly influenced by the Arabic name *Selim* 'peace'.

Selina (f.) English: of uncertain origin. The name first occurs in the 17th century, and it may be an altered form of *Selena* (Greek *Selēnē*), the name of a goddess of the moon, or of *Celina* (Latin *Caelīna*), a derivative of CELIA. The name suddenly became more popular in Britain in the 1980s, partly perhaps because of the familiarity of the television newsreader Selina Scott.

Selma (f.) English: of uncertain origin, probably a contracted form of SELIMA. It has also been occasionally used in Germany and Scandinavia, probably because it occurs as the name of Ossian's castle in Macpherson's poems, once enormously popular there.

Selwyn (m.) English: transferred use of the surname, which is of disputed origin. There was a given name *Selewyn* in use in the Middle Ages, which probably represents a survival of an unrecorded Old English name composed of the elements *sēle* prosperity or *sele* hall + *wine* friend. Alternatively, the surname may be Norman, derived from *Seluein*, an Old French form of Latin *Silvānus* (from *silva* wood; cf. SILAS).

Variant: **Selwin.**

Semyon (m.) Russian form of SIMON (actually from the form *Simeon*).

Pet form: **Senya.**

Senan (m.) Irish: Anglicized form of the Gaelic name **Seanán**, originally a byname representing a diminutive of *sean* old, wise. This name was borne by numerous early Irish saints, including a 6th-century bishop and a 7th-century hermit.

Sender (m.) Jewish: Yiddish form of ALEXANDER.

Senga (f.) Scottish: common in the north-east of Scotland, this name is popularly supposed to represent AGNES spelled backwards (which it undeniably does). However, it is more likely to have originated from the Gaelic vocabulary word *seang* slender.

Senya (m.) Russian: pet form of both ARSENI and SEMYON.

Seocan (m.) Scottish Gaelic: pet form of JOCK.

Seoirse (m.) Irish Gaelic form of GEORGE.

Seonag (f.) Scottish Gaelic form of JOAN.

Seònaid (f.) Scottish Gaelic form of JANET.

Anglicized forms: **Seona, Shona.**

Seòras (m.) Scottish Gaelic form of GEORGE.

Variants: **Seòrsa, Deòrsa.**

Seòsaidh (m.) Scottish Gaelic form of JOSEPH.

Seosaimhín (f.) Irish Gaelic form of JOSEPHINE.

Seosamh (m.) Irish Gaelic form of JOSEPH.

Sepp (m.) German (esp. Bavarian): short form of JOSEPH.

Septimus (m.) English: from a Late Latin name derived from Latin *septimus* seventh. It was fairly commonly used in large Victorian families for the seventh son or a male seventh child, but is now rare.

Seraphina (f.) Latinate derivative of Hebrew *seraphim* 'burning ones', the name of an order of angels (Isaiah 6: 2). It was borne by a rather shadowy saint who was martyred at the beginning of the 5th century in Italy, Spain, or Armenia.

Variant: **Serafina.**

Cognate: Russian: **Serafima.**

Short form: English: **Fina.**

Pet forms: Russian: **Sima, Fima, Fimochka.**

Masculine form: Italian: **Serafino.**

Serena (f.) From a Latin name, representing the feminine form of the adjective *serēnus* calm, serene. It was borne by an early Christian saint, about whom little is known. In her *Life* she is described as a wife of the Emperor Domitian (AD 51–96), but there is no mention of her in any of the historical sources that deal with this period.

Serge (m.) French form of SERGEI, brought into use at the beginning of the 20th century. There is no connection with the type of material called *serge* (Old French *sarge*, from Latin *sericum* silk).

Sergei (m.) Russian: from the old Roman family name *Sergius*, which is of uncertain, though probably Etruscan, origin. (It was borne, for example, by the conspirator denounced by Cicero, Lucius Sergius Catilina.) St Sergius of Radonezh (*c.*1314–92) is one of the most famous of all Russian saints, hence the great popularity of the name.

Pet form: **Seryozha.**

Servaas (m.) Dutch: from the Late Latin name *Servātius*, a derivative of *servātus* saved, i.e. 'redeemed'. This was the name of a 4th-century saint, bishop of Tangres in the Low Countries.

Sessy (f.) English: pet form of CECILY.

Sesto (m.) Italian form of SEXTUS.

Seth (m.) Biblical: name (from a Hebrew word meaning 'appointed, placed') of the third son of Adam, who was born after the murder of Abel (Genesis 4: 25, 'And Adam knew his wife again; and she bare a son, and called his name Seth: For God, said she, hath appointed me another seed instead of Abel, whom Cain slew'). It was popular among the Puritans (particularly for children born after the death of an elder sibling), and has been occasionally used since. By the 20th century it had become rare. It was used for the darkly passionate rural character Seth Starkadder in Stella Gibbons's comic novel *Cold Comfort Farm* (1932). In Scotland it has been used as an Anglicized form of SEAGHDH.

Seumas (m.) Scottish Gaelic form of JAMES, also an older Irish Gaelic form.

Seumus (m.) Irish Gaelic: older spelling of SÉAMAS.

Seva (m.) Russian: pet form of both VSEVOLOD and SEVASTIAN.

Variant: **Syova.**

Sevastian (m.) Russian form of SEBASTIAN.

Variant: **Sevastyan.**

Seve (m.) Spanish: pet form of SEVERIANO and SEVERINO.

Severiano (m.) Italian, Spanish, and Portuguese: from Latin *Sevēriānus*, a further elaboration of *Sevērīnus* (see SEVERINO). The name was borne by several early minor saints, but is not now in common use.

Severino (m.) Italian, Spanish, and Portuguese: from the Latin family name *Sevērīnus*, a derivative of *Sevērus* (see SEVERO). This name was borne by a large number of early saints, including a 5th-century apostle of Austria and a 6th-century bishop of Santempeda (now *Sanseverino*).

Cognates: Polish: **Seweryn.** Danish: **Søren.** Hungarian: **Szörény.**

Feminine forms: Latinate: **Severina.** French: **Sévérine.**

Severo (m.) Italian, Spanish, and Portuguese: from Latin *Sevērus*, an old Roman family name, originally a byname meaning 'severe, stern'. This name was borne by a large number of early saints, including bishops of Ravenna (d. *c.*348), Naples (d. 409), and Barcelona (d. 633).

Sextus (m.) Traditional Latin given name, meaning originally 'sixth'. It was taken up in England during the Victorian period, often for a sixth son or a male sixth child, but it is now little used. The form *Sixtus* borne by three early popes is most likely a variant of this name, although it is often associated with the Greek word *xystos* polished.

Cognates: Italian: **Sesto, Sisto**.

Seymour (m.) English: transferred use of the surname, originally a Norman baronial name from *Saint-Maur* in Normandy. This place was so called from the dedication of its church to St Maurus, whose Latin name means 'Moor', i.e. North African. The identity of this saint is not known.

Sgàire (m.) Scottish Gaelic: traditional name, probably in origin a borrowing of the Old Norse byname *Skári* 'sea-mew'. It has sometimes been Anglicized as ZACHARY.

Shabbetai (m.) Jewish: Hebrew name derived from *shabbāth* sabbath (itself a derivative of *shābath* rested). It has been given to boys born on this day of the week.

Variant (contracted form): **Shabtai**.

Shahar (m.) Jewish: modern Hebrew name meaning 'dawn'.

Shalom (m.) Jewish: from the Hebrew vocabulary word *shalom* peace.

Shamus (m.) Anglicized spelling of *Séamus* (see SÉAMAS). It has sometimes been used in Ireland, but is now rare.

Shane (m., f.) English and Irish: early Anglicized form of SEÁN, representing a Northern Irish pronunciation of the Gaelic name. In recent years it has also been used as a female name.

Shanee (f.) English: apparently an Anglicized form of Welsh *Siani* (see SIÂN).

Shannah (f.) English: rare name of uncertain origin. It would seem to represent a short form of *Shoshannah*, the original Hebrew form of SUSANNA. However, the even rarer spelling **Shannagh** would seem to suggest association with the Irish surname *Shannagh*, from Gaelic *Ó Seanaigh* 'descendant of Seanach'. *Seanach* is a Gaelic personal name derived from *sean* old, wise (cf. SENAN).

Shannon (f.) English (chiefly U.S.): from the name of a river in Ireland. It is not clear why it has become so popular as a given name, but it combines a similar phonetic shape to SHARON, an Irish reference as in ERIN, and a river name as in CLODAGH. It is not used in Ireland itself.

Shari (f.) English (esp. U.S.): Anglicized spelling of *Sári* (see SARAH).

Sharman (f., m.) English: 1. (f.) Altered form of CHARMIAN.

2. (m.) Transferred use of the surname, a variant of SHERMAN.

Sharon (f.) English: a 20th-century coinage, from a biblical placename. The derivation is from the phrase 'I am the rose of Sharon, and the lily of the valleys' (Song of Solomon 2: 1). The plant name 'rose of Sharon' is used for a shrub of the genus *Hypericum*, with yellow flowers, and for a species of hibiscus, with purple flowers. *Rosasharn* (Rose of Sharon) is the name of one of the characters in John Steinbeck's novel *The Grapes of Wrath* (1936).

Variant: **Sharron**.

Sharona (f.) Latinate elaborated form of SHARON, now quite often used in the English-speaking world.

Sharonda (f.) English: less frequent elaboration of SHARON, with the suffix *-da* apparently abstracted from names such as GLENDA and LINDA.

Sharron (f.) English: variant spelling of SHARON.

Shaughan (m.) English and Irish: variant spelling of SHAUN, probably influenced by VAUGHAN.

Shaun (m.) Anglicized spelling of SEÁN, somewhat less common than SHAWN in America, but more so in Britain.

Shauna (f.) A feminized form of SHAUN, unknown in Ireland and rare in Britain, but reasonably common in America.

Shaw (m.) 1. Scottish: Anglicized form of SEAGHDH.

2. English: transferred use of the surname, which originated as a local name meaning 'wood, copse' (Old English *sceaga*, Old Norse *skógr*).

Shawn (m.) Anglicized spelling of SEÁN, found mainly in America.

Shayna (f.) Jewish: Yiddish name meaning 'beautiful' (modern German *schön*). See also BEILE and YAFFA.

Variant: **Sheine.**

Sheena (f.) Anglicized spelling of *Sìne* (Scottish) or *Síne* (Irish), the Gaelic forms of JANE (see SÍNE).

Sheila (f.) Anglicized spelling of Irish Gaelic SÍLE, now so common that it is hardly felt to be Irish any longer. In Australia since the 19th century it has been a slang generic term for any woman.

Sheine (f.) Jewish (Yiddish): variant of SHAYNA.

Shelagh (f.) Another Anglicized form of SÍLE (see also SHEILA). The final consonants in the written form seem to have been added to restore a Gaelic feel to the name, since they occur at the end of many Gaelic words and are silent. However, they do not have any historically justified place in the name.

Variant: **Sheelagh.**

Sheldon (m.) English: transferred use of the surname, which originated as a local name from any of various places so called. Examples occur in Derbyshire, Devon, and the West Midlands; they all have different origins.

Shell (f.) English: 1. Normally a short form of MICHELLE.

2. In some cases it may be a back-formation from SHELLEY (as if this contained the hypocoristic suffix *-(e)y*) or simply a shortened form of SHELLEY.

Shelley (f., occasionally m.) English: transferred use of the surname, the most famous bearer of which was the English Romantic poet Percy Bysshe Shelley (1792–1822). The surname is a local name from one of the various places (in Essex, Suffolk, and Yorkshire) named in Old English as the 'wood (or clearing) on (or near) a slope (or ledge)'. The name is now almost exclusively female, in part no doubt as a result of association with SHIRLEY (the actress Shelley Winters was born in 1922 as Shirley Schrift), and in part due to the characteristically feminine ending *-ie*, *-y*.

Shelomit (f.) Jewish: derived from Hebrew *shalom* peace. It is both a male and a female name in the Bible, but in modern Hebrew it is only used as a female name.

Sheree (f.) English: respelled form of *Chérie* (see CHERRY), used especially in America.

Sheridan (m.) English: transferred use of the surname made famous by the Irish playwright Richard Brinsley Sheridan (1751–1816). The surname is from Gaelic *Ó Sirideáin* 'descendant of *Sirideán*', a personal name of uncertain origin, possibly connected with *sirim* to seek.

Sherman (m.) English: transferred use of the surname, which originated in the Middle Ages as an occupational name for someone who trimmed the nap of woollen cloth after it had been woven. It represents a compound of the Old English elements *scēara* shears + *mann* man.

Sherry (f.) English: probably in origin a respelled form of *Chérie* (see CHERRY). It is now more closely associated with the fortified wine, earlier *sherry wine*, so named from the port of Jérez in southern Spain.

Variant: **Sherrie.**

Sheryl (f.) English: variant of CHERYL.

Variants: **Sherill, Sherrill.**

Shevaun (f.) Irish and English: Anglicized form of Gaelic SIOBHÁN.

Shifra (f.) Jewish: from Hebrew *shifra* beauty, grace. Spelled *Shiphrah* in the Authorized Version, it was the name of one of the midwives who defied Pharaoh's order to drown all newborn Hebrew boys (Exodus 1: 15–19).
Variant: **Shiphrah**.

Shilla (f.) English: modern name, apparently an altered spelling of SHEILA.

Shimon (m.) Jewish: modern Hebrew form of SIMON.

Shiphrah (f.) Jewish: variant of SHIFRA.

Shireen (f.) English: variant of SHIRIN, by association with the productive suffix *-een*.

Shirin (f.) Muslim name of Persian or Arabic origin now beginning to be fairly commonly used in the English-speaking world.
Variant: **Shirrin**.

Shirley (f., formerly m.) English: transferred use of the surname, which is a local name from any of the various places (in the West Midlands, Derbyshire, Hampshire, and Surrey) named in Old English from the elements *scīr* county, shire or *scīr* bright + *lēah* wood or clearing. It was given by Charlotte Brontë to the heroine of her novel *Shirley* (1849). According to the novel, her parents had selected the name in prospect of a male child and used it regardless. *Shirley* had earlier been used as a male name (Charlotte Brontë refers to it as a 'masculine cognomen'), but this literary influence fixed it firmly as a female name. It was strongly reinforced during the 1930s and 1940s by the popularity of the child film star Shirley Temple (b. 1928).
Variant: **Shirlee** (rare).

Shlomo (m.) Jewish: modern Hebrew form of SOLOMON.

Shmuel (m.) Jewish: modern Hebrew form of SAMUEL.

Shneur (m.) Jewish: Yiddish name, apparently derived from Latin *senior* elder. Alternatively, it may have a Hebrew origin meaning 'two lights', a reference to illustrious ancestors on both sides of the child's family.

Sholto (m.) Scottish: apparently an Anglicized form of a Gaelic name, **Sìoltach**, originally a byname meaning 'sower', i.e. 'fruitful' or 'seed-bearing'. This name is traditional in the Douglas family.

Shona (f.) Scottish: Anglicized form of Gaelic SEONAG or SEÒNAID.

Shprinze (f.) Jewish: of uncertain origin, probably a Yiddish form of ESPERANZA.

Shraga (m.) Jewish: Aramaic name meaning 'fire, lantern'. It is usually paired with the Yiddish equivalent FAIVISH.

Shula (f.) As a Jewish name this is a short form of SHULAMIT. It has been adopted by non-Jews in the English-speaking world as an independent given name.

Shulamit (f.) Jewish: Hebrew name meaning 'peacefulness', a derivative of *shalom* peace. The name occurs as a personification in the Song of Solomon (6: 13): 'Return, return, O Shulamite; return, return, that we may look upon thee'. It is a popular modern Hebrew name.
Variants: **Shulamith, Shulamite**.

Shura (m., f.) Russian: short form of *Sashura*, itself an elaborated version of SASHA, a pet form of ALEXANDER. Occasionally it is found as a female name, ultimately from ALEXANDRA.

Siân (f.) Welsh form of JANE, derived from Anglo-Norman *Jeanne*. In the English-speaking world it is often used without the accent (**Sian**).
Pet form: **Siani**.

Siarl (m.) Welsh form of CHARLES.

Sibb (f.) English: short form of SIBYL, popular in the Middle Ages, but now rare.
Pet form: **Sibby** (used in Ireland as an Anglicized form of Gaelic SIBÉAL).

Sibéal (f.) Irish Gaelic form of ISABEL, derived in the early Middle Ages from the Anglo-Norman name.

Sibyl (f.) English: variant spelling of SYBIL. Even in classical times there was confusion between the vowels in this word.

Variants: **Sibylla** (Latinate form, common in Denmark and Sweden); **Sibilla**; **Sibella** (by association with the Italian feminine diminutive suffix *-ella*).

Sidney (m., occasionally f.) English: transferred use of the surname, which is usually said to be a Norman baronial name from *Saint-Denis* in France. However, at least in the case of the family of the poet and soldier Sir Philip Sidney (1554–86), it appears to have a more humble origin, being derived from lands in Surrey named as the 'wide meadow' (Old English *sīdan* wide (dative case) + *ēg* island in a river, riverside meadow). The popularity of the male name increased considerably in the 19th century, probably under the influence of Sidney Carton, hero of Dickens's novel *A Tale of Two Cities* (1859). As a female name it is perhaps in part a contracted form of SIDONY, and coincidentally represents a metathesized form of SINDY, but this use is quite rare.

Variant: **Sydney**.

Short form: **Sid**.

Sidony (f.) English: from a Latin ethnic name, *Sidōnius* (m.) or *Sidōnia* (f.) 'person from Sidon' (in Phoenicia). This quite early came to be associated with the Greek word *sindon* winding-sheet. Two saints called Sidonius are venerated in the Catholic Church: Sidonius Apollinaris, a 4th-century bishop of Clermont, and a 7th-century Irish monk who was the first abbot of the monastery of Saint-Saëns (named with a much mutilated form of his name). *Sidonius* does not seem to have been used as a given name in the later Middle Ages, but the feminine form *Sidonia* (English *Sidony*) was comparatively popular and has continued in occasional use ever since.

Variant: **Sidonie**.

Sieffre (m.) Welsh form of GEOFFREY.

Siegbert (m.) German (esp. Jewish): from an old Germanic personal name composed of the elements *sige* victory + *berht* bright, famous. The name was borne by a 7th-century French king, regarded as a saint because of his foundation of numerous hospitals, churches, and monasteries. An Old English cognate was borne by a contemporary who was the first Christian king of East Anglia. The reason why the name should have become particularly popular among Jews is not clear.

Siegfried (m.) German: from an old Germanic personal name composed of the elements *sige* victory + *frid*, *fred* peace. This was a relatively common given name in the Middle Ages, but its modern use dates from the latter part of the 19th century, and reflects the revival of interest in Germanic legend, culminating in Wagner's operatic treatment in his *Ring* cycle.

Sieglinde (f.) German: from an old Germanic female personal name composed of the elements *sige* victory + *lind* weak, tender, soft.

Siegmund (m.) Usual modern German form of SIGMUND.

Siemen (m.) Dutch and Low German form of SIMON.

Siencyn (m.) Welsh spelling of JENKIN.

Sigbjörn (m.) Swedish: from an Old Norse personal name composed of the elements *sigr* victory + *björn* bear.

Cognate: Norwegian: **Sigbjørn**.

Pet form: Swedish: **Sigge**.

Sigge (m.) Swedish: pet form of SIGURD and, occasionally, of the less common SIGBJÖRN.

Sigi (m.) German: pet form of any of the various male names of Germanic origin containing the first element *sige* victory, as, for example, SIEGBERT, SIEGFRIED, and SIEGMUND.

Sigismund (m.) German: variant of SIGMUND, with the first element representing an extended form of the Germanic element *sige* victory. St Sigismund (d. 523) was a king of the Burgundians, murdered by political enemies but honoured as a martyr because he died in a monk's habit adopted for disguise.

Sigiswald (m.) German: from an old Germanic personal name composed of the elements *sige* victory + *wald* ruler.

Sigmund (m.) English and German: from an old Germanic personal name composed of the elements *sige* victory + *mund* protector. It was introduced to Britain both before and after the Conquest, from Scandinavia and Normandy, but there was much confusion with SIMON (final *-d* being added and dropped in the Middle Ages with great abandon) and it eventually fell out of use. As a modern given name in the English-speaking world, it is a recent reintroduction from Germany.

Variants: German: **Siegmund**, SIGISMUND.

Cognate: Polish: **Zygmunt**.

Signy (f.) Scandinavian: from an Old Norse female personal name composed of the elements *sigr* victory + *ný* new.

Variants: **Signi, Signe**.

Sigrid (f.) Scandinavian: from an Old Norse female personal name composed of the elements *sigr* victory + *fríðr* fair, beautiful. The name is now also fairly commonly used in the English-speaking world.

Pet form: **Siri**.

Sigrun (f.) Scandinavian: from an Old Norse female personal name composed of the elements *sigr* victory + *rūn* secret lore. The name was borne in Scandinavian mythology by one of the Valkyries, and was revived as a given name in the late 18th century.

Sigurd (m.) Scandinavian: from an Old Norse personal name composed of the elements *sigr* victory + *vörðr* guardian. According to Scandinavian legend, a character of this name slew the dragon Fafnir, who was guarding an accursed treasure; according to Wagner's treatment in the *Ring* cycle, this role is taken by Siegfried.

Variant: Norwegian: **Sjurd**.

Pet form: Swedish: **Sigge**.

Sikke (m.) Frisian: pet form of any of the various names of Germanic origin containing the first element *sige* victory; cf. SIGI.

Silas (m.) New Testament: Greek name, a short form of *Silouanus* (Latin *Silvānus*, from *silva* wood). This name was borne by a companion of St Paul, who is also mentioned in the Bible in the full form of his name. The Eastern Church recognizes two separate saints, Silas and Silvanus, but honours both on the same day (20 July).

Síle (f.) Irish Gaelic form of CECILY, derived in the early Middle Ages from the Anglo-Norman form *Cecile*.

Anglicized forms: SHEILA, **She(e)lagh**.

Cognates: Scottish Gaelic: **Sìle, Sìleas, Sìlis**.

Silja (f.) Finnish (used also in Denmark, Norway, and Sweden): vernacular form of *Cecilia* (see CECILY). The name was made famous by the novel *The Maid Silja* (1931) by Frans Eemil Sillanpää, winner of the Nobel Prize for literature.

Silke (f.) Low German and Frisian: pet name derived from a short form of CELIA or *Cecilia* (see CECILY). The name is now also more widely popular in the German-speaking world.

Silvana (f.) Italian: feminine form of SILVANO, now also used in Germany and occasionally in the English-speaking world.

Silvano (m.) Italian: from Latin *Silvānus*; see SILAS. The name Silvanus was also borne by over a dozen other early saints, including a 6th-century abbot of Bangor in Ireland. In his case, the name is probably a classicized form of some faintly similar Celtic original.

Cognate: French: **Sylvain**.

Silver (f., m.) English: from the name of the precious metal (Old English *siolfor*), sometimes given to babies born with very fair, silvery white hair.

Silvester (m.) English and German: from a Latin name, meaning 'of the woods'. It was borne by various early saints, most notably by the first pope to govern a Church free from persecution (314–35). His feast is on 31 December, and in various parts of Europe the New Year is celebrated under his name. The name has been continuously, if modestly, used from the Middle Ages to the present day.

Variant: **Sylvester.**

Cognates: Italian: **Silvestro**. Spanish: **Silvestre**. Polish: **Sylwester**.

Silvestra (f.) Latinate feminine form of SILVESTER.

Silvia (f.) Italian and English: from Roman legend. Rhea *Silvia* was, according to mythological tradition, the mother of the twins Romulus and Remus, who founded Rome. Her name probably represents a reworking, by association with Latin *silva* wood, of some pre-Roman form. It was borne by a 6th-century saint, mother of Gregory the Great, and has always been relatively popular in Italy. Shakespeare used it as a typically Italian name in his *Two Gentlemen of Verona*, but it is now completely established in the English-speaking world.

Variant: English, Scandinavian: **Sylvia**.

Cognate: French: **Sylvie**.

Silvio (m.) Italian: from Latin *Silvius*, a masculine form of SILVIA. Several of the legendary kings of Alba Longa bore this name, and a St Silvius was martyred at Alexandria in Egypt in one of the early persecutions of the Christians.

Sima (f.) Russian: pet form of *Serafima* (see SERAPHINA).

Simcha (m., f.) Jewish: Hebrew name meaning 'joy'. It was orignally a female name, but is now more commonly given to males among Ashkenazic Jews.

Simeon (m.) Biblical: from Hebrew, meaning 'hearkening'. It is borne by several Old and New Testament characters, rendered in the Authorized Version variously as *Shimeon*, *Simeon*, and SIMON. In the New Testament, it is the spelling used for the man who blessed the infant Christ (Luke 2: 25).

Simon (m.) Usual English form of SIMEON. This form of the name is borne in the New Testament by various characters: two apostles, a brother of Jesus, a Pharisee, a leper, a tanner, a sorcerer (who offered money for the gifts of the Holy Ghost, giving rise to the term *simony*), and the man who carried Jesus's cross to the Crucifixion.

Cognates: Irish Gaelic: **Síomón**. Scottish Gaelic: **Sìm, Simidh**. Dutch, Low German: **Siemen**. Polish: **Szymon**. Czech: **Šimon**. Russian: **Semyon**. Hebrew: **Shimon**.

Pet forms: Czech: **Ši(on)ek, Simůnek, Simeček**.

Simone (f.) French: feminine form of SIMON, now also quite commonly used in the English-speaking world.

Sina (f.) German and Scandinavian: short form of various Latinate female names ending in these syllables, for example *Thomasina* (see THOMAS).

Variant: Danish: **Sine**.

Sinclair (m.) English and Scottish: transferred use of the Scottish surname, which originated as a Norman baronial name borne by a family that held a manor in northern France called *Saint-Clair*, probably Saint-Clair-sur-Elle in La Manche. It is an extremely common Scottish surname: the Norman family received the earldoms of Caithness and Orkney. They merged with the Norse- and Gaelic-speaking inhabitants of their domains to form one of the most powerful of the Scottish Highland families. The name of the novelist Sinclair Lewis (1885–1951) may have had some influence on the choice of this as a twentieth-century given name.

Sinda (f.) 1. English: variant of SINDY.
2. Spanish: short form of various names ending in this element, of Visigothic origin, as, for example, GUMERSINDA.

Sindy (f.) English: variant spelling of CINDY that came into use in about 1950 and is most common in America.

Sine (f.) Danish: variant of SINA.

Síne (f.) Irish Gaelic form of JANE, derived from Anglo-Norman *Jeanne*.
Cognate: Scottish Gaelic: **Sìne** (Anglicized as **Sheena**).
Pet form: Scottish Gaelic: **Sìneag**.

Sinéad (f.) Irish Gaelic form of JANET, derived from Anglo-Norman *Jeannette*.
Diminutive: **Sinéidín**.

Siobhán (f.) Irish Gaelic form of JANE, derived from the Anglo-Norman disyllabic form *Jehanne*. It became widely known in the English-speaking world as a result of the fame of the actress Siobhán McKenna (1923–86), and has recently come to be a popular given name.
Anglicized forms: **Shevaun, Chevonne** (modern).
Cognate: Scottish Gaelic: **Siubhan**.

Siôn (m.) Welsh form of JOHN, derived from Anglo-Norman *Jean*.
Pet form: **Sionym**.

Sioned (f.) Welsh form of JANET.

Siôr (m.) Welsh form of GEORGE.
Variants: **Sior(y)s**.

Siothrún (m.) Irish Gaelic form of GEOFFREY.

Siri (f.) Scandinavian: simplified form of SIGRID, often used as a pet form of that name.

Sissel (f.) Scandinavian form of CICELY.

Sissy (f.) English: pet form of CICELY that came into use about 1890 but disappeared again after about 1920, no doubt because of the homonymous slang word *sissy* 'effeminate' (which is probably from the kinship term *sister*). In recent years it has undergone something of a revival.
Variants: **Sissey, Sissie**.

Sisto (m.) Italian: variant of *Sesto* (see SEXTUS).

Siubhan (f.) Scottish Gaelic form of JANE, derived from the Old French disyllabic form *Jehanne* (see JEAN). This name is usually Anglicized as JUDITH.

Siùsan (f.) Scottish Gaelic form of *Susan* (see SUSANNA).
Variant: **Siùsaidh**.

Siv (f.) Scandinavian: originally a byname meaning 'bride, wife'. It is borne in Scandinavian mythology by the wife of Thor.

Sive (f.) Irish: Anglicized form of Gaelic SADHBH. *Sive* is the title of a popular contemporary play by John B. Keene.

Sixten (f.) Swedish: from an Old Norse personal name composed of the elements *sigr* victory + *steinn* stone.

Sjurd (m.) Norwegian: contracted form of SIGURD.

Skipper (m.) English: originally a nickname from the vocabulary word *skipper* boss (originally a ship's captain, from Middle Dutch *schipper*), or else representing an agent derivative of *skip* to leap, bound (probably of Scandinavian origin). It is now sometimes used as an independent given name, especially in America.
Short forms: **Skip, Skipp**.

Slava (m.) Russian: pet form of the numerous compound names containing the Slavonic element *slav* glory, as, for example, *Mstislav* (see MŚCISŁAW), ROSTISLAV, *Stanislav* (see STANISLAS), and VYACHESLAV.

Sławomierz (m.) Polish: from an old Slavonic personal name composed of the elements *slav* glory + *meri* great, famous (see CASIMIR). The same elements appear in the reverse order in the name MIROSŁAW.
Cognate: Czech: **Slavomír**.

Sly (m., f.) English (mainly U.S.): modern name. The reasons for its adoption as a given name are not clear. In the case of the American actor Sylvester Stallone, it is used as a contracted pet form of his given name. The fact that it coincides in form with the vocabulary word *sly* 'cunning, devious' does not seem to have been a bar to its use as a given name.

Sobiesław (m.) Polish: from an old Slavonic personal name composed of the elements *sobi* to appropriate, usurp + *slav* glory (cf. ROŚCISŁAW).

Cognate: Czech: **Soběslav**.

Feminine form: Czech: **Soběslava**.

Pet forms: Czech: **Sobík, Sobeš** (m.); **Soběna, Sobeška** (f.).

Socorro (f.) Spanish: from a title of the Virgin Mary, *Nuestra Señora del Socorro* 'Our Lady of Perpetual Succour', alluding to her readiness to intercede for her devotees in distress.

Sofia (f.) Norwegian and Swedish form of SOPHIA.

Sofie (f.) Low German, Dutch, and Danish form of SOPHIA.

Sol (f., m.) 1. (f.) Spanish: from Spanish *sol* sun (Latin *sol*), apparently alluding to the beauty and purity of the celestial body. This was a common given name in the Middle Ages, being borne, for example, by one of the daughters of El Cid, and it is still in use today; in part it may now be taken as a short form of SOLEDAD.

2. (m.) Jewish: short form of SOLOMON used in the English-speaking world. The pet form **Solly** is also used.

Solange (f.) French: vernacular form of the Late Latin name *Sollemnia*, a derivative of *sollemnis* solemn, religious. St Solange was a poor shepherdess from Bourges who was killed in the 9th century by her master for resisting his attempts on her virtue; in consequence she came to be regarded as a martyr for the faith.

Soledad (f.) Spanish: from a title of the Virgin Mary, *Maria de Soledad* (from Spanish *soledad* solitude, Late Latin *sōlitās*, a derivative of *sōlus* alone). The allusion is to the Christian virtue of solitude, or separation from the distractions of the world.

Pet form: **Chole**.

Solita (f.) Spanish: pet form of the female name SOL.

Solly (m.) Pet form of the male name SOL, used mainly by Jews in the English-speaking world.

Solomon (m.) Biblical: name (Hebrew *Shlomo*, derived from *shalom* peace) of a king of Israel, son of David and Bathsheba, who was legendary for his wisdom (2 Samuel 12–24; 1 Kings 1–11; 2 Chronicles 1–9). The books of Proverbs and Ecclesiastes were ascribed to him, and the Song of Solomon, otherwise known as the Song of Songs, bears his name. It has been sporadically used among Gentiles since the Middle Ages, often by parents who wished wisdom for their child, but is still largely a Jewish name.

Other forms: Jewish: **Shlomo** (Hebrew); **Zalman** (Yiddish). Gaelic: **Solamh**.

Short form: SOL.

Solveig (f.) Norwegian: from an Old Norse female personal name composed of the elements *salr* house, hall + *veig* strength. The usual Swedish spelling of the name is **Solvig**, the Danish **Solvej**. The name Solveig is borne by the heroine of Henrik Ibsen's *Peer Gynt* (1867, first performed 1876); although abandoned by Peer without warning, she patiently waits several years for his return, and at the last redeems him from doom by her love and forgiveness.

Somerled (m.) Scottish (Highland): from the Old Norse personal name *Sumarlíðr*, probably originally a byname meaning 'summer traveller'. This was the name of the founder of the powerful and widespread Clan Macdonald, Lords of the Isles from the 12th to the 15th century, and it is still occasionally bestowed on Macdonalds and members of septs of the various branches of the clan. The Somerled in question was Lord of Argyll from about 1130 to 1164. The clan actually takes its name from his grandson.

Variants: **Summerlad** (altered by folk etymology); **Somhairle** (Gaelic form, also used in Ireland; Anglicized as **Sorley**).

Sonya (f.) Russian: pet form of *Sofya* (see SOPHIA), popular as a given name in its own right in Britain and elsewhere since the 1920s.

Variants: **Sonia** (English spelling); **Sonja**, **Sonje** (German and Scandinavian spellings).

Soo (f.) English: fanciful variant spelling of SUE.

Sondra (f.) English: of recent origin, apparently an altered form of SANDRA.

Sophia (f.) From the Greek word meaning 'wisdom'. The Eastern cult of St Sophia seems to be the result of misinterpretation of the phrase *Hagia Sophia* 'holy wisdom' as if it meant 'St Sophia'. The name became popular in England in the 17th and 18th centuries. The heroine of Fielding's novel *Tom Jones* (1749) is called Sophia Weston. In recent years, its popularity has been further increased by the fame of the Italian film actress Sophia Loren (b. 1934). In the Scottish Highlands it has been used as an Anglicized form of the Gaelic name *Beathag* (see BEATHAN).

Derivatives: French, English, German: **Sophie**. Low German, Danish, Dutch: **Sofie**. Norwegian, Swedish: **Sofia**. Polish: **Zofia**. Czech: **Žofie**. Hungarian: **Zsófia**.

Pet forms: Low German: **Fieke**. Russian: **Sonya**. Polish: **Zosia**. Czech: **Žofka**.

Sophie (f.) Variant, of French origin, of SOPHIA. In the English-speaking world, where it has been popular since the 18th century, it is often taken as a pet form of *Sophia*, and is sometimes spelled **Sophy**.

Sorcha (f.) Irish and Scottish Gaelic name derived from an Old Celtic element meaning 'brightness'. In Ireland it has long been considered a Gaelic form of SARAH, and Anglicized as *Sarah* and *Sally*, but this is based on no more than a slight phonetic similarity. In Scotland the meaning of the name has resulted in its being translated as *Clara*.

Sören (m.) Scandinavian (Danish) form of *Severinus* (see SEVERINO).

Sorley (m.) Scottish (Highland) and Irish: Anglicized form of Gaelic *Somhairle*; see SOMERLED.

Sorne (f.) Basque equivalent of CONCEPCIÓN.

Sorrel (f.) English: from the plant, so named in the Middle Ages from Old French *surele*, apparently a derivative of *sur* sour (of Germanic origin), alluding to the acid taste of its leaves. The spellings **Sorrell** and **Sorell** also occur; the rare **Sorel** is used in Noel Coward's *Hay Fever* (1925).

Spencer (m.) English: transferred use of the surname, originally an occupational name for a 'dispenser' of supplies in a manor house. This is the name of a great English noble family, traditionally supposed to be descended from someone who performed this function in the royal household. Its popularity as a given name was increased in the mid-20th century by the fame of the American film actor Spencer Tracy (1900–67).

Spike (m.) English: normally a nickname, but occasionally bestowed as an official given name. As a nickname it seems usually to refer to an unruly tuft or 'spike' of hair.

Spiridon (m.) Russian: from the Late Greek personal name *Spiridion*, a diminutive formation from Latin *spiritus* spirit, soul. This name was borne by a 4th-century saint much venerated in the Eastern Church. He was a bishop of Tremithus in Cyprus and was persecuted under the Emperor Diocletian, but survived to play a major role at the Council of Nicaea (325). See also DUŠAN.

Sroel (m.) Jewish: Yiddish form of ISRAEL.

Staaf (m.) Dutch: short form of *Gustaaf* (see GUSTAV).

Staas (m.) Frisian: derived from a short form of *Anastasius* (see ANASTASIA), and perhaps also the rarer *Eustasius* (see EUSTACE).

Stacey (f.) English: of uncertain derivation, perhaps originating as a pet form of ANASTASIA, and respelled as a result of association with EUSTACE. It is not clear why this name, together with its variants **Stacy** and **Stacie**, should have become so common in the 1970s and 1980s. It is now also occasionally used as a male name.

Staffan (m.) Swedish form of STEPHEN, now rather less common than STEFAN.

Stafford (m.) English: transferred use of the aristocratic surname, which originated as a local name from any of various places, so called from Old English *stæð* landing place + *ford* ford, most notably the county town of Staffordshire. This was the surname of the family that held the dukedom of Buckingham in the 15th and 16th centuries.

Stan (m.) English: short form of STANLEY, not commonly used as an independent given name.

Stanislas (m.) Latinized form of an old Slavonic personal name composed of the elements *stan* government + *slav* glory. St Stanislas Szczepanowski (1030–79) was a bishop of Cracow who was killed by King Bolesław the Cruel of Poland.

Variant: **Stanislaus.**

Cognates: Polish: **Stanisław**. Czech, Russian: **Stanislav.**

Feminine forms: Polish: **Stanisława**. Czech: **Stanislava.**

Pet forms: Polish: **Stasiak** (m.). Czech: **Stáňa** (m., f.); **Stanek, Stanko, Staní(če)k, Stanouš(ek)** (m.); **Stánička, Stanuška** (f.).

Stanley (m.) English: transferred use of the surname, derived from any of numerous places (in Derbys., Durham, Gloucs., Staffs., Wilts., and Yorks.) named in Old English from *stān* stone + *lēah* wood or clearing. This is well established as a given name, and has been widely used as such since the 1880s. It had been in occasional use earlier. Its popularity seems to have stemmed at least in part from the fame of the explorer Sir Henry Morton Stanley (1841–1904), who was born in Wales as John Rowlands but later took the name of his adoptive father, a New Orleans cotton dealer.

Short form: **Stan.**

Star (f.) English: modern given name, a vernacular equivalent of STELLA.

Stasiak (m.) Polish: pet form of *Stanisław* (see STANISLAS).

Steaphan (m.) Scottish Gaelic form of STEPHEN.

Stefan (m.) German and Scandinavian form of STEPHEN. This form is also in use in Russia and Poland, beside the more common respective forms STEPAN and SZCZEPAN.

Stefania (f.) Italian form of STEPHANIE. This form of the name is also used in Poland.

Short form: Italian: **Fania.**

Stefano (m.) Italian form of STEPHEN.

Steffan (m.) Welsh form of STEPHEN.

Steffany (f.) English: variant spelling of STEPHANIE.

Steffen (m.) Low German form of STEPHEN.

Steffi (f.) German: pet form of STEPHANIE.

Stella (f.) English: from Latin *stella* star. This was not used as a given name before the 16th century, when Sir Philip Sidney seems to have been the first to use it (as a name deliberately far removed from the prosaic range of everyday names) in his sonnets supposedly addressed by Astrophel to his lady, Stella.

Cognate: Spanish: **Estrella**. See also ESTELLE.

Sten (m.) Swedish: from an Old Norse personal name, originally a short form of the various compound names containing the element *steinn* stone (cf. e.g. TORSTEN). Numerous names of Old Norse origin containing this as a first element are still in limited used today, as, for example, **Stenbjörn, Stenfinn, Stenkil,** and **Stenulf**.

Cognates: Norwegian: **Stein**. Danish: **Ste(e)n**.

Stenya (m.) Russian: pet form of STEPAN. The form **Styopa** is also used.

Stepan (m.) The usual Russian form of STEPHAN.

Štěpán (m.) Czech form of STEPHEN.

Pet forms: **Štěpanek, Štěp(k)a, Štěpek, Štěpík, Stepoušek**.

Feminine form: **Stěpánka** (formally a diminutive).

Steph (f.) English: informal short form of STEPHANIE.

Stephan (m.) German and English: variant of STEPHEN, preserving the vowels of the Greek name.

Stéphane (m.) French: learned form of STEPHEN, in occasional use beside the vernacular ÉTIENNE.

Stephanie (f.) English and German: from French **Stéphanie**, vernacular form of Latin *Stephania*, a variant of *Stephana*, which was in use among early Christians as a feminine form of *Stephanus* (see STEPHEN).

Variant: English: **Steffany**.

Cognates: Italian, Polish: **Stefania**. Spanish: **Estefanía**.

Pet form: English: **Stevie**.

Stephen (m.) Usual English spelling of the name of the first Christian martyr (Acts 6–7), whose feast is accordingly celebrated next after Christ's own (26 December). His name is derived from the Greek word *stephanos* garland, crown.

Variants: **Steven, Stephan**.

Cognates: Irish Gaelic: **Stiofán, Stiana**. Scottish Gaelic: **Steaphan**. Welsh: **Steffan**. French: **Étienne, Stéphane**. Provençal: **Estève**. Italian: **Stefano**. Spanish: **Estéban**. Catalan: **Esteve**. Portuguese: **Estévão**. German: **Stefan, Stephan**. Low German: **Steffen**. Scandinavian: **Stefan; Staffan** (Swedish). Polish: **Szczepan, Stefan**. Czech: **Stépan**. Russian: **Stepan, Stefan**. Hungarian: **István**.

Short form: English: **Steve**.

Pet form: English: **Stevie**.

Sterling (m.) English: transferred use of the surname, which may represent a hypercorrected form of the nickname *Starling* (referring to the bird). As a given name, however, *Sterling* is likely to have been chosen because of its association with the vocabulary word occurring in such phrases as 'sterling qualities' and 'sterling worth'. This word is derived from the Middle English word *sterrling* 'little star': some Norman coins had a little star on them.

Variant: **Stirling** (respelled as if derived from the Scottish placename, which is of uncertain derivation, possibly from Welsh *ystre Velyn* 'dwelling of Melyn').

Steve (m.) English: short form of STEPHEN and STEVEN.

Steven (m.) English: variant of STEPHEN, reflecting the normal pronunciation of the name in the English-speaking world.

Stevie (m., f.) English: pet form of STEPHEN and of STEPHANIE. A well-known recent female bearer was the poet Stevie Smith (1902–71), whose baptismal name was Florence Margaret Smith.

Variant: **Stevi** (f.).

Stewart (m.) English: variant of STUART, less common as a given name, although more common as a surname.

Stian (m.) Scandinavian: from the Old Norse personal name *Stígandr*, originally a byname meaning 'wanderer'. This is currently a very popular given name in Norway.

Stiana (m.) Irish Gaelic form of STEPHEN (see also STIOFÁN).

Stig (m.) Scandinavian: from the Old Norse personal name *Stígr*, a short form of *Stígandr* (see STIAN).

Stina (f.) German and Scandinavian: short form of any of the Latinate female given names that end in these two syllables, principally CRISTINA.

Stìneag (f.) Scottish Gaelic form of CHRISTINA.

Stiofán (m.) Irish Gaelic form of STEPHEN.

St John (m.) English: name expressing devotion to St John; it has been in use in the English-speaking world, mainly among Roman Catholics, from the last two decades of the 19th century up to the present day.

Stoffel (m.) German: pet form of *Christoph* (see CHRISTOPHER), with the addition of the hypocoristic suffix -*(e)l*.

Storm (m., f.) English: apparently a 20th-century coinage, although it may have been in use slightly earlier. The name is presumably derived from the climatic phenomenon, although it is hard to see why it should be chosen. It derives perhaps from the Romantic commitment to emotional drama, and may sometimes have been given in the hope that a child would have a dramatic personality. In other cases, it may have been used for a child born during a storm.

Stuart (m.) Scottish and English: from the French version of the surname *Stewart*. This form was introduced to Scotland in the 16th century by Mary Stuart, Queen of Scots, who was brought up in France. The surname originated as an occupational or status name for someone who served as a *steward* in a manor or royal household. The Scottish royal family of this name are traditionally supposed to be descended from a family who were hereditary stewards in Brittany before the Conquest. Use as a given name originated in Scotland, but is now widespread throughout the English-speaking world.

Variant: **Stewart**.

Short forms: **Stu, Stew**.

Sture (m.) Scandinavian (Swedish): from a medieval byname derived from the verb *stura* to be contrary, self-willed. This is now a common given name in Sweden as it has been borne by several great personalities in Swedish history.

Sue (f.) English: short form of SUSAN and, less commonly, of SUSANNA and SUZANNE. In the past couple of decades it has sometimes been used as an independent name.

Variants: **Su, Soo**.

Suelo (f.) Spanish: short form of CONSUELO.

Sukie (f.) English: pet form of SUSAN, very common in the 18th century, but now rare.

Variant: **Sukey**.

Summer (f.) English (esp. U.S.): from the name of the season (Old English *sumor*), used in modern times as a given name because of its pleasant associations.

Summerlad (m.) Scottish: variant spelling of SOMERLED, being taken by folk etymology as derived from the words *summer* and *lad*.

Sunniva (f.) Scandinavian: Latinized form of the Old English female name *Sunngifu*, composed of the elements *sunne* sun + *gifu* gift. According to legend, St Sunniva was a 10th-century British princess who was shipwrecked off the coast of Norway and murdered by the inhabitants as she struggled ashore.

Cognates: Swedish: **Synnöve**. Danish, Norwegian: **Synnøve**.

Susan (f.) English: Anglicized form of SUSANNA, and always the most common of this group of names.

Variant: **Suzan**.

Short form: **Sue**.

Pet forms: **Susie, Sukie**.

Susanna (f.) New Testament form (Luke 8: 3) of the Hebrew name *Shoshana* (from *shoshan* lily, in modern Hebrew also 'rose'). The name is also spelled **Susannah**, a transliteration used in the Old Testament. The tale of Susannah, wife of Joachim, and the elders who falsely accused her of adultery, is to be found in the apocryphal book that bears her name, and was popular in the Middle Ages and later.

Variant: **Suzanna.**

Cognates: English: **Susan.** Scottish Gaelic: **Siùsan, Siùsaidh.** French: **Suzanne.** German: **Susanne.** Polish: **Zuzanna.** Czech: **Zuzana.** Hungarian: **Zsuzsanna.**

Short form: Scandinavian: **Sanna.**

Susie (f.) English: pet form of SUSAN and SUSANNA.

Variants: **Suzie, Suzy.**

Suzanne (f.) French version of SUSANNA, now also used in the English-speaking world.

Suzette (f.) French: pet form of SUZANNE.

Svanhild (f.) Scandinavian spelling of SWANHILD. This is the name borne by the daughter of Sigurd and Gudrun in the Edda.

Svante (m.) Swedish: short form, dating from the Middle Ages, of the Slavonic name ŚWIĘTOPEŁK; cf. DAGMAR and GUSTAV.

Svatomír (m.) Czech form of ŚWIĘTOMIERZ.

Svatopluk (m.) Czech form of ŚWIĘTOPEŁK.

Svatoslav (m.) Czech form of ŚWIĘTOSŁAW.

Svea (f.) Swedish: patriotic name formed in the 19th century from the former name of Sweden, *Svearike* (now *Sverige*). The second element of the national name is from Old Norse *ríki* kingdom; the first is of uncertain derivation.

Sven (m.) Swedish: from the Old Norse byname *Sveinn* 'boy, lad'. It is now also used in the German-speaking world and to some extent in the United States.

Cognates: Danish: **Svend.** Norwegian: **Svein.**

Sverre (m.) Norwegian: from the Old Norse personal name *Sverrir*, originally apparently a byname for a wild or restless person, and connected with the dialectal term *sverra* to spin, swing, swirl about.

Svetlana (f.) Russian: vernacular loan translation (from the Slavonic element *svet* light) of the Greek name *Phōtinē* (from Greek *phōtos* light). St Photine was an early saint martyred at Rome in the 1st century; in the Eastern Church she has been identified with the 'Samaritan woman' mentioned in St John's gospel, chapter 4.

Cognate: Czech: **Světlana.**

Pet forms: Czech: **Světla, Světlanka, Světluše, Světluška.**

Svyatopolk (m.) Russian form of ŚWIĘTOPEŁK. This was the name of the brother of Sts Boris and Gleb at whose behest they were murdered in 1015.

Svyatoslav (m.) Russian form of ŚWIĘTOSŁAW.

Swanhild (f.) Low German: from an Old Saxon female personal name composed of the elements *swan* swan + *hild* battle.

Variants: **Swanhilda, Swanhilde.**

Cognate: Scandinavian: **Svanhild.**

Świętomierz (m.) Polish: from an old Slavonic personal name composed of the elements *svyanto* bright, holy + *meri* great, famous (see CASIMIR).

Cognate: Czech: **Svatomír.**

Świętopełk (m.) Polish: from an old Slavonic personal name composed of the elements *svyanto* bright, holy + *polk* people, race.

Cognates: Czech: **Svatopluk.** Russian: **Svyatopolk.**

Świętosław (m.) Polish: from an old Slavonic personal name composed of the elements *svyanto* bright, holy + *slav* glory.

Cognates: Czech: **Svatoslav.** Russian: **Svyatoslav.**

Sybil (f.) English: from the name (Greek *Sibylla* or *Sybilla*, with confusion over the vowels from an early period) of a class of ancient prophetesses inspired by Apollo. According to medieval theology, they were pagans denied the knowledge of

Christ but blessed by God with some insight into things to come and accordingly admitted to heaven. It was thus regarded as a respectable name to be borne by Christians. The classical form **Sybilla** and the French form **Sybille** are also occasionally used in the English-speaking world.
Variants: **Sibyl**, SIBILLA.

Sydney (m., occasionally f.) English: variant of SIDNEY. It was a medieval practice to write *y* for *i*, for greater clarity since *i* was easily confused with other letters.

Sylvain (m.) French form of *Silvanus* (see SILVANO).

Sylvester (m.) English: variant of SILVESTER.

Sylvia (f.) English: variant, respelled for elegance, of SILVIA. It is now rather more common than the plain form.

Sylvie (f.) French form of SILVIA, now also used in the English-speaking world.

Sylwester (m.) Polish form of SILVESTER.

Synnöve (f.) Swedish: vernacular form of SUNNIVA. In Denmark and Norway the form **Synnøve** is used.

Szczepan (m.) The usual Polish form of STEPHEN.

Szczęsny (m.) Polish: name meaning 'happy, fortunate', used as a vernacular equivalent of FELIX.

Szerény (m.) Hungarian: name representing a loan translation of MODEST.

Szilárd (m.) Hungarian: from the vocabulary word *szilárd* firm, steadfast. The name is used as a loan translation of CONSTANT.

Szörény (m.) Hungarian form of *Severinus*; see SEVERINO.

Szymon (m.) Polish form of SIMON.

T

Taavi (m.) Finnish form of DAVID.

Tabitha (f.) Aramaic name, meaning 'doe' or 'roe', borne in the New Testament by a woman who was restored to life by St Peter (Acts 9: 36–41). In the biblical account this form of the name is given together with its Greek equivalent, DORCAS. It was one of the names much favoured by Puritans and Dissenters from the 17th to the 19th century, and is still occasionally used as a girl's name in the English- and German-speaking world. However, in Britain it is more commonly bestowed on cats.

Pet forms: English: **Tabby** (obsolete). German: **Tabea** (at present a fashionable name in German-speaking countries).

Tad (m.) English and Irish: normally an Anglicized form of TADHG, but sometimes a short form of THADDEUS. It is fairly commonly used as an independent given name, in particular in America.

Taddeo (m.) Italian form of THADDEUS.

Tadeo (m.) Spanish form of THADDEUS.

Tadeu (m.) Portuguese form of THADDEUS.

Tadeusz (m.) Polish form of THADDEUS.

Tadhg (m.) Irish and Scottish Gaelic: traditional name, originally a byname meaning 'poet, philosopher'. This was a very common given name throughout the Middle Ages, and Protestants in modern Northern Ireland use *Taig* or *Teague* as a generic derogatory term for a Catholic Irishman.

Variant: Scottish Gaelic: **Taogh**.

Anglicized forms (Irish): **Tad**, **Teague**, **Teigue**, THADDEUS, **Thady**, **Tim**.

Tadzio (m.) Polish: pet form of TADEUSZ.

Tage (m.) Scandinavian (Danish): from Old Danish *Taki*, originally a byname meaning 'guarantor, surety' or 'receiver' (from *taka* to take).

Talfryn (m.) Welsh: modern given name, originally a local name, from Welsh *tal* high, end of + a mutated form of *bryn* hill.

Taliesin (m.) Welsh: composed of the elements *tâl* brow + *iesin* shining. This was the name of a legendary 6th-century Welsh poet, and has been revived in recent times.

Talitha (f.) New Testament: from an Aramaic word meaning 'little girl'. Jesus raised a child from the dead with the words 'Talitha cumi; which is, being interpreted, Damsel, I say unto thee, arise' (Mark 5: 41).

Tallulah (f.) English: rare name, chosen occasionally as a result of the fame of the American actress Tallulah Bankhead (1903–68). In spite of its exotic appearance, her given name was not adopted for the sake of her career but inherited from her grandmother. It may be a variant of TALULLA; or it may be taken from the placename Tallulah Falls, Georgia, which is of American Indian origin.

Talulla (f.) Irish: Anglicized form of the Gaelic name **Tuilelaith**, composed of elements meaning 'abundance' and 'lady, princess'. This name was borne by at least two Irish saints of the 8th and 9th centuries.

Talya (f.) Russian: pet form of NATALYA.

Variant: **Talia** (an Anglicized spelling).

Tam (m.) Scottish: short form of THOMAS.

Tamar (f.) Jewish: very popular modern Hebrew name; see TAMARA.

Variant: **Tama**.

Tamara (f.) Russian: probably derived from the Hebrew name *Tamar* 'date palm', with the addition of the feminine suffix *-a*. The name Tamar is borne in the Bible by two female characters: the daughter-in-law of Judah, who is involved in a somewhat seamy story of sexual intrigue (Genesis 38), and a daughter of King David (2 Samuel 13), the full sister of Absalom, who is raped by her half-brother Amnon, for which Absalom kills him. It is rather surprising, therefore, that it should have given rise to such a popular given name. However, Absalom himself later has a daughter named Tamar, who is referred to as 'a woman of a fair countenance' (2 Samuel 14: 27), and the name may derive its popularity from this reference.

Tammaro (m.) Italian: of Germanic origin, composed of the elements *thank* thought + *mār*, *mēr* fame. St Tammarus was an African priest who, together with St Priscus, landed in southern Italy in the 5th century after being cast adrift in a rudderless boat by the Arian Vandals.

Tammy (f.) English: pet form of TAMARA and TAMSIN.

Tamsin (f.) English: contracted form of *Thomasina* (see THOMAS), relatively common throughout Britain in the Middle Ages, but confined to Cornwall immediately before its recent revival.

Tancredo (m.) Italian: of Germanic origin, composed of the elements *thank* thought + *rād* counsel. The name has become known in Italy through Torquato Tasso's *Gerusalemme Liberata* (1581), in which a prominent part is played by Tancred, hero of the First Crusade (1199).

Taneli (m.) Finnish form of DANIEL.

Tansy (f.) English: a flower name, derived from Greek *athanasia* immortal. It has enjoyed some popularity as a given name in the 20th century.

Tanya (f.) Russian: pet form of TATIANA, now quite commonly also used as an independent given name in the English-speaking world.

Variants: **Tania** (an English spelling); **Tanja** (a German spelling).

Tara (f.) English: from the name (meaning 'hill') of a place in Meath, seat of the high kings of Ireland. It has been used as a female given name in America since around 1940, probably as a result of the success of the film *Gone with the Wind*, in which the estate of this name has great emotional significance. In Britain it was not much used before the 1960s, and its popularity since then seems to be the result of its use for the character Tara King in the television series *The Avengers*.

Taras (m.). Russian: from Greek *Tarasios* or *Tharasios*, a name of uncertain origin, possibly connected with the town or river of *Taras* (Latin *Tarentum*) in southern Italy. St Tarasius (d. 806) was bishop of Constantinople during a period of considerable religious and political upheaval, and he is much venerated in the Orthodox Church. The form *Tarasi* is less common.

Tárlach (m.) Irish Gaelic: a modern shortened form of TOIRDHEALBHACH.

Tarquin (m.) The name borne by two early kings of Rome, Tarquinius Priscus 'the Old' (616–578 BC) and Tarquinius Superbus 'the Proud' (534–510 BC). It is of uncertain, probably Etruscan, origin; many of the most ancient Roman institutions and the vocabulary associated with them, as well as many Roman family names, were borrowed from the Etruscans. The name is now occasionally used in the English-speaking world.

Tasgall (m.) Scottish Gaelic: traditional name, originally a borrowing of the Old Norse personal name *Ásketill*, composed of the elements *ǽs* god + *ketill* sacrificial cauldron. This name is in use among the MacAskills in the Isle of Berneray, whose surname derives from a patronymic form of the same name. It is sometimes Anglicized as **Taskill**.

Tasha (f.) Short form of NATASHA, now quite commonly used in the English-speaking world (especially in America) as an independent given name.

Tatiana (f.) Russian: of early Christian origin. This was the name of various early saints honoured particularly in the Eastern Church. In origin it is a feminine form of Latin *Tatiānus*, apparently a derivative of *Tatius*, a Roman family name of obscure origin. Titus Tatius was, according to tradition, a king of the Sabines who later shared with Romulus the rule over a united population of Sabines and Latins.
Pet form: **Tanya**.

Tauno (m.) Finnish form of AUGUSTINE.

Tawny (f.) English: from the vocabulary word descriptive of hair colour (Anglo-Norman *tauné*, Old French *tané* tanned). This is a modern name created on the lines of examples such as GINGER and SANDY.
Variant: **Tawney**.

Taylor (m.) English: transferred use of the surname, which originated as an occupational name for a tailor, from Anglo-Norman French *taillour*, a derivative of *taillier* to cut (Late Latin *tāleāre*).

Teague (m.) Irish: Anglicized form of Gaelic TADHG.
Variant: **Teigue**.

Teal (f.) English: one of the female names taken from birds in the past couple of decades. The teal is a kind of small duck; its name is attested since the 14th century and seems to be connected with Middle Low German *tēlink*, Middle Dutch *tēling*.
Variant: **Teale**.

Teàrlach (m.) Scottish Gaelic: a modern shortened form of TOIRDHEALBHACH.
Feminine form: **Teàrlag**.

Teasag (f.) Scottish Gaelic form of JESSIE.

Techomír (m.) Czech: from an old Slavonic personal name composed of the elements *tech* consolation + *meri* great, famous (see CASIMIR).

Techoslav (m.) Czech: from an old Slavonic personal name composed of the elements *tech* consolation + *slav* glory.

Ted (m.) English: short form of EDWARD, also used for THEODORE.
Pet form: **Teddy**.

Teda (f.) Polish: pet form of TEODORA.

Teddy (m.) English: pet form of TED. Teddy bears were so named from the American president Theodore Roosevelt (1858–1919).

Tegwen (f.) Welsh: modern name composed of the elements *teg* fair, lovely + *(g)wen*, feminine form of *gwyn* white, fair, blessed, holy.

Teigue (m.) Irish: variant of TEAGUE.

Teive (m.) Jewish (Yiddish): variant of TEVYE.

Tekla (f.) Scandinavian form of THECLA.

Tel (m.) English: altered short form of TERRY or TERENCE, of recent origin. For the substitution of *-l* for *-r*, cf. HAL.

Teleri (f.) Welsh: extension of the name ELERI, with the addition of the honorific prefix *ty-* your. Teleri, daughter of Peul, is mentioned in the *Mabinogi*.

Telesforo (m.) Italian and Spanish: from Greek *Telesphoros*, a compound derived from *telos* end, completion + *pherein* to bring, bear. This was originally an epithet of Zeus or of the personified abstraction, Justice. Later it came to be understood as the name of an independent deity concerned with health, a companion of Aesculapius and Hygiea. In the Late Greek period it was used as a personal name, and in early Christian times it was borne by an early pope who was martyred under Hadrian in 136; he was a Calabrian Greek by origin.
Cognate: French: **Télésphore** (rare).

Teodora (f.) Italian, Spanish, Portuguese, Swedish, and Polish form of THEODORA.
Pet form: Polish: **Teda**.

Teodosio (m.) Italian, Spanish, and Portuguese: from the Latin name *Theodosius*,

Greek *Theodosios*, composed of the elements *theos* god + *dōsis* giving (and so a doublet of THEODORE). The name was borne by several early saints, most notably Theodosius the Cenobiarch (423–529), a Cappadocian who founded several monasteries in Palestine.

Cognate: Russian: **Fe(o)dosi**. See also DOSIFEI.

Teofilo (m.) Italian, Spanish, and Portuguese form of THEOPHILUS.

Tere (f.) Spanish: short form of TERESA.

Terence (m.) English and Irish: from the Latin name *Terentius*, which is of uncertain origin. It was borne by the Roman playwright Marcus Terentius Afer (who was a former slave, and took his name from his master, Publius Terentius Lucanus), and later by various minor early Christian saints. As a modern given name it is a 'learned' back-formation from the supposed pet form TERRY. It has become common in Ireland through being used as an Anglicized form of the Gaelic name TOIRDHEALBHACH 'instigator'.

Variants: **Terrance, Terrence**.

Short form: **Tel**. See also TERRY.

Teresa (f.) Italian and Spanish form of THERESA. In the English-speaking world the name is often chosen in this spelling by Roman Catholics, with particular reference to the Spanish saint, Teresa of Ávila (Teresa Cepeda de Ahumada, 1515–82).

Short form: Spanish: **Tere**.

Pet forms: Spanish: **Teresita, Tete**.

Terje (m.) Norwegian: vernacular form of *Torgeir* (see TORGER).

Terrance (m.) The most common American spelling of TERENCE. The spelling **Terrence** is also frequent.

Terri (f.) English (esp. U.S.): name that seems to have originated either as a pet form of THERESA, or directly as a feminine spelling of TERRY.

Terry (m.) English: in the Middle Ages this was a Germanic name (composed of elements meaning 'tribe' and 'power'; see DIETRICH) introduced to England by the Normans in the form *T(h)ierri*. (A fuller form is represented by the name of the Emperor *Theodoric*, where the spelling has been influenced by association with THEODORE; see also DEREK and DERRICK.) In modern English use *Terry* seems at first to have been a transferred use of the surname, which is derived from the medieval given name, and later to have been taken as a pet form of TERENCE.

Short form: **Tel**.

Terryl (f.) English: modern coinage, apparently an elaboration of TERRI with the suffix *-yl* seen in names such as CHERYL.

Tessa (f.) English: this name and its shortened form **Tess** are generally considered to be pet forms of THERESA, although now often used independently. However, the formation is not clear, and *Tessa* may be of distinct origin. Literary contexts of the late 19th century show that the name was thought of as Italian, although it is in fact unknown in Italy.

Pet form: **Tessie**.

Tete (f.) Spanish: pet form of TERESA.

Tetty (f.) English: pet form of ELIZABETH, common in the 18th century (when it was borne, for example, by Samuel Johnson's wife) but now little used.

Variant: **Tettie**.

Teunis (m.) Dutch: short form derived from *Antonius* (see ANTHONY).

Tevye (m.) Jewish: Yiddish form of TUVIA.

Tex (m.) English (U.S.): short form of the ethnic name *Texan*, now used as a given name along the lines of DEX, LEX, and REX.

Thaddeus (m.) Latin form of a New Testament name, the byname used to refer to one of Christ's lesser-known apostles, whose given name was *Lebbaeus* (Matthew 10: 3). It is of uncertain origin. It may be a Greek spelling of an Aramaic version of a short form of a Greek name, perhaps *Theodōros* 'gift of God' (see THEODORE) or *Theodotos* 'given by God'. In Ireland this has been used as an Anglicized form of TADHG.

Derivatives: Italian: **Taddeo**. Spanish: **Tadeo**. Portuguese: **Tadeu**. Polish: **Tadeusz**. Russian: **Faddei**.

Short form: English, Irish: **Tad**.

Pet forms: Polish: **Tadzio**. Irish: **Thady**.

Thalia (f.) Name borne in classical mythology by the Muse of comedy; it is derived from Greek *thallein* to flourish, and has occasionally been chosen in recent years by parents in the English-speaking world in search of novelty.

Thea (f.) English: short form of DOROTHEA, now to some extent used as an independent given name.

Thecla (f.) English: contracted form of the Greek name *Theokleia*, composed of the elements *theos* god + *kleia* glory. The name was borne by a 1st-century saint (the first female martyr), who was particularly popular in the Middle Ages because of the lurid details of her suffering recorded in the apocryphal 'Acts of Paul and Thecla'.

Cognate: Scandinavian: **Tekla**.

Theda (f.) German: Latinate short form of the various old Germanic female names containing the element *theod* people, race, as, for example, *Theodelinde* 'people + tender' and *Theodegunde* 'people + strife'. The name enjoyed a brief popularity in America from about 1915 to 1920, due to the popularity of the silent-film actress Theda Bara (1890–1955), the original 'vamp'. Her real name was Theodosia Goodman.

Thelma (f.) English: first used by the novelist Marie Corelli for the heroine of her novel *Thelma* (1887). She was supposed to be Norwegian, but it is not a traditional Scandinavian name. Greek *thelēma* (neuter) means 'wish, (act of) will', and the name could perhaps be interpreted as a contracted form of this.

Thelonius (m.) Latinized form of the name of St Tillo (see TILL). The spelling **Thelonious** is particularly associated with the American jazz pianist Thelonious Monk (1920–82).

Theo (m.) English: short form of THEODORE and, less commonly, of THEOBALD.

Theobald (m.) English: from a Latinized form, first found in medieval documents, of a Norman name of Germanic origin, composed of the elements *theud* people, race + *bald* bold, brave; the first element has been altered under the influence of Greek *theos* god.

Cognates: Irish Gaelic: **Tiobóid**. Scottish Gaelic: **Tiobaid**.

Theodoor (m.) Dutch form of THEODORE.

Theodor (m.) German form of THEODORE.

Theodora (f.) Feminine form of THEODORE, borne most notably by a 9th-century empress of Byzantium, the wife of Theophilus the Iconoclast. It has frequently been used as an English given name. The elements are the same as those of DOROTHEA, but in reverse order.

Derivatives: Italian, Spanish, Portuguese, Swedish, and Polish: TEODORA. Russian: **Feodora**.

Theodore (m.) English: from the French form of the Greek name *Theodōros*, composed of the elements *theos* god + *dōron* gift. The name was popular among early Christians and was borne by several saints.

Cognates: French: **Théodore**. German: **Theodor**. Dutch: **Theodoor**. Hungarian: **Tivadar**. Russian: **Fyodor**. Jewish (Aramaic): **Todos**.

Short forms: English: **Theo, Ted**.

Theodosia (f.) Greek: derived from the elements *theos* god + *dōsis* giving. It was borne by several early saints venerated mostly in the Eastern Church, and is only very occasionally used in the English-speaking world today.

Theophilus (m.) New Testament: Latin form of the name of the addressee of St Luke's gospel and the Acts of the Apostles; also borne by various early saints. It is composed of the Greek elements *theos* god + *philos* friend, and was popular among early Christians because of its well-omened meaning: 'lover of God' or 'beloved by God'.

Derivatives: French: **Théophile**. Italian, Spanish, Portuguese: **Teofilo**. Russian: **Feofil**.

Thera (f.) English: of uncertain derivation. It could either represent a shortened form of THERESA, or be derived from the name of the Greek island of *Thēra*.

Theresa (f.) English: of problematic origin. The name seems to have been first used in Spain and Portugal, and, according to tradition, was the name of the wife of St Paulinus of Nola, who spent most of his life in Spain; she was said to have originated (and to have derived her name) from the Greek island of *Thēra*. However, this theory is neither factually nor etymologically reliable.

Cognates: Irish Gaelic: **Treasa**. French: **Thérèse** (also sometimes used in the English-speaking world in honour of St Thérèse of Lisieux, Marie Françoise Thérèse Martin, 1873–97). Spanish, Italian: TERESA. German: **Theresia** (much used in the combination **Maria Theresia** in families claiming connection with the royal Habsburg line; also occasionally used in the English-speaking world).

Short form: Spanish: **Tere**.

Pet forms: English: **Terri**; TESSA, **Tess**. Spanish: **Teresita**, **Tete**. German: **Resi**, **Reserl**, **Resli**.

Thierry (m.) French form of the Germanic name *Theodoric*; see also TERRY, DIETRICH, and DEREK.

Thijs (m.) Dutch: aphetic short form of *Matthijs* (see MATTHEW), now used as an independent given name.

Thomas (m.) New Testament name, borne by one of Christ's twelve apostles, referred to as 'Thomas, called Didymus' (John 11: 16; 20: 24). *Didymos* is the Greek word for 'twin', and the name is the Greek form of an Aramaic byname meaning 'twin'. The given name has always been popular throughout Christendom, perhaps because St Thomas's doubts and reassurance have made him seem a very human character.

Derivatives: Irish Gaelic: **Tomás**. Scottish Gaelic: **Tòmas**; **Tàmhas** (a dialectal variant, from which comes the surname *Mac Thàmhais*, Anglicized as *MacTavish*). Welsh: **Tomos**. Italian: **Tommaso**. Polish: **Tomasz**. Czech: **Tomáš**. Russian: **Foma**. Finnish: **Tuomo**.

Short forms: English: **Tom**. Scottish: **Tam**. Italian: **Maso**. Dutch: **Maas**.

Pet forms: English: **Tommy**. Scottish Gaelic: **Tòmachan**, **Tòmag**.

Feminine forms: English: **Thomasina**, **Thomasine**, TAMSIN.

Tia (f.) English: apparently in origin a short form of the various given names ending thus, as, for example, CRESCENTIA and LAETITIA.

Tibor (m.) Hungarian: from Latin *Tiberius*, a derivative of the name (of obscure origin) of the River Tiber. It was borne by the second Roman emperor and by a martyr who was executed in 303 under the Emperor Diocletian, together with Modestus and Florence.

Tiede (m.) Dutch: pet form of DIEDERIK.

Tiernan (m.) Irish: Anglicized form of the Gaelic name **Ti(ghe)arnán**, originally a byname representing a diminutive form of *tighearna* lord.

Tierney (m.) Irish: Anglicized form of the Gaelic name **Ti(ghe)arnach**, a derivative of *tighearna* lord. The name was borne by a 6th-century saint who served as abbot of Clones and later as bishop of Clogher.

Tiffany (f.) Usual medieval English form of Greek *Theophania* 'Epiphany', from *theos* god + *phainein* to appear. This was once a relatively common name, given particularly to girls born on the feast of the Epiphany (6 January), and it gave rise to an English surname. As a given name, it fell into disuse until revived in the 20th century under the influence of the famous

New York jewellers, Tiffany's, and the film, starring Audrey Hepburn, *Breakfast at Tiffany's* (1961). In 1982 this was the most popular of all female names in use among American Blacks, and thirty-third most popular among Whites.

Tikhon (m.) Russian form of TYCHO.

Tikvah (f.) Jewish: Hebrew name meaning 'hope'. The name is borne in the Bible by a male character mentioned in passing (2 Kings 22: 14), but is now a female name chosen for the sake of its good omen.

Variant: **Tikva**.

Tilda (f.) English and Swedish: short form of MATILDA.

Cognate: Danish: **Tilde**.

Till (m.) Low German: from a medieval pet form of DIETRICH and other Germanic personal names with the same first element. St Tillo evangelized the district around Tournai and Courtrai in Belgium during the 8th century.

Extended forms: **Til(l)man**; **Thelonius** (Latinized).

Tilly (f.) English: pet form of MATILDA, much used from the Middle Ages to the late 19th century, when it also came to be an independent given name. It is rare in either use nowadays.

Variant: **Tillie**.

Tim (m.) English: short form of TIMOTHY, also used in Ireland as an Anglicized form of TADHG.

Pet form: **Timmy** (normally used only for young boys).

Timothy (m.) English form, used in the Authorized Version of the Bible (alongside the Latin form *Timotheus*), of Greek *Timotheos*, composed of the elements *tīmē* honour + *theos* god. This was the name of a companion of St Paul; according to tradition, he was stoned to death for denouncing the worship of Diana, but there is no historical evidence for this. Surprisingly, the name was not used in England at all before the Reformation.

Cognates: French: **Timothée**. Italian, Spanish, Portuguese: **Timoteo**. Polish: **Tymoteusz**. Russian: **Timofei**.

Pet form: Russian: **Tyoma**.

Tina (f.) Short form of CHRISTINA and, less commonly, of other female names ending in *-tina*. This is a relatively common given name in the English-speaking world, and elsewhere. It was the most common of all female names bestowed in Denmark in the mid-1960s.

Tiobóid (m.) Irish Gaelic form of THEOBALD, derived in the early Middle Ages from Anglo-Norman *Thebaud*.

Cognate: Scottish Gaelic: **Tiobaid**.

Tirion (f.) Welsh: modern given name, from the vocabulary word meaning 'kind, gentle'.

Tirso (m.) Spanish: from the Greek name *Thyrsos*. A *thyrsos* was a characteristic vine-decked staff carried by devotees of the god Dionysus; the word seems to have been introduced, together with the cult of Dionysus, from the Orient. St Thyrsos was martyred at Apollonia in Phrygia in *c.*251, together with Lucius and Kallinikos. Their relics were brought to Spain in the early Middle Ages, and Thyrsos was honoured with a full office in the Mozarabic liturgy.

Cognates: Catalan: **Tirs**. Russian: **Firs**.

Tita (f.) English: short form of MARTITA, or else perhaps a feminine form of TITUS.

Titty (f.) English: pet form of LAETITIA that has now become obsolete because of its unfortunate coincidence in form with the slang word for a female breast.

Titus (m.) From an old Roman given name, of unknown origin. It was borne by a companion of St Paul who became the first bishop of Crete, and also by the Roman emperor who destroyed Jerusalem in AD 70. It is not commonly used as a given name in the English-speaking world.

Derivative: Italian, Spanish, Portuguese: **Tito**.

Tivadar (m.) Hungarian form of THEODORE.

Tiziano (m.) Italian: name borne in honour of the famous medieval painter Tiziano Vecellio (?1490–1576), known in English as Titian. The medieval name *Tiziano* derives from Latin *Titiānus*, a double derivative of TITUS that was borne by a 6th-century bishop of Brescia and a 7th-century bishop of Oderzo.

Tjalf (m.) East Frisian form of DETLEV.

Tjark (m.) East Frisian form of DEREK.

Toal (m.) Irish: Anglicized form of TUATHAL.

Tobbe (m.) Swedish and Danish: pet form of TORBJÖRN and *Torbjørn*.

Tobias (m.) Biblical: Greek form of Hebrew *Tobiah* 'God is good'. This name is borne by several characters in the Bible (appearing in the Authorized Version also as *Tobijah*), but in the Middle Ages it was principally associated with the tale of 'Tobias and the Angel'. According to the Book of Tobit in the Apocrypha, Tobias, the son of Tobit, a rich and righteous Jew of Nineveh, was lucky enough to acquire the services of the archangel Raphael as a travelling companion on a journey to Ecbatana. He returned wealthy, married, and with a cure for his father's blindness. A historical St Tobias was martyred (*c.*315) at Sebaste in Armenia, together with Carterius, Styriacus, Eudoxius, Agapius, and five others.

Cognates: Jewish: **Tuvia** (Hebrew); **Tevye, Teive** (Yiddish).

Toby (m.) English: vernacular form of TOBIAS.

Todd (m.) English: transferred use of the surname, which was originally a nickname from an English dialect word meaning 'fox'.

Todos (m.) Jewish: Aramaic form of Greek *Theodōros* (see THEODORE). The name has been in use among Jews since the Hellenistic period.

Toinette (f.) English and French: short form of ANTOINETTE.

Toini (f.) Finnish form of ANTONIA.

Toirdhealbhach (m.) Irish Gaelic: probably originally a byname meaning 'instigator', from *toirdhealbh* prompting + the Gaelic suffix *-ach*. The belief that this is a derivative of the name of the Norse god of thunder, *Þorr*, is probably no more than folk etymology.

Cognate: Scottish Gaelic: **Teàrlach**.

Anglicized forms: TURLOUGH, **Turley**; TERENCE.

Toivo (f.) Finnish: meaning 'hope', this is a loan translation of Latin *spes*, Greek *elpis*.

Toltse (f.) Jewish: Yiddish name, probably from the Italian affectionate nickname *Dolce* 'sweet, lovely' (cf. DULCIE).

Tom (m.) English: short form of THOMAS, in use since the Middle Ages, and recorded as an independent name since the 18th century.

Pet form: **Tommy**.

Tòmas (m.) Scottish Gaelic form of THOMAS.

Tomás (m.) Irish Gaelic form of THOMAS.

Tomáš (m.) Czech form of THOMAS.

Pet forms: **Tomášek, Tomoušek, Tomík, Toman**.

Tomasz (m.) Polish form of THOMAS.

Tommaso (m.) Italian form of THOMAS.

Short form: **Maso**.

Tomos (m.) Welsh form of THOMAS.

Tonete (m.) Spanish: pet form of ANTONIO.

Toni (f.) English (mainly U.S.): either a pet form of ANTONIA or a supposedly feminine spelling of TONY.

Variants: **Tonia, Tonie** (less common).

Tonio (m.) Italian: short form of ANTONIO.

Tönjes (m.) Low German and Frisian: short form of *Antonius* (see ANTHONY).
Variant: **Tönnies.**

Toño (m.) Spanish: short form of ANTONIO.

Tony (m.) English: short form of ANTHONY, now sometimes used as an independent name in the English-speaking world.

Topaz (f.) English: one of the rarer examples of the class of modern female names taken from vocabulary words denoting gemstones. The topaz gets its name via French and Latin from Greek; it is probably ultimately of oriental origin. In the Middle Ages this was sometimes used as a male name, representing a form of TOBIAS.

Tor (m.) Scandinavian: originally the name of the god of thunder in Norse mythology, Thor (Old Norse *Þórr*). This was not used as a personal name during the Middle Ages. The modern name is either a late 18th-century revival of the divine name or else a vernacular development of TORD.
Variant: **Thor** (chiefly Danish).

Torbjörn (m.) Swedish: from an Old Norse personal name composed of the name of the god Thor (*Þórr*) + Old Norse *björn* bear.
Cognates: Danish: **T(h)orbjørn, Torbe(r)n.** Norwegian: **Torbjørn.**
Pet form: Swedish, Danish: **Tobbe.**

Torborg (f.) Scandinavian: from an Old Norse female personal name composed of the name of the god Thor (*Þórr*) + Old Norse *borg* fortification.
Variants: **Thorborg.** Norwegian: **Torbjørg.**

Tord (m.) Scandinavian: contracted form of the Old Norse personal name *Þorfriðr*, composed of the name of the god Thor (*Þórr*) + Old Norse *friðr* peace.

Tordis (f.) Scandinavian: from an Old Norse female personal name composed of the name of the god Thor (*Þórr*) + Old Norse *dís* goddess.

Tore (m.) Scandinavian: from the Old Norse personal name *Þórir*, apparently originally composed of the name of the god Thor (*Þórr*) + Old Norse *verr* man. It has also been interpreted as a derivative form from *Þórr*. As early as the Viking period, however, the form *Þóri* was being used as a short form of all the compound names with the first element *Þórr*.
Variant: **Ture.**

Torger (m.) Swedish: from an Old Norse personal name composed of the name of the god Thor (*Þórr*) + Old Norse *geirr* spear.
Cognates: Norwegian: **Torgeir, Terje.**

Toribio (m.) Spanish: from Latin *Turibius*, a name of extremely uncertain derivation. It may represent a Latinized form of an indigenous Iberian name. The name was borne by a 5th-century bishop of Astorga and by the 6th-century founder of the abbey of Liébana in Asturias.

Torkel (m.) Swedish: from a contracted form of the Old Norse personal name *Þorketill*, composed of the name of the god Thor (*Þórr*) + Old Norse *ketill* kettle, helmet.
Variants: **Torkil, Thorkel.**
Cognates: Norwegian: **Torkjell.** Danish: **Torkil(d).** See also TORQUIL.

Tormod (m.) Scottish Gaelic: traditional name, originally a borrowing of the Old Norse personal name *Þórmóðr*, composed of the name of the god Thor (*Þórr*) + Old Norse *móðr* mind, courage.
Variant: **Tormailt** (a dialectal form).
Anglicized form: NORMAN (chosen because of the similarity in sound and because the Gaelic name is generally known to be of Norse origin).

Torolf (m.) Swedish and Danish: from an Old Norse personal name composed of the name of the god Thor (*Þórr*) + Old Norse *úlfr* wolf.
Variant: **Torulf.**
Cognate: Norwegian: **Torolv.**

Torquil (m.) Scottish: Anglicized form of the traditional Gaelic name **Torcall,** originally a borrowing of the Old Norse personal name *Þorketill* (see TORKEL). The earlier uncontracted form of the Gaelic name is preserved in the surname *Mac Thorcadail*, Anglicized as *MacCorquodale*.

Torsten (m.) Swedish and Danish: from an Old Norse personal name composed of the name of the god Thor (*Þórr*) + Old Norse *steinn* stone.
Variant: **Thorstein(n)**.
Cognate: Norwegian: **Torstein**.

Torvald (m.) Scandinavian: from an Old Norse personal name composed of the name of the god Thor (*Þórr*) + Old Norse *valdr* ruler.
Variant: **Thorwald**. See also TOVE.

Tory (f.) English: pet form of VICTORIA.

Totty (f.) English: pet form of CHARLOTTE, representing a rhyming variant of LOTTIE. The name was most common in the 18th and 19th centuries, like TETTY.
Variant: **Tottie**.

Toussaint (m.) French: name chosen by parents who wish to invoke the blessing and protection of 'all the saints' (French *tous* (*les*) *saints*) for their son. The name is also often given to a boy born on the feast of All Saints (cf. SANTOS).

Tova (f.) 1. Jewish: modern Hebrew name meaning 'good' (cf. TOBIAS).
2. Swedish: from the Old Norse female personal name *Tōfa*, a short form of *Þorfríðr* (see TURID).

Tove (f., m.) 1. (f.) Danish and Norwegian: from the Old Norse female personal name *Tófa*, a short form of *Þorfríðr* (see TURID).
2. (m.) Swedish: short form, used as early as the Viking period, of TORVALD.
Variant (of 2): **Tuve**.

Tracy (f., formerly m.) English: transferred use of the surname, which is derived from a Norman baronial name from places in France called Tracy 'place of Thracius'. In former times, *Tracy* was occasionally used as a male given name, as were the surnames of other English noble families. Later, it was also used as a female name, generally being taken as a pet form of THERESA. In recent years, it has become an immensely popular female name. A strong influence was the character of Tracy Lord, played by Grace Kelly in the film *High Society* (1956).
Variants: **Tracey, Tracie** (f.).

Trahaearn (m.) Welsh: traditional name composed of the intensive prefix *tra-* + *haearn* iron.

Traolach (m.) Irish Gaelic: a dialectal form of TOIRDHEALBHACH.

Travis (m.) English: transferred use of the surname, which is derived from a Norman French occupational name (from *traverser* to cross) for someone who collected a toll from users of a bridge or a particular stretch of road. It is now regularly used as a given name, especially in America and Australia.

Treasa (f.) Irish: Gaelic form of THERESA.

Treena (f.) English: modern variant spelling of TRINA.

Treeza (f.) English: modern contracted spelling of THERESA.

Trevelyan (m.) English: transferred use of the surname, which is of Cornish origin, a local name from a place named in the Domesday Book as *Trevelien*, i.e. 'homestead or settlement (Cornish *tref*) of *Elian*'.

Trevor (m.) Welsh and English: transferred use of the Welsh surname, which in turn is from a placename. There are a large number of places in Wales called *Trefor*, from the elements *tref* settlement + *fôr*, mutated and unaccented form of *mawr* large. In recent years, *Trevor* has also become popular as a given name among people who have no connection with Wales.
Welsh form: **Trefor**.
Short form (informal): **Trev**.

Tricia (f.) English: short form of PATRICIA.

Trina (f.) English: short form of KATRINA.

Trine (f.) Danish: short form of KATRINE.

Trinette (f.) English: modern elaboration of TRINA, using the originally French feminine diminutive suffix *-ette*.

Trinidad (f.) Spanish: name taken in honour of the Holy Trinity (Latin *trīnitas*, genitive *trīnitātis*, from *trīni*, a distributive numeral from *trēs* three).

Cognate: Portuguese: **Trindade**.

Short form: Spanish: **Trini**.

Tríona (f.) Irish Gaelic: short form of CAITRÍONA.

Anglicized form: **Triona**.

Trisha (f.) English: phonetic respelling of TRICIA, comparatively recent in origin. It is currently fairly popular, and sometimes bestowed as a given name in its own right.

Tristan (m.) English, Welsh, and French: variant of TRISTRAM. Both forms of the name occur in medieval and later versions of the legend.

Variant: **Trystan** (mainly Welsh).

Tristram (m.) English: from Celtic legend, the name borne by a hero of medieval romance. There are many different versions of the immensely popular and tragic story of Tristram and his love for Isolde. Generally, they agree that Tristram was an envoy sent by King Mark of Cornwall to bring back his bride, the Irish princess Isolde. Unfortunately, Tristram and Isolde fall in love with each other, having accidentally drunk the love potion intended for King Mark's wedding night. Tristram eventually leaves Cornwall to fight for King Howel of Brittany. Wounded in battle, he sends for Isolde. She arrives too late, and dies of grief beside his bier. The name *Tristram* is of unknown derivation, though it may be connected with Pictish *Drostan*; it has been altered from an irrecoverable original as a result of transmission through Old French sources that insisted on associating it with Latin *tristis* sad, a reference to the young knight's tragic fate.

Variants: **Tristrand, Tristan, Drystan**.

Trixie (f.) English: pet name derived from a short form of BEATRIX, occasionally used as an independent given name.

Variant: **Trixi**.

Trofim (m.) Russian: from the Greek name *Trophimos*, a derivative of *trophos* nurseling. It was borne by half a dozen early Christian saints, martyred under the Emperors Probus and Diocletian and much venerated in the Eastern Church.

Trond (m.) Scandinavian: originally an ethnic byname for someone who came from the Trøndelag region in central Norway. The name was in use in the Viking period, and was revived in the early 20th century.

Troy (m., f.) English: probably originally a transferred use of the surname, which is derived from *Troyes* in France. Nowadays, however, the given name is principally associated with the ancient city of Troy in Asia Minor, whose fate has been a central topic in epic poetry from Homer onwards. The story tells how Troy was sacked by the Greeks after a siege of ten years; according to classical legend, a few Trojan survivors got away to found Rome (and, according to medieval legend, another group founded Britain).

Trudeliese (f.) German: combination of the names *Trude* (see TRUDI) and LIESE.

Trudi (f.) German (esp. Swiss): pet form of the various female names ending in *-trud*; see, for example, GERTRUDE and ERMINTRUDE. It is now also used to some extent in the English-speaking world, under the influence of the many other female names now spelled with a final *-i*.

Trudy (f.) English: respelling of TRUDI.

Variant: **Trudie**.

Truman (m.) English: in the main, a transferred use of the surname. This is in part of English origin, representing a nickname derived from Old English *trēowe* true, trusty + *mann* man, but in America it is more commonly an Anglicized version of the German cognate *Treumann*. The favourable meaning of the elements has no doubt influenced its choice as a given name to some extent. A further possible influence may have been the fame of Harry S. Truman (1884–1972), president of the United States (1945–52), but the given name was in use before he became president.

Variant: **Trueman**.

Tryggve (m.) Scandinavian: from an Old Norse personal name, originally a byname derived from the adjective *tryggr* true, trusty (cf. TRUMAN).

Variant: **Trygve**.

Trystan (m.) Variant (mainly Welsh) of TRISTAN.

Tuathal (m.) Irish Gaelic: name meaning 'ruler of a tribe'.

Anglicized form: **Toal**.

Tudur (m.) Welsh: traditional name derived from the Old Celtic form *Teutorix*, composed of elements meaning 'people, tribe' + 'ruler, king'. The name has been widely believed to be a Welsh form of THEODORE, but there is in fact no connection between the two names.

Variants: **Tudyr** (an earlier spelling); **Tudor** (an Anglicized spelling).

Tullio (m.) Italian: from the old Roman family name *Tullius*, borne, for example, by the orator Marcus Tullius Cicero (106–43 BC).

Tuomo (m.) Finnish form of THOMAS.

Ture (m.) Scandinavian: variant of TORE, formerly used mainly in Denmark and southern Sweden.

Turid (f.) Scandinavian: from an Old Norse female personal name composed of the name of the god Thor (*Þórr*) + Old Norse *fríðr* fair, beautiful.

Turiddu (m.) Italian (Sicilian): local pet form of *Salvatore* (see SALVADOR).

Turlough (m.) Irish: Anglicized form of Gaelic TOIRDHEALBHACH.

Tuvia (m.) Jewish: modern Hebrew form of TOBIAS.

Cognates: Yiddish: **Tevye, Teive**.

Tybalt (m.) English: the usual medieval form of THEOBALD, rarely used nowadays. It occurs in Shakespeare's *Romeo and Juliet* as the name of a brash young man who is killed in a brawl.

Tycho (m.) Latinized form of the name of St Tychon (d. *c.*450), bishop of Amathus in Cyprus, who worked to suppress the last remnants of the cult of Aphrodite on the island. The Greek name *Tychōn* means 'hitting the mark', and was chosen for the sake of its good omen. The most famous modern bearer of the given name was the Danish astronomer Tycho Brahe (1546–1601).

Derivatives: Swedish: **Tyko**. Danish: **Tyge** (vernacular). Russian: **Tikhon**.

Tyler (m.) English: transferred use of the surname, which originated as an occupational name borne by someone who tiled roofs.

Tymoteusz (m.) Polish form of TIMOTHY.

Tyoma (m.) Russian: pet form of ARTEMI and of *Timofei* (see TIMOTHY).

Tyrone (m.) English (esp. U.S.): from the name of a county in Northern Ireland and a town in Pennsylvania. Its use as a given name seems to be entirely due to the influence of the two film actors (father and son) called Tyrone Power.

Txomin (m.) Basque form of DOMINIC.

U

Ualan (m.) Scottish Gaelic form of the male name VALENTINE.

Variant: **Uailean**.

Uarraig (m.) Scottish Gaelic: traditional name composed of the elements *uall* pride + *garg* fierce. It has been Anglicized as KENNEDY, apparently because it was a common given name in kindreds with that surname.

Udo (m.) German: an old Germanic personal name derived from the element *uod(al)* prosperity, riches, fortune. It probably originated as a short form of the various compound names containing this element. It is still in comparatively common use in Germany.

Ughtred (m.) English: from the rare Old English personal name *Uhtrǣd*, composed of the elements *uht* dawn + *rǣd* counsel, advice. This is a very uncommon given name in the English-speaking world, but remains in use in the Shuttleworth family.

Ugo (m.) Italian form of HUGH.

Uilleam (m.) Scottish Gaelic form of WILLIAM.

Pet forms: **Uilleachan, Uillidh**.

Uinseann (m.) Irish Gaelic form of VINCENT.

Ùisdean (m.) Scottish Gaelic: traditional name, originally a borrowing of the Old Norse personal name *Eysteinn*, composed of the elements *ei*, *ey* always, for ever + *steinn* stone.

Variant: **Hùisdean**.

Anglicized form: HUGH.

Ulf (m.) Danish and Swedish: cognate of WOLF, from the Old Norse personal name or byname *Úlfr*.

Cognate: Norwegian: **Ulv**.

Ulick (m.) Irish: Anglicized form of Gaelic **Uilleac** or **Uilleag**. This name probably derives from Old Norse *Hugleikr*, composed of the elements *hugr* heart, mind, spirit + *leikr* play, sport. Alternatively, it may represent a diminutive derived from a short form of *Uilleam*, a Gaelic version of WILLIAM (cf. LIAM).

Ulises (m.) Spanish form of ULYSSES.

Ulisse (m.) Italian form of ULYSSES, taken up as a given name during the Renaissance, and permitted as a baptismal name by the Roman Catholic Church even though it had been borne neither by a New Testament character nor by an early saint.

Ulla (f.) Scandinavian: pet form of ULRIKA.

Ulric (m.) English: in the Middle Ages, this represented an Old English name composed of the elements *wulf* wolf + *rīc* power. In its occasional modern use, it is probably an Anglicized spelling of ULRICH.

Variant: **Ulrick**.

Ulrich (m.) German: from an old Germanic personal name composed of the elements *uodal* prosperity, riches, fortune + *rīc* power. This name was borne by two major German saints, Ulrich of Augsburg (d. 973) and Ulrich of Cluny (*c.*1018–93), as well as by the Blessed Ulrich of Einsiedeln in Switzerland (d. *c.*980).

Cognates: Scandinavian: **Ulrik**. Polish: **Ulryk**. Czech: **Oldřich**.

Pet form: German: **Utz**.

Ulrika (f.) Scandinavian form and German variant of ULRIKE.

Pet form: Scandinavian: **Ulla**.

Ulrike (f.) German and Danish: feminine form of ULRICH. The name is now also occasionally used in the English-speaking world.

Cognate: Czech: **Oldřiška**.

Ultan (m.) Irish: Anglicized form of the Gaelic name *Ultán*, a diminutive form of the ethnic name *Ultach* 'Ulsterman'.

Ulysses (m.) Latin form of the Greek name *Odysseus*, borne by the famous wanderer of Homer's *Odyssey*. The name is of uncertain derivation (it was associated by the Greeks themselves with the verb *odyssesthai* to hate); moreover, it is not clear why the Latin form should be so altered (mediation through Etruscan has been one suggestion). As an English given name it has occasionally been used in the 19th and 20th centuries, especially in America (like other names of classical origin such as HOMER and VIRGIL). It was the name of the 18th president of the United States, Ulysses S. Grant (1822–85). It has also been used in Ireland as a classicizing form of ULICK.

Derivatives: Italian: **Ulisse**. Spanish: **Ulises**.

Umberto (m.) Italian form of HUMBERT. The former Italian royal family is descended from the Blessed Umberto of Savoy (1136–88).

Úna (f.) Irish Gaelic: traditional name of uncertain derivation. It is identical in form with the vocabulary word *úna* hunger, famine, but may rather be connnected with *uan* lamb. The Anglicized form *Una* is sometimes taken to be from the feminine of Latin *unus* one, and therefore a doublet of UNITY. It is the name used by Edmund Spenser as that of the lady of the Red Cross Knight in *The Faerie Queene*: he almost certainly had Latin rather than Irish in mind, even though he worked in Ireland for a while.

Cognate: Scottish Gaelic: **Ùna**.

Anglicized forms: **Una**; **Oona(gh)** (Irish); **Euna** (Scottish); UNITY, JUNO, WINIFRED, AGNES.

Unity (f.) English: from the quality (Latin *unitās*, a derivative of *unus* one). It achieved some currency among the Puritans, but has been mainly used in Ireland as a kind of Anglicized extended form of ÚNA.

Urban (m.) English, Danish, Swedish, Polish, and Czech: from the Latin name *Urbānus* 'city-dweller'. This was borne by numerous early saints, and was adopted by several popes (who may have felt it to be particularly appropriate since they ruled from the city of Rome).

Cognate: Hungarian: **Órban**.

Pet forms: Czech: **Ur(b)a**, **Ur(b)ek**.

Uri (m.) Jewish: from a Hebrew word meaning 'light' (cf. URIAH and URIEL). There is no connection with the Russian name YURI.

Uriah (m.) Biblical: name (from Hebrew, meaning 'God is light') borne by a Hittite warrior treacherously disposed of by King David after he had made Uriah's wife Bathsheba pregnant (2 Samuel 11). The Greek form *Urias* occurs in the New Testament (Matthew 1: 6). The name was popular in the 19th century, but is now most closely associated with the character of the obsequious Uriah Heep in Dickens's *David Copperfield* (1850) and has consequently undergone a sharp decline in popularity.

Uriel (m.) Biblical: Hebrew name composed of the elements *uri* light (cf. URI) + *'el* God, and so a doublet of URIAH. It is borne by two minor characters mentioned in genealogies (1 Chronicles 6: 24; 2 Chronicles 13: 2), and is relatively common among modern Jews.

Urien (m.) Welsh: name borne by a character in the *Mabinogi*, Urien of Rheged. He is probably identical with the historical figure Urien who fought against the Northumbrians in the 6th century. The name may be composed of the Old Celtic elements *ōrbo* privileged + *gen* birth.

Urs (m.) German (esp. Swiss): vernacular form of the Latin name *Ursus* 'bear'. Victor and Ursus were two soldiers of the Theban legion who were martyred in 286 and are particularly venerated in Switzerland.

Ursula (f.) English, German, and Scandinavian: from the Latin name *Ursula*, a diminutive of *ursa* (she-)bear (cf. URS). This was the name of a 4th-century saint martyred at Cologne with a number of companions, traditionally said to have been eleven thousand, but more probably just eleven, the exaggeration being due to a misreading of a diacritic mark in an early manuscript.

Uschi (f.) German: common pet form of URSULA.

Usko (f.) Finnish: meaning 'faith', this is a loan translation of the Latin name *Fides* or the Greek *Pistis*.

Ute (f.) German: from a medieval given name derived from the Germanic element *uod(al)* prosperity, riches, fortune. It is therefore a feminine equivalent of UDO.
Variants: **Ude, Ode** (both rare).

Utz (m.) German: pet form of ULRICH.

Uwe (m.) Low German and Frisian: equivalent form of OVE.

Uzi (m.) Mainly Jewish: name, meaning 'power' or 'might' in Hebrew, borne in the Bible by six minor characters mentioned in genealogies. In the Authorized Version the spelling **Uzzi** is used. The name seems to represent a short form of the theophoric names UZZIAH and UZZIEL.

Uzziah (m.) Biblical: Hebrew name meaning 'power of Yahweh (God)'. It is borne by several characters in the Old Testament, including one of the kings of Judea.
Variant: **Uziah**.

Uzziel (m.) Biblical: Hebrew name meaning 'power of God'. It is borne by several minor characters mentioned in Old Testament genealogies and has enjoyed some popularity as a given name among Jews.
Variant: **Uziel**.

V

Vaast (m.) Flemish: borne by a 6th-century saint, bishop of Arras-Cambrai. His name appears in medieval sources in the Latinized form *Vedastus*, and is of uncertain origin. It is probably a contracted form of the name *Widogast* (or *Widigast*), which is also found in medieval documents; it is composed of the Germanic elements *widu* wood + *gast* guest.

Václav (m.) Czech form of WENCESLAS.

Feminine form: **Václava**.

Vadim (m.) Russian: of uncertain origin. The name has been in use since the Middle Ages, and would seem to represent a reduced form of VLADIMIR, but this may be too simple an explanation.

Val (f., occasionally m.) English: 1. (f.) Short form of VALERIE.

2. (m.) Short form of VALENTINE.

Valda (f.) English: a 20th-century coinage, representing a fanciful elaboration of VAL with the suffix *-da*, extracted from names such as GLENDA and LINDA.

Valdemar (f.) Scandinavian: variant spelling of WALDEMAR,

Valene (f.) English: a 20th-century coinage, apparently of Australian origin, representing a fanciful elaboration of VAL with the productive feminine suffix *-ene*.

Valentine (m., occasionally f.) English form of the Latin name *Valentīnus*, a derivative of *valens* healthy, strong. This was the name of a Roman martyr of the 3rd century, whose feast is celebrated on 14 February. This was the date of a pagan fertility festival marking the first stirrings of spring, which has survived in an attenuated form under the patronage of the saint.

Cognates: Scottish Gaelic: **Ualan, Uailean**. Welsh: **Folant**. French, Danish, Swedish: **Valentin**. Italian: **Valentino**. Spanish: **Valentín**. Portuguese: **Valentim**. German: **Valentin**. S. German: **Velten**. Polish: **Walenty**. Czech: **Valentin**. Hungarian: **Bálint**.

Short form: English: **Val**.

Feminine forms: Latinate: **Valentina** (used esp. in Eastern Europe). Polish: **Walentyna**.

Valère (m.) French form of the Latin name *Valērius* (see VALERIE). There are several early saints of this name who have connections with France: a Roman missionary martyred at Soissons in 287, the first bishop of Conserans, an early bishop of Trèves, and a 5th-century bishop of Antibes.

Valeri (m.) Russian form of the Latin name *Valērius* (see VALERIE).

Valerie (f.) English: from the French form of the Latin name *Valēria*, the feminine form of the old Roman family name *Valērius*, which was apparently derived from *valēre* to be healthy, strong. The name was popular in France in the Middle Ages as a result of the cult of a 3rd-century saint (probably spurious) converted by Martial of Limoges.

Cognate: French: **Valérie**.

Short form: English: **Val**.

Valéry (m.) French: often taken to be a variant of VALÈRE, but in fact of Germanic rather than Latin origin. It is composed of the Germanic elements *walh* foreign, strange + *rīc* power. St Valéry or Walericus was the 7th-century founder of the abbey of Lencone at the mouth of the Somme.

Valetta (f.) English: a 20th-century coinage, representing an elaboration of VAL with the suffix *-etta*, originally an Italian feminine diminutive suffix. Valetta or Valletta is coincidentally the name of the capital of Malta.

Valter (m.) Scandinavian: variant spelling of WALTER.

Vanessa (f.) English: name invented by Jonathan Swift (1667–1745) for his intimate friend Esther Vanhomrigh. It seems to have been derived from the first syllable of her (Dutch) surname, with the addition of the suffix *-essa* (perhaps influenced by the first syllable of her given name).
Short form: **Nessa.**

Vanja (f.) Scandinavian: from the Russian name VANYA, but used as a girl's name because in the Scandinavian languages the ending *-a* is typical of female names.

Vanya (m.) Russian: pet form of IVAN.

Varda (f.) Jewish: modern name meaning 'rose' in Hebrew.
Variant: **Vardah.**

Varfolomei (m.) Russian form of BARTHOLOMEW.

Varvara (f.) Russian form of BARBARA.
Pet form: **Varya.**

Vasco (m.) Spanish, Portuguese, and Italian: contracted form of the medieval Spanish given name *Velasco* or *Belasco*, from which is derived the Spanish surname *Velázquez*. The medieval name is of uncertain origin; it may be connected with a Basque element meaning 'crow'. In form the modern given name coincides with the Spanish adjective *vasco* Basque (cf. GASTON).

Vasili (m.) Russian form of BASIL.

Vaughan (m.) Welsh and English: transferred use of the Welsh surname, which derives from the mutated form (*fychan* in Welsh orthography) of the Welsh adjective *bychan* small. This was originally a nickname or descriptive name.

Vavřinec (m.) Czech form of LAURENCE.
Short form: **Vavro.**
Pet forms: **Vavřík, Vavřiniček.**

Veerle (f.) Belgian: vernacular Flemish form of the old Germanic female personal name *Farahilda*, composed of the elements *fara* to go, travel + *hild* battle. The 8th-century St Farahilda, who was mistreated by her husband because of her extreme Christian zeal, has long been venerated as a patron saint of Ghent.

Veit (m.) 1. German: vernacular form of VITUS.
2. Dutch form of GUY.

Veleslav (m.) Czech form of WIELISŁAW.
Feminine form: **Veleslava.**
Pet forms: **Vela** (m., f.); **Velek, Veloušek** (m.); **Velka, Veluška, Velin(k)a** (f.).

Velma (f.) English (esp. U.S.): of modern origin and uncertain derivation, possibly based on SELMA or THELMA.

Velten (m.) South German form of VALENTINE.

Venceslao (m.) Italian form of WENCESLAS, occasionally borne in honour of the Bohemian saint.
Cognates: Spanish: **Venceslás.** Portuguese: **Venceslau.**

Věnceslav (m.) Older Czech form of WENCESLAS; cf. VÁCLAV.
Feminine form: **Věnceslava.**
Pet forms: **Věna** (m., f.); **Věnek, Venoušek** (m.); **Venka, Venuška** (f.).

Vendelín (m.) Czech form of WENDELIN.

Venedikt (m.) Russian form of BENEDICT.

Venessa (f.) English: modern altered form of VANESSA.

Venetia (f.) English: of uncertain origin, used occasionally since the late Middle Ages. In form the name coincides with that of the region of northern Italy.

Venyamin (m.) Russian form of BENJAMIN.
Pet forn: **Venya.**

Vera (f.) Russian name, meaning 'faith', introduced to Britain at the beginning of the 20th century. It coincides in form with the feminine form of the Latin adjective *vērus* true, and this has no doubt enhanced its popularity as a given name in the English-speaking world and in Scandinavia.

Cognates: Polish: **Wera, Wiera**. Czech: **Věra**.
Pet forms: Czech: **Věrka, Veruška**.

Vere (m.) English: transferred use of the surname, which originated as a Norman French baronial name, from any of the numerous places in northern France so called from the Gaulish element *ver(n)* alder.

Verena (f.) Characteristically Swiss name, first borne by a 3rd-century saint who lived as a hermit near Zurich. She is said to have come originally from Thebes in Egypt, and the origin of her name is obscure.

Pet form: **Vreni**.

Vergil (m.) English (esp. U.S.): variant of VIRGIL.

Verina (f.) English: variant of VERENA, with the common feminine name ending *-ina*.

Verity (f.) English: from the archaic abstract noun meaning 'truth' (coming via Old French from Latin *vēritās*, a derivative of *vērus* true; cf. VERA). It was a popular Puritan name, and is still occasionally used in the English-speaking world.

Verna (f.) English: a name that originated in the latter part of the 19th century, perhaps as a contracted form of VERENA or VERONA, or as a deliberately formed feminine equivalent of VERNON.

Verner (m.) Scandinavian: variant spelling of WERNER.

Vernon (m.) English: transferred use of the surname, which originated as a Norman French baronial name, from any of various places in Normandy so called from Gaulish elements meaning 'place of alders' (cf. VERE).

Verona (f.) English: of uncertain origin. It seems to have come into use towards the end of the 19th century, and may either represent a shortened form of VERONICA or be taken from the name of the Italian city. It became more widely known from Sinclair Lewis's novel *Babbitt* (1923), in which it is borne by the daughter of the eponymous hero.

Veronica (f.) Latin form, somewhat garbled, of BERENICE, influenced from an early date by association with the Church Latin phrase *vera icon* 'true image', of which this form is an anagram. The legend of the saint who wiped Christ's face on the way to Calvary and found an image of his face imprinted on the towel seems to have been invented to account for this derivation.

Cognates: French: **Véronique** (sometimes also used in the English-speaking world). German: **Veronike**. Scandinavian: **Veronika**.

Pet form: English: **Ronnie**.

Vessa (f.) English: modern creation, representing a contracted form of VENESSA or an assimilated form of VESTA.

Vesta (f.) English: from the Latin name of the Roman goddess of the hearth, cognate with that of a Greek goddess with similar functions, *Hestia*, but of uncertain derivation. It is only rarely used as a given name in the English-speaking world, but was borne as a stage name by the Victorian music-hall artiste Vesta Tilley (1864–1952).

Vester (m.) German: short form of SILVESTER.

Vi (f.) English: short form of VIOLET or VIVIAN/VIVIEN as a female name.

Vibeke (f.) Danish and Norwegian form of WIBEKE, also in use in Sweden.

Vicenç (m.) Catalan form of VINCENT.

Vicente (m.) Spanish form of VINCENT.

Vicky (f.) English: pet form of VICTORIA.

Variants: **Vickie, Vicki, Vikki**.

Victoire (f.) French form of VICTORIA.

Victor (m.) English: from a Late Latin personal name meaning 'conqueror'. This was popular among early Christians as a reference to Christ's victory over death and sin, and was borne by several saints.

Cognates: German, Scandinavian, Polish, Czech: **Viktor**. Italian: **Vittore**. See also GWYTHYR.

Equivalent: Hungarian: **Győző**.

Victoria (f.) English and Spanish: feminine form of the Latin name *Victōrius* (see VITTORIO), also perhaps a direct use of Latin *victōria* victory. It was little known in England until the accession in 1837 of Queen Victoria (1819–1901), who got it from her German mother, Mary Louise Victoria of Saxe-Coburg. It did not begin to be a popular name among commoners in Britain until the 1940s, reaching a peak in the 1970s.

Cognates: German, Scandinavian: **Viktoria**. Italian: **Vittoria**. French: **Victoire**; **Victorine** (an elaborated form). Scottish Gaelic: **Bhictoria**.

Pet form: English: **Vicky**.

Vidal (m.) Spanish form of VITALE that has been adopted in particular by Sefardic Jews as a translation of the Hebrew name *Hayyim* 'life' (see CHAIM and HYAM).

Vidkun (m.) Scandinavian: from an Old Norse personal name composed of the elements *víðr* wide + *kunnr* wise, experienced. It was borne by Vidkun Quisling (1887–1945), the Norwegian collaborator with the Nazis, whose surname has become a byword for treachery. Consequently, it is now completely out of fashion.

Vidor (m.) Hungarian: name representing a loan translation of HILARY.

Vigdis (f.) Scandinavian: from an Old Norse female personal name composed of the elements *víg* war + *dís* goddess.

Viggo (m.) Scandinavian: Latinized form of the Old Danish personal name *Vigge*, a short form of various compound names with the first element *víg* war.

Vigilio (m.) Italian (characteristic of the Trentino region): borne in honour of the local saint, *Vigilius*, bishop of Trent (d. 405), who was stoned to death for overturning a statue of Saturn. The name is probably a derivative of Latin *vigil* wakeful, watchful (cf. GREGORY).

Viktoria (f.) German and Scandinavian form of VICTORIA.

Vilém (m.) Czech form of WILLIAM.

Pet forms: **Vilémek**, **Vile(če)k**, **Vilík**, **Viloušek**.

Vilfred (m.) Scandinavian form of WILFRID.

Vilhelm (m.) Scandinavian form of WILLIAM.

Vilhelmina (f.) Swedish form of WILHELMINA.

Cognate: Danish, Norwegian: **Vilhelmine**.

Pet form: Danish: **Mine**.

Vilmos (m.) Hungarian form of WILLIAM.

Feminine form: **Vilma**.

Vilppu (m.) Finnish form of PHILIP.

Vince (m.) 1. English: short form of VINCENT, in use at least from the 17th century, and probably earlier, since it has given rise to a surname.

2. Hungarian form of VINCENT.

Vincent (m.) English, French, Dutch, Danish, and Swedish: from the Old French form of the Latin name *Vincens* 'conquering' (genitive *Vincentis*), from *vincere* to conquer. This name was borne by various early saints particularly associated with France, most notably the 5th-century St Vincent of Lérins.

Cognates: Irish Gaelic: **Uinseann**. Italian: **Vincente**; **Vi(n)cenzo** (from the elaborated form *Vincentius*). Spanish: **Vicente**. Catalan: **Vicenç**. German: **Vinzenz** (from *Vincentius*). Polish: **Wincenty** (from *Vincentius*). Czech: **Vincenc** (from *Vincentius*). Hungarian: **Vince**.

Short form: English: **Vince**.

Pet forms: Czech: **Vinca**, **Vinc(en)ek**, **Čenek**.

Viola (f.) English, Italian, and Scandinavian: from Latin *viōla* violet. The name is relatively common in Italy and was used by Shakespeare in *Twelfth Night* (where most of the characters have Italianate names). However, in England it seems to have been used in modern times mainly as a result of its association with the somewhat larger flower so called in English (a single-coloured pansy).

Violet (f.) English: from the name of the flower (Old French *violette*, Late Latin *violetta*, a diminutive of *viōla*). This was one of the earliest flower names to become popular in Britain, being well established before the middle of the 19th century, but it is now out of favour.

Cognates: French: **Violette**. Italian: **Violetta**.

Short form: English: **Vi**.

Virág (m.) Hungarian: originally an affectionate nickname meaning 'flower', now a given name in its own right.

Virgil (m.) Usual English form of the name of the most celebrated of Roman poets, Publius Vergilius Maro (70–19 BC). The correct Latin spelling is *Vergilius*, but it was early altered to *Virgilius* by association with *virgo* maiden or *virga* stick. Today the name is almost always given with direct reference to the poet, but medieval instances may have been intended to honour instead a 6th-century bishop of Arles or an 8th-century Irish monk who evangelized Carinthia and became archbishop of Salzburg, both of whom also bore the name. In the case of the later saint, it was a classicized form of the Gaelic name *Fearghal*; see FERGAL.

Variant: **Vergil**.

Cognate: Italian, Spanish: **Virgilio**.

Virginia (f.) English, Italian, Spanish, Portuguese, Danish, and Swedish: from the feminine form of Latin *Virginius* (more correctly *Verginius*; cf. VIRGIL), a Roman family name. It was borne by a Roman maiden killed, according to legend, by her own father to spare her the attentions of an importunate suitor. It does not seem to have been used as a given name in the Middle Ages. It was bestowed on the first American child of English parentage, born at Roanoke, Virginia, in August 1587. It has since become very popular. Both child and province were named in honour of Elizabeth I, the 'Virgin Queen'.

Cognate: French: **Virginie** (sometimes also used in the English-speaking world).

Pet form: English: **Ginny**. See also GINGER.

Virtudes (f.) Spanish: name given as a reference to the Seven Christian Virtues (Spanish *virtudes* virtues, Latin *virtūtes*, originally a derivative of *vir* man, meaning 'manly qualities').

Visitación (f.) Spanish: name recalling the New Testament story of the visit by the Virgin Mary to her cousin Elizabeth, the mother of John the Baptist (Luke 1: 39–56). This event is commemorated in the Catholic Church with a feast on 2 July, recognized since 1389.

Cognate: Portuguese: **Visitação**.

Vissarion (m.) Russian: from Greek *Bessarion*, a name of extremely uncertain derivation (probably a transliteration of a non-Greek original). A 2nd-century saint of this name lived as a hermit in the Egyptian desert, and he is still greatly venerated in the Orthodox Church.

Vít (m.) Czech form of VITUS.

Vita (f.) English and Danish: 19th-century coinage, either directly from Latin *vita* life, or else as a feminine form of VITUS. It has been borne most notably by the English writer Vita Sackville-West (1892–1962), in whose case it was a pet form of the given name *Victoria*.

Vitale (m.) Italian: from the Late Latin name *Vitālis*, a derivative of *vita* life. There are over a dozen early saints of this name, including Vitalis of Milan, the father of Gervasius and Protasius.

Cognate: Russian: **Vitali**.

Vittore (m.) Italian form of VICTOR.

Vittoria (f.) Italian form of VICTORIA.

Vittorio (m.) Italian: from the Latin name *Victōrius*, a derivative of VICTOR borne by a 5th-century bishop of Le Mans and by two obscure early martyrs.

Vitus (m.) The name of a child saint martyred in Sicily at an unknown (but early) date, together with his nurse Crescentia and her husband Modestus. His name seems to derive from Latin *vita* life (cf. VITA), and his two companions bear unmistakably Latin names, but there has been some confusion with forms of GUY.

Derivatives: German: **Veit.** Polish: **Wit.** Czech: **Vít.**

Viv (f., m.) English: short form, usually feminine, of VIVIAN and VIVIEN.

Viveka (f.) Swedish form of WIBEKE.

Variants: **Viveca, Vivica.**

Vivi (f.) English and Scandinavian: feminine pet form of VIVIAN or VIVIEN.

Vivian (m., occasionally f.) English: from an Old French form of the Latin name *Viviānus* (probably a derivative of *vivus* alive). The name was borne by a 5th-century bishop of Saintes in western France, who protected his people during the invasion of the Visigoths. As a woman's name it has sometimes been used as an Anglicized form of the Irish Gaelic name **Béibhinn** meaning 'white lady'.

Variant: **Vyvyan.**

Short forms: **Vi, Viv, Vivi.**

Vivien (f., formerly m.) Originally the more common Old French form of VIVIAN, but used by Tennyson in his poem *Merlin and Vivien* (1859) as a female name in place of the usual feminine form VIVIENNE; in this case, it may represent an altered form of some Celtic name. The actress Vivien Leigh (1913–67) was originally christened *Vivian*.

Variants: **Viviann(e)** (also used in Scandinavia), **Vivean.**

Short forms: **Vi, Viv, Vivi.**

Vivienne (f.) French: feminine form of VIVIEN, popular also in the English-speaking world.

Vladilen (m.) Russian: modern name constructed from that of the founder of the Soviet state, Vladimir Ilyich Lenin (1870–1924). Cf. NINEL and MELOR.

Variant: **Vladlen.**

Feminine form: **Vladilena.**

Vladimir (m.) Russian: from an old Slavonic personal name composed of the elements *volod* rule (cognate with Germanic *wald*) + *meri* great, famous (see CASIMIR). The stress is on the second syllable. St Vladimir (956–1015) was Great Prince of Kievan Russia and the father of Sts Boris and Gleb; he is honoured as the ruler, 'equal to the apostles', who brought Russia into the Christian Church. See also VADIM.

Cognates: Polish: **Włodzimierz.** Czech: **Vladimír.** German, Dutch: **Waldemar.** Scandinavian: **Waldemar, Valdemar.**

Pet forms: Russian: **Volodya, Volya.**

Feminine forms: Russian: **Vladimira.** Czech: **Vladimíra.**

Vladislav (m.) Czech form of WŁADYSŁAW.

Variant: **Ladislav.**

Feminine forms: **Vladislava, Ladislava.**

Vlas (m.) Russian form of BLAISE. The learned variant **Vlasi** is also used.

Vojtěch (m.) Czech form of WOJCIECH.

Pet forms: **Vojta, Vojtek, Vojtík, Vojtíšek.**

Volf (m.) Jewish: Yiddish form of WOLF.

Volker (m.) German: from an old Germanic personal name composed of the elements *folk* people + *heri*, *hari* army, warrior. The English surname *Fulcher* derives from a Norman form of this.

Volkmar (m.) German: from an old Germanic personal name composed of the elements *folk* people + *māri*, *mēri* famous.

Volodya (m.) Russian: pet form of VLADIMIR (via the colloquial form *Volodimir*) and of VSEVOLOD.

Volya (m.) Russian: contracted form of VOLODYA.

Vreni (f.) Swiss: contracted pet form of VERENA.

Vsevolod (m.) Russian: from an old Slavonic personal name composed of the

W

Wacław (m.) Polish form of WENCESLAS.

Variants: **Więcesław, Wieńczysław, Wenczesław** (all archaic).

Wade (m.) English: transferred use of the surname, which is derived either from a medieval given name or from the medieval vocabulary word *wade* ford. The former represents an Old English personal name, derived from *wadan* to go, which according to legend was borne by a great sea-giant.

Walburg (f.) German: from a Germanic personal name composed of the elements *wald* rule or *wal* foreign, strange + *burg* fortress. St Walburg was of Anglo-Saxon origin, the sister of St WILLIBALD, and the original form of her name was *Wealdburh* or *Wealburh*. She became abbess of Heidenheim and her relics are preserved at Eichstatt.

Waldemar (m.) German, Scandinavian, and Dutch: from an old Germanic personal name composed of the elements *wald* rule + *māri*, *mēri* famous. This was the name of four kings of Denmark, in particular Waldemar the Great (ruled 1157–82). The name itself is ultimately a cognate of VLADIMIR and has been used as a Germanic equivalent or translation of that name.

Variants: Scandinavian: **Valdemar**; German, Dutch, Danish: **Woldemar**.

Waldo (m.) English and German: a short form of any of several old Germanic personal names containing *wald* rule as a first element (possibly also as a second element). This gave rise in the early Middle Ages to a surname, borne notably by Peter Waldo, a 12th-century merchant of Lyons, who founded a reformist Catholic sect known as the Waldensians, which in the 16th century joined the Reformation movement. In America the name is particularly associated with the poet and essayist Ralph Waldo Emerson (1803–82), whose father was a Lutheran clergyman.

Walenty (m.) Polish form of VALENTINE.

Feminine form: **Walentyna**.

Wallace (m.) Scottish and English: transferred use of the surname, which was originally an ethnic byname from Old French *waleis* meaning 'foreign, Celtic', used by the Normans to denote members of various Celtic races in areas where they were in the minority—Welshmen in the Welsh Marches, Bretons in East Anglia, and surviving Britons in the Strathclyde region. The given name seems to have been first used in Scotland, being bestowed in honour of the Scottish patriot William Wallace (?1272–1305).

Wally (m.) English: informal pet form of WALTER or, less commonly, of WALLACE. It has dropped almost completely out of fashion, especially since the slang word *wally* is used in Britain for a stupid or incompetent person.

Walter (m.) English, German, and Scandinavian: from an old Germanic personal name composed of the elements *wald* rule + *heri*, *hari* army, warrior. There was a native Old English form of the name, *Wealdhere*, but it was replaced at the time of the Conquest by the Continental forms in use among the Normans. In medieval Germany, the most famous bearer was the minnesinger Walther von der Vogelweide (*c.*1170–*c.*1230).

Variants: German: **Walther**. Scandinavian: **Valter**.

Cognates: Scottish Gaelic: **Bhàtair, Bhaltair**. Welsh: **Gwallter**. Dutch: **Wouter, Wolter**. Low German: **Wolter**. French: **Gaut(h)ier**. Italian, Spanish: **Gualtiero**. [*cont.*]

Short forms: English: **Wat** (medieval, occasionally revived); **Walt** (esp. U.S.). Dutch: **Weit**.
Pet form: English: **Watkin**.

Waltraud (f.) German: from an old Germanic female personal name composed of the elements *wald* rule or *walh* foreigner, stranger + *thrūd* strength. St Waltraud was a 7th-century nun who founded a convent at the place that grew to be the town of Mons in Belgium.
Variants: **Waltrud(e)**.

Wanda (f.) English: of uncertain origin. Attempts have been made to derive it from various Germanic and Slavonic roots: it was certainly in use in Poland in the 19th century, and is found in Polish folk-tales as the name of a princess. The derivation may well be from the ethnic term *Wend*, denoting the Slavonic people who inhabited what is now northern East Germany in the Middle Ages. The name was introduced to the English-speaking world by Ouida (Marie Louise de la Ramée), who used it for the heroine of her novel *Wanda* (1883).

Wandelin (m.) Polish: variant of WENDELIN.

Ward (m.) English: transferred use of the surname, originally an occupational name from Old English *weard* guard or watchman.

Warner (m.) English: transferred use of the surname derived from the medieval English given name corresponding to WERNER.

Warren (m.) English: transferred use of the English surname, which is of Norman origin, derived partly from a place in Normandy called *La Varenne* 'the game-park' and partly from a Germanic personal name (cf. WERNER). In America it has sometimes been bestowed in honour of General Joseph Warren, the first hero of the American Revolution, who was killed at Bunker Hill (1775).

Warwick (m.) English: transferred use of the surname, which is taken from the town in the West Midlands. The place-name is probably from Old English *wær(ing)*, *wer(ing)* weir, dam + *wīc* dairy farm.

Washington (m.) English (esp. U.S.): from the surname of the first president of the United States, George Washington (1732–99), whose family came originally from Northamptonshire in England. They had been established in Virginia since 1656. The surname in this case is derived from the village of Washington in Co. Durham (now Tyne and Wear), so called from Old English *Wassingtūn* 'settlement associated with Wassa'. Use as a given name is well established, especially in the United States, where it was borne, for example, by the writer Washington Irving (1783–1859).

Wat (m.) English: the usual medieval short form of WALTER, based on the normal vernacular pronunciation, *Water*, with a short 'a'.

Watkin (m.) English: either a revival of the medieval pet name (WAT + the hypocoristic suffix *-kin*), or a transferred use of the surname derived from it.

Wawrzyniec (m.) Polish form of LAURENCE.

Wayne (m.) English: transferred use of the surname, originally an occupational name for a carter or cartwright, from Old English *wægen* cart, wagon. It was adopted as a given name in the second half of the 20th century, mainly as a result of the popularity of the American film actor John Wayne (1907–82), who was born Marion Michael Morrison; his screen name was chosen in honour of the American Revolutionary general Anthony Wayne (1745–96).

Webster (m.) English: transferred use of the surname, which originated as an occupational name for a weaver, Old English *webbestre* (a derivative of *webb* web). The *-estre* suffix was originally feminine, but by the Middle English period the gender distinction had been lost. Use as a given name in America no doubt owes something to the politician and orator Daniel Webster (1782–1852) and the lexicographer Noah Webster (1758–1843).

Wenceslas (m.) Latinized form of an East European Slavonic name, composed of the elements *ventie* more, greater + *slav* glory. St Wenceslas was a 10th-century duke of Bohemia noted for his piety, the grandson of St Ludmilla. He is regarded as the patron of Bohemia, which now forms part of Czechoslovakia. This was also the name of four kings of Bohemia in the period covering the 13th to the 15th century.

Cognates: German: **Wenzeslaus**, WENZEL. Polish: WACŁAW. Czech: **Věnceslav**, **Václav**. Russian: **Vyacheslav**. Italian: **Venceslao**. Spanish: **Venceslás**. Portuguese: **Venceslau**.

Wenda (f.) English: apparently an altered form of WENDY (cf. e.g. *Jenna* from *Jenny*), since it does not appear in modern use until the vogue for that name. In the early Middle Ages, however, a name of identical form was in occasional use on the Continent as a short form of various female names (such as *Wendelburg* and *Wendelgard*) containing as their first element the ethnic name of the Wends (cf. WENDEL). It may well have been partly influenced by WANDA.

Wendel (m.) German: from an old Germanic personal name, in origin an ethnic byname for a Wend, a member of the Slavonic people living in the area between the Elbe and the Oder, who were overrun by Germanic migrants in the 12th century. In part it was also used as a short form of various compound names with that first element (cf. WENDA). St Wendel was a 6th- or 7th-century shepherd and confessor, who is venerated especially at Sanktwendel on the River Nahe.

Wendelin (m.) German and Polish: from an old Germanic personal name, a derivative of the ethnic byname *wend* Wend (see WENDEL).

Variant: Polish: **Wandelin**.

Cognate: Czech: **Vendelín**.

Wendell (m.) English (esp. U.S.): from the surname derived in the Middle Ages from the Continental Germanic personal name WENDEL. It has been adopted as a given name as a result of the fame of the American writer Oliver Wendell Holmes (1809–94) and his jurist son, also Oliver Wendell Holmes (1841–1935), members of a leading New England family.

Wendy (f.) English: invented by J. M. Barrie for the 'little mother' in his play *Peter Pan* (1904). He took it from the nickname *Fwendy-Wendy* (i.e. 'friend') used for him by a child acquaintance, Margaret Henley. It has achieved widespread popularity in its short lifespan.

Variant: **Wendi** (rare).

Wenzel (m.) German: medieval pet form of *Wenzeslaus*, the German version of WENCESLAS. This was in common use in the heavily Slavonic regions of eastern Germany and is still occasionally chosen today as an independent given name.

Wera (f.) Polish form of VERA.

Werner (m.) German, Dutch, and Scandinavian: from an old Germanic personal name composed of the tribal name *Warin* + the element *heri*, *hari* army, warrior. See also WARNER.

Variant: Scandinavian: **Verner**.

Pet forms: German: WETZEL. Low German, Dutch, Frisian: **Wessel**.

Werther (m.) German: found in the early Middle Ages in the Latinized form *Wertharius*. It probably derives from the Germanic elements *wert* worthy + *heri*, *hari* army, warrior. The name had become comparatively rare in Germany by the later Middle Ages, but was chosen by Goethe for the hero of his early novel *Die Leiden des jungen Werther* ('The Sorrows of Young Werther', 1774), since when it has been quietly popular.

Wesley (m.) English: from the surname of the founder of the Methodist Church, John Wesley (1703–91), and his brother Charles (1707–88), who was also influential in the movement. Their family must have come originally from one or other of the various places in England called *Westley*, the 'western wood, clearing, or meadow'. The given name was at first confined to members of the Methodist Church, but is now very widely used among English-speaking people of many different creeds, often without reference to its religious connotations.

Short form: **Wes.**

Wessel (m.) Low German and Frisian: pet form of WERNER.

Wetzel (m.) German: from a medieval pet form of WERNER, now occasionally chosen as an independent given name.

Whiltierna (f.) Irish: Anglicized form of the Gaelic name **Faoiltiarna**, composed of the elements *faol* wolf + *tighearna* lord.

Whitney (f., m.) English (mainly U.S.): transferred use of the surname, originally a local name from any of various places in England named with the Middle English phrase *atten whiten ey* 'by the white island'. In the 1980s its popularity as a female name has been increased by the fame of the American singer Whitney Houston.

Wiara (f.) Polish form of VERA.

Wibeke (f.) Low German, Dutch, and Frisian: pet form derived from the medieval given name *Wibe*, in origin a short form of various Germanic compound names, such as *Wigburg*, composed of the elements *wig* war + *burg* fortress.

Variants: **Wi(e)bke.**

Cognates: Danish, Norwegian: **Vibeke**. Swedish: **Viveka, Viveca, Vivica.**

Więcesław (m.) Archaic Polish form of WACŁAW. See WENCESLAS.

Wieland (m.) German: from an old Germanic personal name of uncertain derivation. It was borne in Germanic legend by Wieland the Smith, king of the elves, and was revived to a limited extent as a result of the 19th-century interest in this group of tales. The name was borne by a grandson of the composer Richard Wagner.

Wielisław (m.) Polish: from an old Slavonic personal name composed of the elements *vele* great + *slav* glory.

Variant: **Wiesław.**

Cognate: Czech: **Veleslav.**

Pet forms: Polish: **Wiesi(ul)ek.** Czech: **Vela, Velek, Veloušek.**

Wiera (f.) Polish form of VERA.

Wiga (f.) Polish: short form of JADWIGA.

Pet form: **Wisia.**

Wilberforce (m.) English: transferred use of the surname, which originated as a local name from *Wilberfoss* in North Yorkshire. This place is so called from the Old English female personal name *Wilburg* (see WILBUR) + Old English *foss* ditch (from Latin *fossa*). It may have been taken up as a given name in honour of the anti-slavery campaigner William Wilberforce (1759–1833), or perhaps because it is thought of as an extended form of *Wilbur*.

Wilbur (m.) English: transferred use of a comparatively rare surname, which is now a fairly common given name, especially in America. The surname probably derives from a medieval female name composed of the Old English elements *will* will, desire + *burh* fortress.

Wilfrid (m.) English: from an Old English personal name composed of the Germanic elements *wil* will, desire + *frid, fred* peace. This name was borne by two saints. There is some doubt about the exact form of the name of the more famous, who played a leading role at the Council of Whitby (664); it may have been *Walfrid* 'stranger peace' or 'peace to the Welsh', from Old English *walh* stranger, Welshman. Wilfrid the Younger was an 8th-century bishop of York. The name was not used in the Middle Ages, but was revived in the 19th century, and enjoyed great popularity then and in the first part of the 20th century.

Variant: **Wilfred.**

Cognates: German: **Wilfried**. Scandinavian: **Vilfred.**

Short form: English: **Wilf.**

Wilhelm (m.) German form of WILLIAM.

Wilhelmina (f.) German: feminine version of WILHELM, formed with the Latinate suffix *-ina*. This name was introduced to the English-speaking world from Germany in the 19th century. It is now very rarely used.

Variant: **Wilhelmine.**

Cognates: Swedish: **Vilhelmina**. Danish, Norwegian: **Vilhelmine.**

Short forms: German: **Wilma, Helmine, Helma, Mine**. Danish: **Mine.**

Pet forms: German: **Minna, Minne**. English: **Minnie.**

Will (m.) English: short form of WILLIAM, in use since the early Middle Ages, when it was occasionally used also for various other given names containing as their first element Germanic *wil* will, desire (e.g. *Wilbert* and WILMER).

Willa (f.) English: a feminine form of WILLIAM, created by appending the characteristically feminine final letter *-a* to the short form WILL.

Willard (m.) English (esp. U.S.): transferred use of the surname, which seems itself to have derived from the Old English personal name *Wilheard*, composed of the elements *will* will, desire + *heard* hardy, brave, strong. The modern given name is sometimes taken as an elaborated form of WILL.

Willem (m.) Low German and Dutch form of WILLIAM.

Willi (m.) German: pet form of WILHELM.

William (m.) English: the most successful of all the Germanic names introduced to England by the Normans. It is composed of the elements *wil* will, desire + *helm* helmet, protection. The fact that it was borne by the Conqueror himself does not seem to have inhibited its favour with the 'conquered' population: in the first century after the Conquest it was the commonest male name of all, not only among Normans. In the later Middle Ages it was overtaken by JOHN, but continued to run second to that name until the 20th century, when the picture became more fragmented. It was a royal name not only in England, but also in Germany and the Netherlands.

Cognates: Irish Gaelic: **Liam**. Scottish Gaelic: **Uilleam**. Welsh: **Gwilym**. French: **Guillaume**. Italian: **Guglielmo**. Spanish: **Guilermo**. Catalan: **Guillem**. Portuguese: **Guilherme**. German: **Wilhelm**. Low German, Dutch: **Willem**. Scandinavian: **Vilhelm**. Czech: **Vilem**. Hungarian: **Vilmos**. Finnish: **Vilppu.**

Short forms: English: **Will**, BILL. German: **Wim.**

Pet forms: English and Scottish: **Willy, Willie**. German: **Willi.**

Feminine forms: English: **Willa, Wilma**, BILLIE. German: **Wilhelmina, Wilhelmine, Helmine, Helma, Mine**. Hungarian: **Vilma.**

Willibald (m.) German: from an old Germanic personal name composed of the elements *wil* will, desire + *bald* bold, brave. St Willibald (*c.*700–*c.*786) was of Anglo-Saxon origin, and aided his cousin Boniface in evangelical missions in Germany.

Willoughby (m.) English: transferred use of the surname, which was originally a local name from any of various places in northern England so called from Old English *welig* willow + Old Norse *býr* settlement.

Willow (f.) English: from the tree, Old English *welig*, noted for its grace and the pliancy of its wood.

Wilma (f.) 1. German: contracted form of WILHELMINA.

2. English: either a borrowing of the German name, or an independent coinage, formed as a feminine equivalent of WILLIAM.

Wilmer (m.) English: formally it is possible that this could represent an old Germanic personal name composed of the elements *wil* will, desire + *mēri*, *māri* famous, but it is more likely to have arisen as a masculine form of the similarly pronounced WILMA (cf. *Peta*, derived from *Peter* by the reverse process).

Wilmette (f.) English (esp. U.S.): a recent coinage, originating as an elaborated form of WILMA with the productive feminine ending (originally a French diminutive) *-ette*.
Variant: **Wilmetta**.

Wilmot (m.) English: transferred use of the surname, which is derived from a medieval pet form of WILLIAM. It is possible from the form of the medieval name that it could represent an old Germanic personal name composed of the elements *wil* will, desire + *muot* mind, courage, but this is no evidence for the existence of such a name.

Wim (m.) German: contracted form of WILHELM.

Win (f.) English: short form of WINIFRED.

Wincenty (m.) Polish form of VINCENT.

Windsor (m.) English: transferred use of the surname, which is derived from a place in Berkshire, originally named in Old English as *Windels-ōra* 'landing place with a windlass'. It is the site of a castle that is in regular use as a residence of the royal family. Its use as a given name dates from the mid-19th century and was reinforced by its adoption in 1917 as the surname of the British royal family (from their residence at Windsor in Berkshire). It was felt necessary to replace the German name *Wettin*, which had been introduced by Queen Victoria's husband Albert, in deference to anti-German feeling during the First World War.

Winifred (f.) English and Welsh: from the Welsh personal name GWENFREWI, altered by association with the Old English name elements *wynn* joy + *frið* peace. In Ireland and Scotland it has been used as an Anglicized form of ÚNA and *Ùna*.
Short forms: **Win, Freda**.
Pet form: **Winnie**.

Winston (m.) English: transferred use of the surname. Although there was an Old English personal name, *Wynnstan*, composed of the elements *wynn* joy + *stān* stone, which would have had this form if it had survived, the modern given name originated in the Churchill family. The first Winston Churchill (b. 1620) was christened with the surname of his mother's family, who had come originally from the hamlet of Winston in Gloucestershire. The name has continued in this family ever since, and has recently been more widely used in honour of the statesman Winston Spencer Churchill (1874–1965).

Winthrop (m.) English (esp. U.S.): from the surname of a leading American pioneering family, and still more or less completely confined to America. John Winthrop (1588–1649) was one of the first governors of the Massachusetts Bay Colony, and his son (1606–76) and grandson (1638–1707), who bore the same name, were also colonial governors. Their family probably came originally from one of the places in England called *Winthorpe* (named in Old English as the 'village of Wynna').

Winton (m.) English: transferred use of the surname, which originated as a local name from any of the various places so called. One in Cumbria gets its name from Old English *winn* pasture + *tūn* enclosure, settlement; another in the same county is from *wiðig* willow + *tūn*; the one in North Yorkshire is from the Old English personal name *Wina* + *tūn*.

Wisia (f.) Polish: pet form of *Wiga*, a short form of JADWIGA.

Wit (m.) Polish form of VITUS.

Witold (m.) German, Polish: as a German name, this derives from the Germanic elements *wīda* wide or *witu* wood + *wald* ruler. As a Polish name, it represents an assimilation to this form of the Lithuanian name *Vytautas*, borne in the 14th century by the first Christian ruler of Lithuania.
Variant: Polish: **Witołd**.

Władysław (m.) Polish: from an old Slavonic personal name composed of the elements *volod* rule + *slav* glory. This was the name of four kings of Poland, and was an aristocratic name long before it was a royal name. The Blessed Władysław (1440–1505) is revered as an evangelist.

Variant: **Włodzisław**.

Cognates: Czech: **Vladislav, Ladislav**. Latinate: LADISLAS. Hungarian: LÁSZLÓ. Italian: **Ladislao**.

Włodzimierz (m.) Polish form of VLADIMIR.

Wmffre (m.) Welsh form of HUMPHREY.

Wojciech (m.) Common Polish name, from an old Slavonic personal name composed of the elements *voi* soldier, warrior + *tech* consolation.

Cognate: Czech: **Vojtěch**.

Pet forms: Polish: **Wojtek, Wojteczek**. Czech: **Vojta, Vojtek, Vojtík, Vojtíšek**.

Wojsław (m.) Polish: from an old Slavonic personal name composed of the elements *voi* soldier, warrior + *slav* glory.

Wojtek (m.) Polish: pet form of WOJCIECH.

Variant: **Wojteczek**.

Woldemar (m.) German, Dutch, and Danish: variant of WALDEMAR.

Wolf (m.) German and Jewish: short form of WOLFGANG and WOLFRAM, or else an independent given name going back to an old Germanic byname meaning 'wolf' (Old High German *wolf*). Wolves were plentiful in the forests of northern Europe throughout the Middle Ages, and played an important part in Germanic folklore. As a Jewish name it has been used as an equivalent to ZEEV.

Cognates: Danish, Swedish: **Ulf**. Norwegian: **Ulv**.

Wolfgang (m.) German: common name from an old Germanic personal name composed of the elements *wolf* wolf + *gang* going. The name is often bestowed, sometimes even in the English-speaking world, in honour of the composer Wolfgang Amadeus Mozart (1756–91).

Wolfram (m.) German: from an old Germanic personal name composed of the elements *wolf* wolf + *hramn* raven. The name was borne in the Middle Ages by the poet Wolfram von Eschenbach (*c.*1170–*c.*1220).

Wolter (m.) Low German and Dutch form of WALTER.

Woodrow (m.) English: transferred use of the surname, originally a local name given to someone who lived in a row of houses by a wood. It is occasionally bestowed as a given name in the English-speaking world in honour of the American president Woodrow Wilson (1856–1924).

Woody (m.) English (chiefly U.S.): pet form of WOODROW, or in some cases perhaps a nickname bestowed because of some imagined similarity to the cartoon character Woody Woodpecker. It has been borne by the American folk singer Woody (Woodrow Wilson) Guthrie (1912–67) and the 1940s band leader Woody (Woodrow Charles) Herman (1913–87). The American humorist Woody Allen was born Allen Stewart Konigsberg in 1935.

Wouter (m.) Dutch form of WALTER.

Wyn (m.) Welsh: originally a byname from the Welsh vocabulary word *(g)wyn* white, fair, blessed, holy. The name is found in this form from the early Middle Ages. It is at present extremely popular in Wales.

Wyndham (m.) English: transferred use of the surname, which is derived from a contracted form of the placename *Wymondham* in Norfolk, originally named in Old English as the 'homestead of Wigmund'.

Wynne (m., f.) 1. (m.) English: transferred use of the surname, which is derived from the Old and Middle English personal name *Wine* 'friend'.

2. (m.) Welsh: elaborated spelling of WYN.

3. (f.) English: apparently an 'elegant' respelling of *Win*, a short form of WINIFRED.

Variant (of 1): **Wynn**.

Wystan (m.) English: from an Old English personal name composed of the elements *wīg* battle + *stān* stone. St Wistan was a 9th-century prince of Mercia, murdered by his nephew Bertulf. The modern given name is rare, being best known in the name of the poet Wystan Hugh Auden (1907–73).

X

Xaime (m.) Galician form of JAMES; see also JAIME.

Xanthe (f.) English: from the feminine form of the classical Greek adjective *xanthos* yellow, bright. The name was borne by various minor figures in classical mythology and is occasionally chosen by parents in search of an unusual given name for a daughter.

Xavier (m.) From the surname of the Spanish soldier-saint Francis Xavier (1506–52), one of the founding members of the Society of Jesus (the Jesuits). He was born on the ancestral estate at Xavier (now Javier) in Navarre, which in the early Middle Ages was an independent Basque kingdom. *Xavier* probably represents a Hispanicized form of the Basque place-name *Etcheberria* 'the new house' (*x* was pronounced in the Middle Ages as *sh*, now as *h*). The given name is used almost exclusively among Roman Catholics.

Other forms: Italian: **Saverio**. Spanish, Portuguese: **Javier**. German: **Xaver**. Polish: **Ksawery**.

Xaviera (f.) Feminine form of XAVIER.

Xenia (f.) English: comparatively rare given name, coined from the Greek vocabulary word *xenia* hospitality, from *xenos* stranger, foreigner.

Xoán (m.) Galician form of JOHN; see also JUAN.

Xosé (m.) Galician form of JOSEPH; see also JOSÉ.

Y

Yael (f.) Jewish: from a Hebrew word denoting a female wild goat. The name is borne in the Bible by a Kenite woman who killed Sisera, the Canaanite general and an enemy of the Israelites (Judges 4: 17–22). It has remained extremely popular among Jews to the present day.

Variant: **Jael**.

Yaffa (f.) Jewish: variant of JAFFE. It has become very popular as a modern Hebrew translation of SHAYNA.

Yakim (m.) The usual Russian form of JOACHIM; see also AKIM.

Pet form: **Kima**.

Yakov (m.) Jewish: the modern Hebrew form of JACOB. This is also the form of the name in Russian.

Variant: Jewish: **Yaakov**.

Pet forms: Jewish: **Yankel** (Yiddish). Russian: **Yasha**.

Feminine form: Jewish: **Yakova**.

Yann (m.) Breton form of JOHN.

Pet form: **Yannic(k)**.

Yaropolk (m.) Russian form of JAROPEŁK.

Yaroslav (m.) Russian form of JAROSŁAW.

Yasha (m.) Russian: pet form of YAKOV.

Yasmin (f.) English: variant of JASMINE, representing a 'learned' re-creation of the Persian form.

Yayone (f.) Basque: variant spelling of IAIONE.

Yefim (m.) Russian: from the Greek name *Euphēmios*, composed of the elements *eu* well, good + *phēnai* to speak, say; cf. EUPHEMIA.

Yefrem (m.) Russian form of EPHRAIM.

Pet form: **Rema**.

Yegor (m.) Russian: popular form of GEORGE.

Yehiel (m.) Jewish: Hebrew name, meaning 'God lives', borne in the Bible by an early Levite appointed to play the psaltery in sacred processions (1 Chronicles 15: 20). In the Authorized Version the name is transliterated *Jehiel*. It is a popular modern Hebrew name.

Yehuda (m.) Jewish: modern Hebrew form of JUDAH.

Yehudi (m.) Jewish: modern Hebrew name, originally an ethnic byname meaning 'Jew'.

Yehudit (f.) Jewish: modern Hebrew form of JUDITH.

Yekatarina (f.) Russian form of KATHERINE.

Pet form: **Katya**.

Yelena (f.) Russian form of HELEN.

Pet form: **Nelya**.

Yelisaveta (f.) Russian form of ELIZABETH.

Yelisei (m.) Russian form of ELISEO.

Yente (f.) Jewish: Yiddish name, probably a back-formation from **Yentl** (apparently from the French nickname *Gentille* 'kind, nice'), the *-l* being interpreted as a Yiddish hypocoristic suffix. The Yiddish vocabulary word *yente*, derived from the name, denotes a gossipy woman.

Yered (m.) Jewish: Hebrew form of JARED.

Yermolai (m.) Russian: from the Greek name *Hermolaos*, composed of the elements *Hermēs* (the name of the messenger god; cf. ERMETE) + *lāos*, *leōs* people, tribe. St Hermolaos (d. *c.*300) was martyred in Nicomedia together with his brothers Hermippos and Hermocrates, who shared the first element of his name (combined respectively with *hippos* horse and *kratein* to rule), according to a pattern common in the classical period and later.

Yetta (f.) Jewish: of uncertain origin, possibly a variant of ETTA originating in dialects of Yiddish subject to Slavonic influence, or else a derivative of YEHUDIT or ESTHER.

Yevgeni (m.) Russian form of EUGENE.

Yigael (m.) Jewish: traditional Hebrew name of uncertain derivation, probably meaning 'he shall be redeemed'.

Yitzhak (m.) Jewish: modern Hebrew form of ISAAC.

Yngvar (m.) Scandinavian: variant of INGVAR.

Ynyr (m.) Welsh: traditional name of uncertain derivation, probably from Latin *Honōrius* (see HONORIA). There is a passing reference in the *Mabinogi* to 'the battle between the two Ynyrs'.

Yolande (f.) English and French: of uncertain origin. It is found in Old French in this form, and seems to be ultimately of Germanic origin, but if so it has been changed beyond recognition by attempted associations with various Greek and Latin elements. It is also sometimes identified with the name of St *Jolenta* (d. 1298), daughter of the king of Hungary; her name is also occasionally rendered as HELEN.

Variant: English: **Yolanda.**

Cognates: Italian: **Jolanda.** Polish: **Jolanta.** Czech: **Jolan(t)a.** Hungarian: **Jolán.**

Pet form: Polish: **Jola.**

Yon (m.) Basque: variant spelling of ION.

Yoram (m.) Jewish: Hebrew name, meaning 'Yahweh is high', borne in the Bible by an evil king of Israel. This has not stopped it from becoming a moderately popular given name in modern Israel.

Yorath (m.) English and Welsh: Anglicized form of the Welsh personal name IORWERTH or, in some cases, a transferred use of the surname derived from it.

Yorick (m.) English: the name of the (defunct) court jester in Shakespeare's *Hamlet*. It is apparently a respelling of *Jorck*, a Danish form of GEORGE.

York (m.) English: in most cases, probably a transferred use of the surname, which originated as a local name for someone who came from the city of York in northeastern England. The placename was originally *Eburacon*, a derivative of a British element meaning 'yew'. The Anglo-Saxon settlers changed this to Old English *Eofor-wīc* 'boar farm', which in Old Norse became *Iorvík* or *Iork*. The given name may also have been influenced by Scandinavian forms of GEORGE (e.g. Danish *Jorck*).

Yosef (m.) Jewish: modern Hebrew form of JOSEPH.

Yrjö (m.) Finnish form of GEORGE.

Ysanne (f.) English: of uncertain origin, apparently composed of *Ys-* (as in YSEULT) + *Anne*.

Yseult (f.) Medieval French form of ISOLDE, still occasionally used as a given name in the English-speaking world.

Yuri (m.) The usual Russian form of GEORGE, beside *Georgi*. This form is also found in Poland, with the spelling **Juri**.

Yves (m.) French: from a Germanic personal name representing a short form of various compound names containing the element *iv-* 'yew' (cf. Old Norse *ýr*, as in IVOR). The final *-s* is the mark of the Old French nominative case. The name was introduced to Britain from France at the time of the Norman Conquest, and again in the 20th century.

Cognates: German: **Ivo.** Polish: **Iwo.**

Yvette (f.) French: feminine diminutive form of YVES, now also used in the English-speaking world.

Yvonne (f.) French: feminine diminutive form of YVES (or simply a feminine form based on the Old French oblique case *Yvon*), now also widely used in the English-speaking world and in Scandinavia.

Z

Zachary (m.) English form (pre-dating the Authorized Version) of the New Testament Greek name *Zacharias*, a form of Hebrew ZECHARIAH. In the New Testament it is the name of the father of John the Baptist, who underwent a temporary period of dumbness for his lack of faith (Luke 1), and of a more obscure figure, Zacharias son of Barachias, who was slain 'between the temple and the altar' (Matthew 23: 35; Luke 11: 51). Like many biblical names, it is now out of fashion, although in the United States it is familiar as the name of a 19th-century president, Zachary Taylor. In the Highlands of Scotland it has been used as an Anglicized form of the Gaelic name SGÀIRE.

Variants: **Zacharias, Zachariah,** ZECHARIAH.

Cognate: Scottish Gaelic: **Sachairi.**

Zack (m.) English (esp. U.S.): short form of ZACHARY, also occasionally used as an independent given name.

Variant: **Zak.**

Zadok (m.) Jewish: Hebrew name meaning 'just' or 'righteous'. It was borne in the Bible by one of the chief priests of King David, who later anointed Solomon king of Israel (1 Kings 1: 39), and it has been used ever since, no doubt partly because of its auspicious meaning.

Zahava (f.) Jewish: modern Hebrew name, from the vocabulary word *zahav* gold.

Zalman (m.) Jewish: Hebraicized form of *Zalmen*, itself a Yiddish form of SOLOMON.

Zanna (f.) English: modern coinage, apparently originating as a short form of *Suzanna* (see SUSANNA).

Zara (f.) Name occasionally used in the 20th century in Britain, and to a lesser extent in Italy, Spain, and Portugal. It is said to be of Arabic origin, from *zahr* flower. It was given by Princess Anne and Mark Philips to their second child (b. 1981), which aroused considerable comment at the time as a departure from the traditional patterns of royal nomenclature. It has no doubt been influenced by SARAH.

Zaylie (f.) English: rare name of uncertain derivation, perhaps a respelling of ZÉLIE.

Zbigniew (m.) Common Polish name, from an old Slavonic personal name composed of the elements *zbit* to get rid of + *gniew* anger.

Cognate: Czech: **Zbyhněv.**

Feminine form: Czech: **Zbyhněva.**

Pet forms: Czech: **Zbyňa** (m., f.); **Zbyněk, Zbyšek** (m.); **Zbyhně(uš)ka, Zbyša** (f.).

Zdeněk (m.) Common Czech name, in origin a diminutive derived from a much contracted form of Latin *Sidōnius* (see SIDONY).

Feminine forms: **Zdeňka, Zdenka, Zdena.**

Pet forms: **Zdenko, Zdeněček, Zdení(če)k, Zdenoušek** (m.); **Zdenička, Zdenuška, Zdenin(k)a** (f.).

Zdzisław (m.) Polish: from an old Slavonic personal name composed of the elements *zde* here, present + *slav* glory.

Cognates: Czech: **Zdislav, Zdeslav.**

Feminine forms: Polish: **Zdzisława.** Czech: **Zdislava, Zdeslava.**

Pet forms: Polish: **Zdziś, Zdzi(e)ch, Zdzisiek, Zdziesz(ko)** (m.). Czech: **Zdík, Zdišek** (m.); **Zdiš(k)a** (f.).

Zeb (m.) English (esp. U.S.): short form of the much rarer full name **Zebulun,** borne in the Bible by the sixth son of Leah and Jacob. The name may mean 'exaltation', although Leah derives it from another meaning of the Hebrew root *zabal*, namely 'to dwell': 'now will my husband dwell with me, because I have borne him six sons' (Genesis 30: 20). It appears in the New Testament (Matthew 4: 13) in the form *Zabulon*.

Zechariah (m.) Biblical: name (meaning 'God has remembered' in Hebrew) of several figures in the Bible, most notably one of the twelve 'minor' prophets, author of the book that bears his name. It was also the name of an earlier prophet, who was stoned by the people because of his preaching (2 Chronicles 24: 20–3), and of the last Israelite king of the race of Jehu, who was overthrown by Shallum the son of Jabesh (2 Kings 15: 8–10). See also ZACHARY.

Zed (m.) English (esp. U.S.): short form of the much rarer full name **Zedekiah**. This name, meaning 'justice of Yahweh' in Hebrew, is borne in the Bible by three separate characters.

Zeev (m.) Jewish: Hebrew name meaning 'wolf'. It has become popular as a translation of European names with this meaning. The wolf is traditionally associated with the tribe of *Binyamin* or BENJAMIN, because in his dying blessing the patriarch Jacob said 'Benjamin shall ravin as a wolf' (Genesis 49: 27).

Zeke (m.) English (esp. U.S.): short form of EZEKIEL, still occasionally used as an independent given name.

Zelah (f.) Biblical: name (meaning 'side' in Hebrew) of one of the fourteen cities of the tribe of Benjamin (Joshua 18: 28). It is far from clear why it should have come to be used, albeit rarely, as a female given name in the English-speaking world. It may simply be a variant of ZILLAH under the influence of the placename. However, for evidence that biblical placenames did yield English given names, cf. EBENEZER.

Zelda (f.) English: modern name of uncertain origin, possibly a short form of GRISELDA. It came to prominence in the 1920s as the name of the wife of the American writer F. Scott Fitzgerald (1896–1940). **Zelde**, however, is a traditional Yiddish given name, derived from a Middle High German vocabulary word meaning 'happiness, good fortune' (cf. SELIG).

Zélie (f.) French and English: apparently an altered form of *Célie* (see CELIA).

Zelig (m.) Jewish: variant of SELIG.

Żelisław (m.) Polish: from an old Slavonic personal name composed of the elements *zhelit* to desire + *slav* glory.

Cognate: Czech: **Želislav**.

Pet forms: Polish: **Żelek**, **Żelusz**. Czech: **Želek, Želí(če)k, Želoušek**.

Zelma (f.) English: altered form of SELMA.

Zena (f.) 1. English: of uncertain origin. It may be a variant spelling of ZINA, a coinage as a feminine equivalent of ZENO, a shortened form of ZENOBIA, or a simplified variant of XENIA.

2. Scottish (Highland): short form of ALEXINA.

Zeno (m.) From the classical Greek name *Zēnōn*, a short form of any of several names having as their first element *Zēn-*, the stem form of the name of Zeus, king of the gods, for example *Zēnodōros* 'gift of Zeus'. Zeno was the name of two major Greek philosophers and a Christian Eastern Roman emperor (d. 491). Zeno of Elea (*c.*490–430 BC) was an original thinker who challenged common-sense notions like motion and number with sophisticated logical arguments. Zeno of Citium (*c.*334–262 BC) was the founder of the Stoics.

Zenobia (f.) Classical Greek name: feminine form of *Zēnobios*, a personal name composed of the elements *Zēn-* (see ZENO) + *bios* life. This was the name of a queen of Palmyra (*fl.* AD 267–72), who expanded her empire in the eastern Mediterranean and Asia Minor, but eventually came into conflict with Rome and was deposed by Aurelian. She was noted for her beauty and intelligence, but was also ruthless: she appears to have had her husband and his eldest son murdered.

Derivative: Russian: ZINOVIA.

Zenzi (f.) South German: pet form of KRESZENZ.

Zeph (m.) English (esp. U.S): short form of the much rarer full name **Zephaniah**, meaning 'hidden by God' in Hebrew. This was the name of one of the minor biblical prophets, author of the book of the Bible that bears his name.

Zephyrine (f.) English: Anglicized form of French **Zéphyrine**, an elaborated name derived from Latin *Zephyrus*, Greek *Zephyros* west wind (apparently a derivative of Greek *zophos* darkness). St Zephyrinus was pope 199–217, but there is no equivalent female saint, so it is rather surprising that this name should occur only in a female form.

Zhenya (m., f.) Russian: pet form of both YEVGENI and its rarer feminine form *Yevgenia*.

Zillah (f.) Biblical: name (from a Hebrew word meaning 'shade') of one of the two wives of Lamech (Genesis 4: 19). The name was taken up in the first place by the Puritans, and again by fundamentalist Christian groups in the 19th century, partly because Zillah is only the third woman to be mentioned by name in the Bible, and her name was therefore prominent to readers of the Book of Genesis. She is not remarkable for any special qualities of character. ADAH, the name of Lamech's other wife, may in part lie behind ADA, which was also a popular 19th-century female name.

Zina Russian: short form of ZINAIDA and of ZINOVIA. This name is also occasionally used in the English-speaking world.

Zinaida (f.) Russian: from the Greek name *Zēnais* (genitive *Zēnaidos*), derived from the name of *Zeus* (genitive *Zēnos*), king of the gods. At least two saints of this name are revered in the Orthodox Church as 1st-century martyrs.

Zinovia (f.) Russian form of ZENOBIA. A St Zenobia was martyred in Asia Minor, together with her brother Zenobios, probably at the beginning of the 3rd century.

Zipporah (f.) Jewish: common female form of the rare Hebrew male name **Zippor** meaning 'bird'. The female name is borne in the Bible by the wife of Moses and mother of Gershom and Eliezer (Exodus 18: 2–4).

Zissi (f.) German: pet form of *Franziska* (see FRANZ).

Zita (f.) Italian and English: from the name of a 13th-century saint from Lucca in Tuscany, who led an uneventful life as a domestic servant; she was canonized in 1696, and is regarded as the patroness of domestic servants. Her name was probably a nickname from the medieval Tuscan dialect word *zit(t)a* girl, although efforts have been made to link it with Greek *zētein* to seek.

Žitomír (m.) Czech: from an old Slavonic personal name composed of the elements *zhit* to live + *meri* great, famous (see CASIMIR).

Feminine form: **Žitomíra.**

Pet forms: **Žit(ouš)ek** (m.); **Žitka, Žituše** (f.).

Živan (m.) Czech: from an old Slavonic byname derived from the element *zhiv* living.

Feminine form: **Živ(an)ka.**

Pet forms: **Živ(an)ek, Živko** (m.); **Živuše, Živuška** (f.).

Zlatan (m.) Czech: derivative of the element *zlato* gold, used as a vernacular loan translation of the Latin name *Aurēlius* (see AURÈLE).

Feminine form: **Zlata.**

Pet forms: **Zlatek, Zlatko, Zlatí(če)k, Zlatoušek** (m.); **Zlat(uš)ka, Zlatuše, Zlatin(k)a, Zlatun(k)a** (f.).

Zoë (f.) English: from the Greek name meaning 'life'. This was already in use in Rome towards the end of the classical period (at first as an affectionate nickname), and was popular with the early Christians, who bestowed it with refer-

ence to their hopes of eternal life. It was borne by martyrs of the 2nd and 3rd centuries, but was taken up as an English given name only in the 19th century.
Variant: **Zoe**.

Zofia (f.) Polish form of SOFIA.
Pet form: **Zosia**.

Žofie (f.) Czech form of SOFIA.

Zola (f.) English: apparently a late 20th-century creation, formed from the first syllable of ZOË with the ending *-la* common in female names. It coincides in form with the surname of the French novelist Émile Zola (1840–1902), who was of Italian descent, but it is unlikely that he had any influence on the popularity of the name.

Zoltán (m.) Hungarian: of uncertain derivation, possibly from an honorific title of Turkic origin and ultimately connected with modern English *sultan*.

Zosia (f.) Polish: pet form of ZOFIA.

Zsófia (f.) Hungarian form of SOFIA.

Zsuzsanna (f.) Hungarian form of SUSANNA.

Zula (f.) English: modern name, apparently derived from the tribal name of the Zulus. The Zulu people of Southern Africa formed a powerful warrior nation under their leader Chaka in the 19th century, and controlled an extensive empire. In 1838, under the leadership of their ruler Dingaan, they ambushed and slaughtered a group of some 500 Boers. Not surprisingly, this given name is chosen mainly, if not exclusively, by Blacks proud of their African origins.

Zuzana (f.) Czech form of SUSANNA.

Zuzanna (f.) Polish form of SUSANNA.

Zvi (m.) Jewish: Hebrew name meaning 'hart, deer'. It has become a popular modern Hebrew name as a translation of Yiddish HIRSH and HERSHEL. The deer is traditionally associated with the name NAPHTALI, because in his dying blessing the patriarch Jacob says 'Naphtali is a hind let loose' (Genesis 49: 21). In this verse the Hebrew word for 'hind' is *ayala*, but since this is a feminine noun (see AYALA and HINDE), the masculine noun *zvi* is substituted as a male given name.
Variant: **Zwi** (German, Dutch, and Polish spelling).

Zwaante (f.) Frisian: pet derivative of a short form of any of various old Germanic female personal names containing the first element *swan* swan, such as SWANHILD and *Swanburg*.

Zygmunt (m.) Polish form of SIGMUND.

SUPPLEMENT I

COMMON NAMES IN THE ARAB WORLD

INTRODUCTION

This short supplement gives an account of the personal names that are most widely used in the Arab world. These form a comparatively homogeneous set, largely because of the unifying influence of Islam. Ideally, one would want to start an account of the subject by referring to previous work. Unfortunately this is impossible, because the subject seems to be so totally neglected. To the best of my knowledge, there does not exist a scholarly tradition of studying names in Arabic. Partly for this reason, the views expressed below must be regarded as both preliminary and tentative.

Similarly, the range of names selected for inclusion here is itself restricted, not only by the available space but also by the compiler's own limitations: one tends to be more familiar with names used in one's own immediate culture and environment. The Arab world covers a vast area: according to the *Cambridge Encyclopaedia of the Middle East and North Africa* (1988), Arabic is the chief language in eighteen countries (with a total population of over 180 million people) and is the sixth most common first language in the world. A comprehensive dictionary of names used in the Arab world, showing the many variations in form and choice, could only be compiled by a team rather than by a single individual.

Names in the Arab world are part and parcel of the Arabic language. Apart from a few borrowings, mainly from Turkish and Persian, Arabic names on the whole consist of vocabulary words. Although a few vocabulary words have been used as given names in the West, for example *Joy* and *Prudence*, most Western European names come from dead languages such as Germanic, Latin, and biblical Hebrew. The meaning of an English name is often not readily accessible to its bearer, but Arabs more often than not know what their names mean. If they do not, they can look them up in an ordinary dictionary, like any other vocabulary word. This may well have contributed to the apparent lack of interest in the study of names in the Arab world. More importantly, it suggests that the meaning of a name is an important element in its choice. However, as this supplement makes clear, the most popular Arabic names are associated with famous personalities of the past, and this factor has had a significant effect on the popularity of names.

Arabic names have had a strong influence on the names of other cultures, mainly of course in Islamic countries.

THE INFLUENCE OF ISLAM ON THE ARABIC NAMING TRADITION

It is no exaggeration to say that the rise of Islam in the 7th century was the single most important event in the history of the Arab world. The birth of Muḥammad, Prophet of Islam, in 570 marks the beginning of what was to become a major and enduring transformation of the political, linguistic, and cultural identity of the area and its peoples. By far the richest source of given names in the Arab world has been, and remains, the historical and moral legacy of Islam. *Muḥammad* remains undoubtedly the most popular male name in the whole of the Islamic world. Names such as *Maḥmūd* and *Aḥmad*, which are derived from the same root, *ḥamida* (to praise), are also among the most popular. Equally popular for boys are *ʿAbd-Allāh* (servant of Allah) and other compound names which consist of *ʿAbd* 'servant of' plus one of the ninety-nine attributes of Allah, for example *ʿAbd-al-ʿAzīz* and *ʿAbd-al-Raḥīm*. In view of the fact that there are potentially ninety-nine such compound names, only the more popular of these have been included in this supplement. A well-known saying attributed to the Prophet suggests that the best names are those derived from the root *ḥamida* and the compound names beginning with *ʿAbd*. This contributed significantly to the enduring popularity of these names.

Another group of popular names are associated with the Prophet's immediate family and his close companions. These include, for boys, *Ḥasan*, *Ḥusayn*, *ʿAli*, and *ʿUmar*, and, for girls, *Khadīja*, *ʿĀʾisha*, and *Zaynab*. Among the most common names for boys are also those of famous Muslim military and political leaders, for example *ʿAmr*, *Khālid*, *Saʿd*, and *Ṭāriq*.

Islam recognizes Judaism and Christianity, and many of the stories told in both the Old and the New Testament appear in the Koran, sometimes with minor variations. Some of the most common Arabic names are direct derivations from the Koran and have counterparts in the Bible, for example *Ibrāhīm* (Abraham), *Ismāʿīl* (Ishmael), *Maryam* (Mary), and *Yūsuf* (Joseph). Other derivations from the Bible, such as *Dawūd* (David), *ʿĪsa* (Jesus), *Isḥāq* (Isaac), *Mūsa* (Moses), and *Yaʿqūb* (Jacob) are also used, but mostly by Christian Arabs: they therefore tend to be much less common. They have not all been included in this supplement.

The influence of Islam and its teachings remains evident even among names that seem to be relatively recent coinages, such as *ʿAfāf* (chastity), *Hādi, Hadya, Huda* (all derived from *hada* to guide, in a religious sense), *Khayri, Khayriyya, Khayrat* (related to charity), *Rashād, Rashīd, Rushdi* (to guide, in a religious sense), and *Ṭāhir* (pure, virtuous). These all express Islamic themes: chastity, charity, and following the right path—that of Islam. Moreover, the importance of 'praise' as a theme in the Islamic naming tradition (cf. *Muḥammad, Aḥmad* and *Maḥmūd*) has given rise to more recent variations on the same root, *ḥamida*: *Ḥāmid* and *Ḥamdi*, as well as derivations from other roots with similar meanings: *Mamdūḥ, Midḥat, Madīḥa*; *Thanā'*.

THE PRE-ISLAMIC TRADITION

A significant number of names which were common prior to the rise of Islam and which reflect the interests and beliefs of the Arab community at that time have survived into present-day use, even though some of them cannot be directly associated with any leading Muslim religious figures. These include a few male names, such as *ʿAdnān*, and many female names, such as *ʿAbla, ʿAzza, Layla,* and *Lubna.* The latter remain popular largely because they are associated with ancient legends of romantic love, recorded in literature. Often, the themes found in these names are quite different from those of typical Islamic names, which generally reflect a concern with virtues such as chastity, charity, praiseworthiness, and so on. Names such as *ʿAbla* meaning 'having a full, fine figure', and *Layla*, meaning 'wine' or its intoxicating effect, clearly have little to do with Islamic virtues. Many male names that date back to pre-Islamic times are vocabulary words denoting ferocious animals, symbolizing courage and power: examples are *Fahd* (panther) and *Haytham* (young eagle). Various nicknames of the lion are particularly popular; they include *ʿAbbās*, *'Usāma*, and *Ḥārith*. For girls, names of tamer animals were chosen; they include *Arwa* (young goat) and *Rīm* (white antelope).

Another important symbol in the male naming tradition, both pre- and post-Islamic, is the sword: for example *Ḥusām* and *Muhannad.* The sword is a symbol not only of power but also of decisiveness and of the ability to make a sharp, uncompromising division between right and wrong. This theme underlies several derivations, all used as male names: for example *Farūq, Fayṣal, Ḥāsim,* and *Ḥātim.*

The hot, arid environment of many parts of the Arab world inspired and continues to inspire a series of names, both male and female, which revolve around the theme of water. For boys, these include *Ghayth* (rain), *Jaʿfar* (small river), *Māzin* (rain clouds), and *Ṭalāl* (fine rain). For girls, they include *Dīma* (thunder-free rain), *Ghadīr* (a brook), *Nada* (dew), *Nadya* (moist with dew), *Nahla* (a drink of water), and *Nihāl* (sated with drink).

The use of diminutives to suggest endearment is widespread in the Arabic naming tradition. Examples of diminutive names include *Ḥusayn* (little beauty) and *Zuhayr* (little flower) for boys, and *Lujayn* (small piece of silver), *Thuhayba* (small bar of gold), and *Umayma* (little mother) for girls. The use of comparatives is also common for boys' names, for example *Aḥmad* (more commendable), *Amjad* (more glorious), *Ashraf* (more honourable), and *Asʿad* (luckier/happier).

CURRENT TRENDS

Although, as suggested above, a significant number of recent coinages do reflect Islamic values, some express different themes, which cannot be said to have a particularly Islamic character. Examples of such themes are 'nightly chats' (*Samar, Sāmir, Samīr/Samīra*), and, for female names, 'physical beauty' (*Nāhida, Jāthibiyya, Hayfā', Fātin, Ghāda*), and 'coquettishness' (*Dalāl*). Many female names are now chosen because they suggest delicacy rather than chastity or virtue, for example *Sarāb* (mirage), *ʿAbīr* (fragrance), *Hadīl* (cooing of pigeons), *Aḥlām* (dreams), and *Malak* (angel). The names of various flowers are also now popular as female names, for example *Sawsan* and *Dalia*.

The influence of the media on the choice of names, particularly female names, is becoming increasingly noticeable. Names of film stars, such as *Fātin* and *Hind*, as well as of famous singers, such as *Shadya*, *Ṣabāḥ*, and *Fayrūz*, have risen in popularity over the past few decades.

Another noticeable trend seems to be a preference for foreign-sounding names, particularly among the upper and middle classes. Among the more fashionable female names are *Nivīn*, *Mirvat*, *Shahināz*, and even *Susan* and *Nancy*. These, however, tend to be restricted to rather small areas within the Arab world, and are mainly borne by city girls. They have therefore not been included in this supplement.

At a time when the Bible and Christian tradition seem to be playing a diminishing role in the choice of a name in the West, the influence of the Islamic tradition in the Arab world has, by contrast gained momentum in recent decades. The Arab world is currently witnessing a revival of interest in all things Islamic and a strong movement against all forms of Westernization. This is likely to have an effect on the choice of names. It would be difficult to substantiate any statements on current trends without the support of a much larger study, but it seems reasonable to suggest that the popularity of traditional Islamic names such as *Khadīja* and *Zaynab*, as well as old Arabic names such as *Walīd* and *ʿAdnān*, has certainly not diminished and may well have increased. At the same time, however, the trend towards liberalization and Westernization, though denounced by many, has continued unabated, resulting in a form of polarization which has guaranteed that both Islamic tradition and modern themes remain equally rich sources for names and are likely to remain so for the forseeable future.

Mona Baker
January 1990

BIBLIOGRAPHY

Abaza, A.: *Qays-wa-Lubna* (Qays and Lubna; Cairo: Dār-al-Maʿārif, 1979).

ʿAbd-al-Rahmān, A. (Bint-al-Shati): *Tarājim Sayidāt Bayt-al-Nubwwa* (Biographies of the Ladies in the Prophet's Household; Beirut: Dār-al-Kitāb Al-ʿArabi, 1982).

Al-Fayyoumi, A.: *Al-Miṣbāḥ Al-Munīr* (8th-century Arabic dictionary; reissued Beirut: Al-Maktaba al-ʿilmiyya, no date).

Al-Jurr, K.: *Al-Muʿjam Al-ʿArabi Al-Ḥadīth* (Modern Arabic Dictionary; Larousse, 1973).

Al-Muʿjam Al-ʿArabi Al-Asāsi (Elementary Arabic Dictionary; ALECSO/Larousse, 1989).

Al-Munjid fi al-Lugha wa al-Aʿlām (Al-Munjid Language Dictionary, with a Biographical Appendix; Beirut: Dār Al-Mashraq, 27th edn, 1984).

Al-Rāzi, M.: *Mukhtār Alṣaḥāḥ* (Arabic Dictionary; Beirut: Dār-al-Kitāb al-ʿArabi, 1981).

Baʿalbaki, M.: *Al-Mawrid* (Modern English-Arabic Dictionary; Beirut: Dār-al-ʿIlm Lil-Malayīn, 1985).

Barāniq, M.A.: *Ṣāliḥ* (Cario: Dār-al-Maʿārif, 1971).

Cambridge Encyclopaedia of the Middle East and North Africa (Cambridge University Press, 1988).

Encyclopaedia of Islam (Leiden: E. J. Brill, 1960–).

First Encyclopaedia of Islam (Leiden: E. J. Brill, 1913–36).

Glubb, J. B.: *The Course of Empire: the Arabs and their Successors* (London: Hodder and Stoughton, 1965).

——: *The Great Arab Conquests* (London: Hodder and Stoughton, 1963).

Hindley, G.: *Saladin* (London: Constable, 1976).

Howat, G. M. D., and A. J. P. Taylor: *Dictionary of World History* (London: Nelson, 1973).

Lewis, B.: *The Arabs in History* (London: Hutchinson, 1966).

Surūr, N.: *Yasīn-wa-Bahiyya* (Yasin and Bahiyya; Cairo: Maktabat-Madbuli, no date).

Wehr, H.: *A Dictionary of Modern Written Arabic* (Beirut: Libarie du Liban and London: Macdonald & Evans, 1961).

Who's Who in the Arab World (Publitec Publications).

The World Almanac and Book of Facts (New York: Newspaper Enterprise Association, 1985).

The World Book Encyclopedia, vols. 7 and 13 (Chicago: World Books, 1983).

A

ʿAbbās (m.) From *ʿabbās* sullen, austere, from *ʿabasa* to frown, look sternly at. Sternness seems to have once been regarded by the Arabs as a desirable quality for men. *ʿAbbās* is also a nickname for the lion. ʿAbbās ibn-ʿAbd-al-Muṭṭalib (*c.*566–652) was the Prophet's uncle and the ancestor of the dynasty of Abbasid caliphs, who ruled the Islamic world between 750 and 1258. They were noted for their strict religious orthodoxy and their patronage of scholarship. ʿAbbās remained a polytheist until the Muslims' final victory, when they took Mecca in January 630. It is alleged that he stayed in Mecca to act as a spy for Muḥammad and that he warned him of the plans of his opponents, the Quraish tribe, before the Battle of Uḥud (625). There is some dispute among historians as to the sincerity of his Islam: he may well have been a sincere supporter of Islam, but he could also have been merely playing safe until a decisive outcome became clear.

ʿAbd-al-ʿĀṭi (m.) Compound name consisting of *ʿabd* servant (of) + *al* the + *ʿāṭi* donor, giver. *Al-ʿĀṭi* 'the Giver' is an attribute of Allah. See also ʿABD-AL-MUʿṬI.
Variant: **ʿAbdel-ʿĀṭi.**

ʿAbd-al-ʿAzīz (Abdul Aziz) (m.) Compound name consisting of *ʿabd* servant (of) + *al* the + *ʿazīz* powerful, mighty. *Al-ʿAzīz* 'the All-Powerful' is an attribute of Allah. ʿAbd-al-ʿAzīz II (ibn-Saʿūd) (*c.*1880–1953) was the founder of modern-day Saudi Arabia. In 1902 he defeated the Rashidis and recovered Riyadh. By 1926 he had extended his control over most of the Arabian Peninsula. His kingdom became known as Saudi Arabia in 1934.
Variant: **ʿAbdel-ʿAzīz.**

ʿAbd-al-Fattāḥ (m.) Compound name consisting of *ʿabd* servant (of) + *al* the + *fattāḥ* opener (i.e. of the gates of sustenance and profit). *Al-Fattāḥ* 'the Opener' is an attribute of Allah.
Variant: **ʿAbdel-Fattāḥ.**

ʿAbd-al-Hādi (m.) Compound name consisting of *ʿabd* servant (of) + *al* the + *hādi* one who guides or leads. *Al-Hādi* 'the Guide' is an attribute of Allah.
Variant: **ʿAbdel-Hādi.**

ʿAbd-al-Ḥakīm (m.) Compound name consisting of *ʿabd* servant (of) + *al* the + *ḥakīm* wise, judicious. *Al-Ḥakīm* 'the Wise' is an attribute of Allah.
Variant: **ʿAbdel-Ḥakīm.**

ʿAbd-al-Ḥalīm (m.) Compound name consisting of *ʿabd* servant (of) + *al* the + *ḥalīm* mild-tempered, patient. *Al-Ḥalīm* 'the Patient' is an attribute of Allah.
Variant: **ʿAbdel-Ḥalīm.**

ʿAbd-al-Ḥamīd (m.) Compound name consisting of *ʿabd* servant (of) + *al* the + *ḥamīd* commendable, praiseworthy. *Al-Ḥamīd* 'the Praiseworthy' is an attribute of Allah.
Variant: **ʿAbdel-Ḥamīd.**

ʿAbd-al-Jawwād (m.) Compound name consisting of *ʿabd* servant (of) + *al* the + *jawwād* generous, magnanimous. *Al-Jawwād* 'the Magnanimous' is an attribute of Allah.
Variant: **ʿAbdel-Gawwād.**

ʿAbd-al-Karīm (m.) Compound name consisting of *ʿabd* servant (of) + *al* the + *karīm* generous, kind. *Al-Karīm* 'the Generous' is an attribute of Allah. ʿAbd-al-Karīm Al-Khaṭṭabi (1882–1963) was a Moroccan nationalist leader. He fought against the invasion of his country by French and Spanish forces.
Variants: **ʿAbdel-Kerīm.**

ʿAbd-Allāh (Abdullah) (m.) Compound name consisting of *ʿabd* servant (of) + *Allāh* God. Although this is one of the most popular names in the Islamic world and is therefore commonly believed to be an Islamic name, it was in fact common in Arabia prior to the rise of Islam. Monotheistic religions, Christianity and Judaism, did exist among Arabs before the birth of Muḥammad, and subscribed to the idea of the one God, or Allah. ʿAbd-Allāh ibn-ʿAbd-al-Muṭṭalib (*c.*545–70) was the Prophet's father. He died shortly before Muḥammad was born. In Arabic tradition a story is told of ʿAbd-Allāh that is similar to the story of Isaac in biblical tradition (or Ishmael in Islamic tradition): ʿAbd-Allāh is said to have been offered by his father as a sacrifice to the gods, but was saved at the last minute when the gods graciously accepted one hundred camels in his place.

Variant: **ʿAbdalla.**

ʿAbd-al-Laṭīf (m.) Compound name consisting of *ʿabd* servant (of) + *al* the + *laṭīf* kind, gentle. *Al Laṭīf* 'the Kind' is an attribute of Allah.

Variant: **ʿAbdel-Laṭīf.**

ʿAbd-al-Malik (m.) Compound name consisting of *ʿabd* servant (of) + *al* the + *malik* king, sovereign. *Al-Malik* 'the Sovereign' is an attribute of Allah. ʿAbd-al-Malik ibn-Marwān (647–705) was the fifth, and perhaps the greatest, Umayyad caliph (685–705). He came to the throne at a time of intense danger to the Umayyads, with several factions in open revolt and with a powerful opponent, ʿAbd-Allāh ibn-al-Zubayr, attempting to seize the caliphate and winning the allegiance of the major part of the Muslim Empire. In 689 ʿAbd-al-Malik concluded a truce with Byzantium, which allowed him to concentrate on his internal problems. By 701 he had crushed all opposition. ʿAbd-al-Malik is also remembered for centralizing the administration of the empire, making Arabic the official language throughout the nation, and introducing a new Islamic gold coin (the dinar).

Variant: **ʿAbdel-Malik.**

ʿAbd-al-Muʿṭi (m.) Compound name consisting of *ʿabd* servant (of) + *al* the + *muʿṭi* donor, giver. *Al-Muʿṭi* 'the Donor' is an attribute of Allah. See also ʿABD-AL-ʿĀṬI.

Variant: **ʿAbdel-Muʿṭi.**

ʿAbd-al-Qādir (m.) Compound name consisting of *ʿabd* servant (of) + *al* the + *qādir* able, powerful, capable. *Al-Qādir* 'the Capable' is an attribute of Allah. ʿAbd-al-Qādir Al Jazā'iri (1808–83) was one of the principal leaders of Algerian resistance to French occupation. After several years of fighting the French, he concluded a treaty with them in 1837 that kept wide areas of Algeria under his control. His struggle against them reached its climax in 1846, when they finally managed to overcome his forces. In 1847 he surrendered to the French: they kept him in prison for five years before fulfilling the terms of his surrender by allowing him to reside freely in an Arab country. He settled in Damascus where, in spite of his long struggle against the French forces, he saved the French consul and several thousand Christians from being massacred by the Druzes. For this, he was awarded a medal by the French government bearing the words 'Amir of North Africa: Defender of Arab Nationality: Protector of Oppressed Christians'. ʿAbd-al-Qādir Al-Jailāni (d. 1166), founded a Muslim brotherhood, known as *Al-Qādiriyya*. It still exists in India, Yemen, and some parts of Africa.

Variant: **ʿAbdel-'Ādir.**

ʿAbd-al-Raḥīm (m.) Compound name consisting of *ʿabd* servant (of) + *al* the + *raḥīm* merciful, compassionate. *Al-Raḥīm* 'the Compassionate' is an attribute of Allah.

Variant: **ʿAbder-Riḥīm.**

ʿAbd-al-Raḥmān (m.) Compound name consisting of *ʿabd* servant (of) + *al* the + *raḥmān* merciful. *Al-Raḥmān* 'the All-Merciful' is an attribute of Allah. ʿAbd-Al-Raḥmān Al-Dākhil (d. 780) was an Umayyad leader who escaped Abbasid persecution and fled to Spain, where in 756 be founded the Umayyad dynasty at

Cordoba, which lasted for almost three centuries. ʿAbd-al-Raḥmān III (891–961) was perhaps the greatest Umayyad ruler in Spain (912–61). In 929 he assumed the caliphate and turned Andalus (the Arabic name for Spain) into a major power in the Mediterranean. He also made Cordoba a leading centre of learning in Western Europe.

Variant: **ʿAbder-Raḥmān**.

ʿAbd-al-Rāziq (m.) Compound name consisting of *ʿabd* servant (of) + *al* the + *rāziq* provider. *Al-Rāziq* 'the Provider' is an attribute of Allah. See also ʿABD-AL-RAZZĀQ.

Variant: **ʿAbder-Rāzi'**.

ʿAbd-al-Razzāq (m.) Compound name consisting of *ʿabd* servant (of) + *al* the + *razzāq* provider. *Al-Razzāq* 'the Provider' is an attribute of Allah. See also ʿABD-AL-RĀZIQ.

Variant: **ʿAbder-Razzā'**.

ʿAbd-al-Salām (m.) Compound name consisting of *ʿabd* servant (of) + *al* the + *salām* peace. *Al-Salām* 'Peace (i.e. the Peaceable)' is an attribute of Allah. The expression *ʿAlayhi al-Salām* 'Peace be on him' is conventionally used after the name of an angel or prophet has been mentioned.

Variant: **ʿAbd-es-Salām**.

ʿAbd-al-Wahāb (m.) Compound name consisting of *ʿabd* servant (of) + *al* the + *wahāb*, shortened form of the adjective *wahhāb* giving. *Al-Wahhāb* 'the Giver' is an attribute of Allah. Muḥammad ibn-ʿAbd-al-Wahāb (1703–92) was the founder of the religious movement known as the *Wahhabiyya*. With the aid of ibn-Saʿūd and his son, ʿAbd-al-ʿAzīz, the movement gradually gained ground in Saudi Arabia, mainly by force. With the fall of Riyadh to ibn-Saʿūd in 1773, most of the Nejd area came under the control of the Wahabis. The main doctrines of *Wahhabiyya* consist of the worship of God alone, and opposition to any form of innovation in Islam.

Variant: **ʿAbdel-Wahāb**.

ʿAbīr (f.) Apparently a comparatively recent coinage from the vocabulary word *ʿabīr* fragrance, aroma.

ʿAbla (f.) From *ʿabla*, a word denoting a woman possessing a full, fine figure, from *ʿabula* to be big or full. This is an ancient Arabic name, which was used in pre-Islamic times and is still common today. ʿAbla was the name of the cousin of ʿAntarah ibn-Shaddād (*c.*525–615), a pre-Islamic Arab poet known for his chivalry. He was in love with her, and most of his poetry, which is still widely read and taught in many Arab schools to this day, was dedicated to her. This has perhaps helped to keep the name perennially popular.

ʿĀdil (m.) From *ʿādil* just, fair, from *ʿadala* to act justly. This name is very popular in most Arab countries, particularly in Egypt. See also IʿTIDĀL.

ʿAdnān (m.) Possibly from *ʿadana* to settle down (in a place or a country). This is an old Arabic name, in use since pre-Islamic times. Tradition relates that the ʿAdnāniyūn, the Arabs who lived in the north of the Arabian Peninsula, are descended from a certain ʿAdnān who in turn is descended from Ismāʿīl, son of the patriarch Ibrāhīm (Abraham). The name is still popular in most Arab countries.

ʿAfāf (f.) From *ʿafāf* chastity, virtuousness, from *ʿaffa*, to refrain (from forbidden or indecent things).

Aḥlām (f.) From *aḥlām* dreams, visions, fantasies, from *ḥalama* to dream. It implies perfection or a state of bliss.

Aḥmad (Ahmed) (m.) From *aḥmad* meaning 'more commendable', from *ḥamida* to praise. This is one of the most popular names in all Muslim countries. See also MUḤAMMAD, MAḤMŪD, ḤĀMID, ḤAMDI for names derived from the same root. Aḥmad ibn-Ḥanbal (780–855) was a celebrated theologian, the founder of the Hanbaliya school of Islamic law (one of four recognized schools). His teachings are thought to have had much influence on the *Wahhabiyya* religious movement, which started in Saudi Arabia in the 18th century. Aḥmad ʿUrābi (1839–1911), known as ʿUrābi Pasha, led the Egyptian army to mutiny against Ottoman rule in 1881. In 1882 he became minister of War. He is considered to be one of the principal figures in the history of the Egyptian nationalist movement.

Use of the name in the Indian subcontinent has been influenced by *Ahmadiyya*, a religious movement that started in Qadiyan, in the eastern Punjab, in 1889. It was founded by Ghulam Ahmad (*c.*1839–1908) and is regarded by most orthodox Muslims as heretical. It is split into two groups. The first and bigger group regards Ghulam Ahmad as a divine prophet and claims membership of over one million people spread throughout the Muslim world, especially in Pakistan, India, and West Africa. The second group, based in West Pakistan, considers Ghulam Ahmad only as a reformer: it is mainly engaged in missionary work.

ʿĀ'isha (f.) From the feminine adjective *ʿā'isha* alive and well, from *ʿāsha* to live. This is one of the best-established traditional female names in the Arab world. ʿĀ'isha bint-Abi-Bakr (*c.*613–78) was Muḥammad's third and favourite wife. She was the daughter of Abu-Bakr al-Ṣiddīq, who later became the first 'guided' caliph (632–4). According to tradition, she was only nine years old when Muḥammad married her. She is said to have had a strong personality, becoming a very jealous wife. After Muḥammad's death, she strongly opposed ʿAli ibn-Abi-Ṭālib, fourth 'guided' caliph, and called on the Muslim community to depose him. In the Battle of the Camel (656), ʿĀ'isha led the rebels' forces herself against ʿAli, but was defeated and sent back to Medina, where she devoted the rest of her life to religious tuition.

Variant: ʿ**Āisha**.

ʿAlā' (m.) From *ʿalā'* elevation, excellence, supremacy, from *ʿala* to rise or ascend. *ʿAlā'* is a shortened form replacing the older names *ʿAlā'-al-Dīn* and *Abu-al-ʿAlā'*. See also ʿALI, ʿALYĀ', and ʿALYA for other names derived from this root. Abu-al-ʿAlā' Al-Maʿarri (973–1057) was a poet who lived in north Syria during the Abbasid rule.

ʿAli (Ali) (m.) From *ʿaliy, ʿali* sublime, elevated, from *ʿalā* to rise or ascend. *Al-ʿAliy* 'the Sublime' is an attribute of Allah. See also ʿALĀ', ʿALYĀ', and ʿALYA. ʿAli ibn-Abi-Ṭālib (*c.*600–61) was the Prophet's cousin, brought up by Muḥammad in his own house. He was the first male convert to Islam and married Fāṭima, Muḥammad's daughter. After Muḥammad's death, ʿAli became the fourth caliph to rule the Islamic world (656–61), following the assassination of ʿUthmān. He was strongly opposed by ʿA'isha, the Prophet's widow. Having defeated her at the Battle of the Camel (656), he went on to meet the forces of an even stronger opponent, Muʿāwiya, in the Battle of Siffin (657). Although ʿAli's forces were winning, he consented to formal arbitration, which reduced him from the position of a legitimate caliph to that of a candidate like Muʿāwiya. This move lost him the support of many of his followers, known as Kharijites, who later fought against him at the Battle of Nahrawan. In 661 ʿAli was stabbed to death by a Kharijite assassin, leaving behind him a legacy of unresolved conflicts and the beginning of what was to become the major division in Islam, that between Shiites and Sunnis. ʿAli was the last legitimate caliph to rule the Islamic community, and his death marked the end of a period known as that of the *Khulafā' Rāshidūn*, the 'rightly guided caliphs' (632–61). According to Shiite Muslims, ʿAli was the only legitimate successor to

Muḥammad and only his descendants are recognized as caliphs.

ʿAlya (f.) Variant of *ʿāliya* sublime, elevated, from *ʿalā* to rise or ascend. See also ʿALI, ʿALĀʾ, and ʿALYĀʾ.

ʿAlyāʾ (f.) From *ʿalyāʾ* high position, loftiness, sublimity, from *ʿalā* to rise or ascend. See also ʿALI, ʿALYA, and ʿALĀʾ.

Amal (f., m.) From *amal* hope, expectation, from *amala* to hope. This is a predominantly female name but is also occasionally used as a male name. See also AMĀL.

Amāl (f., m.) From *amāl* hopes, from *amala* to hope. This is an exclusively female name in Egypt, but is occasionally used as a male name in Syria and Lebanon. See also AMAL.

Amāni (f.) From *amāni* wishes, desires, aspirations, from *mana* to desire or to find by good luck. See also UMNIYA and MUNA.

Amīn (m.), **Amīna** (f.) From *amīn* honest, trustworthy, from *amuna* to be reliable or faithful. This name is popular throughout the Islamic world. See also ĀMINA, IMĀN, and MAʾMŪN. Al-Amīn (787–813), sixth Abbasid caliph (809–13), was the son of the famous caliph of Baghdad, Harūn Al-Rashīd. He was killed by his brother Al-Maʾmūn, who became seventh Abbasid caliph.

Āmina (f.) From *āmina* peaceful or feeling safe, from *amina* to be or feel safe. See also AMĪN/AMĪNA, IMĀN, and MAʾMŪN. Āmina bint-Wahab (d. 576), of the Beni-Zuhra clan of the Quraish tribe, was the Prophet's mother. She died when Muḥammad was only six years old.
Variant: **Amna**.

Amīr (m.), **Amīra** (f.) From *amīr* prince or emir, from *amara* to command or to become an emir. In Abbasid times, the title of *Amīr* was granted to rulers of provinces. Some emirs had the right to establish dynasties, provided that they paid allegiance to the ruling caliph by mentioning his name in the *khutba*, the Friday sermon, and perhaps also by inscribing his name on their coins. In 935 the title *Amīr-al-Umarāʾ* 'Prince of Princes' came into use in Baghdad, indicating the pre-eminence of the emir even over the caliph. Over the years, the title of *Amīr* came to be used quite frequently for a whole range of appointments, mostly military. The title *Amīr-al-Muʾminīn* 'Commander of the Faithful' was first bestowed on ʿUmar ibn-al-Khaṭṭāb, second 'guided' caliph (634–44), and thereafter was reserved exclusively for caliphs.

ʿĀmir (m.) From *ʿāmir* populous, flourishing, prosperous. See also ʿUMAR, ʿAMR, and ʿAMMĀR.

Amjad (m.) From *amjad* meaning 'more glorious', from *majada* to be praiseworthy. See also MĀJID and MAJDI.
Variant: **Amgad**.

ʿAmmār (m.) From *ʿammār* long-lived, from *ʿamara* to live long. See also ʿUMAR, ʿAMR, and ʿĀMIR. ʿAmmār ibn-Yāsir was one of the earliest converts to Islam. As a slave, he was severely persecuted for his conviction, but was eventually saved by the well-to-do Abu Bakr, first 'guided' caliph, who bought him from his master and then set him free. Thereafter, ʿAmmār lived in strict piety until he reached a very advanced age. In 642 ʿUmar ibn-al-Khaṭṭāb, second 'guided' caliph, impressed by ʿAmmār's piety, appointed him governor of Kufa, but was compelled to dismiss him soon after when he realized that his old age and weakness made him ill suited for the post.

ʿAmr (m.) Variant of *ʿUmar*. See also ʿĀMIR and AMMĀR. ʿAmr ibn-al-ʿĀṣ (d. 663), often referred to as 'the conqueror of Egypt', was a brilliant military leader and an astute politician. He fought with Khālid ibn-al-Walīd at the battles of Ajnadayn (634) and Yarmuk (636), but is mostly remembered for his conquest of Egypt, which he seized from the Byzantines between 639 and 642. Historians tend to give him much credit for promoting a spirit of tolerance towards the Copts in Egypt. In particular, a speech he gave in the spring of 644 seems to have had a significant influence on the relationship between Copts and Muslims, for he laid a specific injunction on his fellow Muslims: 'take good care of your neighbours the Copts, for the messenger of God himself gave orders for us to do so'.

Anwar (m.) From *anwar* clearer, brighter. See also NŪR, MUNĪR/MUNĪRA, MANĀR, and NŪRA. Anwar al-Sadāt (1918–81) was president of Egypt (1970–81). He started his political career as a member of the Free Officers' Group, who overthrew the monarchy and took control of Egypt in 1952. He served as vice-president twice during Nāṣir's (Nasser's) term of presidency, and became president following the death of Nāṣir in 1970. He is remembered in the West for taking the initiative to conclude a peace agreement with Israel in 1979, a move that resulted in the political and moral isolation of Egypt in the Arab world for several years. In 1978 al-Sadāt was awarded the Nobel Prize jointly with Menachem Begin. He was assassinated in October 1981 by a group of Muslim extremists during a military parade.

Arwa (f.) Possibly derived from the plural noun *arwa* female mountain goats. This name is particularly popular in Saudi Arabia, the Gulf States, and Jordan.
Variant: **Ruwa**.

Asʿad (m.) From *asʿad* happier or luckier, from *saʿida* to be lucky or happy. See also SAʿD, SAʿĪD, MUSʿAD, and MASʿŪD for other names from this root.

Ashraf (m.) From *ashraf* more honourable, from *sharafa* to be distinguished, noble, or honourable. See also SHARĪF/SHARĪFA.

ʿĀṣim (m.) From *ʿāṣim* protector, guardian, from *ʿaṣama* to protect. See also ʿIṢĀM, ʿIṢMAT, and MUʿTAṢIM.

Asmā' (f.) From *asmā'* meaning 'appellations' or 'prestige'. Asmā' was the daughter of Abu-Bakr, first 'guided' caliph (632–4). She is remembered for her courage in helping the Prophet and her father to escape from Mecca in 622, when the Prophet's opponents were planning to murder him. Asmā' smuggled parcels of food to her father and Muḥammad while they were hiding in a cave on Mount Thor, south of Mecca. She split her belt and used it to tie the parcels of food to one of the saddles: because of this she became known as *Thāt al-Niṭāqayn* 'Lady of the Two Belts'. A brave and determined girl, she later refused to give information on the whereabouts of the Prophet and her father to their enemies, in spite of their threats.

ʿĀṭif (m.) From *ʿāṭif* compassionate, loving, sympathetic, from *ʿaṭafa* to sympathize. See also ʿAWĀṬIF. This name is particularly popular in Egypt.

ʿAwāṭif (f.) From the plural noun *ʿawāṭif* affection, compassion, from *ʿaṭafa* to sympathize or be fond of (someone). See also ʿĀṬIF. This name is particularly popular in Egypt.

ʿAyda (f.) Derivative of *ʿā'ida* benefit, advantage, from *ʿāda* to return.

Ayman (m.) From *ayman* blessed, prosperous, from *yamana* to be fortunate. The Prophet Muḥammad had a nanny by the name of *Um-Ayman* 'Mother of Ayman'. She accompanied the Prophet and his mother on their trip to Yathrib to visit his father's grave and was with the Prophet (six years old at the time) when his mother died near the end of the journey. Muḥammad often referred to Um-Ayman as his 'second mother'.

ʿAzīz (m.), **ʿAzīza** (f.) From *ʿazīz* invincible or beloved, from *ʿazza* to be powerful or be cherished. Although both interpretations are possible, the meaning of endearment is generally taken to be more characteristic of the name in modern Arabic than that of power. See also ʿAzza and Muʿtazz. *Al-ʿAzīz* is one of the attributes of Allah, see ʿAbd-al-ʿAzīz. Al-ʿAzīz (955–96) was the fifth Fatimid caliph of Egypt (975–96). A capable ruler, he gave Egypt twenty-one years of peace, during which the wealth of the Fatimids and the luxuries of their courts and palaces were almost beyond belief. One of Al-ʿAzīz's major achievements lay in devoting the famous Al-Azhar mosque to the teaching of students. It has remained ever since one of the most famous Islamic institutions in the world. He was also known for his tolerance towards Christians and Jews.

ʿAzza (f.) Probably a derivative of *ʿizza* pride or power, but possibly also influenced by or derived from *ʿuzza* female baby gazelle. See also ʿAzīz/ʿAzīza and Muʿtazz. The Umayyad poet Kuthayyir-ʿAzza (d. 723) devoted much of his verse to a girl named ʿAzza, with whom he was in love and by whose name he became known.

B

Badr (m., f.) From *badr* full moon, from *badara* to come up unexpectedly, take by surprise. See also Budūr. This is one of the few Arabic names that are used for both sexes. However, it is more common as a male name.

Bahā' (m.) From *bahā'* splendour, magnificence, glory, from *baha* to be beautiful or glorious. This is possibly a shortened form of the earlier names *Bahā'u-Allāh* 'Glory of God' or *Bahā'u-iddīn* 'Glory of Religion'. In Iraq *Bahā'* is a female name, but it is used exclusively as a male name in most other Arab countries. See also Bahiyya. Bahā'ullāh (1817–92) was the founder of the worldwide religious movement known as Baha'ism.

Bahīja (f.) From *bahīja* joyous, delightful, from *bahija* to be glad or happy. See also Bahjat.

Variant: **Bahīga.**

Bahiyya (f.) From the feminine form *bahiyya* beautiful, radiant, from *baha* to be beautiful. See also Bahā'. According to Egyptian folklore, the story of Yasīn and Bahiyya was played out in a small village in Upper Egypt during the early part of the 20th century. They were engaged to be married when the pasha, the feudal lord of the village, sent for Bahiyya to be brought to his house, a gesture that endangered her honour and alarmed her lover, Yasīn. The details of the story remain rather vague, but it is thought that Yasīn started a rebellion in the village against the pasha. During the ensuing struggle, the pasha's house was burnt and Yasīn was killed. The story of the heartbroken Bahiyya has been told in many different ways, on stage, in songs, and in various other art forms. It is cited as an example of the social injustice and oppression that were prevalent in Egypt prior to the 1952 revolution. Bahiyya has come to be regarded as a symbol of Egypt in art and literature.

Bahjat (m.) From *bahja* joy or delight. See also Bahīja.

Variant: **Bahgat.**

Bakr (m.) From *bakr* a young camel. This name is common in both Saudi Arabia and the Gulf States. Abu-Bakr al-Ṣiddīq (573–634) was the first successor to the Prophet Muḥammad and hence the first 'guided' caliph (632–4). He was also the father of ʿĀ'isha, one of the Prophet's wives.

Bāsim (m.) From *bāsim* smiling, from *basama* to smile. See also Basma and Ibtisām.

Basma (f.) From *basma* a smile, from *basama* to smile. See also Bāsim and Ibtisām.

Budūr (f.) From *budūr*, plural form of *badr* full moon, from *badara* to come up unexpectedly, take by surprise. *Badr-al-Budūr* is a complimentary expression used to indicate outstanding beauty. See also BADR.

Buthayna (f.) A diminutive of *bathua*, which in classical Arabic meant 'flat land, easy to cultivate'. Jamīl-Buthayna, originally Jamīl ibn-Muʿammar (d. 701), is a well-known Arab poet. He was in love with his cousin Buthayna and devoted much of his poetry to her, so that her name was added to his as a byname. Prevented by Buthayna's parents from marrying her, Jamīl left his home and travelled to the Levant and then to Egypt, where he died. His poetry is still widely read and studied in many Arab schools.

Variant: **Busayna**.

D

Dalāl (f.) From *dalāl* coquettishness, from *dalla* to dally or be coquettish. This is a fairly recent coinage as a personal name, but it is now quite popular in Egypt and Syria.

Dalia (f.) Possibly from *dalia* meaning 'dahlia', the flower. It is a fairly recent coinage as a personal name.

Dawūd (m.) Arabic form of *David*. Dawūd (*c.*1000–961 BC) was a Hebrew king and the father of Solomon.

Dīma (f.) From *dīma* meaning 'downpour, continuous rain with no thunder or lightning'. The word *dīma* has positive connotations in Arabic, no doubt because it contrasts with the usual intense heat and dryness of a desert climate. This name is particularly popular in Saudi Arabia, the Gulf States, and Jordan.

Ḍiyā' (m.) From *ḍiyā'* brightness, glow, from *ḍā'* to gleam or shine.

Variant: **Ḍiya**.

Duʿā' (f.) From *duʿā'* prayer, supplication, from *daʿa* to invoke or pray to God.

Ḍuḥa (f.) From *ḍuḥa* forenoon, from *ḍaḥa* to appear, become visible.

F

Fādi (m.), **Fadia** (f.) From *fādi* redeemer, saviour, from *fada* to redeem, sacrifice. *Al-Fādi* 'the Saviour' is an attribute of Jesus Christ in Arabic.

Fāḍil (m.) From *fāḍil* virtuous, generous, or distinguished, from *faḍala* to excel or surpass. See also FAḌĪLA and FAḌL.

Faḍīla (f.) From *faḍīla* moral excellence, virtue, from *faḍala* to excel or surpass. See also FĀḌIL and FAḌL.

Faḍl (m.) From *faḍl* grace, favour, generosity, from *faḍala* to excel or surpass. See also FĀḌIL and FAḌĪLA.

Fahd (m.) From *fahd* panther, leopard, implying fierceness and courage. Fahd ibn-ʿAbd-al-ʿAzīz Āl-Saʿūd (b. 1923) became King of Saudi Arabia in 1982. From 1953 to 1960 he was Saudi Arabia's first minister of Education, and in 1967 he became second deputy prime minister. He was crown prince to his half-brother, Khālid, from 1975–82.

Fakhr-al-Dīn (m.) Compound name consisting of *fakhr* pride, glory + *al* the + *dīn* religion, i.e. 'Glory of Religion'. See also FAKHRI/FAKHRIYYA. Fakhr-al-Dīn II (1572–1635) was a Lebanese emir who fought to make Lebanon independent from the Ottoman Empire.

Variant: **Fakhrid-Dīn**.

Fakhri (m.), **Fakhriyya** (f.) From *fakhri* meritorious, honorary, from *fakhara* to be proud, to glory. See also FAKHR-AL-DĪN.

Faraj (m.) From *faraj* remedy, improvement, from *faraja* to remedy, drive away (worries or grief).

Variant: **Farag**.

Fardoos (f.) Derivative of *firdaws* paradise.

Farīd (m.), **Farīda** (f.) From *farīd* unique, unrivalled, from *farada* to be unique. *Farīda* also denotes a precious pearl or gem.

Farūq (m.) From *farūq* meaning 'person capable of distinguishing right from wrong or truth from falsehood', from *faraqa* to make a distinction, separate. *Al-Farūq* is an epithet of 'Umar ibn-al-Khaṭṭāb, second 'guided' caliph (634–44), who was known for his uncompromising execution of justice. The Koran is sometimes referred to as *Al-Furqān* because it makes clear distinctions between right and wrong. *Farūq* was also the name of the last king of Egypt (1920–65; reigned 1936–52). He was deposed by the Egyptian army and sent into exile in 1952.

Variant: **Farū'**.

Fatḥi (m.), **Fatḥiyya** (f.) Possibly derived from *fātiḥ* releaser or conqueror, from *fataḥa* to open or conquer.

Fāṭima (f.) From *fāṭima*, denoting a woman who weans an infant or who abstains from forbidden things, from *faṭama* to wean or abstain. This name is very popular in all Muslim countries and can be interpreted either from the weaning aspect, implying motherly care, or from the abstaining aspect. Abstention, especially where women are concerned, is considered very desirable in Muslim societies as it implies chastity. Fāṭima bint-Muḥammad (*c.*606–32) was the Prophet's favourite daughter. She married 'Ali ibn-Abi-Ṭālib, fourth 'guided' caliph, and became mother of his sons Ḥasan and Ḥusayn (venerated as a saint by the Shiites). She died less than six months after her father. Because she was the only one among Muḥammad's daughters who left children to continue the family line, she is sometimes referred to as 'the Mother of all Muslims'. The Fatimid dynasty, which ruled Egypt and North Africa between 909 and 1171, claimed to be descendants of 'Ali and Fāṭima, hence the name Fatimid.

Variant: **Faṭma**.

Fātin (f.) From *fātin* charming, seductive, from *fatana* to enamour, enchant. This is a fairly recent coinage as a given name. The Egyptian actress Fātin Ḥamāma (b. 1932), ex-wife of the film star 'Umar al-Sharīf (Omar Sharif), is considered by many to be the most outstanding actress in the history of the Arab cinema. She is referred to in Egypt as 'the Lady of the Arab Screen'.

Fawzi (m.), **Fawziyya** (f.) Possibly from *fawz* triumph, victory, accomplishment, from *fāza* to achieve or win. See also FĀYIZ/FAYZA.

Fāyiz (m.), **Fayza** (f.) From *fā'iz* victor, winner, from *fāza* to achieve or win. See also FAWZI/FAWZIYYA.

Fayrūz (f.) From *fayrūz* turquoise (the precious stone). This name is probably of Persian origin. The last king of the Sassanid dynasty, King Yezdegird of Persia (d. 652), had a son by the name of Fayrūz. In Arab countries, however, the name is now exclusively female. Fayrūz is the name of a leading contemporary Arab singer, who is of Lebanese origin.

Fayṣal (m.) From *fayṣal* a judge (literally meaning 'separator between right and wrong'), from *faṣala* to separate or set apart. *Fayṣal* also denotes a sharp sword. Fayṣal I (1883–1933), King of Iraq (1921–33), was the son of Al-Sharīf Ḥusayn of Mecca. He led the northern forces in the Arab Revolt (1916–18) and actively supported the Arab nationalist cause in Syria. Having failed to obtain British support against the French forces, his Syrian army was eventually defeated, and France assumed a mandate over Syria in 1920. In July 1921 Fayṣal was elected King of Iraq in a referendum. As a strong and practical leader, he was able to maintain a balance between the nationalists and the British forces and to guide Iraq gradually to independence. Another Fayṣal (1905–75) was King of Saudi Arabia (1964–75). He adopted a policy of internal modernization coupled with adherence to Islamic tradition.

Variant: **Feiṣal**.

Fiḍḍa (f.) From *fiḍḍa* silver. This name is particularly popular in Jordan.

Variant: **Fiẓẓa**.

Fihr (m.) An ancient Arabic name of uncertain meaning. It may be related to *fihr*, a type of stone pestle used for pounding the ingredients of medicines. The name is popular mainly in Syria and Lebanon. In the 3rd century it was borne by one of the great-grandfathers of Muḥammad, who was also head of the Quraish tribe.

Fikri (m.), **Fikriyya** (f.) From *fikri* intellectual, relating to the mind, from *fakara* to meditate, ponder. This name is particularly popular in Egypt and Syria.

Fu'ād (m.) From *fu'ād* heart.

G

Ghāda (f.) From *ghāda* a graceful young girl or lady, from *ghayada* to walk gracefully.

Ghadīr (f.) From *ghadīr* a brook or stream. Words referring to fresh water usually have favourable connotations in Arabic, and this is one of several that are used as personal names.

Ghālib (m.) From *ghālib* conqueror, victor, from *ghalaba* to subdue or defeat. The expression *lā ghālib illa Allāh* 'God is the only conqueror' is often inscribed on entrances to mosques, and can be found on the walls of old palaces such as the Alhambra in Granada, Spain.

Ghassān (m.) From *ghassān* prime of youth. *Ghassāniyy* means 'very beautiful'. *Ghassān* is a popular name in most Arab countries. In the 6th century, which saw the birth of the Prophet, Banu-Ghassān (sons of Ghassān) were a local tribe situated in the north-west of Arabia. They acted as a satellite Arab state under the control of the Byzantine Empire. Their princes enjoyed a high status under Byzantine rulers and were engaged in endless warfare against the Lakhm dynasty, which was allied to Persia. The Ghassān princes and the Arabs on the Syrian border were Christians. By around 540, the relations between Banu-Ghassān and their Byzantine allies had deteriorated considerably. The Byzantines proceeded to persecute them as monophysites (the Arabs believed that Christ had only a divine nature, while the Orthodox Church believed he partook of the divine and the human). In 581 the Banu-Ghassān dynasty was finally abolished by the Byzantines.

Ghayth (m.) From *ghayth* rain, from *ghātha* to water with rain. Several Arabic words that refer to rain are used as personal names, rain being especially prized in the arid environment of a desert culture. Cf. also, for example, the female name *Dīma*.

Variant: **Ghaith**.

Ghufrān (f.) From *ghufrān* forgiveness, remission, from *ghafara* to forgive. This name is particularly popular in Iraq.

H

Ḥabīb (m.), **Ḥabība** (f.) From *ḥabīb* beloved, dear, from *ḥabba* to love.

Hādi (m.), **Hadya** (f.) From *hādi* meaning 'one who leads or guides' (mainly in a religious sense), from *hadā* to guide, lead (i.e. to the true faith). This name may also be a shortened form of *hādi'* calm, of a quiet nature, from *hada'a* to be calm. Both interpretations are possible in modern Arabic. See also HUDA.

Hadīl (f.) From *hadīl*, denoting the soft, murmuring sounds made by pigeons, cooing, from *hadala* to coo (of a pigeon). According to tradition, *hadīl* was the name of a particular bird that existed at the time of Noah. It was eaten by a bird of prey, and was mourned by other pigeons and doves. This name is particularly popular in Jordan, Syria, and Lebanon.

Ḥāfiẓ (m.) From *ḥāfiẓ* custodian, guardian, from *ḥafaẓa* to guard or memorize. *Ḥāfiẓ* used to be an honorific epithet denoting any person who knew the Koran by heart.

Ḥafṣa (f.) The origin and meaning of this name are uncertain, but it probably derives from a word meaning a brooding hen, and indicates motherly tenderness. It is an old Arabic name, which has been in use since pre-Islamic times. Ḥafṣa (d. 665) was the daughter of ʿUmar ibn-al-Khaṭṭāb, second 'guided' caliph, and one of the Prophet's wives. After Muḥammad's death, she was chosen by Abu-Bakr, first 'guided' caliph, to hold the only written copy of the Koran. She is therefore known as *Ḥāfiẓat Al-Qur'ān* 'the Koran Keeper'.

Variant: **Ḥafẓa**.

Hājar (f.) Possibly derived from *hājara* to emigrate. According to Arab tradition, Hājar was the Egyptian concubine given to Ibrāhīm (Abraham) by his wife Sarah, who could not bear children. When Hājar gave birth to Ismāʿīl (Ishmael), Sarah became jealous with the result that Ibrāhīm decided to take mother and son to the desert where he left them without food or water. In her attempt to find water for her infant son, Hājar is thought to have run several times between the mounts of Al-Safa and Al-Marwa near Mecca. God soon took pity on her and sent a bird which bored a hole in the ground, uncovering the well of Zamzam. To this day, when Muslims visit Mecca for pilgrimage, they drink from Zamzam and walk the distance between Al-Safa and Al-Marwa seven times as part of the pilgrimage rites. Hājar is often referred to as 'the Mother of the Arabs', since Arabs believe they are descended from Ismāʿīl, son of Ibrāhīm by Hājar, while Hebrews are descended from Isaac, his son by Sarah.

Variant: **Hāgir**.

Ḥakīm (m.) From *ḥakīm* wise, judicious, from *ḥakama* to pass judgement. See also Ḥikmat.

Hāla (f.) From *hāla* a halo around the moon. This is an old Arabic name, which seems to have been in use since pre-Islamic times. Khadīja, the Prophet's first wife, had a sister by the name of Hāla. It is alleged that when Khadīja died the Prophet was always keen to see Hāla and hear her voice, which reminded him of Khadīja's.

Ḥamdi (m.) From *ḥamdi*, which means 'having to do with praise and gratitude', particularly for God's favours. See also Aḥmad, Ḥāmid, Maḥmūd, and Muḥammad.

Ḥāmid (m.) From *ḥāmid* thankful, praising, from *ḥamida* to praise or commend. Praise is usually conferred on God, hence the expression *Al-Ḥamdu Lillāh* 'Praise be to God'. See also Aḥmad, Ḥamdi, Maḥmūd, and Muḥammad for other names from the same root.

Ḥamza (m.) Possibly derived from *ḥamuza* to be or become strong or steadfast. It is an old Arabic name, which dates back to pre-Islamic times. Ḥamza was the Prophet's uncle. He was a well-respected member of his clan, noted for his great physical strength and his courage as a warrior. An early convert to Islam, he fought with Muḥammad against his own tribe at Badr (624) and Uhud (625). He was killed and his body mutilated in the Battle of Uhud.

Hanā' (f.) From *hanā'* bliss, happiness, wellbeing, from *hani'a* to take pleasure in, be delighted. See also Hāni/Haniyya.

Ḥanān (f.) From *ḥanān* tenderness, affection, from *ḥanna* to feel compassion, sympathize.

Hāni (m.), **Haniyya** (f.) From *hāni'* happy, delighted, from *hani'a* to be happy or contented. See also HANĀ'.

Ḥārith (m.) From *ḥaratha* to be a good provider, be able to make money. *Al-ḥārith* is also an appellation of the lion.

Ḥasan (m.) From *ḥasan* good, beautiful, from *ḥasuna* to be good. See also ḤUSAYN, ḤUSNI, IḤSĀN, MAḤĀSIN, and MUḤSIN/MUḤSINA for other names derived from the same root. This is one of the most popular names in all Islamic countries and has strong religious associations. Al-Ḥasan (*c*.625–69) was the grandson of the Prophet, son of ʿAli ibn-Abi-Ṭālib, fourth 'guided' caliph, and Fāṭima bint-Muḥammad. Ḥasan is said to have resembled the Prophet in physical appearance. He was thirty-seven years of age when his father was assassinated. The men of the city of Kufa swore allegiance to him in January 661. Six months later, he was forced to abdicate by Muʿāwiya, who became the fifth caliph and founded the first dynasty of caliphs, the Umayyads, who ruled the Islamic community from 661 to 750. Ḥasan died eight years later from a poison given to him by one of his wives. The Shiites, those who supported ʿAli and his descendants as the only legitimate successors to Muḥammad, claim that Muʿāwiya paid a large sum of money to Ḥasan's wife to administer the poison and promised to marry her to his son Yazīd, who later became caliph. No such marriage ever took place. Ḥasan is venerated as a martyr by Shiite Muslims.

Hāshim (m.) From *hāshim* crushing, destroying, from *hashama* to smash or crush. See also HISHĀM. In classical Arabic *hāshim* denotes one who breaks up bread and dunks it in meat stock. Hāshim ibn-ʿAbd-Manāf of the Quraish tribe was a great-grandfather of the Prophet and one of the most eminent members of his clan. He was in charge of the pilgrims who came to visit the holy temple of Kaʿba every year, and was responsible for providing them with food and drink. He initiated the two annual trading caravan trips to the Yemen and the Levant, the first in winter and the second in summer. On his return from one of those trips, he brought with him some bread, which he crushed for his tribe; he therefore became known as *Al-Hāshim* 'the Crusher'. His original name was ʿAmr. Muslims are sometimes referred to as 'Hashemites' because they are regarded as the descendants of Hāshim.

Ḥāsim (m.) From *ḥāsim* decisive, from *ḥasama* to decide, separate, or cut off. Decisiveness, and in particular the ability to make a swift and clear distinction between right and wrong, are qualities greatly prized among Muslims. See also ḤUSĀM.

Ḥātim (m.) From *ḥātim* decisive, determined, from *ḥatama* to decide. Ḥātim ibn-ʿAbd-Allāh (d. 605) of the tribe of Ṭā'i (Ḥātim Al-Ṭā'i), who lived in the years immediately preceding Islam, was famous for his generosity. He is referred to in the *Rubaiyat* of Omar Khayyam:

> Let Rustum lay about him as he will
> Or Hatim Tai cry 'Supper!'—heed them not.

So famous was he that the name *Ḥātim* has come to be associated more with generosity than with decisiveness.

Hayfā' (f.) From *hayfā'* slender or delicate.

Variant: **Hayfa.**

Haytham (m.) From *haytham* a young eagle, bestowed as a given name because of the proud and imperious qualities attributed to the eagle.

Hiba (f.) From *hiba* a gift or grant, from *wahaba* to give or donate. This name also occurs in the compound form *Hibatu-Allāh* 'Gift of God'. See also IHĀB and WAHĪB.

Ḥikmat (m., f.) From *ḥikma* wisdom, sagacity, from *ḥakama* to pass judgement. This is one of the few Arabic names widely used for both sexes. See also ḤAKĪM.

Hind (f.) An ancient Arabic name of obscure origin and meaning, which seems to have been in common use since pre-Islamic times. It was at one time used for both sexes, but is now exclusively a female name. Hind ibn-Abi-Hāla was the Prophet's stepson by Khadīja. Hind bint-abi-Umayya (known as Um-Salma) was one of the Prophet's wives. She was a widow when he married her. It is said that her beauty caused a great deal of jealousy among the Prophet's other wives.

Hishām (m.) From *hishām* meaning 'generous by nature', originally derived from *hashama* to smash or crush. The idea of crushing or breaking up bread became associated with generosity, because the Arabs who went on caravan trips to the Yemen and the Levant brought with them bread, which they crushed and served to fellow members of their clan. In classical Arabic, therefore, *hishām*, literally 'crushing', is used to suggest that the man to whom it refers is extremely generous. See also HĀSHIM. Hishām ibn-ʿAbd-al-Malik (691–743) was a strong Umayyad caliph (724–43). During his reign the Arab armies invaded France, but were defeated by the Franks at Tours on the Loire (732). He is also remembered for his agricultural reforms.

Huda (f.) From *huda* right guidance (especially in a religious sense), from *hada* to lead on the right path. See also HĀDI/HADYA.

Ḥusām (m.) From *ḥusām* sword, from *ḥasama* to cut, sever, decide finally. See also ḤĀSIM.

Ḥusayn (m.) Diminutive of *ḥasan* good, beautiful, exquisite, from *ḥasuna* to be good. Diminutive forms are used for various reasons in Arabic, in this instance to express endearment. This name bears strong religious associations and is therefore one of the most popular names in all Muslim countries. See also ḤASAN, ḤUSNI, IḤSĀN, MAḤĀSIN, and MUḤSIN/MUḤSINA. Al-Ḥusayn (*c.*626–80) was the grandson of the Prophet from his daughter Fāṭima and ʿAli ibn-Abi-Ṭālib, fourth 'guided' caliph. His brother, Al-Ḥasan, was fifth caliph. The Prophet's great love for Al-Ḥasan and Al-Ḥusayn and their ensuing tragic careers have proved of great significance in the history of Islam. Ḥusayn and his followers were massacred in 680 at the city of Kerbelā' in Iraq by the Umayyad governor, which resulted in a violent reaction against the Umayyads. During the twelve years of civil war that followed, the supporters of Ḥusayn and his father ʿAli organized their forces and emerged as the Shīʿa party, dedicated to working for the elevation of ʿAli's descendants to the caliphate. This is the sect known today as the Shiites. The day of Ḥusayn's defeat at Kerbelā' (10 Muḥarram in the Hajīra year 61: 10 October 680) became a holy day for the Shiites, who commemorate it with extensive mourning rituals. The tomb of Ḥusayn at Kerbelā' is a holy place of pilgrimage to many Muslims.

In more recent times, the present King of Jordan, Ḥusayn ibn-Ṭalāl (b. 1935) is perhaps the most famous bearer of the name. He became king in 1953, following the abdication of his father in 1952.

Variant: **Ḥisein**.

Ḥusni (m.) Derived from *ḥusn* beauty, excellence, from *ḥasuna* to be beautiful or good. See also ḤASAN, ḤUSAYN, IḤSĀN, MUḤSIN/MUḤSINA, and MAḤĀSIN. Ḥusni Mubārak (b. 1928) became president of Egypt in 1981, following the assassination of Anwar Al-Sadāt by Muslim extremists in October 1981. He was commander of Egypt's air force before becoming vice-president in 1979. He has undertaken to continue Al-Sadāt's policies, in spite of strong opposition from Islamic fundamentalists.

I

Ibrāhīm (m.) Arabic form of *Abraham*, the biblical patriarch and father of Ismāʿīl and Isḥāq (Ishmael and Isaac). It is one of the most popular names in the Islamic world. According to Arab tradition, Ibrāhīm (in the 19th century BC) begot Ismā'īl by Hājar, and Isḥāq by Sarah. Muslims are believed to be the descendants of Ismā'īl, while the Jews are the descendants of Isḥāq. Ibrāhīm, with the help of his son Ismā'īl, built the temple of Ka'ba in Mecca, which is the centre of all pilgrimage rites and the point that all Muslims face when they perform their daily prayers.

Ibtisām (f.) From *ibtisām* smiling, from *basama* to smile. See also Basma and Bāsim.

Ihāb (m., f.) From *ihāb* gift or donation, from *wahaba* to give or donate. See also Wahīb and Hiba.

Iḥsān (m., f.) From *iḥsān* charity, benefaction, from *aḥsana* to do good. See also Ḥasan, Ḥusayn, Ḥusni, Maḥāsin, and Muḥsin/Muḥsina.

Imām (m.) From *imām* leader (especially one who leads the congregation at prayers in a mosque), from *amma* to lead in prayer. In Islam, *imām* is used to describe a recognized leader. For Sunnis, it refers only to the leader of prayers in a mosque; any pious Moslem can act as imam. For Shiites, however, *imām* has come to be synonymous with caliph. It refers to the successors of Muḥammad as recognized by the Shiites, i.e. only the descendants of 'Ali and Fāṭima, the last of whom was for some Shiite sects the seventh, and for others the twelfth, imam after 'Ali. Shiites generally believe that imams are guided directly by Allah and are therefore infallible.

Imān (f.) From *imān* faith, belief, from *āmana* to believe (in God). See also Amīn/Amīna, Āmina, and Ma'mūn.

In'ām (f.) From *in'ām* benefaction, bestowal, from *an'ama* to bestow. See also Mun'im, Na'īma, and Ni'mat.

'Iṣām (m.) From *'iṣām* strap (implying protection), pledge, security, from *'aṣama* to protect or guard. *'Iṣām* also denotes a self-made man. This is a shortened version of the earlier form *'Iṣām al-Dīn* 'Protector of Religion'. See also 'Āṣim, 'Iṣmat, and Mu'taṣim for other names derived from the same root.

Ismā'īl (m.) Arabic form of *Ishmael*, name borne in the Old Testament by a son of the patriarch Abraham. It is popular throughout the Islamic world. According to Arab tradition, Ismā'īl was son of Ibrāhīm (Abraham) by Hājar, the Egyptian concubine given to him by his wife Sarah, who could not bear children. When Hājar gave birth to Ismā'īl, Sarah became jealous and forced Ibrāhīm to take mother and son to the desert, where he left them without food or water. God took pity on them and sent a bird which bored a hole in the ground, uncovering the well of Zamzam, which saved their lives and encouraged other travellers to settle in the area. Ibrāhīm later returned to see his son and together they built the Ka'ba, the temple in Mecca that all Muslims face towards when they pray. It is the centre of Muslim pilgrimage. Arabs believe that they are descended from Ismā'īl, so that they are sometimes referred to as 'Ismailites', while the Hebrews are descended from Isaac, son of Ibrāhīm by Sarah. In Muslim tradition, the same legend is told of Ismā'īl as of Isaac. Because Ibrāhīm was spared the sacrifice of his son Ismā'īl, Muslims still sacrifice a sheep or a goat in commemoration of this event on the tenth day of the Arab month of Thu-al-Ḥijjah, known as *'Īd-al-Aḍḥa* 'feast of sacrifice'. The meat, or at least a portion of it, is shared among the needy.

Ismā'īl al-Ṣiddīq was the son of Ja'far al-Ṣiddīq (699–765), the sixth Shiite imam. The quarrel between Ismā'īl and his brother Mūsa led to a split in the Shiite ranks. The minority, who believed that the divine spirit passed from Ja'far to

Ismāʿīl rather than to Mūsa, became known as the Ismailis. In 909 the Ismailis established the Fatimid caliphate, which ruled Egypt and North Africa until 1171. The Ismailis adopt several doctrines that differ considerably from those of other Muslim sects.

ʿIṣmat (m., f.) From *ʿiṣma*, which means 'safeguarding, sinlessness, or infallibility', from *ʿaṣama* to guard or preserve. See also ʿĀṢIM, ʿIṢĀM, and MUʿTAṢIM.

Isrā' (f.) From *isrā'* nocturnal journey, from *sarā* to travel by night. The word *isrā'* is used in particular to refer to the story of Muḥammad's midnight journey to Jerusalem, where he is said to have visited the mosque and the church and to have met Jesus and Moses before returning to Mecca the same night.

Iʿtidāl (f.) From *iʿtidāl* temperance, moderation, from *ʿadala* to be moderate or to straighten. See also ʿĀDIL.

ʿIzz-al-Dīn (m.) Compound name consisting of *ʿizz* power, glory, honour + *al* the + *dīn* religion, i.e. 'power (or glory) of religion'. ʿIzz-al-Dīn Aybak was the first Mamluk sultan of Egypt (1250–7). He acted as *atabeg* (adviser) to Shajarat-al-Durr, widow of the Ayyubid sultan who died in 1249. In 1250 ʿIzz-al-Dīn became sultan and married Shajarat-al-Durr. During his period of rule, he strengthened the Mamluk regime in Egypt, keeping the country under Mamluk control against the attempts of the Ayyubids in Syria and the crusaders, then in Palestine. In 1257, fearing that ʿIzz-al-Dīn intended to renounce her, Shajarat-al-Durr had him killed. Having lost his support, she herself lost her life soon after.

Variant: **ʿIzz-ed-Dīn**.

J

Jābir (m.) From *jābir* comforter, one who assists in time of need, from *jabara* to restore, bring back to normal. See also JABR.

Variant: **Gābir**.

Jabr (m.) From *jabr* consolation or assistance in time of need, from *jabara* to restore (originally, broken bones), bring back to normal. See also JĀBIR.

Variant: **Gabr**.

Jaʿfar (m.) From *jaʿfar* small river, stream. Jaʿfar ibn-Abi-Ṭālib (d. 629) was brother of ʿAli, fourth 'guided' caliph. He died heroically, fighting against the Byzantines in the Battle of Mota (629). Jaʿfar held aloft the Muslim banner proclaiming 'Paradise!' until he lost both his hands. He then held the staff between his stumps and kept the banner raised until he was struck by a mortal blow. The Prophet is alleged to have had a vision of Jaʿfar in paradise, appearing as an angel with two wings bearing the blood of martyrdom. He has since been referred to as *Jaʿfar al-Ṭayyār* 'Jaʿfar the flyer'. In the area where the Battle of Mota took place, in present-day Jordan, a mosque with two tall minarets now stands marking the grave of Jaʿfar. Jaʿfar al-Ṣiddīq (699–765) was the sixth Shiite imam. He had two sons, Ismāʿīl and Mūsa. After his death, a split occurred in the Shiite ranks between those who believed that the divine spirit passed from Jaʿfar to his son Ismāʿīl, who became known as the Ismailis, and the majority of Shiites, who believed that the divine spirit passed to Mūsa and then to his descendants. These became known as the Twelvers, because the last survivor of Mūsa's line of descendants was the twelfth imam starting with ʿAli, fourth 'guided' caliph, whose descendants are recognized as imams by the Shiites.

Variant: **Gaʿfar**.

Jalāl (m.) From *jalāl* greatness, veneration, glory, from *jalla* to be great or illustrious. See also JALĪLA.

Variant: **Galāl**.

Jalīla (f.) From *jalīla* important, honourable, exalted, from *jalla* to be great or illustrious. See also JALĀL.

Variant: **Galīla**.

Jamāl (m., f.) From *jamāl* beauty, from *jamula* to be handsome or comely. This is not one of the traditional Islamic names but is popular in most Arab countries. It is used as a female name in some parts of the Arab world, such as Syria, but is exclusively used as a male name in others, such as Egypt. See also JAMĪL/JAMĪLA. Jamāl al-Dīn al-Afghāni (1839–97), of Persian origin, was the principal advocate of pan-Islamism. He travelled widely in India, Egypt, Afghanistan, Iran, Europe and throughout the Ottoman Empire calling on all Muslims to reunite against the encroachments of Europe. Jamāl ʿAbd-al-Nāṣir, i.e. Nasser, (1918–70) was president of Egypt (1956–70). He helped in establishing the nationalist Free Officers' Group, which overthrew the monarchy in 1952. His nationalization of the Suez Canal was followed by an unsuccessful Israeli and Anglo-French attack on Egypt in 1956, after which he was established as leader of the Arab world. His socialist and Arab nationalist policies had much effect on shaping the recent history of the area and brought him into frequent conflict with the West.

Variant: **Gamāl**.

Jamīl (m.), **Jamīla** (f.) From *jamīl* beautiful, graceful, handsome, from *jamula* to be beautiful. See also JAMĀL.

Variant: **Gamīl**.

Jāthibiyya (f.) From *jāthibiyya* attractiveness, charm, from *jathaba* to attract.

Variants: **Gathbiyya, Gazbiyya**.

Jawāhir (f.) From *jawāhir* jewels.

Variant: **Gawāhir**.

Jawdat (m.) From *jawda* excellence, goodness, from *jāda* to be or become good. See also JŪDA.

Variant: **Gawdat**.

Jinān (m., f.) From *jinān* garden or paradise. This name is used mainly in Syria, Lebanon, and Iraq.

Jūda (m.) From *jawda* goodness, excellence, from *jāda* to be or become good. See also JAWDAT.

Variant: **Gūda**.

K

Kamāl (m.) From *kamāl* perfection, from *kamula* to be or become perfect. See also KĀMIL.

Kāmil (m.) From *kāmil* perfect, complete, from *kamula* to be or become perfect. See also KAMĀL.

Karam (m., f.) From *karam* generosity, magnanimity, noble nature, from *karuma* to be noble or generous. See also KARĪM/KARĪMA and MAKRAM.

Karīm (m.), **Karīma** (f.) From *karīm* noble, generous, from *karuma* to be noble or generous. The vocabulary word also denotes precious stones and so means 'valuable'. See also KARAM and MAKRAM.

Khadīja (f.) From *khadīja* premature child. This is an old Arabic name, in use since pre-Islamic times. Khadīja bint-Khuwaylid (d. 619) was the Prophet's first wife, and mother of all his children. A rich Meccan widow, some fifteen years his senior and about forty years of age at the time of the marriage (595), Khadīja was an ardent supporter of her husband. Her wealth, maturity, and unquestioning belief in Muḥammad provided him with the strength he needed to launch his religion against an unsympathetic and often dangerously hostile environment. Khadīja was the first convert to Islam. In spite of the difference in their ages, she seems to have enjoyed more respect and love from Muḥammad than any other woman in his life. He never married another woman while she was alive and always remembered her with great affection after her death. Because of the important role she played in the Prophet's life and the fact that she was the mother of all his children, the name remains perennially popular among Muslims everywhere, especially conservatives, irrespective of nationality.

Variant: **Khadīga.**

Khālid (m.) From *khālid* undying, eternal, from *khalada* to last for ever, enjoy a long life. This is one of the most popular names in the Arab world. Khālid ibn-al-Walīd (d. 642) was a brave and brilliant military leader, instrumental in accomplishing many of the great Islamic conquests. It is said that the Prophet Muḥammad himself nicknamed him 'the unsheathed sword of God'. In spite of disagreements between him and ʿUmar ibn-al-Khaṭṭāb, second 'guided' caliph, ʿUmar acknowledged him as 'a prince among men'. After mercilessly quelling the rebellion of some Arab tribes (known as Al-Ridda) in 632–3, he went on to defeat the Zoroastrian Persians in 633 and the Christian Byzantines in 634–6. His most famous victories over the Byzantines were at Al-Ajnadayn and on the Yarmuk River. Judging by his style of life, Khālid was not a religious man; he is said to have become extremely rich from his conquests, to have acquired many wives and concubines, and even to have indulged in wine, contrary to Islamic teaching. Nevertheless, it was largely Khālid's military genius and strong leadership that brought about the defeat of the Byzantine Empire and its expulsion from Syria. In recent times, the name has been borne by the king (1913–81) who ruled Saudi Arabia between 1975 and 1981, in the aftermath of the assassination of his brother Fayṣal.

Feminine form: **Khālida** (rare).

Khalīfa (m.) From *khalīfa* caliph or successor, from *khalafa* to succeed, replace. *Khalīfa* is a word with strong religious associations. It originally referred to the successors of Muḥammad, as elected by the Muslim community. The first four caliphs (Abu-Bakr, ʿUmar, ʿUthmān, and ʿAli) had both spiritual and temporal authority. They are known as *Al-Khulafā' al-Rāshidūn* 'the rightly guided caliphs'. Following the death of ʿAli in 661, the caliphate was seized by Muʿāwiya, who founded in Damascus the first dynasty of caliphs, the Umayyads, who ruled the Arab Empire from 661 to 750. In 750 the Shiites managed to gain control over the Muslim community, and the Abbasid dynasty was established. This lasted until the fall of Baghdad to the Mongols in 1258. When the Ottomans captured Egypt in 1517, their sultans assumed the title, which by then had come to bear very little religious significance. The caliphate was formally abolished in 1924.

Khalīl (m.) From *khalīl* bosom friend. *Al-Khalīl* is an epithet of Ibrāhīm (Abraham).

Khayrat (m.) From *khayra* good deed. See also KHAYRI/KHAYRIYYA and MUKHTĀR.

Khayri (m.), **Khayriyya** (f.) From *khayri* charitable, benevolent. See also KHAYRAT and MUKHTĀR.

L

Lamyā' (f.) From *lamiā'*, which means 'possessing beautiful, brownish lips'.

Variant: **Lamya.**

Lawāḥiẓ (f.) From *lawāḥiẓ* glances, from *lahaẓa* to look at, notice.

Variant: **Lawāḥiz.**

Layla (f.) From *layla* wine, alcohol, or its intoxicating effect. Qays ibn-al-Mulawwaḥ (d. 688) was a well-known Arab poet, most of whose poetry is dedicated to his cousin Layla. The story of Qays and Layla is as famous as that of Romeo and Juliet, and their names have come to be associated with romantic love and devotion. The story of their love inspired the well-known Arabic expression *kullun yabki/yughanni ʿala laylāh* ('Each mourns/sings for his own Layla', i.e. each follows his own fancy).

Līna (f.) From *līna*, a type of palm tree.

Lubna (f.) From *lubna* storax, a tree with a sweet honey-like sap, used for making incense and perfume and still popular in most Arab countries. According to Arab tradition, Lubna bint-al-Ḥubāb Al-Kalbiyya was very happily married to Qays ibn-Thurayḥ, but was unable to bear children. Having failed to force his son to divorce her and marry another, Qays's father decided to sit in the intense heat of the sun every day until he died. The story goes that Qays followed his father wherever he went and shielded him from the sun for a whole year, after which time he finally consented to divorce his beloved Lubna. To ease his passion for his first wife, his father then arranged for him to marry a very beautiful woman, again by the name of Lubna, but Qays refused to touch her. In one version of the story, Qays and the first Lubna eventually get back together and live happily ever after, while in another they die separated, each married to another. The events of the story probably occurred during the 7th century. It is alleged that Al-Ḥasan and Al-Ḥusayn, the Prophet's grandsons, were asked to intervene to bring the two lovers back together. The story has been told many times in various forms of literature.

Lujayn (f.) A diminutive of *lujayn* silver. This name is mainly popular in Jordan, Saudi Arabia, and the Gulf States.

M

Madīḥa (f.) A variant of *madīḥ* praise, commendation, or eulogy, from *madaḥa* to praise. See also MAMDŪḤ and MIDḤAT.

Maha (f.) From *maha* wild cow. Wild cows are admired for their large and beautiful eyes, hence the expression *ʿuyyūn al-maha* 'eyes of a wild cow', which is often used in Arabic literature in association with female beauty.

Maḥāsin (f.) From *maḥāsin* charms, good qualities, from *ḥasuna* to be beautiful or good. See also ḤASAN, ḤUSAYN, ḤUSNI, IḤSĀN, and MUḤSIN/MUḤSINA.

Māhir (m.) From *māhir* skilful, proficient, from *mahara* to be skilled.

Maḥmūd (m.) From *maḥmūd* praiseworthy, commendable, from *ḥamida* to praise. See also AḤMAD, ḤĀMID, ḤAMDI, and MUḤAMMAD. Maḥmūd of Ghazna (971–1030), Ghaznevid sultan (997–1030) was the first Muslim leader to conquer India. Although he was a Turk, all his battles were fought in the name of Islam and his army included Muslims of all nationalities. He is considered one of the strongest military leaders of all time, but his desecration and destruction of Hindu temples in India are thought to have sown the seeds of enmity between Muslims and Hindus, the effects of which are still evident to this day.

Majdi (m.) From *majdi* praiseworthy, laudable, from *majada* to be glorious, illustrious. See also MĀJID/MĀJIDA and AMJAD.

Variant: **Magdi**.

Mājid (m.), **Mājida** (f.) From *mājid* glorious, illustrious, from *majada* to be glorious. See also MAJDI and AMJAD.

Variants: **Māgid, Magda**.

Makram (m.) From *makram* generous, noble, from *karuma* to be noble or magnanimous. See also KARAM and KARĪM/KARĪMA.

Malak (f.) From *malak* angel.

Mamdūḥ (m.) From *mamdūḥ* praised, commended, from *madaḥa* to praise. See also MADĪḤA and MIDḤAT.

Ma'mūn (m.) From *ma'mūn* reliable, trustworthy, from *amuna* to be faithful or reliable. See also AMĪN/AMĪNA, ĀMINA and IMĀN. Al-Ma'mūn (786–833) was the seventh Abbasid caliph (813–33) and son of the famous caliph of Baghdad, Harūn al-Rashīd. In 830 Al-Ma'mūn established *Dār Al-Ḥikma* 'the House of Wisdom', an institution that promoted many scholarly activities, especially translation of Greek works into Arabic.

Manāl (m., f.) From *manāl* attainment, acquisition, from *nāla* to obtain or achieve. See also NĀ'IL/NĀ'ILA.

Manār (m., f.) From *manār* lighthouse, beacon, from *nawara* to illuminate. See also ANWAR, MUNĪR/MUNĪRA, NŪR, and NURA.

Manṣūr (m.) From *manṣūr* victorious, triumphant, from *naṣara* to render victorious, assist. See also NAṢR and NĀṢIR. Al-Manṣūr, Abu-Jaʿfar (*c.*712–75) was the second Abbasid caliph (754–75). He built the city of Baghdad (762), which then became the Abbasid capital. He is considered the real founder of the Abbasid caliphate.

Marwa (f.) From *marw/marwa*, a word denoting a fragrant plant or a shiny type of pebble used as flint. Al-Marwa is one of the two mounts in Mecca marking the spot where Hājar is thought to have run backwards and forwards in her attempt to find water for her infant son Ismāʿīl (Ishmael). The ritual of walking the distance between the mounts of Al-Safa and Al-Marwa seven times is adopted by Muslim pilgrims to this day.

Maryam (f.) The origin of this name is uncertain, but it is probably derived from a Syriac word meaning 'elevated'. It is the Arabic form of *Miriam*, the Hebrew form of *Mary*, and is common among both Christians and Muslims in the Arab world.

Masʿūd (m.) From *masʿūd* lucky, fortunate, from *saʿida* to be lucky. See also ASʿAD, MUSʿAD, SAʿD, and SAʿĪD.

Maysa (f.) Possibly a variant of *mayyas* 'to walk with a graceful, proud gait', from *mayasa* to swing from side to side, walk proudly.

Mayy (f.) An old Arabic name of uncertain meaning and origin. It is popular mainly in Jordan, Syria, and Lebanon.

Māzin (m.) Possibly a variant of *muzn* rain clouds.

Midḥat (m.) A variant of *midḥa* commendation, eulogy, from *madaḥa* to praise. See also MADĪḤA and MAMDŪḤ.

Mubārak (m.) From *mubārak* blessed, fortunate, from *bāraka* to bless.

Muḥammad (m.) From *muḥammad* praiseworthy, possessing fine qualities, from *ḥamida* to praise. This is probably the most popular name in the Islamic world. See also AḤMAD, ḤĀMID, ḤAMDI, and MAḤMŪD. Muḥammad ibn-ʿAbd-Allāh ibn-ʿAbd-al-Muṭṭalib (570–632) was the Prophet of Islam. Muslims believe that he was the last of God's inspired prophets. He was born in Mecca (in what is now Saudi Arabia) into the Beni-Hāshim clan of the Quraish tribe. Brought up as an orphan by his grandfather and then his uncle, he married Khadīja, a wealthy Meccan widow, in 595. He received his first revelation on Mount Hira at the age of forty. He gained few converts, but his teachings soon alarmed members of his tribe, who feared that the new religion would undermine the pre-eminence of Mecca as a centre of pilgrimage. In 622, following persecution by the Quraish, Muḥammad and his adherents left for Medina, where he settled until his death in 632. The Muslims, whose numbers were now steadily increasing, encountered the forces of the Quraish at Badr (624), Uhud (625), and Medina (627). In 628 they concluded the Hudaibiya Truce with the Meccans. Two years later, in 630, they marched on Mecca, where they achieved their final victory over the Quraish tribe and then set about expanding their influence throughout Arabia.

Muḥammad brought a new religion to the world, a religion that was to unite many people under its banner irrespective of race, colour, or nationality. The bases of this religion are a belief in the sole sovereignty of God (*Allāh*), a belief in Muḥammad as the Prophet of Allah, and a belief in an afterlife in which Allah punishes sinners and rewards believers. It is estimated that one-seventh of the world's population today are Muslims.

Variants: **Miḥammad**; **Mahomet** (non-Arab version).

Muhannad (m.) From *muhannad*, a word denoting a sword made of Indian steel.

Muḥayya (f.) From *muḥayya* face, countenance, from *ḥayya* to greet or salute. See also TAḤIYYA.

Muḥsin (m.), **Muḥsina** (f.) From *muḥsin* charitable, beneficent, from *aḥsana* to do right, be charitable, give alms. This is a fairly old but still popular name in most Arab countries. See also ḤASAN, ḤUSAYN, ḤUSNI, IḤSĀN, and MAḤĀSIN.

Mukhtār (m.) From *mukhtār* chosen, preferred, from *khāra* to choose. See also KHAYRAT and KHAYRI/KHAYRIYYA.

Muna (f.) From *muna* meaning 'hope' or 'object of desire', from *maniya* to desire, have hope. *Maniya* also means 'to shed blood'. See also AMĀNI and UMNIYA. *Muna* is also a variant of *Mina*, a valley near Mecca through which Muslims pass as part of the *haj* pilgrimage, so called because it is the place where sacrifice is performed during pilgrimage.

Munʿim (m.) From *munʿim* benefactor, donor, from *anʿama* to bestow. See also INʿĀM, NAʿĪM/NAʿĪMA, and NIʿMAT.

Munīr (m.), **Munīra** (f.) From *munīr* luminous, bright, shining, from *nawara* to illuminate. See also ANWAR, MANĀR, NŪR, and NURA.

Musʿad (m.) From *musʿad* lucky, favoured by fortune, from *saʿida* to be lucky. See also ASʿAD, MASʿŪD, SAʿD, and SAʿĪD.

Variant: **Misʿid**.

Muṣṭafa (m.) From *muṣṭafa* chosen, selected, from *ṣafa* to be pure or select. For Muslims, *Al-Muṣṭafa* 'the Chosen One', is an epithet of Muḥammad; for Christians, it is an epithet of St Paul. This is one of the most popular names in the Islamic world. See also ṢAFĀ', ṢAFIYYA, and ṢAFWAT. Muṣṭafa Kamāl (1881–1938) was the founder of modern Turkey. He became first president of Turkey in 1922, and came to be known as *Atatürk*, which means 'father of the Turks' in Turkish. Muṣṭafa Kamāl (1874–1908) was an Egyptian nationalist leader who led many campaigns against the British occupation of Egypt.

Muʿtaṣim (m.) From *muʿtaṣim* meaning 'adhering to (God)' or 'seeking refuge in (God)', from *ʿaṣama* to protect or defend. This is a shortened version of the earlier name *Muʿtaṣim Billāh* 'seeking refuge in God'. See also ʿĀṢIM, ʿIṢĀM, and ʿIṢMAT. Al-Muʿtaṣim Billāh (795–842) was the eighth Abbasid caliph (833–42).

Muʿtazz (m.) From *muʿtazz* proud, powerful, from *ʿazza* to be powerful. See also ʿAZZA and ʿAZĪZ/ʿAZĪZA.

N

Nabīl (m.), **Nabīla** (f.) From *nabīl* noble, honourable, from *nabula* to be noble or high-born.

Nada (f.) From *nada*, which can mean 'morning dew' or 'generosity', from *nada* to be moist with dew or to be generous. See also NADYA.

Nadīm (m.) From *nadīm* drinking companion, confidant, from *nādama* to drink with (someone).

Nādir (m.), **Nādira** (f.) From *nādir* rare, precious, from *nadara* to be rare.

Variants: **Nadra**, **Nādra** (f.).

Nadya (f.) From *nada* moist with dew, from *nada* to be moist. In a generally dry environment such as that of many Arab countries, moisture and morning dew are appreciated. See also NADA. Although *Nadya* has an Arabic interpretation, it may have been borrowed from the Russian name *Nadia*, a diminutive of *Nadezhda* 'hope'.

Nāhida (f.) From *nāhida*, denoting a young girl with swelling breasts, from *nahada* to have round swelling breasts. See also NIHĀD. This does not seem to have been used as a name during the early days of Islam.

Variant: **Nāhid**.

Nahla (f.) From *nahla* a drink of water, draught, from *nahala* to quench one's thirst: an important concept for desert-dwellers. See also NIHĀL.

Nā'il (m.), **Nā'ila** (f.) From *nā'il* attainer (of one's desires or aims), acquirer, winner, from *nāla* to attain or procure. See also MANĀL. Nā'ila was a wife of ʿUthmān ibn-ʿAffān, third 'guided' caliph. In 656 ʿUthmān was besieged in his house for forty days by a group of rebels. When they finally broke in, Nā'ila threw herself in front of her husband's body in a vain attempt to save him from their swords, and lost several of her fingers in doing so. Having failed to save her husband's life, she ran screaming to the roof to announce the murder of the caliph.

Naʿīm (m.), **Naʿīma** (f.) From *naʿīm* contented, tranquil, happy, from *naʿima* to live in comfort, be carefree. See also INʿĀM, MUNʿIM and NIʿMAT.

Najāḥ (f.) From *najāḥ* success, progress, from *najaḥa* to succeed.

Variant: **Nagāḥ**.

Najāt (f.) From *najāh* salvation, redemption, safety, or escape (from danger), from *naja* to be rescued, escape from danger. See also NĀJI.

Variant: **Nagāt**.

Nāji (m.) From *nāji* saved, rescued, from *naja* to escape, be saved. See also NAJĀT.

Variant: **Nāgi**.

Najīb (m.), **Najība** (f.) From *najīb* of noble descent, distinguished, high-minded, from *najuba* to be of noble birth, be distinguished. In modern Arabic, *najīb* also means 'bright, intelligent'.

Variants: **Nagīb** (m.); **Nagība** (f.).

Najlā' (f.) From *najlā'* having large and beautiful eyes.

Variants: **Naglā'**; **Nagla**.

Najwa (f.) From *najwa* meaning 'intimate confidential conversation' or 'heart-to-heart talk', from *nāja* to confide in.

Variant: **Nagwa**.

Nāṣir (m.) From *nāṣir* helper or supporter, particularly one who helps to secure victory, from *naṣara* to assist or render victorious. See also MANṢŪR and NAṢR.

Naṣr (m.) From *naṣr* victory, triumph, from *naṣara* to render victorious. See also MANṢŪR and NĀṢIR.

Nawāl (f.) From *nawāl* gift or benefit, from *nawala* to donate, bestow.

Nibāl (f.) From *nibāl* arrows.

Nihād (f.) Possibly derived from *nahd*, which can mean either 'elevated piece of ground' or 'female breasts'. *Nahd* also denotes a lion. See also NĀHIDA.

Nihāl (f.) Plural form of *nāhil* 'one whose thirst is quenched'. See also NAHLA.

Niʿmat (f.) A variant of *niʿmah* boon, favour, blessing, from *naʿima* to live in comfort or be happy. It is a shortened, more common form of the compound name *Niʿmatu-Allāh* 'Grace of God'. See also MUNʿIM, INʿĀM, and NAʿĪM/NAʿĪMA.

Nizār (m.) The meaning of this name is uncertain. It may be derived form *nazīr* to be little. Nizār Al-Qabbāni (b. 1923) is a famous contemporary Arab poet. Born in Damascus, Syria, he started his career as a diplomat. His poetry is very popular but controversial. Whether about love or politics, his verse tends to be remarkably daring and outspoken in comparison to the generally conservative environment of the Middle East. Among his most famous collections of poems is *Hawāmesh ʿAla Daftar Al-Naksah* ('Marginal Notes in the Book of Defeat'), published in 1967 following the defeat of the Arabs by Israeli forces. In this collection, he strongly criticizes the political leaders of the region and the Arab way of life as the causes of defeat.

Nuha (f.) From *nuha* mind, intellect.

Nūr (f., m.) From *nūr* light, from *nawara* to illuminate. This is one of the few names used for both sexes in Arabic. See also ANWAR, MANĀR, MUNĪR/MUNĪRA, and NURA for other names from the same root.

Nura (f.) Of uncertain origin, perhaps derived from an altered form of *nūr* light, from *nawara* to illuminate. *Nura* also means 'a characteristic'. See also ANWAR, MANĀR, and MUNĪR/MUNĪRA.

Q

Qāsim (m.) From *qāsim* 'one who divides or distributes (money or food, for instance) among his people', from *qasama* to share or divide. Muḥammad is thought to have had a son by Khadīja by the name of Qāsim, who died in infancy.

Quṣay (m.) Possibly a variant of *qaṣiy* distant, remote, from *qaṣā* to be far away. This is a very ancient Arabic name, which has been in use since pre-Islamic times. Quṣay ibn-Fihr of the Quraish tribe was the great-great-great-grandfather of the Prophet. Around 420 he married the daughter of the then chief of Mecca, who was in charge of the idol temple, or Kaʿba. Quṣay became involved in performing some of the duties related to the Kaʿba, which was the centre of pilgrimage. When his father-in-law died, Quṣay seized the guardianship of the temple for himself and proceeded to introduce a number of modernizations. He changed the Arab lunar year, which showed no set relationship between the months and seasons, by inserting a thirteenth intercalary month in every third year, thus making it possible to set the pilgrimage for the autumn season. He also organized a tribal council, built a council hall and ordered the tent-based tribes to build houses around the Kaʿba. The calendar introduced by Quṣay was later abolished by the Muslims, who reverted to the Arab lunar year.

R

Rabāb (f.) From *rabāb*, a word denoting a stringed musical instrument resembling the fiddle. The instrument is more commonly known as the *rabābah*. Rabāb (d. 681) was the wife of Ḥusayn (the grandson of the Prophet and venerated saint of the Shiites); she died one year after the massacre of Kerbelā' (680), in which her husband and her son were killed.

Raʿd (m.) From *raʿd* thunder, from *raʿada* to thunder. This name is particularly popular in Iraq.

Raḍwa (f.) From *Raḍwa*, the name of a hill in Mecca, the birthplace of the Prophet Muḥammad.

Raḍwān (m.) A variant of *riḍwān* pleasure or consent, from *raḍiya* to be satisfied or content. See also RIḌA.

Ra'fat (m.) A variant of *ra'fah* mercy, compassion, from *ra'afa* to show mercy. See also RA'ŪF.

Rafīq (m.) Either from *rafīq* companion, comrade, friend (from *rāfaqa* to accompany, be friends with) or from *rafīq* kind, gentle (from *rafaqa* to be gentle).

Variant: **Rafī'**.

Raghīd (m.), **Raghda** (f.) From *raghīd* carefree, pleasant (life), from *raghuda* to be comfortable, to enjoy a carefree life.

Rajā' (f.) From *rajā'* hope, anticipation, from *raja* to anticipate. See also RĀJYA.

Variant: **Ragā'**.

Rajab (m.) From *rajab*, the seventh month of the Arab lunar calendar and one of the four holy months during which no fighting was allowed in pre-Islamic times, from *rajaba* to glorify, treat with awe.

Variant: **Ragab**.

Rājya (f.) From the feminine form *rājya* hopeful, from *raja* to hope for or anticipate. See also RAJĀ'.

Variant: **Ragya**.

Ramaḍān (m.) From *ramaḍān*, the ninth month in the Arab calander, from *ramiḍ* very hot. Ramaḍān is the holiest month in Islam, during which Muslims fast from dawn until sunset. It is thought that when the Arabs were in the process of naming the various months of their calendar, the month of Ramaḍān happened to fall in a period of intense heat, hence the name. It is now used both as a first name and as a surname in several Arab countries.

Rana (f.) From *rana* meaning 'an eye-catching, beautiful object', from *rana* to gaze or look at. See also RANYA. This name is particularly popular in Saudi Arabia and the Gulf States.

Randa (f.) Possibly from *ranad* or *randa*, denoting a sweet-smelling tree that grows in the desert.

Ranya (f.) From *ranya*, which means 'looking or gazing at (the beloved)', from *rana* to gaze. See also RANA.

Rashād (m.) From *rashād* good sense or good guidance (especially in religious matters), from *rashada* to follow the right course. See also RASHĪD/RASHĪDA and RUSHDI.

Rashīd (m.), **Rashīda** (f.) From *rashīd* rightly guided, mature, from *rashada* to follow the right course. See also RASHĀD and RUSHDI.

Ra'ūf (m.) From *ra'ūf* merciful, compassionate, from *ra'afa* to show mercy, be gracious. *Al-Ra'ūf* 'the Compassionate' is an attribute of Allah. This name also occurs in the compound form, *'Abd-al-Ra'ūf* 'servant of the Compassionate'. See also RA'FAT.

Rāwiya (f.) From *rāwiya* narrator, transmitter (especially of ancient Arabic poetry), or storyteller, from *rawa* to relate or quote.

Variant: **Rawya**.

Riḍa (m., f.) From *riḍa* contentment, satisfaction, approval (of God), from *raḍiya* to be content. See also RAḌWĀN. This name is used for both sexes but is predominantly a male name.

Rīm (f.) From *rīm* a white antelope.

Ruqayya (f.) Most likely derived from *ruqiy* ascent, progress, or promotion, from *raqiya* to ascend or rise. It could also be related to *ruqyah*, which derives from the same root and means 'spell, charm, incantation'. Ruqayya was one of Muḥammad's daughters. She married 'Uthmān ibn-'Affān, third 'guided' caliph, and emigrated with him to Ethiopia during the early days of Islam to escape persecution. They later returned to Mecca for a short period of time before joining the Prophet on his trip to Yathrib (Medina). Ruqayya is therefore referred to as *Thāt al-Hijratayn* 'the Lady of the Two Migrations'. She died in 624, just as the Muslims won their first victory in the Battle of Badr.

Rushdi (m.) A variant of *rushd* sensible conduct, maturity (of the mind), from *rashada* to follow the right course. See also RASHĀD and RASHĪD/RASHĪDA.

S

Ṣabāḥ (f.) From *ṣabāḥ* morning, from *ṣabaḥa* to happen in the morning or to become morning. Ṣabāḥ is a contemporary Lebanese singer and actress who started her career in Egypt. She is very popular in all Arab countries, and her fame may well have contributed to the popularity of the name in recent times.

Ṣābir (m.) From *ṣābir* patient, enduring, persevering, from *ṣabara* to endure. See also ṢABRI/ṢABRIYYA.

Ṣabri (m.), **Ṣabriyya** (f.) A variant of *ṣabr* patience, endurance, from *ṣabara* to endure. See also ṢĀBIR.

Saʿd (m.) From *saʿd* good luck, fortune, from *saʿida* to be lucky or happy. See also ASʿAD, MASʿŪD, MUSʿAD and SAʿĪD. Saʿd ibn-Abi-Waqqāṣ was a cousin of the Prophet and one of the earliest converts to Islam. He became commander-in-chief of the Arab forces in Iraq during the reign of ʿUmar ibn-al-Khaṭṭāb, second 'guided' caliph, and led the Muslims to victory in the decisive Battle of Qadisiyya (637). In 639 he settled with his troops at a site near Hira, where they erected a mosque and then other buildings until the city of Kufa gradually took shape, a city that was to play a very important role in Islamic history, witnessing and provoking the emergence of the Shiite sect.

Saʿd Zaghlūl (1857–1927) was one of the leading Egyptian nationalists whose efforts are thought to have led to the eventual expulsion of the British from Egypt. He was one of the founders of the Wafd Party and was arrested by the British and sent into exile in 1919. When the 1922 treaty was concluded, giving Egypt limited independence, he was released and became prime minister of Egypt in 1924 but was forced by the British to resign shortly afterwards. The 1919 revolution, inspired by the leadership of Saʿd Zaghlūl, is considered an important landmark on the road to Egyptian independence.

Ṣafā' (f., m.) From *ṣafā'* purity, sincerity, from *ṣafa* to be pure. See also MUṢṬAFA, ṢAFIYYA, and ṢAFWAT.

Ṣafināz (f.) Most probably comes from Turkish or Persian; its meaning is obscure. In Egypt, it is strictly an upper- to middle-class type of name and is rarely, if ever, used by the working classes.

Ṣafiyya (f.) From the feminine form *ṣafiyya* confidante or bosom friend. *Ṣafiyya* also denotes the best part or lion's share of something, from *ṣafa* to be pure or select. See also MUṢṬAFA, ṢAFĀ', and ṢAFWAT.

Ṣafwat (m.) A variant of *ṣafwah* the choicest or best, from *ṣafa* to be pure or select. See also MUṢṬAFA, ṢAFĀ', and ṢAFIYYA.

Saḥar (f.) From *saḥar* early morning, dawn.

Saʿīd (m.) From *saʿīd* happy, lucky, from *saʿida* to be lucky or happy. See also ASʿAD, MASʿŪD, MUSʿAD, and SAʿD.

Ṣakhr (m.) From *ṣakhr* solid rock. This name is particularly popular in Saudi Arabia. The poetess Al-Khansā' (d. ?630), whose work was much admired by the Prophet Muḥammad and is still widely read and studied in Arab schools, had a brother by the name of Ṣakhr whom she loved dearly. When he was killed in battle she devoted much of her poetry to lamenting his death.

Ṣalāḥ (m.) From *ṣalāḥ* goodness, righteousness, from *ṣaluḥa* to be pious or good. *Ṣalāḥ* is a shorter version of the compound name *Ṣalāḥ al-Dīn* 'Righteousness of Religion' (often Anglicized as *Saladdin*). It is a very popular name throughout the Arab world. See also ṢĀLIḤ. Ṣalāḥ al-Dīn al-Ayyūbi (*c.*1137–93) was a Muslim military and political leader. He took over Egypt from the Fatimid dynasty and became sultan in 1175, founding the Ayyubite dynasty. He then extended his control over Syria and captured the kingdom of Jerusalem following his great victory over the Christian crusaders at the Battle of Hattin (1187). He also succeeded in repelling the Third Crusade (1190–2), led by Richard I of England. Ṣalāḥ Al-Dīn had a reputation among Christians for his generosity and chivalry, and he seems to have regarded Richard I as a worthy opponent. The conflict between the two leaders and their admiration for one another has been celebrated in chivalric romance.

Salāma (m.) From *salāma* safety, well-being, from *salima* to be unharmed. See also SALĪM, SĀLIM, and SALMA.

Ṣāliḥ (m.), **Ṣālḥa** (f.) From *ṣāliḥ* virtuous, devout, from *ṣaluḥa* to be righteous. See also ṢALĀḤ. According to Islamic tradition, Ṣāliḥ was a prophet sent to the people of Thammud to call them to God's worship. They refused to believe him and asked him to prove that he was a messenger of God by producing a big, red-skinned, black-eyed she-camel capable of providing enough milk for the whole village. This Ṣāliḥ is said to have done. He advised his people to look after the camel as, if it were to come to any harm, God would destroy the whole village. Some of the people who did not believe in Ṣāliḥ conspired to kill the camel to prove him a liar. They did this and the village was struck by an earthquake: only Ṣāliḥ and a small number of believers were saved.

Salīm (m.) From *salīm* safe, sound, from *salima* to be unharmed. See also SALĀMA, SĀLIM, and SALMA.

Variant: **Selīm**.

Sālim (m.) From *sālim* secure, safe, from *salima* to be unharmed. See also SALĀMA, SALĪM, and SALMA.

Salma (f.) Possibly a variant of *sālima* safe, unhurt, from *salima* to be unharmed. This is an old Arabic name, which has been in use since pre-Islamic times. See also SALĀMA, SALĪM, and SĀLIM.

Salwa (f.) From *salwa* consolation, solace, from *sala* to help forget, comfort, distract. This name is particularly popular in Egypt.

Samar (f.) From *samar* 'intimate night talk', from *samara* to chat in the evening or at night. See also SAMĪR/SAMĪRA.

Sāmi (m.), **Samya** (f.) From *sāmi* elevated, sublime, from *sama* to rise high, be elevated.

Samīḥ (m.), **Samīḥa** (f.) From *samīḥ*, *sāmiḥ* generous, tolerant, magnanimous, from *samuḥa* to forgive, be tolerant of.

Variant: **Sāmiḥ** (m.)

Samīr (m.), **Samīra** (f.) From *samīr*, *sāmir* 'companion in nightly talk, one who entertains with lively conversation at night', from *samara* to chat in the evening or at night. See also SAMAR.

Variant: **Sāmir** (m.)

Sanā' (f.) From *sanā'* brilliance, radiance, from *sana* to gleam or shine. See also SANIYYA and THANĀ'.

Saniyya (f.) From *saniyya* radiant, resplendent, brilliant, from *sana* to gleam or shine. See also SANĀ'.

Sāra (f.) Arabic form of *Sarah* (see main dictionary), common in most Arab countries, especially Saudi Arabia and the Gulf States. Sāra was the wife of the patriarch Abraham and the mother of Isaac.

Sarāb (f.) From *sarāb* mirage, from *sariba* to flow, escape, steal away.

Sawsan (f.) From *sawsan* lily of the valley.

Sayyid (m.) From *sayyid* master, lord, from *sāda* to rule, prevail. *Sayyidi*, or *sīdi* in colloquial usage, i.e. 'my lord', is an honorific title used before the names of Muslim saints. Sayyid Darwīsh (1893–1923) was an Egyptian composer and singer. Many of his songs expressed the suffering and hardship of the working classes under British rule. His most famous song, *Bilādi, Bilādi* ('My Country, My Country'), has been repeatedly used by Egyptian patriots in demonstrations against British rule, against the Egyptian monarchy before 1952, and even against the Sadāt regime as recently as 1972–3. It has also been adopted as the national anthem of Egypt. Sayyid Darwīsh is regarded as the undisputed leader of the modern Egyptian musical renaissance.

Sha'bān (m.) From *sha'bān*, the eighth month of the Muslim calender.

Shādi (m.), **Shadya** (f.) From *shādi* singer, from *shada* to sing. Shadya is a well-known contemporary Egyptian singer and actress.

Shafīq (m.), **Shafīqa** (f.) From *shafīq* compassionate, sympathetic, from *shafaqa* to sympathize or pity.
Variant: **Shafī'**; **Shafī'a**.

Shahīra (f.) From *shahīra* renowned, famous, from *shuhira* to be or become well-known.

Shahrazād (f.) A borrowing from Persian *shahr* meaning 'city' and *zād* meaning 'person'. The story of Shahrazād (Sheherazade) is told in the *Thousand and One Nights*. Having been betrayed by his wife and having seen his brother suffer from the same predicament, King Shahrayār marries a virgin every night and has her beheaded before dawn. After a period of three years, his vizier fails to find him any more virgins, but the vizier's daughter, Shahrazād, begs her father to give her to the king in marriage so that she can put an end to these murders. She then proceeds to relate an enthralling story to the king every night, for a thousand and one nights, thus lulling him to sleep before he can give the order to behead her. The story goes that the king eventually falls in love with Shahrazād and they live happily ever after.
Variant: **Shahrizād**.

Shākir (m.) From *shākir* thankful, grateful, from *shakara* to thank. See also SHUKRI/SHUKRIYYA.

Sharīf (m.), **Sharīfa** (f.) From *sharīf* eminent, honourable, virtuous, from *sharafa* to be high-bred or distinguished. See also ASHRAF. *Sharīf* is the title given to the descendants of the Prophet Muḥammad. In Ottoman times, it used to be the title of the governor of Mecca.
Variant: **Sherīf**; **Sherīfa**.

Shatha (f.) From *shatha* fragrance, perfume.

Shukri (m.), **Shukriyya** (f.) From *shukri* of thanks, thanking, from *shakara* to thank. See also SHĀKIR. Shukri Al-Quwaṭli (1891–1967) was a Syrian nationalist leader and became president of Syria (1943–9, 1955–8). He formed the United Arab Republic (Syria and Egypt) with Nāṣir (Nasser) in 1958.

Sihām (f.) From *sihām* arrows, from *sahama* to cast or draw.

Sonya (f.) Russian form of *Sophia*, which has become popular in some Arab countries, particularly in Egypt. The presence of a fairly large Armenian community in Egypt may help to account for the popularity of the name there.

Su'ād (f.) Of unknown meaning and origin. It may be a variant of *sa'āda* happiness.

Suha (f.) From *suha* a star. It may also be a variant of *sahw* absent-mindedness, distractedness, from *saha* to forget or be inattentive.

Suhād (f.) From *suhād* sleeplessness, from *sahida* to find no sleep.

Suhair (f.) Possibly a variant of *suhar* meaning sleeplessness, from *sahira* to find no sleep.

Suhayl (m.) From *suhayl*, which refers to the star known in English as Canopus. This name is particularly popular in the Levant. Suhayl ibn-'Amr, a Meccan noted as an orator and persuasive diplomat, was chosen by the Quraish tribe to negotiate the Hudaibiya Truce with the Prophet Muḥammad, when the Muslims marched on Mecca in February 628. The Muslims agreed to observe a ten-year truce, during which they were allowed to visit Mecca for pilgrimage and form alliances with tribes but were bound to send back any Meccans who attempted to join them. As the truce was concluded, Suhayl's son arrived, expressing his wish to join the Muslims. However, bound by the new agreement, the Muslims had no alternative but to send him back to Mecca.
Variant: **Suhail**.

Sulaymān (m.) Arabic form of *Solomon*. Sulaymān (*c.*961–922 BC), the Israelite king celebrated for his honesty and fairness, built the great temple in Jerusalem.

His reign marked a time of great prosperity in Palestine, due to his control over rich trade routes and copper mines. According to Arab tradition, Sulaymān was gifted with a special talent that enabled him to converse with birds and animals.
Variants: **Silimān, Suleimān.**

Surayya (f.) Variant of THURAYYA.

T

Taghrīd (f.) From *taghrīd* meaning 'the singing or warbling of birds'; from *gharada* to sing or warble.

Ṭāha (m.) The Arabic letters *ṭ*, pronounced 'ṭa', and *h*, pronounced 'ha', which form this name, are the opening letters of the twentieth sura in the Koran. In some Arab countries, *Ṭāha* is used to refer to the Prophet Muḥammad.

Ṭāhir (m.) From *ṭāhir* pure, virtuous, chaste, from *ṭahura* to be pure, clean.

Taḥiyya (f.) From *taḥiyya* greeting, salutation, from *ḥayya* to greet. See also MUḤAYYA.

Ṭalāl (m.) Derives from *ṭalla*, a root rich in meanings, one of which is 'dew, fine rain'. It may also be a variant of *ṭalālah* meaning 'joy, rejoicing' as well as 'good looks'. This name is particularly popular in Saudi Arabia.

Tāmir (m.) From *tāmir* meaning 'possessor of many dates'. Dates, *tamr*, at one time used to be the staple diet of Arabs. *Tāmir* would therefore also imply being rich or well off.

Ṭāriq (m.) From *ṭāriq* one who knocks at the door, a nocturnal visitor, from *ṭaraqa* to knock or to come by night. *Ṭāriq* is also the name of the morning star. Ṭāriq ibn-Ziyād (d. ?720), one of the most outstanding military leaders in the history of Islam, was the Berber leader responsible for the invasion and rapid conquest of Spain. In the spring of 711, he crossed the straits and landed in Spain near the mountain that bears his name to this day, *Jabal-Ṭāriq* (i.e. Gibraltar).
Variant: **Ṭāri'**.

Ṭarūb (f.) From *ṭarūb* enraptured, merry, from *ṭariba* to be moved with the joy of music or to be delighted.

Tawfīq (m.) From *tawfīq* good fortune, prosperity, from *wafiqa* to be successful or lucky. Tawfīq Al-Ḥakīm (1898–1987) was an eminent Egyptian playwright and author.
Variant: **Tawfī'**.

Thanā' (f.) From *thanā'* praise, commendation, from *athna* to praise. Although this is often pronounced identically with SANĀ', it is an independent name in its own right.

Thheiba (f.) From a variant of the diminutive *thuhayba* a small bar of gold, from *thahab* gold. It is a particularly common name in Jordan.

Thurayya (f.) From *thurayya* the Pleiades, the seven visible stars in the neck of the constellation Taurus, so called because there are many of them within a small area, from *thariya* to be abundant.
Variant: **Surayya.**

U

'Umar (Omar) (m.) A variant of *'āmir* populous, flourishing, from *'amara* to thrive, prosper, or live long. This is one of the most popular names throughout the Islamic world. See also 'AMR, 'ĀMIR, and 'AMMĀR. 'Umar ibn-al-Khaṭṭāb (*c.*581–644), second 'guided' caliph (634–44), became one of the strongest supporters of the Prophet Muḥammad following his conversion to Islam in 618. An able and just ruler, 'Umar is considered by many to be the founder of the Muslim state, having laid the administrative base of the empire during his period of office. In spite of the great military conquests and vast expansion of the Muslim Empire during his caliphate, ʿUmar remained simply clad and extremely frugal in his own house. During the drought in 639, he set an example to other Muslims by refusing to have anything but the most meagre diet, such as was available to the poorest of his subjects. ʿUmar was stabbed to death in Medina by a foreign slave in 644.

ʿUmar Al-Khayyam (*c.*1048–*c.*1122), the famous Persian poet born in Nishapur, was also an accomplished astronomer and mathematician. His most famous work is the *Rubaiyat*, a long poem written in quatrains. It was translated into English by Edward Fitzgerald in 1859, and enjoyed great popularity throughout the English-speaking world.

'Umayma (f.) Diminutive of *'umm* mother, i.e. 'little mother'. This is an old Arabic name, which has been in use since pre-Islamic times. One of the Prophet's aunts was called 'Umayma.

'Um-Kalthūm (f.) Compound name consisting of *'um* mother (of) + *kalthūm* 'one who has plump cheeks'. 'Um-Kalthūm (d. 630) was one of the Prophet's daughters. She married ʿUthmān ibn-ʿAffān, third 'guided' caliph.

Variant: **'Um-Kalsūm**.

'Umniya (f.) From *'umniya* wish, desire, from *mana* to desire, wish for, or find by good luck. See also AMĀNI and MUNA.

'Usāma (m.) From *'usāma*, a nickname for the lion. 'Usāma ibn-Munqiz (1095–1188) was an Arab prince and poet. He led several campaigns against the crusaders. His memoirs provide a fascinating and detailed picture of life in 12th-century Palestine.

ʿUsmān (m.) Turkish form of ʿUTHMĀN, common in Egypt.

ʿUthmān (m.) From *ʿuthmān* a baby bustard (a bird similar to the crane). This name is popular throughout the Islamic world. It was originally bestowed in honour of ʿUthmān ibn-ʿAffān (*c.*574–656), third 'guided' caliph (644–56) and one of the earliest converts to Islam. He married Ruqayya, Muḥammad's daughter, and when she died he married her sister, thus becoming twice over the Prophet's son-in-law. Muḥammad was often heard praising ʿUthmān for his generosity and loyalty; perhaps the highest praise of all was the remark that 'even the angels stood abashed before ʿUthmān'. ʿUthmān was called to the caliphate at the age of seventy. Once caliph, he fell under the control of his clan of rich Meccan merchants, who usurped for themselves the highest imperial posts. This gave rise to much protest, and in June 656, after a siege of his house lasting forty days, he was murdered by a group of rebels. The murder of ʿUthmān is considered a turning point in the history of Islam: the assassination of a caliph by rebellious Muslims seriously weakened the religious and moral authority of the office as a bond uniting the Islamic community. In recent history the name has come to be associated with the Ottoman Empire, which ruled almost the whole Arabic-speaking world from 1517 until the 20th century.

Variant: **ʿUsmān**.

W

Wafā' (f.) From *wafā'* loyalty, fidelity, from *wafa* to fulfil or live up to (a promise).

Wahīb (m.), **Wahība** (f.) From *wahīb* donor, generous giver, from *wahaba* to give. See also HIBA and IHĀB. *Al-Wahīb* 'the Giver' is an epithet of Allah.

Wā'il (m.) From *wā'il* one who reverts back to God, from *wa'ala* to revert. Wā'il was the name of a famous Arab tribe, Wā'il ibn-Qasit. It is now popular as a first name in most Arab countries.

Wajīh (m.) From *wajīh* distinguished, notable, from *wajuha* to be a man of distinction.

Variant: **Wagīh.**

Walīd (m.) From *walīd* a newborn baby, from *walada* to give birth. Al-Walīd ibn-ʿAbd-al-Malik (d. 715) was the Umayyad caliph (705–15) during whose reign the glory of Arab military conquests reached its pinnacle. His armies conquered Spain and made an ambitious attempt to conquer Constantinople. In spite of the eventual failure of this attempt, the Arabs, under Walīd I, became the strongest military force in the world.

Wasīm (m.) From *wasīm* handsome, graceful, good-looking, from *wasama* to distinguish or mark.

Widād (f.) From *widād* affection, friendship, from *wadda* to love, be fond of.

Y

Yaḥya (m.) Arabic form of *John*, common in most Arab countries but particularly popular in Egypt. Yaḥya (John the Baptist), the son of Zacharias, was the cousin of Jesus Christ.

Variant: **Yiḥya.**

Yasīn (m.) The Arabic letters *y*, pronounced 'yā', and *s*, pronounced 'sīn', which form this name, are the opening letters of the thirty-sixth sura of the Koran. According to Egyptian tradition, the story of Yasīn and Bahiyya took place in a small village in Upper Egypt during the early part of the 20th century. They were engaged to be married when the pasha, the feudal lord of the village, sent for Bahiyya to be brought to his house, a gesture that endangered her honour and angered her lover, Yasīn. The details of the story are rather vague, but it is thought that Yasīn organized a rebellion against the pasha. During the ensuing struggle, the pasha's house was burnt and Yasīn was killed. The story of the two lovers has been told on stage, in songs, and in various other art forms. It is cited as an example of the social injustice and oppression which were prevalent in Egypt prior to the 1952 revolution.

Yāsir (m.) From *yāsir* to be rich or be easy, from *yasira* to make easy, facilitate. See also Yusra and Yusri/Yusriyya. Yāsir ʿArafāt (b. 1929) is the leader of the PLO (Palestine Liberation Organization) and of its major component, Al-Fatḥ. He was born in Jerusalem and was educated in Cairo. He became president of the League of Palestinian Students (1952–6), formed Al-Fatḥ in 1956, and has been its president since 1968.

Yasmīn (f.) From *yasmīn* jasmine, a sweet-smelling bush that bears small white flowers.

Variant: **Yasmīna** (singular form of the noun).

Yusra (f.) From *yusra* prosperity, affluence, ease, from *aysara* to be or become rich or lucky. See also Yāsir and Yusri/Yusriyya.

Yusri (m.), **Yusriyya** (f.) Possibly a variant of *yāsir* prosperous, well-off, from *yasira* to make easy, facilitate. See also Yāsir and Yusra.

Yūsuf (m.) Arabic form of *Joseph*, popular in most Arab countries.

Variant: **Yūsif.**

Z

Zāhir (m.) From *zāhir* shining, radiant, flourishing, from *zahara* to shine or blossom. See also Zahra and Zuhayr.

Zahra (f.) From *zahra* flower, blossom, from *zahara* to shine or blossom. See also Zāhir and Zuhayr. Zahra was the family name of the Prophet's mother. There is some dispute among early Arab historians as to whether this was originally a male or female name. Some say it was a female name adopted as a family name, while others maintain that it was the name of the Prophet's grandfather, adopted by his mother. In any case, it is now an exclusively female name and is widely used in many parts of the Arab world.

Variant: **Zuhra**.

Zaki (m.), **Zakiyya** (f.) From *zakiy* pure, virtuous, chaste, from *zaka* to be pure or righteous. It may also be a variant of *thakiy* intelligent. The sound /ð/ (transcribed into English as *th*) is often altered to /z/, particularly in Egyptian Arabic.

Zayd (m.) Possibly derived from *zāda* to become greater, increase. This is an old Arabic name, which was common before the rise of Islam and is still widely used by Arabs today. See also Ziyād. Zayd ibn-Ḥāritha (d. 629) was a slave of Khadīja's, Muḥammad's first wife. He had been kidnapped by bandits as a child and sold in Mecca. As Muḥammad became increasingly attached to him, Khadīja gave Zayd to him as his personal slave. Soon afterwards, Zayd's father arrived in Mecca looking for his son. It is alleged that Muḥammad gave the youth a choice between leaving with his father or staying with him. Zayd chose to stay with the Prophet, who immediately freed him from slavery and adopted him as his son. Zayd later became one of the earliest converts to Islam and strongest supporters of Muḥammad. He was killed by Byzantine forces in the Battle of Mota (629).

Variant: **Zaid**.

Zaynab (f.) Possibly from *zaynab*, the name of a beautiful, fragrant plant. This is one of the most popular names in the Arab world, perhaps because it featured several times in the life of the Prophet Muḥammad. The first Zaynab in his life was his daughter by Khadīja. The second was Zaynab bint-Khuzayma, who married the Prophet in 625 but died a few months later. She was reputed to be charitable and pious. The third was Zaynab bint-Jaḥsh, cousin of the Prophet. Muḥammad married her after his adopted son, Zayd ibn-Ḥāritha, agreed to divorce her. The Prophet was granted special permission (by Koranic verse) to marry her, a fact that delighted Zaynab, as it set her apart from his other wives, God himself having blessed the marriage.

The last Zaynab in Muḥammad's life, and the most revered by Muslims, was his granddaughter by Fāṭima, the sister of Al-Ḥusayn (the third imam of the Shiites). She witnessed the massacre of Kerbelā' (680), in which her brother and many of her relatives were killed. Following the massacre, she was forced by the Umayyads (the ruling family responsible for the massacre) to go to Egypt, where she died approximately eighteen months later. Many historians claim that it was largely due to her efforts that the murder of the Prophet's grandson was not forgotten. Her courage in speaking out against the Umayyads and calling for revenge seem to have been instrumental in eventually bringing down their regime. She is known to Muslims as *Al-Sayyida Zaynab*. Al-Sayyida Zaynab district in Cairo, and the mosque that bears her name, are the centre of annual Muslim rituals commemorating her death.

Variant: **Zainab**.

Ziyād (m.) Possibly a shortened form of *ziyāda* increase, growth, from *zāda* to increase. See also Zayd.

Zuhayr (m.) Diminutive of *zahr* flowers, blossoms, from *zahara* to shine or blossom. See also Zahra and Zāhir. Zuhayr ibn-Abi-Sulma (*c.*520–609) was a well-known pre-Islamic poet. His poetry is still widely read and taught in most Arab schools.

Variant: **Zuhair**.

SUPPLEMENT 2

COMMON NAMES OF THE INDIAN SUBCONTINENT

INTRODUCTION

PRINCIPLES

The naming of a child is as important in the Indian subcontinent as elsewhere, and the principles by which a name is chosen are often similar to those in other cultures, though the specific reasons given for the choice may differ. Thus children are often named after ancestors, especially grandparents, but among Hindus in particular the motive for this is often the belief in reincarnation or rebirth: the children are their ancestors reborn. The normal household in the subcontinent usually consists of an extended family unit, and the sense of family identity is often strengthened by giving a child a similar name to its father, mother, brother or sister (for example, a name with the same prefix or suffix, or, among Hindus, a different name of the same god or goddess).

The main source of personal names in the subcontinent is religion, and variations in the popularity and forms of a particular name are usually caused by regional and language differences. However, place-names, names of professions, and ordinary vocabulary words, such as names of plants and animals and words denoting qualities, are also often used as personal names. Children are given names with positive connotations, such as names of deities or names derived from words for good qualities, in the belief that this will encourage them to try to live up to them.

The names of deities are especially popular among Hindus because of the widespread belief in the non-dual or monist view of life: we are all parts or manifestations of the divine. Also, by giving a child the name of a deity, we are in a way praying every time we call the child. The eternity of sound is an ancient doctrine, and even the individual syllables of a deity's name or the written characters representing them are considered powerful enough to invoke the totality.

LANGUAGES

Of the principal language groups represented in the subcontinent, by far the largest is the Indo-European group, of which the oldest language for which records survive is Sanskrit. The main modern languages in this group are all ultimately derived from Sanskrit: they include Hindi, Gujarati, Punjabi, Bengali, and Marathi. These are spoken in northern and central parts of the subcontinent by over 500 million people or about 70 per cent of the population as a whole. Bengali is the main language of Bangladesh. Sinhalese, spoken in Sri Lanka, also derives from Sanskrit and belongs to this group.

The Dravidian languages—Tamil, Telugu, Kannada, and Malayalam—are spoken only in southern India, by over 100 million or 20–25 per cent. Tamil is also spoken in Sri Lanka. However, even among speakers of Dravidian languages, many personal names tend to be of Sanskrit origin because of the influence of Hinduism. Conversely, virtually no names of Dravidian origin are established widely in the subcontinent: for this reason, no names of Dravidian origin are included here.

The main language of Pakistan, Urdu, is also spoken by many people in north-west India, especially by Muslims. Urdu is very similar to Hindi and is therefore primarily an Indo-European language derived from Sanskrit, but it has a high proportion of Arabic and Persian loan-words (Persian belongs to the Indo-Iranian branch of the Indo-European group). The fact that it is written in Arabic script shows the strong Islamic influence.

Most of the Islamic names used in the subcontinent are derived from Arabic. The most frequent of these are included here, in their normal Roman-alphabet spelling or spellings, usually in the form of a cross-reference to Supplement 1, 'Common Names in the Arab World'. There are also a few names common among Muslims that are of non-Arabic origin, especially those derived from Persian: these are explained in full here.

SPELLING VARIATIONS, REGIONAL VARIATIONS, AND COMPOUND NAMES

Most of the languages of the subcontinent have their own scripts, and there is no standard system of transliterating these into Roman script, except among academics. For this reason, in everyday usage names from the subcontinent are rendered into English in a variety of forms, largely according to the preference of the individual concerned. For example, *Sita* is also written *Seeta* or *Seetha*. Only the most important spelling variations can be shown in the selection of names presented here.

The standard academic transliteration is used for Sanskrit words cited as etymons, and this involves the use of a small set of diacritics: length marks distinguish the long vowels *ā, ī, ū* from their short counterparts; *ṛ* denotes Sanskrit vocalic *r* as distinct from consonantal *r*; *ṅ* and *ñ* stand for velar *n* and palatal *n* respectively; *ṭ, ḍ, ṇ* and *ṣ* mark the retroflex consonants; *ś* represents palatal *s*; *ḥ* denotes a final aspirate and *ṃ* the homorganic nasal. In addition, *kh, gh, ch, jh, ṭh, ḍh, th, dh, ph* and *bh* distinguish the aspirated consonants from their unaspirated counterparts. The transliteration for Arabic etymons is the same as in Supplement 1. For etymons from Persian or Urdu, three extra diacritics have been used for *k͟h*, *g͟h*, and *s͟h*.

Names also acquire different forms as a result of differences in regional pronunciation or by moving from an Indo-European language area to a Dravidian one. Hence the Sanskrit name *devadāna* 'gift of the gods' is usually written *Devdan* in the north but sometimes *Deodan*, and is normally written *Debdan* in Bengali-speaking areas. Similarly, the Sanskrit name *kṛṣṇa* is usually written *Krishna*, but also occurs as *Kishen* (north), *Kistna* (central), and *Kannan* (south).

Some general statements can be made about these regional variations. In the north, the final *-a* of a Sanskrit element in a name is usually omitted (e.g. Sanskrit *rāja* 'king' becomes *Raj*), whereas in the south the *-a* is not only retained but often strengthened by the addition of an *-n* or *-m* (e.g. Sanskrit *rāja* usually becomes *Rajan* or *Rajam*). In eastern areas, especially in Bengal, an *a* in a Sanskrit name is usually written *o*, a *v* becomes a *b* (e.g. the Bengali name *Aurobindo* is from Sanskrit *aravinda*; see *Arvind*), and a Sanskrit *ṣ* is often rendered *sh*. A Sanskrit *j* can become *y* (cf. Sanskrit *rāja* and the modern form *Ray*), and *kṣ* can be written as *x* (cf. *Lakshmi* and *Laxmi*). A final *-ra* in Sanskrit commonly becomes *-er* in many parts of the subcontinent (compare *Chandra* and *Chander*, *Indra* and *-inder* at the end of compound names such as *Jitinder*).

The tendency towards compound words in classical Sanskrit, emphasized in the creation of numerous compound epithets for deities during the Bhakti, or devotional, period of medieval Hinduism, remains evident in modern times in the popularity of compound names, especially in southern India. However, these compound names are often written as separate words, e.g. *Ram Gopal* for *Ramgopal*.

PERSONAL NAMES AND OTHER NAMES

Most people in the subcontinent typically bear several names: for example a personal name, a patronymic, a village name, a caste name, and so on. These occur in a different order in different parts of the subcontinent. Care is therefore needed in deciding which of an individual's names is the personal name. Many names refer to the bearer's religious or sectarian affiliations, geographical origins, profession, or honorific titles granted to his or her family for religious or secular achievements, etc. For example, a male Sikh will usually have three names: the first of them is the personal name, the second—usually *Singh*—represents his Sikh identity, and the third denotes his clan or sub-sect. The third name of female Sikhs, however, is often *Kaur*, which merely informs us that she is female. In southern India many people, males and females alike, still observe the tradition of having three names, which represent the name of their village, their father's name, and their personal name, in that order. As many families in the subcontinent and abroad gradually convert to the Western tradition of personal name and family surname, different strategies are adopted and often confuse matters further.

RELIGIONS OF THE SUBCONTINENT

Hinduism

The main source of personal names in the subcontinent is religion. Within each religious tradition names are given not only at birth but at various stages in a person's life, for example to mark rites of passage or the performance of a particular ceremony or pilgrimage. The predominant religion is Hinduism, which is a complex and varied mixture of ideas and practices that have been developed over many centuries. The main historical phases of the Hindu religion may be summarized by reference to the chief texts of each phase, which were written mainly in Sanskrit until the medieval period. These phases may be summarized as follows: the Vedic period (up to *c.*800 BC), the late Vedic period (*c.*800–*c.*400 BC), the epic period (*c.*300 BC–*c.* AD 300), the classical period (*c.* AD 100–*c.*800), the Puranic period (*c.* AD 500–*c.*1000), and the medieval period (*c.*1000–*c.*1600).

The Vedic period

The main text of the Vedic period (up to *c.*800 BC) is the Rig-Veda (from Sanskrit *ṛk* a type of verse + *veda* knowledge). This is a collection of hymns in an old form of Sanskrit. Some of these hymns were probably composed by nomadic Aryan tribes towards the end of the

2nd millenium BC, before they arrived in the subcontinent and settled there. It is thought likely that they brought with them the concepts of the sacred fire; solar, elemental and ethical deities such as Indra, Agni, Rudra, Varuna, Vishnu, and Mitra; and large-scale public rituals involving the use of the intoxicating plant soma. They probably introduced the horse into the subcontinent as well, and it too was the focus of a major rite. The names of many of the deities of the Rig-Veda are still in use as personal names today, for example *Saraswati* and *Vishnu*, and many vocabulary words from this period later became used as personal names (e.g. *Arun*, *Jyoti*, *Madhu*, *Mani*, *Tarun*, and *Uttam*).

After the Aryans had settled in the north-west of the subcontinent, their priests increased in importance at the expense of their tribal chiefs. The priests gathered together the Rig-Vedic hymns (around 800 BC), developed domestic rituals, and established the caste system, which helped them to maintain their position. The Yajur-Veda uses mainly Rig-Vedic material to elaborate on the public rituals, and the Sama-Veda recasts the material for chanting purposes.

The late Vedic period

In the late Vedic period (*c.*800–*c.*400 BC) Hinduism gradually assimilated beliefs and customs now thought to be of non-Aryan origin, such as the worship of the supreme deity in female form; the sacredness of particular places, rivers, and trees; the use of the phallic symbol and idols in temples; and various ascetic and magical practices such as yoga. The Atharva-Veda incorporates many of these. Modern Hindu names probably having their sources in the Atharva-Veda include *Anuradha*, *Kishore*, *Nanda*, *Samant*, and *Sharada*.

The Brahmana texts (*c.*600 BC) seek to explain the public and domestic Vedic rituals in metaphysical terms, and the Upanishads (500 BC) emphasize and expand on their philosophical aspects. One of the central features of Hinduism of this period is the concept of karma, the natural law by which a person's deeds are responsible for his or her subsequent destiny, including his or her rebirth in further lives. This is an elaboration of the cyclical conception of the universe which is found from the Rig-Veda onwards. The goal of religion is seen as escape from this cycle of rebirth, and various new methods are developed, such as philosophical investigation, meditation, physical yoga, good works, and devotion to a particular god, although the power of Vedic rituals is never denied. Modern Hindu names such as *Bala*, *Madhav*, and *Vinayak* probably have their origin in the Brahmanas, and *Om* and *Prasad* in the Upanishads.

Also compiled during this period, sutras are texts dealing with specific areas of knowledge such as astrology, medicine, and language, and include Panini's famous grammar of *c.*400 BC.

The epic period

The epic period (*c.*300 BC–*c.* AD 300) is dominated by the compilation of the Hindu epics, the *Mahabharata* and the *Ramayana*, although the core stories probably have their origin in much earlier times.

The *Mahabharata* is the older, probably compiled *c.*300 BC. Primarily, it tells the story of a war between two closely related royal families, the Pandavas and the Kauravas. However, it also includes various myths about Hindu divinities. Modern names such as *Baldev*, *Damodar*, *Karan*, and *Sanjay* have their origins in the *Mahabharata*.

Within the *Mahabharata* is found the famous religious text called the *Bhagavad Gita*, which is probably a later interpolation. In it Krishna reveals himself as the godhead incarnate to Prince Arjuna. Because of the continuing popularity of the text, the names *Krishna* (with its numerous variants) and *Arjun* are among the most frequently occurring names among Hindus in modern times.

The central story of the *Ramayana* (probably compiled in about the 1st century AD) concerns Prince Rama's exile, the abduction of his wife Sita by a demon king, and Rama's rescue of her, but it also includes much material extraneous to this plot. Many modern Hindu names are primarily connected with characters from the *Ramayana*, especially *Rama*, *Sita*, *Janaki*, and *Lakshman*.

The classical period

The classical period (AD *c.*100–*c.*800) includes numerous works of prose, poetry, and drama, as well as some Buddhist texts. Kalidasa is considered to be the greatest author in this period. Classical works deal extensively with secular themes for the first time in Sanskrit literature. Modern Hindu names particularly associated with this period include *Kalidas*, *Shakuntala*, *Raghu*, and *Vikram*. Many vocabulary words from this period also gave rise to personal names, for example *Dipak*, *Kamal*, *Madhukar*, *Malati*, *Pravin*, *Saroja*, and *Vinod*.

Religious texts continued to be compiled in the classical period. Gradually, they began to transcend the traditional schools of religious practice and address themselves to the entire Hindu community: *śāstra* texts codify rules of behaviour for daily life. The most famous of these is the text compiled by Manu in the early centuries AD.

Many modern Hindus still follow in essence the rules laid down by Manu for caste names: 'Brahmins (the priestly caste) should bear auspicious names that connote spiritual prosperity; Ksatriyas' (warriors') names should be full of power and connote safeguard; the names of Vaisyas (merchants) should imply wealth; and those of Sudras (peasants and labourers) should denote servitude.' Thus *Kalyan* 'beautiful or auspicious' would be a good choice for a Brahmin child, *Ajit* 'invincible' for a Ksatriya, *Shripati* 'lord of fortune' for a Vaisya, and a name ending in *-dās* 'servant' for a Sudra. The recommendations for women's names, which are not subject to caste in Manu's rules, are that they should be 'pleasant-sounding, plain in meaning, auspicious, and end in long vowels so that they sound like benedictions' (see, for example, *Asha*, *Radha*, and *Shanta*).

The Puranic period

The Puranic period (AD *c.*500–*c.*1000) laid the basis for medieval Hinduism in the form of numerous texts called Puranas. They include retellings of myths and legends from the Vedas and epics and information on religious practices and daily life. In particular, they serve to accentuate the sectarian divisions between the worshippers of Vishnu and those of Shiva, already evident in the epics. The Puranas and the slightly later Tantric texts also establish a major role for the worship of goddesses in Hinduism. It is this period that is particularly fertile as a source of modern Hindu female names such as *Sushila*, *Shyama*, *Shakti*, *Parvati*, *Mohini*, *Meena*, and *Kanti*. Interspersed in the Puranic texts are accounts of historical events and lists of kings.

The medieval period

In the medieval period (*c.*1000–*c.*1600) Hindu texts gradually came to be written in vernacular languages as well as Sanskrit. They include a wide variety of material, much of it derived from earlier periods. Earlier works were gathered together, and extracts from them were grouped under subject headings in vast compendia. The practice of accumulating epithets and names of the gods, evident from the Rig-Veda onwards, reached its apogee in works called *Namastotras*, hymns consisting entirely of the names of a particular deity, which are recited as a devotional practice. Many modern compound names can be traced back to such works.

The Bhakti, or devotional, movement gave rise to a great deal of fresh religious material such as the *Gita Govinda*, which tells of the love of the god Krishna and his mistress Radha. This material served to bring names of minor importance in earlier periods into greater prominence. The Bhakti movement also did much to reduce the importance of caste, although it heightened sectarian identity. Modern names that can be traced back to this period probably include *Devdan*, *Harish*, *Jayakrishna*, *Nataraj*, *Raghuvir*, *Ramakrishna*, *Ramnarayan*, *Sriram*, *Umashankar*, and *Vishwanath*, all of which are compounds, and most of which reflect their sectarian origins.

Buddhism

Two major reform movements arose around the middle of the 1st millenium BC, rejecting the prevailing Hindu systems of theism, caste, and ritual, and advocating instead atheism, egalitarianism, non-violence, and morality. These later developed into the distinct religions of Buddhism and Jainism.

The Buddha was born a Hindu prince, probably in the late 6th century BC, but rapid disillusionment in childhood led him to embark on an ascetic and errant life. He engaged in philosophic disputes with various Hindu and non-Hindu religious teachers but, gaining little satisfaction from them, he eventually sought and achieved enlightenment in solitude at Gaya, near Benares. His main teachings were later codified in the Pali language. Pali was a vernacular language derived from Sanskrit and was deliberately used so that ordinary people could understand the Buddha's teachings, which form the basis of all schools of Buddhism. In modern times early epithets of the Buddha such as *siddhārtha* 'one who has achieved the goal (of enlightenment)' and *amitābha* 'of immeasurable splendour' (see *Siddhartha* and *Amitabh*), are fairly commonly used as personal names. The same is true of his personal or clan name *Gautama* (see *Gautam*). Other epithets such as *jayavardhana* 'promoting (the) victory (of Buddhism)' and *vikramasiṃha* 'a lion in valour' (usually written *Jayawardene* and *Wickramasinghe* respectively in modern times) are common only in Sri Lanka, where Buddhism still flourishes. Qualities highly regarded in Buddhism such as *śīla* 'good character or conduct' (see *Sheela*) are also in frequent use as personal names.

In the 3rd century BC the Emperor Asoka, in deep remorse after a particularly bloody campaign in eastern India, renounced warfare and, impressed by the emphasis laid on non-violence by the Buddha, converted from Hinduism to Buddhism. He sent missionaries all over the subcontinent, including Sri Lanka, where, as in Burma and south-east Asia, the principal religion today is the early form of Buddhism known as Hinayana. Early Buddhist texts are among the oldest sources of reliable historical information in the subcontinent, and the selection of a name such as *Ashok* in modern times must be connected in the minds of most people in the subcontinent with the Emperor Asoka rather than with the Sanskrit vocabulary word for the tree. The name *Nanda* no doubt gains much of its modern popularity from the king of that name who founded a dynasty in the 4th century BC. The Nandas were renowned for their wealth, and much of the information about them is known from Buddhist sources.

By about AD 500, Buddhism had started to be strongly influenced by the mystical or Tantric movement and developed a pantheon of symbolic deities. It also began accepting the idea that one could not only attain enlightenment for oneself but also help others to achieve it. The historical Buddha came to be seen as one of a long line of Bodhisattvas or teachers, who were human embodiments of enlightened beings. It is this form of Buddhism, called Mahayana, that spread to Tibet, China, and Japan.

Modern personal names that have probably gained greater prominence as a result of these developments in Buddhism include the female name *Tara*, which is borne by a Mahayana goddess, and the names *Mani* and *Padma*, which are both contained in the Tantric mantra *oṃ maṇi padme huṃ* 'The jewel is in the lotus', which became a cornerstone of Mahayana teaching and practice.

In most parts of the subcontinent, the influence of Buddhism was severely curtailed towards AD 1000 by Hun invasions, the advent of Islam, and the incorporation of the Buddha into Hinduism as an incarnation of Vishnu. In modern times it is often hard to distinguish Buddhist names from Hindu ones, partly because of this incorporation of the Buddha into Hinduism and partly because names in both religions ultimately derive from the same Sanskrit forms.

Jainism

Jainism was founded about the same time as Buddhism (6th century BC), and its history has many parallel features to Buddhism. Its founder, Mahavira, like the Buddha, was a member of the Hindu warrior caste. He achieved spiritual enlightenment by severe personal austerity, and his teachings laid particular emphasis on non-violence. He too won many disciples, and eventually came to be seen as the latest in a long line of spiritual teachers. However, Jainism never attained the popularity of Buddhism, and did not spread very far geographically. It went into severe decline by AD 1000, but remains a steady but influential minority religion, especially in the west and north-west of India, where Jains are prominent in the business community. Most extant Jain literature is in Sanskrit, and many primarily Jain names are also used by members of other religions. *Mahavir* is almost exclusively a

Jain name in modern times, and some epithets of Mahavira, such as *puruṣottama* and *narottama*, both meaning 'best of men', are used as personal names among Jains (see *Purushottam* and *Narottam*).

Parsees

Also mainly in the west and north-west of India are the members of another important minority religion, the Parsees, who fled from Persia (hence their name) when it was conquered by the Arabs around AD 800. They are followers of Zoroaster (also known as Zarathustra). Zoroaster (*fl.* 6th century BC) was a priest in the ancient Persian religion that involved a fire cult and animal sacrifices. Like the Vedic religion, it originated among nomadic Aryan tribes. Zoroaster introduced many reforms, especially abolishing the use of intoxicants (cf. soma in the Vedic religion). His teachings survive in the text known as the Zend-Avesta, which is composed in a language very similar to Vedic Sanskrit. In it, the key concepts of deva and asura are reversed: in the Veda, deva means god and asura means demon, in the Avesta the opposite. In modern times it is often difficult to distinguish Parsee names such as *Firoz* from similar Islamic names in Urdu, because both names ultimately derive from the same Persian form. Like the Jains, the Parsees are noted for having established large commercial organizations.

Islam

Islam, founded in the Arabian peninsula by Muhammad in the 7th century AD, was first brought to the subcontinent by Arabs, who occupied Sind in 712. However, they were at first restricted to a small area of the west coast by the neighbouring Hindu kings. Extensive and repeated raids during the 11th and 12th centuries by Turkish chiefs based in Afghanistan served to spread Islamic influence in the north. The Delhi sultanate, founded in 1206, gradually accrued vast territories in the subcontinent, and even parts of southern India came under Islamic rule. Islam reached the peak of its influence in the subcontinent under the Mogul empire (i.e. between the 16th and the 19th centuries). Founded by Babar in 1526, the empire was at its height until the death of Aurangzeb in 1707. Thereafter, it fragmented and most of its parts gradually came under British control, though it officially survived until 1857. In 1947, at the end of the British period in India, Muslims demanded and obtained a separate Islamic nation, Pakistan. Islamic influence remains strong in India, which is still the home of many millions of Muslims, although by far the greater majority now live in the neighbouring states of Pakistan and Bangladesh. Most of the personal names borne by Muslims in Pakistan, Bangladesh, and India are of Arabic origin, and for this reason frequent reference is made here to Supplement 1.

Sikhism

The most recent major religion to arise in the subcontinent is Sikhism, founded in the 15th century by Guru Nanak, with the aim of combining elements of Hinduism and Islam. Sikhism accepts Hindu ideas of karma and rebirth, but rejects the caste system. It shares some of the mystical ideas of Islamic Sufis and some of the devotional aspects of the Hindu Bhakti movement. Sikhs attach great sacredness to their holy book, the Granth, which is a compilation of the teachings of the first five gurus. They hold the ten gurus of the tradition in great reverence. There is considerable emphasis on the martial aspects of religion, combining Hindu Ksatriya (warrior-caste) ideals and the Islamic concept of jihad (holy war).

Sikhism predominates in the Punjab, in the north-west of the subcontinent. Modern Sikh names are most commonly compound names, and often end in *-inder*, from the Vedic deity *Indra* whom the Indo-Aryans invoked for aid in battle. Such combinations as *Surinder*, *Jitinder*, and *Harinder* thus serve to stress the martial aspect of the Sikh religion. This suffix is even found in some female names such as *Rupinder* and *Jaswinder*. Compound names beginning with *bal-*, from Sanskrit *bala* 'strength', are also common (see *Baldev*).

Sikhism lays special stress on the name of God (as does Islam), sabad 'sound' being termed the medium of communication and nam 'name (of God)' being the object of communication. Hence the naming of a child acquires a heightened significance, and children are named by consulting the priest, who opens the Granth, the Sikh holy book, at random. The first syllable on the opened page determines the initial syllable of the child's name.

Christianity

Christianity may have been brought to the subcontinent by the disciple Thomas himself, if the numerous local legends are to be believed. It is more likely that Nestorian missionaries from Persia introduced it from the 6th century onwards. During the period of European colonization many missionary groups, Catholic and Protestant, were active in the subcontinent, and many conversions took place. There are now several Christian Churches in the subcontinent and several million practising Christians. Over the centuries many Christian practices have been affected by local customs—for example, crucifixes and statues of Jesus are often garlanded and ornamented with vermilion and sandalwood paste like Hindu idols, and many people remove their shoes to enter Christian churches. Christian names are not dealt with here, as Christians in the subcontinent choose names from the same sources as Christians elsewhere. Old and New Testament names, such as *Abraham* and *Sarah*, *John* and *Mary*, are common. Saints' names are also frequent, but the specific choice and form may reflect either British, French, or Portuguese influence. A few interesting local developments are found in the subcontinent: for example, the compound name *Yesudas*, which combines the name of Jesus with the common Hindu suffix *-dās* 'servant of' (cf. *Kalidas*).

CONCLUSION

From this brief survey of the culture of the Indian subcontinent, it will be readily seen that many diverse influences are at work in the choosing of personal names, and a wide variety of forms exist. It has only been possible here to give a modest selection of the most important names. An attempt has been made to identify principles and patterns in the choosing of personal names, but it is often misleading to ascribe a particular religious affiliation or social identity to a person purely on the basis of his or her personal name. For example, because Islam acknowledges much of the Judaeo-Christian tradition, a biblical name such as *Zakaria* may be borne by a Christian or by a Muslim in the subcontinent.

Over the centuries, the traditional stock of names in the subcontinent has been extended by variations on old names, for example *Devi* and *Devika*, and hypocoristic forms such as *Balu*, *Raju*, and *Ramu*. Nowadays new names are sometimes coined, often by analogy with older names (e.g. *Mukesh* and *Naresh*; cf. *Ganesh* and *Dinesh*), and especially by popular figures such as film stars and pop singers. As people from the subcontinent are increasingly exposed to foreign cultures, by improved travel opportunities and the greater availability of television programmes from abroad, the stock of names is likely to be extended still further.

I gratefully acknowledge the assistance of Mr Saiyid Muinuddin Shah in the preparation of the Islamic entries in this section.

Ramesh Krishnamurthy
January 1990

BIBLIOGRAPHY

Auboyer, J.: *Daily Life in Ancient India* (London: Weidenfeld and Nicolson, 1965).

Basham, A. L.: *The Wonder that was India* (London: Sidgwick and Jackson, 1967).

Brough, J.: *Poems from the Sanskrit* (London: Penguin Books, 1972).

Chaudhuri, N. C.: *Hinduism* (Oxford: Oxford University Press, 1980).

Coulson, M.: *Three Sanskrit Plays* (London: Penguin Books, 1978).

Dawood, N. J.: *The Koran* (London: Penguin Books, 1982).

Dowson, J.: *A Classical Dictionary of Hindu Mythology and Religion* (London: Routledge and Kegan Paul, 1968).

Humphreys, C.: *Buddhism* (London: Penguin Books, 1951).

Mascaro, J.: *The Bhagavad Gita* (London: Penguin Books, 1962).

—— *The Upanishads* (London: Penguin Books, 1965).

Monier-Williams, M.: *A Sanskrit-English Dictionary* (Oxford: Oxford University Press, 1899).

Narayan, R. K.: *The Ramayana* (New Delhi: Vision Books, 1987).

—— *The Mahabharata* (New Delhi: Vision Books, 1987).

Nehru, J.: *Discovery of India* (London: Meridian Books, 1960).

Nilakanta Sastri, K. A.: *A History of South India* (Oxford: Oxford University Press, 1955).

O'Flaherty, W. D.: *Hindu Myths* (London: Penguin Books, 1975).

—— *The Rig Veda: An Anthology* (London: Penguin Books, 1981).

Pathak, R. C.: *Standard Illustrated Dictionary of the Hindi Language* (Varanasi: Bhargava Book Depot; repr., 1967).

Piggott, S.: *Prehistoric India* (London: Penguin Books, 1961).

Rajagopalachari, C.: *The Mahabharata* (Bombay: Bharatiya Vidya Bhavan, 27th edn, 1986).

—— *The Ramayana* (Bombay: Bharatiya Vidya Bhavan, 25th edn, 1987).

Ramanujan, A. K.: *Speaking of Siva* (London: Penguin Books, 1973).

Rowland, B.: *Art and Architecture of India* (London: Penguin Books, 1970).

Sen, K. M.: *Hinduism* (London: Penguin Books, 1961).

Zimmer, H.: *Myths and Symbols in Indian Art and Civilization* (New York: Harper and Row, 1962).

A

Abbas (m.) From Arabic: see ʿABBĀS in Supplement 1.

Abdul Hafeez (m.) See HAFIZ.

Abdul Hakim (m.) From Arabic: see ʿABD-AL-ḤAKĪM in Supplement 1.
Variant: **Abdul Hakeen.**

Abdul Hamid (m.) From Arabic: see ʿABD-AL-ḤAMĪD in Supplement 1.

Abdul Jabbar (m.) See JABBAR.

Abdul Karim (m.) From Arabic: see ʿABD-AL-KARĪM in Supplement 1.

Abdullah (m.) From Arabic: see ʿABD-ALLĀH in Supplement 1.
Variant: **Abdulla.**

Abdul Latif (m.) From Arabic: see ʿABD-AL-LAṬĪF in Supplement 1.
Variant: **Abdul Lateef.**

Abdul Majid (m.) See MAJID.

Abdul Qadir (m.) From Arabic: see ʿABD-AL-QĀDIR in Supplement 1.
Variant: **Abdul Kadir.**

Abdur Rahim (m.) From Arabic: see ʿABD-AL-RAḤĪM in Supplement 1.

Abdur Rahman (m.) From Arabic: see ʿABD-AL-RAḤMĀN in Supplement 1.
Variant: **Abdul Rehman.**

Abdur Rashid (m.) See RASHID.

Abdur Razzak (m.) From Arabic: see ʿABD-AL-RAZZĀQ in Supplement 1.
Variants: **Abdul Razzak, Abdur Razzaq.**

Abdus Salam (m.) From Arabic: see ʿABD-AL-SALĀM in Supplement 1.
Variant: **Abdul Salam.**

Abid (m.) Muslim name, from Arabic *ʿābid* server, worshipper, adorer (of God), from *ʿabada* to worship, adore. It also denotes a recluse.

Aftab (m.) Muslim name, from Persian *āftāb* sunshine, the sun.

Afzal (m.) Muslim name, from Arabic *afẓal* most excellent, pre-eminent, best.

Agha (m.) Muslim name, from the eastern Turkish word *āg͟hā* meaning 'older brother'. It was used as an honorific among the Mongols and applied especially to the imperial princes. It was an honorary title at the court of the Shahs of Persia during the Kajar dynasty (1794–1925), founded by Agha Muhammad Khan. It was borne by Hasan Ali Shah, who revolted against the Kajars in 1838 but was defeated and fled to Sind. In Bombay in 1866 he was legally acknowledged as the Imam of the Ismailis, a Shiite Muslim sect with adherents in Syria, central Asia, Iran, and East Africa, as well as in the Indian subcontinent. Hasan Ali's descendants continue to be the spiritual leaders of the Ismailis and to bear the hereditary title *Agha Khan*. These have included Ali Shah, Sir Sultan Muhammad Shah, and Prince Karim, the present Agha Khan.
Variant: **Aga.**

Ahmad (m.) From Arabic: see AḤMAD in Supplement 1.

Aisha (f.) From Arabic: see ʿĀʾISHA in Supplement 1.
Variant: **Ayesha.**

Ajaz (m.) Muslim name, from Arabic *ʿajāz* wonder, surprise, miracle.

Ajit (m.) From Sanskrit *a-* not + *jita* conquered (i.e. 'invincible'). *Jita* is the past participle of the verb *ji* to conquer, from which numerous other names are also derived, e.g. JAY, JAYANT, JAYASHREE, JITENDRA, and VIJAYA. Various Sanskrit lexicons give *ajita* as the name of the god Vishnu, the god Shiva, and of a future Buddha, but the earliest attestation is in the compound name *ajitāpīḍa* 'having an unconquered crown', the name of a king in *Rajatarangini*, a historical chronicle of the kings of Kashmir written in the 12th century AD. The form **Ajit** is of fairly recent origin.

Variant: **Ajeet**.

Ali (m.) From Arabic: see ʿALI in Supplement 1.

Alka (f.) Of uncertain origin, perhaps from Sanskrit *alaka*, attested in classical texts, meaning 'a lock of hair', and therefore denoting a curly-haired girl. The word is also attested in the same period meaning 'an eight- to ten-year-old girl', and may therefore denote youthfulness (compare KUMARI). *Alakā* occurs in classical and epic texts as the name of the city of Kubera (the god of wealth) and also denotes an inhabitant of this city, so the personal name may be given for this connotation with wealth.

Allahbukhsh (m.) Muslim name consisting of a compound of Arabic *Allāh* God + Persian *bukhsh* giving or giver (i.e. 'God is the giver').

Allahditta (m.) Muslim name consisting of a compound of Arabic *Allāh* God + Urdu *ditta* given (i.e. 'God-given').

Allahrakha (m.) Muslim name consisting of a compound of Arabic *Allāh* God + Urdu *rakhā* preservation, protection (i.e. 'having the protection of God').

Amin (m.), **Amina** (f.) From Arabic: see AMĪN/AMĪNA in Supplement 1.

Variant: **Ameena** (f.).

Amir (m.) From Arabic: see AMĪR in Supplement 1.

Amitabh (m.) From Sanskrit *amitābha* meaning 'of unmeasured splendour', from *a-* not + *mita* (from the verb *mā* to measure) + *ābhā* splendour. *Amitabha* is the name of a deity or of one of the five aspects of the Buddha in Mahayana Buddhism. Its earliest attestation is in the *Buddhacarita*, a poetic work by Ashvaghosha, probably written in the 2nd century AD. The plural denotes a class of Hindu deities found in the Puranas.

Amjad (m.) From Arabic: see AMJAD in Supplement 1.

Amrit (m., f.) From Sanskrit *amṛta* immortal, from *a-* not + *mṛta*, past participle of the verb *mṛ* to die. In the Vedas the word also means 'that which gives immortality', i.e. the water of life, the divine soma juice, nectar or ambrosia. In the epics *amṛta* is a name of Shiva and Vishnu. The epics and Puranas recount frequently and in detail the legend of the 'churning of the ocean', which explains the origin of ambrosia, *amṛta*. The gods were losing in their interminable war against the demons and sought Vishnu's aid. He instructed them to churn the primeval Ocean of Milk. Mount Mandara was used as the churning stick, the serpent Vasuki as the rope, and Vishnu himself consented to act as the base or pivot in the form of a giant tortoise. The churning produced numerous 'lost' treasures (the churning is a periodically repeated event) including the cow of plenty, the goddess of wine, a magic tree, the moon, a terrible poison, and ambrosia. The gods drank the ambrosia and defeated the demons. The feminine form *amṛtā* is the name of a goddess in the Vedas, and of numerous female characters in the epics and Puranas.

Variant: **Amrita** (f.)

Anand (m.) From Sanskrit *ānanda* happiness, joy. In the Vedas the word refers to sensual pleasure, but in later texts it especially signifies the spiritual bliss of mystical enlightenment through meditation. It also came to be used as a name of Shiva, and Buddhist and Jain works use it as the name of a deity in their pantheons.

Feminine form: **Ananda**.

Anil (m.) From Sanskrit *anila* air, wind. This is one of the commonest names of the wind-god Vayu from the earliest texts onwards. It is also the name of one of the eight demigods called the Vasus. Various the number 49 in mystical texts (there being forty-nine winds according to one tradition). In the Vedas the wind-god is Indra's charioteer, driving a golden chariot pulled by a thousand horses. Various legends speak of him being born from the breath of purusha, or cosmic man, and he is regarded as regent of the north-western quarter, and king of the gandharvas (celestial musicians). One legend ascribes to him the creation of Sri Lanka, when he broke off the summit of Mount Meru and hurled it into the sea. He is also the reputed father of Bhima (a mighty warrior in the *Mahabharata* war) and of Hanuman, the semi-divine monkey chief who greatly assisted Rama.

Feminine form: **Anila**.

Anima (f.) From Sanskrit *aṇiman* minuteness, used in yoga texts to refer to one of the eight Siddhis or superhuman powers that can be obtained as a result of meditation, namely the power to make oneself infinitely small and thereby invisible. These Siddhis are personified in mystical texts as female aides of gods and masters of meditation. The name may therefore refer to the physical attribute of petiteness in a woman.

Anuradha (f.) Probably from Sanskrit *anurādhā*, seventeenth of the 28 naksatras (asterisms or lunar mansions), said to mean 'a stream of oblations', first attested in the Atharva-Veda. In the same work the form *anūrādha* also occurs, meaning 'causing welfare or happiness', but is used to denote the same asterism. The word later serves as an adjective to describe a person born under this asterism. As such, it is the name of a Buddhist who founded the ancient capital of Sri Lanka, Anuradhapura. Another derivation is possible, from *anurāddha* effected, accomplished, from *rādh* to succeed, not attested until the Puranic period.

Anwar (m.) From Arabic: see ANWAR in Supplement 1.

Variant: **Anver**.

Arjun (m.) From Sanskrit *arjuna* meaning 'white: the colour of dawn, lightning, milk, and silver', which is attested from the Vedas onwards. This is a name of Indra in Vedic texts, but it is most famous as the name of the noblest of the five Pandava princes in the *Mahabharata*, the son of Indra and Kunti. Arjuna was the successful suitor of Princess Draupadi, who became the common wife of the five princes. During a voluntary twelve-year exile, Arjuna studied warfare under Parasurama (the sixth incarnation of Vishnu) and made a pilgrimage to the Himalayas, where he unwittingly fought against Shiva. The gods were so impressed by his prowess that they rewarded him with special weapons. Before the *Mahabharata* war, when offered the choice of Krishna (the eighth incarnation of Vishnu) as his non-combatant charioteer or Krishna's entire army, Arjuna chose Krishna's services. One of the most celebrated texts in the Sanskrit language, the *Bhagavad Gita*, was recited by Krishna to Arjuna just before the battle, in order to overcome Arjuna's reluctance to fight. Arjuna, recognizing Krishna as the godhead incarnate, was accorded the vision of his cosmic form.

Arun (m.) From Sanskrit *aruṇa*, attested from the Rig-Veda onwards, meaning 'reddish-brown: the colour of dawn, gold, and rubies'. In post-Vedic texts *Arun* is the personification of the dawn, the charioteer of the sun, and the son of Kasyapa and Kadru. Arun is also the name of a famous religious teacher in the Vedas and in later texts. In the epics the name is borne by various characters, for example by a son of Krishna, and by the father of Jatayu (king of the vultures and ally of Rama).

Variant: **Aroon**.

Aruna (f.) The feminine form of ARUN and the name of various plants, including the madder and the bitter apple. It is also the name of the red-and-black berry which is used as a jeweller's weight.

Arvind (m.) From Sanskrit *aravinda* lotus, attested in Panini's grammar and the classical drama *Sakuntala* by Kalidasa. It denotes both *Nelumbium speciosum* and *Nymphaea nelumbo*. Panini derives it from *ara* spoke of a wheel + *vinda*, from *vid* to contrive, i.e. 'seeming to have spokes like a wheel'. **Aurobindo** is a modern Bengali variant of this name, borne by the famous Indian nationalist leader and religious teacher, Aurobindo Ghose (1872–1950).
Variant: **Aravind.**

Asad (m.) From Arabic: see AS'AD in Supplement 1.

Asha (f.) From Sanskrit *āśā* meaning 'wish, desire, hope', attested from the Atharva-Veda onwards. In the *Harivamsa*, a classical text appended to the *Mahabharata*, *āśā* is personified as the wife of one of the eight demigods called the Vasus. In a later philosophical drama she is regarded as the daughter-in-law of Manas (the personification of mind).

Ashish (m.) Of uncertain origin: probably from Sanskrit *āśis* prayer, wish. *Āśis* is attested from the Rig-Veda onwards and is used more specifically in epic and classical texts to mean 'blessing, benediction', but is not found as a name before modern times.

Ashok (m.) From Sanskrit *aśoka*, attested in a Brahmana text, meaning 'without heat', but in classical times said to mean 'not causing or feeling sorrow' from *a-* not + *śoka* sorrow, from the verb *śuc* to burn or grieve. The adjective is used in modern Hindi to mean 'cheerful or tranquil'. It is attested from the epics onwards as the name of a common Indian tree with bright red flowers. In the Ramayana, Asoka is the name of a minister of King Dasaratha. In the *Mahabharata* it is the name of a king of Pataliputra. The latter is probably identical with the historical King Asoka of the Maurya dynasty, grandson of its founder Candragupta. Asoka ruled *c.*269–232 BC over an empire which eventually stretched from Afghanistan to Ceylon. He converted from the Brahmanical religion to Buddhism after a particularly bloody military campaign. Asoka held a famous Buddhist assembly, *c.*250 BC, after which he sent missionaries to Ceylon and all over his empire, and had 84,000 columns erected with inscriptions declaring his peaceful aims. These inscriptions are also found on rocks in various places in the subcontinent. He became noted for his good works and his tenderness for all living creatures. In the inscriptions he is called *piyadasī* 'of fond regard' (i.e. looking with kindness on all creatures), or *devānaṃ piya* 'beloved of the gods'.

Ashraf (m.) From Arabic: see ASHRAF in Supplement 1.

Aziz (m.) From Arabic: see 'AZĪZ in Supplement 1.

Azra (f.) Muslim name, from Arabic *'azrā* virgin. This was the name of the mistress of the legendary lover Wamiq, who is a stock character in Persian and Urdu poetry.

B

Babar (m.) Muslim name, from Turkish *bābar* lion. This was the byname of Zahir ud-Din Muhammad (*c.*1482–1530), first of the Mogul rulers in India. He was a descendant of Timur (Tamerlaine, *c.*1336–1405). He succeeded as Mirza (prince) of Ferghana in central Asia in 1495. After capturing Kabul in 1504 and establishing a kingdom in Afghanistan, he was invited into India by relatives of Ibrahim Lodhi, Sultan of Delhi, to assist in their conspiracy against him. Though his forces were small, Babar's brilliant tactics won him victory against Ibrahim at Panipat in 1526. He soon extended his empire over most of northern India and as far east as Bengal. He is also reputed to have been a highly cultured monarch, and a poet in his own right.
Variant: **Baber.**

Babu (m.) From the Brij word *bābū*. Brij is a language spoken in northern India around Mathura and Agra. *Bābū* was originally a title of respect for a gentleman of rank, meaning 'Sir, young master, father'. It is used as a term of endearment to children, and as a name in its own right. It also denotes a clerk in an office.

Badar (m.) From Arabic: see BADR in Supplement 1.

Bala (m., f.) From Sanskrit *bāla* young, attested from late Vedic texts onwards. In classical texts it is often used to describe the sun just after it has risen, and the new or waxing moon. The noun *bāla* is used in epic and classical texts, meaning 'child or boy'. In later texts it often occurs as the first element in compound names, especially in epithets relating to Krishna's infancy, such as *bālakṛṣṇa* and *bālagopāla*. Both of these are used as personal names in modern times, especially in southern India. As a feminine name, *bālā*, it was borne by the mother of the two monkey chiefs, Vali and Sugriva, in the *Ramayana*.
Variants: (m.) BALU, **Balan**.

Baldev (m.) From Sanskrit *bala* strength + *deva* god and meaning 'god of strength'. Baladeva was the name of the elder brother of Krishna, also called Balarama and Balabhadra, who first appears in the *Mahabharata*. In that text Vishnu is said to have taken two of his hairs, one white and one black, and transformed them into Baladeva and Krishna respectively. Baladeva is regarded as the seventh incarnation of Vishnu, or sometimes as the incarnation of Sesha, the serpent on which Vishnu reclines. He is described as wine-loving and irascible, and teaches the warriors Duryodhana and Bhima the use of the mace, but takes no active part in the *Mahabharata* war. In the Puranas he often shares the childhood exploits of Krishna. In one legend Baladeva gets drunk and orders the River Yamuna to come to him so that he can bathe. It refuses, and he plunges his ploughshare into it and drags the river with him wherever he goes until it takes the form of a woman and begs his forgiveness. The name *Baldev* is particularly popular among Sikhs, as are other compound names with the same first element, such as **Balraj** and **Balwant,** because of their preference for names with warrior-like connotations.

Balu (m.) Variant of BALA, or an abbreviation of any of the compound names with *Bāla-* as first element (such as **Balakrishna**, **Balagopal**, and **Balachander**, which are especially popular in the south of India) with the hypocoristic terminal vowel *-u*. Its use as a pet name and as a name in its own right is of recent origin.

Bano (f.) Muslim name, from Persian *bāno* lady, princess, bride.

Baqar (m.) From Arabic: see BAKR in Supplement 1.

Bharat (m.) From Sanskrit *bharata* 'being maintained', from the verb *bhṛ* to bear, maintain. In the Rig-Veda, *bharata* is an epithet of Agni, the god of fire, who is maintained by the care of men and is the bearer of their oblations to the gods. Bharata is also the name of a celebrated hero, the son of King Dushyanta and the semi-divine maiden Sakuntala. He is the first of twelve cakravartins, or universal emperors, and the ancestor of both the Kauravas and the Pandavas, the opposing parties in the *Mahabharata* war. However, the Pandavas are especially referred to as descendants of Bharata. Another famous bearer of this name appears in the epics, the son of King Dasaratha and the younger brother of Rama. After the machinations of his mother had resulted in Rama's exile, he was offered the throne but refused it. Instead, he dutifully ruled the kingdom in Rama's name until his return, keeping Rama's slippers on the throne as a token of his loyalty. In the Puranas the name applies to a manu or ancient sage and ruler, who gave his name to the country of India (Bharat was adopted as the official name of India at Independence.) This person is in modern times identified with the son of King Dushyanta in the Rig-Veda. The name is also borne by various teachers and authors, especially the author of the *Natyasastra*, the primary text on Sanskrit dramaturgy.

Bharati (f.) The feminine form of BHARAT, name of a deity in the Rig-Veda who is later identified with Saraswati, the goddess of speech and learning. The name is also that of one of the ten orders of religious mendicants, founded by the famous religious teacher Sankara (see SHANKAR), whose members append it to their own names.

Bhaskar (m.) From Sanskrit *bhās* light + *kara* making, meaning 'shining, bright'. As a noun *bhāskara* denotes the sun from late Vedic texts onwards, and is used as a name of Shiva in the epics. The name was borne by the most celebrated astronomer and mathematician in Indian history, also known as Bhaskaracarya, or 'Bhaskara the teacher', who wrote a famous text in the 12th century.

Bibi (f.) Muslim name, from Persian *bībī* lady, wife, mistress of the house.

Bishen (m.) Variant of VISHNU in northern India, especially among Sikhs.

C

Chandan (m.) From the Sanskrit *candana* sandal (*Sirium myrtifolium*), which refers to the tree, its fragrant wood, and especially to the paste made from the wood. The paste was used as a perfume and a medicinal ointment on the human body, and is now widely used in Hindu ceremonies to anoint images of deities and to make an auspicious mark on the forehead of participants. In epic and classical texts it is the name of various characters: a divine being, a prince, and an ape in the monkey army which helps Rama.

Chander (m.) Variant of CHANDRA.

Chandra (m., f.) From Sanskrit *candra* moon, from the verb *cand* to shine. It is attested in Vedic texts meaning 'shining' and is used to describe gold, gods, water, and soma, but in late Vedic texts denotes the moon, which is its commonest meaning from then on, often personified as a deity. Candra is also the name of a demon in the epics and of a son of Krishna in the Puranas. Though the moon is always regarded as a male deity in Hinduism, the feminine form *candrā* is a popular female name. The name also appears as the second element in compound names such as RAMACHANDRA.

Variants: **Candra, Chander.**

Chandrakant (m.) From Sanskrit *candra* moon + *kānta* beloved (from the verb *kam* to desire), meaning 'beloved of the moon'. As such, it is the name of a mythical gem, the Moonstone, which is supposed to be formed by the congelation of the moon's rays. The Moonstone is a recurring concept in classical texts, where it is said to have a cooling effect on the human body. *Candrakanta* also denotes the white edible water-lily, which blossoms at night and is therefore regarded as the beloved of the moon.

Chandrakanta (f.) The feminine form of CHANDRAKANT, regarded as the wife of the moon and therefore used to denote night in classical texts.

D

Damayanti (f.) From Sanskrit *damayanti* present participle of *dam* to subdue, meaning 'subduing (men by beauty or personality)'. In a famous classical legend, Damayanti is the name of a beautiful and intelligent princess. She and Prince Nala fall in love merely on hearing of each other, and their courting is conducted by the mediation of magic swans. When the time comes for Damayanti to choose a husband, four gods disguised as Nala are among Nala's rival suitors. Astutely perceiving their divine traits, the princess chooses the real Nala. After several years of happy marriage, the demon Kali lures Nala into gambling and tricks him into losing his kingdom and all his possessions, and the faithful Damayanti insists on following him into exile. Nala abandons her and she returns to her father. An official search for Nala proves vain, so Damayanti announces her intention to remarry. One of her suitors brings an ugly dwarf with him as his cook. Damayanti recognizes the dwarf as Nala by his cooking, and learns that he has been transformed into this state by a serpent's curse. They are reunited, Nala regains his kingdom in another gambling session, and the serpent's curse is revoked.

Damodar (m.) From Sanskrit *dāma* rope + *udara* belly, meaning 'having a rope round his belly'. This is an epithet of Krishna in the epics and stems from the legend in which, as a child, he stole butter and broke pots of milk and curds in his foster-mother's house. She tied him up to a large vessel by means of a rope round his waist in order to prevent him getting up to more mischief. Being an incarnation of Vishnu, he used his superhuman strength to drag the vessel along until it finally got caught between two trees, which were uprooted in the process. The legend is often repeated in the Puranas and became a favourite subject of Indian painters. The name Damodara is borne by two kings of Kashmir in the historical chronicle *Rajatarangini*, written in the 12th century. It is also the name of the ninth arhat, or enlightened being, in the Jain religion.

Feminine form: **Damodari**.

Daud (m.) From Arabic: see DAWŪD in Supplement 1.

Dayaram (m.) From Sanskrit *dayā* compassion + RAM (a variant of RAMA), meaning 'a veritable Rama in his compassion for others'. This compound name first occurs in late classical texts, at a time when the worship of Rama as an incarnation of Vishnu increased, and various attributes were prefixed to the name *Ram* in chants and hymns.

Deb (m.) A variant of DEV, particularly common in Bengal.

Debdan (m.) A variant of DEVDAN, particularly common in Bengal.

Deepak (m.) An older variant of DIPAK.

Deo (m.) A variant of DEV, particularly common in northern India.

Deodan (m.) A variant of DEVDAN, particularly common in northern India.

Dev (m.) From Sanskrit *deva* god. The gods are often reckoned as thirty-three in number from the Rig-Veda onwards, eleven for each of the three worlds. In the epics *deva* frequently refers to Indra as the god of the sky and the giver of rain. From classical times *deva* is the standard term of address for kings and princes, equivalent to 'Your Majesty' or 'Your Highness', and for Brahmins and priests, equivalent to 'Your Reverence'.

Variants: DEB, DEO.
Feminine form: DEVI.

Devdan (m.) From Sanskrit *deva* god + *dāna* gift, meaning 'gift of the gods' . The name is not attested in Sanskrit literature before medieval times and is probably a re-formulation of the name *Devadatta* 'given by the gods', which is well attested in epic, classical and Puranic texts.

Variants: **Deodan, Debdan**.

Devdas (m.) From Sanskrit *deva* god + *dāsa* slave, servant, meaning 'servant of the gods'. The compound is of late attestation, denoting a servant of a monastery in Buddhist texts. It is the name of a merchant's son in the *Kathasaritsagara*, or 'Ocean of Stories', a late classical compilation of folk-tales. It is also the name of various authors in an early medieval compilation of religious texts. The suffix *-dāsa* originally identified the bearer as a member of the Sudra caste, a peasant or servant. But in medieval times it acquired a positive spiritual connotation, because the Bhakti, or devotional, movement in Hinduism encouraged worshippers to see themselves as servants of God.

Devi (f.) The feminine form of DEV, attested in the Rig-Veda denoting a female deity or goddess. The name is especially used to refer to the wife of Shiva from epic texts onwards. She is regarded as having both a mild aspect and a fierce aspect and is worshipped under different names accordingly. *Bhavani*, GAURI, PARVATI, and UMA stand for the mild form and DURGA, *Kali*, and SHYAMA for the fierce form. As with *deva* (see DEV), *devī* is the standard form of address for queens and princesses, representing 'Your Majesty' or 'Your Highness'.

Devika (f.) From Sanskrit *devī* goddess + the diminutive or assimilative suffix *-kā*, meaning 'little goddess' or 'like a goddess'.

Dilip (m.) Of uncertain etymology, but probably from Sanskrit *dilī* Delhi + *pa* protecting. Dilipa is the name of various kings in epic and classical texts. It especially refers to the son of King Amsumat and father of King Bhagiratha, a member of the solar race of kings and an ancestor of Rama, the eponymous hero of the *Ramayana*. The legend often related is that Dilipa was once rude to Surabhi, the cow of plenty, and was placed under a curse of sterility. When he saved her daughter Nandini from the god Shiva's lion, the curse was revoked and he became the father of Raghu, another famous king. Another King Dilipa, also a prince of the solar race, is said to have helped the gods in their interminable war against the demons, in return for which he was granted a boon. He asked to know how long he would live and was told that he would die within the hour. He hurried back to the world of mortals and by earnest prayer attained union with the god Vishnu and thus escaped the predicted fate.

Variant: **Duleep**.

Dinesh (m.) From Sanskrit *dina* day + *īśa* lord, meaning 'lord of the day' (i.e. the sun) and widely attested from classical texts onwards as a vocabulary word for the sun.

Dipak (m.) From Sanskrit *dīpa* light, lamp + the diminutive or assimilative suffix *-ka*, meaning 'little lamp' or 'like a lamp'. It is well attested from classical times onwards and is the name of a son of Garuda (the father of all birds, and the vehicle of Vishnu) in the *Mahabharata*. It is also used as an epithet of Kama, the god of love, in its original meaning of 'kindling, exciting'.

Variant: **Deepak**.

Duleep (m.) An older and less common variant of DILIP.

Durga (f.) From Sanskrit *durga* difficult of access, unattainable. From late Vedic texts onwards, it is a name of the wife of Shiva in her fierce form (see DEVI) as the inaccessible or terrifying goddess. She is inaccessible because of her propensity for prolonged and deep meditation, and terrifying because of her anger when disturbed and the awesome powers she has acquired by meditation. She is usually depicted with twelve arms, each holding a terrible weapon, and mounted on the back of a lion. A festival held annually in her honour called 'Durgapuja' is celebrated especially in Bengal.

E

Ebrahim (m.) From Arabic: see IBRAHĪM in Supplement 1.

Variant: **Ibraheem**.

F

Fahim (m.) Muslim name, from Arabic *fahīm* meaning 'a person of great understanding or intellect, a learned man', from *fahima* to understand.

Fahmida (f.) Muslim name, the Urdu feminine form of Arabic FAHIM.

Faiz (m.), **Faiza** (f.) From Arabic: see FĀYIZ /FAYZA in Supplement 1.

Fakhruddin (m.) From Arabic: see FAKHR-AL-DĪN in Supplement 1.

Fareed (m.) Muslim name, from Arabic. See FARĪD in Supplement 1. This name is especially popular in the subcontinent because of its association with the Persian poet and Sufi mystic of Nishapur, Farid ud-Din Attar (died *c.*1229). Surnamed Attar because he was a chemist, he was converted to Sufism and became an expounder of the faith, hence his byname Farid ud-Din 'pearl of the faith'. His masterpiece was the *Mantiq ut-Tair*, 'Language of the Birds', a long allegorical survey of Sufism.

Fareeda (f.) From Arabic: see FARĪD in Supplement 1.

Variant: **Faridah**.

Faruq (m.) From Arabic: see FARŪQ in Supplement 1.

Variants: **Farook, Farooq**.

Fatima (f.) From Arabic: see FĀṬIMA in Supplement 1.

Variant: **Fatma**.

Firdos (m.) Muslim name, from Arabic *firdaws* paradise. This name is especially popular in the subcontinent because of its association with Firdausi (*c.*940–1020), the Persian poet and historian. He was the author of the epic *Shah Namah*, 'The Book of Kings', which relates and glorifies in 60,000 verses the history of Persia until the arrival of the Arabs. He wrote it at the court of Mahmud of Ghazni (*c.*971–1030), who underpaid him for his work. Firdausi wrote a fierce satire of the king and fled. After wandering from court to court, he returned home to die.

Variants: **Firdose, Firdoze, Firdaus**.

Firoz (m.) Muslim name, from Arabic *firoz* meaning 'victorious, prosperous, successful'. It was the name of one of the Prophet Muhammad's companions, who killed the pseudo-prophet Aswad. In the subcontinent, the name was most famously borne by Firuz Shah Tughluq (*c.*1307–88), a younger cousin of Muhammad Tughluq, Sultan of Delhi (1325–51). Firuz was a prolific builder, founding several cities, erecting mosques, palaces, and public buildings, and preserving old monuments such as the Qutb Minar in Delhi. The many gardens he laid out around Delhi substantially increased the supply of flowers and fruit to the city.

Variants: **Firuz, Feroz, Feroze**.

G

Ganesh (m.) From Sanskrit *gaṇa* host or horde + *īśa* lord, meaning 'lord of the hosts'. *Gaṇeśa* was originally a title in the *Mahabharata* of the god Shiva, who is renowned for having hosts of demigods in his retinue. These often have semi-animal forms and some demonic attributes, but some texts say that they are human beings who achieved semi-divine status by worship. In the *Mahabharata* and especially in the Puranas, Ganesh is also the name of the elder son of Shiva. Numerous legends are recounted about his origins: he was born from the sweat and dust on the body of Shiva's wife, or was a clay doll that was brought to life; he was born of the mystical syllable *oṃ*, or born of Shiva and his wife mating in the form of elephants. Ganesh has the head of an elephant. His body is that of a short fat man with a huge belly, and he often has a large rat as his vehicle. He is regarded as the god of obstacles and is therefore propitiated at the beginning of all Hindu ceremonies and at the beginning of literary works. He is said to have written down the *Mahabharata* at the dictation of the sage Vyasa, using his broken tusk as a stylus. He is also the god of wisdom, often outwitting his brother Skanda or Kartikeya. He is widely worshipped in India and has his own festival when clay images are used.

Gauri (f.) From Sanskrit *gaurī* white, a name of Shiva's wife from late Vedic times. It is said to have originated after Shiva had teased her for being rather dark in complexion. She then engaged herself in deep meditation in the Himalayas (she is regarded as the daughter of Mount Himavat, the 'snow-laden') and acquired a brilliant white complexion.
Variant: **Gowri**.

Gautam (m.) From the Sanskrit male patronymic *gautama*, 'descendant of Gotama' (see GOTAM), attested from late Vedic texts onwards. The patronymic is especially famous as applied to Sakyamuni, the Buddha, hence the name is popular among Buddhists. Gautama is also the name of the first pupil of the last 'Jina', or Jain saint, and is therefore also borne by many Jains. In modern usage the name is often merely a variant of *Gotam*.

Gita (f.) From Sanskrit *gīta* song, from *gai* to sing, attested from Vedic texts onwards and used especially in the names of religious works. The most famous is the *Bhagavad Gita*, or 'Song of the Lord', related to Arjuna by Krishna (see ARJUN). The name is probably used to mean 'whose praises are sung'.
Variant: **Geeta**.

Gobind (m.) A variant of GOVIND, especially popular among Sikhs. One of the ten supremely venerated teachers of Sikhism was Guru Gobind Singh (Sanskrit *Govindasiṃha*). This variant is also common in Bengal.

Gopal (m.) From Sanskrit *go* cow + *pāla* protector (i.e. 'cowherd'), attested in Vedic texts. In classical texts it is also used to mean 'king', the earth being regarded fancifully as the milch-cow of kings, who are its protectors. In the *Mahabharata* it is a name of Krishna, who spent his childhood in a cowherding community, and the name was taken up enthusiastically in the Puranas and by the medieval Bhakti, or devotional, movement of Hinduism as Krishna-worship developed. The compound name *Gopalakrishna* is also popular, especially in southern India.

Gotam (m.) From Sanskrit *go* cow, ox + the superlative suffix *-tama*, meaning 'the best ox, the most powerful ox'. Gotama is the name of an ancient sage to whom several hymns in the Rig-Veda are attributed. In ancient Indian literature cattle are a symbol for wealth, or for anyone or anything that provides good things in abundance. Gotama is also the name of the founder of the Nyaya system of philosophy, one of the six major ancient Indian systems. In Jain literature the name is borne by the chief disciple of Mahavira, and hence is popular among Jains.
Variant: GAUTAM.

Govind (m.) From the Sanskrit *go* cow + the suffix *-vinda* finding, gaining (from *vid* to find), meaning 'one who is (good at) finding cows'. The Vedic form *govid* is an epithet of the god Indra. In the *Mahabharata*, *govinda* is an epithet of Krishna, and this became very popular as a name of Krishna in the Puranas and in medieval devotional texts, especially in the *Gita Govinda* written by Jayadeva, probably in the 12th century.
Variant: GOBIND.

Gowri (f.) A variant of GAURI.

Gulzar (m.) Muslim name, from Persian *gulzār* rose-garden, blooming, flourishing.

H

Habib (m.), **Habiba** (f.) From Arabic: see ḤABĪB/ḤABĪBA in Supplement 1.

Hafiz (m.) From Arabic: see ḤĀFIẒ in Supplement 1.
Variant: **Hafeez**.

Haidar (m.) Muslim name, from Arabic *ḥaidar* lion. Its use as a name stems from the titles of Ali (the son-in-law of the Prophet Muhammad), who was called *Ḥaidar-ul-Llah* 'the Lion of the Lord' and *Ḥaidar-i-Karrar* 'the Lion of repeated attack'. The name was famously borne by Haidar Ali (1722–82), the first Sultan of Mysore. He won victories over the British in 1769 and 1780, but was eventually defeated by them near Madras in 1781.

Variants: **Haider, Hyder, Hayder.**

Hamid (m.) From Arabic: see ḤĀMID in Supplement 1.

Hari (m.) From Sanskrit *hari* denoting a colour variously interpreted as a shade of brown, yellow, or green. It is applied to horses in the Rig-Veda, especially the horses of Indra. In the epics it is used as a noun with widely differing meanings, e.g. 'lion', 'sun', 'monkey', and 'wind'. It is a name of the wind-god Vayu and of Indra in the *Ramayana*, but from epic texts onwards it is most frequently a name of Vishnu or Krishna. As such, it is often taken to be derived from the verb *hṛ* to take or remove, referring to the god's ability to remove evil or sin. The name is also borne by numerous other characters in epic and classical texts, notably by the son of Vishnu's divine bird-vehicle Garuda.

Harinder (m.) From Sanskrit *hari*, a name of Vishnu, + INDRA, the name of the foremost god of the Rig-Veda. A compound name especially favoured by Sikhs, as suggesting the warrior attributes of both these great gods.

Harish (m.) From Sanskrit *hari* (see HARI) + *īśa* lord. The compound is only attested in the *Ramayana*, where it means 'king of the monkeys'. Its current popularity springs from its use in medieval times as a name of Vishnu in devotional texts alongside the epic name *Hari*.

Harun (m.) Muslim name, the Arabic form of the biblical name *Aaron*. The Arabic form *Hārūn* is mostly associated with Harun al-Rashid 'Aaron the Upright' (*c*.764–809), who figures in many of the stories in the *Arabian Nights* or *Thousand and One Nights*. Harun was the fifth and most famous Abbasid caliph. In his youth he was a successful general, leading invasions into Asia Minor against the Byzantine Greeks. When he succeeded to the throne of Baghdad, his empire covered all of south-west Asia and north Africa, and he had ambassadors in China and at the court of Charlemagne. Harun was a generous patron of the arts and learning, and during his reign Baghdad reached its peak as a centre of culture.

Variant: **Haroun.**

Hasan (m.) From Arabic: see ḤASAN in Supplement 1.

Hashim (m.) From Arabic: see HĀSHIM in Supplement 1.

Husain (m.) From Arabic: see ḤUSAYN in Supplement 1.

Variants: **Hussain, Hussein.**

I

Ibrahim (m.) From Arabic: see IBRAHĪM in Supplement 1.

Idris (m.) Muslim name, from Arabic *Idrīs*: the name of a man mentioned twice in the Koran (XIX, 57/56–58/57 and XXI, 85–86), described as 'a true man, a prophet' and 'of the righteous'. He was 'raised up to a high place' and 'admitted to Our mercy'. Idris was also the name of the founder of the first Shiite dynasty (788–974). A descendant of Ali, the Prophet Muhammad's cousin and son-in-law, he fled from Arabia to Morocco and established a state there.

Iman (m.) From Arabic: see IMĀN in Supplement 1.

Inam (m.) From Arabic: see INʿĀM in Supplement 1.

Variant: **Enam.**

Inderjit (m., f.) From Sanskrit INDRA + the suffix *-jit* (from *ji* to conquer), meaning 'conqueror of Indra'. Indrajit is best known as the name of the son of the demon king, Ravana, in the *Ramayana*. Because of the martial connotations of the name, it is very popular among Sikhs, who use it as a female as well as a male name.

Inderpal (m.) From Sanskrit INDRA + the suffix *-pāla* protector, meaning 'protector of Indra' or perhaps 'Indra's bodyguard'. The name is attested from the epics onwards, usually borne by minor personages. In more recent times it has become popular among Sikhs because of its martial connotations.

Indira (f.) From Sanskrit *indirā*, a name of Lakshmi, the wife of Vishnu. It is attested in late classical and Puranic texts and is said to mean 'beauty' or 'splendour', as does *Lakshmi*. It is difficult not to conjecture a connection of the name with that of Indra, the foremost god of the Rig-Veda, and to regard *Indira* as a variant of the attested feminine forms of Indra, namely the Rig-Vedic *indrāṇī*, the Puranic *aindrī*, and the *indrā* given in Sanskrit lexicons. In modern times the name was borne by Indira Gandhi (1917–84), prime minister of India (1966–77 and 1980–4).

Indra (m.) The etymology of this name is uncertain, but it is most likely to be from the Sanskrit verb *ind* to drop, and therefore to be a compound of *indu* a drop (of liquid) + the suffix *-ra* acquiring, possessing, thus meaning 'possessing drops (of rain)'. In the Rig-Veda, Indra is the name of the god of the atmosphere and sky. He is lord of rain and rules over the deities of the intermediate region or atmosphere. He fights and conquers the demons of darkness by using his thunderbolt. He was not originally the lord of the sky-gods, but because his deeds were useful to mankind, more hymns were addressed to him than to any other deity in the Rig-Veda, and he superseded the lofty and spiritual god Varuna. In later mythology Indra is subordinated to the triad of Brahma, Vishnu, and Shiva but remains chief of all the other deities. In modern times *Indra* is rarely used as a name in its own right, but is extremely productive as the first or second element in compound names, usually in the variant form *inder* (e.g. INDERPAL, JASWINDER).

Ismail (m.) From Arabic: see ISMĀʿĪL in Supplement 1.
Variant: **Esmail**.

J

Jabbar (m.) From Arabic: see JĀBIR in Supplement 1.

Jafar (m.) From Arabic: see JAʿFAR in Supplement 1.
Variants: **Jaffer, Jaffar**.

Jagannath (m.) From Sanskrit *jagat* world + *nātha* lord, meaning 'lord of the world'. The epithet *jagannātha* is applied to Vishnu or Krishna in the *Mahabharata*, to Rama in the *Ramayana*, and to Dattatreya (a sage who propitiated the gods Brahma, Vishnu, and Shiva, and is sometimes worshipped as representing this triad) in the Puranas. Since Puranic times the name has been especially that of Vishnu and in particular of his image in the temple at Puri in the Indian state of Orissa. A large cult developed there and continues today, attracting thousands of pilgrims, especially to the two annual festival processions. Temple legend has it that Krishna, an incarnation of Vishnu, was killed by a hunter, and his body was left to rot. King Indradyumna was told by Vishnu to put the bones inside the image of Jagannatha, which the celestial architect Visvakarman had agreed to make on condition that he was not interrupted. The impatient king could not wait, hence the image has only stumps for feet and hands. The desolate king prayed to Brahma, who promised to make the image famous, give it eyes and a soul, and act as its high priest.

Jagdish (m.) From Sanskrit *jagat* world + *īśa* ruler, meaning 'ruler of the world'. The epithet *jagadīśa* is applied to the gods Brahma, Vishnu, and Shiva in late Puranic texts.

Jagjit (m.) A contracted form of Sanskrit *jagajjit* 'conqueror of the world', from *jagat* world + the suffix *-jit* conquering. The name is not attested before medieval times, and is especially popular among Sikhs.

Jahangir (m.) Muslim name, a compound of Persian *jahāṇ* world + *girholder*. It is most famous as the regnal name of the Mogul emperor Nur ud-Din Muhammad (1569–1627), the eldest son of Akbar. Originally named Salim because his birth was attributed to the successful prayers of the dervish Salim Chishti, Jahangir succeeded to the throne after his father's death in 1605. He had dealings with both the Portuguese and the British and granted the East India Company permission to establish trading stations. He is known for his patronage of the arts, especially miniature painting, and his love of hunting and carousing. He was devoted to his wife Nur Jahan, who was later buried alongside him in his mausoleum in Lahore.

Variant: **Jehangir**.

Jai (m.) Variant of JAY.

Jamal (m.) From Arabic: see JAMĀL in Supplement 1.

Jamil (m.), **Jamila** (f.) From Arabic: see JAMĪL/JAMĪLA in Supplement 1.

Variants: **Jameel, Jameela**.

Jamshed (m.) Of uncertain etymology and meaning, the name is borne chiefly by Parsees and Muslims. Jamshed was a legendary king of ancient Persia, of uncertain date, remembered as the founder of Persepolis. He is said to have introduced the solar year and established a festival to celebrate its first day. The Persian poet Firdausi (*c.*940–1020) says that Jamshed's reign lasted 700 years, beginning in about 800 BC. Jamshed is also noted for a wondrous goblet that he possessed, called 'Jam Jamshed', about which many tales are told. It used to dazzle all who looked into it, and hence became the standard poetic comparison for the sparkling eye of a hero or heroine. In modern times *Jamshed* has become a popular name among Parsees. It was borne notably by Jamshed Tata (1839–1904), a leading industrialist. In 1911 his successors built India's first steel mill in a city named Jamshedpur in his honour.

Variant: **Jamshad**.

Janaki (f.) Feminine form of Sanskrit patronymic *jānaka* meaning 'descendant of Janaka', which is attested from late Vedic texts. In epic and classical texts Janaki refers especially to Sita, the daughter of King Janaka and the wife of Rama. A famous late classical poem called *Janakiharana*, 'The Abduction of Sita', relates the episode from the *Ramayana* in which the demon king, Ravana, abducts Sita while she and Rama are in exile in the forest, and takes her to his island kingdom of Lanka.

Jan Muhammad (m.) Muslim name consisting of a compound of Persian *jān* breath, life, essence + Arabic *Muḥammad*, the name of the Prophet of Islam, and therefore meaning 'having Muhammad as the source of life'.

Jaswinder (f.) From Sanskrit *jasu*, the name of Indra's thunderbolt, + INDRA, meaning 'Indra of the bolt'. The name is almost exclusively used by Sikhs, who favour names ending in *-inder* because of the connotation of strength and valour for which the god Indra is noted. However, this name is unusual in applying solely to females, whereas other names in *-inder* are normally masculine.

Javed (m.) Muslim name, from Persian *jawid* meaning 'perpetual, eternal, eternity'.

Variant: **Javaid**.

Jay (m.) From Sanskrit *jaya* victory. The word is attested since late Vedic times, when it was also used to denote verses that promote victory. These verses were sometimes personified as deities. Jaya is the name of a sage in the Rig-Veda; of

Arjuna, the sun, and a serpent in the *Mahabharata*; and of an attendant of Vishnu and numerous other minor characters in the Puranas. From classical times the word was used to greet kings and princes. It is frequently the first element in compound names, for example, *Jaipal*, JAYAKRISHNA, and JAYASHANKAR.

Variant: **Jai**.

Jaya (f.) Feminine form of JAY. *Jayā* is the name of various plants, including *Sesbania aegyptica*, *Premna spinosa*, and *Terminalia chebula*. In epic and classical texts it is an epithet of Durga, the wife of Shiva, sometimes regarded as the daughter of the god Daksha. It is also the name of one of Durga's principal handmaids, a *yogini* or *sakti*, sometimes said to be the wife of the semi-divine Puspadanta, in Puranic and Tantric texts. The name also refers to a female deity in Buddhism.

Jayakrishna (m.) From Sanskrit *jaya* victory + KRISHNA, meaning 'the victorious Krishna'. It is one of many such compounds popularized by the medieval Hindu Bhakti, or devotional, movement in their hymns.

Jayant (m.) From Sanskrit *jayanta* victorious. In epic and classical texts Jayanta is the name of the son of Indra in particular, but also of various minor personages, such as a minister of King Dasaratha, a son of Bhimasena, and a minor deity.

Jayanti (f.) Feminine form of JAYANT. In epic and classical texts this is an epithet of Durga, the wife of Shiva (cf. JAYA), and also the name of Indra's daughter. The word has also been commonly used since that time to denote the anniversary of the birth or death of famous people, as in 'Krishna Jayanti' and 'Gandhi Jayanti'.

Jayashankar (m.) From Sanskrit *jaya* victory + SHANKAR, meaning 'the victorious Shiva'. The name was popularized by the medieval Bhakti, or devotional, movement in Hinduism and is one of several such compounds used in their hymns.

Jayashree (f.) From Sanskrit *jaya* victory + *shree* (see SRI), a name of the goddess Lakshmi, wife of Vishnu, meaning 'goddess of victory' and first attested in *Rajatarangini*, a historical chronicle of the kings of Kashmir written in the 12th century.

Jaywant (m.) From Sanskrit *jayavant*, meaning 'possessing victory', only attested rarely in early medieval literature. The name is popular among Sikhs because of its martial connotations.

Jeetendra (m.) Variant of JITENDRA.

Jitender (m.) Variant of JITENDRA, especially common among Sikhs.

Jitendra (m.) From Sanskrit *jita* conquered + INDRA, meaning 'having conquered Indra' (i.e. so powerful as to have conquered even the mighty god Indra). The name is not attested in Sanskrit literature, so was probably produced by analogy with other compound names having *-indra* as a second element. It may possibly have its origins in a misunderstanding of Sanskrit *jitendriya* 'having one's senses under control', well attested in the epics and in texts on yoga and meditation.

Variants: **Jeetendra**, JITENDER, JITINDER.

Jitinder (m.) Variant of JITENDRA, especially common among Sikhs.

Jyoti (f.) From Sanskrit *jyotis* light, attested from the Rig-Veda onwards, referring to the light of the sun, the dawn, fire, lightning, and the moon. In later texts the word denotes heavenly bodies, in particular the sun and moon, and the science of astronomy. From Vedic times the word also denotes light as a symbol of heaven, intelligence, and liberation. *Jyoti* is not attested as a name until recent times. It is occasionally used as a masculine name.

K

Kadir (m.) See ABDUL QADIR.

Kailash (m., f.) From Sanskrit *kailāsa*, of uncertain etymology and meaning, the name of a mountain in the Himalayas, north of Lake Manasa. It is the site of Shiva's paradise and the abode of Kubera, the god of wealth, according to Sanskrit texts from the epics onwards.

Kalidas (m.) From Sanskrit *kālī* the black one, a name of Shiva's wife in her fierce form (see DEVI), + *dāsa* servant, meaning 'servant of the goddess Kali'. The name was most famously borne by a classical poet and dramatist, author of several plays, including *Sakuntala* (translated into English by Sir William Jones in 1789), and several major poetical works (see SHAKUNTALA). He probably lived in the 2nd or 3rd century AD and was regarded as one of the 'Nine Gems' at the court of King Vikramaditya of Ujjain.

Kalpana (f.) From Sanskrit *kalpanā* making, imagining, fantasy. The word is used to mean 'ornament' in the *Mahabharata* and specifically 'an elephant's finery' in a late classical text. In religious texts it is used to refer to the act of resolution immediately prior to the performance of a ritual, during which the performer concentrates on the solemn purpose of the ritual. Its use as a name is not attested before late medieval times and presumably refers to ideal female beauty in terms of perfect creation or imagination.

Kalyan (m.) From Sanskrit *kalyāṇa* beautiful, auspicious, and attested from the Rig-Veda onwards. It is most widely known as the name of a musical raga which is usually played or sung at night, and is also attested as the name of a gandharva, or divine minstrel, and of a prince.

Kalyani (f.) The feminine form of KALYAN. In the *Mahabharata* it is the name of one of the Krittikas, the Pleiades, who became the foster-mothers of Skanda or Kartikeya, son of Shiva. It is also the name of the ragini, or semi-divine patroness, of the musical raga Kalyan, and a name of Durga, the wife of Shiva, in her mild form (see DEVI).

Kamal (m.) 1. From Sanskrit *kamala* pale-red, attested in late Vedic texts. In classical texts it denotes the lotus *Nelumbium*, and occurs as the name of the pupil of a sage and of an asura, or demon.

2. From Arabic: see KAMĀL in Supplement 1.

Kamala (f.) Feminine form of KAMAL. It is a name of the goddess Lakshmi, wife of Vishnu, in late classical texts; of one of the Krittikas, the Pleiades, who became the foster-mothers of Skanda or Kartikeya, the son of Shiva, in the *Mahabharata*; of Durga, the wife of Shiva, in her mild form (see DEVI) in the Puranas; and of the wife of King Jayapida in *Rajatarangini*, a historical chronicle of the kings of Kashmir written in the 12th century.

Kamil (m.) From Arabic: see KĀMIL in Supplement 1.

Kannan (m.) A variant of KRISHNA, used especially in the south of India.

Kanta (f.) From Sanskrit *kānta* desired, beautiful. In classical texts the word denotes a wife or mistress, and is often used as the second element in compounds (cf. CHANDRAKANTA).

Kanti (f.) From Sanskrit *kānti* beauty, well attested in classical texts, often referring to the shining beauty of the moon. It frequently denotes a lovely woman, and is especially used in late classical and Puranic texts as an epithet of Chandra, the wife of the moon, and of the goddesses Lakshmi and Durga.

Kapil (m.) From Sanskrit *kapila* (attested from the Rig-Veda onwards), which is probably formed from *kapi* monkey (from *kamp* to shake, cause to tremble) + the adjectival suffix *-la*, thus meaning 'monkey-coloured' or 'reddish-brown'. In the *Mahabharata*, Kapila is the name of an ancient sage, identified in some passages with Vishnu. Some texts credit him with founding the Samkhya school of philosophy, one of the six ancient orthodox systems of Indian philosophy. The name is quite commonly used of various other personages in later Sanskrit literature.

Karan (m.) From Sanskrit *karṇa* ear, attested from the Rig-Veda onwards. The name is most famously borne by a king of Anga (modern Bengal) in the *Mahabharata*. The son of Kunti by Surya the sun-god, Karna was born fully equipped with weapons and armour. Being unmarried and afraid of censure, his mother abandoned him on the banks of the River Yamuna. She later married King Pandu and gave birth to the five Pandava princes. Meanwhile, Karna was rescued and brought up by the charioteer of King Dhrtarashtra, the brother of King Pandu and the father of the Kaurava princes. Though knowing the truth of his birth and that he was therefore half-brother to the Pandavas, Karna fought on the side of the Kauravas in the famous war, because they helped him to become King of Anga. There was a special rivalry and enmity between Karna and Arjuna, partly no doubt because the Princess Draupadi had rejected Karna, thinking him to be the son of a charioteer, and married Arjuna and his brothers instead. Eventually Arjuna killed him, and the Pandavas, learning who Karna really was, mourned him and compensated his family, though he had fought against them. In modern times the variant *Karan* is popular in northern India, especially among Sikhs because of its martial connotations.

Karim (m.) From Arabic: see KARĪM in Supplement 1.

Kasi (m.) From Sanskrit *kāśi* shining. This is the name of a celebrated city and place of pilgrimage, attested from late Vedic texts onwards. It was gradually identified with the modern city of Varanasi or Benares, and a late classical text gives Kasi as the name of a prince of the family of Bharata (see BHARAT) who founded the dynasty of kings that ruled over the city. The city is especially famous for its numerous temples to Shiva and for its bathing ghats along the sacred River Ganges, often regarded as the mistress or wife of Shiva, who wears her in his matted locks. *Kāśi* has also been used from late Vedic times to denote an inhabitant of the city, and this may be the origin of its adoption as a personal name.

Kausalya (f.) From the Sanskrit adjective *kausalya* 'belonging to the Kosala people'. The masculine form *kausalya* is attested in a late Vedic text as an epithet of a prince of the Kosalas, but not as a personal name. The feminine form *kausalyā* is widely attested in epic and classical texts as the name of various women, especially three famous queens. The first was the wife of King Puru and the mother of King Janamejaya, and the second was the mother of King Dhrtarashtra and King Pandu, fathers of the princes who fought the *Mahabharata* war. The third, and probably the most famous, was the wife of King Dasaratha and mother of Rama, hero of the *Ramayana*.

Khalid (m.), **Khalida** (f.) From Arabic: see KHĀLID in Supplement 1.

Khalil (m.) From Arabic: see KHALĪL in Supplement 1.

Variant: **Khaleel**.

Khurshid (m.) Muslim name, from Persian *k͟hurshīd* sun. The name suggests a person of bright and dazzling countenance.

Khwaja (m.) Muslim name, from Persian *k͟hwaja* lord, master, owner. Khwaja Khizr was the name of a legendary prophet skilled in divination, who is said to have discovered and drunk of the fountain of life. Hence he is considered as the saint of waters. He is confounded by some with the biblical prophet Elijah, and regarded by others as a companion of Moses, or as Phineas (grandson of Aaron).

Kiran (m.) From Sanskrit *kiraṇa*, attested in the Rig-Veda, meaning 'dust, thread' but later denoting 'a ray of light' and, especially in epic and classical texts, 'sunbeam' or 'moonbeam'. It is not attested as a personal name before late medieval times.

Kishen (m.) Modern variant of KRISHNA, especially common in northern India.

Kishore (m.) From Sanskrit *kiśora*, attested in the Atharva-Veda, meaning 'colt, young horse' and gradually coming to mean 'a young boy' in epic and classical texts, where it also occurs as the name of a *danava*, or demon.

Kishori (f.) Feminine form of KISHORE, attested meaning 'filly' in the *Ramayana* and meaning 'young girl' in the Puranas, but not used as a personal name until late medieval times.

Kistna (m.) A variant of KRISHNA, used especially in central India.

Krishna (m.) From Sanskrit *kṛṣṇa* black, dark, attested from the Rig-Veda onwards. It is also used as a noun denoting the black antelope. In classical religious texts it is also used to denote the dark fortnight or period of the waning moon. In Vedic texts Krishna is the name of a rishi, or ancient sage, but the most famous bearer of the name first appears in the *Mahabharata*. Krishna is now thought to have originally been a tribal hero from Gujarat. By the 3rd century BC he was noticed as the object of a large and growing cult by the Greek Megasthenes, a Seleucid envoy at the court of the Emperor Chandragupta. Accommodated into sectarian Hinduism as an incarnation of Vishnu, from epic and classical times Krishna is often regarded as Vishnu himself. Probably the most popular and most widely worshipped of Hindu deities, many legends have developed around him since Puranic times.

Krishna was the eighth son of King Vasudeva and his wife Devaki. The first six sons were killed by King Kamsa, because of a prediction that a son of Vasudeva would kill him. The seventh, Balarama, was saved by being magically transferred to another woman's womb. The eighth, Krishna, was given away to a cowherd family and many legends exist about his childhood mischief and prodigious strength (cf. DAMODAR). He defeated numerous attempts by King Kamsa to murder him: for example he sucked the life out of the demoness Putana, sent to poison him with her breast-milk, and he eventually killed Kamsa. He killed numerous other demons, notably the serpent Kaliya, whom he destroyed by dancing on its numerous heads.

Krishna's adolescent phase was marked by amorous exploits with the gopis, or cowherdesses: stealing their clothes while they were bathing, enticing them with his flute-playing, and so on, exploits that are still re-enacted today in music and dance dramas. He challenged and defeated Indra, protecting his pastoral community against that god's wrath by lifting up Mount Govardhana on one finger and sheltering them under it.

Krishna's father was the brother of the Pandavas' mother, so he was their natural ally. At the gambling match which was the prelude to the *Mahabharata* war, he preserved the modesty of the Pandavas' wife, Draupadi, when her clothes were demanded in forfeit by the Kauravas. As they pulled her sari off her, new material magically appeared in its place, so that she remained fully clothed. Chosen by Arjuna (see ARJUN) as his charioteer, Krishna delivered the great oration known as the *Bhagavad Gita* to him on the eve of the *Mahabharata* war and revealed himself as the supreme deity incarnate.

Variants: **Kishen, Kistna, Kannan.**

Kumar (m.) From Sanskrit *kumāra* boy, son, attested from the Rig-Veda onwards. This is one of the nine names of Agni the fire-god in the Brahmanas, but in the epics it denotes the beautiful youth Skanda, the son of Shiva. Skanda is the hero of the epic poem *Kumarasambhava*, 'The Birth of Skanda', by Kalidasa. In classical texts *kumāra* is also commonly used to mean 'prince'.

Kumari (f.) Feminine form of KUMAR, attested from the Atharva-Veda onwards, meaning 'maiden, daughter'. It is the name of the warrior Bhima's wife in the *Mahabharata*. In later texts it is an epithet of Durga, Shiva's wife, in her mild form (see DEVI). A famous temple dedicated to *Kanyakumārī*, 'Durga the Virgin', stands at the cape at the southern tip of India. *Kumārī* is used as an epithet of Sita, the wife of Rama, in later texts. In classical texts *kumārī* also denotes a princess.

L

Lakshman (m.) From Sanskrit *lakṣmaṇa*, attested from late Vedic texts onwards, meaning 'having auspicious marks'. The name Lakshmana is borne by the son of Duryodhana, the chief Kaurava prince in the *Mahabharata*, who was slain by Abhimanyu the son of Arjuna. Much more famous is Lakshmana, son of King Dasaratha, who appears prominently in the *Ramayana*. The half-brother of Rama, Lakshmana is often regarded as a partial incarnation of Vishnu, or as the incarnation of Sesha (the serpent on which Vishnu reclines in between the cycles of creation). Lakshmana was the embodiment of fraternal loyalty, willingly sharing Rama's exile and protecting Sita. He fought untiringly at Rama's side in the battle against the demon king, Ravana, who had abducted Sita. He often helped to bring Rama out of his periodic despair, and nursed him after injury. One of the favourite subjects of Indian religious painting is a tableau of Rama and Lakshmana with their bows slung over their shoulders, standing next to Sita and the semi-divine monkey Hanuman, their faithful servant.

Variant: **Laxman**.

Lakshmi (f.) From Sanskrit *lakṣmī* mark, sign, attested from the Rig-Veda onwards. In Vedic texts it usually denotes a good sign or lucky omen. In the Atharva-Veda Lakshmi is the name of good luck personified as a female, and her sister Alakshmi personifies bad luck. In other Vedic texts Lakshmi and Sri (goddess of wealth) are regarded as the wives of Aditya, the supreme solar deity. In epic and classical texts Lakshmi is the goddess of beauty, good fortune, and wealth, and the wife of Vishnu. She is said to have arisen from the 'churning of the ocean' (see AMRIT) with a lotus in her hand, or from the heart-lotus of Vishnu, and hence is often called PADMA or lotus. In the Puranas, she is described as partnering Vishnu in his incarnations, born as Sita to his Rama, and Rukmini to his Krishna. The Mahalakshmi ('Great Lakshmi') temple in Bombay is dedicated to her as the goddess of fortune and is said to account for the city's great prosperity.

Variant: **Laxmi**.

Lal (m.) From Sanskrit *lal* to play, caress. It is only attested in medieval texts as the name of various minor personages, including an author and an astronomer. It is a term of endearment in modern Hindi, meaning 'darling boy', and often applies to Krishna in his childhood. An alternative derivation from Prakrit *lāla* king (derived from Sanskrit *rāja*) is likely in some instances.

Lalita (f.) From Sanskrit *lalita* playful, amorous, charming (from *lal* to play), widely attested in epic and classical texts. It is the name of a gopi, or cowherdess, who is one of the amorous playmates of the adolescent Krishna. She is sometimes identified with his favourite companion, normally called Radha. It is also a name of Durga, Shiva's wife, especially in Tantric texts.

Variant: **Lalit**.

Lata (f.) From Sanskrit *latā*, a creeping plant or a tendril of such a plant, widely attested in epic and classical texts. It is most often used in metaphors describing eyebrows, arms, hair, swords, lightning, and women's bodies, suggesting curves or slimness. It is the name of an apsaras, or semi-divine maiden, in the *Mahabharata*. In the Puranas it is the name of a daughter of Mount Meru, the mythical mountain at the centre of the universe.

Latif (m.) See Abdul Latif.
Variant: **Lateef.**

Laxman (m.) Modern variant of Lakshman.

Laxmi (f.) Modern variant of Lakshmi.

Leela (f.) From Sanskrit *līlā* play, widely attested in epic and classical texts. It is especially associated with amorous sport and with disguise or feigning. *Līlā* often signifies the divine creator's activities, especially in philosophical schools which regard the empirical world of the senses as God's great hoax.
Variant: **Lila.**

Liaqat (m.) Muslim name, from Persian *liaqat* dignity, merit, ability, judgement.

M

Mabarak (m.) From Arabic: see Mubārak in Supplement 1.

Madhav (m.) From Sanskrit *mādhava* vernal, from *madhu* (see Madhu), attested from late Vedic texts. Madhu is the name of a legendary king whose descendants are called *mādhava*, the most famous of these being Krishna. Hence *mādhava* is used widely in epic and classical texts as an epithet of Krishna and of Vishnu, of whom Krishna is an incarnation. It is also used as a name of Shiva and Indra in later texts. The hero of Bhavabhuti's late classical drama *Malatimadhava* is called Madhava.

The name was borne by one of the principal religious scholars and teachers of medieval Hinduism, also known as Madhavacarya 'Madhava the teacher', who assisted his brother Sayana in producing the first edited version of the Vedas and adding copious commentaries. Madhava lived in the 14th century and was prime minister to the king of Vijayanagara. He was also responsible for establishing the major philosophical school of dvaita, or dualism, holding that the supreme soul (or God) and the individual human soul were distinct entities. He thereby refuted the monistic doctrine of Sankara (see Shankar), which had held sway since the 8th century, and facilitated the growth of the Bhakti, or devotional, movement in Hinduism.

Madhavi (f.) Feminine form of Madhav, often used as a name of the goddess Lakshmi, wife of Vishnu. It is also the name of the spring flower *Gaertnera racemosa* in classical texts. In the *Mahabharata* it is a name of Kunti, wife of King Pandu, because she was descended from the legendary King Madhu. In epic texts the name is also borne by one of the Krittikas, the Pleiades, who became the foster-mothers of Skanda, son of Shiva. Elsewhere it is used as a name of Durga, Shiva's wife.

Madhu (f.) From Sanskrit *madhu* sweet, honey, attested from the Rig-Veda onwards. This is the name of the first month of the Indian year, occurring in March/April, and is therefore also used to mean the spring season. It is not attested as a female personal name until late medieval times.

Madhukar (m.) From Sanskrit *madhukara* honey-maker, bee. From the classical analogy between a lover and a bee sipping nectar from a flower, it has connotations of amorousness. It is not used as a personal name until late medieval times.

Madhur (f.) From Sanskrit *madhura* sweet, attested since late Vedic times, being used to describe voices and sounds as well as tastes. It was not adopted as a personal name until recent times.

Mahavir (m.) From Sanskrit *mahā-* great, + *vīra* hero, meaning 'great hero', and attested from the Rig-Veda onwards. The epithet *mahāvīra* is commonly applied to gods, especially to Indra and Vishnu, but is also used contrastively of men as opposed to gods. It is used in epic, classical and later Sanskrit literature as a name of Vishnu and of the Buddha, and is also the name of various kings.

The name is most famous from Jain literature as that of the last arhat, or enlightened being, of the present age. He is thought to have flourished in north-central India in about the 6th century BC. Mahavir is regarded as the founder of Jainism, and his personal history reads very like that of the Buddha. He was a member of the Hindu warrior caste who achieved enlightenment through severe austerities. His teachings laid great emphasis on non-violence. In modern times the name is therefore particularly common among Jains, who form a substantial and influential minority in the west and north-west of the subcontinent, especially in the world of commerce and industry.

Mahendra (m.) From Sanskrit *mahā-* great + INDRA, meaning 'the great god Indra'. *Mahendra* is attested as an epithet of Indra from the Atharva-Veda onwards. It is a name of Vishnu in the *Ramayana* and of Shiva in Tantric texts. In historical times Mahendra was the name of the younger brother of the Emperor Asoka (see ASHOK), who was sent as a Buddhist missionary to Ceylon. It is also the name of one of India's mountain ranges, which runs from Gondwana to Orissa.

Variants: MAHINDER, MOHINDER.

Mahesh (m.) From Sanskrit *mahā-* great + *īśa* ruler, meaning 'great ruler', and attested as a name of Shiva from classical times. It is also the name of a Buddhist deity. *Mahesa* is the name of various authors from Puranic times onwards.

Mahinder (m.) Variant of MAHENDRA, especially common in northern India.

Mahmood (m.) From Arabic: see MAḤMŪD in Supplement 1.

Variants: **Mehmud, Mehmood.**

Majid (m.) From Arabic: see MĀJID in Supplement 1.

Variant: **Majeed.**

Malati (f.) From Sanskrit *mālatī*, the flower *Jasminum grandiflorum*, which has flowers that open towards evening. The word is attested from classical texts onwards, and is later also used to mean 'the night' or 'moonlight'. It is the name of the heroine of the late classical drama *Malatimadhava* by Bhavabhuti.

Mani (m., occasionally f.) From Sanskrit *maṇi* jewel, and attested from the Rig-Veda onwards. It is most well known from the Sanskrit mantra *Oṃ maṇi padme huṃ*, literally meaning 'the jewel is in the lotus'. *Maṇi* in medical texts denotes the penis, and it is often construed with that meaning in some explanations of the mantra, especially in Tantric texts, where the lotus is taken to mean 'vagina' and connubial bliss is used as a metaphor for mystical union with the supreme spirit or godhead. The mantra is a cornerstone of Buddhist religious practices.

In the *Mahabharata* Mani is the name of a naga, or serpent, and also of a companion of Skanda, son of Shiva. The name often carries magical or mystical connotations. It is particularly common in southern India, where it is regarded as an abbreviation of *Subrahmanya*, a popular name for Skanda. It also often occurs as the first element in compound names in northern India, e.g. *Manilal*, *Manibhai*, and the feminine *Manibehn*.

Mansoor (m.) From Arabic: see MANṢŪR in Supplement 1.

Mariam (f.) From Arabic: see MARYAM in Supplement 1.

Masood (m.) From Arabic: see MASʿŪD in Supplement 1.

Meena (f.) From Sanskrit *mīna* fish, attested from epic and classical texts. It also denotes the sign of the zodiac Pisces. In the Puranas it is the name of the daughter of Usha, goddess of the dawn, and the wife of the ancient sage Kasyapa.

It is also the name of a daughter of Kubera, god of wealth. In southern India it is more commonly found in the compound *mīnākṣī* 'having eyes shaped like a fish', which is the name of the deified daughter of a Pandya king. Meenakshi is worshipped especially in the city of Madurai, and has been assimilated into the Hindu pantheon as a manifestation of Durga, the wife of Shiva, in her mild form (see DEVI).

Mehjibin (f.) Muslim name, from Persian: a compound of *mah* moon + *jibīn* the temple, the side of the forehead, i.e. 'a woman with a face as beautiful as the moon'.

Mehmud (m.) Variant of MAHMOOD.

Mirza (m.) Muslim name, from a Persian honorific title *Mirzā*. It was introduced into the subcontinent by the Moguls, and used to address or refer to a prince and placed after his personal name.

Mohan (m.) From Sanskrit *mohana* bewitching, leading astray, attested from the epics. It is a name of Shiva in the *Ramayana*, and of one of the five arrows of Kama, the god of love, in late classical and Puranic texts. It is therefore also used as a name of Kama. It is the name of various men and authors from that period onwards. In the medieval period it is used as an epithet of Krishna, who beguiles the gopis, or cowherdesses, and enchants his devotees.

Mohana (f.) Feminine form of MOHAN, attested in Puranic and Tantric texts denoting a magic spell. It is also the name of an apsaras, or semi-divine maiden, and of one of the saktis, or female attendants of Vishnu.

Mohinder (m.) Variant of MAHENDRA, especially common in northern India.

Mohini (f.) From Sanskrit *muh* to bewitch, lead astray, meaning 'a fascinating or bewitching woman'. In Puranic and Tantric texts it is the name of an apsaras, or semi-divine maiden, and of a daughter of the warrior Rukmangada. In Puranic legend Mohini is the name adopted by Vishnu when he took the guise of a beautiful woman in order to interrupt the meditation of Shiva. The other gods asked him to do this, because if Shiva sinks too deep in meditation, the energy so created can engulf the universe. From that legend, it is also the name of a style of classical dancing said to represent the dance employed by Vishnu as Mohini.

Mostafa (m.) From Arabic: see MUṢṬAFA in Supplement 1.

Variant: **Mustufa.**

Muhammad (m.) From Arabic: see MUḤAMMAD in Supplement 1.

Variants: **Mohammad, Mohammed.**

Muhsin (m.) From Arabic: see MUḤSIN in Supplement 1.

Mujtaba (m.) Muslim name, from Arabic *mujtabā* chosen, from *ijtaba* to pick, choose, elect. It is one of the names of the Prophet Muhammad.

Mukesh (m.) Of uncertain origin; probably formed on the analogy of other names ending in the Sanskrit element *īśa* ruler (cf. DINESH, GANESH). Muka is the name of a demon in the form of a wild boar. He attacked Arjuna (see ARJUN) but was killed by the god Shiva in the guise of a wild mountain-dweller. Hence *Mukesh* may mean 'lord or conqueror of the demon Muka'.

Mukhtar (m.) From Arabic: see MUKHTĀR in Supplement 1.

Muneer (m.) From Arabic: see MUNĪR in Supplement 1.

Murali (m.) From Sanskrit *muralī* flute. Its use as a name is based on various compound epithets of Krishna in Puranic and later texts, especially *muralīdhara* 'bearer of the flute'. These epithets relate to the amorous, adolescent Krishna enticing the gopis, or cowherdesses, with the music of his flute. Krishna is often depicted in flute-playing posture in religious statues and paintings. The name is particularly popular in southern India.

N

Nabibukhsh (m.) Muslim name consisting of a compound of Arabic *nabī* a prophet + Persian *bukhsh* giving, giver (i.e. 'the Prophet is the giver').

Nadim (m.) From Arabic: see NADĪM in Supplement 1.
Variant: **Nadeem.**

Nadir (m.), **Nadira** (f.) From Arabic: see NĀDIR/NADIRA in Supplement 1.

Nagendra (m.) From Sanskrit *nāga* serpent, elephant + INDRA (used as a superlative suffix), meaning 'the mightiest serpent' or 'the mightiest elephant'. It is attested as a vocabulary word denoting a particularly large or powerful snake or elephant in epic and classical texts, but is not found as a name until late medieval times.

Nahid (f.) From Arabic: see NĀHIDA in Supplement 1.

Naim (m.) From Arabic: see NA'ĪM in Supplement 1.

Nanda (m.) From Sanskrit *nanda* joy, attested from the Atharva-Veda onwards. It is very common as a name in epic and Puranic texts, referring especially to the foster-father of Krishna. In the same texts it is also a name of Vishnu, and of various minor characters including an attendant of Skanda (the son of Shiva), a naga, or serpent, and a son of King Dhrtarashtra. In Buddhist texts it is the name of a deity and of the stepbrother and disciple of the Buddha himself. In historical times Nanda was the name of the king who founded a dynasty in Magadha, which was overthrown by Chandragupta Maurya *c.*315 BC and which was renowned for its wealth. Since classical times the word has also meant 'son', sons being highly regarded in the predominantly patriarchal cultures of the subcontinent, and the birth of a son being considered a particularly joyous occasion.

Narain (m.) Variant of NARAYAN, especially common in northern India.

Narayan (m.) From Sanskrit *nara* man + *ayana* path (commonly used as a patronymic suffix). Hence *nārāyaṇa* means 'son of man'. From late Vedic times the name Naryana has signified the deity or sage who is the origin of creation. Narayana soon came to be identified with Brahma, god of creation. Because of the patronymic suffix, the name is used of the sons of various minor personages in Puranic and later texts. Devotees of Vishnu frequently used the name as an epithet of Vishnu or Krishna during the rise of the Bhakti, or devotional, school of Hinduism, and it is now with Vishnu that the name is usually identified.

Narendra (m.) From Sanskrit *nara* man + INDRA, meaning 'a mighty man'. It is attested in epic and classical texts with the meaning 'king, prince' but is not found as a name until medieval times. It also acquired the secondary meanings of 'physician', 'curer of snake-bites', and 'master of charms and antidotes'. The variants **Narender**, **Narendhra**, and **Narinder** are fairly common.

Naresh (m.) From Sanskrit *nara* man + *īśa* ruler, meaning 'ruler of men, king'. The word is attested in the *Mahabharata*, but its use as a name is of fairly recent origin.

Narottam (m.) From Sanskrit *nara* man + *uttama* highest (used as a superlative suffix), meaning 'the best of men'. It is attested in epic and classical texts, but not used as a name until recent times. It is popular in Gujarat, especially among Jains.

Nasir (m.) From Arabic: see NĀṢIR in Supplement 1.
Variant: **Nasr.**

Nasrin (f.) Muslim name, from Persian *nasrin* wild rose. An alternative derivation is possible from Arabic *nasrīn* denoting the constellation The Eagle and the Lyre.
Variant: **Nasreen.**

Nataraj (m.) From Sanskrit *naṭa* dance + *rāja* king, meaning 'king of dancers' or 'lord of the dance'. It is not attested until medieval times, when it became famous as a name of Shiva. He is frequently described in epic, classical, and Puranic texts as dancing to the rhythm of the universe to entertain the gods and his wife. He also dances when he is angry or after defeating a demon, and especially at the cyclic destruction of the universe. Images of Shiva in dancing posture are common, in particular the image of Nataraja at the temple of Chidambaram in southern India.

Natraj (m.) Variant of NATARAJ used in northern India.

Naveed (m.) Muslim name, from Persian *naveed* glad tidings, wedding invitation.

Niaz (m.) Muslim name, from Persian *niāz* prayer, gift, offering.

Noor (m., f.) From Arabic: see NŪR in Supplement 1.

O

Om (m.) From Sanskrit *oṃ*, a mystical and sacred syllable used in religious texts since the Upanishads as an object of meditation. It is regularly prefixed to all mantras or prayers, to all religious ceremonies, and is printed at the head of religious and secular works. In Sanskrit phonetics, *oṃ* represents the combination of the sounds *a*, *u*, and *m*, which in turn stand for the whole range of sounds that the human voice can produce, starting at the back of the mouth and ending at the lips. Thus it represents in a symbolic way every word that can be uttered by the human articulatory system. Hindu tradition identifies the three sounds with the three Vedas or the triad of supreme gods (Vishnu, Shiva, and Brahma). It is often used as the first element in compound names such as *Omprakash*, which are also written as two words, for example *Om Mathur*.

Omar (m.) From Arabic: see 'UMAR in Supplement 1.

Osman (m.) From Arabic: see 'USMĀN in Supplement 1.

P

Padma (m., f.) From Sanskrit *padma* lotus, denoting especially *Nelumbium speciosum* which closes at evening. The word is widely attested from epic and classical texts onwards. It is often used symbolically, for example to denote the cakras, or centres of psychic energy in the human body. It is also the name of one of the nine treasures of the god of wealth Kubera, in which sense it is frequently personified. Padma occurs as the name of numerous minor characters in Sanskrit literature, for example a serpent, a mythical elephant, a demon, an attendant of Skanda (the son of Shiva), a brahmin, and a king. In a later text it is an epithet of Rama. Its use as a male name is commonest in Nepal, Kashmir and northern India. The feminine form *padmā* is attested as a name of the goddess Sri or Lakshmi from epic and classical texts. In modern times *Padma* is commoner as a feminine name.

Padmavati (f.) From Sanskrit *padmā* lotus + the suffix *-vatī* having, resembling, and meaning 'full of lotuses' or 'lotus-like'. In the *Mahabharata* it is the name of one of the Krittikas, the Pleiades, who became the foster-mothers of Skanda, son of Shiva. In later texts it is an epithet of the goddess Lakshmi and the name of various women. It was also the name of a wife of the Emperor Asoka (see ASHOK).

Padmini (f.) From Sanskrit *padma* lotus, + the suffix *-inī* having, meaning 'full of lotuses'. From classical texts onwards the word denotes *Nelumbium speciosum*, or 'a bed of lotuses', or 'a lotus pond'. In late classical texts it is the name of various minor female characters.

Parvaiz (m.) Muslim name, from Persian *parvaiz* meaning 'victorious, fortunate, happy, excellent, precious'. The name was borne by the second son of the Mogul emperor JAHANGIR. Sultan Parwiz (*c.*1590–1626) was noted for erecting many splendid buildings at Sultanpur near Agra, of which sadly only the ruins remain.

Variants: **Parviz, Parvez, Parwiz.**

Parvati (f.) From Sanskrit *pārvatī* '(daughter) of the mountain', and attested from the Upanishads onwards as an epithet of Shiva's wife. She is regarded as the daughter of Himavat, king of the Snowy Mountains (the Himalayas), and is a mild form of the goddess (see DEVI), noted for her predilection for meditation. It is a standard name for Shiva's wife from the Puranas onwards. The name is especially popular in southern India.

Parvin (f.) Muslim name, from Persian *parvīn* denoting the Pleiades or one of the 28 stations of the moon. Parwin was the name borne by Persia's greatest poetess (d. 1941).

Variants: **Parveen, Parwin.**

Pitambar (m.) From Sanskrit *pīta* yellow + *ambara* garment, meaning 'wearing yellow garments'. This is an epithet of Vishnu or Krishna attested in early medieval texts. Yellow or saffron-coloured clothes are traditionally worn at times of worship or pilgrimage by Hindus. The name is often given to children of families of the Vaishnava sect, who regard Vishnu or Krishna as the sole or supreme form of the godhead. It also has associations with the dancing and acting professions from their performances in Vishnu-worship.

Prabhakar (m.) From Sanskrit *prabhā* light + *kara* maker, meaning 'illuminator', and widely attested in epic and classical texts as an epithet of the sun. In the *Mahabharata* the name refers to a serpent-demon. In Puranic and Tantric texts it is a name of Shiva, as well as of several minor characters, such as a sage and a son of King Jyotismat. Prabhakara was the name of a famous medieval religious teacher, who propounded orthodox interpretations of the Vedas.

Prabhu (m.) From Sanskrit *prabhu* mighty, attested from the Rig-Veda onwards. The word came to mean 'king' and was applied to various gods in the Rig-Veda, for example Surya (the sun-god) and Agni (god of fire). It is the name of various minor characters in epic, classical, and Puranic texts. During this period it also began to be used as a term of address for a king or a deity.

Prabodh (m.) From Sanskrit *prabodha* awakening, widely attested in epic and classical texts. It also denoted the blooming of flowers. It is frequently used in religious and philosophical texts as a metaphor for the awakening of consciousness or intelligence. It is not found as a given name until late medieval times.

Pradeep (m.) From Sanskrit *pradīpa* light, lantern, attested from epic and classical texts onwards. It is often the final element in compound epithets meaning 'the glory of (the race, family, etc.)'. Its use as a personal name is of fairly recent origin.

Prakash (m.) From Sanskrit *prakāśa* light, attested from the Rig-Veda onwards. In classical texts it came to mean 'famous'. It is the name of a brahmin in the *Mahabharata* and of an ancient sage in a later text.

Pramod (m.) From Sanskrit *pramoda* joy, attested from late Vedic texts onwards. In epic and Puranic texts it is the name of pleasure personified. It is also the name of an attendant on Skanda (son of Shiva), of a naga, or serpent, of a son of the god Brahma, and of various men.

Pran (m.) From Sanskrit *prāṇa* breath, life-force, widely attested from the Rig-Veda onwards and personified in the Atharva-Veda. It is the name of various minor deities in the epics and Puranas, and is also used as a term of endearment.

Prasad (m.) From Sanskrit *prasāda* brightness, and attested from the Upanishads onwards. It denotes especially 'the grace of God' and suggests tranquillity. In religious rituals, it denotes the offerings which are made to a deity and subsequently distributed among the participants as blessed. Its use as a given name is of fairly recent origin. It often occurs as the second element in compound names such as *Ramprasad*.

Pratap (m.) From Sanskrit *pratāpa* heat, attested in epic and classical texts. It also acquires the meaning 'splendour, majesty, power' and is used to describe kings and warriors.

Pratibha (f.) From Sanskrit *pratibhā* light, image, attested in epic and classical texts. It also denotes 'intelligence, wit, audacity, imagination'. Its use as a name is of late medieval origin.

Pravin (m.) From Sanskrit *pravīṇa* skilful, attested in classical literature. It also occurs as the name of the son of an ancient sage.

Prem (m.) From Sanskrit *prema* love, affection, attested from late Vedic texts onwards. It is also used in classical texts to mean 'jest, joke'. It is found as the name of various men in *Rajatarangini*, a historical chronicle of the kings of Kashmir written in the 12th century. It is frequently the first element in compound names such as *Premchand*, *Premjit*, *Premnath*, and *Premshankar*.

Prema (f.) Feminine form of PREM, used as a name since late medieval times.

Premlata (f.) From Sanskrit *premalatā*, a small creeping plant, attested in late classical texts and sometimes used as a metaphor for love. It has occurred as a name only since late medieval times.

Priya (f.) From Sanskrit *priyā* beloved, dear, attested from the Rig-Veda onwards. In later texts it is often used to denote a wife or mistress. It is the name of a daughter of the legendary King Daksha in the Puranas.

Purnima (f.) From Sanskrit *pūrṇimā* 'the night (or day) of the full moon', attested in early medieval texts. Its use as a name is of late medieval origin.

Purushottam (m.) From Sanskrit *puruṣa* man + *uttama* highest (used as a superlative suffix), meaning 'the best of men' (cf. NAROTTAM). It is attested in epic and classical texts, where it is also a name of Vishnu or Krishna as the highest being or supreme spirit. In Jain texts it is the name of a jina, or deified teacher, and hence is a popular name among Jains.

Q

Qadir (m.) See ABDUL QADIR.
Variants: **Qadeer, Qadar**.

Qasim (m.) From Arabic: see QĀSIM in Supplement 1.
Variant: **Kasim**.

R

Rabab (f.) From Arabic: see RABĀB in Supplement 1.

Radha (f., m.) 1. (f.) From Sanskrit *rādhā* success, and rarely attested in texts but given in some Sanskrit lexicons, where it is also said to denote lightning and be a name of the twenty-first naksatra, or asterism. The name is borne in the *Mahabharata* by the wife of Adhiratha, the charioteer of King Sura. It is most famous as the name of a gopi, or cowherdess, the favourite consort of Krishna. She is the principal personage in the *Gita Govinda*, a poem celebrating the love of Radha and Krishna written by Jayadeva, probably in the 12th century. She is regarded by some people as a symbol of the human soul being drawn towards the supreme spirit, but is more commonly deified as a goddess and identified with Lakshmi.

2. (m.) Abbreviation of various compound names having *Rādhā-* as their first element, such as RADHAKRISHNA, *Radha-*

svami, and *Radhagopal*, which are especially common in southern India.

Radhakrishna (m.) Compound name from the Sanskrit names RADHA + KRISHNA. It was popularized in medieval times by devotees of the Krishna cult. The compound emphasizes the inseparable unity of the male and female principles of godhead, or the androgynous nature of the supreme being (cf. analogous compounds such as *Radhagopal* and *Lakshminarayana*, and SITARAM). The name is especially popular in southern India, usually in the variant form *Radhakrishnan*.

Rafiq (m.) From Arabic: see RAFĪQ in Supplement 1.
Variants: **Rafi, Rafee.**

Raghav (m.) From the Sanskrit patronymic *rāghava* meaning 'descendant of Raghu'. In the *Ramayana* and classical texts *rāghava* is especially an epithet of Rama, and in later texts is used as a name of Rama.

Raghu (m.) From Sanskrit *raghu* swift, attested in the Rig-Veda. In epic and classical texts it is the name of a legendary king of the solar race, ancestor of Rama and the hero of Kalidasa's epic poem *Raghuvamsa*, 'The Lineage of Raghu'. In Buddhist texts it is the name of a son of the Buddha. It frequently occurs as the first element in compound names such as RAGHUVIR and *Raghupati*.

Raghuvir (m.) From Sanskrit *raghuvīra* meaning 'Raghu the hero', an epithet of Rama coined in medieval times with the rise of devotional and sectarian Hinduism.

Rahim (m.) See ABDUR RAHIM.

Rahman (m.) See ABDUR RAHMAN.

Raj (m.) From Sanskrit *rāja* king, attested from the Rig-Veda onwards, where it is applied to various gods, for example Varuna, Aditya, Indra, and Yama. In the Rig-Veda it also frequently denotes soma, the plant and its juice which are prominent in many rituals and sacrifices, and sometimes refers to the moon. In late Vedic texts and thereafter it is used to refer to any ksatriya, or man of the military caste. In the *Mahabharata*, Raja is a name of Yudhisthira, the chief Pandava prince, but is also frequently used as a term of address for any king. It is frequently the first member of compound names such as RAJKUMAR and RAJALAKSHMI. In southern India the variants *Raja*, *Rajan*, and *Rajam* are common.

Rajab (m.) From Arabic: see RAJAB in Supplement 1.

Rajalakshmi (f.) From Sanskrit *rāja* king + LAKSHMI goddess of fortune, attested from classical texts onwards denoting royal majesty or sovereignty. It often signifies the fortune or prosperity of a king, personified as a goddess. The name is particularly popular in southern India.

Rajani (f.) From Sanskrit *rajanī* 'the coloured (or dark) one', hence 'the night'. It is attested from the Atharva-Veda onwards. In the *Harivamsa*, a classical text appended to the *Mahabharata*, it is a name of Durga, the wife of Shiva (cf. her name Kali 'the black one'). Elsewhere it is the name of an apsaras, or semi-divine maiden.

Rajanikant (m.) From Sanskrit *rajanī* night + *kānta* beloved, meaning 'beloved of the night'. This was a medieval epithet of the moon. Its use as a personal name is of late medieval origin.

Rajendra (m.) From the Sanskrit *rāja* king + INDRA (used as a superlative suffix), meaning 'mighty king'. It is attested from epic texts onwards meaning 'emperor', and is the name of various authors and minor characters in medieval times. It is now also common in its variant forms **Rajender** and **Rajinder**.

Rajesh (m.) From Sanskrit *rāja* king + *īśa* ruler (a popular second element in compound names, cf. DINESH and GANESH), meaning 'ruler of kings, emperor'. The name was coined in medieval times.

Raji (f.) Abbreviation of compound names such as RAJALAKSHMI or *Rajashree*, and of recent origin. It is often a pet name but is also used in its own right, and is especially popular in southern India.

Rajiv (m.) From Sanskrit *rājīva* striped, the name of a species of fish and of the blue lotus in classical texts. Its use as a personal name dates from the medieval period. In modern times its most famous bearer is Rajiv Gandhi, prime minister of India (1984–9).

Rajkumar (m.) From Sanskrit *rājakumāra* meaning 'king's son' or 'prince', and attested from late classical texts onwards. It is not found as a personal name before medieval times.
Feminine form: **Rajkumari**.

Rajni (f.) Probably a contracted form of RAJANI. A derivation is also possible from Sanskrit *rājñī* queen, the standard feminine form of *rāja* king, which is attested from late Vedic texts onwards and is used in the Puranas as the name of the wife of the sun.

Rajnish (m.) From Sanskrit *rajanī* night + *īśa* ruler (a popular second element in compound names), meaning 'ruler of the night'. It denotes the moon and is attested from late classical texts onwards. Its use as a given name is of recent origin. The variant **Rajneesh** is also common.

Raju (m.) Variant of RAJ, or an abbreviation of any of the compound names with *Rāja-* as first element, with the hypocoristic terminal vowel *-u*. Its use as a pet name and as a name in its own right is of recent origin.

Rakesh (m.) From Sanskrit *rākā* full-moon day + *īśa* ruler (a popular second element in compound names), meaning 'ruler of the full-moon day'. *Rākā* is attested since the Rig-Veda, and is often personified as the presiding goddess of the day of the full moon. In Puranic and Tantric texts, *rākeśa* denotes the full moon, but is also used as a name of Shiva.

Ram (m.) Variant of RAMA, especially popular in northern India. It also frequently occurs as first element in compound names such as *Ramdas* 'servant of Rama', *Rampal* 'having Rama as protector', and *Ramsunder* 'as handsome as Rama'.

Rama (m.) From Sanskrit *rāma* pleasing, attested from epic and classical texts onwards. Three famous bearers of the name are known. The first is more usually called Parasurama 'Rama of the axe', and is regarded as the sixth incarnation of Vishnu. He was a brahmin, or priest, and legends relate his annihilation of the ksatriyas, or warrior caste. He is particularly associated with the modern Indian state of Kerala. Legend says that he rescued the land of Kerala from the sea, which agreed to relinquish the area spanned by Parasurama's axe when he threw it from the mountains of the Western Ghats. The second is usually known as Balarama, 'the strong Rama', and was the elder brother of Krishna and the eighth incarnation of Vishnu, noted for his fondness for strong drink and his quick temper (see BALDEV).

The third and by far the most famous, also known as RAMACHANDRA, was the eldest son of King Dasaratha of Ayodhya (modern Oudh). He is considered to be the seventh incarnation of Vishnu, and his story is told briefly in the *Mahabharata* and forms the main subject of the *Ramayana*. In his youth Rama and his brother Lakshmana were taught the martial arts by the great sage Visvamitra, and used their skills to protect forest ascetics from rakshasas, or demons, who were defiling their rituals and interrupting their meditation. Rama married the princess Sita after he alone was able to bend the mighty bow of the god Shiva, which none of the other suitors could even lift. Rama's weak stepmother, persuaded by her wicked servant, demanded Rama's banishment so that her own son Bharata could become king. Lakshmana and Sita followed Rama into exile. But the loyal Bharata refused the kingdom and ruled as regent till Rama's return. The demon king, Ravana, abducted Sita and took her to his island kingdom of Lanka. After a long search Rama found her, built a bridge across the sea, and defeated Ravana in battle. His exile completed, he returned to rule at Ayodhya. Rama became a popular figure of worship in medieval times and remains so today. Constant repetition of the name is regarded as a form of worship. The name *Rama* is often found as the first element in compound names such as *Ramachandra* and RAMAKRISHNA.

Variant: RAM.

Ramachandra (m.) From Sanskrit *rāma-candra* 'Rama-moon', the full name of the son of King Dasaratha (see RAMA) and seventh incarnation of Vishnu. Despite his name, he was of the solar race. The name was borne by numerous kings, authors, and religious teachers in the medieval period. The variant **Rama-chander** is popular in southern India.

Ramakrishna (m.) Compound name from RAMA + KRISHNA, probably originating in the rise of Vishnu-worship in medieval times. The name was most famously borne by the Bengali saint and mystic Sri Ramakrishna Paramahamsa (1836–86). Born of a poor brahmin family, he was a devotee of the goddess Kali. After studying Islam and Christianity he became convinced of the validity and essential unity of all religions. By his personal example and by his teaching, he encouraged practical benevolence and attracted a large following. His disciple Swami Vivekananda spread his teachings in the United States and founded the Ramakrishna Mission, which publishes religious texts and organizes meetings. An order of monks follow Ramakrishna's teachings by practising a life of chastity, poverty, and charity.

Ramesh (m.) From Sanskrit *rameśa*, from *Ramā*, a name of Lakshmi (wife of Vishnu), + *īśa* ruler (a common second element in compound names), meaning 'ruler of Lakshmi'. This is a name of Vishnu and is attested from Puranic texts onwards. The name was borne by various authors and minor characters in medieval times.

Rameshchandra (m.) Compound name of recent origin, probably formed by analogy with RAMACHANDRA.

Rameshwar (m.) From Sanskrit *Ramā*, a name of Lakshmi, or RAMA + *īśvara* lord, meaning 'lord of Lakshmi' or 'lord Rama'. Rameshwaram is the name of a famous and holy city on the east coast of southern India. A natural causeway runs from it into the sea, towards Sri Lanka; this is regarded as the remains of the land bridge constructed by Rama in order to rescue his wife Sita from the demon king, Ravana. Tradition states that Rama erected a linga, or phallic symbol, which represents Shiva, at this site in thanksgiving for the success of the bridge-building exploit. That linga is identified with the one now housed in the main temple of the city, which is a popular Hindu pilgrimage centre.

Ramgopal (m.) Compound name from RAM + GOPAL, synonymous with RAMAKRISHNA, *gopal* being originally an epithet of Krishna. The name originated in medieval times with the rise of Vishnu-worship in devotional Hinduism.

Ramnarayan (m.) Compound name from RAM + NARAYAN, originating in medieval times with the rise of Vishnu-worship in devotional Hinduism. The variant **Ramnarain** is common in the north of India.

Ramnath (m.) From Sanskrit RAMA + *nātha* lord, meaning 'lord Rama'. The name originated in medieval times, when it was borne by a king and various religious teachers and authors. Its popularity owes much to the rise of Vishnu-worship in devotional Hinduism.

Ramu (m.) Variant of RAM or RAMA, and abbreviation of compound names in *Rām-* or *Rāma-*, with the hypocoristic terminal vowel *-u*. Its use as a pet name and as a name in its own right is of recent origin.

Rana (m., f.) From Arabic: see RANA in Supplement 1.

Ranjit (m.) From Sanskrit *rañjita* coloured, painted, attested in epic and classical texts. It also means 'affected, moved, charmed, delighted'. It is not found as a personal name until medieval times. The name was borne by Ranjit Singh (1780–1839), the founder of the Sikh kingdom in the Punjab.

Rashid (m.), **Rashida** (f.) From Arabic: see RASHĪD/RASHĪDA in Supplement 1.
Variant: **Rasheed** (m.).

Ratan (m.) From Sanskrit *ratna* jewel, attested from the Rig-Veda onwards. It is not found as a name until medieval times, and even then usually as the first element in compound names. The form *Ratan* has come via Prakrit and is common in most of the subcontinent except the south, where the original Sanskrit form is preserved and a final nasal is added: **Ratnam**.

Rati (f.) From Sanskrit *rati* rest, repose, attested from late Vedic texts onwards. It soon came to mean 'pleasure' (especially sexual pleasure), and is attested with this meaning in the Upanishads and in epic and classical texts. In the same period pleasure is often personified as the wife of Kama, god of love, and she is given the name Rati or Priti. In the epics Rati is also the name of a love potion and an apsaras, or semi-divine maiden. In the Puranas it is also the name of the wife of the minor deity Vibhu.

Ratilal (m.) From Sanskrit *rati* pleasure + Prakrit *lāla* king (derived from Sanskrit *rāja*), meaning 'lord of pleasure'. It is an epithet of Kama, the god of love. The name is of late medieval origin and is especially popular in northern India.

Ravi (m.) From Sanskrit *ravi* sun, attested in epic and classical texts. It is also a name of the sun-god and of a son of King Dhrtarashtra. As the sun is regarded as one of the twelve Adityas, a group of solar deities, *ravi* also comes to denote the number twelve in late classical and Tantric texts.

Ravindra (m.) From Sanskrit *ravi* sun + INDRA (used as a superlative suffix), meaning 'mightiest of suns'. In modern times, in its Bengali variant form **Rabindra** compounded with Sanskrit *nātha* lord, it was the name of the nationalist poet and reformer, Rabindranath Tagore (1861–1941).

Raza (m.) Muslim name, from Arabic *riẓa* contentment, satisfaction, approval (of God), from *raẓiya* to be content. Ali Musi Raza (764–818) was the name of the eighth Shiite imam. Poisoned by the seventh Abbasid caliph al-Mamun, son of Harun al-Rashid (see HARUN), he was buried in Mashed in Iran, now the greatest pilgrimage centre in that country.
Variant: **Riza**.

Razzak (m.) See ABDUR RAZZAK.

Riaz (m.) Muslim name, from Arabic *riyāḍ* meadows, gardens, often denoting the lawns where young colts were trained or broken in. The same word is used in the name of the capital of Saudi Arabia, Al-Riyadh.

Rohan (m.) From Sanskrit *rohaṇa* ascending, attested from Vedic texts onwards. In later texts, the word is also used to mean 'healing' or 'a medicine'. It is the name of the mountain in Sri Lanka known as Adam's Peak. At the summit of this mountain is a gigantic human footprint in stone, which is regarded as the Buddha's footprint by Buddhists, as Shiva's footprint by Hindus, and as Adam's footprint by Muslims, who also believe it to be the site of Adam's fall from paradise.

Roshan (m., f.) Muslim name, from Persian *roshan* meaning 'light, shining, splendid'. It is used in modern Hindi and Urdu to mean 'famous, well-known'.

Roshanara (f.) Muslim name, from Persian *roshanārā* meaning 'light of the assembly', suggesting a woman whose beauty attracts everyone. Roshan Ara Begum was the name of the youngest daughter of the Mogul emperor Shah Jahan (1592–1666). On her death (*c.*1669) she was buried at Shahjahanabad (the new city he had built at Delhi) in his personal garden which was named in her honour the Garden of Roshan Ara.

Rukmini (f.) From Sanskrit *rukmiṇī* 'adorned with gold' (from the verb *ruc* to shine), attested in the Rig-Veda. In the *Mahabharata* is related the story of Rukmini, the daughter of King Bhishmaka. She was betrothed by her father to King Sisupala, but became the secret lover of Krishna. Krishna defeated her brother Rukmin in battle and carried her off. She is regarded as the mother of Krishna's son Pradyumna, who is sometimes identified with Kama, the god of love. In later mythology she is identified with Lakshmi, wife of Vishnu.

Rupchand (m.) From Sanskrit *rūpa* form, beauty + *candra* moon, meaning 'of moonlike radiance' or 'as beautiful as the moon'. Rupacandra is the name of a medieval author.

Rupinder (f.) From Sanskrit *rūpa* form, beauty + INDRA (used as a superlative suffix), meaning 'of the greatest beauty'. The name is especially popular among Sikhs.

S

Saba (f.) From Arabic: see ṢABĀḤ in Supplement 1.

Sabir (m.) From Arabic: see ṢĀBIR in Supplement 1.

Sachdev (m.) From Sanskrit *satya* truth + *deva* god, meaning 'of impeccable honesty'. Satyadeva was the name of a late classical poet.

Saeed (m.) From Arabic: see SA'ĪD in Supplement 1.

Variants: **Saiyid, Syed.**

Safdar (m.) Muslim name, from Arabic *ṣafdar* meaning 'one who breaks ranks'. Therefore the name suggests a brave man or a gallant commander.

Safia (f.) From Arabic: see ṢAFIYYA in Supplement 1.

Salah (m.) From Arabic: see ṢALĀḤ in Supplement 1.

Variant: **Saleh.**

Salim (m.) From Arabic: see SALĪM in Supplement 1.

Variant: **Saleem.**

Salma (f.) From Arabic: see SALMA in Supplement 1.

Variant: **Salima.**

Samant (m.) From Sanskrit *samanta* universal, whole, attested from the Atharva-Veda onwards. The name is probably a short form of various compound names (such as *Samantabhadra*, a Buddhist deity) which are common in Mahayana Buddhism.

Sami (m.) From Arabic: see SĀMI in Supplement 1.

Sandhya (f.) From Sanskrit *sandhyā* junction, twilight, attested from late Vedic texts onwards. It is used to denote the rituals performed three times daily by Brahmins and members of the other twice-born castes. The evening twilight came to be regarded as especially important, and is personified in the epics and Puranas as a daughter of the god Brahma. She is often said to be the consort of Shiva, but some texts refer to her as the wife of the sun, of Kala (the personification of time), of Pulastya (an ancient sage), or of the god Pusan. In the Puranas the legend is related that Brahma attempted incest with his daughter Sandhya. She changed into a deer, so Brahma changed into a stag and followed her through the sky. Shiva saw this and struck off the stag's head with an arrow. Brahma resumed his own form, paid homage to Shiva, and begged forgiveness. The arrow became the sixth lunar mansion, and the stag's head remained transfixed in the fifth mansion, which is called Mrgasiras, or 'Deer-head'.

Sanjay (m.) From Sanskrit *saṃjaya* triumphant, attested in the Vedas and Brahmanas. The word also came to mean 'victory' and is the name of a particular battle array. In the epics and Puranas it is the name of various personages, but especially of a minister and charioteer of King Dhrtarashtra, who was sent as ambassador to the Pandava princes before the great *Mahabharata* war. He later related the events of the war to the king. In modern times the name was borne by Sanjay Gandhi, son of Indira Gandhi, prime minister of India (1966–77 and 1980–4).

Sanjeev (m.) From Sanskrit *saṃjīva* reviving, attested from the Atharva-Veda onwards. It is found as a name from late classical texts onwards, usually in suffixed forms such as *saṃjīvaka*, *saṃjīvana*, and *saṃjīvin*.

Variant: **Sanjiv**.

Sankar (m.) Variant of SHANKAR.

Sara (f.) From Arabic: see SĀRA in Supplement 1.

Sarala (f.) From Sanskrit *sarala* straight, honest, widely attested in classical and medieval texts. It also denotes the pine tree *Pinus longifolia*.

Saraswati (f.) From Sanskrit *saras* fluid, lake, (from the verb *sṛ* to flow) + the possessive suffix *-vatī*, meaning 'having or possessing waters'. In the Rig-Veda *Sarasvati* is the name of a river (sometimes identified with the Indus) deified as a goddess. She is said to move along a golden path, is praised for slaying the demon Vrtra (a feat usually ascribed to Indra), and is connected with various gods, including Indra. In late Vedic texts she is identified with Vac, the goddess of speech. In epic and classical texts and in the Puranas, she is regarded as the goddess of eloquence and learning and the daughter or wife of the god Brahma. She is sometimes identified with Durga the wife of Shiva, and sometimes regarded as the wife of Vishnu or of the ancient sage and primeval man Manu. In modern Hinduism she is the patroness of education, the arts and sciences, and the wife of Brahma.

Sardar (m.) Mainly a Muslim name, from Persian *sardār* headman, general, nobleman. It was adopted as an honorific title by the Sikhs. In modern times it is also occasionally a Hindu name.

Variant: **Sirdar**.

Sarfaraz (m.) Muslim name, from Persian *sarfarāz* meaning 'having the head raised, proud'.

Variant: **Sarfraz**.

Saroja (f.) From Sanskrit *saras* lake + the suffix *-ja* born, meaning 'born in a lake'. It is widely attested in classical texts meaning 'lotus', but is not found as a name until late medieval times.

Sarojini (f.) From Sanskrit *saroja* lotus + the possessive suffix *-inī*, meaning 'having lotuses'. It is attested in classical texts meaning 'lotus-pond'. The name is of recent origin; it was borne by Sarojini Naidu (1879–1949), a close associate of Mahatma Gandhi in the Indian Independence movement and the first woman president of the Indian National Congress.

Satish (m.) From Sanskrit *Satī*, a name of Durga (wife of the god Shiva), + *īśa* lord (a common second element in compound names), meaning 'lord of Durga'. *Satī* is from the present participle of the verb *as* to be, meaning 'being, enduring', hence 'real, true'. Durga is sometimes regarded as truth personified. Both the form *Satish* and its use as a personal name are of recent origin, but the synonymous *Satīśvara* is attested in medieval literature as the name of a linga, or phallic symbol, sacred to the god Shiva.

Savitri (f.) From Sanskrit *sāvitrī*, meaning 'relating to the sun-god Savitr'. It is used especially to describe prayers addressed to that god. From late Vedic texts onwards it specifically denotes one such prayer, which has come to be the most important prayer in modern Hindu ceremonies. The illuminating and vivifying power of the sun is personified as his wife or daughter Savitri. In epic and classical texts Savitri is the name of the wife or daughter of Brahma, and represents the deification of the prayer or the mother of all twice-born Hindus. In the *Mahabharata* Savitri was the lover of King Satyavan, whom she married despite the warning that he was doomed to die in one year's time. On the fated day she accompanied him everywhere until his collapse. Yama, king of the underworld, came to collect Satyavan's spirit but Savitri followed him. Impressed by her devotion to her husband, Yama offered her any boon except the life of Satyavan. She eventually accepted three boons, but still pleaded for her husband's life to be restored. Finally, Yama was obliged to consent. This story is often repeated in classical and Puranic texts, and Savitri has come to be regarded as the symbol of conjugal love and fidelity. The name is also borne by numerous minor personages in epic, classical, and medieval texts.

Seeta (f.) Variant of SITA.

Seetha (f.) Variant of SITA.

Sekar (m.) From Sanskrit *śekhara* peak, crest, and attested in late classical and Puranic texts, describing the summit of mountains and also the top of the human head. It also denotes any ornament worn on top of the head such as a crown or wreath, and is commonly used as the second element of compounds, with the meaning 'the best of'. Hence, it is commonly the abbreviated form of compound names such as *Chandrasekhar* 'moon-crested', an epithet of the god Shiva, who wears the crescent moon in his matted locks.

Variant: **Shekhar**.

Seth (m.) Of uncertain origin, but given in dictionaries of Hindi and other modern Indian languages as being derived from Sanskrit *setu* bridge, or *śveta* white. *Setu*, attested in the Rig-Veda, came to signify the sacred syllable *oṃ* (see OM) in Puranic and Tantric texts, but is not found as a name in Sanskrit literature. However, *śveta*, also attested in the Rig-Veda, is the name of various characters from late Vedic texts onwards, including a solar deity, an attendant of Skanda (son of Shiva), a son of King Sudeva, a mythical elephant, and an incarnation of Shiva. From the epics onwards it is also the name of a range of mountains and an island in Hindu cosmography.

Shabbir (m.) Muslim name, the Arabic form *Shabbīr* of the name of a son of the biblical Aaron. The Prophet Muhammad is said to have called his grandson Husain, son of Ali, by this name.

Shafiq (m.) From Arabic: see SHAFĪQ in Supplement 1.

Variants: **Shafi, Shafee**.

Shah (m.) Muslim name, from Persian *s̲h̲āh* king, emperor. It is assumed as a title by Muslim Sufis (mystics) in the subcontinent.

Shahjahan (m.) Muslim name, from Persian *s̲h̲āh* king, emperor + *jahāṇ* world (i.e. 'king of the world'). The name was most famously borne by the Mogul emperor Shah Jahan (1592–1666). His reign represented the golden age of Mogul art and architecture. The Taj Mahal and the Pearl Mosque at Agra were built during his reign. He then moved the Mogul capital to Delhi and founded a new city, named Shahjahanabad in his honour. Its main buildings still stand today: the Red Fort, the Palace, and the Great Mosque (Jama Masjid). The Palace contains the famous Peacock Throne, consisting of two peacocks fashioned in sapphires, emeralds, rubies, and other jewels. On his death Shah Jahan was buried in the Taj Mahal close to the grave of his favourite wife Mumtaz Mahal.

Variant: **Shahjehan.**

Shahnawaz (m.) Muslim name, from Persian *shāh* king, emperor + *nawāz* cherisher (i.e. 'a cherisher of kings').

Shahnaz (f.) Muslim name, from Persian *shāh* king, emperor + *nāz* glory, pride, grace. The name denotes a woman so beautiful that she would be the pride and glory even of a king.

Shahzad (m.) Muslim name, from Persian *shahzād* meaning 'king's son, prince'.

Shakil (m.) Muslim name, from Arabic *shakīl* meaning 'well-formed, handsome'.

Shakir (m.) From Arabic: see SHĀKIR in Supplement 1.

Shakti (f.) From Sanskrit *śakti* power, faculty, attested from the Rig-Veda onwards. In later texts it denotes regal power, the power of a word to designate a thing, the power of a mantra or prayer, and the creative power of a poet. In classical and Puranic texts it specifically means 'the active power of a deity', personified as his wife. Hence Lakshmi is regarded as the sakti of Vishnu, and Durga as that of Shiva. In Tantric texts the saktis of the gods receive the highest worship, the gods being deemed powerless without them. The name *Sakti* is especially used to refer to the wife of Shiva.

Shakuntala (f.) From Sanskrit *śakuntalā*, the name of the heroine of Kalidasa's classical drama. Her name is said to derive from *śakunta* a bird, because she was abandoned in a forest soon after birth and reared by the birds. King Dushyanta met her while hunting in the forest, and they fell in love and married. The king gave her his ring and returned to his capital. The lovesick Sakuntala neglected a visiting sage, who laid on her a curse that she should be forgotten by Dushyanta, but later agreed that the curse would expire when the king saw her ring. Sakuntala, now pregnant, went to the capital but lost the ring on her journey, so Dushyanta was unable to remember her. Later, a fisherman found the ring in a fish and was arrested as a thief. At the trial the king saw the ring, regained his memory, and became grief-stricken at losing Sakuntala. After helping the god Indra to defeat some demons, Dushyanta was reunited with Sakuntala and his son Bharata, who later founded a famous dynasty of kings (see BHARAT).

Shamim (m., f.) Muslim name, from Arabic *shamīm* fragrant, perfume.

Shamshad (m., f.) Muslim name, from Persian *shamshād* denoting the box tree or any tall and upright tree. The name suggests a person with a graceful and slender figure.

Shankar (m.) From Sanskrit *śam* auspicious (attested only in the Rig-Veda) + *kara* making, meaning 'one who confers happiness and welfare'. *Śaṃkara* is a name of the god Rudra or Shiva in Vedic texts, but in later texts it is also the name of Skanda (son of Shiva). In historical times, the name was borne by a famous religious teacher (also known as *Sankaracarya* 'Sankara the teacher'). He lived in the 8th or 9th century AD and propounded the non-dualistic philosophy of Vedanta, which is very influential in modern Hinduism. Born in Malabar in south-west India, he is said to have led a nomadic life, preaching, disputing with heretics, writing commentaries on religious texts, and composing hymns in praise of Shiva and Parvati. It is claimed that he travelled as far as Kashmir and died at Kedarnath in the Himalayas at the age of 32. He was soon regarded by many people as an incarnation of Shiva. He established monasteries in the four corners of India, which survive to this day. He is the hero of two famous medieval texts which relate his arguments with the heretics.

Variant: **Sankar.**

Shanta (f.) From Sanskrit *śānta* pacified, calm, attested from the Atharva-Veda onwards. In the Upanishads and texts on meditation or yoga, it describes particularly someone who has gained control of their senses and emotions. In the *Mahabharata* it is the name of the daughter of King Dasaratha, who was adopted by King Lomapada and married to the sage Rsyasrnga.

Shanti (f.) From Sanskrit *śānti* tranquillity, attested from the Atharva-Veda onwards. It is frequently used in the Upanishads and texts on meditation or yoga to denote the mental state achieved by successful practitioners. It is used in religious texts as a peace invocation. In late classical texts and the Puranas, Santi is personified as the daughter of Sraddha (faith), as the wife of Atharvan (the primeval priest), or as the daughter of the deity Daksha and the wife of Dharma (religion).

Sharada (f.) From Sanskrit *śārada* autumnal, mature, and attested from the Atharva-Veda onwards. It is a name of Durga, the wife of Shiva, in Puranic and Tantric texts.

Sharif (m.) From Arabic: see SHARĪF in Supplement 1.
Variant: **Shareef.**

Sharma (m.) From Sanskrit *śarman* protection, refuge, attested from the Rig-Veda onwards. In epic and classical texts it comes to mean 'joy' or 'comfort'. In this period it is also traditionally appended to the names of brahmins, or priests, indicating their obligation to provide spiritual protection and refuge to the rest of the population. Its use as a personal name in its own right is of recent origin.

Sharmila (f.) From Sanskrit *śarman* protection, refuge. It is only attested in a Sanskrit lexicon in the compound *pāṇḍu-śarmilā*, meaning 'the joy of the house of King Pandu' and used as an epithet of Draupadi (wife of the Pandava princes in the *Mahabharata*). It is given in Hindi dictionaries as meaning 'bashful, modest'. Its use as a name is of fairly recent origin.

Shashi (m.) From Sanskrit *śaśin* 'having a hare', an epithet of the moon attested from the Rig-Veda onwards. The epithet derives from the Indian interpretation of the visible features of the moon as resembling a hare. It occurs as the name of a man in a late classical text. It is also found as the first element in compound names such as *Shashikant* 'beloved of the moon' (cf. CHANDRAKANT) and *Sashichand* 'the hare-marked moon'.
Variant: **Sashi.**

Sheela (f.) From Sanskrit *śīla* character, conduct, attested from late Vedic texts onwards. In epic and classical texts it came to mean specifically 'good character and conduct' and hence 'piety'. It is the standard term in Buddhism for one of the six perfections to be striven for, and is also found in Buddhist texts as a man's name. It is the name of a king in *Rajatarangini*, a historical chronicle of the kings of Kashmir written in the 12th century. Its use as a feminine name is of late medieval origin. The variant **Sheila** is found in modern times as a result of Western influence.

Shekhar (m.) Variant of SEKAR.

Sher (m.) Muslim name, from Persian *s̲h̲er* lion. It was famously borne by Sher Shah (1486–1545), emperor from 1540 to 1545. Named Farid at birth, he entered the service of the king of Bihar and received the title Sher Khan after killing a tiger. He gradually asserted his own authority and conquered Bihar in 1533. When he extended his sway into Bengal in 1537, the Mogul emperor Humayun was forced to attack him. However, Sher Khan completely outwitted Humayun and defeated him in Bihar in 1539 and more crushingly at Kanauj in 1540. Humayun fled to Sind and thence to Persia. Meanwhile, Sher Khan assumed the Mogul throne as Sher Shah and proved an able administrator. He initiated many reforms and public works of lasting benefit, including the construction of the Grand Trunk Road from Peshawar to Calcutta. His reign is remembered for its effective maintenance of law and order.

Shirin (f.) Muslim name, from Persian *shirīn* meaning 'sweet, charming, agreeable'. The name is mostly associated with the daughter of the Byzantine emperor Maurice (*c.*539–602). She is celebrated in numerous Persian and Turkish romances, which tell of the rivalry for her love between Khusrao, the Sassanid king of Persia, and Farhad, a lowly but extremely handsome youth. Khusrao promises Shirin to Farhad if he digs a canal through a certain mountain. Just as Farhad is about to complete this task, Khusrao sends a messenger to him with false news of Shirin's death, whereupon Farhad takes his own life.

Shiv (m.) Variant of SHIVA, especially popular in northern India.

Shiva (m.) From Sanskrit *śiva* benign, auspicious, attested in the Rig-Veda. From the Yajur-Veda onwards, it was used as a euphemistic epithet of the terrifying god Rudra. In the *Ramayana* Shiva is a personal god rather than the supreme deity. He receives worship alongside Brahma, Vishnu, and Indra, but acknowledges Rama's divinity and seems lower in status than Vishnu. In the *Mahabharata* though the supreme position is once again usually given to Vishnu or Krishna, there are passages where those gods pay homage to Shiva. Shiva's connection with the Vedic god Rudra is evident in the terrifying aspects of his character. As Bhutesvara 'lord of ghosts', he frequents cemeteries and cremation grounds. As Kala 'the black one', he is the personification of Time the Destroyer. Shiva performs a dance of destruction (see NATARAJ), and his third eye is capable of destroying the universe. However, Shiva is also the great ascetic. He sits in the Himalayas, scantily clad and with matted locks, deep in meditation. This is the source of his immense power, which can be creative as well as destructive. His generative power is symbolized by his most popular image in worship, the linga, or phallic emblem. In most Shiva temples this stands on a circular podium called the yoni, a symbolic vagina.

Shiva is the centre of numerous myths which explain his iconographical features. His blue throat comes of drinking the poison which was produced at the 'churning of the ocean' (see AMRIT). He wears the River Ganges in his hair because he had to break her fall from heaven in order to give the earth the benefit of her life-giving waters. The bull Nandi is his vehicle and the trident his weapon. Durga is his wife, and Ganesh and Skanda are his sons.

Shiva is worshipped throughout India, but Benares is regarded as particularly sacred to him (see KASI). The name is also found in variant forms such as **Sib** and **Sheo** in northern India, and also in numerous compound names such as *Sivaram*, *Sivakrishna*, *Sivamurti*, *Sivakumar*, and *Sivaraj*, which are especially common in the south.

Shivaji (m.) From Sanskrit, SHIVA + the honorific suffix *-ji*. The name was most famously borne by the Marattha chieftain Shivaji (1627–80), who fought against the Mogul empire from his capital at Poona and succeeded in carving out a large empire of his own in central India. He is still a very popular hero in the state of Maharashtra. The name is also used in its more general connection with the god Shiva.

Shobha (f.) From Sanskrit *śobhā* brilliance, beauty, attested from late Vedic texts onwards. It is not found as a personal name until late medieval times.

Shobhana (f.) From Sanskrit *śobhanā* brilliant, beautiful, attested from late Vedic texts onwards. In epic and classical texts it is often used as a term of endearment addressed to a mistress or wife. In the *Mahabharata* it is also the name of one of the Krittikas, the Pleiades, who became the foster-mothers of Skanda, son of Shiva.

Shri (f.) Variant of SRI, also found as *Shree.*

Shripati (m.) From Sanskrit *Śrī*, a name of the goddess of fortune, prosperity, and beauty (also called Lakshmi), + *pati* husband or lord. Taken as 'husband of the goddess Sri', it is a name of Vishnu or Krishna attested in late classical and Puranic texts. Vishnu is especially worshipped under this name at Tirupati (*tiru* being the Tamil for *śrī*) in the south of India, a major pilgrimage centre. In the meaning 'lord of fortune', it denotes a king or prince.

Shyam (m.) From Sanskrit *śyāma* black, dark, attested from the Atharva-Veda onwards, often suggesting 'beauty'. In some early texts it denotes a black bull, and in others a particular musical raga. In epic and classical texts it is especially the name of the sacred fig tree at Prayaga (modern Allahabad). In the Puranas it is the name of a brother of Vasudeva, the father of Krishna, and is sometimes used as a synonym for Krishna himself. The variants **Sham** and **Sam** are also found, as well as the compound *Shyamsunder* (emphasizing the suggestion of beauty; see SUNDER).

Shyama (f.) Feminine form of SHYAM, attested from epic and classical texts onwards. It sometimes denotes night, or any of various dark-coloured birds and plants. It is the name of various women, especially a daughter of Meru (the mythical mountain at the centre of the universe) who is regarded as an incarnation of the river Ganges. In Tantric texts it is usually a name of Durga, the wife of Shiva. It is also the name of a goddess in the Jain religion.

Siddhartha (m.) From Sanskrit *siddha* accomplished + *artha* aim, goal, meaning 'one who has accomplished his goal'. It is attested in epic and classical texts, where it is the name of various people, including an attendant of Skanda (son of Shiva), a king, and a counsellor of King Dasaratha. The name is most widely known as an epithet of the Buddha. A late classical text uses it as the name of the father of Mahavira, founder of Jainism. The name was also borne by a late classical poet.

Sita (f.) From Sanskrit *sītā* furrow, attested in the Rig-Veda, where the goddess Sita is the personification of agriculture and the harvest. In later Vedic texts she is also called Savitri in rituals and is sometimes regarded as the wife of Indra. In the epics Sita is the daughter of King Janaka, and her name is explained by the story that she sprang from a furrow made by his plough. She is usually regarded as an incarnation of the goddess Lakshmi, because she marries Rama, an incarnation of Vishnu. Her story is related briefly in the *Mahabharata*, and forms a central part of the *Ramayana* (see also RAMA). She married Rama when he won the marriage contest by bending the great bow of Shiva. The embodiment of purity, tenderness, and conjugal fidelity, she followed Rama into exile. She was abducted by the demon king, Ravana, and spent many years as a prisoner in his island kingdom of Lanka, but resisted all his attempts to woo her. After her rescue and Rama's restoration to the throne, public opinion doubted her virtue, so she entered the fire to prove her purity. The god of fire, Agni, restored her to Rama, but Rama had to yield to public pressure and banished her. She lived in a hermitage with her twin sons until Rama accidentally came across her. Relinquishing her sons to him, she was taken back by her spiritual mother the earth. She is still the supreme symbol of wifely virtues for Hindus, and receives worship alongside Rama.

Variants: **Seeta, Seetha.**

Sitaram (m.) Compound name from SITA + RAMA, formed in medieval times with the rise of devotional and sectarian Hinduism. It is an epithet of Rama, meaning 'Rama whose wife was Sita', and also denotes godhead as the union of male and female principles.

Sneh (f.) From Sanskrit *sneha* oiliness, oil, attested from late Vedic texts. In philosophical texts it denotes viscidity, one of the properties of physical matter. It also comes to mean 'affection' or 'tenderness' in the Upanishads, epics, and classical texts. It is not found as a personal name before late medieval times.

Sri (f.) From Sanskrit *śrī* light, beauty, prosperity, attested from the Rig-Veda onwards. In later Vedic texts it means 'rank, power, royal majesty' and is sometimes personified. From then onwards it is a name of Lakshmi as the goddess of prosperity and beauty. The goddess Sri is usually said to have arisen from the 'churning of the ocean' by the gods and demons to produce the nectar of immortality (see AMRIT). In epic and classical texts Sri is also a name of the goddess Saraswati, patroness of learning and the arts. From late Classical times *Sri* is widely used as an honorific and placed before the names of deities (e.g. Sri Rama, Sri Krishna, Sri Durga), kings, religious teachers, and other eminent persons. It is often written at the beginning and end of religious texts, official documents, letters and manuscripts, rather like the syllable *oṃ* (see OM).
Variant: **Shree, Shri**.

Sridhar (m.) From Sanskrit, SRI + *dhara* bearing, possessing, meaning 'bearing or possessing the goddess Lakshmi'. This is an epithet of the god Vishnu attested from the epics onwards, and used as a name since medieval times.

Srikant (m.) From Sanskrit *śrī* beauty + *kaṇṭha* throat, meaning 'having a beautiful throat'. It is attested as an epithet of the god Shiva from epic texts onwards. The epithet derives from the myth in which Shiva swallows the poison that arises when the gods and demons churn the ocean to produce the nectar of immortality (see AMRIT). Shiva thereby saves the universe, but his throat turns blue from the poison. It was a name of the classical poet and dramatist Bhavabhuti, and of various authors and men in medieval times, as well as of a musical raga. An alternative derivation is possible: from SRI, the goddess Lakshmi, + *kānta* beloved, meaning 'the beloved of Sri'. This is an epithet of Vishnu attested since medieval times.

Srinivas (m.) From Sanskrit, SRI, the goddess Lakshmi, + *nivāsa* abode, meaning 'the abode of the goddess Sri'. This is attested in classical and Puranic texts as an epithet of Vishnu, which derives from the myth that Sri resides in a lotus in the heart of Vishnu. *Śrīnivāsa* is by extension also used to denote heaven or paradise. The name is especially popular in southern India.

Sriram (m.) From the Sanskrit honorific *śrī* (see SRI) + RAMA, meaning 'the divine Rama'. The name is of medieval origin. It is also used as a salutation by Rama devotees and is considered by many to constitute a mantra, or prayer, in itself.

Subhash (m.) From the Sanskrit prefix *su-* good + *bhāṣā* speech, meaning 'eloquent'. It is attested as a personal name only in the Puranas, in the derivative form *subhāṣaṇa*. In modern times the name was borne by Subhash Chandra Bose (1897–1945), the Indian nationalist. He was president of the National Congress Party in 1938, but was forced to resign by Gandhi because of his militancy. In the Second World War he courted the Axis powers and organized an 'Indian National Army' to fight the British.

Sudhir (m.) From the Sanskrit prefix *su-* good + *dhīra* wise, resolute, attested in late classical and medieval texts. Its use as a personal name is of late medieval origin.

Suhail (m.) From Arabic: see SUHAYL in Supplement 1.

Sujata (f.) From the Sanskrit prefix *su-* good + *jāta* born. It is attested from the Rig-Veda onwards with the meaning 'born of noble parents' or 'of an excellent nature'. In the masculine form, it is the name of a son of King Dhrtarashtra in the

Mahabharata, and of a son of Bharata in the Puranas. In the feminine form it is the name of various women in the epics and Puranas. It is rarely used as a masculine name nowadays.

Sulaiman (m.) From Arabic: see SULAYMĀN in Supplement 1.

Sultan (m.) Muslim name, from Arabic *sulṭān* king, emperor, from *salṭāna* to proclaim (or establish) as ruler.

Sultana (f.) Muslim name, the feminine form *sulṭānā* of Arabic *sulṭān*, hence empress, queen.

Suman (m.) From the Sanskrit prefix *su-* good + *manas* mind, attested from the Rig-Veda onwards with the meaning 'well-disposed, cheerful'. It comes to mean 'wise' in classical and later texts. It is the name of various personages in epic, classical, and Puranic texts, such as a son of the mythical sage Uru, a grandson of Balarama (the eighth incarnation of Vishnu), and a son of King Haryasva.

Sumanjit (m.) From Sanskrit *Sumana*, the name of a minor demon, + the suffix *-jita* conquered, meaning 'the conqueror of the demon Sumana'. The name is not attested before recent times, but is now used especially in Bengal.

Sumantra (m.) From the Sanskrit prefix *su-* good + *mantra* advice, meaning '(giver of) good advice'. It is attested as the name of a minister of King Dasaratha in the *Ramayana* and of a counsellor of King Harivara in a late classical text. In later literature it becomes an archetypal name for a minister. In modern times the name is used especially in Bengal.

Sumati (f.) From the Sanskrit prefix *su-* good + *mati* mind, meaning 'intelligent' and attested from the Rig-Veda onwards. It also denotes benevolence or prayer, and is widely used as a name in epic, classical, and Puranic texts, but more commonly as a masculine name than a feminine name. In modern times the situation has been reversed, and the masculine name has almost entirely disappeared. The feminine name was borne in epic legend by the wife of King Sagara, who bore 60,000 sons.

Sunder (m.) From Sanskrit *sundara* beautiful, attested from epic and classical texts onwards. It is the name of several minor characters. In modern times the variants **Sundar, Sundara, Sundaram,** and **Sundaran** are also found, especially in southern India. In the south it is also often the first element in compound names such as *Sundararaja* and *Sunder Ram*.

Sunil (m.) From the Sanskrit prefix *su-* good, very + *nīla* dark blue, meaning 'very dark blue'. It is attested only in Sanskrit lexicons, where it is said to denote the pomegranate tree or the common flax plant. Though not found as a name before modern times, *Sunil* is now especially popular in northern India.

Sunita (f.) Probably from the Sanskrit prefix *su-* good + *nīta* led, conducted, and meaning 'of good conduct'. This is attested from epic and classical texts onwards and is found as a masculine name in the Puranas. An alternative derivation is possible from *su-* + *nītha*, attested in the Rig-Veda with the meaning 'giving good guidance, righteous' and used as a masculine name in the Rig-Veda and in epic and classical texts. It is also found as a feminine name in epic and classical texts, referring especially to the daughter of King Anga of Bengal. In modern times it is exclusively a feminine name.

Suniti (f.) From the Sanskrit prefix *su-* + *nīti* conduct, meaning 'of good conduct', and attested from the Rig-Veda onwards. In the Puranas it occurs as the name of the wife of the star Uttanapada and the mother of the pole-star, Dhruva. In modern times it is especially popular in Bengal.

Suresh (m.) From Sanskrit *sura* god + *īśa* ruler, lord (a popular second element in compound names), meaning 'ruler of the gods'. It is attested in epic and Puranic texts as the name of a distinct god, but occurs more commonly as an epithet of Indra, Shiva, or Vishnu.

Surinder (m.) From Sanskrit *sura* god + INDRA (used as a superlative suffix), meaning 'the mightiest of gods'. It is attested in epic and classical texts as an epithet of various gods, but especially of Indra. The form *Surinder* is especially popular among Sikhs, but **Surendra** is also common.

Surjit (m.) From Sanskrit *sura* god + *jita* conquered, meaning 'one who has conquered the gods', and attested as the name of various authors in medieval times.

Surya (m.) From Sanskrit *sūrya* sun, attested from the Rig-Veda onwards. It also denotes the sun-god in his physical form as against Savitr, the sun-god as divine influence and vivifying power (see SAVITRI). In the Vedas he is regarded as one of the original triad of gods: Surya ruled the sky, Agni (the fire-god) ruled the earth, and Indra ruled the atmosphere. Surya has a chariot pulled by seven horses and driven by Aruna, dawn personified. He is the husband of Ushas, female personification of the dawn, and the father of the Asvins, the heavenly twins. In the epics the myth is related that he was too bright, so his wife gave him Chaya, or shade, for his handmaid, and Vishvakarma, the divine architect, trimmed him on a lathe and used the fragments to make the weapons of the gods. Other epic myths refer to him as the father of various heroes, and he is credited with founding the solar race of kings. The twins Yama and Yami, primal man and woman, are also said to be his offspring. The name is frequently found in compounds such as *Suryakant* in northern India and *Suryanarayana* in the south.

Sushil (m.) From the Sanskrit prefix *su-* good + *śīla* conduct, nature, meaning 'well-disposed, good-tempered'. It is attested from epic and classical texts onwards and is the name of various minor kings and other personages in these texts.

Sushila (f.) Feminine form of SUSHIL, attested as the name of a wife of Krishna or a female attendant of Krishna's mistress Radha in Puranic texts. The variant **Susheela** is also common in modern times.

Swapan (m.) From Sanskrit *svapna* sleep, dream, attested from the Rig-Veda onwards. It is not found as a personal name until late medieval times.

Swaran (m.) From the Sanskrit prefix *su-* good + *varṇa* colour, meaning 'beautiful in colour', 'golden', and attested from the Rig-Veda onwards. It is often found contracted to *svarṇa* in epic and classical texts, where it is frequently used as a name, for example that of an ascetic, a gandharva or celestial musician, a minister of King Dasaratha, and a son of Antariksha, personification of the atmosphere.

T

Tahir (m.) From Arabic: see ṬĀHIR in Supplement 1.

Taqi (m.) Muslim name, from Arabic *tuqā* piety, fear of God. The name *Taqī* was famously borne by Muhammad Taqi (811–35), also called Muhammad-al-Jawad, the ninth Shiite imam.

Tara (m., f.) 1. (m.) Probably from Sanskrit *tāra* carrying, saviour. It is attested from late Vedic texts as an epithet of Rudra, and is found as an epithet of Vishnu in the *Mahabharata*. An alternative derivation is possible from the homonym *tāra* shining, probably from the verb *stṛ* to spread or scatter. This is attested from classical texts and is found as a name in epic and Puranic texts, of a demon, a monkey general in Rama's army, and a member of a class of gods.

2. (f.) From Sanskrit *tārā* star, asterism (cognate with Latin *stella*), attested from epic and classical texts onwards. It is the name of Durga (the wife of Shiva) in her guise of yogini or meditational adept and magical being, and as such she is the protectress of the ancient sage Grtsamada. In the Puranas Tara is the wife of Brhaspati, preceptor of the gods. She was abducted by Soma, or the moon, and this led to a war between the gods and the demons. The conflict was eventually ended by Brahma, who restored Tara to Brhaspati. She subsequently had a child, which she claimed was Soma's. The child was named Budha and is the Indian equivalent of the god Mercury. In Mahayana Buddhism, Tara is the name of the wife of the Buddha and of a Buddhist goddess. Tara is a sakti, or female deity, in Jain texts.

Tariq (m.) From Arabic: see ṬĀRIQ in Supplement 1.

Tarun (m.) From Sanskrit *taruṇa* young, tender. It is attested from the Rig-Veda onwards and used especially of the newly risen sun and of young plants. In epic and classical texts the word often also suggests tenderness of feelings or affection. It is also found as the name of a rishi, or sage, and of a mythical being.

Tulsi (m.) From Sanskrit *tulasī* holy basil, attested from Puranic texts onwards. Basil is regarded as sacred to Vishnu, and is said to have been produced at the 'churning of the ocean' by the gods and demons in their quest for the nectar of immortality (see AMRIT). Some texts say it was produced from the hair of the goddess Tulasi, personification of the plant. The plant is still used in the worship of Vishnu and is sometimes itself the object of worship, as a symbol of Vishnu. The name is most famous in the compound form *Tulsidas* 'servant of Tulasi', a late medieval Hindi poet and composer of a new version of the *Ramayana*.

U

Uma (f.) From Sanskrit *umā* flax (*Linum usitatissimum*) or turmeric (*Curcuma longa*), attested from late Vedic texts. In the Kena-Upanishad, Uma appears as a goddess and a mediatrix between Brahma and the other gods. She is identified with the goddess Vac, the personification of speech. In the epics and Puranas Uma is the name of various women, but most commonly of Parvati, wife of Shiva (see PARVATI). In the myths the origin of the name is said to be from the words addressed to Parvati by her mother (*u mā* 'O do not') when trying to dissuade her from constantly practising austerity and meditating.

Umar (m.) From Arabic: see 'UMAR in Supplement 1.

Umashankar (m.) Compound name from UMA + SHANKAR, formed in medieval times with the rise of devotional and sectarian Hinduism. Its meaning can be either 'Shankar whose wife is Uma' (i.e. the god Shiva), or 'Uma and Shankar', referring to the godhead as the union of male and female principles.

Usha (f.) From Sanskrit *uṣā* dawn. It is attested from the Rig-Veda onwards, where dawn is personified as the daughter of heaven, the sister of the Adityas, or solar gods, and the sister of night. She is said to be very beautiful, the friend of men, the bringer of wealth, and always young although she makes men grow old. She is the wife of the god Bhava or Rudra in the Puranas. A famous Puranic legend tells the story of another Usha, a demon princess. Her father Bana was a favourite of Shiva and an enemy of Vishnu. Usha fell in love with a prince whom she saw in a dream. Her companion Citralekha eventually identified the prince in her dream as Aniruddha, grandson of Krishna (an incarnation of Vishnu), and used her magic powers to bring him to Usha. Usha's irate father Bana could not kill Aniruddha, but succeeded in binding him with magic serpents. Although Bana was helped by Shiva, Aniruddha and Usha were rescued by Krishna and eloped.

Usman (m.) From Arabic: see ʿUSMĀN in Supplement 1.

Uttam (m.) From Sanskrit *uttama* highest, furthest, last, best, attested from the Rig-Veda onwards. It is the term for the first person form in grammatical texts, and occurs in the Puranas as the name of a brother of Dhruva, the pole-star.

V

Vasant (m.) From Sanskrit *vasanta* spring season (from the verb *vas* to shine), attested from the Rig-Veda onwards. In later literature spring is often personified, and is regarded as the friend or attendant of Kama, the god of love. *Vasanta* is found as a personal name from medieval times, and often occurs as the first element in compounds such as *Vasantakumar* or *Vasantarao*, which are especially popular in southern India. In Bengal the variant **Basant** is common.

Feminine form: **Vasanta.**

Vasu (m.) From Sanskrit *vasu* bright, beneficent, excellent, attested from the Rig-Veda onwards. It commonly occurs as an epithet of various gods, eight of whom are classed together as a group called the Vasus, including Indra, Agni, and Vishnu. It is also the name of one of the seven great ancient sages, author of some of the hymns of the Rig-Veda. In later literature it is the name of a son of Krishna and various other personages. It is commonly used as an abbreviation of *Vasudeva*, a name of Vishnu and of the father of Krishna. Hence it is often attested as an epithet or patronymic of Krishna. In Bengal the variant **Basu** is common.

Venkat (m.) From Sanskrit *veṅkaṭa*, of uncertain etymology and meaning, the name of a very sacred hill near Madras in southern India. It is also called Tirupati (see SHRIPATI), from the name of the god Vishnu in the temple at its summit. The hill is referred to in classical Tamil texts of the early centuries AD as the northern boundary of the Tamil kingdoms. Its sacredness is attested in the Puranas, by which time it was already a major centre of pilgrimage. It is now one of the most famous shrines in India. One of the kings of the famous Vijayanagara empire in medieval times was named Venkata. The name is also frequently found as the first element in compounds such as *Venkatesh*, *Venkateswara*, *Venkataraghavan*, *Venkataraman*, etc., which are very popular in southern India.

Vijay (m.) From Sanskrit *vijaya* victory, attested from the Rig-Veda onwards. In later texts it also means 'booty' or 'a military array'. It sometimes denotes a particular time of day, especially the time of Krishna's birth. It is the name of a province in eastern India, famous later as the centre of the medieval Vijayanagara empire. In epic and Puranic texts it is widely used as a name, being borne by a grandson of Indra, a son of Krishna, an attendant of Vishnu, a son of King Dhrtarashtra, and a counsellor of King Dasaratha among others. It is also an epithet of Arjuna. It has occurred since medieval times in such compound names as *Vijayakumar*, and *Vijayashankar*. In Bengal the variants **Bijay** and **Bijoy** are common.

Vijaya (f.) Feminine form of VIJAY, attested from late classical times as the name of various plants, of a particular day (especially Krishna's birthday), and of a magic formula. In epic and Puranic texts it is a name of the goddess Durga, wife of Shiva, or an attendant of Durga, and of various other female characters.

Vijayalakshmi (f.) From Sanskrit *vijaya* victory + LAKSHMI. It is attested from classical texts onwards as a particular form of Lakshmi regarded as the goddess of victory. In modern times the name has been borne by Vijayalakshmi Pandit, sister of the first prime minister of India, Jawaharlal Nehru. She was Indian high commissioner to Britain in the 1950s and 1960s.

Vijayashree (f.) Another name for VIJAYALAKSHMI, *Shree* being a variant of SRI, a goddess usually identified with the goddess Lakshmi. See also JAYASHREE.

Vikram (m.) From Sanskrit *vikrama* stride, pace, attested in late Vedic texts. It is found in epic and classical texts with the meanings 'heroism' and 'strength'. It is a name of Vishnu in the *Mahabharata*, probably derived from *trivikrama* 'thrice stepping', a frequent epithet of his in the Vedas. This refers to the myth in which he encompasses the three worlds of the universe in three steps. The exploit is repeated by Vishnu in his incarnation as Vamana, a dwarf, when his mission is to destroy the demon Bali. Bali laughingly grants his request for all that he can cover in three strides. The dwarf then expands to Vishnu's cosmic proportions, takes in the rest of the universe in two strides, and with the third places his foot on Bali's head.

In historical times Vikram has become famous as the name of the king of Ujjain also known as Vikramaditya, who is said to have driven the Sakas, or Scythian invaders, out of India. He may also have been the founder of the Vikrama era, which began in 58 BC. A king of the same name is famous for having at his court the 'Nine Gems' of the artistic world, including the classical poet and dramatist Kalidasa. Other kings were also given the name as a title, which makes precise historical identification difficult.

Vimal (m.) From Sanskrit *vimala* stainless, pure, attested from epic and classical texts onwards. It is also used as a name in these texts, being borne by several minor characters. The name is especially frequent in Buddhist literature. In Bengal the variant **Bimal** is common.

Vimala (f.) Feminine form of VIMAL, attested in late classical texts as the name of various minor goddesses, and occasionally also as a name of Durga, wife of Shiva.

Vinay (m.) From Sanskrit *vinaya*, attested in the Rig-Veda meaning 'leading asunder'. In epic and classical literature it is commonly used but only with the meaning 'guidance, training, education', often with specific connotations of good breeding, propriety, and decency. In the Puranas *vinaya* (propriety) is sometimes personified as a son of Kriya (religious ritual) or of Lajja (modesty). The term is generally used in Buddhist texts to mean conduct appropriate to monks, and one of the three main sections of the Buddhist canon is entitled *Vinaya*.

Vinayak (m.) From Sanskrit *vināyaka* 'one who leads asunder', attested in late Vedic texts and in the *Mahabharata* as the name of a class of demons that cause despondency, failure, and even madness. They are loosely connected with Rudra, god of destruction. In later texts Vinayaka is a name of the elephant-headed god Ganesh, who is regarded as the son of Shiva (a euphemistic epithet of Rudra). Both as a name of Ganesh and as a personal name, it is used mainly in southern India.

Vinod (m.) From Sanskrit *vinoda* driving away, removal, attested in classical texts. It frequently carries the suggestion of diversion, sport, or pleasure. It is not attested as a name before late medieval times and is more common in northern India.

Vishnu (m.) From Sanskrit *viṣṇu*, the god Vishnu, attested from the Rig-Veda onwards. This is thought to derive from the verb *viṣ* to be active. In the Rig-Veda he was a secondary god, frequently invoked with other gods and especially with Indra, whom he helped to kill the demon Vrtra and with whom he drank the divine soma juice. He was a personification of the sun, especially in the myth of the three paces with which he strode over the heavens (see VIKRAM), representing the three stages of the sun's daily course. Gradually he came to be included in the group of solar gods known as the Adityas, and eventually to be regarded as their chief. In late Vedic texts he was identified with the soma sacrifices by which the brahmins or priests thought the universal order was maintained.

Vishnu rose to supremacy in the epics, where his rivalry with Shiva began to emerge. In Puranic literature the concept grew of him as the supreme deity Narayana, reclining on the cosmic ocean on the body of the serpent Sesa, with Brahma the god of creation arising from a lotus in his navel. Lakshmi, Sri and even Saraswati were regarded as his wives, and Kama, god of love, as his son. His heaven was named Vaikuntha, his vehicle was the king of birds Garuda, his weapons were the conch, discus, and mace. Myths of his incarnations increased, but these are now usually numbered as ten: fish, tortoise, boar, man-lion, dwarf, Parasurama, Rama of the *Ramayana*, Krishna, the Buddha, and Kalki (who is yet to come). Of these only Rama and Krishna, especially the latter, receive full worship as Vishnu. Like Shiva, Vishnu has numerous other names.
Variant: **Bishen.**

Vishwanath (m.) From Sanskrit *viśva* all, whole, universal + *nātha* lord, meaning 'lord of all'. This is a medieval formation by analogy with the synonyms *viśveśa* and *viśveśvara*, which are attested from the Upanishads and epic and classical texts as the name of Brahma, Vishnu, or Shiva. *Vishwanath* especially comes to denote Shiva, and is the name under which he is mainly worshipped at Benares, a major centre of Hindu pilgrimage.

W

Wasim (m.) From Arabic: see WASĪM in Supplement 1.
Variant: **Waseem.**

Y

Yadav (m.) From the Sanskrit patronymic *yādava*, meaning 'descendant of Yadu'. It is attested from epic and classical texts onwards, usually as an epithet of Krishna. The ancient hero Yadu is frequently mentioned in the Vedas, where he is rescued by Indra from a flood. In the epics Yadu is the son of King Yayati of the lunar race and behaves rather badly towards his father. His descendants, the Yadavas, were a pastoral race before Krishna's birth, but under Krishna's leadership they established a kingdom in Dwaraka in Gujarat. The capital city was submerged by the ocean after Krishna's death, and the few Yadavas who were elsewhere at the time continued the race. The kings of the medieval Vijayanagara empire claimed to be Yadavas. In modern times Yadu the bad son of the epics is almost totally forgotten, and the name is chosen mainly for its association with Krishna. It is popular among Krishna devotees in northern India, especially in Gujarat.

Yahya (m.) From Arabic: see YAḤYA in Supplement 1.

Yaqub (m.) Muslim name, the Arabic form *Ya'qūb* of the biblical name *Jacob*.
Variant: **Yaqoob.**

Yashpal (m.) From Sanskrit *yaśas* splendour, fame + *pāla* protector, meaning 'protector of splendour'. It is attested only in medieval times as the name of a prince and of an author. An alternative derivation is possible from *yaja* sacrifice + *pāla* (formed by analogy with the synonym *yajñapati*), and attested in the Rig-Veda and later Vedic texts meaning 'lord of sacrifice', a title given to anyone who instituted and bore the expense of a sacrifice.

Yasin (m.) From Arabic: see YASĪN in Supplement 1.

Yasmin (f.) From Arabic: see YASMĪN in Supplement 1.

Yunus (m.) Muslim name, the Arabic form *Yūnis* of the biblical name *Jonah*.
Variants: **Yunis, Younis.**

Yusuf (m.) From Arabic: see YŪSUF in Supplement 1.

Z

Zafar (m.) Muslim name, from Arabic *ẓafar* victory, triumph, from *ẓafira* to succeed. Zafar is mostly remembered as the poetic name of Bahadur Shah II (1755–1862), the last Mogul emperor. Abdul Muzaffar is the chronogram of his date of birth. Succeeding to the throne in 1837, he was merely a figurehead for the East India Company. However, he was an excellent Persian scholar and an elegant Urdu poet, and wrote four *Diwans*, or books of odes, under the poetic name Zafar. In 1857–8 nationalist troops used him as a figurehead in their rebellion. Convicted of complicity in the affair by the British, he was sent as a prisoner to Calcutta and then to Rangoon, where he died.

Zahir (m.) From Arabic: see ZĀHIR in Supplement 1.
Variant: **Zaheer.**

Zahra (f.) From Arabic: see ZAHRA in Supplement 1.

Zaibunissa (f.) Muslim name, a compound of Persian *zaib* ornament, beauty + Arabic *nisā* woman (i.e. 'woman of beauty'). It is mostly associated with Zaib-un-Nisa (1673–1702), the eldest child of the Mogul emperor Aurangzeb. She was celebrated both for her own literary attainments and for her liberal patronage of men of learning. Her *Diwan* (collected poetic works) was lithographed in Cawnpore (1851) and Lucknow (1867), and a manuscript copy of it is in the British Library in London.

Zainab (f.) From Arabic: see ZAYNAB in Supplement 1.

Zakaria (m.) Muslim name, the Arabic form *Zakariyya* of the biblical name *Zachariah*. It was famously borne by Baha-ud-Din Zakaria Shaikh (1170–1266), a Muslim saint of Multan. After his initial studies, he journeyed to Baghdad to complete his education. He is highly revered in the subcontinent. This form of the name is also used by some Christians.

Zakiyya (f.) From Arabic: see ZAKI in Supplement 1.
Variant: **Zakia.**

Zamir (m.) Muslim name, from Arabic *ẓamīr* mind, thought, sense.

Zarina (f.) Muslim name, from Persian *zarina* meaning 'golden, a golden vessel'.

Zia (m.) Muslim name, from Arabic *ẓiyā* light, splendour. The name was famously borne by the historian Zia ud-Din Barni (1282–1356), who flourished during the reigns of Muhammad Shah Tughlaq and Firoz Shah Tughlaq, sultans of Delhi. Zia gives an account of eight reigns from 1266 to 1356. In modern times the name has been borne by Zia-ul-Haq (1924–88), president of Pakistan from 1977 to 1988.
Variant: **Ziya.**

Zubaida (f.) Muslim name, from *zubaidā* marigold (*Calendula officinalis*). The name is remembered as that of the wife (died 831) of the fifth Abbasid caliph Harun al-Rashid (*c.*764–809). She was noted for her chastity and virtue, and is said to have built the city of Tabriz in 806.
Variant: **Zubeda.**

Zulekha (f.) Muslim name, the Arabic form *zulekhā* of the name of Potiphar's wife in the Bible. Her passion for Joseph is much celebrated in the East, particularly in the elegant Persian works by Firdausi (*c.*940–1020) and Jami (1414–92).